A History of Western Mus

D0547369

Date Due

AUG 2009

EDWARD LIPPMAN

A HISTORY OF WESTERN

MUSICAL AESTHETICS

UNIVERSITY OF NEBRASKA PRESS

LINCOLN & LONDON

© 1992 by the University of Nebraska Press
All rights reserved
Manufactured in the United States of America
First paperback printing: 1994
Most recent printing indicated by the last digit below:
10   9   8   7   6   5   4   3   2   1

Library of Congress Cataloging-in-publication data
Lippman, Edward A.
A history of Western musical aesthetics / Edward Lippman.
p.   cm.
Includes bibliographical references and index.
ISBN 0-8032-2863-5
ISBN 0-8032-7951-5 pa.
1. Music—Philosophy and aesthetics.   I. Title.
ML3845.L565   1992
781.1'7—dc20
91-47076   CIP

∞

To Vi and our family

CONTENTS

ONE: TRADITIONAL CONCEPTIONS OF MUSIC

1. Harmonic and Ethical Views   3

TWO: THE EMERGENCE OF AESTHETIC ISSUES

2. Music as a Fine Art   19
3. Expression and Rhetoric   26
4. Seventeenth-Century Views of Opera   42

THREE: THE EIGHTEENTH CENTURY

5. Galant Aesthetics   59
6. Imitation and Expression   83
7. Operatic Aesthetics   137

FOUR: THE NINETEENTH CENTURY

8. Romantic Aesthetics   203
9. Emotional Realism   239
10. Formalism and Autonomy   291
11. The Idealist Tradition   320

FIVE: THE TWENTIETH CENTURY

12. Theories of Meaning   351
13. Conceptions of Objectivity   393
14. The Phenomenology of Music   437
15. The Sociology of Music   470

NOTES   511

BIBLIOGRAPHY   519

INDEX   531

PART ONE

TRADITIONAL CONCEPTIONS OF MUSIC

CHAPTER ONE

HARMONIC AND ETHICAL VIEWS

I f we examine the fundamental views of the nature of music that are found in Western thought from Greek antiquity to the seventeenth century, two major types seem to emerge, which we can call *metaphysical* and *ethical*. Both of these present us with puzzles, for each in its own way strains our credulity. Is it really possible, we wonder, that music or harmony was seriously believed to extend to all of the cosmos and to the constitution of man? And could music really have been thought to form and control the character and behavior of the individual, not to mention his state of health, and indeed the health of society as well? Each of these two spheres of thought clearly calls for closer examination, not only because of their connection with aesthetic views of music, but also because they are difficult to accept without some attempt to understand their foundation and their more exact meaning.

At the end of Plato's *Republic*, in book 10, there is a vivid description of cosmic harmony that forms part of the tale of the hero Er. Twelve days after having been slain in battle, Er returns to life and tells what he has seen in the otherworld. In a highly poetic account, Plato takes up his theme of justice, for the vision of Er concerns the judgment of the soul, the ultimate rewards and punishments. Since this vision follows a prolonged condemnation of art as a corruption of truth and morality, Plato can be understood as presenting an alternative: a clairvoyant art that sees the truth and leads us to virtue through its inspirational power—art as an adjunct of philosophy. Sensory experience plays a prominent role, in the colors of the cosmic whorls and the song of the sirens and the Fates:

Now when the spirits which were in the meadow had tarried seven days, on the eighth they were obliged to proceed on their journey, and, on the fourth day after, he said that they came to a place where they

3

could see from above a line of light, straight as a column, extending right through the whole heaven and through the earth, in colour resembling the rainbow, only brighter and purer; another day's journey brought them to the place, and there, in the midst of the light, they saw the ends of the chains of heaven let down from above: for this light is the belt of heaven, and holds together the circle of the universe, like the number-girders of a trireme. From these ends is extended the spindle of Necessity, on which all the revolutions turn. The shaft and hook of this spindle are made of steel, and the whorl is made partly of steel and also partly of other materials. Now the whorl is in form like the whorl used on earth; and the description of it implied that there is one large hollow whorl which is quite scooped out, and into this is fitted another lesser one, and another, and another, and four others, making eight in all, like vessels which fit into one another; the whorls show their edges on the upper side, and on their lower side all together form one continuous whorl. This is pierced by the spindle, which is driven home through the centre of the eighth. The first and outermost whorl has the rim broadest, and the seven inner whorls are narrower, in the following proportions—the sixth is next to the first in size, the fourth next to the sixth; then comes the eighth; the seventh is fifth, the fifth is sixth, the third is seventh, last and eighth comes the second. The largest is spangled, and the seventh is brightest; the eight coloured by the reflected light of the seventh; the second and fifth are in colour like one another, and yellower than the preceding; the third has the whitest light; the fourth is reddish; the sixth is in whiteness second. Now the whole spindle has the same motion; but, as the whole revolves in one direction, the seven inner circles moved slowly in the other, and of these the swiftest is the eighth; next in swiftness are the seventh, sixth, and fifth, which move together; third in swiftness appeared to move according to the law of this reversed motion the fourth; the third appeared fourth and the second fifth. The spindle turns on the knees of Necessity; and on the upper surface of each circle is a siren, who goes round with them, humming a single tone or note. The eight together form one harmony; and round about, at equal intervals, there is another band, three in number, each sitting upon her throne; these are the Fates, daughters of Necessity, who are clothed in white robes and have chaplets upon their heads, Lachesis and Clotho and Atropos, who accompany with their voices the harmony of the sirens—Lachesis singing of the past, Clotho of the present, Atropos of the future. Clotho from time to time assisting with a touch of her right hand the revolution of the outer circle of the whorl or spindle, and Atropos with her left hand touching and

4

guiding the inner ones, and Lachesis laying hold of either in turn, first with one hand and then with the other.[1]

It is instructive to compare this description with the account of cosmic harmony that is given in Plato's *Timaeus* (34–47), where we find, not music itself, but the theory of music. In making the soul of the world, the Creator mixes together three elemental constituents—the same, the other, and an intermediate constituent. He then separates from the mixture a series of portions related to one another according to the powers of two and three (1, 2, 4, 8; 1, 3, 9, 27). The intervals of each of these frameworks are then filled in with additional portions of the mixture equal to the arithmetic and harmonic means of each interval. Where octaves result that are filled in with two fourths spaced one tone apart, each fourth is filled in ("downward") with two successive tones, leaving a small remainder, 256:243. Plato's description is given in purely arithmetic terms; there is no reference to music; but the intervals involved are the perfect octave, fifth, and fourth and the tone 9:8—the ratios of Pythagorean tuning. The human soul, with the mixture of the elements now somewhat diluted, is then ordered in the same proportions. World and man are thus composed according to a musical, or "harmonic," principle, for their order contains the harmony par excellence, the *harmonia*, which designated the basic scalar system of the octave. (In antiquity, "harmony" was a "fitting together" successively.) *Harmonia* also designated the octave itself, as a fitting together of two tones or as a fitting together of two intervals, the fifth and the fourth.

Now the first thing we can say about Plato's conception is that music, or at least the musical system, provides a model for the soul. Thus, Pythagorean musical theory—which is a speculative rather than a practical type of theory—is an investigative tool, or has an epistemological value, in cosmology and in anthropology and indeed, as it turns out, in physics generally and in the study of society as well. But how can this be? Where can such a belief, or evidence for such a belief, have come from?

To begin with, it is of interest to observe that beliefs similar to this have been found throughout ancient civilizations. There were correlations between tones and intervals and musical instruments, on the one hand, and natural manifestations such as the seasons, on the other, in ancient China, Babylonia, and India. The basic role of correlation in thought does not seem sufficient to explain this persistent connection. Neither does transmission of the idea from a single place of origin. In mythological and religious thought, however, such as that of the Veda, sound and tone often play a fundamental generative role in cosmology, and perhaps a prehistoric conception of this kind, based on the creative or magical power of utterance, taken together with the influence of hearing on vision and with the universal tendency of correlative thinking, can account for the coupling of music and cosmos.

More important for our purpose, however, is the development of Pythagorean mathematics that took place in this context, for the discovery of the relation between string length and pitch made intervallic relations the main basis of the study of proportion and reinforced the belief that all things were composed of number. It also secured a place for harmonics (or "music") in the quadrivium as one of the four mathematical disciplines (arithmetic, geometry, music, and astronomy) dealing with being—with magnitude and multitude. The quadrivium was the Pythagorean equivalent of science, and it was an essential preparation for philosophy. Music was the most general of the quadrivial studies, permeating all the others and occupying a summary and culminating position. This becomes evident in the *Republic*. And the quadrivium as a whole is not just preparatory to philosophy in Plato's dialogues but really a part of philosophy also, an instrument of philosophy.

Thus, Plato presents two contrasting conceptions of cosmic harmony, both of which became the bases of impressive traditions in Western thought. In the earlier of these—that of the *Republic*—aesthetic properties are prominent, but, considered in their larger context, their appeal to sense is subservient to ethics. In the description of the *Timaeus*, aesthetic properties are eliminated in favor of science and metaphysics. The scalar ordering of the soul is followed directly in the *Timaeus* by a picture of astronomical revolutions essentially the same as that presented in the *Republic*, but there are no colors and no sounding tones. In both cases, the description of cosmic harmony is clearly governed by the larger purpose of the dialogue—in the one the nature of justice, in the other the nature of the universe. But there is another logic to the distinction also, for the description in the *Republic* is of the physical body of the universe, while the description in the *Timaeus* is of its impalpable soul.

The myth of Er was imitated by Cicero in the last book of his *Republic*, but the vision after death is replaced by a dream. The general Scipio Africanus tells of being up among the stars, where he converses with his grandfather, Scipio Africanus the Elder, the conqueror of Carthage, as they look down on the celestial spheres from their heavenly vantage point. Cicero's account replaces the sirens and the Fates with a more scientific view of the production of the tones, together with a consideration of the different pitches and their arrangement:

> I stood dumbfounded at these sights, and when I recovered my senses I inquired: "What is this great and pleasing sound that fills my ears?"
> "That," replied my grandfather, "is a concord of tones separated by un-

equal but nevertheless carefully proportioned intervals, caused by the rapid motion of the spheres themselves. The high and low tones blended together produce different harmonies. Of course such swift motions could not be accomplished in silence and, as nature requires, the spheres at one extreme produce the low tones and at the other extreme the high tones. Consequently the outermost sphere, the star-bearer, with its swifter motion gives forth a higher-pitched tone, whereas the lunar sphere, the lowest, has the deepest tone. Of course the earth, the ninth and stationary sphere, always clings to the same position in the middle of the universe. The other eight spheres, two of which move at the same speed, produce seven different tones, this number being, one might almost say, the key to the universe."

The account also makes explicit the idea that earthly music is an imitation of the music of the spheres, and it undertakes to explain why we do not hear this music (although this would seem to make it impossible to imitate):

"Gifted men, imitating this harmony on stringed instruments and in singing, have gained for themselves a return to this region, as have those who have devoted their exceptional abilities to a search for divine truths. The ears of mortals are filled with this sound, but they are unable to hear it. Indeed, hearing is the dullest of the senses: consider the people who dwell in the region about the Great Cataract, where the Nile comes rushing down from lofty mountains; they have lost their sense of hearing because of the loud roar. But the sound coming from the heavenly spheres revolving at very swift speeds is of course so great that human ears cannot catch it; you might as well try to stare directly at the sun, whose rays are much too strong for your eyes." [2]

The presence of proportions in the cosmos that are the same as those in music means that there is a cosmic harmony in a larger and figurative sense of the word *harmony*. For a Pythagorean perspective, this sense of the word will be the essential one, although, more accurately speaking, it will not be figurative, for it will designate the fundamental mathematical nature of harmony (or music). If cosmic harmony is taken literally, however, the result is either poetry or problematic science. It can also be both of these at once, as it is in Cicero's *Dream of Scipio*. But there is a more basic problem than audibility: the component tones of the harmony sound together and must therefore be mutually consonant, or harmonious in a modern sense, but if they produce harmony in the sense of a scale (*harmonia*), their simultaneity is disconcerting. The description in Plato's *Republic* is not decisive on this point, and the Fates present a further musical enigma. Cicero's description is hardly more definite, but the fact that the harmony is imitated by human singing, together with the emphasis on seven different tones, suggests a scale. The *Timaeus*, which also describes seven circles, gives the ratios separating them, as we might expect, and these designate the consonant relations of the octave and fifth. The audibility of the tones, however, is not part of the conception.

Macrobius's *Commentary on the Dream of Scipio* (ca. A.D. 400) and Chalcidius's *Commentary on Plato's Timaeus* (fifth century A.D.), both of which were of fundamental importance in the intellectual life of the Middle Ages, ensured the currency of the conception of cosmic harmony for a millennium. The combination of the two traditions—of the *Dream of Scipio* and the *Timaeus*—can be seen in Macrobius's *Commentary*, which uses the passage on the world soul in the *Timaeus* to help clarify the meaning of Cicero's description of the cosmic spheres. The harmony of the spheres is nothing less than a myth of Western civilization. It is found in the poetry and literature of every age, in innumerable commentaries on Plato, and in astronomical tracts. It plays a part in theoretical treatises on music: in Ptolemy, Aristides Quintilianus, Athanasius Kircher. It is predictably present in Neoplatonic writings: in Marsilio Ficino, Robert Fludd, Schelling. It is a basic source of inspiration and in fact a governing principle in the celestial mechanics of Kepler.

But the harmony of the spheres is only a particularly compelling example of a general conception of harmony that is apprehended purely intellectually, of harmony that is suprasensible, or noetic. It is indeed so compelling an example that it took on the concrete interpretation of tones that actually sounded. But this interpretation obscures its noetic aspect, which makes it one of a family of conceptions of suprasensible harmony. These conceptions endow countless features of man, society, and the world with a musical character that is sometimes distinct and sometimes vague, or merely suggested. As early as the *Timaeus*, the human soul is described as a microcosm of the world soul, and in various places Plato also describes bodily health and the health of society as harmonies. Noetic harmony, as a basic ingredient of Neoplatonism and of *musica mundana* and *humana,* is prominent in countless tracts of the Middle Ages and the Renaissance: in Boethius, Scotus Erigena, Othlo of St. Emmeram; in Nicholas of Cusa, Marsilio Ficino, Agrippa of Nettesheim, Franciscus Venetus. And it is not confined solely to the harmony of the spheres. Architectural proportions are harmonic in Vitruvius and in Alberti. Hans Kayser, in this century, finds harmonic principles in crystals, plants, and the earth itself. Indeed, there is apparently no end to the diffusion and persistence of the idea of harmony or to the variety of its manifestations.

The universality of harmony is the product of a mode of thought so fundamental that it is Christian as well as Neoplatonic, mythical as well as scientific. Harmony finds its expression more in poetry and in poetic prose than in reasoned discourse. Endless varieties of subject matter suggest a harmonic interpretation, which manifests itself even in the sonorities of poetic language. In Latin, the Greek *harmonia* and *symphonia* are replaced by *concordia* and *consonantia,* and these, in conjunction with many other words having the prefix *con-,* provide a powerful resource for reflecting harmonic ideas in language and, conversely, for "harmonizing" many concepts represented by words that have only this prefix in common.[3]

The combination of the ideas with their harmonious or resounding verbal formulation can produce, in modern languages as well as Latin, a powerful expression of harmony that unites poetic conceptions with the actual sonorities of "verbal harmony." Often the subject matter itself combines musical harmony with conceptual. A well-known example of such poetry in English is Milton's "On the Morning of Christ's Nativity" (1629), which contains a number of musical descriptions, among them a depiction of the harmony of the spheres, crowned—as it is characteristically in Christian conceptions— by the music of angels:

> Ring out ye crystal spheres,
> Once bless our human ears,
> (If ye have power to touch our senses so)
> And let your silver chime
> Move in melodious time;
> And let the bass of heaven's deep organ blow,
> And with your ninefold harmony
> Make up full consort to the angelic symphony.

In "At a Solemn Music" (1630–33), Milton presents a more complex series of images:

> Blest pair of sirens, pledges of heaven's joy,
> Sphere-born harmonious sisters, voice, and verse,
> Wed your divine sounds, and mixed power employ
> Dead things with inbreathed sense able to pierce,
> And to our high-raised phantasy present,
> That undisturbed song of pure concent,
> Aye sung before the sapphire-colored throne
> To him that sits thereon
> With saintly shout, and solemn jubilee,
> Where the bright seraphim in burning row

Their loud uplifted angel trumpets blow,
And the cherubic host in thousand choirs
Touch their immortal harps of golden wires,
With those just spirits that wear victorious palms,
Hymns devout and holy psalms
Singing everlastingly;
That we on earth with undiscording voice
May rightly answer that melodious noise;
As once we did, till disproportioned sin
Jarred against nature's chime, and with harsh din
Broke the fair music that all creatures made
To their great Lord, whose love their motion swayed
In perfect diapason, whilst they stood
In first obedience, and their state of good.
O may we soon again renew that song,
And keep in tune with heaven, till God erelong
To his celestial consort us unite,
To live with him, and sing in endless morn of light.[4]

That music possesses ethical properties and has ethical influence is a second traditional view of music that seems to extend indefinitely into the past—especially if its medical antecedents are considered. Like the idea of harmony, this idea is also not without parallels outside the West; ancient Chinese conceptions in particular are quite similar to those of ancient Greece. And again, ethical views secure their definitive form in the dialogues of Plato. There are extended discussions in the *Republic* and the *Laws* concerning the various types of music and their power for good or ill in the formation of the character of the individual and of society as a whole. In book 3 of the *Republic*, musical modes and instruments and rhythms are considered in regard to their ethos, or ethical character; some are to be used and some prohibited. In addition, simplicity is commended and the mixture of modes and rhythms censured. Books 2, 3, and 7 of the *Laws* extend these considerations, discarding pleasure as a criterion of musical value and installing truth in its place. But if an artistic imitation is a true one, an imitation of good should be a moral force for good and an imitation of evil the opposite.

About the actual efficacy of music Plato has not the slightest doubt. This is particularly clear in book 3 of the *Republic*, when Socrates talks to Glaucon about musical education:

And therefore, I said, Glaucon, musical training is a more potent instrument than any other, because rhythm and harmony find their way into the inward places of the soul, on which they mightily fasten, imparting grace, and making the soul of him who is rightly educated graceful, or of him who is ill-educated ungraceful; and also because he who has received this true education of the inner being will most shrewdly perceive omissions or faults in art and nature, and with a true taste, while he praises and rejoices over and receives into his soul the good, and becomes noble and good, he will justly blame and hate the bad, now in the days of his youth, even before he is able to know the reason why; and when reason comes he will recognize and salute the friend with whom his education has made him long familiar. . . .

And when a man allows music to play upon him and to pour into his soul through the funnel of his ears those sweet and soft and melancholy airs of which we were just now speaking, and his whole life is passed in warbling and the delights of song; in the first stage of the process the passion or spirit which is in him is tempered like iron, and made useful, instead of brittle and useless. But, if he carries on the softening and soothing process, in the next stage he begins to melt and waste, until he has wasted away his spirit and cut out the sinews of his soul; and he becomes a feeble warrior.[5]

The effect of music on society is equally drastic. It is described in book 3 of the *Laws* by the Athenian protagonist:

And then, as time went on, the poets themselves introduced the reign of vulgar and lawless innovation. They were men of genius, but they had no perception of what is just and lawful in music; raging like Bacchanals and possessed with inordinate delights—mingling lamentations with hymns, and paeans with dithyrambs; imitating the sounds of the aulos on the lyre, and making one general confusion; ignorantly affirming that music has no truth, and, whether good or bad, can only be judged of rightly by the pleasure of the hearer. And by composing such licentious works, and adding to them words as licentious, they have inspired the multitude with lawlessness and boldness, and made them fancy that they can judge for themselves about melody and song. And in this way the theatres from being mute have become vocal, as though they had understanding of good and bad in music and poetry; and instead of an aristocracy, an evil sort of theatrocracy has grown up. For if the democracy which judged had only consisted of educated persons, no fatal harm would have been done; but in music there first arose the universal conceit of omniscience and general lawlessness;— freedom came following afterwards, and men, fancying that they knew what they did not know, had no longer any fear, and the absence of fear begets shamelessness. For what is this shamelessness, which is so evil a thing, but the insolent refusal to regard the opinion of the better by reason of an over-daring sort of liberty? . . . Consequent upon this freedom comes the other freedom, of disobedience to rulers; and then the attempt to escape the control and exhortation of father, mother, elders, and when near the end, the control of the laws also; and at the very end there is the contempt of oaths and pledges, and no regard at all for the Gods,—herein they exhibit and imitate the old so-called Titanic nature, and come to the same point as the Titans when they rebelled against God, leading a life of endless evils.[6]

Conceptions of the ethical power of music have had as varied and complex a history as harmonic conceptions. In Roman times they were connected with oratory, in which musical elements were considered partly responsible for persuasiveness. In this role, and in connection with the character of the various modes in the Middle Ages and the Renaissance, the power of music to shape moral nature devolved into an expressive quality that had at most a temporary force on feeling. Yet ancient stories of the irresistible effect of music on behavior as well as on feeling were told and retold as a topos in orations in praise of music and in hortatory introductions to musical treatises, where they persisted until the seventeenth century and even beyond. Tales of the miraculous effects of music in the cure of disease were part of this traditional material. In terms of Western musical history, the most impressive outcome of the belief in the influence of music was the aesthetics of opera that developed in the late Renaissance, and even opera itself. A more recent outcome is the use and regulation of music by totalitarian governments to reinforce political ideology and arouse a militant nationalism. A lesser evil, but also corrupt, is the public use of selected types of music to increase the purchasing of goods or food. On the other hand, it is difficult to find fault with the use of music in dental offices or restaurants. Certainly, the purgation of fear and the facilitation of the digestion have always been approved effects of music. But the most highly regarded influence of music, of course, has been the promotion of piety and reverence. While views of the harmonic or musical nature of the world and man and society may very well fade or even vanish, theories of the influence of music—its power both to arouse and to soothe—are doubtless so well grounded in the nature of the art itself that their persistence in one form or another is highly probable.

Like conceptions of harmony, conceptions of the power of music are mythical as well as scientific, and they are similarly expressed to a great extent in poetry and in opera. The most familiar of the operatic myths is the tale of Orpheus, which was an almost inevitable choice in a musical art de-

voted to moving its audience. A long series of musical influences is presented
by Dryden in the ode "Alexander's Feast" (1697), which was set to music by
Handel in 1736. There are numerous references to the influence of music in
Shakespeare, among them the well-known discourse of Lorenzo to Jessica
in act 5, scene 1, of *The Merchant of Venice* (ca. 1596), in which cosmic
harmony also plays a part:

> *Lor.* How sweet the moonlight sleeps upon this bank!
> Here will we sit, and let the sounds of music
> Creep in our ears. Soft stillness and the night
> Become the touches of sweet harmony.
> Sit, Jessica. Look how the floor of heaven
> Is thick inlaid with patens of bright gold.
> There's not the smallest orb which thou behold'st
> But in his motion like an angel sings,
> Still quiring to the young-ey'd cherubins;
> Such harmony is in immortal souls;
> But whilst this muddy vesture of decay
> Doth grossly close it in, we cannot hear it.
> [*Enter* Musicians.]
> Come ho, and wake Diana with a hymn,
> With sweetest touches pierce your mistress' ear,
> And draw her home with music.
> [*Play music.*]
>
> *Jess.* I am never merry when I hear sweet music.
> *Lor.* The reason is, your spirits are attentive;
> For do but note a wild and wanton herd
> Or race of youthful and unhandled colts,
> Fetching mad bounds, bellowing and neighing loud,
> Which is the hot condition of their blood,
> If they but hear perchance a trumpet sound,
> Or any air of music touch their ears,
> You shall perceive them make a mutual stand,
> Their savage eyes turn'd to a modest gaze,
> By the sweet power of music; therefore the poet
> Did feign that Orpheus drew trees, stones, and floods;
> Since naught so stockish, hard, and full of rage,
> But music for the time doth change his nature.
> The man that hath no music in himself,
> Nor is not moved with concord of sweet sounds,
> Is fit for treasons, stratagems, and spoils;

The motions of his spirit are dull as night,
And his affections dark as Erebus:
Let no such man be trusted. Mark the music.[7]

Thus Shakespeare juxtaposes and even combines a Christianized harmony of the spheres with the power of sounding music, yet an important relation between the two does not appear, for the basis of the musical influence on human beings is provided by the motions of "vital spirits" rather than by the restoration of a microcosmic harmony.

In spite of their very different contexts of thought, which seem to permit no point of contact, the harmonic and the ethical conceptions of music have a deep-seated connection with one another. Not only is harmony in the soul or the state clearly ethical in nature, but the harmony of the spheres itself also has an ethical property; its inspirational force can be seen at once in the myth of Er and in the *Dream of Scipio*. It is also evident, both in the *Republic* and in the *Timaeus*, that the conception of the quadrivial sciences, particularly as it is permeated by manifestations of harmony, contains a powerful tendency toward the ultimate study of philosophy. This ethical value was subsequently directed to rhetoric and then still more strongly to theology, as Augustine makes clear in his treatise on the liberal arts.

From the opposite point of view, the effect of music in calming the passions, in soothing and moderating the feelings, has its explanation in the structural equivalence of cosmos, soul, and music that is described in the *Timaeus*, for Plato explains later in the dialogue the effect of sense impressions and emotional disturbances on the soul as disrupting the even course of its revolutions and introducing various kinds of irregularities and confusion. Thus, the effect of music of the Dorian mode and the diatonic genus, which are the musical counterparts of the structure of the cosmos and the soul, will be to restore the normal order, eliminating the perturbations created by disturbing impressions and emotions. A corollary of this conception is that, in producing various alterations in the soul that correspond to them structurally, various modes and rhythms will provoke the various emotions that are characteristic of different musical styles. This essentially mechanical picture of the effect of music, which is clearly implied and even made partly explicit in the *Timaeus*, was apparently never worked out in detail and in the course of time was supplanted by a theory that was quite different.

With the disruption of the circular regularity of the cosmos by Galileo and Kepler, the conception that music acted on the material but tenuous spirits of the body became dominant in the seventeenth century. These "vital spirits" flowed through the nerves and by way of the brain affected the balance of the humors (blood, phlegm, yellow bile, black bile) and the vapors (wetness, dryness, heat, cold). Natural temperament was in this way altered by the influence of the music being listened to, and the new proportions of the bodily fluids and vapors, which were determined by the proportions ingredient in the music, represented a changed emotional disposition. This explanation of the action of music was just as mechanical as that based on the harmonic circles of the soul. What is more, proportion was again a crucial part of the conception, and connected with proportion was the idea of harmony, even if not the particular idea of the harmony of the spheres.

In spite of the general resemblance between the Greek and the Baroque descriptions of the effects of music, closer consideration reveals important differences. The ancient description is more mathematical, the Baroque description more physical. The perceived qualities of consonance and dissonance are closely related to the emotional effects of modes, rhythms, and melodic intervals, and seventeenth-century explanations of these qualities were concerned less with mathematics than with the physical picture of vibrations impinging on the ear drum, and through this, of course, on the same physiological mechanisms that accounted for the effects of music on the emotions. The process in both cases was physical, even if largely imagined. It is interesting that Kepler himself, who more than anyone else was responsible for the change in explanatory basis, still adhered to the belief in cosmic harmony, faith in which played a vital role in his search for the true laws of planetary motion. Indeed, some such faith in mathematical simplicity continued to underlie science through Einstein and beyond and is doubtless intrinsic to the very idea of science. The change necessitated in Kepler's case by empirical discoveries manifested a new kind of simplicity: the constant tones of the circular system became slowly undulating ones, in step with the varying angular velocity of the planets, and there were new laws to take the place of the old ones.

That the ethical effects of music described in ancient Greek literature and philosophy have been increasingly difficult to believe or to take at face value in more recent times may very well be due to our neglect of certain important features of ancient music that we easily overlook in the perspective that has been produced by the independence of instrumental music, the autonomy of aesthetic apprehension, and the predominance of listening over amateur performance. Inherent in the nature of ancient music was its existence in the context of a specific social or ritual occasion, the presence of words as an intrinsic part of the music, and the prevalence, finally, of participation over listening. When these features are taken into account, the ethical and emotional force of music, together with the defined character of this force, is not difficult to understand.

While the traditional conceptions of harmony and of musical influence are not specifically or primarily aesthetic and are rarely subjected to extended consideration in written documents, they both border on aesthetics and in some measure, in fact, are literally aesthetic. Harmonic order, whether visual, auditory, envisioned, or purely conceptual, has its own immediate beauty—of symmetry, of euphony, or of mathematical perfection or simplicity. It also occasions feelings of aspiration and sublimity. And the feelings produced by music are not only literal perceptions aroused in the listener but can also be imagined as qualities and forms in their own right or even perceived as objective properties of the music. As imagined or especially as intrinsic properties, they cannot be denied an aesthetic status. The distinctive concerns of aesthetics, however, became the primary object of interest in art and music only during the course of the Renaissance.

PART TWO

THE EMERGENCE OF

AESTHETIC ISSUES

CHAPTER TWO

MUSIC AS A FINE ART

T he sixteenth century in Italy saw the beginning of a number of features of music and of musical thought that were of decisive importance to the development of aesthetics. The variety and range of these manifestations are remarkable: music printing, the musical work of art, the study of composition (*musica poetica*), the conception of genius, stylistic diversity (including first of all the historical duality of a traditional style and a novel one), an increasing interest in expressiveness, and a concern with the physical and sensuous nature of tonal experience rather than with the primarily mathematical comprehension of music that had prevailed previously.

To be sure, isolated discussions of aesthetic properties and concepts can be found throughout the history of musical thought, but the fundamental new factors that made their appearance in the sixteenth century constitute a constellation that becomes more coherent and more prominent with time and that can therefore be regarded as the first stage in the generation of a new complex of thought and ultimately of a new discipline. The question of the beginnings of aesthetics and of musical aesthetics is a vexed one, but the weight of evidence points to the time of the Italian Renaissance and to its clearly appropriate context of secularism, sensuousness, and individual expression. This formative period of the subject was completed only during the course of the eighteenth century, when the field of thought was given its name by Baumgarten (1750) and its autonomy and philosophical grounding by Kant (1790). Also in the eighteenth century a continuous literature came into existence that dealt specifically with aesthetic problems. It is only from that time on, therefore, that the use of the term *aesthetics* is justified in its full sense, as a continuous tradition of thought devoted to explicit issues. Its use in the sixteenth and seventeenth centuries must be a qualified one in that it refers not to independent writings in an established field but to particular conceptions or occasional discussions that are found in works devoted to other matters and that are typically brief and unsystematic. The adjective *aesthetic* is of course correctly applied to various artistic ideas and perceptual qualities whenever they occur and is in no way anachronistic in view of the Greek origins of the word. But to speak of "medieval aesthetics," for example, is misleading.

The field of musical aesthetics clearly depends on the conception of music as an art; this in turn is connected with the modern notion of art in general. Thus, musical aesthetics and general aesthetics are intrinsically related, and they both rest on the conception of "fine art." Now the fine arts are perhaps best understood by distinguishing them from the much older liberal arts, which in spite of various alterations have existed continuously from antiquity to the present. The fine arts, on the other hand, are a much newer group of fields, which began its process of formation in the sixteenth century. They did not replace the liberal arts, but neither are they wholly distinct from them. Common to both groups is a certain claim on characteristically human capacities of a superior order: of intellect and social status in the one case and of skill, inventiveness, and perceptual sensitivity in the other. From their inception, the liberal arts were a curriculum for the aristocracy and for the leaders of society. Although Plato regarded the quadrivium in particular as preparatory for philosophy, the liberal arts came to subserve oratory in Roman times and theology in the Christian world.

Although the arts are even older than the liberal arts, before the Renaissance they were devoted more to their use and their role in social life than to beauty and expressiveness for their own sake. And in spite of their common character as types of making, their community as fine arts awaited an emphasis on contemplation rather than formative activity. For the production of art is a specific technical fabrication peculiar to each art, while in the perceptual activity that characterizes their reception there are features and qualities that are common to all the senses and that suggest more strongly the applicability of a general aesthetic. The activity of making, in any event, suggests primarily the use of the hands, and since manual activities were not on the same level as purely mental ones, belonging more to labor than to leisured pursuits, the static arts of space were too different from the arts of time for a thoroughgoing resemblance to be conceived, and the general community of the arts was not easily recognized. This heritage of ancient Greek thought had to be repudiated in the Renaissance in order for the construction of a system of fine arts and of aesthetic thought to proceed. Ancient Greece had placed a higher value on the arts in which contemplation played a conspicuous role—the arts of performance and participation—yet these arts belonged not to the sphere of making (*poiein*) but to the same sphere as conceptual thought, that of "theory" (*theorein*), as is still evident in the word *theater*. Thus, in music itself, both Plato and Aristotle will tolerate instrumental performance only insofar as it conduces to the higher activity of cultivated listening; as an end in itself it is not worthy of a freeman. In general, the theoretical character that ennobles the liberal arts acted to divide the fine arts, obstructing the conception of their unity.

A crucial event in the Renaissance unification of the arts was the publication in Venice, around the beginning of the sixteenth century, of Aristotle's *Poetics* both in Greek and in Latin. The *Poetics* discusses a group of "musical arts"—chiefly epic, drama, dithyrambic poetry, instrumental music, and dance—that are shown to be unified in fundamental ways. This discussion became a model for a generalized approach to the arts. The basis it provided for the unity of the arts is really a double one: it consists first of all in the functional unity constituted by the joint action of the individual arts in composite arts, particularly in the drama; but it consists also in the fact that all these arts imitate the ethical character, passions, and practical intentions of human beings. The joint action and the feature of imitation are bound together in the very nature of Greek poetry and drama. This is most clearly evident in the drama, which combines, now successively and now simultaneously, the three means of imitation—rhythm, melody, and words—and in which the original nature of imitation (*mimesis*) is revealed as mimicking, corporeal duplication. The drama is a bodily duplication, a re-presentation of an action, but of an action that is the expression of character, passion, and intention. And the arts singly, as Aristotle points out, partake of the same nature.

Although the static spatial arts—except for architecture—are also imitative, they do not possess the educative and ethical potency of the musical arts; indeed, their ethical and emotive effect is often entirely absent. This deficiency, added to their ignoble employment of the hands, separated them distinctly from the musical arts. They seemed to belong more to the common arts of utility—which were devoid of both imitation and ethical influence—than they did to the arts of aristocratic leisure.

During the course of the sixteenth century, as far as art was concerned, the low esteem attached to manual activity gave way to a positive attitude. If artists belonged largely to the middle class, the nobility, for whom art was produced, could confine themselves to enlightened contemplation. Of considerable importance in improving the attitude toward the spatial arts was the increasing role played by scientific knowledge in the creation of art, for while the useful arts might very well sustain themselves with traditional and uninformed productive activity, the demands of verisimilitude alone that were placed on painting and sculpture necessitated a detailed knowledge of mathematical perspective for painting and of anatomy for both sculpture and painting. Both these arts, and architecture as well, took music as a model in this new emphasis on scientific underpinning, for music had a strong and flourishing tradition of mathematical theory, both for its elemental structures and for contrapuntal composition, and it was mathematics that was the most distinctive manifestation of science. Indeed, not only composers but even singers required a well-defined body of technical knowledge. New mathematical discoveries motivated by a new need were thus of considerable importance in producing an ever greater equivalence of the spatial arts to the musical ones.

Within the musical or, more properly, temporal arts, the influence of rhetoric in the Renaissance represented a new factor of interconnection, for not only did rhetoric exert a strong influence on the language of poetry and drama, but it influenced the structure and effects of music as well, particularly because music was also an art of language. This reversed the ancient influence that is evident in the rhetorical treatises of Cicero and Quintilian, in which music played an important part in rhetorical education and in oratorical delivery. In any event, the pervasive effect of rhetoric in the sixteenth century produced a certain resemblance between the arts of music, poetry, and drama in addition to their similarity as arts of imitation and their concrete unity as parts of a composite art. The temporal arts had indeed always constituted a unified group both in practice and in theory, but in the Renaissance the spatial arts also came to constitute a special group. This occurred because each of them possessed a foundation in mathematics or science, and they were also brought together conceptually as a group of "arts of design" (*arti del disegno*), a term that signified their elevation to the status of fine arts.

Another and more general factor in the growing equivalence of the fine arts, which both furthered and expressed the equivalence, was the practice of comparing one art with another. The locus classicus for this practice, "a poem is like a picture" (*ut poesis pictura*), or "as a picture, so a poem," is verse 361 of Horace's *Ars poetica* (ca. 20 B.C.). In the sixteenth century comparison (*paragone*) of the arts, painting is often compared to music and to poetry, thus producing the crucial bridge between the temporal arts and the spatial ones. Painting emulated music because of its mathematical theory, just as it did centuries later, but for a different reason, in Whistler's thesis that "all arts aspire to the condition of music." Another prominent *paragone*, which is more a contrast than a comparison, is that of painting and sculpture. Comparisons of the arts, both within each group and across groups, become popular once again in the eighteenth century, when they are the more immediate predecessors of formal systems of the arts.

For the full confirmation of the status of music as a fine art, one further development was required. To be truly an art, music had to give rise to works of art. It had to move more emphatically from music making to a fully made and preserved definitive form. There must be a musical text, as there was a text in poetry and verbal art in general, particularly in view of the gradual separation, over the course of centuries, of the individual arts of the musical complex, a separation completed in the sixteenth century by the more visible independence of purely instrumental music.

The required notational foundation of the musical work of art was immeasurably strengthened by the invention of music printing, which achieved its complete form in the *Od hecaton* in Venice in 1501. This development—so vastly superior to hand copying—permitted a circulation of the musical work to a larger public that was at least potentially comparable to the public for printed verbal art, which antedated the printing of music by about half a century. Accompanying the advent of music printing was the increased use of the score arrangement of polyphonic music, as opposed to the arrangement by individual parts, a practice that eventually found its way from the composer's workshop to the published work. Notation in score form facilitated the elaboration and complexity of the musical work, thus completing the equation of the musical work of art to the verbal or spatial work. By the beginning of the seventeenth century, music had clearly achieved a medium of formulation that was definitive and permanent and that proved equal to the demands of every style.

Nicolas Listenius, in his *Musica* (1537), a Lutheran textbook of the rudiments of music, is generally considered to be the first to record the new conception of the musical work. A prerequisite for such a conception was the recognition of musical composition as an independent endeavor. The study of counterpoint alone was still a matter of pedagogy, of training in the technique and principles of compositional activity from an abstract and analytic point of view, rather than a concrete consideration of properties of the musical composition as a whole. But starting with Volcyr, at the beginning of the sixteenth century, German theorists in particular revived a division of musical study that had been recognized in antiquity, notably in the treatise of Aristides Quintilianus, and thus filled out a scheme that corresponded with the Aristotelian division of human activity into theoretical, practical, and constructive. Musical composition—which, prior to the 16th century, as an activity of music making, belonged to the sphere of practice in the established two-part scheme of *theorica* and *practica*—now became—as a corollary of the recognition of the musical work itself—the independent *musica poetica*. Thus, when Listenius mentions the musical work, his conception is appended to the definition of *musica poetica,* in his short characterization of the three branches of musical study.[1] Composers seek to produce a completed and perfect work, he tells us; after their death, they leave behind this perfect and absolute work (*opus perfectum et absolutum*). In a word, labor is converted into a durable product.

Unequivocally announced here is the idea of a form of music that is independent of the composer or performer or listener—a form that is therefore objective and both capable and deserving of becoming the embodiment of the care and skill and genius of the composer in his distinctive style. The musical work is a nucleus for the group of properties that became an essential concern of the field of aesthetics. In addition, the musical work is the basis that is required if the notion of contemplation is to be applied to music as well as to the other arts. Indeed, it is the objectivity of the musical work, grounded in the objectivity of the score, that gives music its full status as an art. It is instructive to compare instrumental music with dance in this respect, for dance is the only part of the complex of musical arts that has persisted until recently purely as a "performing art"—a status that began to change only with the development of dance notation.

Finally, the preliminary cluster of aesthetic conceptions that is found in the sixteenth century includes the idea of the resemblance of art and nature, as conveyed in the phrase "imitation of nature" (*imitazione della natura*). This idea may have made more for confusion than for intellectual advance, yet it persisted tenaciously in aesthetics in the most varied forms. It had a sanction in the original meaning of the word *aesthetics* itself, as pertaining to sensation and perception and their objects, without the implication of any restriction on the objects that may be perceived or contemplated. But the resemblance of art and nature went beyond this, to the conviction that the universe was made by an artificer or by God and to the equally undisputed belief in its consequent perfection and beauty as well as its mathematical structure. From antiquity to the Renaissance the universe was not a process but a cosmos, an eternal, revolving realm of order and beauty. Thus, beauty—in a somewhat lesser degree, to be sure—almost automatically became a property of art as well. This had always been implied in the case of music by the traditional conception of cosmic harmony, and in the nineteenth century there was the further outcome that the composer took on an aspect of divinity in his work of creation. Naive as this conception may seem to the prevailing mentality of the twentieth century, it was doubtless of influence in giving aesthetics one of its central concepts—that of beauty—and in producing, in the later eighteenth century, an emphasis on the autonomy and coherence of the musical work of art: the eventual elaboration—at a considerable remove in time—of Listenius's conception of the musical work.

Originally, nevertheless, and still in the Renaissance, beauty was a characteristic of the world of nature, of the eternal Platonic Forms, and of the human form; only in the Renaissance was it explicitly applied to the visual arts. But music, of course, because it sounded in the harmony of the spheres and even in its earthly manifestation shared the same harmonic structure, was in such intimate relation to beauty that only the novelty and paradoxical nature of the musical work can explain why it was not until the later eighteenth century that beauty was seen to reside in the individual work as well as in music in general—and then only because of the additional influences of the opera and of purely instrumental music. Music in performance resembled the cyclical motion of the cosmos, especially when its rhythm was modal or metrical, but this repetition was in principle infinite. It was the cosmos in its finished perfection, then, that was the counterpart of the work of art as a changeless conceptual entity, whether spatial or musical.

CHAPTER THREE

EXPRESSION AND RHETORIC

any of the conceptions we have considered fundamental in the development of aesthetics seem to have had their exemplification in music at the very time that they were formulated. This is hardly surprising since artistic experience is doubtless the chief source of aesthetic ideas. In the *ars perfecta* from Josquin to Palestrina and Willaert and in the international Flemish style that disseminated this musical achievement throughout Europe, a vast body of motets and masses came into being that embodied impressively the ideal of the objective and durable work of art, reflective of the composer's individuality of style and detached from the transient activity of performance through notational fixation. Yet in this extraordinarily complex and perfected style, the mathematical rules of which were codified definitively by Zarlino, there were contained the seeds of novelties and departures from the prevailing ideal that would eventually become new worlds of musical experience competing with and threatening the very existence of the established art. Most if not all of these novel developments grew out of a preoccupation with the sung text: with the sound and rhythm of the text, with its structure, and with its meaning, both conceptual and emotional. This concern with language was quite different from the concern with mathematical structure and regulated dissonance; the two ideals had very little in common and were potentially incompatible; they were the musical representatives, in fact, of mathematics and rhetoric and thus of the two contrasted groups of studies of the liberal arts—the quadrivium and the trivium. It was the conflict between these two principles that produced the first documents of the modern history of musical aesthetics. Indeed, aesthetics has thrived on controversy throughout its history, which is to a great extent a history of polemics.

The conflict of aesthetic principles in the sixteenth century was clearly of a fundamental nature, and its ramifications were felt in every area of musical experience and musical thought. On the most basic level, the contest of mathematics and rhetoric was a contest of beauty and expressiveness—ideals that doubtless in one form or another always represent a potential conflict in art. The connection of music and oratory, in particular, had been made quite explicit in antiquity, in the rhetorical treatises of Cicero and Quintilian. The time-honored roster of the miraculous curative and persuasive powers of music was too similar to the goals of oratory for the resemblance to escape attention. Indeed, this similarity of music and language goes back to the literal union of the two in medical magic. But the connection of music and mathematics, if not quite as old, was even more intimate since music was a sensible embodiment of number and ratio. In vocal music, clearly, these two traditions could lead in different directions, each threatening to suppress or destroy the other.

The polyphonic *ars perfecta* of the sixteenth century was a particularly impressive example of mathematics in musical form, based as it was on the ratios provided by the *senario*—the integers from one to six—and on the regulated treatment of dissonance, which was given a subordinate role and limited to specified unobtrusive types. The *senario* itself had displaced the still more abstract Pythagorean tuning, starting in the early part of the century. The demands of euphony led to thirds that were purely tuned and thus also to a harmonious triad (the *armonia perfetta*) in the ratio $4:5:6$. These new tunings took precedence definitively over the medieval tuning when they were endorsed by Gioseffo Zarlino in Le istitutioni harmoniche (Venice, 1558). Sensuous pleasure and mathematics seemed to have reached a perfect accord. But the ideal they represented was timeless and static and thus subject to destruction in a world of history and changing experience.

A growing interest in expression gradually overcame the rules of dissonance during the course of the century, breaking through the mathematical perfection of the older art. Theorists around the middle of the century—Henricus Glareanus (*Dodecachordon* [Basel, 1547]), Nicola Vicentino (*L'antica musica ridotta alla moderna prattica* [Rome, 1555]), and Zarlino (*Le istitutioni harmoniche*)—allow for the new aesthetic and permit a relaxation of the established stylistic rules for the purpose of the expression of the concepts and affects represented by the words or, as it was then formulated, for the purpose of the "imitation" of these concepts and affects. Authority for these innovations was found in ancient Greek writings on music. The discussions in Plato's *Republic* and *Laws* and in Aristotle's *Poetics* and *Politics* were of particular importance. (The *Poetics* had been published in Latin and in Greek, as we have seen, at the beginning of the century.) The object of the musical imitation had to be clear, and this was possible only if the text controlled the other aspects of musical expressiveness and only, of course, if it was clearly audible. Ancient musical writings even prompted the revival, most notably by Vicentino, of the ancient chromatic and enharmonic genera, this too in the service of expressing the text.

The *ars perfecta* was generally supposed to have reached its culmination in the first half of the sixteenth century, in the works of Josquin and his pupils and in those of Willaert. Yet even at the time of its full realization it contained excesses in the expression of the words that threatened the beauty and the mathematical perfection of the style. Glareanus has fault to find even with Josquin. Although he says of him, "No one has more effectively expressed the passions of the soul in music than this symphonist," he also points to defects:

> But moderation was wanting for the most part and, with learning, judgment; thus in certain places in his compositions he did not, as he should have, soberly repress the violent impulses of his unbridled temperament. . . . Zarlino has a similar attitude towards expression: In so far as he can, the musician must take care to accompany each word in such a way that, if it denotes harshness, hardness, cruelty, bitterness, and other things of this sort, the harmony will be similar, that is somewhat hard and harsh, but so that it does not offend. In the same way, if any word expresses complaint, grief, affliction, sighs, tears, and other things of this sort, the harmony will be full of sadness.[1]

He proceeds to explain exactly how this may be done, but always without infringing the established principles of polyphonic style.

Vicentino, to be sure, is more radical. He maintains that music is made "solely to express the conceits, passions, and affections of the words with harmony."[2] What comes first in his view is expression (or imitation), not harmoniousness. Zarlino's attitude and emphasis are quite different. Even though his words seem to contain an invitation to disregard harmonic perfection, the expressiveness he calls for is carefully controlled: it is either within the range of the qualities available within the *senario* or—like the use of the tritone—a specified exception. Vicentino's radicalism, on the other hand, is as fundamental a principle of his style as harmonic rule; indeed, it is more fundamental, for expression can take precedence over harmony whenever the words demand it and in any way that seems appropriate. Even at mid-century, then, the *ars perfecta* found itself challenged by an opposing approach to style, and in the last few decades of the century the conflict erupted into open warfare.

Fundamental to Vicentino's theory and practice of expression was the idea of reviving and even exceeding the miraculous effects—the *effeti meravi-*

gliosi—of ancient music, of "reducing ancient music to modern practice." The novel effects he endorses and produces in his music are bound up in particular with the revival of the ancient melodic genera—diatonic, chromatic, and enharmonic—and even with the mixture of these within a single composition to evoke greater astonishment and emotion. He was notorious, in particular, for his use of microtonal, or "enharmonic," intervals and for the construction of a keyboard instrument on which these could be produced. There could be no question that he represented a stylistic alternative and a challenge to the *ars perfecta*.

The new polyphonic practices and principles came into open conflict in the famous dispute between the theorist Giovanni Artusi and the composer Claudio Monteverdi. Since the new style was most evident in the madrigal, the dispute rested to some extent on the contrast between progressive secular music in Italian and established religious music in Latin. The *ars perfecta*, however, was a paradigmatic style for polyphony of every kind; mathematically grounded, it was not restricted to any single country or genre. In his *L'Artusi, ovvero, Delle imperfezioni della moderna musica* (Venice, 1660), Artusi presents a discussion between Luca and Vario that is focused on two of Monteverdi's madrigals. Luca, who has heard the madrigals the day before, offers Vario a description of them. "The texture was not unpleasing," he admits, but,

> insofar as it introduced new rules, new modes, and new turns of phrase, these were harsh and little pleasing to the ear, nor could they be otherwise; for so long as they violate the good rules—in part founded upon experience, the mother of all things, in part observed in nature, and in part proved by demonstration—we must believe them deformations of the nature and propriety of true harmony, far removed from the object of music, which, as Your Lordship said yesterday, is delectation.

Vario then presents the offending passages to Luca, who finds them "harsh to the ear, rather offending than delighting it, and to the good rules left by those who have established the order and the bounds of this science they bring confusion and imperfection of no little consequence. . . . But how can they excuse and palliate these imperfections, which could not possibly be more absurd?" "Absurd?" Luca exclaims.

> I do not know how you can defend that opinion of yours. They call absurd the things composed in another style and would have it that theirs is the true method of composition, declaring that this novelty and new order of composing is about to produce many effects which ordinary

music, full of so many and such sweet harmonies, cannot and never will produce. And they will have it that the sense, hearing such asperities, will be moved and will do marvelous things.[3]

The discussion moves on to the technical details of the passages; there is no consideration of the text. Artusi continued his criticism in *Seconda parte dell'Artusi* (Venice, 1603), and Monteverdi responded to him in 1605, in the foreword to his fifth book of madrigals:

> Do not marvel that I am giving these madrigals to the press without first replying to the objections that the *Artusi* has brought against some very minute details in them, for being in the service of His Serene Highness, I have not at my disposal the time that would be required. Nevertheless, to show that I do not compose my works at haphazard, I have written a reply which will appear, as soon as I have revised it, bearing the title, *Seconda Pratica, ovvero, Perfezioni della Moderna Musica*. Some, not suspecting that there is any practice other than that taught by Zarlino, will wonder at this, but let them be assured that, with regard to the consonances and dissonances, there is still another way of considering them, different from the established way, which, with satisfaction to the reason and to the senses, defends the modern method of composing.
>
> I have wished to say this to you in order that the expression "Second Practice" may not be appropriated by any one else, and further, that the ingenious may reflect upon other secondary matters concerning harmony and believe that the modern composer builds upon the foundation of truth.[4]

The promised reply did not appear, however, and the nature of the *seconda prattica* was revealed by Monteverdi's brother Giulio in the form of annotations to this foreword that were published at the end of Monteverdi's *Scherzi musicali* (1607). It had been his brother's intention, Giulio explains, "to make the words the mistress of the harmony and not the servant." This is the point of view from which his work is to be judged "in the composition of the melody." In support of this position, Giulio cites Plato's *Republic*, which states that song is composed of three things, the words, the harmony, and the rhythm; that the manner of the diction and the words follow and conform to the disposition of the soul; and that the rhythm and the harmony follow the words. "But in this case," Giulio continues,

> Artusi takes certain details, or, as he calls them, "passages," from my brother's madrigal "Cruda Amarilli," paying no attention to the words, but neglecting them as though they had nothing to do with the music,

later showing the said "passages" deprived of their words, of all their harmony, and of their rhythm. But if, in the passages noted as false, he had shown the words that went with them, then the world would have known without fail where his judgment had gone astray, and he would not have said that they were chimeras and castles in the air from their entire disregard of the rules of the First Practice.

Madrigals "whose harmony obeys their words exactly . . . would indeed be left bodies without soul if they were left without this most important and principal part of music." By passing judgment on such passages without words, Giulio maintains, Artusi implies "that all excellence and beauty consists in the exact observance of the aforesaid rules of the First Practice, which makes the harmony mistress of the words." Harmony as such, however, has no power over the mind. This is conceded even by Zarlino, whom Giulio cites: "If we take harmony absolutely, without adding to it anything else, it will have no power to produce any extrinsic effect. . . . In a certain way, it intrinsically prepares for and disposes to joy or sadness, but it does not on this account lead to the expression of any extrinsic effect."[5]

More striking than this conflict between two types of polyphony was the fateful dispute between polyphony and monody. The same fundamental problem of expression and its conflict with harmonic law was responsible for both, and the same decisive concern with the importance of the sung text and the new approach to music this entailed. But the style advocated by the monodic theorists was radically different from that of the *ars perfecta*. While the *prima* and *seconda prattiche* were gradually fused during the course of the seventeenth century by the absorption of the new into the old, polyphony and monody resisted this process and generally formed a combined style in which they remained somewhat distinct in spite of the mixture.

It was of the essence of this new controversy, and not a partly external circumstance, that it revolved around the revival of ancient musical effects, as these were described by Plato and Aristotle. Indeed, it involved an effort to duplicate the impact of ancient Greek tragedy, at least in its essential features. But this revival took place in an arena in which various kinds of accompanied singing were already in evidence. Sixteenth-century musical practice included first of all the monodic performance of polyphonic compositions, and of madrigals in particular, in which the top melodic line was sung and the other voices combined in an instrumental performance, usually on the lute, which became the accompaniment of the melody sung. Needless to say, the sung melody generally differed somewhat from the soprano part of the original polyphonic performance. It could hardly forgo added embellishment (a change that also took place in the purely instrumental versions of polyphonic vocal works) or even the addition of phrases borrowed from other voices originally sung for the purpose of enrichment, for added expressiveness, or to fill in silences.

Quite different from this was the less known and less frequent practice of vocal improvisation to instrumental accompaniment. There was recitation in speech to an instrumental background but also the use of intoned speech— of a type of recitative or of repeated conventional melodic phrases—to construct a performance in which an existent poetic text was employed or else a narrative or a poem improvised. Finally, of course, there were lute songs, as an established genre of accompanied song, subject once again—like the solo performance of polyphonic compositions—to embellishment. The new monodic practices can be understood best against this background of related older types of solo song. What was distinctive about them was that, in spite of their appeal to antiquity, they were conceived as new. They were striking and dramatic in style and moving in their effect. And they were explained and justified in writing. They were the occasion, in short, of an early body of aesthetic literature, aesthetic because of the types of stylistic issue involved: the effects and the expressiveness of music.

The first extended consideration of the controversy over monody and polyphony seems to have been written in 1572, as the first in a series of letters addressed to Vincenzo Galilei by Girolamo Mei, a highly respected classical scholar. In response to Galilei's request, Mei's letter presents the results of his investigation into the nature of ancient Greek music. He writes that not only the solo songs but also the choruses of the ancients were monophonic. He had undertaken his investigation because ancient music possessed "a powerful means of exciting the affections," while that of his own time, as is commonly said, "is more readily adapted to everything else." The different effects of the voice, Mei decides, are due to differences in pitch, which in turn arise from differences in the speed of the motion producing them. The differences in pitch are the sign of different affections and thus become routes by which an initial affection produces a similar one in another person through the medium of the voice.[6]

With book 3 of Plato's *Republic* in mind, Mei divides affections into three categories based on low, intermediate, and high pitch—dispirited, calm, and agitated—which reveal, respectively, an indolent, a tranquil, and an aroused soul. He points out that Plato followed the same procedure with rhythms. Referring to the mixture of boiling water and iced water, which produces intermediate quantities of heat and cold, he maintains that the powerful affections produced by ancient music were due to the fact that all the singers together sang the same words, the same mode, the same melody, and the same rhythm at the same speed. No ancient writer, Mei continues, mentions different voice parts, such as bass, tenor, alto, and soprano, which alone suffices to confirm the monophonic character of their music. Modern music, on the other hand, seeks a varied harmony of diverse melodies; it aims at auditory delight, not at arousing affections or impressing concepts on the mind. Thus, there was no limit to the power of ancient music, while modern music can achieve nothing comparable. The mind of the listener is subjected by the diverse and contrary parts of modern music to diverse and contrary affections and is like a column with ropes harnessed to its capitol and pulled on with equal forces in equally spaced directions.

Mei goes on to attack the complexity and artifice of modern music, which he contrasts with the simplicity and naturalness and singleness of purpose of ancient music. He introduces another illustration, this time contrasting the effect of coming on a group of people who are engaged in the most diverse behavior, ranging from weeping to laughing, with the effect of coming on a group in which everyone is weeping. Modern music is censured at length for its faults—diverse and contrary parts; pitch, rhythms, and speed that contradict the concept signified by the words; different parts of the text sung at the same time; erratic melodic leaps; chopping up of words; and so on. In contrast, the action of ancient music, in which everything reinforces a single effect, is compared to the constant dripping of water in the same place on a stone, which finally hollows it out.

In Mei's picture of music, pitch is a sign of certain affections, which are then excited in the soul of the listener, who represents them to himself as present, either actually or in memory. At the same time, the text conveys a certain concept that in itself may excite the same affection in the listener. It is clear that the original affections, which are those of the poet, the composer, or the performer, or perhaps of all three, have their natural signs in pitch and that the effective character of these affections may also be conveyed by the concepts expressed by the words. The listener responds both spontaneously (the affections are excited in his soul) and conceptually (he represents the affections to himself as present). There is also no doubt that the affections in question are real ones; they are not merely apparent, and not merely thought of, but experienced in their actuality. In aesthetic theory—and doubtless also in the musical experience of the time—we are confronted with both an initial expression (in pitch) and an initial formulation (in words) of an affection and thus with music as both a sign and a symbol of this affection, with both a musical effect and a musical meaning. The ambiguity of the idea of "expression" is quite evident, but Mei makes clear what he means in each phase of the musical experience.

Apart from this central matter, Mei distinguishes in passing the sensuous delight of hearing, the emotional effect of music, and the concept conveyed by the sung text. There is even a suggestion of the moral value that attaches to the emotion and concept that are imparted and the lack of value or the negative value connected with auditory pleasure. Indeed, in antiquity it was the value of music in influencing character and behavior that was notable; its emotional effect was less important and generally not even discussed. As for auditory pleasure, it was connected with complexity and censured in Plato also and similarly associated with a mixture of styles and a consequent confusion of ethical qualities. The influence of ancient ideals is quite evident in Mei's thought.

Although much of Mei's criticism of modern music applies to the traditional polyphony of the *ars perfecta,* what he has mostly in mind is the expressive madrigal and perhaps the expressive novelty that entered sacred music as well. It is clear, then, that another new ideal is being espoused, one radical enough in its total rejection of polyphony to supersede not only the traditional *ars perfecta* but modern expressive polyphony as well. The logic of Mei's argument is incontrovertible. But what accompanies it is an ability to see music from only one perspective, and this condition or viewpoint blinds him to any other values that may exist in polyphony apart from its expressive shortcomings. It even gives his attitude toward auditory pleasure a moralistic character that disdains a limitless area of musical beauty and enjoyment. Apart from this, of course, Mei's argument is fallacious in attaching emotional qualities so unequivocally to the various regions of pitch. This attachment may indeed be true for various rhythms and tempos, but musical pitch, a constituent of art, is no longer an unvarying sign of different kinds of feeling; it is rather symbolic, to some degree figurative, and capable of conveying qualities that escape any realistically defined expressive types.

Several of the ideas that Mei expressed in this first letter to Galilei are presented again in the *Discorso . . . sopra la Musica antica, e il cantar bene,* which was written about 1580 by Giovanni de' Bardi, or perhaps for him by Galilei.[7] Bardi was a wealthy amateur whose home was the meeting place of the Florentine Camerata, of which Galilei was a member, and the letters of Mei unquestionably supplied material for the discussions of the group. While both Bardi and Galilei drew on Mei's ideas, Bardi takes a more moderate position than either Galilei or Mei. To be sure, because it mixes different octave species, rhythms, and melodic registers, polyphony cannot move the mind to a particular moral quality, and this purpose is also obstructed by chopped up words and two or more texts sung at the same time. But the textual abuses, at any rate, can be avoided in polyphony, as is shown by the madrigals of Cipriano de Rore. Furthermore, music cannot be reformed all at once.

Bardi's position can be made clear in his own words.

But since we are so much in the dark, let us at least endeavor to give poor unfortunate Music a little light, for from her decline until now, and this means ever so many centuries, she has had not one artificer who has at all considered her case, but has been treated in another way, inimical to her, that of counterpoint. This light may be permitted to reach her only little by little, just as a man who has been afflicted with a very serious illness ought properly to be restored step by step to his former state of health.

For the present, Bardi urges, we should endeavor not to spoil the verse. Polyphony ("counterpoint") may be retained, but the primary emphasis in polyphony as well as monody must be the imitation of speech:

> Rejecting the improper practices employed today by those who search for unusual sounds, you will seek to use only a few, turning about the *mese* [middle note of the Greek scalar system] of the mode and employing it as often as you can, bearing in mind that, in speaking, man seeks to use few sounds and seldom, perhaps never uses wide leaps unless stirred up by anger or some other violent passion.[8]

What Bardi proposes is clearly a kind of recitation or intonation, and he subsequently censures excessive ornamentation as well. But instead of discarding polyphony, he would purge it of its abuses and thus lead it toward the true end of music. Fundamentally, however, he scorns the *contrapuntisti* and believes that their music is suitable only for instruments—specifically *stringed* instruments, for these, he says, are most distant from the human voice.

The manifesto that brought widespread attention to the cause of monody was Galilei's *Dialogo della musica antica e della moderna* (1581).[9] Galilei gives credit to Mei and adopts his ideas extensively. His tone, however, is strongly polemical and his rejection of polyphony unqualified. Forgotten are his own polyphonic madrigals and his respect for the teachings of Zarlino. Galilei's *Dialogo* provoked a response by Zarlino, in his *Sopplimenti musicali* of 1588. "What has the musician to do with those who recite tragedies and comedies?" he asks.[10] Music does not imitate speech, in Zarlino's view, whether of the actor or of the orator; rather, it imitates the laws of nature, as these are manifested by the ratios of the integers from one to six. The two objects of imitation at stake here are the clearest possible expression of the antagonistic quadrivial and rhetorical conceptions of music. Yet it is well to remember that in the *Istitutioni* (1558) Zarlino had also cited Plato, also spoken of the imitation of the text, and also found fault with polyphony for the barbarism of cutting up words and contradicting the length of syllables. The sharply different views of the *Sopplimenti*, which do not, however, literally contradict these, were of course provoked by Galilei's defection and by his uncompromising attitude. The conflict nevertheless was an inevitable consequence of historical change.

About twenty years after Galilei's *Dialogo*, when the next extant discussions of the new expressive style appear, it is in connection with the practical application of the style in the presentation of operas. Although the theoretical and humanistic context of ideas is still very much in evidence, the focus on practice provides the discussions with a new medium of presentation: they now appear in the dedications and prefaces of publications of operatic scores, and they are written by publishers, librettists, and composers.

In his dedication to *Euridice* of 1600,[11] Ottavio Rinuccini, the poet of the libretto, refers directly at the outset to ancient tragedy, as sung throughout. He also refers to his earlier fable *Dafne*, which he had written, as he says, "solely to make a simple trial of what the music of our age could do" and which "gave pleasure beyond belief to the few who heard it." Rinuccini mentions Jacopo Peri as the composer of both *Dafne* and *Euridice*.

Giulio Caccini's dedication to his own setting of *Euridice*,[12] which was also written in 1600 and bears a date only slightly later than Rinuccini's dedication, similarly refers at the outset to ancient tragedy and also mentions earlier compositions, "madrigals," in which he had used the same new style. Caccini does not seem to regard monody as the central matter here, for he mentions the "harmony of the parts reciting in the present Euridice." More essential, evidently, is the presence of the (partly improvised) *basso continuo*. Related to the disregard of parallel octaves and fifths is the central characterization of the new style of singing: "In this manner of singing I have used a certain neglect which I deem to have an element of nobility, believing that with it I have approached that much nearer to ordinary speech." Caccini promises a discussion of this new manner of singing and of his new style of ornamentation as well, and these are indeed discussed in the foreword to his collection of songs, *Le nuove musiche*, of 1602. In the *Euridice* dedication, he seeks to establish his priority in these new inventions: "This manner appears throughout my other compositions, composed at various times going back more than fifteen years, as I have never used in them any art other than the imitation of the conceit of the words, touching those chords more or less passionate which I judged most suitable for the grace which is required for good singing."[13]

Deriving his ideas partly from Rinuccini's dedication, Jacopo Peri's foreword to his score of *Euridice* (1600) contains a more extended consideration of the new dramatic style. It occupies a position between speech and song:

> Seeing that dramatic poetry was concerned and that it was therefore necessary to imitate speech in song (and surely no one ever spoke in

song), I judged that the ancient Greeks and Romans (who, in the opinion of many, sang their tragedies throughout in representing them upon the stage) had used a harmony surpassing that of ordinary speech but falling so far below the melody of song as to take an intermediate form. And this is why we find their poems admitting the iambic verse, a form less elevated than the hexameter but said to be advanced beyond the confines of familiar conversation. For this reason, discarding every other manner of singing hitherto heard, I devoted myself wholly to seeking out the kind of imitation necessary for these poems.

Whereupon Peri appeals to the distinction between intervallic and continuous "speech," saying that the former

> could in part be hastened and made to take an intermediate course, lying between the slow and suspended movements of song and the swift and rapid movements of speech, and that it could be adapted to my purpose (as they adapted it in reading poems and heroic verses) and made to approach that other kind of speech which they called "continuata."

He then describes in more technical terms how he accomplished his purpose:

> I knew likewise that in our speech some words are so intoned that harmony can be based upon them and that in the course of speaking it passes through many others that are not so intoned until it returns to another that will bear a progression to a fresh consonance. And having in mind those inflections and accents that serve us in our grief, in our joy, and in similar states, I caused the bass to move in time to these, either more or less, following the passions, and I held it firm throughout the false and true proportions until, running through various notes, the voice of the speaker came to a word that, being intoned in familiar speech, opened the way to a fresh harmony.

Peri concludes his description as follows:

> And therefore, just as I should not venture to affirm that this is the manner of singing used in the fables of the Greeks and Romans, so I have come to believe that it is the only one our music can give us to be adapted to our speech.[14]

The idea governing Caccini's foreword to his *Le nuove musiche* (1602) is not the rejection of polyphony and its replacement by monody but the improvement of solo singing itself, the replacement of poor practices by good ones. He claims to have introduced at some earlier time two important innovations into solo singing: the expressive use of certain types of ornamentation and the new style of expressive recitative over a sustained bass.

Both innovations are brought under the general Platonic theory of the dominant position of the words, to which the musical aspects are subservient, and the discussions of the Camerata of Giovanni de' Bardi are specified as seminal in the appearance of the new style. The reason for the publication of the collection of songs and particularly for the foreword is given as the lack of understanding and the misuse of his manner of singing and the persistence of reprehensible practices.

Caccini has devised his new ornaments, he says, "to avoid that old manner of running division which has been hitherto used, being indeed more proper for wind and stringed instruments than for the voice." The criticism of divisions is amplified somewhat further on in the foreword. They have been used, Caccini maintains, not because they are necessary to a good style of singing, "but rather for a certain tickling of the ears of those who do not well understand what it is to sing passionately; for if they did, undoubtedly divisions would have been abhorred, there being nothing more contrary to passion than they are." Ornamentation is justified, then, only if it is expressive. But the indiscriminate use of expressive ornamentation is also reprehensible, for it should be used only where the words require it, only where it reinforces "the conceit and meaning" of the text.[15]

In addition to the affective use of ornamentation, Caccini discusses the use of the new monodic style, referring to "a certain noble neglect of the song, passing now and then through certain dissonances, holding the bass note firm." Toward the end of the foreword, he says, "I call that the noble manner of singing which is used without tying a man's self to the ordinary measure of time, making many times the value of the notes less by half, and sometimes more, according to the conceit of the words, whence proceeds that excellent kind of singing with a graceful neglect, whereof I have spoken before." This is of course the technique that singers subsequently rediscovered or reinvented time and again during the course of operatic history so that they might become vocal actors rather than simply singers. Caccini gives the aim of the new style as the imitation of the concepts and character of the words. This is to be accomplished with passionate chords and passionate expression in singing. He has made little use, he says, of the art of counterpoint. But he does not concern himself with denouncing polyphony as such. What he is critical of instead is the "common practice" of performing polyphonic madrigals with a single voice, for "the single part of the soprano, sung as a solo, could have no effect by itself." Caccini tries to establish his priority in the actual creation and use of the new expressive style, which obviously was regarded as an extremely important innovation by those active in originating it.[16]

There are thus three aesthetic controversies taking place more or less simultaneously: one within polyphony itself, under the head of *seconda prattica;* another between polyphony and monody, under the head of *stile rappresentativo* or *stile recitativo;* and a third within solo song, which concerns both ornamentation and the derivation of solo song from polyphony. This third sphere contains two separate issues—the indulgence of virtuosity, with its aim of purely auditory delight, and the performance of polyphonic works as accompanied song. The reforms of both these practices have the same basis; indeed, all the innovations of this decisive period rest on common principles and values: the primacy of the words, in respect of both rhythm and meaning, and, based on this, the primacy of affective expression.

But there were also expressive features of sixteenth-century polyphony that did not provoke aesthetic controversy. In the view of Joachim Burmeister, as presented in his *Musica poetica* (Rostrock, 1606), the polyphonic motets of Orlandus Lassus contain a variety of "figures" that in part parallel those of formal rhetoric and in part are peculiar to music. This conception, like the conception of *musica poetica* itself, is found in German treatises starting in the seventeenth century rather than in Italian ones, and it is to be distinguished from the Italian appeal to expressive speech and the recitation of poetry as models to be imitated by dramatic monody in respect of their inflection and accent. The Italian conception, unlike that of the German theorists, is not really a rhetorical one. Burmeister is apparently an innovator in this field, and the music he finds exemplary was in fact written by a Netherlandish composer, not an Italian one.

The figures Burmeister uncovers in Lassus's music are both expressive and structural. An analysis of a motet presented by the theorist reveals the figures as devices of structural elaboration and shows that the musical form is composed in its entirety of a succession of figures. But the expressive character of the figures is also evident. A figure such as the *climax,* for example—a rising sequential repetition—is obviously both structural and expressive. For the most part, the figures are types of repetition applied to a short homophonic passage, and again there can be no question that the types of repetition— like the homophonic section itself—are expressive as well as structural. For homophony, with its syllabic treatment of words and its environment of imitative polyphony, provides a striking contrast to the prevailing texture. The figures, in fact, are suggestive of two other manifestations of expressiveness. They seem similar to *musica reservata,* an esoteric or arcane style of music and performance that was restricted to a circle of connoisseurs or initiates. They also seem akin to the use of *musica ficta* in the Netherlands motet, which was "secret" in the view of Edward Lowinsky—which could very well be what *musica reservata* signifies.[17] In any event, neither *musica reservata* nor the symbolic use of *musica ficta* produced any descriptive account or written theory at all, while the "rhetorical" figures were followed, belatedly, by an extensive theoretical literature, although hardly an aesthetic one.

Vincenzo Giustiniani's *Discorso sopra la musica* (1628) allows us to see how the monodic "revolution" appeared in the whole context of Italian music after a lapse of a quarter century. The new recitative style is seen as one type of music among many, a particular innovation in a series of expressive innovations due to individual singers and composers. The historical perspective, which is Giustiniani's explicit purpose but which was attached from the beginning to new styles of expression, tells of a succession of novelties that appeared in different cities and courts as well as at different times. Indeed, it may be Gesualdo whom Giustiniani regards as the most important of the innovators:

> And from all these things there can be seen clearly what I have said above; that is, that the mode and manner of singing varies from time to time according to the various tastes of the gentlemen and great princes who delight in them, just as happens in the mode of dress, in which fashions are constantly renewed, according to what is introduced in the courts of the great; as, for example, in Europe, dress in the mode of France and of Spain.
>
> Besides the variations mentioned in the mode of singing, we see by experience that every nation, every province, indeed every city, has a mode of singing that is as different as possible from the one to the other, and from which comes that saying, *Galli cantant, Hispani ululant, Germani boant, Itali plorant* (the Gauls sing, the Spaniards howl, the Germans bellow, the Italians weep). What is more, in this same Italy, from one place to another, we see variety in style and air, as, for example, the air *Romanesca* is singular and reputed most beautiful and sung with great delight by everyone, as exquisite and suited to receive all kinds of ornament and accompanied richly and with great facility; and similarly the air called *Fantinella*. In Sicily there are particular and different airs according to the different localities, so that in Palermo there will be one air, in Messina another, another in Catania, and another in Syracuse. Similarly in the other cities of that realm; and so in other localities in Italy, such as Genoa, Milan, Florence, Bergamo, Urbino, Foligno and Norcia.[18]

What has become conspicuous to Giustiniani is nothing less than stylistic diversity. This appears—with the question of taste that it entailed—in nearly all its various forms during the sixteenth century, from the styles of individual composers and of older times, through the expressive styles of the dramatic recitative and the *seconda prattica*, to national styles, which had already been described in the medieval epigram cited by Giustiniani and which were to become the occasion of a prolonged debate over taste in the eighteenth century.

Giustiniani, finally, is a man interested in the qualities and values of all the arts; he is a cultivated connoisseur and represents the sensitive but somewhat detached attitude that underlies the whole development of aesthetics.

CHAPTER FOUR

SEVENTEENTH-CENTURY VIEWS

OF OPERA

Italy

lthough the poets and composers who wrote prefaces to librettos and operas early in the seventeenth century refer to various aspects of the whole work they are introducing, these references—which generally pertain to performance and production—are brief and not systematically presented. The chief concern is obviously with the new monodic style itself and—to an increasing extent—also with its origins and early history. But in the writings of Giovanni Battista Doni, particularly in the important *Trattato della musica scenica*[1] (1633–35), there is a systematic and general concern with the overall economy of opera and even with the use of music in types of drama that are largely spoken. With continual reference to the dramatic genres of ancient Greece and Rome and to the various dramatic representations of his own time, Doni discusses such questions as the types of dramatic action to which music is appropriate, the types of music that are applicable, the sections of a given dramatic genre that call for music, the length of dramatic poems in which music is to be used, the length and character of the individual lines of poetry, the use of vocal ornamentation, and the use of instrumental accompaniment. The *favola pastorale,* with its nymphs and stylized shepherds, is particularly suited to music, he says, and music should be used throughout, inclusive of traditional kinds of polyphonic song. Other genres call variously for music; indeed, dialogue is often best spoken rather than sung. Furthermore, if dialogue were spoken, operas would be shorter as well as more varied, their dramatic interest would be enhanced, their acting would be improved, and composers could concentrate on the expression of emotion.

An important feature of Doni's aesthetics is his interest in variety, which is based on a fear of monotony and boredom. This is grounded in a tendency of opera that was evident from the beginning and often commented on, especially when it adhered closely to its original aesthetic of creating an emotionally intensified speech. The traditional appeal to the standard of ancient tragedy is also an important feature of Doni's thought, particularly because of his authoritative scholarship in the field.

Making use of the term *monodia* (monody), probably for the first time, Doni distinguishes three types that are devoted, respectively, to narration, recitation, and expression. Narration is employed for conveying or imitating spoken dialogue, recitation for presenting epic narrative, and expression for conveying affective passages. Song formally regulated in rhythm and phrase structure is not considered as such, although it may be subsumed under expressive monody. Clearly, however, it constitutes a further category of solo singing, for monody really designates dramatic singing and is governed more by verbal than by musical principles.

During the last half of the seventeenth century, Venetian operas were characterized by complexity, confusion, and even incoherence of plot, together with numerous and highly varied roles. The aria became longer and more prominent, sacrificing dramatic quality to purely musical values and to vocal display. These developments stood in striking contrast to the dramatic simplicity and poetic quality of early librettos, and they were accompanied by a new aesthetic that made its appearance in the prefaces of Venetian librettos. Instead of the serious emotional and moral effects sought for originally, the later aesthetic stressed the values of delight and astonishment; it aimed at entertainment rather than edification and emotional impact. From a social point of view, the change was a consequence of a public rather than an aristocratic genre.

In his preface to his libretto *Giasone* (1649), Giacinto Andrea Cicognini tells us that he writes "from mere caprice. My caprice aims simply at delight. To cause delight is in my opinion to adapt oneself to the genius and taste of one's listener or reader." This conveniently, and doubtless correctly, places the blame for the nature of the libretto on the audience. Francesco Sbarra's preface to his libretto *Alessandro vincitor* (1651) maintains similarly that "this species of poetry has today no aim other than to delight, whence one is obliged to accommodate oneself to the custom of the times; if the recitative style was not relieved by *scherzi* . . . it would induce more disgust than delight."[2] Here the roots of the aesthetic are found not only in the social context but in the very nature of operatic recitative, in which boredom was a threat from the very beginning. In the early operas, this danger could be mitigated if not circumvented soberly by a talented composer through recourse to stylistic diversity, just as Doni later recommends. In any event, the new aesthetic of entertainment is characteristic of libretto prefaces throughout the second half of the century, particularly in those of Aurelio Aureli.

In the essay published with his libretto *L'Epulone* (1675), Francesco Frugoni subjected Venetian opera to an extended criticism, thus inaugurating a large critical and satirical literature in operatic aesthetics.[3] The project of criticizing and reforming operatic abuse becomes the chief concern of Italian writings in the field and continues with increasing momentum in the eighteenth century.

The means of expression in opera have become more important than the dramatic purpose, Frugoni maintains. Machines and scenery are overemphasized, and the singers are unconcerned with the dramatic character of their roles. The librettist is unable to further any dramatic values. A central dramatic idea is often not in evidence or is buried under continual episodic diversions. The mixture of serious and comic elements, he recommends, and of serious and comic characters should be carefully regulated. The dialogue should be enjoyable to read throughout, but farcical stage business should play no part in the action. As to the unities of time and place, they need not be strictly adhered to, but they should not be ignored altogether by continual changes of place or by a temporal prolongation that goes on for decades.

Some of the relevance of Frugoni's discussion to the opera of his time can be explained by the fact that his essay is attached to a specimen of the characteristic genre of tragicomedy. But *L'Epulone* is cast nevertheless in the conservative form of a prologue and five acts, and Frugoni also makes the traditional references to Aristotle's *Poetics* to justify his critical position, while in no way elevating this problematic work to the status of a rigid and inviolable set of rules. What obstructed the adoption of the libretto was not only its length and its traditional form but also the length of its lines, which made an attractive musical treatment extremely difficult, if not impossible.

In his *Poetica toscana all'uso* (1691), Giuseppe Salvadori includes a full discussion of the composition of poetry that is written specifically for musical setting.[4] His poetics in general reveals that the aesthetics of entertainment could be found not only in the prefaces of librettos but in a treatise on poetics as well. Drama in general should be brief, Salvadori maintains; dwelling on morality in particular is tiresome. The approval of the audience, however, will justify the deus ex machina, lack of verisimilitude, episodic diversion, exaggeration, and departure from historical accuracy.

Poetry for musical setting, he prescribes, should treat sublime and magnificent subjects in a style that is clear, polished, and sonorous. Dramatic poetry for music is of two kinds: recitative and aria. Recitative is to be set without repetition of words or syllables; it employs blank verse in lines seven and eleven syllables long. Since it is not devised to give pleasure, it should be as short as possible—as few as six lines will often suffice. Although recitative is necessary, he continues, the aria is what the audience enjoys. "Natural" arias consist of rhymed verses of four, six, or eight syllables each—but usually of four verses that make up two sentences, each of which is a complete thought, so that the first may also be restated as the final section. There are also *arie cavate* ("scooped-out" arias): one or two lines that the poet intends as recitative but that the composer treats as an aria, perhaps because they contain a rhymed couplet.

Salvadori counsels the librettist to subordinate himself to the composer and to be familiar with the abilities of the singers. Every scene is to contain an aria, he prescribes, preferably not at the beginning. Sentences should be short and accents should fall on *a* or *o*; this is especially important in aria texts. The libretto as a whole should require between four and seven actors.

These recommendations reflect the radical change that had taken place in opera during the course of the seventeenth century. Recitative had lost its position as the foundation of the drama and was regarded as a necessary but potentially tiresome constituent. Its place was taken by the aria, which was increasingly dedicated to purely musical pleasure and to virtuosity, whereas, originally, pieces defined by musical values had been admitted primarily to relieve the intensity or the impending monotony of dramatic recitation. Thus, in response to a new purpose, operatic dramaturgy was completely transformed, and accompanying the transformation was a new aesthetic, which gradually gave way to a satirical and critical reaction.

The shift from acceptance and endorsement to criticism can in fact be witnessed in the writings of one man, Gianvincenzo Gravina, whose favorable attitude toward operatic practices, expressed in a late seventeenth-century essay, became disapproval in the eighteenth century, when he was a critic of unparalleled severity. In 1692, the text of a musical pastorale, *L'Endimione*, was published, written largely by Alessandro Guidi but calling also on the collaboration of Queen Christina of Sweden.[5] Guidi was an Arcadian, a member of an academy with pastoral ideals, and his pastorale had been performed in 1691 at a meeting of the Arcadians in Rome. When the publication appeared the following year, it included Gravina's essay, which may very well have been influenced in its views by the surrounding circumstances but which in any event gave no indication of its author's subsequent advocacy, based on the standard of Greek tragedy, of unrhymed verse and of quantitative poetry. No fault was found with the accentual meter and rhyme of *L'Endimione*. Nor was any objection raised to the use of love as the central theme, or to changes made in the myth on which the poem was based, or to the use of only three characters, which limited the possibility of a complex action, or to the mixture of comedy and tragedy, or even to the combination of good and evil intentions in the individual characters—all features repeatedly censured in operatic criticism.

At the very end of the century, the Neapolitan librettist and producer

Andrea Perrucci provides a final instance of the acceptance of entertainment as the controlling purpose of drama and opera. His treatise *Dell'arte rappresentativa premediatata ed all'improviso* (1699), however, is concerned primarily with practical techniques for avoiding mishaps on stage and for securing a smooth performance.[6] It is characteristic of the Italian theatrical perspective that both spoken drama and opera are included, as are improvised drama as well as that which is fully written out. The state of the Italian theater at the end of the century, which the treatise reveals incidentally, seems to cry out for reform, but Perrucci's purely practical purpose is unconcerned with aesthetic improvement. His objections to obscenity, for example, or to the use of forty or fifty characters in a single drama are purely practical: obscenity will provoke objections by the upper classes and the church, and numerous characters spell high costs and create confusion in entrances and exits. When aesthetic factors are involved in the recommendations, they are simply by-products of practices that are introduced for other purposes.

An aesthetics of entertainment, then, persisted in Italian operatic writings until the end of the century, not seriously contested by pleas or programs for reform. Although French drama became an important source of operatic plots, French neoclassical aesthetics, with its uncompromising hostility toward opera, had relatively little effect on the prevailing Italian attitudes. French criticism of Italian poetry, however, directed mostly and originally against the ornate, complex, mannered, and erotic style made prominent by Giambattista Marino (1569–1625), may have played a part in the simplification of Venetian opera that seems to have begun during the last quarter of the century. Starting in 1690, French criticism was seconded by the foundation of the Arcadian Academies, first in Rome and subsequently throughout Italy, which similarly combatted Marinism and urged the adoption of a simple style, attaching their ideal to the fancied simple life of ancient shepherds and fostering the adoption by Italian poets of pastoral pseudonyms and pastoral costumes. Ancient tragedy and precepts supposedly derived from Aristotle's *Poetics* represented other important Arcadian ideals that were comparable to the neoclassical thought that shaped French drama and opera. One concrete outcome of the Arcadian movement was the increased importance of the lyrical pastorale, which had played a central part in the creation and the early history of Italian opera. But the full effect of the Arcadian movement, and of French criticism as well, was felt only in the eighteenth century.

France

French views of opera until about 1660 are necessarily views of Italian opera since French opera did not exist before that time. But even subsequently, operatic aesthetics in France is centered less on French opera than on a comparison of this opera with that of Italy. This can easily be understood not only by the priority of Italian opera and the attention it attracted but also by its export, which imposed a foreign art and foreign musicians on the other countries of Europe. Thus, Italian opera was known to Frenchmen not only through the isolated reports of travelers in Italy but also through the performance of Italian operas in Paris. What reaction these performances produced, however, especially during the tenure of Cardinal Mazarin (Mazzarino) as prime minister in the 1640s and 1650s, was not really aesthetic but political and financial. Although Italian opera embodied an emotional extravagance that was foreign to the French temperament, it was seen mostly as an insult to French national pride and an insupportable financial burden. The complex political, literary, and artistic history of French and Italian interaction made it inevitable that, when French opera appeared, it would provoke primarily an endless aesthetic controversy, with Italian opera as its antagonist.

In 1659 the *Pastorale d'Issy* was performed, with a libretto by Pierre Perrin and music by Robert Cambert. Two years later, Perrin wrote an extended letter that was sharply critical of Italian opera and of course highly favorable to his pastorale.[7] The librettists of Italian opera, he states, are simply poets, with no special knowledge of how to write lines suitable for musical setting, and recitative is made unavoidable for them because of large amounts of dialogue and complexities of plot. But the *Pastorale d'Issy* shows that a drama can be made up entirely of scenes that call only for singing and the expression of the passions. Italian singing, he continues, allows too many liberties, the ornaments are affected and too frequent, and the whole style has a vulgar effect. French singing, in contrast, is more reasonable and regular, more fashionable and finer. Italian operas last six or seven hours, and a single number can contain fifty or sixty lines. The *Pastorale d'Issy*, however, lasts only an hour and a half, and the numbers contain only ten or twelve lines each; thus, there is greater variety, and none of the voices becomes monotonous. He has also fostered variety, Perrin adds, by not allowing any of the roles to dominate the singing unduly and by employing varied ritornellos and symphonies. As far as poetic style is concerned, not only are Italian librettos unintelligible to the French, but they also make use of affected figures of speech and transpositions of syntax, while the *Pastorale* is written in French that is pure and direct and that presents a beautiful and natural expression of the passions. Finally, Perrin asserts, castrati are horrible to women and laughable to men. They present a striking contrast to the singers of the *Pastorale d'Issy*, whose behavior is entirely natural.

The most influential of all French pronouncements on opera in the seventeenth century is Charles de Saint-Evremond's "Letter to the Duke of Buckingham" (1677 or 1678). "Now how is it possible," Saint-Evremond asks, "to avoid being tired with the Recitativo, which has neither the Charm of Singing, nor the agreeable Energy of Speech?" He finds opera tedious in general because it does not occupy the mind. In this respect, both the action and the poetry are objectionable. To have everything sung, furthermore, is unnatural:

There is another Thing in Operas so contrary to Nature, that I cannot be reconciled to it; and that is the singing of the whole Piece, from beginning to end, as if the Persons represented were ridiculously match'd, and had agreed to treat in Musick both the most common, and most important Affairs of Life. Is it to be imagin'd that a Master calls his Servant, or sends him on an Errand, singing; that one Friend imparts a Secret to another, singing; That Men deliberate in Council, singing; That Orders in time of Battle are given, singing; and That Men are melodiously kill'd with Sward and Darts. This is the downright way to lose the Life of Representation, which without doubt is preferable to that of Harmony. . . .

I pretend not, however, to banish all manner of singing from the Stage: There are some things which ought to be Sung, and others that may be Sung without trespassing against Reason or Decency; Vows, Prayers, Praises, Sacrifices, and generally all that relates to the Service of the Gods, have been Sung in all Nations, and in all times; Tender and Mournful Passions express themselves naturally in a sort of querulous Tone; the Expressions of Love in its Birth; the Irresolution of a Soul toss'd by different Motions, are proper Matters of Stanzas, as Stanzas are for Musick. . . . The Grecians made admirable Tragedies, where they had some singing; the Italians and the French make bad ones, where they sing all. . . .

It remains that I give you my Advice in general for all Comedies, where any singing is used; and that is to leave to the Poet's Discretion the whole Management of the Piece. The Musick must be made for the Words, rather than the Words for the Musick. The Musician is to follow the Poet's Directions; only, in my Opinion, Baptist Lulli is to be exempted, who knows the Passions better, and enters farther into the Heart of Man than the Authors themselves.[8]

Saint-Evremond goes on to discuss national differences in operatic style and in style of singing, notably the differences between Italy and France. He concerns himself finally with the matter of machines and gods, disapproving of both. As for machines, "The more they surprize, the more they divert the Mind from attending to the Discourse; and the more admirable they are, the less Tenderness and exquisite Sense they leave in us, to be touch'd and charm'd with the Musick." As for gods, the Italians have returned to plays that are not so fabulous, while French opera must appear very extravagant to those who are true judges of the probable and the wonderful. "That which vexes me most," he concludes, "at this our Fondness for Operas, is, That they tend directly to ruin the finest Thing we have, I mean TRAGEDY, than which nothing is more proper to elevate the Soul, or more capable to form the Mind."[9]

What are we to make of this rather severe view of opera? For one thing, Saint-Evremond is not nearly so uncompromising as he was generally thought to be; it was common to cite only the most negative sentiments of his letter. But almost every criticism he presents is modified by a more positive attitude that is revealed shortly afterward. Thus, it turns out that music and singing are not always objectionable in drama, that a great composer (Lully) can even tell the poet what to do, that the wonderful has a place in opera if it is used with discretion. While singing will not do for mundane affairs, it is peculiarly appropriate for expressing the passions.

After the qualifications and modifications are taken into account, however, there remains a core of fundamental disapproval that calls for explication. In strange contradiction to his conversance with music, Saint-Evremond clearly has a limited tolerance for it. He finds it appropriate and even pleasing in some of its uses and for a short time, but it occupies a low place in his scale of values, which awards the highest rank to language and reason. As a matter of sensory delight, music cannot be taken very seriously. It then follows, in the combination of the two realms, that language and reason must be dominant and music must know its place. Only a strict alternation of speech and song is acceptable, and indeed opera has often adopted such a dramaturgy. Otherwise, music will distract us from mental activity and then bore us because it cannot sustain our interest. The chief implication of this view of opera is that recitative should be eliminated.

Intrinsic to Saint-Evremond's conception of opera is the idea that it is a type of tragedy, but a type subject to the aesthetics of spoken drama rather than one with its own principles. Thus, an aesthetics of entertainment, inclusive of spectacle and divertissement, is ruled out. Opera is in competition with tragedy, of which it is a corruption, for it is morally as well as intellectually inferior. That it can be an intensification of tragedy, or an alternative but equally powerful form of tragedy, is a possibility of which Saint-Evremond cannot conceive.

The attack on opera by Boileau (Nicolas Boileau-Despréaux) was directed against Philippe Quinault, Lully's librettist. Boileau found fault primarily with the use of love as a central theme. This represented a corruption of the nature of tragedy, in his view, and at the same time a threat to public morality. In his *Satire X* (1692–93), Boileau describes the danger of taking to the opera a lady brought up in maidenly virtue and taught to regulate her desires according to the dictates of her duty:

> How will she react to the seductive strains of soft music, to the suggestive dances, to the heroes' sweet enchanting voices? To discourses that treat only of love, spoken in the sugary tones of sweet Rinaldo or sighed by some mad Roland? Telling her that to Love and Love alone, like some supreme deity, she must sacrifice all, even unto her most carefully guarded virtue? That never too soon can she be fired with passion, that she has been given a tender heart solely that it may be sacrificed on the altar of Love, and other such commonplaces of moral lubricity that Lulli's music instilled with life? [10]

Germany

Views of opera in seventeenth-century Germany were in general not restricted by a purely verbal tradition of drama as they were in France. German authors—although for the most part they belonged to literary societies—gave more weight to music and, instead of finding interference and conflict between the verbal and the musical components of opera, developed theories of a synthesis of all the operatic components. What negative criticism there was had a completely different source, namely, the religious condemnation of theatrical entertainment, which was a more severe counterpart of the secular French concern with the corruption of morals.

Nuremberg's literary society was called the Shepherds of the Pegnitz, a name that indicates that the pastoral tradition was of central importance in Germany, just as it was in Italy. But in the prolonged battle between ancient and modern ideals and achievements, operatic thought in Germany was identified more with the modern world than with the ancient one. The ideas of the Shepherds of the Pegnitz are presented by its leading member, Georg Philipp Harsdörffer, in the conversations of his *Frauenzimmer Gesprächspiele*, which was published in eight volumes from 1641 to 1649.[11] Harsdörffer takes issue with the imitation of the ancients, the authority of Aristotle, and the dramatic unities, espousing instead an aesthetic of theatrical effectiveness based on the synthesis of music, poetry, dance, painting, and stage design. Opera is regarded as the highest form of theater.

Harsdörffer embodied his theories in the spiritual pastorale *Seelewig* (1644), for which music was written by Sigmund Gottlieb Staden.[12] Since

Italian opera was incompatible with the strong German spirit, Harsdörffer maintained, it had to give way to a true German opera that dealt with heroic deeds and Christian virtues. He compared the desired synthesis of the arts with the Pythagorean idea of world harmony, in which divine music harmonizes the dissonances of the world. In opera, similarly, music unites poetry and painting into one whole. But there are not many people, he believes, who are sufficiently talented in all three arts to achieve a perfect synthesis. The novelty and variety of opera, in any event, make it distinctly superior to spoken drama.

Another member of Shepherds of the Pegnitz, Sigmund von Birken, who also wrote librettos, reveals the close connection between the ideal of operatic synthesis and the conception of an ancient or primeval shepherd's art. In his *Teutsche Rede- bind- und Dicht-Kunst*, published in 1679 but written decades before, this primeval art becomes the origin of poetry, of pastoral musical plays, then successively of comedy and tragedy, and ultimately of modern forms of musical drama in which the pure dramatic genres were superceded by generic mixture.[13]

Concern with the historical background of opera took a more characteristically scholarly form in the writings of Hamburg literary figures. Konrad von Höveln, a member of two literary societies in Hamburg, was interested in how opera resembled spoken drama and in how it differed from it. In his *Eren- Danz- Singe Schauspiele-Entwurf* (1663), published under the name Candorin, he developed the view that opera was akin to the ancient Greek dithyramb.[14] Significantly, he found that, in the Aristotelian categories of poetry, epic, lyric, and dithyrambic, all types of drama were classified under dithyramb. It was logical, then, for the composer to be the chief architect of an opera. It was the composer who would know, for one thing, how to write recitative so that the text was not obscured.

A much broader historical picture of literature was presented by Daniel Georg Morhof, a professor of poetry and rhetoric at Kiel, in his *Unterricht von der Teutschen Sprache und Poesie* (1682).[15] He saw opera as an attempt to re-create the ancient unity of poetry, music, dance, and pantomime, which had come apart at the end of antiquity. Because of the complexity of modern music, he believed, this attempt was doomed to fail, but it resulted in a new form of dramatic unity that did not suffer by comparison with the ancient one.

It was not only the popularity of opera but also its complexity that worked to its advantage, for the elaborate nature of the productions necessitated the construction of permanent theaters, while spoken drama was in general presented by itinerant groups. Thus, opera easily advanced to the position of the leading variety of theatrical entertainment, and it was this prominence and popularity, together with its high cost, which made it the object of criticism by Pietist spokesmen. Like the Calvinist critics of theatrical entertainment, the Pietists were particularly incensed by the presentation of pagan myths and of erotic subject matter. Reviving the views and attitudes of the church fathers, they saw opera as the work of the devil, closely comparable to the orgiastic spectacles of Rome. Catholics and orthodox Lutherans came forward to defend the value of opera and even its amenability to moral purposes. In Hamburg in particular, where opera flourished, the conflict was a prolonged and bitter one, particularly in the 1680s. The municipal government intervened, and the faculties of law and theology of the universities of Wittenberg and Rostock debated the question. Their decision was that opera was an acceptable secular form of entertainment under the jurisdiction and control of the government. Patristic writings were therefore not applicable to it, even though it had faults that called for reform. In spite of its resolution in Hamburg, however, the controversy spread to other cities and was carried on well into the eighteenth century.

At the same time, the Hamburg opera won new successes in the 1690s with the operas of Reinhard Keiser and the librettos of Christian Heinrich Postel. In the prefaces to his librettos, Postel presented an influential and diversified series of essays bearing on operatic aesthetics. His fundamental principles were that the taste of the audience was of decisive importance and that opera was a free poetic creation subject neither to the unities of time and place nor to a literal adherence to the source of its plot. Thus, historical, mythological, or religious sources could be altered by omissions or additions for the sake of dramatic effect. Opera was a mixture of fact and fiction in accordance with the laws of poetic fancy; it was a fictional kind of reality. Since its time and space were imaginary, they were not subject to the rules of dramatic unity. Postel used as much of the unities as he felt were applicable or called for by the nature of a given action. Instead of uniformity, therefore, he was able to produce variety. But just as he did not accept the binding force of the dramatic unities, so he did not accept the kind of action that was exemplified by Chinese plays that presented the entire story of a man's life in a performance lasting several days. Opera was to steer a course midway between prescriptive rules and epic discursiveness.

For the most part, Postel's prefaces are devoted understandably to the process of adaptation by which he derived a given libretto from its source. Thus, he discusses the necessity of condensation in respect to a narrative source, the need to shorten a plot or to add a comic figure, the adaptation of classical sources to make them meaningful to modern audiences, and the shortening of Euripides' monologues so that they could be used for singing. His aim in going to any source of the past was to penetrate to the idea or the hidden meaning that underlay the details of the story or drama and to convey this spirit in terms of modern musical-dramatic form.

Views of opera in Germany are fundamentally similar to those in Italy. Both countries are characterized by a frank acceptance of the nature of opera, by a delight in its musical values, and by a primary concern with the pleasure of the audience. The conception is more one of theater than of drama. French operatic thought, in contrast, considers opera chiefly from the viewpoint of spoken drama; opera is more a deviant or corrupt variety of the tragic genus than a type of drama or theater in its own right, with its own characteristics. Such a view easily entails a failure to enjoy or even to accept the constant presence of music, an inability to accept the conventions of the form or to grasp its power. At the same time, in an aristocratic rather than a popular art, comparable in this to Florentine rather than Venetian opera, the audience did not contain the diversity that would raise entertainment to the status of a dominant purpose.

Negative views of opera are found in all three countries, but with characteristic differences. There are moral scruples in France, in addition to a general aesthetic disapproval; in Germany there is religious hostility; while in Italy the critical reactions are really to abuses that can be corrected rather than to opera as such.

Doubtless the most well-founded and forward-looking aesthetic is contained in the German conception of the synthesis of the arts, although some attention is given in all three countries to the character that the operatic action and poetry must assume if they are directed to the success of the resultant combination. A fairly elaborate discussion of this problem can be found in the preface John Dryden wrote to his libretto for *Albion and Albanius* (1685). Dryden's recognition of opera as a separate genre is revealed by his basic principle of following the pattern defined for each poetic genre by its founders. He thus turns to Italian opera as his model. The heart of his discussion, however, is the evaluation of the different properties and qualities of various languages and the study of how English may be adapted to operatic use. As an outstanding example of considerations of this kind, the preface deserves citation at length:

It is almost needless to speak anything of that noble language in which this musical drama was first invented and performed. All who are conversant in the Italian cannot but observe that it is softest, the sweetest, the most harmonious, not only of any modern tongue, but even beyond any of the learned. It seems indeed to have been invented for the sake of poetry and music; the vowels are so abounding in all words, especially in terminations of them, that, excepting some few monosyllables, the whole language ends in them. Then the pronunciation is so manly, and so sonorous, that their very speaking has more of music in it than Dutch poetry and song. It has withal derived so much copiousness and eloquence from the Greek and Latin, in the composition of words and the formation of them, that if, after all, we must call it barbarous, 'tis the most beautiful and most learned of any barbarism in modern tongues. . . . This language has in a manner been refined and purified from the Gothic ever since the time of Dante, which is above four hundred years ago; and the French, who now cast a longing eye to their country, are not less ambitious to possess their elegance in poetry and music; in both which they labour at impossibilities.'Tis true indeed, they have reformed their tongue, and brought both their prose and poetry to a standard; the sweetness, as well as the purity, is much improved by throwing off the unnecessary consonants, which make their spelling tedious, and their pronunciation harsh; but, after all, as nothing can be improved beyond its own species, or farther than its original nature will allow . . . so neither can the natural harshness of the French, or their perpetual ill accent, be ever refined into perfect harmony like the Italian. The English has yet more natural disadvantages than the French; our original Teutonic, consisting most in monosyllables, and those encumbered with consonants, cannot possibly be freed from those inconveniences. The rest of our words . . . are some relief in Poetry, and help us to soften our uncouth numbers; which, together with our English genius, incomparably beyond the trifling of the French, in all the nobler parts of verse, will justly give us the pre-eminence. But, on the other hand, the effeminacy of our pronunciation (a defect common to us and the Danes), and our scarcity of female rhymes, have left the advantage of musical composition for songs, though not for recitative, to our neighbors. . . .

'Tis no easy matter, in our language, to make words so smooth, and numbers so harmonious, that they shall almost set themselves. . . . The necessity of double rhymes, and ordering of the words and numbers for the sweetness of the voice, are the main hinges on which an opera must move; and both of these are without the compass of any art to teach another to perform, unless Nature, in the first place, has done her part by enduing the poetry with that nicety of hearing that the discord of sounds in words shall as much offend him as a seventh in music would a good composer. . . . The chief secret is the choice of words; and, by this choice, I do not here mean elegancy of expression, but propriety of sound, to be varied according to the nature of the subject. . . .

The same reasons which depress thought in an opera have a stronger effect upon the words, especially in our language; for there is no main-taining the purity of English in short measures, where the rhyme returns so quick, and is so often female, or double rhyme, which is not natu-ral to our tongue, because it consists too much of monosyllables, and those, too, most commonly clogged with consonants; for which reason I am often forced to coin new words, revive some that are antiquated, and botch others; as if I had not served out my time in poetry, but was bound apprentice to some doggerel rhymer, who makes songs to tunes and sings them for a livelihood.[16]

To be sure, Dryden's deliberations conclude with a feeling that the oper-atic libretto subjects the poet to foreign aims. Just as Beethoven was to feel relieved, after his struggle with opera, to be able to return to "his art," so Dryden continued his reflections as follows:

It is true, I have not been often put to this drudgery; but where I have, the words will sufficiently show that I was then a slave to the composition, which I will never be again: it is my part to invent, and the musician's to humour that invention. I may be counselled, and will always follow my friend's advice where I find it reasonable; but will never part with the power of the militia.[17]

Indeed, any poet or dramatist will necessarily feel the restrictions he must accept in writing a libretto, unless of course he is also writing the operatic score in its entirety, as Wagner was to do. But it is possible for the libret-tist not to resent or be irked by his task and instead to regard the essential restrictions as the welcome rules of his artistic project. Then he will incor-porate them as part of the problem to be solved and therefore as part of the intrinsic framework that is indispensable to a creative project of any kind.

Since operatic aesthetics is understandably produced by literary figures rather than composers—by librettists, poets, dramatists, literary historians, scholars, and essayists—it is concerned continually with the special demands that opera makes on poetry and on drama. Yet when an author becomes a librettist, a change often occurs in his attitude, and his originally hostile evaluation of opera gives way to a positive consideration of the possibilities and the character of the synthesis.

PART THREE

THE EIGHTEENTH

CENTURY

CHAPTER FIVE

GALANT AESTHETICS

T he dominant aesthetic ideal in eighteenth-century music is one of expressive vocal melody that has a direct and wide appeal. The new conception seems in some ways to be a repetition of the Italian ideas of around 1600. Both the earlier and the later aesthetics are concerned with vocal expressiveness, for example, and both take issue with an older polyphonic art that is connected with mathematical rules. But while the earlier aesthetic is directed to the intense expression of passions, the later, galant aesthetic has its aim in clearly articulated melody that is sensuous, elegant, and moving.

The chief spokesman in Germany for this new aesthetics of melody is Johann Mattheson, the prolific Hamburg theorist and aesthetician. Mattheson's treatises and articles cover a remarkably wide variety of musical matters. The general point of view that runs through them all is first made evident in *Das Neu-Eröffnete Orchestre* (1713), for the full title of the work proposes to reveal "how a cultivated man (*Galant Homme*) may achieve a complete conception of the nobility and dignity of music, shape his taste (*Gout*) in this way," and so on. The influence of French culture on the German Enlightenment is at once apparent. But since the influence of Italian music and of English ideas was also of great importance, Mattheson's *galant homme* was a gentleman of international breadth of culture. Indeed, *galanterie,* which is acquired by "good taste" and "sound judgment," Mattheson finds to be as essential to a musical composition as melody and harmony.

The galant is illuminated continually by its antithesis, the traditional learned polyphony of the German church musicians. To a great extent, then, the conflict of new and old is grounded in a contrast of secular and religious, of an urbane, basically international style and a specifically German, more provincial, contrapuntal complexity. The ideal Mattheson espouses and expounds is really derived from opera, the genre, itself international, that was favored both by Mattheson and by Hamburg. But aesthetics seems to thrive on controversy, even to demand it: on the conflict, typically, of new and old and of simplicity and complexity. Thus, Germany, with its powerful tradition of church polyphony on which there impinged the attractive newer style of secular melody, was fertile ground for aesthetics. Contrapuntal technique and complexity continually called forth critical attacks that served as the foil for newer ideals. Mathematics was pitted against rhetoric, craft against taste, and learning against the galant. Behind the aesthetic conflict there was often a contest of social ideals—of the church with the aristocracy, of the town cantor with the court kapellmeister. And much as in the later sixteenth century and the earlier seventeenth, the foundation of the new musical style could not be provided by training and rules. Instead, the traditional contrapuntal curriculum had its competitor in auditory experience, taste, and judgment, and the composer turned for guidance to principles of rhetoric and aesthetics.

Thus, galant aesthetics was closely associated with musical poetics. The two fields share the same treatises, and their kinship can be traced to the treatises on *musica poetica* that began to appear in the later part of the sixteenth century. These treatises represented a new type of *musica practica* that was occasioned by the advent of the printed and preserved musical work, which in turn produced a new conception of the autonomy of the activity of composition. The science of counterpoint was enlarged into the theory of the musical work, an expansion that took place under the auspices of rhetoric, which similarly had long since become the sponsor of poetry and the literary arts. The compositional methods of an oration as well as its formal and expressive techniques were all gradually applied to musical composition, a process that took place essentially in Germany, where rhetorical tradition and education were particularly well established and vigorously pursued. It is in the treatises on *musica poetica*, then, that rhetoric gave rise first to a theory of musical composition and subsequently to an aesthetics closely related to composition.

It is important to note, however, that the rhetorical conception of music was applied originally to polyphony and continued to influence polyphonic composition throughout the Baroque. But it played a prominent role in the aesthetics of dramatic monody as well, and it must in fact be regarded as a general feature of musical thought, applicable to self-conscious musical art of every type. The only specification that may be valid is that rhetorical ideas seem to possess a positive connotation in music. Thus, in galant aesthetics, rhetoric is connected with melodic style and contrasted with the mathematics of polyphony as good taste is to bad.

The basic priority of sense over reason becomes an explicit issue in *Das*

Neu-Eröffnete Orchestre in Mattheson's discussion of the interval of the fourth.[1] From a mathematical point of view, the fourth is a consonance since it is a product of the ratio 4:3. But Mattheson refuses to make mathematics decisive in music, appealing instead to hearing. The fourth thus becomes either a consonance or a dissonance, depending on its musical context.

The importance of depicting the affections in music is another consequence of Mattheson's appeal to hearing rather than reason. His concern with affections can be seen readily in his discussion of style and genre, particularly in the area of secular music. He distinguishes and describes not only church, chamber, and theater styles but those of Italy, France, England, and Germany as well. His treatment of opera, the genre he prefers to all others, includes a long series of affections: "There a composer has a true opportunity to give free reign to his inventions! There he can depict in a highly natural way and in numberless diversity love, jealousy, hatred, gentleness, impatience, horror, dignity, baseness, splendor, despair, storm, tranquillity, even heaven, earth, sea, hell."[2] The outstanding German composer, in Mattheson's view, was Reinhard Keiser, whose skill was manifest mostly in the newer musical styles and genres and in opera in particular. It was Keiser, the leading Hamburg opera composer, who led the way in the modernization and enlightenment of German music so that it might be freed of its subjection to foreign styles.

Das Neu-Eröffnete Orchestre also contains a description of the affective properties of the various keys. Mattheson starts with an acceptance of the basic distinction of the major and minor thirds as joyous and sad and adds to this a closer characterization of the sixteen most common scales.[3]

The chief opponent of Mattheson's ideas was Johann Heinrich Buttstedt, who took issue with *Das Neu-Eröffnete Orchestre* in a treatise entitled *Ut, mi, sol, re, fa, la, tota musica* (1717). Buttstedt bases his discussion on a traditional mathematical conception of musical theory, which he cites from Andreas Werckmeister's translation (1699–1700) of Agostino Steffani's *Quanto certezza habbia da suoi principii la musica* (1695). This mathematical conception of theory is then turned against Mattheson's idea of the galant: "Then how can a tyro of the present, much less a mere amateur and galant *homme,* conform to rules that were in use over a hundred years ago and that belong only to theory but not so much to practice, and learn music from them or form an adequate conception of it?"[4] Buttstedt subsequently objects in turn to Mattheson's method of judging the fourth, to his evaluation of national styles, and to his description of the affective properties of the keys. In response to the criticism, Mattheson defended his views in *Das Beschützte Orchestre* (1717). The brief *Reflexions* of 1720 reaffirms the affective character of the keys. The keys are necessary to the beauty of melody, Mattheson maintains, for each melody has its particular, appropriate key.

In *Das Forschende Orchestre* (1721), Mattheson opposes the mathematical conception of musical theory and investigates the foundation of the system of the affections. The first part of the treatise deals with the sensory basis of music, with its auditory effect, and the second part with theories of the interval of the fourth. In the first part, Mattheson maintains that music is perceived through sense, that it belongs to the realm of sensation and has essentially nothing to do with understanding. He appeals to John Locke in support of the conception that sensation is the source of all ideas. By means of sensuous feeling, our emotional disposition teaches us to know things and then arranges its ideas accordingly. There is not even a knowledge of virtue and thus a science of morality that is inherent in the soul and does not arise from the senses. Instead, morality depends on time and place, on people and circumstances. The senses are the primary and unique source of feelings. Understanding can only supplement, make abstractions, develop these through complex ideas, or devise additions to them. Music in particular is addressed to the ear. Musical knowledge comes originally from the senses, has its foundation in them, and achieves in them its action and its goal. Thus, the true goal of music is an honest pleasure that resides in hearing. Understanding participates in the judgment of music, but hearing must play the first, best, greatest, and final role.

Music accordingly contains its own sensuous purpose of loveliness and grace, which is not to be identified with its moral purpose; the first is its external aim, the second its inner one, which is more an effect than a true intention. The pleasure of hearing in itself, Mattheson believes, inclines the soul to virtue.[5] As this section of *Das Forschende Orchestre* reveals, Mattheson believes in the cosmic harmony and divine provenance of music and in its ethical and religious effect, both of which remained characteristic of the German outlook even into the nineteenth century; but he has clearly separated out from these traditional conceptions a specifically aesthetic viewpoint that exists alongside them.

In *Kern Melodischer Wissenschaft* (1737), Mattheson undertakes programmatically to establish the priority of melody over harmony, taking explicit issue with Rameau, the most important representative of the opposite point of view. Melody is "natural," Mattheson maintains, harmony "artificial." In this treatise, which was expressly intended as an initial study for *Der vollkommene Capellmeister* (1739), Mattheson explicitly established melody as the heart of galant style.

To be sure, the scope of *Der vollkommene Capellmeister* transcends the single aim of defining the properties of melody, but to develop an aesthetics of melody remains its central purpose. The foreword of the treatise contains an extended discussion of the mathematical view of music. Mattheson combats the belief that all changes in mood have their basis in the various external relations of the tones. "The beloved monochord," he maintains, "is incapable of establishing a single musical truth, but only some harmonic ones of moderate significance, yet which always are appealed to the ear." Ethical truths also cannot be derived from the pure size or sound of intervals, nor can we explain the affections and their cause in this way: "However one defines the mathematical relations of sounds and their quantities, no real connection with the passions of the soul can ever be drawn from this alone. For besides natural science and pure philosophy, other arts are needed here, moral and rhetorical relations."[6]

We should examine not ratios, Mattheson urges, but musical works, from which we can understand the composer's soul and his mastery of the human mind and emotions:

> A perfect understanding of the human emotions, which certainly are not to be measured by the mathematical yardstick, is of much greater importance to melody and its composition than the understanding of tones. . . . It is not so much good proportion but rather the apt usage of the intervals and keys that establishes the beautiful, moving, and natural quality in melody and harmony. Sounds, in themselves, are neither good nor bad; but they become good and bad according to the way in which they are used.

Mattheson turns to painting to reinforce his argument:

> We do not praise the brush, but the painter. Just as paint and brushes, mathematics then has also been able to offer its services in love; but even if a person has totally correct proportions in facial and bodily features, so that one might call her mathematically beautiful, she could still be without charm and compassion. . . .
>
> I have seen many portraits painted, but I have never seen a ruler used therewith. There are countless subjective proportions that are painted by great artists but that can be measured by none. I mean human affections, which are revealed and altered in the most minute facial features and the slightest turnings of the eyes, muscles, lines, etc., in an inexplicable manner. There mathematics ceases entirely, and true beauty really first begins.[7]

Not a single famous actor, musician, or composer, Mattheson concludes, has been able to construct even a simple melody that was of any value on the feeble foundations of mathematics or geometry.

Der vollkommene Capellmeister is divided into three parts, of which the first is devoted to preliminaries, the second to melodic composition, and the third to counterpoint and polyphony. Rhetorical concepts and modes of thought can be found throughout the work, but they are particularly evident in part 2, in which the striking interrelation of the poetics and aesthetics of melody is clearly fostered by the pervasive influence of rhetoric on both fields. In part 1, the discussion of styles (chapter 10) is dependent on rhetorical stylistic categories, and the discussion of gesture (chapter 6) makes explicit reference to oratory. In part 3, the last section (chapter 26) is conceived as a treatment of *elocutio*, under the head of *executio*. The other rhetorical functions all appear in the course of part 2, *inventio* in chapter 4 and *dispositio, elaboratio,* and *decoratio* most explicitly in chapter 14 (although there is also a discussion of melodic ornaments in chapter 3). The parts of an oration—*exordium, narratio, propositio, confirmatio, confutatio,* and *peroratio*—come under the function of *dispositio* and are accordingly treated in chapter 14.

Chapter 5, which is entitled "The Art of Composing a Good Melody," is really an extended discussion of melodic aesthetics. To Mattheson, melody is the foundation of the entire art of composition. He is therefore particularly upset "when it is insistently maintained against all reason *that melody arises from harmony and all rules for the first must be derived from the second"*— a clear reference to Rameau. Pursuing his argument, Mattheson supports it with the notion of imitation. "A piece for one voice even without accompaniment can very well exist, but a so-called harmony without melody is only an empty sound and no vocal piece at all. All arrangement of sound without imitation means little or nothing, but this imitation is grounded in individual melodies." Subsequently, *"Natural patterns give rise to artificial ones.* Art is a servant of nature and appointed for its imitation."[8] While even the most beautiful harmony is often insipid without melody, Mattheson maintains, almost all the force of ideas, passions, and their expression depends on nothing other than simple melody.

In the detailed discussion of melodic beauty, which makes up the largest part of the chapter, Mattheson takes up four basic properties in turn: accessibility, clarity, fluidity, and loveliness. To these there must be added an affecting or moving nature, which the four properties help produce. For each property Mattheson gives a number of rules, for a total of thirty-three in all, each of which he undertakes to explain briefly.

In connection with accessibility, every melody should contain something familiar so that it will be pleasing and easy for the ear to grasp. But familiar passages should be mixed with others that are appropriate but less familiar. Everything forced, farfetched, and difficult in nature must be avoided.

Passages of this kind are often written by composers who become eccentric because they lack natural fertility of invention. For the most part, nature should be followed, and in this the composer can learn from the amateur. Artifice should be set aside or concealed, or it should be introduced skillfully and unobtrusively. Here the French are to be followed more than the Italians, and Lully is an excellent model. We should also keep melodies within the range of an octave or even less so that every moderate voice can sing them and so that the various passages may be well connected. Brief melodies, finally, are easier to retain than long ones, although they should have value as well as brevity. In general, ease refers to the listener; the composer may have secretly perspired in producing it.

As far as clarity is concerned, the articulations of speech must be observed exactly, a rule that applies to instrumental melody as well as vocal. It is also important that an emotion be set up as a principal goal in each melody. Mattheson emphasizes this rule at length. The composer must direct his intent continuously and particularly to his passion, and he must feel it himself and know how to imitate it naturally, or he will not be able to excite it in others. Without such a representation the melody will be only "an empty singing and sounding" (p. 141). Even technical skill such as correct emphasis and accurate rendition of the words arises from emotion. This is quite evident in oratory. "What do our teachers in the pulpit do; do they not perspire; do they not rejoice; do they not weep; do they not clap their hands together; do they not threaten? Who will say that this belongs much more to mere cold instruction than to vital emotion? Who can contradict Plato and David in this?" (p. 142). Rhetoric and music can hardly be separated here.

Mattheson continues with the rules for clarity. The meter, or syllabic rhythm, as the soul of the melody, must be single; the composer should not alter it lightly, "for it would be as though he also wanted to arouse at the same time another passion in an unexpected way" (p. 143). Also, the divisions of a melody should have the same number of measures, especially in short and lively movements, and cadences should fall on accented beats. In addition, we must carefully observe verbal accent. And just as there is a verbal accent, Mattheson states, so is there a tonal accent in instrumental pieces; verbal prosody has a counterpart in tonal prosody. Furthermore, we must reinforce the stress of emphatic words with some kind of musical stress. The verbal emphasis may be discovered, Mattheson suggests, by recasting a proposition as question and answer: "Our life is a journey" becomes "What is our life?" "A journey." Thus, the stress is to fall on "journey" (p. 145).

The following rule, to apply all embellishments with great discretion, is obviously of central importance in galant style, and Mattheson cites a few examples to emphasize it. Closely related to this is the admonition to strive for a noble simplicity in expression. Noble simplicity is uncontrived, undecorated, and natural, with only a single aim. It is necessary also to differentiate different types of style. Vocal style should not be mixed with instrumental either in church, theater, or chamber music, nor should the style of one instrument be confused with that of another. Finally, we should attend not to words but to their significance and in instrumental melody to clarity and speaking tones rather than to multitudes of notes, for "no melody should be without sense, without intent, without emotion, even if without words" (p. 148).

With respect to fluidity, rhythmic patterns or tonal feet should be varied, but the different patterns must be compatible with one another. In addition to this, a given succession of tonal feet should reoccur at corresponding places in the melody. There should be few cadences and sections so as not to obstruct the flow of the melody, and each cadence should be well placed and well prepared. Cadences should also have some connection with what follows them, showing the way, for example, in which the composer plans to continue. Continuity or skillful connection helps melodic flow a great deal, just as transitions do in a good oration. Dotted rhythms are not flowing and should not be used in vocal melodies. Chromaticism and melodic dissonances should also be avoided. Finally, the melody should not be interrupted or held back in its natural progress so that a subordinate voice may take up the theme.

As far as loveliness is concerned, the melody should employ more steps and in general more small intervals than large leaps. But these small intervals should be of different kinds rather than all the same. It is well to search for unmelodic or unsingable passages, classify them into groups, notice what is bad about them, and investigate the cause of their poor sound so that such things can be avoided. Mattheson takes up a number of examples in this connection and derives general rules from them. Similarly, passages that are good should be selected, compiled, and studied as models, and general rules should also be extracted from them. In these recommendations, which are put into practice persuasively in his discussion, Mattheson is really adopting methods used in rhetoric, where there was a tradition of learning and imitating model passages.

Just as in the case of intervals, so in the case of all the parts of a melody—of its phrases, sections, and divisions—the relation of one to another must be coherent; there should be no gross inequalities of parts. Pleasing repetitions, both exact and approximate, should be introduced, but not too frequently. Exact repetitions in direct succession have their place more at the beginning of a melody than in its continuation. Also, a good melody should start by defining the key, either by melodic leaps or preferably by steps, according to whether the melody is fresh and cheerful or suffering and calm. Finally, a lovely melody will make only moderate use of running passages.

The leading representative of galant aesthetics in Berlin is Christian Gottfried Krause, whose influential treatise *Von der Musikalischen Poesie* (1752) was submitted to his fellow members of the Berlin literary society known as the *Montagsklub* (Monday Club) and subjected to four years of discussion and editing before publication. The treatise is devoted to the problem of combining poetry and music, but the understanding of this task involves the investigation of the nature of the two arts considered individually. Krause discusses first the combination of poetry and music in the past and in his own time, but before proceeding to his task of how poetry intended for musical setting should be written, he devotes some space to examining the intrinsic properties of music.

The second chapter of the work deals essentially with the effects of music, which he maintains must be both pleasing and moving. Thus, the song of the nightingale does not qualify as music because, even though it is pleasing, it is not moving. In order for music to be moving, it must be produced and listened to by "thinking beings," for only then will it possess the necessary expressive inflections and provoke the corresponding impressions, or "ideas," of feeling.

It is possible to write a melody to every discourse, Krause continues, for we pronounce all words with certain sounds. It seems, therefore, that music could be connected with any thought expressed in words. But since it can produce only impressions of delight and emotion, only moving words can be united with it.

It is necessary also that the listener be attentive and be musically sensitive. He need not have heard much music or have a knowledge of its technical principles. Krause projects an experiment with such a person and excludes the influence of words by using either an instrumental piece or one sung in a foreign language:

> If it is joyous his blood begins to move more rapidly than before, he comes out of the inactive state which let us say he was in, his eyes and gestures change, he speaks more cheerfully and loudly, he forgets what he otherwise had to do, and is not aware of much that goes on around him. . . . With less cheerful music other conditions occur in his body, which just as much as the former, however, are accompaniments of the passions.[9]

It is difficult, however, to justify the emotional content of music, even though it can be felt clearly. Krause considers two ways in which the clarity of impressions can be increased: by extension, which adds new characteristics to the melody, and by repetition, which occurs when a theme is developed. But repetition is less moving than the addition of new ideas, and it can result in lack of attention. Extension, however, can stray from the principal idea and its feelings. Thus, it is best to combine both kinds of clarity.

Krause regards extension as a source of pleasure and repetition as a display of learning. He favors a galant ideal, which in turn rests on the preference for a certain type of listener. Composers should be pleasing rather than learned. Developmental artifice is acceptable only so long as a work still produces emotion and enjoyment:

> For the most part, however, it is not so much musicians, but rather only musical amateurs who must be taken as judges of this; amateurs who, to be sure, can have heard a lot of music and can also have good taste, but who neither know much of the rules of harmony nor are biased in any other way. They must leave things to the decision of their ears, and for such listeners music is normally made. What pleases them or even moves them will also please and move the musicians themselves.

Intellectual music will please musicians, but not amateurs, "who judge only the impressions of the ears and of the heart" (p. 166).

In a revealing passage, Krause outlines the development of "harmonic" art:

> It was seen that many melodic passages could also be introduced in the bass. There was an awareness that it sounds pleasing when various voices take up a given theme and through its repetition and segmentation set up a competition over it among themselves. It was noticed that when all the voices are active, as the musicians say, this expresses a grandeur, an astonishment, a general delight, and a great zeal, and the heart is filled by it with certain elevated and strong feelings. Musicians moreover found the opportunity to show their skills and their diligence. They went so far in this, however, that they wanted to express all the other affections and not only those we have mentioned, or in their concern they even forget the affections altogether. . . . There are certain countries and places in which we find more taste for pieces that are harmonically filled out than for those that carry us along by means of melody, perhaps because in those places people look only to the ostensibly large and splendid in other things also, and do not know much of the natural and nobly simple. (p. 166)

Learned pieces are admirable, however, in church music, if they are introduced at the right time, in the right place, and with moderation and if affection is not totally absent from them. They also demand practiced listeners and several hearings to be fittingly understood and to delight or move the soul. But there are certain feelings that cannot be depicted without new and difficult melodic passages. And what is instantly comprehended and enjoyed is not for that reason preferable to something difficult.

After weighing the relative merits of immediately appealing music and difficult music, Krause turns to the celebrated effects of music on the feelings and the character. Music is an important moral force because virtue derives not from reason but from emotional inclinations, which music has the power to affect. Yet the power of music has its limitations. The musician produces only general impressions, while the orator can produce not only satisfaction in general but also satisfaction with particular circumstances: "An adagio makes me sad, an allegro joyful; but I know not why and over what" (p. 170). Some affections, in addition, such as greed, cannot be characterized as well as others.

As far as understanding is concerned, music cannot provide insight into detail or widen our knowledge: "No one says: that was an instructive piece of music. The most adept musician will not be able to express merely in tones the sentence: A patient man is better than a strong one. Strive as you will to convince some one in tones that he is to love his neighbor; you will not be successful" (p. 170). With each word we hear we automatically think of a concept, while in hearing a tone we think of nothing except whether it sounds pleasant or unpleasant. Thus, the language that tones contain is only one of desires and passions. Yet Krause finds that music in its own way fulfills the purpose of all imitation, which is to instruct us or to stir us with favor or aversion. It cannot instruct us the way a science does, but its representations nevertheless satisfy our understanding and our desire to learn. And in the arousal of affections and the effort to please it is a powerful moral force: "Shaftesbury maintains as something undeniable that the admiration and love of order and proportion, be it where it may, naturally improves the character, is productive of social inclination, and offers a very great aid to virtue, which last is itself nothing other than love of order and beauty in society; in the smallest things in the world the sight of order takes possession of the soul and draws our inclination after it." In none of the fine arts, Krause insists, is there as much order, symmetry, and proportion as in music:

> All conjunctions of tone, in harmony as well as in melody, are measured out and measured off. Thus music delights quite exceptionally, indeed it moves, although we often do not clearly recognize its object. But because our understanding always seeks to be active along with the movements of the soul, and accordingly distinct thoughts seek to participate also in music, we connect words and tones with one another.

69

Instructive, fiery words still more exalted by a persuasive melody are of great benefit and of incomparable effect. If the former illuminate the understanding and at once in themselves besiege the heart, the latter come to their aid with their ravishing power; and through this the truth is made more pleasant, more forcible, and the love of virtue stronger. The text contains the ideas in a vocal piece, and their sequence and arrangement in general. The music as well as the words works towards the clarification of the ideas and towards the persuasion and activation of the listeners, and it lends to words to which many hearts are closed such charms as unlock the heart and provide an entrance to truth. In this there also consists the greatest superiority that vocal music has over instrumental music. (pp. 171–72)

In the third chapter of his treatise, Krause seeks to determine the kind of subject matter poetry should have if it is intended for musical setting. Again, the properties of music will obviously be decisive. Although all the fine arts imitate nature, Krause remarks, each one does so in its own way. Painting, for example, can express the affections only insofar as they make themselves visible in countenance, gesture, and posture. But neither the painter nor the sculptor can imitate the movement of the feelings, the growth and complexities of the passions, while the poet and the musician can. Besides imitating a storm or the rippling of a brook or the whispering of a breeze, the musician can produce movements of the soul that agitate us with powerful passions: "And this is the true and highest purpose of music. If the musician imitates the song of a nightingale, he is doing what a landscape painter does or a poet in a graphic description. But just as this is not the most admirable pursuit of these arts, so is music of this kind also only a prism that projects the most beautiful colors on paper, all of which, however, do not compose a picture."[10]

Moving music calls for no practiced listener. It is not necessary even to have heard a joyful or sad person sing, but merely to possess sound hearing and to have no natural antipathy toward music: "Then it will be possible for the musician to imbue us with joy and sorrow. The expression of a picture and the posture of a statue, however, has to be very moving and reveal the most intense affection if it is to move us also; and still it will do so only if we consider the state of the person it depicts and after we imagine ourselves in that state. Music, in contrast, moves us directly and infinitely exceeds painting in this." Thus, external descriptions are not the chief work of music, and they are musical only to the extent that they contribute to the arousal of an affection or to a particular pleasure; otherwise they are only oddities: "In listening to a musical work, we do not trouble ourselves about whether it imitates an occurrence in the physical world, but only about whether it is beautiful, whether it pleases and moves. Our inner self, our whole soul, desires to be part of it. . . . But that we become neither wiser nor more learned by listening to music is not the fault of the composers; the reason lies in the nature of their art" (pp. 53–54).

The musician says to our heart only, This is pleasing, this is touching. What will happen, then, when a poetic text is set? Krause considers the verse

> An eye that art and wisdom sharpen.
> (Ein Aug, das Kunst und Weisheit schärfen.)

Our imagination can compose no image here without understanding, reflection, and knowledge conveyed through language. But with the verses

> Oh, that at once I might kiss you,
> Beloved woods and lovely meadow
> (Ach, dass ich dich schön jetzund küssen könte,
> Beliebter Wald und angenehmes Feld)

the musician can express not only this longing in general, but also very clearly the flight of thought in such an exclamation. He can even mark and express in particular, to some extent in touching tones, the contents of the words *ach, schön, itzund, küssen, beliebt, angenehm*. In this way, Krause observes, we can hear what musical passages are trying to say, and there are what the French call "speaking tones." Similarly, music cannot really be instructive in itself; it can only make instructive words stronger and more insistent.

The beauties of music, however, and the affections that can best be expressed in it, are principally those grounded in the noble sentiments that nature has implanted in us, namely, in love, kindness, thankfulness, pleasure in agreement, and so on. These inclinations have the purpose of making us happy, and it is precisely these that tonal successions and their content can comprehend. Thus, he who prizes these will also value highly the pleasure that music provides.

Just as the sight of a beautiful countenance or a well-formed body gives us pleasure without our knowing why, so beautiful melodies produce various impressions and motions, which like all natural feelings are connected with inclination and avoidance, pleasure and antipathy: "And these are the objects of music, but by no means those impressions of the soul that either do not activate these tendencies of the heart at all or do so only very faintly and indirectly" (p. 58). Thus, it is natural for a woman to express in song her wish for the return of an absent lover or her hope that he will soon arrive. But pleasure in singing or playing will never take hold of a young person who is reflecting on metaphysical truths. We sing and make music only when our ideas and feelings awaken pleasure or displeasure in us and when certain motives cause a desire for something or an aversion to it. It is justly said, then, that music arises from reverence, pleasure, rejoicing of the heart, the praise of heros, the language of the affections, and similar things. No one doubts, for example, that there are affections connected with reverence. Reverence is indeed the moving of the heart toward God. Thankfulness, love, joy, longing, hope, and trust in turn enter the heart of one who is reverent.

Krause devotes the fourth chapter of his treatise to the various affections that music represents. "We sing and make music," he says, "when joy and hope, love, sadness, pain, and longing take hold of us. We do not do so, however, when fear, despair, faintheartedness, anger, and envy agitate us" (p. 69). Is it natural and permissible for singing to turn also to these passions? The explanation is to be found in imitation, which is natural to us and gives us pleasure. But since we never sing spontaneously in states of great sadness, anger, and despair, for example, the representation of such passions is not really suited to music. Nor can music imitate such things as simulated sympathy, which demands knowledge for its perception, for this has really nothing to do with music as such. "Everything that awakens fear and horror, the entirely too violent passions of anger and revenge, bickering, murderous actions, frenzy, and everything forcible in nature, is also not in the least musical. Coarse scolding and abuse, crude pranks, and similar things are nowhere beautiful and thus also not in music" (p. 74).

Krause's principal concern is with the restriction of music to the tender passions. Tone painting, similarly, should not seek to depict noisy and ugly sounds and in general is not the true purpose of music. Even though the violent and ugly passions can to some extent be imitated or expressed musically, they should be avoided since they are not natural to music or intrinsically suited to it. Their depiction is best undertaken in dramatic works, where it is supported by vision and by the context of the action: "To represent howling, shrieking, roaring, hissing, rattling, and so on, with beautiful human voices and with pleasing instruments, with measure and with art, is also a contradiction. . . . At all times music has been considered as something beautiful and pleasing" (pp. 74–76).

The foundation of Krause's aesthetics is a belief in the reality of represented feelings, a reality that is reinforced by the physiological events that accompany the representations. The viewpoint is such that no interest is shown in whether the imitation differs from the original and in precisely how it might do so:

> We call something moving, the presence of which, even in imagination, sets our heart in motion. Men communicate their passions, and even the fabricated representation of an angry person stirs our blood and makes

us angry directly. The soul is like a stringed instrument that sounds when a tone is presented to which one of its strings is tuned, although the string itself is not touched. In the previous century, a man traveled around in Europe who smashed all kinds of glasses with his voice. He perceived in a glass what force and what motion of the air it could not withstand. Just in this way many people cannot endure certain tones, and in the opposite way I know a few people who prefer the key of E major to all others. The relation in which the motion of the air and the strings stand in this key must agree perfectly with the natural tension of the veins in their ear. In general, it is because of this proportion that we are affected and moved by music. (p. 79)

The connection of music with morality is subject to two basic considerations that exert opposite influences. On the one hand, moral truths are grasped by the understanding and by reason, which Krause finds foreign to music. On the other hand, however, the virtues cannot really exist without the affections; contentment, for example, is actually an affection as much as a virtue. In contrast, however, unselfishness is dependent on the understanding and thus cannot be directly conveyed by music. Yet inclinations of the heart, Krause asserts, are the true source of virtue and vice; virtue itself is nothing other than a well-ordered and wisely moderated inclination of the heart:

> In this, music is very fortunate. All the noblest virtues and inclinations are accompanied by affections that it can best express. Pious feelings, the raptures of reverence, elevated contemplations, religious zeal, acceptance of God's will, are tied to the most ardent and pleasant affections. Love, as the most prominent among the virtues, natural inclinations, and passions, either takes an exceptional pleasure in others in general or is the special affection that rules the whole world and yet cannot truly be described, although it perhaps ultimately might be directed to the drive of propagation. The range of inclination of love is astonishingly great and its charm uncommonly potent. (pp. 89–90)

Krause describes the vast variety of feelings to which love gives rise, indicating how well suited music is to convey them. He then considers first the other positive passions individually, then the various sad affections, showing frequently how they may be imitated in music. The natural vocal expression of each passion or affection is the basis of its musical imitation:

> Joy . . . can be expressed by cheerful, clear, free tones and with a flowing and rather rapid composition. . . . Hope describes its blessing in measured, manly, somewhat proud and exultant tones. . . . Often it

becomes a restless desire, and a rather powerful, very perceptible, and at times somewhat throbbing and obstinate voice expresses it, just as for longing and desire weak and drawn-out tones are good. . . . The tone of someone sad is weak and tremulous and its expression short and slow. . . . Someone sympathizing . . . employs dark, flexible, and often imploring tones. Groaning, trembling, broken-off tones express fear and anxiety. Since in fright the blood and the vital spirits recede and draw themselves together, the mouth is speechless for a time and the tone afterward broken. (pp. 92–94)

As the emotions become distant from those for which singing is natural, Krause remarks, tones lose their intelligibility and must turn to words and external circumstances. Also, arias containing such emotions are less pleasing and contain dissonances and tones that are harsh and violent. Krause finally states as a general principle: "The more natural an inclination, emotional disposition, and passion is to us, the more it has to do with love and gentle feelings, or at least manifests itself in various gestures and postures of the body, the more musical it is, and the more easily and clearly it can be expressed in tones. In contrast, the less the circumstances mentioned are met with, the more must words contribute the clarity" (p. 101).

While the galant style was European—it appeared in Germany, France, Italy, and England—galant aesthetics was essentially German. Apart from the question of any native German preference for musical speculation and analysis, the galant in Germany developed side by side with a mature polyphonic art, with which it formed a striking contrast. This juxtaposition of new and old almost inevitably produced aesthetic controversy since aesthetics unquestionably thrives on conflicting artistic currents. In addition to the elaborated aesthetics of Mattheson and Krause, whose influence was remarkably widespread and lasting, galant musical qualities are discussed or mentioned in countless German writings. Of particular importance are the Hamburg journal *Der Critische Musikus* (1737–40; published in an enlarged edition in 1745) of the influential theorist and aesthetician Johann Adolf Scheibe and the *Versuch einer Anweisung die Flöte traversière zu spielen* (1752) of Johann Joachim Quantz. Also notable, because of their early date, are the influential treatises of Johann David Heinichen: *Anweisung zum Generalbass* (1711) and its greatly enlarged second edition, *Der Generalbass in der Composition* (1728).

Perhaps the best known characterization of the galant is provided by Scheibe's criticism of J. S. Bach in 1737:

This great man would be the wonder of entire nations if he were more pleasing and if he did not deprive his pieces of naturalness by a swollen and intricate style and obscure their beauty by all too great art. . . . In short, he is in music what Herr von Lohenstein formerly was in poetry. Pomposity has led both of them from the natural to the artificial and from the sublime to the obscure, and one admires in both the laborious work and exceptional pains, which yet are applied in vain because they conflict with reason. . . .

He who manifests musical rules ever so well with respect to purity and art, but does not at the same time think naturally and straightfor-wardly, will doubtless arouse admiration through his painstaking work but by no means touch his audience.[11]

This criticism inaugurated a prolonged controversy between Scheibe and Johann Abraham Birnbaum, professor of rhetoric at the University of Leip-zig, who undertook the defense of Bach. A central issue in the disagreement was the relation of nature and art: Scheibe maintained that the beauty of nature could not be improved, that art could only imitate nature; Birnbaum believed that art could improve and beautify nature. What was involved stylistically was really the property of artifice, which Scheibe found distaste-ful and Birnbaum enjoyed. The controversy is reminiscent of the quarrel between Mattheson and Buttstedt many years earlier.

Thus, polyphony, as an older, sacred style, became a foil for the galant, the newer, secular style. But the antithesis is also one, as we have seen, of provincial and German art as opposed to cosmopolitan. Germany's route to an urbane style was clearly through the music of Italy and France. The Ger-man galant was the result, basically, of the impact of foreign style, and it was defined originally, during the early part of the century, by the homophonic music of Italy and France.

Fundamental musical polarities underlie the contrast of learned and galant, giving it depth of meaning and an apparent inevitability. As basic as the contrast of sacred and secular is that of instrument and voice. Polyphony, with its heavier "harmonic" texture, was the music of instruments, in a sense, even when sung, while galant melody, even when instrumentally performed, was subject to a vocal standard that governed its structure and its sensory appeal. It is continually made explicit—Mattheson's discussion of instru-mental style in *Der vollkommene Capellmeister* is a prominent example— that instrumental melody must emulate vocal. An aesthetic adequate to the peculiar properties of instrumental music was slow to develop.

Polyphony called for understanding; it addressed the mind rather than the heart. Thus, it was compatible with the conception of music as an imitative art rather than an expressive one, and it called forth once again by its abuses of imitation the same criticism that had been voiced long before by Girolamo Mei and Vincenzo Galilei: music should not depict individual words but express the feeling of the text as a whole.

As music of the mind, polyphony was considered devoid of expression. It might evoke admiration or wonderment, however, which in the conception of Descartes was a purely intellectual interest connected with knowledge. It was produced by the surprise of the new and unexpected, the strange and extraordinary. Thus, music that was not an imitation of nature and not an expression of feeling could still be accounted for in some measure as an object of intellectual interest intrinsically deserving of admiration. This adumbration of specifically musical values was found not only in polyphony but also—and probably even earlier—in the idiomatic and virtuosic instrumental music of the Italian concerto as represented by Tartini. Italian music, which had been a model exemplification of galant style, subsequently moved outside the scope of this style and developed antithetical properties.

Wonder, or astonishment, was thus provoked both by German polyphony and by Italian instrumental music. Quantz, for example, writes of the German composers of the seventeenth century that

> they had reached a very high point, not only in correct harmonic composition, but also in the playing of many instruments. Of good taste, however, and of beautiful melody we should find little trace. . . .
>
> In composition they were, as indicated, harmonious and many voice, but not melodious or charming.
>
> Their writing was more artful than intelligible or pleasing, more for the eye than for the ear.

To arouse and still the passions was something unknown to them. Through their artful workmanship and learned works "they sought more to arouse astonishment than to touch and to please." Shortly before this in his *Versuch*, however, Quantz characterizes Italian instrumental music in terms that are not too different: "The Italian way of playing is arbitrary, extravagant, artificial, obscure, likewise frequently audacious and bizarre, difficult in performance; it permits a considerable addition of embellishments and requires a fair knowledge of harmony; in the uninstructed it arouses less pleasure than astonishment." [12]

Astonishment, however, had an equivocal status. While Descartes had considered it to be an affection, Spinoza had not. It was in any event incompatible with the galant affective gamut, which was defined by the concept of "touching" (*rührend*), a concept drawn, like most of the basic ideas of galant aesthetics, from France (*toucher*), in particular from Jean Baptiste Du Bos's influential *Réflexions critiques* of 1719. Galant affections were graceful, gentle, playful, pleasing, joyous, and tender; they represented chiefly the various sentiments expressive of love. Contrasting with this realm of the beautiful was the realm of the sublime. But since music was believed to have its origin in pleasure and joy, galant aestheticians regularly excluded the powerful passions, such as grandiosity, tragedy, pain, despair, rage, grief, fear, and terror.

Galant music sought to be pleasing as well as touching. It was directed to the ear, to the sensuous pleasure of sonority, while the artifice and speculation of polyphony existed only for the eye. The learned style was pedantic, concerned with rules, counterpoint, and harmony, while the galant was euphonious and based on the sensuous beauty of simple and immediately appealing melody. Indeed, the vocal, cantabile nature of this melody stood in contradiction not only to the complexity and inexpressiveness of polyphony but also to the conspicuously instrumental style of Tartini and the later Vivaldi.

The demand that music be pleasing is related to the interest in its appeal to a wider audience: to the musically untutored—the amateur or *Liebhaber*—as well as to the musician—the connoisseur or *Kenner*. The democratic tendency of the Enlightenment was manifested in a more accessible musical style, and the properties desired in this style—variety, clarity, naturalness, and noble simplicity—were logically called for if music was to be pleasing.

Variety made its appearance somewhat later than the other properties; it is rarely mentioned, for example, in the detailed discussion of the *Der vollkommene Capellmeister* in 1739. It presages the advent of the *empfindsamer Stil*, with its rapid changes of feeling. Uniformity, as exemplified by the learned style of Baroque polyphony, began to seem monotonous and tiring. In order to please, music had to provide diversity; it had to appeal to the different temperaments of different listeners. The demand is clearly expressed by Quantz in a discussion of solo instrumental pieces:

The second Allegro may be either very gay and rapid, or moderate and aria-like. In this, the composer must be guided by the first movement. If this is serious, the last movement may be gay. But if it is lively and rapid, the last movement may be moderate and aria-like. With regard to variety of measure, what was said of the concertos must also be observed here, lest one movement be like the other. In general, if a solo is to please everyone, it must be so contrived that it affords nourishment to each listener's temperamental inclinations. It must be neither purely cantabile nor purely lively from beginning to end. And just as each movement must be very different from any other, the individual movements must be in themselves good mixtures of pleasing and brilliant ideas. For the most beautiful melody will in the end prove a soporific if it is never relieved, and continuous liveliness and unmitigated difficulty arouse astonishment but do not move particularly. Indeed, such mixtures of contrasted ideas should be the aim, not merely in the solo, but in all kinds of music. If a composer knows how to hit this off properly and thereby to set in motion the passions of his listeners, one may truly say of him that he has attained a high degree of good taste and found, so to speak, the musical philosopher's stone.[13]

The same purpose can be served in performance also, by variety in phrasing and in ornamentation. The "mixed style," which draws on characteristics of different countries, is discussed in detail by Quantz at the end of his treatise. It is related to variety, but it refers to a mixture of constituents that are present simultaneously rather than successively.

Variety of affections is often described as rapid change; Quantz even connects it with the play of dissonance and consonance. The purpose of music is "to constantly arouse and still the passions," he asserts. "To excite the different passions the dissonances must be struck more strongly than the consonances." Without this succession of agreeable and disagreeable sounds, he says, music would no longer be able "now to arouse the different passions instantly, now to still them again." In spite of this rapid change, however, the passions aroused or expressed by music are thought of most characteristically as real: "The performer of a piece must seek to enter into the principal and related passions that he is to express. And since in the majority of pieces one passion constantly alternates with another, the performer must know how to judge the nature of the passion that each idea contains, and constantly make his execution conform to it." Again, "The passions change frequently in the Allegro just as in the Adagio. The performer must therefore seek to transport himself into each of these passions, and to express it suitably." At times the reality of the feelings of the performer is unequivocally described. "To play an Adagio well," Quantz counsels, "you must enter as much as possible into a calm and almost melancholy mood, so that you execute what you have to play in the same state of mind as that in which the composer wrote it. . . . For that which does not come from the heart does not easily reach the heart."[14]

Surprisingly, however—and inconsistently—the performer's feelings are also at times described as fictional or simulated. Speaking of the changes of affective ideas in music, Quantz states, "Hence you must, so to speak, adopt a different sentiment at each bar, so that you can imagine yourself now melancholy, now gay, now serious, etc. Such dissembling is most necessary in music." In another passage of the treatise he maintains still more explicitly that the performer

> must apply himself well to the art of simulation. This art of simulation is not only permissible, but most necessary, and it does no offence to morals. He who strives all his life to master his passions as fully as possible will not find it difficult to counterfeit in himself the passion required in the piece to be performed. Only then will he play well and as though from the soul. Whoever does not understand this commendable art of simulation is no musician in the true sense.[15]

Clearly Quantz is not consistent in matters of aesthetics. He has a considerable breadth of interest in music, which often extends to aesthetics and style, but his treatise is of course primarily devoted to performance.

This concern with performance is much more narrowly focused in C. P. E. Bach's *Versuch über die wahre Art das Clavier zu spielen* (1753). Yet considerations of affective variety and change are occasionally present here also, along with the conception of the mixed style. Bach occasionally manifests a more dramatic conception of variety as well, which reflects his style as a composer. His treatise, however, reveals the *empfindsamer Stil* as an aspect of the galant rather than as a contrast to it. Bach calls for noble simplicity, for example, and for restraint in the use of embellishments in order to preserve clarity.[16]

The reality of the feelings attached to music is particularly evident in the Bach *Versuch*, both in the feelings expressed by the performer and in those aroused in the listener:

> A musician cannot move others unless he too is moved. He must of necessity feel all of the affects that he hopes to arouse in his audience, for the revealing of his own humor will stimulate a like humor in the listener. In languishing, sad passages, the performer must languish and grow sad. Thus will the expression of the piece be more clearly perceived by the audience. Here, however, the error of a sluggish, dragging performance must be avoided, caused by an excess of affect and melancholy. Similarly, in lively, joyous passages, the executant must again put himself into the appropriate mood.

In spite of their reality, these feelings are subject to abrupt changes in character, especially in fantasias and improvisations:

> And so, constantly varying the passions, he will barely quiet one before he rouses another. Above all, he must discharge this office in a piece which is highly expressive by nature, whether it be by him or someone

else. In the latter case he must make certain that he assumes the emotion which the composer intended in writing it. It is principally in improvisations or fantasias that the keyboardist can best master the feelings of his audience. . . .

As stated earlier, it is especially in fantasias, those expressive not of memorized or plagiarized passages, but rather of true musical creativeness, that the keyboardist more than any other executant can practice the declamatory style, and move audaciously from one affect to another. . . . Unbarred free fantasias seem especially adept at the expression of affects, for each meter carries a kind of compulsion within itself. At least it can be seen in accompanied recitatives that tempo and meter must be frequently changed in order to rouse and still the rapidly alternating affects.[17]

Musical clarity, another major value of galant aesthetics, was seen to be furthered by restraint in ornamentation and by distinct phrasing. It was dependent also, as Mattheson maintained, on the definite expression of an affection. It applied both to composition and to performance. Clarity had been a criterion of truth and knowledge for Descartes, who spoke of clear and distinct perception, and it had been adopted and made into a principle of poetry by Boileau. For Leibnitz, ideas were clear if they were adequate for our adjustment in the world of sense; they were distinct, on the other hand, if they gave us knowledge of the cause of a thing, of its elements and how it is determined by them. Empiricism was contrasted with rigorous science. Krause maintained similarly that music produced clear affects but not distinct ones since the constitution of the cause of these affects and the circumstances of any individual experiencing them were both unknown. Apart from this theory, however, clarity and distinctness were not separately defined in music.

Naturalness in music has two prerequisites: musical expressiveness and sensuous beauty. Natural music is therefore touching and pleasing. In the first characteristic, galant aesthetics comes together with the theory of imitation, which is discussed in the following chapter. Music touches us, it can be said, because it reveals the character, or conveys the quality, of some affection it expresses. Its naturalness consists in its spontaneous expressiveness. But it can also be natural in its direct auditory appeal, as simple lyricism that arises purely from musical experience. Naturalness is a theme of French aesthetics as well as German—particularly in Rousseau and Gui de Chabanon—but it is best understood in France in connection with the problem of imitation and expression.

In the property of noble simplicity, finally, musical aesthetics anticipates the aesthetics of visual art. This idea was introduced into art history by Winckelmann in his *Gedanken über die Nachahmung der griechischen Werke in der Malerei und Bildhauerkunst* of 1755, but it was common shortly before that in the musical aesthetics of Berlin, and it was clearly characterized by Mattheson in *Der vollkommene Capellmeister* (1739).[18] Like galant musical aesthetics in general, however, noble simplicity has its roots in the neoclassical aesthetic of Boileau, who is cited in this connection by both Mattheson and Krause.

Underlying galant aesthetics was a scientific theory of affections and temperaments that accounted for both these manifestations in terms of the vibrations of "inner air" (*pneuma*) or "vital spirits," which act on the bodily vapors of warmth, cold, dryness, and dampness. These vapors in turn act on the four humors, which are bodily manifestations of the four elements. It is the humors that are correlated with the four temperaments. The activating force of this mechanism is the influence of sound waves, which mirror the rhythms, tempos, intervals, and dynamics of music. The system went back to ancient medicine, to the theories of Hippocrates (fourth century B.C.) and Galen (second century A.D.), and it was very much in evidence in the seventeenth century, buttressed simultaneously, in 1650, by Descartes's *Les Passions de l'ame* and Athanasius Kircher's *Musurgia universalis*. Its explanatory power was considerable. Not only states of physical health but also emotions and dispositions were reduced to a rational system that was at once physical and mathematical.

Something of the ancient origins of the theory may be revealed by its scope. Affections and temperaments, which seem to us so radically divided as temporary and permanent, respectively, were traced to a cause that was fundamentally the same for both. But the same equation existed in the ancient theory of ethos. The effects of music, as we know them from Plato's views, were applied without comment both to momentary emotional states, as in many traditional stories of the power of music, and to the permanent shaping of disposition and character, although it must be taken into account that the permanent effects in antiquity were due to musical participation— not to listening—and thus to indoctrination that arose from habitual social activity. As a special case of the theory, both emotional moderation and an equable temperament were manifestations of the balance and harmony of the humors.

But vital spirits could explain a great deal more: most important, the positive effect of musical variety and the apparently irreducible aspects of taste. As far as variety was concerned, the broad appeal it had for audiences was due simply to the conformability of different sections of music to the physiological constitution of different temperaments. There was something for everyone. The same explanation was applicable to the ideal of the mixed style, which Quantz discusses at the end of his *Versuch*, for the combination of the styles characteristic of different nations would satisfy a greater diversity of taste and tend toward universality in its appeal. National taste itself—the center of ceaseless discussion and analysis—was only individual taste writ large and therefore subject to the same explanation in the form of national temperament, which was often believed to be a consequence of climate.

CHAPTER SIX

IMITATION AND EXPRESSION

I mitation and expression are generally considered to represent successive conceptions of the nature of music, the one giving way to the other starting around 1750. This description of the course of musical thought obviously leaves out of account a number of important considerations that are essential to a more accurate understanding. For one thing, we often encounter a third musical idea, that of the effects of music, which went under the name of "musical pathology," a term that serves to remind us today of the medical ancestry of this theory. Another factor of importance in the circle of musical problems is the ambiguity of the concept of "expression," which can refer to the feelings of the composer or the performer or to the intrinsic expressiveness of music itself. This in turn can be identified either with the specific tonal sensuousness of the music or with its presentation of feelings. And these feelings, in turn, may be either peculiar to the music or familiar to us from experience outside music—or even peculiar and familiar at the same time. To add to the complexity of the situation, two or more of these ideas are regularly considered to be applicable simultaneously, or to be actually equivalent, so that music that "expresses" sadness, for example, is also provocative of sadness in the listener.

Bound up with these problems are the questions of realism and rationalism. The musical provocation of feelings would necessarily refer to real feelings, generally to those known outside music. Musical imitations of feeling, like any imitations, would seem to be different from but also similar to their models. The expression of the feelings of the composer or performer would again refer to real feelings, while the expressiveness of music itself could be that of feelings also observed in behavior, countenance, and utterance or of feelings that are very different—otherwise unknown, nameless, ideal, fictional, poorly defined or peculiarly subtle, and so on. Finally, whatever feelings are in question could be rationally cataloged as "affections" or regarded as foreign or opposed to reason in their nature. The physiological theory of affections, however, which is the substructure of the conception of feeling during most of the century, will favor both rationalism and "realism."

France

The concept of imitation was fundamental to the musical aesthetics of the eighteenth century. It provided a basis of explanation for vocal music in particular and to some extent also for instrumental music. French writers accept it as axiomatic during the first half of the century, offering at most an explanation of how it applies to music. During the second half of the century, imitation called for extended discussion, for it clearly needed modification and qualification, and it became the center, in addition, of polemics that undertook to demonstrate that it was of limited importance in the case of music, or even essentially inapplicable. Musical thought turned instead to the concept of expression, although this notion again, like that of imitation, was fraught with ambiguity. There are writers, in fact, who do regard imitation and expression not as contrasted explanatory principles but as identical in meaning.

In Aristotle's *Poetics*, the imitative arts had been connected with drama, which combined them in a common purpose, and it is chiefly writers with an interest in opera and drama, or those devoted to the cultivated enjoyment of the arts in general, who are concerned with the tradition of imitation. Composers and performers, by way of contrast, and amateurs devoted not to all the arts but to music in particular, often take music on its own terms and show no interest in the idea of imitation.

The prominence of imitation in the aesthetic thought of the eighteenth century finds its explanation in the prevailing reliance on reason and objectivity in human experience, with a corollary mistrust of feeling, which was often connected with immorality. This "scientific" attitude found its highest values in clarity and distinctness, and these could be exemplified best in music by its fidelity to a clearly defined model that was being represented. This not only satisfied the condition placed on art in Aristotle's *Poetics* and his *Politics* but connected music at once with the charted realm of objectivity and knowledge. Indeed, even feeling gained admission to this realm, for Descartes had subjected it to his new method and developed a logical classification of the passions of the soul (*Les Passions de l'âme*, 1650). It was not really feelings themselves, however, that became a model for musical imitation but their objective manifestation in impassioned utterance and in vocal cries.

84

In what seems to have been the first treatise in the modern field of aesthetics—the *Traité du beau* (1715) of Jean Pierre de Crousaz—imitation has not yet become a central concern, for the primary traditions in which the work is grounded are not those of Aristotle's *Poetics*, which is really devoted to temporal art, but those of general philosophy and spatial art. Crousaz was a professor of mathematics and philosophy in Lausanne, and his conception of beauty is an essentially mathematical one in which beauty is characterized by unity in multiplicity and by symmetry, regularity, order, and proportion. This view takes up a tradition that can be found, for example, in Augustine's *De ordine*, and since it applies primarily to organic symmetry and to visual art, it leads to a "general aesthetics" that is concerned almost exclusively with nature and the visual arts and that often slights literature and music or overlooks them entirely.

But Crousaz was subject to the more immediate influence of Cartesian thought, which among other things emphasized the criterion of clarity. For Descartes, clarity was a criterion of scientific truth, but Boileau made it a criterion of beauty also, as a consequence of his principle, "Nothing is beautiful but the true." This principle was peculiarly appropriate to art, for, in emphasizing "imitation" as the distinguishing feature of art, Aristotle had, in effect, subjected art to the standard of truth.

But the Cartesian influence extended to the method of Crousaz and to his more detailed conception of beauty. In the letter of dedication of his treatise, Crousaz's discussion of his method is clearly in the vein of Descartes: "I have put out of mind all the impressions that I had received," he writes, "in order to withdraw into myself and to reduce my ideas to the most simple and indubitable notions." As far as the conception of beauty is concerned, Crousaz inherits the problem of the Cartesian duality of soul and body, of reason and sense experience.

The position of seventeenth-century rationalism in general was not too dissimilar to that of Plato: truth resided primarily in reason; the senses— and the feelings they provoke—were unreliable. If we call an object beautiful, Crousaz asserts, it is because we approve of it or because it gives us pleasure. Descartes had held that our ideas of beauty depend solely on the senses and that they were therefore confused and unreliable. But beauty does not depend solely on pleasure or feeling, Crousaz maintains. There are, in fact, beautiful objects that do not please or move, and there is thus a purely intellectual recognition of beauty. More specifically, beauty designates the relation between objects, or the feelings they arouse, and our ideas. And an object is beautiful if our feelings and our ideas are in agreement. The immediate verdict of feeling in response to an operatic aria, for example, will have its confirmation in the objective properties of the music, as these are discovered by reason. The ideas cannot influence the feelings, however, or the feelings the ideas, for body and soul, being totally different in nature, cannot act on one another. Their agreement, then, must be the result of divine intervention. In this way, Crousaz was able to advance beyond the French distrust of feeling, for he provided beauty—as well as *bon goût*—with a rational and thus a universal basis.

A brief but influential discussion of musical imitation is presented by Jean Baptiste Du Bos in his widely read *Réflexions critiques sur la poësie et sur la peinture* (1719), which was translated into English by Thomas Nugent as *Critical Reflections on Poetry, Painting and Music* (1746). "Just as the painter imitates the forms and colors of nature," he writes, "so the musician imitates the tones of the voice—its accents, sighs and inflections. He imitates in short all the sounds that nature herself uses to express the feelings and passions."[1] Du Bos then distinguishes these "signs" of the passions, which are the work of nature, from spoken words, which are arbitrary "symbols" of the passions. Continuous melody, and harmony and rhythm as well, serve to make the imitation more pleasing and more moving, and rhythm also adds reality to the imitation since it has an imitative capacity in its own right. Thus, Du Bos is able to direct every aspect of music to the single end of imitation and its effects. There is an imitative truth in instrumental music also, for this imitates the sounds we hear in nature, many of which are particularly impressive when they occur in the context of a dramatic work. If we are concerned about a person who is about to be engulfed by a tempest, for example, the imitation of its sound will affect us "in much the way" that the sound of a tempest would. But this endorsement of Aristotle (*Politics* 1340a) is followed directly by the only important qualification that Du Bos imposes on imitation, that it "can never be as effective as the thing itself"— a reference to Cicero (*De oratore*, bk. 3).

The community of the arts, which we have recognized as an important feature of aesthetics, is used as an additional argument in support of musical imitation: "The basic principles that govern music are thus similar to those that govern poetry and painting. Like poetry and painting, music is an imitation. Music cannot be good unless it conforms to the general rules that apply to the other arts on such matters as choice of subject and exactness of representation" (p. 21).

Du Bos finally separates the pleasure art gives from its emotional expression and effect. Pleasure can be derived from sensuous qualities and technical excellence, but art will not move us if it is not imitative. Sensory pleasure and technical excellence should in fact be used solely to create and embellish imitation. It is significant that Du Bos does not value art that is not imitative. "Musical compositions that fail to move us can unequivocally be equated with pictures that have no merit other than their coloring, or with poems that are no more than well-constructed verses." The low esteem that is evident here is connected with the separation of feeling from pleasure, a separation we come on continually in aesthetic thought. Feeling can arise only when there is imitation: "Just as some people are more attracted to the color of pictures than to the expression of passions, so others are only sensible to the pleasures of melody or even to the richness of harmony, and pay not the slightest attention to whether the melody is an effective imitation" (p. 21).

In his influential *L'Essai sur le beau* of 1741, Yves Marie André is concerned primarily, as Crousaz was, with demonstrating the objectivity of beauty. "There is an essential musical beauty," he maintains, "that is absolute, wholly independent of human institutions, and even divine." Mathematics again represents the traditional foundation for this view. Referring to a concert he has just attended, André finds order, regularity, proportion, precision, propriety, and unity in the music. He says to a member of the audience, "But such beauty is neither the sound that reached your ear, nor the pleasant sensation that it aroused in your soul, nor the satisfaction that you experienced in your heart upon reflection." The man he has addressed responds as follows: "It must be that in the concert there is a purer pleasure than the sweetness of the actual sounds, and a beauty that does not have its roots in the senses, a particular beauty that charms the mind and which the mind alone perceives and judges." In the course of the conversation, André elucidates: "These principles are grounded in order, in the structural beauty of the piece, in harmonic numbers, in the rule of proportion and harmonious progression, and in the idea of propriety, a sacred law that allots each part its position, its conclusion and the right path by which to reach its end."[2]

André subsequently extends his observations from mathematics to the physics of sound and to human anatomy, finding everywhere the same objective evidence of harmony. He insists above all on the central place of unity, citing Augustine's view that "every form of beauty is a unity." This great principle, André proceeds to argue, is more certain in music than in any other form of sensible beauty.

When he compares music and painting, André abruptly abandons mathematics and states, as a universally recognized fact, that imitation is the basis of the two kinds of beauty represented by these two arts. In a treatise on beauty, imitation understandably can become a subsidiary matter. But André takes "imitation" to be equivalent to "expression," and in the musical discussion as a whole, somewhat inconsistently, in addition to mathematical harmony, he deals with properties of music that are more accurately described as expressive than as imitative.

At least as early as the 1740s, it becomes evident that the concept of imitation is inadequate as a basic principle for the aesthetics of music, however well it might serve in that capacity for other arts. Even in Charles Batteux's important *Les Beaux-arts réduits à un même principe* (1746), which undertakes expressly to demonstrate that imitation is the basis of all the fine arts, the discussion of music does not consistently appeal to the imitative principle. Batteux changes the principle from "the imitation of nature" to "the imitation of beautiful nature" and thus rests his case on a nature that has been subjected to selection and idealization. Even in this modified form, however, imitation is unable to account for the nature of musical experience, and Batteux appeals to the term "expression" instead, which he takes, however, to be equivalent somehow to "imitation."

He begins his discussion of music with the assertion that melodic lines are only imitations, but he does not mean imitations of actual feelings. Instead, he stresses their fabricated character; they are imitations because they seem real, even though they literally imitate no real model. The passions in melody are imaginary or fictitious. They are "wholly the creation of genius and taste: nothing about them is true, everything is artificial. . . . Art is created only to deceive. . . . We shall speak here only of expression." This seems to mean that, since the passions in melody have no actual model, it is better to speak of expression rather than imitation, for tones remain the same, Batteux goes on to say, whether the passions are real or simulated. Indeed, the language of tones is natural to us. The implication is that the tonal configurations of a melody will necessarily express passions but that these passions will be creations, not imitations. Yet Batteux continues his discussion as follows: "A musical composition must be judged in the same way as a picture. . . . What would we think of a painter who was content to throw on the canvas bold shapes and masses of the liveliest color without reference to any known object? The same argument can be applied to music." Thus, after an anticipation of the later conception of fictitious feelings, imitation is reaffirmed, and Batteux's position becomes equivocal. "There is not a musical sound," he now insists, "that does not have its model in nature."[3]

The truth, of course, is almost exactly the opposite, for tone is notoriously rare in the natural world. But in trying, almost automatically, to retain imitation, Batteux succeeds in finding room in music for both imitation and expression: "There are two kinds of music. The one merely imitates unimpassioned sounds and noises and is equivalent to landscape painting. The other expresses animated sounds and relates to the feelings. This corresponds to portrait painting" (p. 49). Yet the account is far from clear or consistent: "The musician is no freer than the painter: he is continuously subject in every way to comparison with nature." This is clear in itself. But we read shortly afterward: "If he paints some ideal object, one that has never really existed, such as the groanings of the earth or the shuddering of a ghost as it rises from its tomb, he must do as the poet does: '*Aut famam sequere, aut sibi convenientia finge*' [Either follow tradition, or invent what is self-consistent]." The citation of Horace (*Ars poetica* 119) makes it quite evident that imitation does not enter here even in connection with the ideal object, but only in the very different sense of imitating other composers. With a similar lack of precision Batteux accepts the fact "that a melodic line can express certain passions: love, for instance, or joy, or sadness." Now the "expression" here certainly qualifies as imitation. "But for every passion that can be identified," he continues, "there are a thousand others that cannot be put into words" (p. 50). Are we still dealing with imitation? Or in what sense are these nameless passions even expressions?

In making use of the term "expression" as well as the term "imitation," Batteux is faced with the difficult problem, which he is unable to solve, of sorting out two spheres of ambiguity. What can be seen clearly enough, however, is that the concept of imitation has become problematic and can no longer be regarded without question as a satisfactory key to the understanding of music.

In the following chapter, Batteux considers the resources that art adds to nature. Sounds have natural expressive qualities, but music makes use also of measure, tempo, melody, and harmony. These things "in no way alter or destroy the natural meaning of sounds.... They serve only to strengthen that meaning, adding lustre to it and giving it greater energy and charm" (p. 52). Their effect, in other words, is to contribute to and enhance the expression. Batteux follows Du Bos here, as he does throughout his discussion of music. And it is still clearer in Du Bos that the realm of beauty, the pleasure that music provides in its own right, is not accepted for its own sake but only because of its effect on the expression or on the purpose of the expression. It is thus expression, or imitation, or, as Batteux further adds, "meaning," that is the dominant value of musical aesthetics.

Although musical imitation was continually called into question in the 1750s and 1760s, a number of writers continue to accept it without qualification. Some of the encyclopedists, surprisingly, still regard it as a self-understood principle and therefore find no need to investigate its nature or to consider it at length. This is the attitude we find in d'Alembert, in the "Discours préliminaire" (1751) of the *Encyclopédie*; in Rousseau, in the chapters on melody and harmony of his *Essai sur l'origine des langues* (1753) and in the article "Imitation" in his *Dictionnaire de musique* (1767); and in Diderot, in *Le Neveu de Rameau* (ca. 1760–64). Of these, Diderot's discussion is doubtless the most interesting:

A tune is an imitation, by means of the tones of a scale, (invented by art or inspired by nature, as you please), of the physical sounds or accents

of passion. And you see that by changing the variables the same definition would apply exactly to painting, eloquence, sculpture or poetry.
Now to come to your question: what is the model for a musician or
a tune? Speech, if the model is alive and thinking; noise, if the model
is inanimate. Speech should be thought of as a line, and the tune as
another line winding in and out of the first. The more vigorous and true
the speech, which is the basis of the tune, and the more closely the tune
fits it and the more points of contact it has with it, the truer that tune
will be and the more beautiful. . . . Go and listen to the piece when the
young man, feeling himself on the point of death, cries: *Mon coeur s'en
va*. Listen to the air, listen to the instrumental setting, and then try and
tell me the difference there is between the real behavior of a dying man
and the turn of this air. You will see whether the line of the melody does
not coincide exactly with that of speech.[4]

In 1753 and 1754, a deep-seated disagreement between Rousseau and
Rameau concerning the nature of musical expression found its definite form
in Rousseau's *Essai* and in Rameau's *Observations sur notre instinct pour
la musique, et sur son principe* (1754). Rousseau saw music as akin to language, with its expressive force embodied in melody, which was an imitation
of impassioned speech. Rameau viewed music as essentially mathematical,
with its foundation in harmony; thus, it was really harmony from which
musical expression arose. The scandalous thesis of Rousseau's *Lettre sur la
musique française* (1753) is that the nature of the French language makes
any acceptable kind of French music impossible. His view of the relation
of melody and harmony, however, is a considered one, although it leaves
no doubt that harmony is essentially an accessory of melody. In his *Essai*,
harmony is given a still more restricted role (chap. 14), as an outcome of its
lack of any imitative function:

Though one calculated the relationships of tones and the laws of harmony for a thousand years, how would one ever make of that art an
art of imitation? Where is the principle of this supposed imitation? Of
what is the harmony a sign? And what is there in common between
chords and our passions?

If we apply the same question to melody, the response comes automatically, it is already in the reader's mind. Melody, in imitating vocal
inflections, expresses laments, cries of sorrow or joy, threats, moans;
all the vocal signs of the passions are within its province. It imitates
the accents of languages, and the affective turns in every idiom that are
caused by certain movements of the soul; it does not imitate alone, it

speaks, and its language—inarticulate but alive, ardent, impassioned—
has a hundred times more energy than speech itself. From this arises
the force of musical imitation; from this arises the dominion of song
over sensitive hearts.[5]

The issue in this dispute is clearly one of fundamental importance in
eighteenth-century musical aesthetics. It has ramifications that connect it
with all the major aspects of musical thought in that period. For one thing, it
is a French counterpart of the polemic of the German galant against Baroque
polyphony. But it also belongs to operatic aesthetics: to the prolonged French
quarrel between the ancients and the moderns and to the important conflict
of national styles that came to a head in 1752 with the Paris performance of
La serva padrona. Indeed, the contest of melody and harmony encompassed
all the forms then current of the conflict of simplicity and complexity.

The last few decades of the century witnessed an increasing emphasis on
the expressive aspects of music and the unequivocal discard of imitation as
an aesthetic principle. Yet we have to think of the controversy over imitation as a perennial one that continued in some form, as issues tend to do in
aesthetics, well beyond what seemed to be a definitive outcome. But even in
the rejection of imitation in the second half of the eighteenth century, it is
evident that the same facts could be viewed in different ways. What to some
writers was a modified form of imitation was to others clear proof that the
principle was not applicable. Literal imitation was obviously not present in
music, just as it is not present in any art or any reproduction other than the
duplication of a product by machine. "Representation" is an alternative concept not so easily disposed of, for political representatives, for example, bear
no conspicuous resemblance to the people they represent. But the accepted
and time-honored term of the controversy was *imitation*, and this was susceptible of a sufficient variety of interpretations as to provide a justification
for arguments of support as well as denial.

Thus, in his article "Idéal" (1754) for the *Encyclopédie*, which is devoted
to ideal beauty, François Jean de Chastellux takes a position diametrically
opposed to that of d'Alembert and Rousseau. After tracing out "the progress
of music," Chastellux continues as follows:

Now I would very much like to know what part the imitation of nature
has had in this progress. The song of the birds is not measured, their
concerts have no harmony at all and are often very discordant. Who
does not see that the beauties of music are all ideal and produced by
groping, that is to say, by that instinct which makes us enlarge and diminish, retouch and correct until we are content with our work? Let us

then be more just towards the fine arts and restore to them the titles of nobility that have been denied them. They are not merely imitators, but creators; and not content to copy nature, they know how to embellish it, they know how to express the thought of man, thought which is only the result of his ambitious desires, and of the ardor with which he seeks pleasure.

After discussing the inadequacy of imitation as a foundation for painting and drama, he turns to music:

It is the same thing for music. Those who desire that a wholly magical art, totally ideal, be limited to imitation and to expression, are not worthy of hearing the melodious accents with which the Buranellos, the Piccinis, the Sacchinis have filled all of Europe, and which equal Corelli in melting the ice of the north; while they are subjected here to a sterile and pedantic criticism as though it was forbidden to art to have riches, and there existed pleasures that were contraband. Passion has the habit of proffering words without rhyme and reason; poetry numbers them and arranges them; music prolongs them and repeats them: deny these last two their privileges, and you will have neither poetry nor music, there will remain to you only intellect, the most useless furniture in the world when it is deprived of imagination and sensibility.

But it is not enough to show that the ideal has a great share in the most beautiful works of art, it is necessary to go further, and to prove that it constitutes the noblest and most precious part of it; now to achieve that, it is sufficient to show that the ideal genre combines three particular advantages that assure it preeminence over the imitative genre; first, it excites new sensations; secondly, it inspires man with a high idea of his own powers; thirdly, it gives powerful wings to his imagination.[6]

Whereupon Chastellux proceeds to elaborate these three advantages.

The 1770s saw the systematic rejection of imitation as an aesthetic principle in music. André Morellet, an economist and philosophical writer, presented a detailed program modifying the idea of imitation that explicitly retreated from its literal meaning. In an interesting and well-thought-out essay, *De l'expression en musique et de l'imitation dans les arts* (1771), Morellet proposed that imitation and expression were one and the same, even though his title suggests correctly that expression is the musical counterpart of imitation in the other arts. After discussing the imitations that music presents of physical objects, he states that they are due to resemblances or analogies. Music is here largely a metaphoric language based in this respect on resemblances or relations between the impressions of the different sense organs.

The reality of these analogies can in fact be demonstrated by the agreement of different composers in their depictions of a given object, such as a flowing brook or the rising sun.

As far as the passions and affections are concerned, they all have their natural declamation, which consists either of inarticulate vocalizations such as cries, sighs, sobs, and interjections or of the inflections taken on by connected discourse when it expresses feelings. These two types of natural declamation are the models that are imitated by music, not only by vocal music, but by instrumental music also. This imitation again, like the imitation of physical objects, depends on various analogies and relations, such as between slowness of melody and sadness, between chromatic melody and grief, between the ascending major sixth and resolute feelings, or between the major mode and gaiety. Above all, however, musical imitation is imperfect, vague, and slight; it does not really produce likenesses. But this is as it should be, for imitation in the arts should embellish nature; it should give more pleasure than the truth itself. Morellet here contradicts Boileau's dictum, Nothing is beautiful but the truth, for he permits art to deviate from the truth in order to augment the beauty of the imitation. This is done by choosing beautiful features from among those that nature presents, by collecting in a single object beautiful features that have never existed simultaneously in nature, and by offering the perceiver the pleasure of discovering the ingenious artifice that has been employed to seduce him.

Developing this last point, Morellet asserts that the charm of an imitation would disappear if it were taken for the truth. The illusion of art should therefore not be complete, yet we experience the greatest pleasure at the moment when it is strongest:

> I believe one may explain this apparent contradiction by distinguishing two phases in the impression that works of art make on us: there must be a moment at which we are ignorant that we are being deceived, and a moment at which we know that we have been deceived; a moment at which we believe we see nature, and another at which we perceive the art which is fleeing and concealing itself, but which, like the shepherd in Vergil, *Se cupit antè videri* (Prefers to be seen). These moments must succeed one another alternately and at short intervals. . . . It is perhaps to this unceasing alternation of illusions and disabusements (I beg to be pardoned this word, which is the most appropriate that can be employed) that we are indebted for the greatest pleasures the arts afford us; it deploys two of the greatest resources of the soul, sensitivity and sagacity. . . .

And we must not think that the illusion, thus interrupted, will be less strong and less vivid in the moment in which it is exercised. I am persuaded, on the contrary, that in this struggle of truth against it, it gains new forces to subjugate our senses and our imagination. When it returns victorious, we are in collusion with it, and we anticipate its yoke. We lend ourselves to all the suppositions, we set aside everything that could undeceive us and make us forget the errors that are dear to us; and what is easier to art than to deceive us when we make ourselves its accomplices?[7]

Thus, with the aid of an ingenious theory, Morellet turns a deficiency into a virtue. Not only does he retain imitation by acknowledging its imperfection, but he also shows that this imperfection is essential to art.

At the end of the decade, a qualified imitation is no longer sufficient, and imitation loses credibility entirely. This can be seen clearly in the extended essay *L'Expression musicale, mise au rang des chimères* (1779), which was written by an author named Boyé, of whom nothing further is known. Boyé equates expression and imitation as a matter of course and maintains that the model for the imitation of passions would have to be the inflections of the speaking voice. But this he shows to be impossible since tones are fixed and the sounds of speech indeterminate. In addition, the intervals used in speech are much smaller than those used in music. "A good composer who claims to copy the impassioned accents of nature," Boyé concludes, "is thus as ridiculous as someone who desires to form all imaginable words with three letters of the alphabet."[8] If you detach the poem from an opera, each melodic phrase will become an inexplicable hieroglyph.

Talking to a woman who has wept over Gluck's *Armide*, he insists that the cause was the interest of the poem and the feeling of the actor. A true actor will not sing exactly what is written but introduces numerous expressive modifications. Thus, the air "J'ai perdu mon Euridice" from Gluck's *Orpheus* has been found so gay that a jolly contredance has been made of it. Indeed, the text "J'ai trouvé mon Euridice" would be more appropriate. (Boyé gives a parody of the four lines that converts the sadness into joy.) Yet when the singer performs it with its original text, hearts melt and tears flow at the terrible situation he feigns to experience. (This air came to represent an aesthetic problem. The most well-known discussion of it occurs in Hanslick's *Vom Musikalisch-Schönen*.)

Boyé will grant various characters to music: it can be naive, majestic, or gay. But these are not expressive of feeling. Otherwise, "my dressing gown would then have expression, for my cook told me the other day that the design is melancholy" (p. 290). Similarly, the somber exterior of a prison does not express the regret of the prisoners. Boyé is here the victim, as we can easily see, of the ambiguity of the term "expression."

If we consider recitative, he points out, we observe that the music that most approaches expression is the most boring. Melodious airs, in contrast, charm the ear, please people of various nationalities even when the words are not comprehended, and inspire interest even when they are performed on instruments. Indeed, Italians attend only to the bravura arias, which are the least expressive things in the world.

Boyé turns to the warbling of birds and to the sounds of inanimate objects, such as the rustling of leaves. He finds it absurd to claim that music can imitate either of these. Still more absurd is the claim that music can imitate visual effects or that it can imitate sleep, solitude, or silence, referring here to Rousseau's claim in the article "Opera" in his *Dictionnaire*. He apparently refers also to Morellet when he writes, "A modern author believes he has removed all these difficulties in saying that music imitates in its fashion. . . . A pleasant imitation, that of not imitating at all" (p. 293). Indeed, the arguments are very much the same in the two authors; it is their evaluations that differ. The slight imitation that Morellet finds to be the only kind that is artistically valuable Boyé calls a feebleness of means that makes it impossible to believe that music is an imitative art. Such is the difference in attitude between the beginning and the end of the decade.

A still more important development is that Boyé offers an alternative to imitation. The beauty of melody and harmony as such, for example, that was seen by Du Bos and Batteux merely as contributing strength to musical imitation is now seen in its own right as an independent and specifically musical value. "The principal object of music," Boyé writes,

> is to please us physically, without the mind putting itself to the trouble of searching for useless comparisons to it. One should regard it entirely as a pleasure of the senses and not of the intelligence. As much as one strives to attribute the cause of the impressions that it makes us experience to a mental principle, one will only be losing one's way in a labyrinth of extravagances: in vain will one search for music there; it will steal away ceaselessly from the efforts of our reason; but when one acknowledges that a concert is to the hearing what a banquet is to the sense of taste, what perfumes are to the sense of smell, and what fireworks are to the eyes; then one will be able to flatter oneself with having adopted the system of truth, and consequently the only one that is in accord with the principle of musical sensations. (p. 294)

Much as this errs in a direction opposite to that of imitation, it has the advantage, in its pure auditory hedonism, of emphasizing a neglected factor that was capable of making an important contribution to musical aesthetics.

In 1779, the same year in which Boyé's essay appeared, what is certainly the most elaborate and definitive rejection of imitation was also published:

the *Observations sur la musique* of Michel Paul Gui de Chabanon. The basic questions to which he devotes himself first are the following. Is music an art of imitation? Is its principal object to imitate? Chabanon begins his argument with the observation that animals, babies, and savages respond to music without knowing anything about imitation. The songs of savages are totally unreflective of their words and of the occasions on which they are sung.

Chabanon cites Morellet at length to the effect that musical imitation is imperfect and that music is something more than exact imitation. He addresses to Morellet the question, Why are the other arts confined to giving us faithful images, while music is exempt from this? Is it not because music is less an art of imitation than the others? The alternative explanation Chabanon offers is essentially the same as that of Boyé. The ear, just like the other senses, has its voluptuous sensations and immediate pleasures.

Chabanon then takes up this thesis and undertakes a further demonstration that "music pleases independently of imitation." After repeating that the response of animals, babies, and savages has nothing to do with imitation, he cites the prelude in music, which again does not imitate. The same is true of music that comforts people and cures those who are ill. "Music therefore acts immediately on our feelings." But the mind is always active and searches for analogies with various objects. It thus proposes imitation to music as a secondary purpose, and it finds even the slightest relations sufficient. But how does music produce imitations, Chabanon asks? "It assimilates (as far as it is able to) its sounds to other sounds, its movements to other movements, and more than all of that, its sensations to our feelings." [9] But the imitations are weak, and they use worn-out formulas; consequently, the ear loses nearly all that the mind gains. Yet if musical imitation is used together with the stage, both the music and the situation are enhanced.

Chabanon then turns his attention to the affections and passions, showing first that song is not an imitation of speech. For one thing, we do not even know that speech preceded song. Nor can we say that languages themselves were derived from the imitation of objects and impressions, for if they were, the various languages would all have resemblances. Chabanon maintains instead that song and speech were independent and that instrumental music preceded vocal. The intervals of speech can be neither perceived nor calculated, and even among the Greeks song differed entirely from speech. Indeed, all the processes of music, including embellishments, repetition, key changes, and harmony, deviate from and even contradict those of speech. Music imitates neither natural speech nor oratorical or theatrical declamation.

Similarly, the expression of song does not consist in the imitation of the inarticulate cry of the passions. How does one make a song from a cry, or from laughter, or from those of our passions that have no cry at all? And how are we to explain expression in instrumental music? Chabanon answers by citing Quintilian: "Nature has made us sensitive to melody." A pleasing melody makes an impression of a certain character on us, and this impression can be made determinate by setting appropriate words to the melody. Similarly, "the air that we call *tender* does not perhaps constitute in us exactly the same situation of body and mind that we would have in actually pitying a woman, a father, a friend. But between these two situations, the one actual, the other musical . . . the analogy is such that the mind consents to take the one for the other." In this way, a slightly vague sensation can be turned into a distinct feeling. Chabanon then investigates the natural means that give melody its various characters. A few of his observations follow:

> The minor mode produces, in general, a sweeter, softer, and more sensitive impression than the major mode. . . . High tones have some indefinable clarity and brilliance that seems to incite the soul to gaiety. Compare the high strings of the harp with the low strings of the same instrument, and you will feel how the latter more readily dispose the soul to tenderness: who knows whether the large undulations of the long and slightly taut strings do not communicate similar vibrations to our nerves, and whether that propensity of our body is not the one which will give us tender sensations? Man, you may believe me, is only an instrument; his fibers respond to the strings of the lyrical instruments which assail them and interrogate them: each tone has its properties, and each instrument also, from which the melody profits skillfully, but which it also controls at its pleasure; for the most sensitive instrument can articulate joyous melodies with success. . . . Those whose taste inclines to sadness, draw out the tones . . . , their bow is afraid to leave the string; their voice gives to the melody some indefinable indolence and laziness. (p. 314)

Considering again the imitation of speech, Chabanon points out that, if song is made to serve this end and to depend on prosodic inflections, there will be two arts of music rather than one: "The vocal will have its principles; and the instrumental will also." Furthermore, each language will have its separate vocal idiom. By way of contrast, however, Chabanon maintains, "Music is simply melody; melody differs from speech; it has its separate processes, which do not depend upon the pronunciation of words. Consequently instrumental melody is like vocal; music of the concert like that of the dance; that of the theater like that of the church; that of Europe like that of Asia." He then explicates this extreme position by a number of examples, of which the first is particularly telling: "Twenty years ago it was not thought at all at the Opéra that the voice could or should do what the instrument did. A ritornello began and said one thing; the voice unexpectedly arrived afterwards to say another. It is no longer that way; orchestra and the actor speak the same language; the same spirit animates them and identifies them (p. 317).

This remarkably clear-sighted account of music signals the end of imitation as the foundation of a general aesthetic. If music was to be integrated into a family of the arts, some unifying principle other than imitation would have to be discovered.

England

Somewhat similar to Crousaz's *Traité du beau* (1715) was the English treatise *An Inquiry Concerning Beauty, Order, Harmony, Design* (1725) by Francis Hutcheson. Here again in the early part of the century is an important treatise in general aesthetics that is connected primarily with visual art and devoted to beauty rather than imitation. And beauty, characteristically, is associated with mathematical concepts of order and harmony as well as with the criterion of "uniformity amid variety." Another fundamental feature of aesthetics is its kinship with morality. Indeed, Hutcheson's treatise on aesthetics was published together with a treatise on "moral good and evil" that attempts, as Hutcheson says, "to introduce a mathematical calculation in subjects of morality." The overall title of this dual publication of 1725 was *An Inquiry into the Original of our Ideas of Beauty and Virtue; In Two Treatises.*

Although the treatise on beauty seems to inaugurate systematic aesthetics, it has its foundation in the work of Shaftesbury: in the two treatises, the title page states, "the principles of the late Earl of Shaftesbury are explain'd and defended." Basic to Hutcheson's view and central in directing attention to the subjective aspect of aesthetics is the notion of a "sense of beauty"— the power we have of receiving the idea provoked in us by the quality of uniformity amid variety in an external object. Beauty is this provoked idea. Of considerable interest, in addition, is the clear distinction between absolute and relative beauty (or original and comparative beauty). We perceive relative beauty in objects that are "commonly considered as imitations or resemblances of something else," while the perception of absolute beauty is independent of any comparison. Hutcheson is interested primarily in original beauty, which in music is manifested by harmony, but he also acknowledges "another charm" in music "to various persons," for when there is any resemblance of a melody to the sound of the human voice in any passion, that same passion will be excited in us by a kind of sympathy.

Because of the different dispositions of man, however, there will be different preferences in imitative music, which stand in sharp contrast to the uniformity of the sense of beauty. This uniformity can be accounted for by Shaftesbury's Platonic view of the universe as an animate work of art created by God, for it is then natural that the arts of man as well as man himself would reveal the same qualities of beauty and also that man would possess an inner, or internal, sense (in addition to the corresponding external sense of perception) that would be responsive to these qualities. Thus, in addition to hearing, for example, we speak of a "musical ear." Relative beauty is another matter, however, and, starting in the 1740s both in England and in France, treatises appear that are devoted specifically to musical and artistic imitation, and with them an entirely different group of problems comes into view.

English tracts on musical imitation are very similar to those published in France: in connection with other arts, and particularly with poetry, they examine the relative adequacy of the theory of imitation in its application to music. Also like the French tracts they expose the weaknesses of the theory and give increasing weight to conceptions of expression rather than of imitation and increasing attention to the problem of finding alternative theories. The writers of both countries, in addition, are distinguished by their inventiveness and their clarity of thought; their style is uniformly engaging and often quite amusing. The first English essay to attract wide attention in this field was "A Discourse on Music, Painting, and Poetry" by James Harris, an English grammarian who was a nephew of Shaftesbury's. The essay appeared in 1744, in Harris's *Three Treatises Concerning Art*. Harris accepts without question that the three arts of his title are all mimetic, or imitative. His concern is to determine which art is the most excellent of the three. They differ, he says, in accuracy of imitation, in the subjects they imitate, and in the value of these subjects. After discussing the subjects the arts imitate, Harris sets this factor aside and turns to the other two types of difference: "Now, from these two circumstances; that is to say, from the accuracy of the imitation, and the merit of the subject imitated, the question concerning which art is most excellent must be tried and determined." [10]

"In music," he asserts, "the fittest subjects of imitation are all such things and incidents as are most eminently characterized by motion and sound" (p. 181). Thus, music can imitate the accidents of water, thunder, and winds, the sounds of animals and birds, and some motions and sounds of people, particularly the sounds expressive of grief and anguish. It turns out, however, that musical imitation is much inferior to that of painting, and imperfect at best. Harris goes on, therefore, to consider whether the efficacy of music does not have a source other than imitation. He starts with a few assertions, the truth of which he evidently finds obvious. (1) Music can arouse various affections, just as ideas can. (2) Ideas and affections have reciprocal effects (doleful ideas arouse melancholy, e.g., and melancholy arouses doleful ideas). (3) If an affection is already present—let us say, through the action of music—then ideas corresponding to it will make a greater impression since the affection they naturally arouse will be reinforced by the level of that affection already present. Even the ideas will be reinforced by the tendency of the initial affection to produce the same ideas:

> A poet thus assisted finds not an audience in a temper averse to the genius of his poem, or perhaps at best under a cool indifference; but by the preludes, the symphonies, and concurrent operation of the music in all its parts, rouzed into those very affections which he would most desire.
>
> An audience so disposed not only embrace with pleasure the ideas of the poet when exhibited, but in a manner even anticipate them in their several imaginations. . . .
>
> And hence the genuine charm of music, and the wonders which it works through its great professors. A power, which consists not in imitations and the raising ideas, but in the raising affections, to which ideas may correspond. There are few to be found so insensible, I may even say so inhumane, as when good poetry is justly set to music, not in some degree to feel the force of so amiable an union. (p. 183)

Harris seems to be interested in the nature of music and in its effects only with regard to its combination with poetry. In the singing of poetry, he resumes, we give up a certain probability and resemblance to nature for the sake of a noble heightening of the affections that are suitable and for the sake of our interest in the subject and our enjoyment:

> For poetry, when alone, must be necessarily forced to waste many of its richest ideas in the mere raising of affections, when to have been properly relished, it should have found those affections in their highest energy. And music, when alone, can only raise affections, which soon languish and decay, if not maintained and fed by the nutritive images of poetry. Yet must it be remembered, in this union, that poetry ever have the precedence; its utility as well as dignity being by far the more considerable. (p. 184)

Harris's automatic but crucial equation of musical affections with those aroused by ideas, however, was destined to be closely scrutinized by his successors.

An Essay on Musical Expression (1752) by Charles Avison begins with a consideration of "the force and effect of music." Musical sounds—a full chord or a beautiful succession of tones—give pleasure by a peculiar and internal sense. They "divest the soul of every unquiet passion," producing a silent and serene joy and a rational, benevolent, and happy tranquillity. If we add expression to the effect of melody and harmony in themselves, they can excite all the most agreeable passions of the soul. It is indeed a special capacity of music to excite the sociable and happy passions and to subdue the contrary ones, for the natural effect of melody and harmony is to produce a pleasurable state. Thus, Avison connects the two traditional powers of music in such a way that the effect of temperance and balance acts to control the arousal of emotions by favoring the pleasant variety. He thereby provides a foundation for the eighteenth-century avoidance of the more violent and negative passions, which were considered unsuitable for music.

Avison then turns to the analogies between music and painting and undertakes a systematic discussion of their resemblances. They both treat of proportion; melody, harmony, and expression in music resemble design, coloring, and expression in painting; the mixture of concords and discords corresponds to chiaroscuro; the bass, tenor, and treble correspond to foreground, middle ground, and distance; the subordination of other parts to the theme ("subject") corresponds to the subordination of other figures to the principal figure; the coherence of a group of themes that are mutually supporting is like the roundness of a group of figures; the necessity of a listening position from which the sounds fuse and are heard in proper relative strengths is like the necessity of a proper viewing point from which the parts are seen in their just proportions; and, finally, the various styles in music— to which various instruments are suited—are analogous to the various styles in painting, such as the grand, the graceful, and the joyous.

Avison maintains that expression arises from a combination of melody and harmony "and is no other than a strong and proper application of them to the intended subject." He distinguishes expression sharply from certain kinds of imitation: rising or falling pitch used to denote ascent or descent, broken intervals used to denote an interrupted motion, rapid passages to describe swiftness or flying, or sounds resembling laughter used to describe laughter: "Now all these I should choose to stile imitation rather than expression, because it seems to me that their tendency is rather to fix the hearers' attention on the similitude between the sounds and the things which they describe, and thereby to excite a reflex act of the understanding, than to affect the heart and raise the passions of the soul." [11]

Defects in music, Avison continues, arise through too great a concern with melody and a consequent neglect of harmony, by too great an attention to harmony or "fugues" so that melodic beauty is destroyed, and by the use of a forced or "unmeaning" imitation and consequent neglect of both melody and harmony, "on which alone true musical expression can be founded." Some very eminent composers, Avison says,

> seem to think they have exhausted all the depths of expression by a dextrous imitation of the meaning of a few particular words that occur in the hymns or songs which they set to music. Thus were one of these gentlemen to express the following words of Milton, ". . . their songs / Divide the night, and lift our thoughts to heaven," it is highly probable that upon the word divide he would run a division of half a dozen bars, and on the subsequent part of the sentence, he would not think he had done the poet justice, or risen to that height of sublimity which he ought to express, till he had climbed up to the very top of his instrument, or at least as far as a human voice could follow him. (p. 191)

But music has very limited powers as an imitative art. Indeed, it should always be combined with poetry when it tries to be imitative, and then it achieves its purpose by arousing affections that correspond to those produced by the poem. Avison forgoes pursuing these assertions because Harris has already demonstrated them "with the precision and accuracy which distinguishes his writings" (p. 191). He contents himself instead with adding a few practical observations by way of corollary. First, when sounds of the inanimate world are to be imitated, accompanying instruments should be used and the voice reserved for expression, that is, for arousing suitable affections. The voice will be appropriate, of course, for chromaticism expressing grief and anguish since here expression will coincide with imitation. Second, when music imitates motions, both vocal and instrumental parts should join in the imitation. Caution is called for in imitating motion since musical intervals are not strictly similar to physical motions. Third, "as music can only imitate motions and sounds only imperfectly, it will follow that musical imitation ought never to be employed in representing objects of which motion or sound are not the principal constituents" (p. 193). Thus, one property of frost is to make people tremble, but a tremulous movement of semitones will never convey the idea of frost, although it may that of a trembling person. Fourth,

> As the aim of music is to affect the passions in a pleasing manner, and as it uses melody and harmony to obtain that end, its imitation must never be employed on ungraceful motions or disagreeable sounds, because in the one case it must injure the melody of the air, and in the other the harmony of the accompaniment; and in both cases must lose its intent of affecting the passions pleasingly.

Fifth, since musical imitation is of use only when it aids the expression, the composer should not seize on every metaphor or epithet, such as "warbling," to show his imitative power:

> What then is the composer who would aim at true musical expression to perform? I answer, he is to blend such an happy mixture of air and harmony as will affect us most strongly with the passions or affections which the poet intends to raise, and that on this account he is not principally to dwell on particular words in the way of imitation, but to comprehend the poet's general drift or intention, and on this to form his airs and harmony, either by imitation (so far as imitation may be proper to this end) or by any other means. But this I must still add, that if he attempts to raise the passions by imitation, it must be such a temperate and chastened imitation as rather brings the object before the hearer than such a one as induces him to form a comparison between the object and the sound.

A fundamental idea in this recommendation, as Avison points out, is that an awareness of the composer's art will check the passion. Music must work in a secret and unsuspected manner. Similarly, there must be no conspicuous display of the composer's skill. For a general principal that will foster expression, then, Avison turns to the values that dominate musical aesthetics for most of the century—*"an unaffected strain of nature and simplicity"* (p. 194). He suggests also that the observation of fine compositions will reveal the effects that various sounds have on the imagination and the affections.

Like the composer, the performer also should not engage in trifling imitations, such as mimicking flageolets, horns, or bagpipes on the violin. In contrast, however, Avison considers the finest instrumental music to be an imitation of vocal music—a view characteristic of the century. Violins in particular, with their expressive tone and subtle changes in pitch, approach most closely the perfection of the human voice.

Unlike Harris, who makes no use of the concept of expression, Avison regards it as the musical value that should replace imitation. His view of expression, however, is characteristic of the general outlook of his times, for which musical expression is not so much a property or an intrinsic part of music but a matter of its effect or power. Expression is the arousal of passions and affections.

The *Observations on the Correspondence between Poetry and Music* (1769) by Daniel Webb is notable for its investigation of the relation between external feelings and those aroused by music. Like its predecessors, it exerted considerable influence; a German translation by J. J. Eschenburg appeared in 1771. Seeking to uncover the connection between sound and sentiment, Webb observes the prominence of ideas of motion in our characterization of the passions (anger quickens, pride exalts) and maintains that this confirms the view that the passions produce various "proper and distinctive motions in the most refined and subtle parts of the human body." The nerves and the spirits, he says, are generally considered to be those parts. Thus, since music produces vibrations, we can deduce that the agreement of music with passion must arise from a coincidence of movements. Webb cites Kircher to this effect and holds that this mode of operation, whether real or imaginary, enables us to convey more clearly ideas concerning "the several modes of Imitation." He divides the musical impressions that correspond to the passions into four general types, based on the types of motion involved:

> If they agitate the nerves with violence, the spirits are hurried into the movements of anger, courage, indignation, and the like.
> The more gentle and placid vibrations shall be in union with love, friendship, and benevolence.
> If the spirits are exalted or dilated, they rise into accord with pride, glory, and emulation.
> If the nerves are relaxed, the spirits subside into the languid movements of sorrow.
> From these observations it is evident, that music cannot, of itself, specify any particular passion, since the movements of every class must be in accord with all the passions of that class.[12]

Instrumental music will therefore give us no determinate idea of any agreement or imitation, but if words cooperate with music, general impressions become specific indications. Webb endorses and explains the prevailing view that not all passions are open to musical imitation:

> Painting and sculpture, on whatever subjects employed, act simply, as imitative arts; they have no other means of affecting us than by their imitations. But music acts in the double character of an art of impression as well as of imitation: and if its impressions are necessarily, and in all cases pleasing, I do not see how they can, by any modification, be brought to unite with ideas of absolute pain. (p. 204)

A new accuracy of thought is revealed in this passage in the use of the term "impression" in place of "expression." Many supposedly painful passions, Webb continues, are at times accompanied by pleasure, as terror is when it is excited by the sublime, and thus relatively few passions will be excluded from musical expression. In this way, significantly, Webb partially overcomes the established tradition of restricting expression to the pleasing passions, a restriction in theory that doubtless reflected eighteenth-century taste.

Investigating the connection between motion and feeling more closely, Webb takes Shakespeare as a point of departure: "It was from a feeling of an imitative virtue in music, or of its aptness to excite pathetic motions, that Shakespeare attributes to it the power of producing a kind of reverberation in the soul: *Duke.* How dost thou like this tune? / *Viola.* It gives a very echo to the seat / Where love is throned (*Twelfth Night*)." He then applies this idea to the effects of *forte* and *piano* in music: "Loudness is an increased velocity in the vibration, or a greater vibration made in the same time. Music therefore becomes imitative, when it so proportions the enforcement or diminution of sound to the force or weakness of the passion, that the soul answers, as in an echo, to the just measure of the impression" (p. 208). Similarly, the voice becomes louder or softer in accordance with the affection it is expressing.

Much of Webb's treatise is devoted, as we would expect in English aesthetics, to the relative virtues of poetry and music and to the principles of their combination. The difference of the two arts in respect of imitative capacity is a major consideration. One passage employs *imitation* as a general term that includes both expression and description: "Now though the imitations of verse may be applied to the purposes either of expression or of description, it is not the same thing with regard to music, the effects of which are so exquisite, so fitted by nature to move the passions, that we feel ourselves hurt and disappointed, when forced to reconcile our sensations to a simple and unaffecting coincidence of sound or motion" (p. 213). The opposed character of poetry and music can be seen even in the imitations of sounds, for poetry excels in the imitation of harsh sounds and music in the imitation of pleasing ones.

The chief value of the treatise, however, lies not in its comparison of poetry and music or in the theory of their combination; nor does it lie in the theory of the limitations of music in its imitation of external objects. Rather, Webb shows a fine insight into the role of motion in the musical imitation of the passions, and it is in the four types of motion and the four groups of passions that correspond to them that an explanation is offered of the really puzzling "limitation" of music: its inability to express a particular passion.

A brief but cogent essay on artistic imitation by the renowned Orientalist William Jones was included in his publication *Poems, Chiefly Translations from Asiatick Languages, together with Two Essays on the Poetry of Eastern Nations and on the Arts commonly called Imitative* (1772). In direct contradiction to the widespread identification of imitation and expression, the essay conceives them as opposites. Jones undertakes at once to establish a basis for the effect of music other than imitation. "It must be clear to anyone," he maintains, "who examines what passes in his own mind, that he is affected by the finest poems, pieces of music and pictures, upon a principle which, whatever it be, is entirely distinct from imitation."[13] He finds support for this contention in Muhammadan countries, where no kind of imitation is admired and imitative visual art is forbidden. Poetic and musical expression, then, which is cultivated with enthusiasm, would seem to rest on some other principle.

On the theory that poetry and music had their origin in the expression of the passions, Jones considers their various sources: praise of the Creator (including the Dionysian origin of the drama), love, grief, and the detestation of vice, which is responsible for moral poetry (including epic and satire). That the expressive values of music account for its effects Jones illustrates in a discussion of ancient and modern modes. He then distinguishes "the music of sounds" from "the music of the passions," connecting the two types with harmony and melody, somewhat as these were contrasted by Rameau and Rousseau. He sees no value at all, however, in harmony and polyphony.

Painting can be strictly imitative, Jones concedes, but "its most powerful influence over the mind, arises, like that of the other arts, from sympathy." Music, on the other hand, cannot be strictly imitative, for even descriptive music acts "by a kind of substitution, that is, by raising in our minds, affections or sentiments, analogous to those which arise in us when the respective objects in nature are presented to our senses" (p. 146).

Entering on the central problem of taste, Jones maintains that the passions are "differently modified" in different men, with the result that there is great diversity in the pleasure they receive from art. He also asserts that there is one uniform standard of taste since the passions are "generally the same in all men." This phase of the essay is not elaborated, however, so that we do not learn how he might have resolved the dilemma.

Jones finally introduces the concept of the sublime, which he distinguishes from the beautiful in terms of his basic theory, stating "that the expressions of love, pity, desire and the tender passions . . . produce in the arts what we call the beautiful; but that hate, anger, fear and the terrible passions . . . are productive of the sublime" (p. 147). At the same time, beauty is no longer defined traditionally, in terms of order, symmetry, and so on, for such a characterization is contradicted, or at least rendered superfluous, by defining it as a type of expression.

The *Essay on Poetry and Music as They Affect the Mind* (1776) by James Beattie is a lengthy and thoughtful investigation of its subject that not only finds imitation to be quite unimportant in music but also goes on to characterize the art in alternative ways that are more appropriate to its nature. The idea of pleasure plays a central role in the essay. It is the pleasure we take in imitation that impresses Beattie and that he tries to account for, and it is similarly the pleasure we find in music that he seeks to explain, for the value and important role of both imitation and music could hardly exist without this motivation. "Such is the delight we have in imitation," he writes, "that what would in itself give neither pleasure nor pain, may become agreeable when well imitated. . . . No wonder, then, that what is agreeable in itself, should, when surveyed through the medium of skillful imitation, be highly agreeable." [14] This goes considerably further than Aristotle's idea that "the habit of feeling pleasure or pain at mere representations is not far removed from the same feeling about realities" (*Politics* 1340a). Even the imitation of unpleasant things, Beattie contends, may be regarded with delight.

Can it be said of music, then, as it can be of painting and poetry, that an air expressive of devotion, for example, is agreeable because it presents us with an imitation of those sounds by which devotion naturally expresses itself? But, Beattie says, the reader would ask, "What is the natural sound of devotion? Where is it to be heard?" (p. 218). Thus, Beattie would strike music off the list of imitative arts, although he regards it still as a fine art. He finds also that imitation is a property of some music, but not of all. The matter hinges on the definition of imitative music, which, Beattie maintains, quite logically, must put one in mind of the thing imitated. He examines in detail the musical imitation of sounds, motions, and high and low elevation, and his conclusion is the following:

> If we compare imitation with expression, the superiority of the latter will be evident. Imitation without expression is nothing: imitation detrimental to expression is faulty: imitation is never tolerable, at least in serious music, except it promote and be subservient to expression. If then the highest excellence may be attained in instrumental music, without imitation; and if, even in vocal music, imitation have only a secondary merit; it must follow, that the imitation of nature is not essential to this art; though sometimes, when judiciously employed, it may be ornamental. (p. 223)

It can clearly be seen in this passage that Beattie's analysis of musical imitation rests on a sharp distinction between "imitation" and "expression." The equation of the two, which depended to some extent on the ambiguity of both terms, opened the door formerly to a confused expansion of the territory of "imitation" in the interest of preserving its applicability to music, but this is no longer the prevailing interest, for a gradual change is under way in the whole conception of musical values. It is also evident, in connection with this change, that instrumental music has acquired enough significance to play a role in Beattie's conception of music as a whole.

Having disposed of purely physical objects of imitation, Beattie considers the imitation of passions and feelings. Can the tones of even the most pathetic melody be said to resemble the voice of a person speaking from the impulse of passion? Beattie grants only that there is some analogy between certain musical sounds and mental affections: "Soft music may be considered as analogous to gentle emotions; and loud music, if the tones are sweet and not too rapid, to sublime ones." Sometimes, also, nature or custom connects certain instruments with certain places and occasions; the sound of an organ, for example, is connected with a church and with the affections suitable to that place. This may help to account for musical expressiveness, that is, to explain why it is that certain passions are aroused or certain ideas are suggested by certain kinds of music:

> But this does not prove music to be an imitative art, in the same sense in which painting and poetry are called imitative. For between a picture and its original; between the ideas suggested by a poetical description and the objects described, there is a strict similitude: but between soft music and a calm temper there is no strict similitude; and between the sound of a drum or of an organ and the affection of courage or of devotion . . . there is only an accidental connection, formed by custom, and founded rather on the nature of the instruments, than on that of the music. (p. 225)

In the following section of his essay, Beattie considers the question of how the pleasures we derive from music can be accounted for and presents, as Chabanon was to do more fully three years later, a positive aesthetics that he deprecates by describing it as "a few cursory remarks." Even his attitude toward this type of project is surprising, suggesting that a negative critique was not only traditional but also compatible with the spirit of the times while a constructive and creative enterprise was perhaps not sufficiently scholarly or philosophical: "As I have no theory to support, and as this topic, though it may amuse, is not of any great utility, I shall be neither positive in my assertions, nor abstruse in my reasoning" (p. 227).

After stating that the prerequisite for pleasure in music is what is called a "musical ear," Beattie discusses five factors that are responsible for musical pleasure. Part of the pleasure both of melody and of harmony, he proposes first, is due to sounds themselves, especially in the case of prolonged tones. These soothe us, increase our sociability, and stimulate our imagination. The body may be mechanically affected by them, for its "finer fibres" may be excited in the fashion of sympathetic vibration. Sweetness and fullness of tone are valued in an instrument, while loud and mellow sounds are sublime, and swelling and decay of tones first awaken and then compose the faculties. The tones of a man's voice possess mellowness and energy, and a fine female voice has the sweetest and most melting sound in art or nature.

A second source of pleasure is concord and harmony, while discords, although disagreeable in themselves, can help concords produce their best effect. The third source of musical pleasure, "pathos, or expression, is the chief excellence of music" (p. 231). For Beattie this is a matter of virtue as well as pleasure, for the effects of musical expression are permanent and "useful." He presents a series of illustrations of the moral benefits of music that range from ancient Greece and Rome to Christianity. But music would not have been so highly esteemed, Beattie says, if it had been merely instrumental: "For, if I mistake not, the expression of music without poetry is vague and ambiguous; and hence it is, that the same air may sometimes be repeated to every stanza of a long ode or ballad" (pp. 231–32). While melody in itself may provoke certain ideas because of some accidental association, this would be true only for those people who had experienced the connection. Also, even instrumental music can derive significance from external circumstances; a melody sounded on the organ during a church service, for example, may promote religious meditation. Apart from these specific connections, instrumental music can at best prepare the mind in general for being affected and direct it to one group of affections rather than another. Beattie always refers to instrumental music as *mere* instrumental music: he regards it as distinctly inferior to vocal music: "But if you grant me this one point, that music is more or less perfect, in proportion as it has more or less power over the heart, it will follow, that all music merely instrumental, and which does not derive significancy from any of the associations, habits, or outward circumstances above mentioned, is to a certain degree imperfect" (p. 233).

The discussion of musical expression concludes with a series of recommendations designed to make certain that vocal music secures its valued effects. (1) Good music set to bad poetry is as inexpressive and therefore as absurd as harmonious language without meaning. (2) The words of every song should be intelligible and distinctly articulated. (3) Noisy accompaniments are not proper. (4) The frequent repetition of words or long-winded divisions of a syllable in a song confound its meaning and distract the attention. (5) The singer should remember that he has sentiments to utter as well as sounds. (6) Church music is more important than any other. (7) Flourished cadences, whether vocal or instrumental, take our attention from the subject and thus counteract the chief end of music.

The fourth source of pleasure in music Beattie designates as variety and simplicity of structure. Variety is produced by a host of factors, such as changes of key, tempo, register, dynamics, rhythm, and melody, while simplicity, which amounts largely to uniformity, is produced to a great extent by rhythmic articulation and regularity. The fifth and last source of pleasure in music is association, from which music benefits if we have heard it performed in an agreeable place, or by an agreeable person, or in our younger years, or accompanied by words describing agreeable ideas.

Beattie proceeds to a discussion of national styles in music, taking as a central consideration that music, like the visible signs of our passions, is a reflection of the state of mind of the composer—of happiness, melancholy, devotion, or affection—and thus of the character and qualities of his nation as well. But this questionable theory is not an integral or essential part of his basic scheme of aesthetics.

In the second of his *Two Dissertations, on Poetical, and Musical, Imitation* (1789), which was published with his study *Aristotle's Treatise on Poetry Translated, with Notes*, the English classical scholar Thomas Twining examined what seems to be the sole remaining means of discrediting the theory of imitation: he returned to the source of the controversy, Aristotle's *Poetics* and *Politics*. His brilliant essay, easily the equal in its clarity and logic of any of the other English or French tracts on the subject in the eighteenth century, is entitled "On the Different Senses of the Word Imitative, as Applied to Music by the Antients and by the Moderns."

Directly at the opening of his discussion, Twining reveals that a comprehensive view of the field is now a matter of course: "The whole power of music may be reduced, I think, to *three* distinct effects;—upon the *ear,* the *passions,* and the *imagination:* in other words, it may be considered as simply delighting the *sense,* as raising *emotions,* or as raising *ideas.*" In its conception of music, this clear compartmentalization of musical effects is representative of the whole mode of thought of the century; it could not be questioned until the radically different conceptions of music of the twentieth century were formulated. Typically, it was the unquestioned premises of eighteenth-century thought that made a fundamentally divergent view of music impossible. Twining continues to stake out his field:

> The last two of these effects, that is, raising emotions and raising ideas constitute the whole of what is called the *moral,* that is, mental, or *expressive* power of music; and in these only we are to look for anything that can be called *imitation.* Music can be said to imitate no farther than as it *expresses* something. As far as its effect is merely physical, and confined to the ear, it gives a simple, original pleasure; it expresses nothing, it *refers* to nothing; it is no more imitative than the smell of a rose, or the flavor of a pineapple.[15]

Shortly afterward he announces his basic theme: when the Ancients "speak of music as imitation, they appear to have solely, or chiefly, in view its power over the *affections. By imitation,* they mean, in short, what *we* commonly distinguish from imitation, and oppose to it, under the general term of *expression*" (p. 244). Twining obviously accepts the identification of expression and emotional effect that prevailed generally in the eighteenth century. He goes on to cite Aristotle, showing that what the *Poetics* calls *imitation* (*mimesis*) the *Politics* (1340a) calls *resemblance* (*homoima*). The *Politics* tells us also that what is imitated—by rhythm and by melody—is human *ethon* (character, disposition, temper, or manners), and he gives the examples of irascible and gentle character and of fortitude and temperance. Twining's claim, based on this passage, is that "Aristotle differs only in the *mode* of expression from Mr. Harris, when *he* affirms that 'there are sounds to *make us cheerful* or *sad, martial* or *tender*,' etc.:—from Dr. Beattie, when he says, 'Music may *inspire devotion, fortitude, compassion;*—may *infuse* a *sorrow*,' etc." (p. 245). Twining's claim, in other words, is that what we call the arousal of emotions the ancients called imitation. His explanation is that the ancients realized that imitation had to contain resemblance and that, since sounds cannot resemble mental affections, the resemblance had to be one of effect: the feelings produced in us by various rhythms and melodies resemble those produced by various actual feelings. This is of course not a flawless chain of reasoning. What we might deduce instead, reasoning more strictly, is that the *Poetics* and the *Politics* are inconsistent, for *resemblance* hardly seems equivalent to *imitation*.

Nevertheless, Twining tries to show that for the ancients they were equivalent. Music without words can arouse only a general feeling, a "disposition," not a particular one, a "passion," and Aristotle does in fact say that rhythms and melodies resemble dispositions (*ethē*), not passions (*pathē*). But music in ancient Greece almost always included words; therefore, the expression, or emotional effect, was indeed specific, just as a passion is. The idea of resemblance is much more accurately applicable and therefore much more likely to have arisen in this connection of specific feelings rather than general ones. And the resemblance would also be closer to imitation and thus could more readily have been called *imitation*. Both terms could then also have been easily used to describe the general resemblance of music without words to emotional disposition, although in ancient times even instrumental music was doubtless quite specific. Such, at least, is Twining's argument, and it is both ingenious and convincing. He points out, however, in closing his essay, that to group music with painting and poetry as an imitative art in modern times is to "defeat the only useful purpose of all classing and arrangement; and, instead of producing order and method in our ideas, produce only embarrassment and confusion" (p. 253).

In the essay "Of the Imitative Arts," which was published in 1795, the renowned economist Adam Smith includes a discussion of musical imitation that is distinguished by its comprehensiveness and by its clarity and independence of thought. Smith presents a hypothetical evolutionary development of vocal music and dance. Speech preceded dance, he believes, but poetry was then the result of the action of music on speech. Considering the three "sister arts," of which the common essence is rhythm, Smith depicts poetry and dance as clarifying the deficiency of music in respect of meaning. When verse is "blended and united" with a melody, "it would seem to give sense and meaning to what otherwise might not appear to have any, or at least any which could be clearly and distinctly understood, without the accompaniment of such an explication." Pantomimic dance can serve the same purpose: "Poetry, however, is capable of expressing many things fully and distinctly, which Dancing either cannot represent at all, or can represent but obscurely and imperfectly . . . in the power of expressing a meaning with clearness and distinctness, Dancing is superior to Music, and Poetry to Dancing." But the arts also differ in the ability of each to subsist independently of the others: "It is Instrumental Music which can best subsist apart, and separate from both Poetry and Dancing." Vocal music, on the other hand, "is necessarily and essentially imitative." [16]

Smith identifies three species of musical imitation: a general one, by which Music is made to resemble discourse; a particular one, by which it is made to express the sentiments and feelings with which a particular situation inspires a particular person; and a third, in which the singer expresses these sentiments and feelings by his countenance, his attitudes, his gestures, and his motions. In the discussion of the second of these types of imitation, Smith introduces an ingenious rationale of the musical imitation that is found in a vocal air. In the imitation of the passions, he maintains, music has a great advantage over discourse that is not sung:

> In a person who is either much depressed by grief or enlivened by joy, who is strongly affected either with love or hatred, with gratitude or resentment, with admiration or contempt, there is commonly one thought or idea which dwells upon his mind, which continually haunts him, which, when he has chaced it away, immediately returns upon him, and which in company makes him absent and inattentive. He can think but of one object, and he cannot repeat to them that object so frequently as it recurs upon him. He takes refuge in solitude, where he can with freedom either indulge the ecstasy or give way to the agony of the agreeable or disagreeable passion which agitates him; and where he can repeat to himself, which he does sometimes mentally, and sometimes even aloud, and almost always in the same words, the particular thought which either delights or distresses him. Neither Prose nor Poetry can venture to

imitate those almost endless repetitions of passion. They may describe them as I do now, but they dare not imitate them; they would become most insufferably tiresome if they did. The Music of a passionate air not only may, but frequently does, imitate them; and it never makes its way so directly or so irresistibly to the heart as when it does so. It is upon this account that the words of an air, especially of a passionate one, though they are seldom very long, yet are scarcely ever sung straight on to the end, like those of a recitative; but are almost always broken into parts, which are transposed and repeated again and again, according to the fancy or judgment of the composer. (pp. 210–11)

Although instrumental music is extremely limited in its imitative capacity, it may nevertheless produce all the effects of imitation. It does this through its effects. "Music can, by a sort of incantation, sooth and charm us into some degree of that particular mood or disposition which accords with its own character and temper." Unlike vocal music, which imitates a gay or melancholy person, tells us a story, or presents the feeling of some other person, instrumental music

becomes itself a gay, a sedate, or a melancholy object; and the mind naturally assumes the mood or disposition which at the time corresponds to the object which engages its attention. Whatever we feel from instrumental Music is an original, and not a sympathetic feeling: it is our own gaiety, sedateness, or melancholy; not the reflected disposition of another person. (p. 223)

Instrumental music can excite different dispositions, but it cannot imitate them: "There are no two things in nature more perfectly disparate than sound and sentiment; and it is impossible by any human power to fashion the one into any thing that bears any real resemblance to the other" (p. 224).

Smith maintains, then, that instrumental music has certain intrinsic qualities of an emotional nature and that these qualities excite corresponding feelings in the listener. Imitation has no part in the process. With the assistance or accompaniment of other arts, however, music appears to take on remarkable powers of imitation, as we can see in the case of opera. With the accompaniment of scenery, action, and poetry, although music

cannot always even then, perhaps, be said properly to imitate, yet by supporting the imitation of some other art, it may produce all the same effects upon us as if itself had imitated in the finest and most perfect manner. Whatever be the object or situation which the scene-painter represents upon the theatre, the Music of the orchestra, by disposing the mind to the same sort of mood and temper which it would feel from the presence of that object, or from sympathy with the person who was placed in that situation, can greatly enhance the effect of that imitation; it can accommodate itself to every diversity of scene. (p. 226)

Smith thereupon extends his discussion of instrumental music in a logical way by proceeding to a consideration of opera, which we must assign to the following chapter. He then examines instrumental music in its own right, contradicting to some extent his previous conception of its indefinite meaning:

But if instrumental Music can seldom be said to be properly imitative, even when it is employed to support the imitation of some other art, it is commonly still less so when it is employed alone. Why should it embarrass its melody and harmony, or constrain its time and measure, by attempting an imitation which, without the accompaniment of some other art to explain and interpret its meaning, nobody is likely to understand? (p. 232)

Instrumental music arouses the attention by the sweetness of its sounds and holds it by their connection and affinity, for these sounds, Smith explains, all have a relation to the same note—the keynote—and also to the melody:

By means of this relation each foregoing sound seems to introduce, and as it were prepare the mind for the following: by its rhythms, by its time and measure, it disposes that succession of sounds into a certain arrangement, which renders the whole more easy to be comprehended and remembered. Time and measure are to instrumental Music what order and method are to discourse; they break it into proper parts and divisions, by which we are enabled both to remember better what is gone before, and frequently to foresee somewhat of what is to come after: we frequently foresee the return of a period which we know must correspond to another which we remember to have gone before; and, according to the saying of an ancient philosopher and musician, the enjoyment of Music arises partly from memory and partly from foresight. (pp. 233–34)

Without this order and method we could remember very little and foresee still less, and the enjoyment of music would be little more than the effect of particular sounds at each particular instant:

A well-composed concerto of instrumental Music, by the number and variety of the instruments, by the variety of the parts which are performed by them, and the perfect concord or correspondence of all these different parts; by the exact harmony or coincidence of all the different sounds which are heard at the same time, and by that happy variety of measure which regulates the succession of those which are heard at different times, presents an object so agreeable, so great, so various, and so interesting, that alone, and without suggesting any other object, either by imitation or otherwise, it can occupy, and as it were fill up, completely the whole capacity of the mind, so as to leave no part of its attention vacant for thinking of any thing else. In the contemplation of that immense variety of agreeable and melodious sounds, arranged and digested, both in their coincidence and in their succession, into so complete and regular a system, the mind in reality enjoys not only a very great sensual, but a very high intellectual, pleasure, not unlike that which it derives from the contemplation of a great system in any other science. (pp. 234–35)

The meaning of an instrumental composition, Smith continues, may be said to be complete in itself, and its subject, unlike the subject of a poem or a painting, is a part of that composition. And while we may say that the complete art of painting, the complete merit of a picture, is composed of drawing, of coloring, and of expression, we cannot say that the complete art of a musician, the complete merit of a piece of music, is composed or made up of melody, of harmony, and of expression, for expression is simply the immediate and necessary effect of melody and harmony. Smith thus agrees with Charles Avison, who finds that expression arises from the combination of melody and harmony.

Alongside the remarkable and perhaps unprecedented understanding of the nature of instrumental music that is revealed in this section of the essay, there are also more traditional eighteenth-century views. Smith believes, for example, that social feelings of a positive nature have a peculiar and inherent suitability to music and that periodic regularity of melody is their natural expression. In spite of the expansion of musical expressiveness in the later part of the century, certain galant characteristics persist, just as they do in the music of Mozart.

Germany

In Germany, as in France and England, imitation was not posited as an independent object of investigation until about 1740. It was simply understood to apply to music as it did to the other arts. In *Der vollkommene Capellmeister*, in fact, in 1739, Mattheson speaks of "expressing" the passions rather than of "imitating" them, and he is concerned primarily with arousing them, which is in keeping with a rhetorical conception of music. The "affections," and the theory of the physiological activity that underlies them, were in particular a basis for musical invention. For the theory of the affections, Mattheson is indebted to Descartes's *Les Passions de l'ame* (1650) and, for the application of the theory to melodic invention, to Heinichen's *Anweisung zum Generalbass* (1711) and its second edition, *Der Generalbass in der Composition* (1728)

"The fifth aspect of the natural theory of sound," Mattheson writes, "is the most important or significant of all and deals with the effects of well-ordered sounds which serve the emotions and passions of the soul." He begins to treat each affection in detail:

> The experts on nature know how to describe the manner in which our affections actually and so to speak physically function, and it is of great advantage to a composer if he also is not inexperienced in this.
>
> Since for example joy is an expansion of our soul, thus it follows reasonably and naturally that I could best express this affect by large and expanded intervals.
>
> Whereas if one knows that sadness is a contraction of these subtle parts of our body, then it is easy to see that the small and smallest intervals are the most suitable for this passion.[17]

Thus, Mattheson is content to leave the physiological details of the theory to scientists, while any "imitation" involved also remains without mention, for it becomes an explicit concern of musical aesthetics only after the publication of Batteux's *Les Beaux-arts* (1746).

Indeed, the critique of imitation in Germany takes place to a great extent under foreign influence. Batteux's treatise was translated into German in 1751 by Johann Adolph Schlegel as *Einschränkung der schönen Künste auf Einen einzigen Grundsatz*; this was only the first of a series of translations of both French and English tracts. Schlegel appended to the translation several essays of his own on the same subject, and a commentary on the treatise was written by his older brother, Johann Elias, in 1752.

Johann Elias Schlegel had already examined artistic imitation in connection with drama and opera in several essays written during the 1740s. His point of departure was Alexander Baumgarten's conception of beauty as the perfection of sensuous knowledge. This entails unity in variety or the unity of a multiplicity. Multiplicity is needed to arouse interest, but pleasure demands the order and easy comprehensibility of the totality. This order, in turn, consists in the similarity of the artistic whole to its model. Schlegel's interest in imitation, however, was precisely the *difference* between the work of art and its model, for it is the comparison of the two that allows the order and perfection of the artistic image to be perceived more clearly. This is a conception that really makes imitation subordinate to beauty.

Accordingly, in his commentary on Batteaux, Schlegel regards the sensuous beauty of music as a value in its own right. For all the arts, he maintains, we may adopt

> not the principle of imitation as the highest but the principle of the sensuous expression of perfection. . . . That tones can serve the purpose of expression, and actually serve, cannot really be doubted. Everything depends, therefore, on whether tones always must necessarily be considered as expression, on whether they cannot at times be manipulated as mere tones, according to their relation to one another, and also according to their capacity to charm a musical ear.[18]

This subordination of imitation was followed, in 1754, by a still more complete rejection of Batteux's principle in an essay entitled "Sendschreiben eines Freundes an den andern über einige Ausdrücke des Herrn Batteux von der Musik," by Caspar Ruetz, cantor and director of music in Lübeck. Tones are not prefigured in words, Ruetz maintains, not even in recitative, and certainly not in an aria: "How far would a composer get when he wanted to set an aria, let us say, if no other tones were permitted to him than those that the natural character of a passion required?" The province of music extends "not only beyond the poverty of an imitated changeable utterance but beyond everything that sounds and sings." Music is no copy of nature, Ruetz insists, but the original itself; it is a natural language: "Not only are the emotions and passions that are also themes of poetry and oratory subject to music, but also a thousand other feelings that cannot be named and described precisely because they are not themes of eloquence."[19]

This recognition of a specifically musical expressiveness was followed shortly afterward by another essay connected with Batteux's treatise, "Abhandlung von der Nachahmung der Natur in der Musik" (1754) by Johann Adam Hiller, who was later to be regarded as the originator of the singspiel. Hiller's essay takes the form of a review of Batteux's treatise, but it really goes its own way and modifies the conception of imitation extensively. "Let us observe," he proposes,

> what takes place in our heart when we listen to many a musical composition. We are attentive; it is pleasing. It seeks to arouse neither sadness nor joy, neither sympathy nor rage, yet we are moved by it. We are moved so imperceptibly by it, so gently, that we do not know what we feel, or, better, that we can give our feeling no name. This feeling of the tones is unknown to us, but it gives us pleasure, and that is enough.

Indeed, the recipient in music cannot name everything or give it a specific designation. Hence music has always filled its office when it has satisfied our heart.[20]

Hiller cites Batteux to this effect, adding that music can always turn to poetry if we desire it to be understandable or to display its power in the imitation of nature. The association of music and poetry, Hiller continues, is like the association of drawing and color in painting. And the words actually contain a natural melody, he claims, which music works up and adds to.

Hiller proceeds to consider the different basic kinds of music—vocal and instrumental, religious and operatic—and then turns to the different kinds of object that music can imitate and to its power to produce tears when it imitates feelings and passions. In the imitation of natural objects that are perceived by the senses, the power of music almost defies explanation:

> We have so much confidence in this kind of imitation, and we are so little on our guard against it, that we often let one sense give the illusion of another or we let hearing represent things that otherwise would not be at all suitable for it. Things that should be grasped by means of an entirely different sense organ seem suddenly to have changed their nature: we believe we find them in tones, and we really do find them there, as vastly different as they otherwise are. Is this not a kind of magic? I do not know what may make us so obliging that we let ourselves be deceived without becoming aware of it or, if we do notice it, that we do not seek to hold ourselves guiltless in the deception. Is a secret inclination to the strange and foreign perhaps to blame for this? Or do we have too little fortitude to resist the power of tones? This is a riddle that reason will not easily solve because it is presented to it as though only in a dream. (p. 534)

To be sure, Hiller is here considering arias, where the text specifies the object of imitation, but what he is trying to account for is the peculiar power of tones to make this object vivid.

He pursues his inquiry with the help of a particular example:

> The flitting of a shadow, which in the language of opera means the ghost of someone who has died, has also given rise to various and often fortunate imitations.

> Perhaps it is possible here to discover in some measure the trick by which our imagination is deceived, and our heart along with it. The appearance of a ghost, the fluttering of a spirit departed from the body, if it really encountered or could encounter us, would be something fearful for us. Art uses this circumstance as an aid; and as it desires to present

a thing that we do not know from any experience better than from the one it presents us with, it does not seek so very carefully to express the quivering or flitting about the ghost; it seeks to express it only fearfully, only terrifyingly. It succeeds in this strategem. We hear and yet believe we see. The tones tremble before our ears, and we think a ghost flutters about before our eyes.

The composer's invention, however, "must still be comparable to nature and have a certain similarity to it. It must not be too far removed from nature; otherwise the imitation would collapse" (pp. 535–36). Hiller stretches the conception of imitation, but does not break with it.

A somewhat similar situation prevails in his discussion of instrumental music. "There are certain musical pieces," he writes,

> that are not so precisely subjected to imitation and to the expression of passions. Art, occupied with itself alone, seems to have brought them forth without the help of nature and to have invented them solely for the pleasure of instruments or of the artist who plays on them. . . .
>
> The melody of a solo or concerto . . . is not so much an imitated song of the passions and the heart as much more a contrived, artful connection of tones in keeping with the constitution of the instrument that is played on, of the correctness of which we must let art rather than nature be the judge. Perceiving its beauty is more a matter of science than of feeling. The artist seeks to show his skill and the perfection of his instrument in such pieces. The astonishment of the listeners is the only approbation he desires. (pp. 536–37)

Here Hiller launches into a lengthy discussion of the wonderful in art, with all its dangers of exaggeration, pomposity, and virtuosic display. He laments such violations of good taste, yet he will not eliminate the wonderful altogether simply because it is misused. He then introduces the idea that an instrument should imitate the human voice—not the actual tones of passion, but their artistic expression in song. Thus, instrumental music is subject to two different values: the wonderful and the expression of the passions. Hiller is led momentarily into operatic aesthetics and finally into the galant or rococo distaste for violent feelings:

> Our heart is more engaged by the peaceful and gentle feelings; it is too strongly assailed by the powerful ones; it is oppressed by their burden. It constantly demands, therefore, that, the sooner the better, the artist descend from the supernatural and wonderful to the natural and moving, in order to give it the needed peace again. Only certain sallies beyond the boundaries of the natural, into the sphere of the wonder-

ful—in which one must not forget, however, some early return—will secure both the astonishment of the ears and the approbation of the heart. (p. 542)

The essay is particularly valuable for its scope as well as its insight, for it reveals the close connection of the theory of imitation with both the aesthetics of the galant and the aesthetics of opera.

Hiller's abiding interest in the question of imitation is shown by his translation of Chabanon's important *Observations sur la musique* (1779) as *Uber die Musik und ihre Wirkungen*, which was published in 1781. At the same time, the translation is another indication of the progressive character and the influence of French thought, starting with Descartes and extending through the eighteenth century.

In contrast to the innovative Elias Schlegel, Ruetz, and Hiller, there are a number of aesthetic writers in Germany during the 1750s and 1760s who continue to express traditional conceptions of music. Prominent among these are the Berlin authors Krause, Marpurg, and Sulzer.

Krause, for example, gives musical recipes for the description and arousal of various affections, which he regards as real and thus as depending for their effect on the temperament of the listener. Music should be turned literally into a language, in his view, with definite meanings belonging to individual phrases and motifs.

Friedrich Wilhelm Marpurg, in his *Kritische Briefe über die Tonkunst* (1760–64, published originally as a weekly from 1759 to 1763), has a still more realistic view of the affections, including the application of "science" and "pathology":

> Thus it would be no thankless effort if a composer with adequate insight into pathology and also into music, with the help of other qualified men, took on himself the task of collecting sufficient examples of the expression of each affection from the dramatic and epic, sacred and secular, serious and playful pieces, and other works of the most famous composers in the arioso and recitative style, in order to confirm with these the preceding rules.[21]

J. G. Sulzer, the author of *Allgemeine Theorie der schönen Künste*, to which J. P. Kirnberger and J. A. P. Schulz contributed many of the articles on music, is an eclectic author whose views are similar to Marpurg's and often derived from Krause. He sees the purpose of music as the arousal of affections by appropriate successions of tones. Music is an "intelligible language of the feelings." It must also possess a moral force, awakening a vigorous feeling for the good and a strong aversion to the bad.

Quantz and C. P. E. Bach, on the other hand, mix newer views with traditional ones: musical values of sensuousness and expressivity with the concept of particular affections. They also favor change and variety in the affections, as we have seen, in spite of their belief in the realistic nature of these affections—a belief that performance readily produces and reinforces. The eclectic Christoph Nichelmann (*Die Melodie nach ihrem Wesen sowohl als nach ihren Eigenschaften*, 1755),[22] who is also concerned to a great extent with performance, found fault with the highly decorated virtuosity that was so characteristic of music in Berlin. This style ignored the formal organization of music, he pointed out, and subjected harmony to melody instead of integrating the two according to their natural relation.

The criticism of imitation in aesthetics that started at mid-century was understandably accompanied by alternative conceptions of the nature of music and musical feeling. This change in musical thought corresponded to a change in music itself and in instrumental music in particular. The galant style gave way to emotional warmth and expressive intensity. The *empfindsamer Stil* and the Mannheim symphony, followed by the Sturm und Drang and high Classicism, are all evidence that the second half of the century was a time of proto-Romanticism even with regard to instrumental music, and similar manifestations in the field of opera reinforce this conception. In the last few decades of the century, the interest in powerful expression and in new qualities of feeling is unmistakable, and musical aesthetics is a formulation in words of the same concerns.

The new spirit is at once manifest in the ideas of Johann Gottfried Herder and Wilhelm Heinse, and it is manifest also in their impassioned style of writing. In this respect—and in his ideas as well—Herder in particular is very much a German counterpart of Rousseau, and he influenced in turn both Heinse and Wackenroder.

In his "Viertes Wäldchen" (1769), Herder seeks to establish nothing less than a new foundation for musical aesthetics. He sets aside abstract concepts such as beauty and sublimity and adopts instead the fundamental musical experience of tone as a starting point. Much of his discussion consists of polemics, not only against abstract concepts as points of departure, but especially against physics and mathematics, which he finds useless in explaining musical experience. Aesthetics must take a subjective view of tone, not an objective one; it must be psychological and deal with the effects of tone on the listener. Music arose from intensified speech, Herder maintains; it is a language of feeling. Only tone and melody have an influence in this respect; harmony has no connection with feeling at all.

To a great extent, Herder restates what Rousseau had said long before, and his polemic against Rameau recalls the quarrel of Rousseau and Rameau about melody and harmony. But Herder sets the contentions of Rousseau in the larger framework of a systematic approach to aesthetics, and he uses tone as his primary datum rather than melody.

The structure of his aesthetics makes use of two important principles: the contrast of eye and ear and the contrast of sound and tone. The first of these became a recurrent theme of nineteenth-century musical aesthetics, and it continues to be found in the twentieth century also: "The beautiful of the eye is colder, more in front of us, easier to dissect, and remains eternally, permitting itself to be discovered; the voluptuous bliss of music lies deeply hidden in us: it acts as an intoxication."[23] But how can inner feeling be placed outside us to be analyzed—to become the object of systematic thought?

The second principle, the contrast of "sound" (*Schall*) and tone, is unfortunately not very clear, but Herder seems to regard "sound" as external and as composed of an aggregate of tones. It can be a clang (a sound, that is, composed of harmonic frequencies) or the kind of "sound" emitted when all the strings of a keyboard instrument, for example, are activated simultaneously. Herder adheres to an analytic principle, however, that with respect to "sound" he states as follows:

Sound is a corporeal mass of tones, in which these are the essential elements: as different, therefore, as the masses can be in their way, so different must the elements of the masses also be with respect to their type of sensation. All elastic bodies resound; not all are perceptible by us in the same way; thus, there must also be just as many different classes among component individual tones as there are in their sums. (p. 101)

If tone is taken to mean "pure tone," this is of course impossible, but Herder is not aware that timbre, or tone color, arises from tones that are composite. His theory—with its contrast of sound mass and tonal line, of measurable objectivity and inner feeling—could exist in its full form only because of this scientific inaccuracy.

In spite of its rejection of physical and mathematical analysis and its reliance on the immediate aesthetic quality of tonal experience, Herder's aesthetics still suffers from elementalism. Constituents do not possess all the qualities of their combination; nor are melodies adequately explained as the sum of their component tones. Herder neglects all the configurational properties that are closely connected with musical experience in its full sense, yet what he does present is in many ways a novel and suggestive groundwork for a more complete musical aesthetics. His achievement is to make no use at all of physical and mathematical relations or of the theory of imitation and to rely completely on experience that is literally aesthetic. His physiological explanation of tonal experience, finally, is as applicable to instrumental music as to vocal, for he explains the emotional effects of tone by excitation of the nerves, not by any affection that is somehow imitated or expressed musically or first expressed in words and then musically intensified. Indeed, in giving examples of the effects of tone, Herder cites a number of varied instruments but makes no reference at all to the human voice.

Herder subsequently traces the progress of sound through the ear up to the point where it reaches the auditory nerve. Here he applies the principle of specific neural energies. "In the difference of the branches of the hearing nerves," he states, "must lie also the essential specific difference of tones and tonal masses, that is, of sounds, in so far as they are the basis, with respect to quality, of musically pleasant and unpleasant sound" (p. 102). To reduce the qualities considered by Herder as residing in the very nature of tone to quantitative relations between partial frequencies would seriously damage the foundation of his aesthetics, just as Romantic science in general could not have existed if the qualitative comprehension of elemental natural phenomena, together with its mystery, had been quantified.

In the first of Heinse's three *Musikalische Dialogen*, which were written in 1776 or 1777 but published only posthumously in 1805, "Jomelli" undertakes specifically to refute the contention of "Rousseau" (who on this point shares the opinion of the historical Rousseau) that melody is only an imitation of the accents of the speaking or impassioned voice. Referring to an aria of Jomelli's on a Metastasian text, Rousseau asks, "Who taught you this so perfectly natural melody?" "Nature, without any doubt, if it is natural," Jomelli answers. "But how did you receive this melody from nature? Did you have these words declaimed by a charming and feelingful Chammelai and then set down the melody according to them, or how else did you compose it?" Rousseau follows his questions with an impassioned description of the powerful effects of Jomelli's music. Jomelli explains, however, that he made no use of imitation: "There is much too great a leap from declamation to melody. In the declamation of a person who finds himself in passion, I notice nothing further than now slow, now fast delivery; the high and low tone of this is anything but melody."[24]

If the intervals of the voice in natural speech cannot be put into notes, Jomelli asks later, how can you make a melody from them? Rousseau is unable to answer. He does not see a source for pathetic music other than impassioned speech, nor can he see how else it can exercise so great a power over the human heart. "How do you come on your pathetic melodies?" he asks. Jomelli appeals to "genius": "Perhaps it is with me as it is with most of the geniuses in all the arts; we know and are convinced that this melody will produce the effect we desire, but we do not know why?" (p. 54). But Rousseau is not satisfied: "Figure out really why you construct your melodies as they are and not otherwise! Nothing is without a reason! So say all metaphysicians, who often do not even know the reason for the statement, Nothing is without a reason!" (p. 58). "I believe," Jomelli says,

> that the reason by which we can explain all the great wonders of our art is nothing further than the effect of tone on the nerves of the human body and that we should not seek the source of this in the accents of speech, for from these it would follow that Italian music could have no effect on Frenchmen, Turks, Russians, Germans, and so on if they did not understand the Italian language; of the opposite, however, daily experience will convince you. . . . Music is a universal language; the Iroquois understands it as the Italian does, only with the difference that the former does not feel so completely the fine, the tender, and the masterful features. Why? He does not have such fine nerves as the latter. . . . A musical genius must be born; nature must create him; art will never do it. It calls for the finest, the most perfect sensitivity, the most delicate ear. (pp. 58–60)

The same tone has a vastly different effect, Jomelli continues, when it is produced by a flute than when it is produced by a trumpet. It is different with every instrument. But about the effect of tones, and especially the connections of tones, little more can be said than, I like it, or do not; I have become tender, or angry, and so on. One can only feel what is beautiful or excellent. Rules will not help:

> The only rule that can be given is, Study the nature of tones and the effects that the different connections of them have on the human heart. . . . One can soon learn to calculate; no genius is involved, for everything goes according to rules; and, as you said, a genius works only according to unknown rules, for otherwise he would not be called a genius. . . . That the octave is related as $1:2$ and the fifth as $2:3$, and so on, can help the fabricators of instruments, but not a musical genius. The ear is the judge, not the relation of $1:2$; what has this to do with the ears. (pp. 62–64)

This lengthy speech of Jomelli's, which is cited here only in part, reveals the close correspondence of Heinse's views with those of Herder. Heinse was evidently familiar with the ideas of his famous predecessor. Of particular importance is the stress on genius, which tends to replace good taste as a crucial concept. Good taste is a purely receptive capacity, a matter of sensitivity and discrimination. Genius, on the other hand, less literally aesthetic, is a matter of active energy, of formative capacity; it is a creative power connected with inspiration and identified with divine creativity.

The aesthetic views of the musical theorist and historian Johann Nikolaus Forkel are to be found in various reviews he wrote for his *Musikalisch-Kritische Bibliothek* (1778–79).[25] They deal primarily with musical imitation and its relation to the intrinsic properties of music. As we would expect in these final decades of the century, Forkel is strongly opposed to imitation and favors purely musical values, but he overstates his case and at the same time inconsistently retains some trace of older ideas. In opposition to external, pictorial representations in music, he insists that "every musical expression must be brought about by the inner force of art, by the impetus of the ideas, and by a conduct of melody and harmony that is conformable to this impetus."[26] Thus, Forkel rejects any tone painting, and he also rejects any musical presentation of psychological experience that is not fused with specifically musical expressiveness; analogies that depend on a conscious comparison of music and inner experience will not do. This is an extreme position for a historian who is particularly interested in J. S. Bach; it is especially unrealistic in the sphere of vocal music, where conscious symbolism often occurs simultaneously with specifically musical expressiveness and nevertheless does not interfere with it.

A traditional feature of Forkel's thought is his belief that the feelings accompanying music can appear only one at a time. They are "dark" or vague, and their relation to inner experience is difficult to determine. But they are "real"; they have properties that are the same as those of other feelings. Music will therefore seek to sustain a pleasant feeling and to modify and transform an unpleasant one. Only rarely, however, will a pleasant feeling be transformed into an unpleasant one "because the first axiom of the whole of musical aesthetics is to describe pleasant passions and feelings, or, in other words, to please and delight people" (p. 207). It is easy to see that this group of older ideas will act as a restraining influence on the course of musical style. It is antagonistic both to Gluck's operatic achievements and to the instrumental music of the time. Forkel maintains, for example, that

> each of our feelings constitutes . . . in itself, to a certain degree, an individual condition to which is attached an inner striving to sustain itself, that is, not to allow itself to be suppressed . . . by other feelings. If the destruction of any feeling is to take place, therefore, we must do here in the sonata what nature does with bodies . . . namely, we must weaken it little by little and thus gradually introduce its dissolution. (p. 208)

The mixture of old and new in Forkel's thought is characteristic of German musical aesthetics as a whole toward the end of the century.

But musical aesthetics also manifests considerable variety during this period. Different types of "feeling" proliferate. Imitative theories are still common, sometimes in altered form. Instead of specific feelings, music may represent states of feeling, or only the form or rhythm of feelings may be musically duplicated. Modifications of these kinds are found in J. J. Engel's *Über die musikalische Malerei* (1780) and in the *System der Ästhetik* (1790) of the Leipzig philosopher Karl Heinrich Heydenreich. Friedrich von Schiller, as we shall see below, also believed that music conveys only the form of feelings.

In contrast to these modified views of imitation, conceptions characteristic of Romantic aesthetics are found in Johann Friedrich Dalberg's *Blicke eines Tonkünstlers in die Musik der Geister* (1787). Dalberg expounds a Christianized Neoplatonism that has recourse to a dream quite similar to the vision of Er and the Dream of Scipio. Having sung Pergolesi's *Stabat mater*, Dalberg's narrator is filled with reverence and pensive melancholy. He falls asleep and hears cosmic music that is produced by the planets and by the realm of spirits. Of this, our earthly music is only the image. There is thus a type of imitation involved, but not an imitation of human feelings.

An implicit musical aesthetic that is compounded of *Empfindsamkeit* and Romanticism is embedded in the novels of this period, notably in Karl Philipp Moritz's *Andreas Hartknopf* (1786) and Jean Paul's *Hesperus* (1795), both of which combine the sentimental effects of music with its expression of endless yearning. In contrast, the operatic aesthetics in Heinse's novel *Hildegard von Hohenthal* (1795–96), which will be considered in the following chapter, is explicit and detailed. Although in addition to the ideas included in his novels Jean Paul presented his aesthetic conceptions in the *Vorschule der Aesthetik* (1804), Moritz seems to have the unique position of developing, alongside the aesthetic of sentiment and yearning in *Andreas Hartknopf*, a Classical aesthetic of the autonomy and perfection of a work of art. This appeared in his *Über die bildende Nachahmung des Schönen* (1788), but it had been sketched out in 1785, the same year in which the novel appeared, in advance of the date of publication given in the imprint. But while the aesthetic of the novel concerns the expressiveness and effect of music, that of the treatise is general rather than musical and connected more with creation than perception. It has a realization in music, however, in the quartets and symphonies of high Classicism and in Mozart's operas.

In Kant's *Critik der Urteilskraft* (1790), art is set into the context of a general examination of cognition, for it is cognition, in Kant's view, that defines the concern of philosophy in general. The problem that underlies the third *Critik* is the relation between the sensible realm of nature and the supersensible realm of freedom. Since freedom intends to actualize its purposes in the world of sense, "nature must be so thought that the conformity to law of its form at least harmonizes with the possibility of the purposes to be effected in it according to the laws of freedom." [27]

Between the understanding, then—the cognitive faculty that legislates for concepts of nature—and the reason—the cognitive faculty that legislates for freedom—there is the cognitive faculty of judgment. In conformity with these types of cognition, the soul in general contains three capacities: knowledge, desire, and the feeling of pleasure and pain: "Now between the faculties of knowledge and desire there is the feeling of pleasure, just as the judgment mediates between the understanding and the reason. We may therefore suppose provisionally that the judgment likewise contains in itself an *a priori* principle" (p. 15).

Judgment in general, Kant continues, is the faculty of thinking the particular as contained under the universal. If the universal is given, the judgment subsuming the particular under it is determinant. If only the particular is given for which the universal has to be found, the judgment is reflective. The transcendental principle of such a judgment—which must be derived from the judgment itself—is that of the formal purposiveness of nature. Nature is represented "as if an understanding contained the ground of the unity of the variety of its empirical laws":

> This transcendental concept of a purposiveness of nature is neither a natural concept nor a concept of freedom, because it ascribes nothing to the object (of nature), but only represents the peculiar way in which we must proceed in reflection upon the objects of nature in reference to a thoroughly connected experience, and is consequently a subjective principle (maxim) of the judgment. . . .
>
> The judgment has therefore also in itself a principle *a priori* of the possibility of nature, but only in a subjective aspect, by which it prescribes not to nature (autonomy), but to itself (heautonomy) a law for its reflection upon nature. (pp. 20, 22)

Understanding seeks to bring a unity of principles into nature, and the achievement of that purpose is bound up with the feeling of pleasure, which is thus due to the harmony of natural laws with our cognitive faculty.

Now the representation of an object by a subject will have an aesthetic character if it is referred to the subject but a character of logical validity if it is used to determine the object:

> If pleasure is bound up with the mere apprehension (*apprehensio*) of the form of an object of intuition, without reference to a concept for a definite cognition, then the representation is thereby not referred to

the object, but simply to the subject, and the pleasure can express nothing else than its harmony with the cognitive faculties which come into play in the reflective judgment, and so far as they are in play, and hence can only express a subjective formal purposiveness of the object. . . . Such a judgment is an aesthetical judgment upon the purposiveness of the object, which does not base itself upon any present concept of the object, nor does it furnish any such. In the case of an object whose form (not the matter of its representation or sensation), in the mere reflection upon it (without reference to any concept to be obtained of it), is judged as the ground of a pleasure in the representation of such an object, this pleasure is judged as bound up with the representation necessarily, and, consequently, not only for the subject which apprehends the form, but for every judging being in general. The object is then called beautiful, and the faculty of judging by means of such a pleasure (and, consequently, with universal validity) is called taste. (pp. 26–27)

There is thus a harmony between the form of the object and the power of judgment or, more specifically, between the representation of this form and the conformity to law in the use of the judgment. This conformity to law consists in the unity of the imagination with the understanding. In Kant's words,

> he who feels pleasure in the mere reflection upon the form of an object without respect to any concept although this judgment be empirical and singular, justly claims the agreement of all men, because the ground of this pleasure is found in the universal, although subjective, condition of reflective judgments, viz. the purposive harmony of an object (whether a product of nature or of art) with the mutual relations of the cognitive faculties (the imagination and the understanding), a harmony which is requisite for every empirical cognition. (p. 28)

Or as Kant states later in the *Critik*:

> Taste, then, as subjective judgment, contains a principle of subsumption, not of intuitions under concepts, but of the *faculty* of intuitions or presentations (i.e. the imagination) under the *faculty* of the concepts (i.e. the understanding), so far as the former *in its freedom* harmonizes with the latter *in its conformity to law*. (p. 29)

Aesthetic judgment is distinguished from teleological judgment as follows: "By the first we understand the faculty of judging of the formal purposiveness (otherwise called subjective) of nature by means of the feeling of pleasure or pain; by the second, the faculty of judging its real (objective) purposiveness by means of understanding and reason" (p. 30). Teleological judgment proceeds according to concepts. But aesthetic judgment—where the object judged belongs to art rather than nature—will also entail concepts, for in art "we realize a preconceived concept of any object which is a purpose of ours" (p. 29).

After the fundamental introduction of the *Critik*, Kant enters on a detailed analysis of beauty, which examines the judgment of taste according to quality (disinterested satisfaction), quantity (the beautiful pleases universally), purpose (beauty has the form of purposiveness but without purpose), and modality (the beautiful, without any concept, is the object of a necessary satisfaction). In the discussion of purposiveness, Kant shows that the pure judgment of taste (and therefore "free beauty," which it judges) is independent of charm and emotion, of the concept of perfection, and of any definite concept of what the object ought to be. The determining ground of such a judgment is solely the purposiveness of the form of the object. The charms of the object, then, "actually do injury to the judgment of taste if they draw attention to themselves as the grounds for judging of beauty. So far are they from adding to beauty that they must only be admitted by indulgence as aliens, and provided always that they do not disturb the beautiful form" (p. 61).

Many natural objects are free beauties (rather than "dependent beauties"), for they are not determined with respect to their purpose by concepts when they are judged. Objects of art, on the other hand, are generally intended to be objects of a certain kind and are accordingly judged as determined by concepts of what they are supposed to be. But decorative borders or wallpapers, for example, are free beauties. And we can refer to the same class, Kant says, "what are called in music phantasies . . . and in fact all music without words" (p. 66). In this last opinion, Kant seems to ignore the significance of titles in instrumental music, even of such generic titles as "sonata."

Paragraphs 43–54 of the *Critik* are devoted to art. In the "aesthetical" as opposed to the "mechanical" arts, pleasant art is distinguished from beautiful art (or "fine art"): representations are regarded as mere sensations in the first, as modes of cognition in the second. Pleasant art is directed merely to enjoyment, while fine art has reflective judgment as a standard. Beyond this, fine art must seem like nature, for both artificial and natural beauty please in the mere act of judging, not in sensation or by means of a concept. Thus, the purposiveness in fine art must not seem to be designed.

Kant then defines genius as "the innate mental disposition through which nature gives the rule to art" (p. 150). Its first property is originality, and its products are exemplary, serving as a standard or rule for others, just as nature does. Yet an author of genius does not know how he has come by his ideas. Genius is required, however, to produce beautiful objects, just as taste is required to judge them.

The important distinction between natural beauty (a beautiful thing) and artificial beauty (a beautiful representation of a thing) is examined in paragraph 48:

> In order to judge of a natural beauty as such, I need not have beforehand a concept of which sort of thing the object is to be; i.e. I need not know its material purposiveness (the purpose), but its mere form pleases by itself in the act of judging it without any knowledge of the purpose. But if the object is given as a product of art and as such is to be declared beautiful . . . there must be at bottom in the first instance a concept of what the thing is to be. And as the agreement of the manifold in a thing with its inner destination, its purpose, constitutes the perfection of the thing, it follows that in judging of artificial beauty the perfection of the thing must be taken into account. (p. 154)

The following paragraph is devoted largely to the discussion of "aesthetical ideas," doubtless the central conception in Kant's view of art. By an "aesthetical idea," Kant says, he understands

> that representation of the imagination which occasions much thought, without however any definite thought, i.e. any concept, being capable of being adequate to it; it consequently cannot be completely encompassed and made intelligible by language. We easily see that it is the counterpart (pendant) of a rational idea, which conversely is a concept to which no intuition (or representation of the imagination) can be adequate. (p. 157)

Or, as it is stated subsequently,

> the aesthetical idea is a representation of the imagination associated with a given concept, which is bound up with such a multiplicity of partial representations in its free employment that for it no expression marking a definite concept can be found; and such a representation, therefore, adds to a concept much ineffable thought, the feeling of which quickens the cognitive faculties. . . .

> The mental powers, therefore, whose union (in a certain relation) constitutes genius are imagination and understanding. In the employment of the imagination for cognition, it submits to the constraint of the understanding and is subject to the limitation of being conformable to the concept of the latter. On the contrary, in an aesthetical point of view it is free to furnish unsought, over and above that agreement with a

concept, abundance of undeveloped material for the understanding, to which the understanding paid no regard in its concept but which it applies, though not objectively for cognition, yet subjectively to quicken the cognitive powers. (p. 160)

For fine art, Kant concludes, what is required is imagination, understanding, and taste. Taste, however, is more important than genius: "Abundance and originality of ideas are less necessary to beauty than the accordance of the imagination in its freedom with the conformity to law of the understanding" (p. 163).

Beauty in general is then described as the expression of aesthetical ideas. In fine art such an idea must be occasioned by a concept of the object, while in "beautiful nature" the mere reflection on a given intuition, without any concept of the object, is sufficient to awaken and communicate the idea of which that object is regarded as the expression.

Kant divides the fine arts into three kinds: the arts of *speech* (rhetoric and poetry), the *formative* arts (sculpture, architecture, and painting), and the art of the *play of sensations* (music and the art of color). Sensations of tone and color in themselves (apart from their use in the perception of external objects) present Kant with a problem, for he finds it difficult to decide whether they are based on sense or reflection, whether they are merely pleasant sensations or a beautiful play of sensations. This depends on whether they evoke a satisfaction in form—in the form, let us say, of a tonal object, for satisfaction in form is a requisite of beauty. The vibrations of an individual tone are too rapid to be judged in respect of form, but the proportion between different rates of vibration can be judged, and such proportion gives rise to intelligible differences in quality. This is a surprisingly inadequate conception of musical form, but it is sufficient for Kant to conclude that music is either a beautiful play of sensations (altogether a *fine* art) or a beautiful play of *pleasant* sensations (at least in part a *pleasant* art). Sensory pleasure or charm in itself, we must remember, is not simply irrelevant to beauty but a threat that can disturb or injure it.

In comparing the aesthetical worth of the fine arts, Kant places poetry highest. He then divides his evaluation into two separate considerations: first, charm and mental movement, then culture supplied to the mind. With respect to charm and mental movement, music comes directly after poetry:

For although it speaks by means of mere sensations without concepts, and so does not, like poetry, leave anything over for reflection, it yet moves the mind in a greater variety of ways and more intensely, although only transitorily. It is, however, rather enjoyment than cultivation (the further play of thought that is excited by its means is merely the effect of a, as it were, mechanical association), and in the judgment of reason it has less worth than any other of the fine arts. Hence, like all enjoyment, it desires constant change and does not bear frequent repetition without producing weariness. (p. 172)

It can be urged against this view that music would leave things over for reflection even apart from concepts since it leaves behind auditory images. But it is also not devoid of concepts—those of key, mode, instruments, form, and genre, for example.

Kant takes this occasion to inquire into the charm of music and into what he takes to be its universal communicability. He appeals both to speech and to mathematics for an explanation. Every expression of speech, he argues,

> has in its context a tone appropriate to the sense. This tone indicates more or less an affection of the speaker and produces it also in the hearer, which affection excites in its turn in the hearer the idea that is expressed in speech by the tone in question. Thus as modulation is, as it were, a universal language of sensations intelligible to every man, the art of tone employs it by itself alone in its full force, viz. as a language of the affections, and thus communicates universally according to the laws of association the aesthetical ideas naturally combined therewith. Now these aesthetical ideas are not concepts or determinate thoughts. Hence the form of the composition of these sensations (harmony and melody) only serves instead of the form of language, by means of their proportionate accordance, to express the aesthetical idea of a connected whole of an unspeakable wealth of thought, corresponding to a certain theme which constitutes the dominating affection in the piece. (p. 173)

Satisfaction in this mathematical form is the condition of musical beauty, but mathematics has no share, Kant maintains, in the charm and mental movement produced by music. It is the indispensable condition of the proportion of the tonal vibrations, but it disappears in the musical effect.

With respect to culture supplied to the mind, music is assigned the lowest place among the arts, for Kant's standard is the expansion of the faculties that must concur in the judgment for cognition, and music "merely plays with sensations."

Although Kant is primarily concerned with the nature of aesthetic judgment and with the characteristics of art that are involved in this judgment, he is concerned as well with the particular characteristics of the individual arts. It is beauty that is subject to judgment, not expressiveness, although Kant also evaluates the arts with respect to their worth in the cultivation of the mind. Yet music represents not only beauty but also a kind of expression akin to speech, and it arouses the affection it expresses in the listener also. In addition, imitation—another traditional characteristic—plays a role that is more essential than expression, for music imitates the tonal modulation of speech. On the other hand, Kant's view of the play of tonal sensations as a condition for musical beauty suggests a formalist ingredient of aesthetics that belongs to the future. And there is no question, despite his appeal to speech, that Kant conceives music in its own terms, as absolute rather than vocal. He is obviously disturbed, however, as philosophers tend to be, that such music lacks concepts. It is evident, then, that Kant's conception of music is partly forward looking and partly traditional. It was in any event found to be inadequate to the nature of the art, for it became increasingly obvious with every year that passed that instrumental music was a fine art in its own right and that its beauty was not lessened by pleasure in tonal sonority but rather that both its beauty and its significance were deepened by their sensuous element. The gradual growth of this awareness constitutes a fascinating aspect of the history of aesthetic consciousness, and there is no doubt that the low esteem in which Kant held instrumental music had a positive value—because of its inadequacy—in bringing musical aesthetics to fruition.

In the remarkably eclectic aesthetics of Friedrich von Schiller, Kant is doubtless the most important influence. This can be seen in Schiller's conception of beauty (in which form plays a decisive role), in his reliance on the ideas of play and freedom, and in his celebrated definition of beauty as "freedom in appearance" (*Freiheit in der Erscheinung*). Of great influence also are the views of Winckelmann and of Goethe.

In a review of the poems of Matthisson (1794), Schiller emphasizes the idealism of art.[28] It is necessary for art to be related to our emotional capacities, but this relation must be based, not on realistic detail or on the accidental or historical features of an individual person, but on idealized feelings that are purely human—that arise from the nobility of humanity. Because of this attachment of art to human experience, the succession of feelings presented will possess a character of necessity. Now the content of feelings cannot be represented, Schiller continues, but their form can, and it is music that has this form as its object. The whole effect of music consists in accompanying and realizing the inner motions of the soul, and since these proceed according to the strict laws of necessity that belong to human nature, this necessity and definiteness also characterizes their sensible realization.

In the twenty-second letter of his *Briefe über die ästhetische Erziehung des Menschen* (1795), Schiller maintains that, because of its matter, music "has a closer affinity with the senses than true aesthetic freedom allows." The special affinities of the various arts recede, however, as a work of art reaches a higher level. In their perfection, the arts become "increasingly similar to each other in their effect upon our nature":

> Music in its loftiest exaltation must become shape, and act upon us with the tranquil power of the antique. . . . And the artist must not only overcome, by his treatment, the limitations which are inherent in the specific character of his type of art, but also those belonging to the particular material with which he is dealing. In a truly beautiful work of art the content should do nothing, the form everything; for the wholeness of Man is affected by the form alone, and only individual powers by the content. However sublime and comprehensive it may be, the content always has a restrictive action upon the spirit, and only from the form is true aesthetic freedom to be expected. Therefore the real artistic secret of the master consists in his annihilation of the material by means of the form.[29]

Just as subjection to the senses is succeeded, Schiller believed, by the freedom of form, so will aesthetic freedom pave the way for moral and political freedom. Beauty is a necessary stage in the education of man, a conception that was pressed on Schiller by the reign of terror that followed the French Revolution.

Schiller's ideas were applied to music in particular by Christian Gottfried Körner (the father of the poet, Karl Theodor), who was Schiller's closest friend and who helped stimulate his interest in philosophy initially. In his essay "Ueber Charakterdarstellung in der Musik" (1795), Körner makes a basic distinction, as Kant had done and Hanslick was later to do, between pleasure and beauty. Music as a pleasing art is directed solely to the enjoyment of the audience. But musical beauty is subject to entirely different laws. Freed from all the prejudices and fashions of his time, the composer is that much stricter with himself, "and his single endeavor is to give his works an independent, self-contained value."[30] What, Körner asks, is in itself worthy of representation by an art without respect to the receptivity of a particular public?

The imitation of natural sounds has been replaced by the expression of human feeling, but is there not a still higher goal? Körner then presents the alternative of the permanent and the transient, of ethos, or character, and pathos, or an impassioned state. It is the first of these—human moral character—that meets the fundamental and incontrovertible demand of a work of art that it be unified by an ordering power and thus distinct from the results of blind chance:

> The poet and the formative artist by their nature can never represent the state of mind without the person; but with the musician the delusion

can easily arise that it is possible for him to realize motions of the soul as something independent. If he is then satisfied to furnish a chaos of tones that expresses an unconnected mixture of passions, he will not have difficulty, to be sure, but he may not pretend to the name of artist. On the other hand, if he recognizes the need for unity, he will seek it in vain in a series of passionate mental states. Here there is nothing other than multiplicity, constant change, increase, and decrease." (p. 148)

Furthermore, a work of art cannot repeat the actual world unchanged. The artist must idealize his material: "In the creations of his fantasy the dignity of human nature must be seen. From a lower sphere of dependence and limitation he must raise us up to himself and represent the infinite, which outside of art we are permitted only to think, in perceptible form" (p. 148). But in human nature, Körner continues, there is nothing infinite but freedom, and it is this that is depicted in the representation of moral character. The representation of this ideal would not be possible, however, if music as an independent art offered us nothing definite to think about, even though we cannot translate the sense of music into words or shapes.

At one time music manifested simply a drive to express oneself; there was still no thought of representing a definite object. But then the need was felt to go beyond the personal and to create a work that existed in its own right. The realization of this work, Körner seems to feel, is necessarily accompanied by representation. The personal expression of the artist is not entirely superceded, however. It competes with the artistic idea, and a balance is produced between the two.

Now the feeling of the artist in expressing his personal mood is intrinsically dark and indistinct, and this permits the free play of the imagination. But the representation of the artistic idea demands signs with a definite meaning, and the represented object must be given definite limits; it must be conceived in a corporeal shell before it can succeed to appearance. The limits will become perceptible in particular relations, and by means of these we recognize the artistic ideal, reasoning from effects to their cause. The relations must not aim at completeness, or else the artistic appearance will approach reality, and the fantasy of the observer will not be engaged.

We are conscious of both our dependence on the external world and our independence, the argument proceeds. Our independence is manifested both in receptivity and in action, both in being determined and in determining. As a result, we feel ourselves to be in a certain state or condition with respect to the world:

Under the presupposition that an inner impulse to extend our existence and to resist external restriction never entirely loses its activity, the limits of our power are not indifferent to us. Their perception is therefore accompanied by certain feelings, by joy or pain and their manifold intermediate degrees. Through these feelings the inner sense recognizes to what extent that general impulse of life is satisfied by our present relation to the external world, and this belongs to the definite characteristics of our state of mind. (p. 153)

To perceive this characteristic of a mental state in other people also, we recognize certain outer signs that indicate the degree of these feelings. In all the arts, Körner maintains, motion provides such signs. Music does not lack clear signs that designate definite states, and it is possible for it to represent character. A definite and lasting relation between the drives of activity and receptivity is a characteristic of character, and this is given by the relation between the masculine and feminine ideals. But one characteristic is sufficient to determine the representation of character completely; filling in the other characteristics can be left to the free play of the imagination. Thus, differences of roughness and softness in tone, whether of voices or of instruments, are an unmistakable sign of character. So are the differences of duration that play a part in musical motion: "Regularity in the change of duration—rhythm—marks the independence of motion. What we perceive in this rule is what persists in the living creature, what maintains its independence through all external changes" (p. 157).

This rather elaborate theory can be regarded as the counterpart in aesthetics of the mature Classical style of Haydn and Mozart, with which Körner was intimately acquainted. Not only was the aesthetics contemporaneous with the music, but it combines, as Classical instrumental music does, an ideal and edifying moral character with a unity based on thematic workmanship and the integration of motives. This particular combination, distinguished by human freedom in both its aspects and belonging to purely instrumental music that is also free in respect of external function, was achieved for the first time in Viennese Classicism, just as it was adequately described for the first time in Körner's musical aesthetics.

CHAPTER SEVEN

OPERATIC AESTHETICS

Italy

J ust as in the seventeenth century, operatic aesthetics in the eighteenth century continued to be discussed largely by literary figures and librettists rather than composers. Their attention was devoted primarily to questions of reform since the major development in opera itself was the appearance in Venice during the second half of the seventeenth century of several features that were subject to criticism especially when they were viewed in the perspective of traditional dramatic theory. Italian opera had come to be dominated by arias and vocal display at the expense of dramatic coherence and dramatic values. There was a mixture of serious and comic scenes, a profusion of characters, and a disregard of the dramatic unities of time, place, and action. Italian disapproval had its chief source in the Arcadian Academies, the first of which was founded in Rome in 1690. Giovanni Maria Crescimbeni, a poet and literary historian, was the leader of this academy and had played a central role in founding it. In his collection of dialogues entitled *La bellezza della volgar poesia* (1700), one of the characters, "Logisto," finds fault with opera ("melodrama") for ruining the art of acting and for killing off both spoken tragedy and good comedy:

> In order better to attract with novelty the indolent taste of those theater goers to whom the rudeness of the comic and seriousness of the tragic were equally repugnant, the inventor of melodramas (Cicognini) combined elements of both in his works, monstrously linking kings, heroes, and other illustrious persons with buffoons, servants, and characters of the most humble birth. The confounding of character types brought about the total ruin of the rules of poetry, which fell into such disuse that attention was no longer given to the art of tragic declamation which, forced to serve music, lost its purity and became full of idiocy.

The orderly handling of the poetic figures which dignify declamation, now restricted for the most part to the normal and familiar manner of speech more suitable for music, was neglected, and, finally, a combination of the too frequent use of those short poems, popularly called arias, and the excessive impropriety of making a stage personage speak by singing, utterly removed from poetic compositions the power of the *affetti* and the means of stirring an audience. The same Cigognini also manufactured prose comedies which became so popular in Italian theaters that in the end they reduced the art of acting to conversing only with the lowest sorts of people in shop windows and in public squares. This unhappy state of affairs grew worse all over in Italy through the course of forty years or more. Singers succeeded actors with more success than actors had ever enjoyed, and won incredible benefits, favors, and riches.[1]

The idea that opera had killed off spoken drama and the feeling that singing is unnatural both seem to echo Saint-Evremond. Indeed, the influence of France is confirmed subsequently, for Logisto mentions the return of tragedy to Rome in the form of translations from the French. He then continues with a happier picture of his own time:

But in the end, as is happening in other branches of poetry, it seems at present as if Italy is beginning to open her eyes, and to recognize the uselessness which comes from having abandoned her old traditions. And although she still has not reclaimed true comedy, nonetheless, choosing the lesser of two evils, she has corrected many manifestations of the monstrous mixing of character types practiced till now, managing at least to establish entirely serious melodramas like those used today in the theaters of Venice, which do not use comic characters and which, by diminishing the excessive number of arias, allow some opportunity in the recitatives for the *affetti*. (pp. 13–14)

In spite of this encouraging improvement, however, Logisto feels that "the person who invented melodrama would have done better not to have invented it and to have left the world as he found it." One of his respondents points to another possibility of improvement, citing librettos in which "the comic quality interferes in no way with the heroic" (p. 14), with the result that the two genres are united.

Still another solution appears in a letter—dated 24 February 1703—of the famous librettist Apostolo Zeno to Antonfrancesco Marini: "I have read *Griselda*, and am extraordinarily well pleased by the comic scenes which Signor Gigli has made for you with so much skill. They are of so little consequence that they have not bothered me in the least, nor have they made the work appear different from the manner in which I first published it."[2]

Crescimbeni again discusses the improvement of opera around 1700 in his *Comentarii intorno alla sua istoria della volgar poesia* (1702–11).[3] Fewer areas are being used, choruses are returning to comment on the action and to mark the ends of acts in place of intermezzi and dances, the unity of time is observed more frequently, a division into five acts is returning in place of division into three, and fine pastorales are being produced. Crescimbeni's approval is clearly based on Classical norms derived from Aristotle's *Poetics*, which are the characteristic foundation of the aesthetics of operatic reform.

Another Arcadian literary historian, Lodovico Antonio Muratori, was a considerably more severe critic of opera than Crescimbeni. His *Della perfetta poesia italiana* (1706)[4] treats opera from the point of view of spoken drama, just as seventeenth-century French writers did, without considering the possibility that it might constitute a genre in its own right and therefore have its own principles. But the ethical aspect of this literary perspective, which in France seems as urgent an issue as it was in ancient Greece, is reinforced in the case of Muratori by his outlook as a priest and also by his adoption of French ideas and attitudes.

Opera has done great harm to poetry, Muratori complains, quite in the fashion of Saint-Evremond; the Italian theater has lost all hope of glory since opera has taken it over. Citing Cicero, Quintilian, and Plutarch, Muratori asserts that the theatrical music of his time is effeminate and more calculated to corrupt the minds of the audience than to purge and improve them as ancient music did. His criticism is really moral indignation, and it echoes not only Plato and the Roman rhetoricians but also the outcry of the church fathers against theater—the disdain of the Christian for the pagan.

Muratori then turns to dramatic poetry, lamenting that poetry is now the servant of music: "But nothing is more evident than how much poetry obeys music today rather than commanding it" (p. 58). The poet is told the number and kinds of characters, in accordance with the number and kinds of musicians. He is told to add or subtract arias and recitatives, to tailor his parts to the abilities and importance of the singers, to adapt his verses to some machinery that must be introduced. Music alters the vowels and the whole sound of his words, and ignorant singers destroy their sense. The listeners do not understand what is being sung and what the opera is about. They attend the theater solely to hear the singers. The musical directors of opera have no use for dramas that are carefully worked out and contain ingenious ideas because they do not know how to adapt music to the verses and arias of these so easily. They like only sweet and sonorous words, not strong feelings and subtle reflections. The principal object is musical delight; thus, the poet follows musical taste and necessity, not his genius.

Having reviewed at some length all these defects in opera, Muratori mentions two consequences: the poets cannot compose anything fine in the tragic genre, and even if they do, it will not achieve the goal of tragedy when it is sung according to present-day practices. He discusses these in great detail. Indeed, it is difficult to think of a more thorough condemnation of opera. Muratori finds fault with every feature, from arias—which are extraneous to the drama—to word repetition. The chief basis of the whole argument is verisimilitude. The drama must imitate real behavior, and angry or grieving people, or those engaged in serious discussion, do not sing. It is singing itself that is not acceptable. Thus, it is not only operatic abuses that are criticized, as in Benedetto Marcello's famous satire of a few years later, but the fundamental convention of the genre. Opera in its very nature is monstrous; it violates the aesthetic principle of imitation, and it is morally corrupting as well. All the defects it has as drama are secondary to this. But in refusing to accept the medium of song, Muratori is really saying, "I don't like music," and then calling in reason and argument in support of an emotional reaction. For as soon as music finds a response, all objections to opera disappear. Beyond this, Muratori, like Saint-Evremond, does not enjoy having opera secure the popular approval that he would like literary art to enjoy, and since the drama is identified with a powerful influence on morals, it is convenient to depict opera as having a corrupting influence. It is attached, therefore, to the negative tradition of lascivious and theatrical music rather than to the noble musical traditions of worship and public ceremony.

Giovanni Gravina, the literary critic who had written such a favorable evaluation of a musical pastorale in 1692 (see chapter 4), subjected opera to strongly adverse criticism in his essay *Della tragedia* of 1715.[5] The essay of 1692 was written when Gravina was an Arcadian, but it clearly controverted Aristotelian principles. In contrast, the essay of 1715 was written a few years after Gravina had broken with the Arcadians; paradoxically, however, he now follows the plan of Aristotle's *Poetics* and adopts Aristotelian precepts, although he retains the freedom to interpret these in accordance with his own views. Taking as his foundation the basic Aristotelian tenet that the chief purpose of the theater is moral improvement, Gravina examines the practices of his own time and finds them amoral or worse. Ancient Greek tragedy, he maintains, was set to music throughout. It is not in this respect that opera goes wrong. The trouble instead is that the nature of music has changed. Ancient music, Gravina continues, made use of two distinct styles—one for soloists and the other for unison choruses. These styles, however, did not resemble those of modern recitative and aria, and the difference is a profound one. Ancient music was in general a means for projecting texts and for heightening their affective impact, while the music of opera is a decorative element that obscures the meaning of texts and weakens or contradicts the affective aim of the poet. In the one case the poets were also the composers and the stage designers, while in the other the poet, the composer, the designer, and the producer know nothing of each other's problems and have no interest in collaboration. Thus, there is no dramatic effect in the modern Italian theater, while the ancient tragedy was a unified work with a powerful dramatic effect.

Gravina favors the strict observation of the three Aristotelian unities but admits the possibility of tragedies with happy endings. He condemns plots relying too much on love and on unexpected events but accepts the untying of dramatic knots by a deus ex machina. He rejects protagonists embodying conflicting motivations, which he had favored in 1692, and calls for the incorruptible heroes and irredeemable villains coming into favor in the eighteenth century. He finds three acts as acceptable as five and accepts the opinion that horror scenes on stage are too repugnant to be ethically effective. But he opposes scene changes that weaken verisimilitude and insists that all acts end with choruses and that rhyme should be used only in these. Thus, Gravina is not really consistent. Basically, he applies the standard of Greek tragedy to the evaluation of opera, but the disapproval that this entails is tempered by an acceptance of many practices of the early eighteenth century that stand in contradiction to the nature of ancient tragedy.

A constructive as well as entertaining contrast to Gravina's critical essay of 1715 appeared that same year in the *Della tragedia antica e moderna* of the poet and librettist Pier-Jacopo Martello.[6] This work includes an elaborate discussion of opera, which had not been part of the original edition of 1714, entitled *L'Impostore*. Martello's treatise takes the form of six dialogues between the author and an "Impostor," who claims that he is in fact Aristotle, kept alive through the centuries by an elixir. The fifth dialogue, the one added in the second edition, is devoted specifically to opera, for which the Impostor takes as a postulate that music is primary and must be served by poetry and by stage machinery. Indeed, poor poetry, he says, is more suitable for this purpose than the finest. Composers know the kind of poetry they can set best, the Impostor continues, and therefore they should write the poetry as well as the music. Because they generally do not understand poetry or know how to write it, they can easily adapt their verses to musical use: "Seated at their harpsichords, they find facile words abounding in vowels—just what is needed for the coloratura passages—which have little meaning or no meaning at all" (p. 39). The Impostor is obviously adept at mixing truth with sarcasm, and the result is a discourse that is both perceptive and amusing. In spite of the display of wit, however, this description contains a penetrating criticism of the French and Italian literary view of opera—the self-understood separation of the components of opera and the evaluation of the drama in particular as an independent creation. Opera was simply taken to be drama, an understandable prejudice in an aesthetics constructed by poets, dramatists, and literary historians—and understandable also because of the prominent place of ancient Greek tragedy in the conception of opera. As soon as opera is considered to be a type of tragedy, however, or a type of drama, it is necessarily misjudged.

Paradoxically, this was expressed, although not understood, when authors made a distinction between dramas to be read and librettos for the theater. Writing librettos was regarded as a menial task for the poet, and librettists, particularly Zeno and Metastasio, desired to be known only as literary figures, whose dramas would be published in collected editions. An interesting outcome of this distinction was the endeavor to write "dual purpose" dramas, equally well suited for reading and for use as librettos. Another outcome was the "reform" of the libretto, which emphasized a well-developed action and an elevated style. But it was also often observed, as an adumbration of an aesthetic more adequate to opera, that a libretto that was insipid when read became astonishingly effective when performed in the theater.

In the course of Martello's dialogue on opera there begins to be evident some of the principles and theory of an evaluation of the libretto on its own terms. The Impostor favors fable over history as the material for librettos since "the versifier will have complete authority, as did our forefathers, to make one believe nonsense—to add Italian lies to Greek ones, and, abandoning the ancients, to contrive modern supplements that make a story more suitable for machinery and show" (p. 40). In spite of its typically negative form, this reveals an awareness and even an acceptance of the characteristics of opera in its own right.

A more explicit aesthetic, but one still mixing sarcasm with truth, makes an appearance subsequently in a long discourse by the Imposter that amounts to an "Aristotelian" poetics of the libretto:

> Custom demands that your libretto be divided into three acts, since if you were to divide it into five, you would make people believe that you wished to give them a tragedy, senselessly obligating yourself to rules which you could not observe. . . . Forget the modest principles of tragedy and the epic, and bear in mind that when the curtain rises, the audience will grow cool if it sees two characters discoursing gravely about their private affairs. The public wishes an abundance of people on stage—if not of characters, then of supernumeraries. A debarcation scene, the dancing of a *moresca*, a fight, or something similar, will

make your audience raise its eyebrows and bless the money they have left at the door. In the second act you should look to the development both of the action and of the passions. The frivolous misunderstandings, changes of costume, love letters, and portraits, so suspect to your tragedians, are held in highest esteem by your authors of *melodrammi*. Thus, having abandoned the severe verisimilitude of the Greek, French, and indeed Italian tragedy, you will boldly appropriate the ingenious complications of the Spaniards. I do not say that you should omit verisimilitude altogether from your dramatic incidents, but that your precious verisimilitude should not prevent you from preferring the marvelous. (pp. 41–42)

The Imposter calls for various and contrasting passions, but love is to triumph over all the others: "Let the other passions serve only to highlight the amorous, which, since it is common to all mankind, is perceived with the greatest pleasure":

In the third act heed the loosening or untying of the dramatic knot, and let it take place through the use of a machine. If the impresario will permit this, the work will be better received because of the display of the marvelous, even though the dramatic knot perhaps may not merit inconveniencing a god to descend from heaven to untie it. . . . Concerning the vicissitudes of human fortune [peripeties], it is better that those events be actually seen rather than narrated, for whatever strikes the senses is more pleasing to the public, since they come to see, not think. . . .

It is necessary that the whole be divided into recitative and arias— or as we call the latter, *canzonette*. . . . Anything in the way of narration or unimpassioned expression should be expressed in recitative verse. But whatever is motivated by passion or somehow reflects greater vehemence tends toward the canzonetta. The recitative should be brief enough not to put us to sleep with its tediousness, but long enough for us to understand what is happening. Its sentences and constructions should be easy, and concise rather than extended. . . . The recitative, then, ought to limit itself to verses of seven and eleven syllables, alternating and mixed, depending on which falls more suitably and so that, at least with respect to the cadences, there can occur a correspondence of consonances and of rhymes that will be seen more to favor the flowing quality of the music. What I have said about the recitatives bears some limitation in what I have called *scene di forza*, since in these the recitative, the element of greater strength and relevance to the action, ought to predominate over the ariettas. . . .

"Exit" arias should conclude every scene, and a singer ought never leave the stage without exercising his throat on a *canzonetta*. It matters little whether the use of such arias is verisimilar. Be more than certain that your scenes end with spirit and with vigor, and be sure that when you end a scene with an exit aria, you do not begin the next with an "entrance" aria, for then there is no contrast in the music. . . . That is the reason entrance arias should appear only at the beginnings of acts. There is no objection to duets that occur in the midst of scenes, for they give reciprocal action to more than one actor; I would even prefer one of them at the end of the second act. A chorus at the close of the last act is inevitable, since the public enjoys listening to the combination of all those voices, each of which it has applauded separately during the opera. The din of the singers and instruments causes the audience to rise to their feet and to depart satisfied and happy with what they have heard, filled with the desire to return.

These arias or canzonettas ought to be distributed in such a manner that the singers of greater reputation have an equal number of them, since the rivalries of singers are punctilious and unconquerable, and since it is useful for the performance of the drama if the best voices make an equal display of themselves to the ears of the audience. (pp. 42–44)

The Impostor takes up in detail the metrical patterns used most in arias and then describes the poetic style that is desirable in a libretto:

I believe that the moderate and graceful is more appropriate to libretti than the serious and magnificent, for music, an art invented for the delight and soothing of souls, ought to be assisted by words and sentiments which clothe the agreeable nature of the pleasures. This is not to say, however, that the magnificent ought not to be used from time to time, if only as a contrast to the charming. (p. 44)

The constructions must be easy, he continues, the sentences clear and short, the words plain and attractive, the verses fluent and tenderly sonorous. He describes many additional requirements and restrictions. Writing librettos teaches poets to conquer themselves, he says, by renouncing their own wishes; and although rare exceptions are possible, the libretto is generally not acceptable as poetry or drama.

The Impostor's "poetics of opera" is based fundamentally on an acceptance of the operatic status quo. Opera should not be abolished or condemned, he believes, for it provides a salutary pleasure to the audience. It should in any event be judged as a whole. This whole, in the Impostor's view, is dominated by music, which is the essence of opera, while poetry, far from being the primary concern, is really incidental, much like all the other components outside music. He concludes his discourse with a hymn of praise to music, which

> deserves to have voices, instruments, poetry, painting, architecture, mechanics, mimic, and any other art pay court to it and obey it. Deserves . . . that you exclude the operatic poems from the printed collection of your theatrical works, for you should be doing music an injustice by separating a mere accessory from it, while you should reap your punishment in being mocked by your readers.[7]

The dialogues preceding the one on opera are concerned with establishing the value of the modern arts. As far as the modern theater is concerned, it need not imitate ancient models. Aristotle's *Poetics* applied to the theater of his own time and should not be regarded as a timeless standard. The unities of time, place, and action, for example, no longer have to be observed so strictly when stage sets can be quickly and easily changed. And in modern Europe, since the position of women has become so different than it was in ancient Greece and rulers govern with justice and clemency, there is no reason to reject love as dramatic subject matter or to adhere to the themes approved for ancient drama. Thus, the earlier dialogues of Martello's work pave the way for the one on opera by attacking the rigid application of Aristotle's *Poetics* and ancient drama to the modern theater. The final dialogue is devoted to various styles of performance of tragedy and comedy and in particular to the relative merits and deficiencies of France and Italy with respect to acting.

The satirical aspect of the Italian operatic aesthetic, which was manifest in Martello's *Della tragedia* of 1715, becomes an independent genre of criticism in *Il teatro alla moda*[8] (1720) by Benedetto Marcello, a descendent of a patrician family of Venice that can be traced back to the seventh century. The work of a composer rather than a literary figure, Marcello's criticism of opera has its source not in a scholarly concern with dramatic theory but rather in firsthand knowledge of Venetian operatic practice. Here there could be no doubt that the vociferous popular audience controlled the situation. An enormous appetite for opera and an overriding desire for entertainment and for new works as much as dictated the quantity and quality of operatic production and indeed the very nature and constitution of the operas that were served up so rapidly. The central expression of the influence of the audience was of course the dominant position of the virtuoso singer, but another popular feature of opera that worked equally to the disadvantage of specifically dramatic interest and value was the use of machines and spectacular stage effects. It is apparent that Venetian opera was particularly vulnerable to attack, and Marcello's widely read work was followed almost as a matter of course by a series of opera buffas that are devoted to the satire of serious opera. The contents and even the titles of these satirical operas reveal that they are in a sense the successors of the *Teatro alla moda*.

The extended title of Marcello's little book is essentially a list of its contents: "A sure and easy method to compose well and to produce Italian operas in the modern fashion. Containing useful and necessary instructions for librettists, composers, for singers of either sex, for impresarios, orchestra musicians, theatrical engineers, and painters of scenery, for those playing comic parts, for theater tailors, pages, extras, prompters, copyists, for patrons and mothers of female singers, and for other persons connected with the theater" (p. 371).

The author subjects operatic practices to ridicule by presenting them with mock seriousness in the form of advice to the various participants. Some of his instructions to the librettist, for example, are as follows:

Before the librettist begins writing he should ask the impresario for a detailed list giving the number and kind of stage sets and decorations he wishes to see employed. He will then incorporate all these into his drama. He should always be on the lookout for elaborate scenes such as sacrifices, sumptuous banquets, apparitions, or other spectacles. When those are to occur in the opera the librettist will consult with the theater engineer in order to find out how many dialogues, monologues, and arias will be needed to stretch each scene of that type, so that all technical problems can be worked out without hurrying. The disintegration of the drama as an entity and the intense boredom of the audience are of no importance in connection with all this.

He should write the whole opera without any preconceived plan but rather proceed verse by verse. For if the audience never understands the plot their attentiveness to the very end of the opera will be insured. One thing any able modern librettist must strive for is frequently to have all characters of the piece on the stage at the same time, though nobody knows why. They then may leave the stage, one by one, singing the usual canzonetta. . . .

Real life is imparted to the opera by the use of prisons, daggers, poison, the writing of letters on stage, bear and wild bull hunts, earthquakes, storms, sacrifices, the settling of accounts, and mad scenes. The audience will be deeply moved by unexpected events of that kind. If it should furthermore be possible to introduce a scene in which some actors sit down and doze off while an attempt on their lives is being made (which they conveniently thwart by waking up in time), then one would have created something so extremely admirable as has never before been viewed on the Italian stage. . . .

During the rehearsals he must not reveal any of his dramatic intentions to the actors since he rightly assumes that they will do as they please anyway.

If the work should be such that certain characters have little to do or to sing he should immediately comply with the requests of these singers (or of their rich patrons) to add to their parts. He should always keep at hand a supply of a few hundred arias, in case alterations or additions should be wanted. . . .

The librettist might notice that the singers pronounce their words indistinctly, in which case he must not correct them. If the virtuosos should see their mistake and enunciate clearly the sale of the libretto might be seriously impaired.

If some of the actors should ask him from where they are to go on the stage and in which direction they should make their exit, or if they have questions about acting or costumes he will tell them to do all of these things in any way they have a mind to.

The composer might express a dislike for the meter in some of the arias, in which case the librettist must change it at once. To suit the composer's fancy he might also add a breeze, storms, fog, southern, eastern, and northern winds. (pp. 373, 375–76, 378, 379)

Performance is clearly part of Marcello's concern, for he is examining the whole operatic enterprise, and, in any event, performance is inextricably involved with the composition of both the poetry and the music. Some of Marcello's instructions to the composer are the following:

He must not allow himself to read the entire libretto, as that might confuse him. Rather he should compose it verse by verse and insist immediately that all arias be re-written. . . .

He must not forget that happy and sad arias should alternate throughout the opera, from beginning to end, regardless of any meaning of text, music, or stage action.

If nouns such as "father," "empire," "love," "arena," "kingdom," "beauty," "courage," "heart," should appear in the aria the modern composer should write long coloraturas over them. This applies also to "no," "without," and "already" and other adverbs. . . .

He should speed up or slow down the tempo of the arias according to every whim of the singer and he should swallow all their impertinences, remembering that his own honor, esteem, and future are at their mercy. For that reason he will change, if desired, their arias, recitatives, sharps, flats, naturals, etc. . . . .

In a similar vein again is the advice to the castrati:

> The modern Virtuoso should never have practiced solfeggio during his student days or later on in his career; there would be too much danger that he might finish his notes properly, or that he might sing in tune and in time. . . .
>
> To become a virtuoso a singer need not be able to read or write, or to pronounce correctly vowels and diphthongs, nor does he have to understand the text. He must be an expert, however, at disregarding sense and at mixing up letters and syllables in order to show off flashy passages, trills, appoggiaturas, endless cadenzas, etc. . . .
>
> At the performance he should sing with his mouth half-closed and with his teeth firmly pressed together—in short, he should do everything to prevent the understanding of a single word, and in the recitatives he should be sure to disregard periods and commas.
>
> In an ensemble scene, when addressed by another character or while the latter might have to sing an arietta, he should wave greetings to some masked lady-friend in one of the boxes, or smile sweetly to someone in the orchestra or to one of the supers. In that way it will be made quite clear to the audience that he is Alipio Forconi, the famous singer, and not the Prince Zoroastro whose part he is playing. . . .
>
> If the libretto calls for a duel and if the virtuoso is supposed to receive an arm wound he should nevertheless continue to gesticulate with that arm as if nothing had happened. If he is to take poison he should first sing his aria holding the cup in his hand and waving it around to show that it is empty. (pp. 382, 382–83, 384, 388, 389, 392)

As for the prima donna, she should not bother with her arias or cadenzas during the first rehearsals: "Only during the dress rehearsal should she condescend to sing them" (p. 396). Marcello takes up not just the actual participants in the creation and production of an opera but even the countless social relationships and accessory people surrounding these participants. The result is a lively picture of operatic activity in Venice during his time. There is some difficulty, however, in assessing the accuracy of this picture, for there is a certain amount of exaggeration and just plain silliness in his account. The factual foundation is nevertheless greater than we might at first sight believe or even imagine. For most of the instructions correspond to a state of affairs that was lamented in an unmistakably serious tone and with details that correspond by Muratori (1706) and by Martello (1714). That state of affairs continued to be criticized by Quadrio, Metastasio, Algarotti, Planelli, and Arteaga, and it was also ridiculed in numerous opera buffas. Still additional confirmation of the factual basis of Marcello's satire is provided by Tosi's *Opinioni de' cantori* (1723), by the accounts of various travelers who reached Venice from France, and of course by the actual librettos of early eighteenth-century Venetian opera.

The Veronese poet and literary critic Scipione Maffei shows little evidence of the operatic understanding of Martello, nor does he confine himself, as Marcello does, to the abuses of Venetian opera in particular. His condemnation of opera is characteristic of a literary perspective and of an Arcadian interested in establishing the value of Italian spoken tragedy and in defending Italian poetry against French attacks. Purposes of this kind, especially when combined with the goal of the advancement and moral improvement of poetry, almost necessarily entail the view that opera is intrinsically objectionable. It is not an acceptable form of tragedy and simply diverts the drama from its desirable ends. Fundamentally, it is music that is to blame, or the music of his modern times, for "until the present variety of music is moderated, it will never be possible to construct operas so that they do not always appear like one form of art distorted for the sake of another—a situation in which the superior miserably serves the inferior, where the poet occupies the same position as a violinist who plays for dancing."[9] Maffei's remarks are found in the preface of his *Teatro italiano* (1723), an anthology of Italian tragedies. Singing about the passions and activities of modern times lacks verisimilitude, he maintains, while the number of arias necessary in opera obstructs its dramatic effect. In 1753, in his essay *De' teatri antichi e moderni*, Maffei's judgment of opera is equally severe:

> How little the mass of the public knows about poetry these days can be perceived by observing that many people actually read libretti that were written for music. Several worthy gentlemen . . . have accomplished wonders in this genre and have even banished the effeminacies of the past century. But they have not been able to bring it about that operas are ever anything but works in which one form of art is distorted for the sake of another, spurious works that are neither tragedies nor comedies. Whenever music is involved, its charm makes everything suffer. One pays no attention to the passage, in a single evening, of dramatic actions which should require months. The beauty of the scenery results in applause for the frequent changing, without any magical art, of the location. For the sake now of one art, now of another, one is not supposed to feel bored, although dramatic accidents lacking in any sort of verisimilitude are represented, as are developments that are very dif-

ficult to understand. But when reading a libretto, how can one enjoy a genre whose chief value lies in the arias, words that are unnecessary and often artificially joined, words that are principally concerned with such expressions as "the charming little cloud" or "the pretty little turtledove"? (p. 53)

Maffei's censure, finally, is directed against the use of love as the theme of operatic plots: "Of musical dramas that have any moral worth there are only the numerous works by the two most celebrated authors of our day." Maffei cites Zeno, who points to Maffei's *Merope* as an exception: "In my day Marchese Maffei's *Merope* is the only dramatic work I have seen produce the miracle of giving pleasure to everyone without any admixture of amorous interests." And Maffei continues, "But other works without love intrigues have also met with public approval" (p. 53). The acknowledgment that librettos have improved, a positive view that Maffei rarely expresses, does not appreciably mitigate the prevailing severity of his opinion. Plots dealing with love, of course, constitute a prominent issue in the operatic aesthetics of literary critics, those of seventeenth-century France and—unquestionably influenced by them—those of eighteenth-century Italy. Both dramaturgy and morality are involved, for the cathartic effect of pity and fear—indeed, the fundamental nature of tragedy as conceived in the tradition and spirit of ancient Greece—is blatantly contradicted by the thematic employment of love, while the expression and display of amorous feelings is viewed as an influence that corrupts public morals. Thus, the drama acts to weaken and soften the character of the audience instead of ennobling it.

A more positive attitude toward opera was characteristic of the second half of the eighteenth century in spite of ceaseless faultfinding with respect to particular features. The benefits of such a positive approach can be seen at once in the judicious and highly influential *Saggio sopra l'opera in musica* (1755) of Francesco Algarotti. A native of Venice, he spent the 1740s in Berlin, helping Frederick the Great with the translation of opera librettos. Algarotti was a cultivated and cosmopolitan connoisseur. What his theories lacked in profundity they made up in practicality and value. Indeed, he anticipated much of the novel practice and progressive thought of the future. Not only was he knowledgeable about the varieties of opera past and present in both Italy and France, but he also took the broadest possible view of his subject, taking into consideration all the different components of opera and adopting as his underlying principle the cooperation of these components toward a single dramatic purpose. The poet, consequently, is the most important participant in the operatic enterprise and must not be subjected to interference by the composer or anyone else: "The poet is to carry in his mind a comprehensive view of the *whole* of the drama; because those parts which are not the productions of his pen ought to flow from the dictates of his actuating judgment, which is to give being and movement to the whole." [10]

Algarotti's treatment of the history of opera is part of his discussion of the best operatic subject matter. In itself, the history suffers from inaccuracy, particularly in its recourse to an economic explanation of the course of events. Thus, the ills of opera are traced to the institution of public opera in Venice. The conclusions Algarotti draws, however, are just ones:

> The fabulous subjects, on account of the great number of machines and magnificent apparatus which they require, often distress the poet into limits too narrow for him to carry on and unravel his plot with propriety; because he is not allowed either sufficient time or space to display the passions of each character, so absolutely necessary to the completing of an opera. . . . On the other hand, the subjects taken from history are liable to the objection of their not being so well adapted to music, which seems to exclude them from all plea of probability. . . . For who can be brought to think that the trillings of an air flow so justifiably from the mouth of a Julius Caesar or a Cato as from the lips of Venus or Apollo? Moreover, historical subjects do not furnish so striking a variety as those that are fabulous; they are apt to be too austere and monotonous. . . . Besides, it is no easy matter to contrive ballets or interludes suitable to subjects taken from history; because all such entertainments ought to form a kind of social union and become, as it were, constituent parts of the whole. (pp. 660–61)

The poet's purpose, Algarotti states, is to delight the eyes and the ears and to affect the heart, without offending common sense. He should therefore choose an event, from either remote times or distant lands, that, while it can involve the marvelous, is familiar and extremely simple. The marvelous will permit dances, choruses, and scenic display, and the simplicity and familiarity will permit the display of passions, "the main spring and actuating spirit of the stage" (p. 662), without the perplexity and tedium of preparations. To illustrate this excellent analysis, Algarotti discusses a number of appropriate operatic subjects.

He then turns his attention to music, again combining his remarks with a historical account, the theme of which this time is its degeneration from earlier states of excellence. The faults he finds are due principally to the composer's refusal to accept a station subordinate to that of the poet. A proper relation between words and music would remove the improbability, for example, of heroes and heroines singing as they die: "Were all ridiculous quavering omitted when the serious passions are to speak, and were the musical composition judiciously adapted to them, then it would not appear more improbable that a person should die singing, than reciting verses" (p. 664). The twin sisters, poetry and music, no longer go hand in hand, a problem that becomes fundamental in the operatic conceptions of Wagner. Similarly, the overture is regarded as quite detached from the drama, whereas it should presage the whole and prepare the audience to receive the impressions that will result from the whole.

Recitative is discussed by a detailed appeal to the procedures of Peri, who is taken as representative of the early composers of opera: "The recitative in their time was made to vary with the subject and assume a complexion suitable to the spirit of the words. It sometimes moved with a rapidity equal to that of the text and at others with an attendant slowness; but never failed to mark, in a conspicuous manner, those inflections and sallies which the violence of our passions can transfuse into the expression of them" (p. 666). Algarotti recommends in particular a greater use of obbligato recitative. This would have the further advantage of lessening the disproportion between recitative and aria, and the same purpose would be served by moderating the vocal ornamentation of the aria and curbing the instrumental part. The ritornellos are tediously prolix and often superfluous: "Can anything be more improbable than that, in an air expressive of wrath, an actor should calmly wait with his hand stuck in his sword-belt until the ritornello be over to give vent to a passion that is supposed to be boiling in his breast?" (p. 668). As far as the accompaniment is concerned, there should be fewer violins but more bass viols, and more use should be made of bass parts in general. Lutes and harps should be employed, and in the interest of enhancing the harmony, the violas should not be excluded. Algarotti also finds fault with concerted arias featuring an oboe or a trumpet, which exhibit "a kind of musical tilting-match with the utmost exertion on either side" (p. 668).

In a more detailed consideration of the aria, Algarotti condemns brilliant passages except when the words express passion or movement. The repetition of words and their meaningless juxtaposition for the sake of sound alone are also intolerable: "Words are to be treated in no other manner but according as the passion dictates; and when the sense of an aria is finished, the first part of it ought never to be sung over again" (p. 669). Nor should the prevailing expression be contradicted for the sake of a particular word: "The duty of a composer is to express the sense, not of this or that particular word, but the comprehensive meaning of all the words in the air." Finally, just as the text should not be merely a collection of euphonious words, so the melody must be more than merely artfully constructed. An aria must "paint images to the mind or express the passions"; it must be congenial to nature, "which can never be justly imitated but by a beautiful simplicity" (p. 670). The imitation of nature, combined with the value of beautiful simplicity, constitutes the underlying maxim of galant musical aesthetics and is especially characteristic of France. Oliver Strunk traces Algarotti's formulation to d'Alembert,[11] and we have seen that the conception figures prominently in Mattheson's aesthetics of melody considerably earlier. Algarotti himself finds its origin in Italian intermezzi and opera buffa and asserts that it was carried to France by *Serva padrona*.

The powerful and pervasive influence of Algarotti doubtless finds its most conspicuous manifestation in Antonio Planelli's treatise of 1772, *Dell'opera in musica*.[12] In certain respects, Planelli is even more cognizant of the potentialities of opera than his renowned predecessor. It is an independent genre, he insists, not simply sung tragedy, and it has its own requirements and conventions. He is also more insistent than Algarotti on the musical importance of the affections, even to the extent of suppressing the sensuous pleasures of hearing, which he can see only as an alternative to feeling, not as a possible enhancement. A corollary of the antithesis makes music a servant of the text, and its strict subordination to reason entails a rejection of the da capo and of the repetition of words. The emphasis on feeling, on the other hand, leads to a rejection of comparison arias and of sententious texts. There is an adumbration of Wagner in Planelli's view that the aria should present the protagonist's feeling at the time, free from reflective thought: "The style of the arias should be of the utmost simplicity, for the language of the heart will not abide any artificial reflection" (p. 323). Beyond this, there should be no ornamentation at all added by the singer.

Planelli makes other distinctive proposals, including an overture that introduces the general mood of the first scene rather than the general mood of the whole opera, as Algarotti had recommended, and a division of the opera into two or three acts rather than five. Just as Algarotti had forecast Gluck's achievement, so Planelli is impressed by it, although not as a perfect exemplification of his theories, and he admires the effect of unity produced by Calzabigi's *Alceste*. His approval of Gluck's preface to the score is actually an approval of Algarotti, who is the source of Gluck's ideas as well as Planelli's. Indeed, not just the substance of Planelli's treatise, but even the arrangement, is adopted from Algarotti.

France

At the very beginning of the eighteenth century in France, operatic aesthetics becomes a prominent public issue as part of the ongoing controversy over the

relative merits of French and Italian music. Not only do the essays of François Raguenet and Jean-Laurent Lecerf de la Viéville signal a new intensity
in this quarrel of the two national styles, but they also establish the outlook
that remains dominant for most of the century. Discussions of opera, even
when they are directed to French opera alone, cannot seem to pursue their
considerations without reference to Italy, either as a standard or as the target
of criticism, for the controversy belonged to a general habit of thought, with
manifestations in other types of music, in poetry and drama, and, indeed,
in every aspect of culture. As far as opera is concerned, Italy could not be
ignored. It occupied the authoritative position that is often conceded to an
originator, and, in any event, when Italian opera was brought to France, or
when it was viewed in Italy by French travelers, a comparison with French
opera was inevitable.

But how does such a competitive situation produce aesthetics? Apparently, the activity of faultfinding and approbation will have an aesthetic
basis, as any serious criticism must, whether this basis is made explicit or
simply remains implicit. There is in either event a prescriptive or a valua-
tional aesthetics. The outcome may be simply the acknowledgment of different national styles, as part of the general awareness of stylistic diversity that
increased so markedly at the end of the Renaissance. Then Italian opera and
French opera will be legitimated equally as expressions of different national
styles or different tastes. They will become the representatives, therefore, of
a pluralistic aesthetics. Another result, however, can be the rapprochement
of the two types of opera, with the result that one may borrow desirable
features from the other and abandon its own objectionable practices. An improved or ideal opera can then be envisaged. The comparison of two types
of opera, therefore, is not limited to the mere statement of dislikes and preferences but is really a fertile ground for the development of principles of
value, which is to say, for the development of an explicit aesthetics.

The Abbé Raguenet was a cultivated man already respected as a scholar
of church law and a biographer of Oliver Cromwell before his essay on
music appeared. When his duties as a tutor involved a visit to Rome, he took
the opportunity to become familiar with Roman visual art and with Italian
opera as well. His interest and admiration led to a book on the monuments
of Rome (1700), which was well received, and the essay comparing Italian
music with French (1702), which gave rise to a prolonged controversy.[13] The
essay was entitled *Parallèle des Italiens et des François en ce qui regarde
la musique et les opéra*. This title refers to the book by Charles Perrault,
Parallèle des anciens et des modernes (1688–97), that was an important
landmark in the history of the dispute—passed down in various forms from
the Renaissance—between the "ancients" and the "moderns," as the two

opposed groups of partisans were called in France. Thus, Raguenet aligned himself with Perrault, who was the leading representative of the moderns and who insisted on the independent value of opera as a legitimate dramatic genre, a creation of modern times that had no parallel in antiquity.

But Raguenet also connected the quarrel over the relative merits of French and Italian opera with the dispute between the ancients and the moderns, his preference going to the Italian, or modern, type. Clearly, the ancient-modern dichotomy was a pattern of thought, unrestricted by a literal reference to antiquity and applicable to the two sides of any argument, particularly when innovation was contrasted with tradition. Thus, while Perrault had regarded the operas of Quinault and Lully as representative of modern art, Raguenet considered them ancient. Only five years separated the two views, and Lully's *tragédie lyrique* was an art of the past for both writers. The important difference, of course, was that Raguenet was the champion of a newer "modern" opera, and from this station point Lully became an ancient. Even in Galilei's epochal *Dialogo* the two camps were not so simply defined, for *musica antica* designated a *modern* art, and *moderna* similarly a modern one, but more widely known. As the champion of *musica antica,* then, Galilei was really the advocate of an innovative art that was identified with an ancient one.

Raguenet does not take issue with the clearly superior aspects of French opera: the poetic and dramatic values of the librettos, the choruses and recitatives, the dances, and even the costumes and the style of violin playing. But he is enthusiastic rather than sober in extolling the virtues of Italian opera, namely, the power and diversity of the affections, the imagination and boldness of the melody, the astonishing inventiveness of the machinery and staging, the excellence of the singing and acting, the extraordinary accomplishments of the castrati, even the inherently musical character of the Italian language. The essay is aesthetic in the most fundamental sense of the word—that of dealing primarily and almost exclusively with sonority, with sensuous qualities and their emotional impact. Thus, Raguenet provides what is almost a symbolic introduction of the century that is distinguished by a continuous and deep concern with aesthetic problems and by the establishment of both general aesthetics and musical aesthetics as independent fields of thought. He dwells admiringly and with evident pleasure on sonorous properties, whether in Italian music or in French—the charm of the bass voice in France, the sonority of Italian vowels, the firm, piercing voice of the castrato, the dying away, again in Italy, of a sustained tone of the violin or the voice. He writes as follows of the Italian bass viols: "This is certainly an instrument much wanted in France; 'tis a sure foundation, equally firm as it is deep and low; it has a full mellow sound, filling the air with an agreeable harmony in a sphere of activity extending itself to the utmost bounds of the most capacious places." This remarkable display of spatial sensitivity continues: "The sound of their symphonies is wafted by the air to the roof in their churches and even to the skies in open places." [14]

The controversy that ensued on Raguenet's provocation found its first expression in two distinguished periodicals: the *Journal des savants*, the oldest French organ for the discussion of serious issues, and the *Memoires de Trévoux*, an important journal started in 1701 by the Jesuits. Raguenet's rapid notoriety was without question due to the importance of the issue he articulated in such an engaging way, and particularly to his espousal of the cause of the opposition, but it was fostered by the influence of Fontenelle, a highly regarded spokesman for the moderns, who bestowed governmental approval on the *Parallèle* for publication and who was, incidentally, a member of the French Academy, as Raguenet was also. Beyond this, Italian style was fashionable in France at the time; therefore the *Parallèle* easily found a number of sympathetic readers. In any event, the *Journal des savants* and the *Memoires de Trévoux* continued to attend to the issue after the entry of Lecerf on the scene, responding to the principals in the argument and seeking to moderate the dispute.

An extended response to Raguenet appeared in 1704, entitled *Comparaison de la musique italienne et de la musique française*. It was written by a poet and scholar whose full name was Jean-Laurent Lecerf de la Viéville, Seigneur de Freneuse. The *Comparaison* consists of three dialogues along with a letter that reveals Lecerf's basic belief in art that is natural rather than affected. But while Raguenet represents the frank hedonism of a lover of music particularly responsive to its sensuous appeal, Lecerf considers opera from a literary point of view. The different preferences of the two are thus quite predictable. Lecerf essentially applies to opera the values and opinions of the French literary critics of the seventeenth century, notably Boileau and Bouhours. His criticism of Italian opera echoes the criticism of Italian literature. He is akin to Raguenet in an attitude that lies at the heart of aesthetics almost as a condition of its existence and that is a certain polite and really aristocratic viewpoint, one of connoisseurship and delectation. Yet the two opponents differ in that Raguenet is much more general and unconcerned with technical detail; as a matter of fact, he is innocent of theoretical conceptions of art. Lecerf is a much closer and more disciplined inquirer; he even discusses technical details—those, at any rate, in which poetry is involved.

The second edition of the *Comparaison*, published in 1705, includes three additional dialogues, which extend Lecerf's discussion into the fields of music history and musical aesthetics. In the preface to the edition, Lecerf represents himself, with some justice, as an innovator in a new field, for he maintains that musical treatises have been concerned only with mechanics and craftsmanship, with teaching the rules of construction in a dry manner. There have been a sufficient number of these, he feels, but none that teaches a reasonable person "to judge as a whole the worth of a symphony or air. I believe there would be some merit and glory in being the first to write a treatise of this nature." [15] Although Lecerf doubtless has in mind symphonies and airs as parts of operas, he is clearly not addressing himself here to opera as such or to opera as a whole. He does, moreover, present in the sixth dialogue an extended and carefully thought-out "Traité du bon goût en musique." The principles set up in this discourse, he states, are those of ancient music. Indeed, in the first part of the sixth dialogue, Lecerf insists on the value of ancient music and takes a position opposed to that of Claude Perrault, who was a modern, like his brother Charles. Thus, Lecerf not only supports the view that true principles are timeless but also endorses the connection between ancient music and French opera, on the one hand, and modern music and Italian opera, on the other. The aesthetic issues at stake in the quarrel over French and Italian opera are consequently also at stake in the quarrel over ancient and modern music.

Lecerf observes first in the "Traité du bon goût" that there are only two ways of judging good and bad: inner feeling and rules. The first should be corrected and strengthened by the second, and it is their union that constitutes good taste. Or, as Lecerf also formulated it, "Good taste is the most natural feeling, corrected or confirmed by the best rules." [16] Thus, the galant standard of natural feeling and simplicity is combined with the rational and neoclassical recourse to invariant precepts. There are little rules and great ones. The little rules are those of composition. Lecerf takes as an example the use of low or high notes with words representing a low or a lofty object. The great rules call for music to be natural (or simple), expressive, and harmonious (or melodious). A final rule is added, which clarifies and fortifies both the little and the great ones: always to abhor excess. But there is an easier way to judge music: not by reasoning but by comparison with models that have already been evaluated and are used as a standard.

The conversation then turns to the judgment of *degrees* of value. Infringement of the great rules, Lecerf's spokesman maintains, is worse than infringement of the little ones. Second, disregarding the laws that concern the heart, or feeling, is worse than disregarding those that concern the ear. Third, degrees of value can be determined by considering the groups of people that admire a given piece. There are basically three such groups: the people, the learned (or professional musicians), and the connoisseurs. The people judge by natural feeling, the learned by the rules, and the connoisseurs by both, but slightly more by feeling than by the rules. Lecerf then establishes four degrees of beauty. The lowest degree belongs to a piece admired by the learned alone; the next higher is that of a piece admired only by the connoisseurs; next above this is the degree of beauty belonging to a piece admired only by the people; and the highest level of all is occupied by a piece admired both by the people and by one of the other groups. As we can see most readily in the relative positions of the two middle groups, the classification gives more weight to feeling than to the rules; this is indeed grounded in the nature of aesthetics, which looks beyond the technicalities for sources of an equivalence among the arts that can be discovered in perceptual experience itself. Aside from imitation, certainly feeling and expression can provide a common denominator. The priority of feeling over rules, however, would seem to argue the priority of Italian opera over French and the triumph of Raguenet over Lecerf. But the superiority of French opera can be deduced if we remember that the feeling appealed to is natural rather than extravagant; in any event, French opera is the appropriate choice of a method of aesthetics that is rational, just as Italian opera would be the preference of a method relying on enthusiasm and strength of response.

Raguenet's *Défense du Parallèle* (1705) was published after the second edition of the *Comparaison*, but it deals only with the three original dialogues of 1704 and is confined to matters of factual detail. In response to the *Défense*, both the *Journal des savants* and the *Memoires de Trévoux* in essence call for a more adequate examination of the issue.

In a second addition to his *Comparaison* in 1706, Lecerf included a reply to Raguenet's *Défense*. After asserting that Raguenet as well as one of the writers of the *Journal des savants* have not confronted the more substantial questions he has raised, Lecerf explicitly connects Lully with the ancients, maintaining that Lully adheres to ancient values. There was no further reply from Raguenet, but Lecerf had already begun to regard the *Journal* as his opponent. Succeeding exchanges, however, consist essentially of charges of prejudice or incompetence and add nothing of substantial interest to the controversy.

The existence of two opposed national styles need not of course give rise to an argument over which is superior. Other outcomes are possible, such as the recognition that each is a legitimate expression of an idiosyncratic taste, the project of modifying each so as to remove its weaknesses by borrowing from the other, or even the project of formulating some intermediate style that combines the virtues of both. Indeed, suggestions of this kind began to appear as the quarrel between Raguenet and Lecerf came to an end, and the suggestions were followed by concrete changes along the same lines in music and opera themselves, which continually testified to a rapprochement and combination of Italian and French traits over a period of time that extended into the nineteenth century. But in aesthetics itself rather than in opera, the contest between the two styles never disappeared. It flared up repeatedly during the course of the eighteenth century, often accompanied by echoes of the contest between ancient and modern. The explanation of this persistence lies in the fact that the stylistic controversy represented an underlying contest of aesthetic values that at times becomes explicit—of the opposed criteria, that is, of reason and sense, the first identified with rules and the second with the purely musical or tonal provocation of feeling.

Du Bos's influential treatise *Réflexions critiques* (1719) is an outstanding early example of the efforts of aestheticians to reconcile these contrasted values in the definition of artistic taste and the process of judgment.[17] In his discussion of music, Du Bos emphasizes the imitation of nature, which in this case means the tones of the human voice as these express feelings and passions. Thus, music becomes expressive and moving. Because of the imitation of nature, then, reason and the rules are connected with feeling and expressiveness, with the result that feeling enters into both sides of the duality of reason and sense: as the expressiveness of an imitated passion and as the feeling response to sonority and to purely musical configurations, which seems also to be the "inner feeling" by which music is judged. This complicates the duality, whether as one of opposed criteria or as the opposition of ancient and modern or French and Italian. But the one feeling is objective and in conformity with the universality of reason, while the other is subjective and a matter of individual taste. The problem confronted by aesthetics in general starting in the second decade of the century, and by Du Bos in particular in 1719, had been provided with a clear and convincing solution by Lecerf in 1705, although without any attention to the property of imitation.

The question continued to be argued nevertheless, brought to new life and urgency by each change in the character of opera itself. Indeed, Lecerf's "Traité du bon goût" was also brought to life in 1732, disguised by a slightly altered title, by Nicolas Ragot de Grandval. The "author" condenses the original, but he also reveals the new spirit of reconciliation by maintaining that justice must be done to everyone. He embraces the beautiful "wherever it may be found" and has the highest esteem for "the good Italian composers."

The production of *Hippolyte et Aricie* in 1733 precipitated a second operatic controversy in France that to a certain extent revived the views of Raguenet and Lecerf concerning French and Italian opera. In spite of these echoes, however, the actual issues of the dispute between the Lullistes and the Ramistes had changed. To be sure, one camp still supported the opera of Lully, with its "ancient" simplicity and naturalness, and the other the "modern" opera of Rameau, the character of which, according to some of its opponents, derived from Italy. Nevertheless, the two competing styles were both French, and the contest of national styles was therefore not literally present. At stake were qualities more abstractly defined: simplicity versus complexity, melody versus harmony, galant versus learned, moderation and unity versus imagination and variety. It was no longer clear which side could claim the virtue of rationality, for it could be connected with Rameau as much as with Lully.

Much of the more generalized and more specifically aesthetic duality can be seen as early as 1727, in a letter written by Rameau to the poet and librettist Houdart de la Motte:

> Those who speak of learned musicians usually mean men who know everything about the various tone combinations; but in doing so they imply that these men are so preoccupied with them that they sacrifice everything (common sense, feeling, wit, and meaning) for their sake. These composers are the ones trained in the schools, where one speaks of nothing but notes, to the extent that one has good reason for preferring composers who care less about technique than taste. However, he whose taste was formed solely in relation to his own feelings can at best excel in certain genres, namely in those which are suited to his temperament. If he has a gentle nature, he will succeed in expressing tenderness; and if he is lively, jovial, and playful, his music will be correspondingly so. . . . It seems desirable, therefore, to find an operatic composer who has studied nature before painting it, and whose art enables him to choose exactly those shades and colors which his wit and taste suggest as being suited to the required expressions. I am far from believing that I am that composer; but at least I have the advantage over the others of knowing the shades and colors of which they have but a confused notion, and which they use only haphazardly. They possess taste and imagination, but both are confined within the limits of their feelings, where the various objects concentrate in a small range of colors, beyond which they see nothing. Nature has not altogether deprived me of its gifts, and I have not experimented with tone combinations to the point of forgetting their intimate relations with "natural beauty" (le beau naturel).

Rameau also asserts, "I do not parade my knowledge in my works, where I try to hide art by art itself. For I write only for the people of taste, and not for the experts, since there are so many of the former and so few of the latter."[18] The weight that Lecerf gives to the opinion of the connoisseur rather than the professional musician is here explicitly cited as a cause of the concealment of art by art—the ingratiating appearance of the "second nature" that was a characteristic aesthetic value of the later eighteenth century.

In addition to embodying this value in his operas, Rameau filled them to overflowing with varied and attractive music. But the divertissements overshadowed the recitative, and, to make matters worse, Rameau was careless about the poetic and dramatic quality of his librettos. Thus, French taste remained with no fully satisfactory alternative to Lully, who began to seem old fashioned and monotonous when Rameau appeared on the scene. But Rameau also did not provide the peculiarly musical delight of self-contained melody that was at the same time expressive of feeling. His opera was musical, but not musical enough—or at least not musical in the right way. France still remained vulnerable to the intoxicating charm of Neapolitan melody, especially when that melody expressed the direct sentiments of ordinary people rather than the majestic emotions of monarchs and gods.

As though in response to the dissatisfaction with French opera, an essay that appeared in 1741, Toussaint Rémond de Saint-Mard's *Réflexions sur l'opéra*,[19] projected an ideal type of opera that was based on the melodious expression of feeling. Like Raguenet, Rémond viewed the operatic genre in its own terms; he did not approach it from the standpoint of poetry and spoken drama. The expression of the passions and the feelings demanded music, he believed; words were not adequate. But since song is the most important factor in opera and song is suited in particular to the expression of emotion, the action must consist as much as possible of situations that involve feeling. This type of action must proceed rapidly so that the greatest number of opportunities will arise for emotional expression. In addition, however, opera has its own poetic requirements, for song differs from declamation in calling for a special diction, for words intrinsically suited to melody. Quinault does not quite meet these requirements, Rémond finds, for his action does not always call for the expression of feeling throughout. Rémond's aesthetics contains a galant restriction, however; the feelings appropriate for opera are not the noble, grand, and majestic ones: "Du tendre, du passionné, du gracieux, voilà ce qu'il nous faut."[20] His concern with specifically musical expressiveness is also limited to melody; harmonic values are not considered. But pointing to the future again is the fact that melodic feeling and sensuousness are emphasized for their own sake. They are not conceived as an imitation of actual affections and are therefore not limited by any preconceptions of external reference.

The same forward-looking character can be found in Charles Batteux's important treatise *Les Beaux-arts réduits à un même principe* (1746). Among all the treatises on taste that preceded it in France—notably those of Cartaud de la Vilate (1736), André (1741), Pluche (1746), and Bollioud de Mermet (1746)—Batteux's work was disseminated most widely and had the greatest influence. Nominally a definitive statement of the theory of imitation, in fact it substantially modifies the strict construal of the term. But perhaps even more important than its comprehensive presentation of the theory of imitation is the connection that is established between imitation and taste and thus between the traditional, rationalistic view of art and the new, aesthetic view ushered in by the eighteenth century, which was vitally concerned with subjective values. Taste, Batteux maintained, is the ability to discern when art is a true imitation of nature. Since nature presents various facets, there can be a number of different tastes each equally justifiable as "good."

Concerning artistic imitation in itself, Batteux develops the view implicit in Aristotle's *Poetics* that the arts join together naturally in the furtherance of imitative values. Opera is therefore regarded in the highly favorable light of the cooperation of its constituent arts. When the arts join together, furthermore, one of them always dominates the others, determining the nature of the whole. It is of decisive importance, then, that tone and gesture are the instruments of the heart, just as language is the instrument of reason. Thus, the principal object of music and dance should be the imitation of the feelings, while poetry is principally the imitation of actions:

> But since passions and actions are nearly always united in nature, and since they should also be found together in the arts, there will be this difference between poetry on the one hand and music and dance on the other: that, in the first, the passions will be employed as means or motives that prepare the action and produce it and, in music and dance, the action will be only a sort of canvas destined to carry, sustain, conduct, and bind the different passions that the artist desires to express.[21]

Batteux's line of thought leads to an explicit and well-founded aesthetics of opera:

> Also we see that in the majority of the tragedies constructed to be set to music, what interests us most is not the actual substratum of the action, but the feelings that arise from the situations introduced by the action. . . . From this it follows that everything which is only action in itself, only idea, or image, is little appropriate to music. It is for this reason that long recitations, expositions of the subject, transitions, metaphors, plays of wit, in a word, everything that derives from memory or from reflection resists music so strongly. (p. 271)

The feeling best expressed in music, however, is naive and simple. Feeling that is too subtle, at any rate, cannot be rendered in music, or will be rendered only in part, only weakly or obscurely. Batteux's final chapter is devoted to his most cherished aim, the union of the fine arts, and in this context he considers the poetic style that is appropriate for the operatic libretto. When the arts are combined, he states, one should excel, the others taking second place:

> If it is music that displays itself, it alone has the right to spread out all its attractions. The theater belongs to it. Poetry has only the second place, and dance the third. There are no longer those magnificent and high-flown verses, those bold descriptions, those striking images; it is a simple, naive poetry, which runs along softly and with negligence, which simply lets the words fall into place. The reason is that the verses must follow the melody, not precede it. The words in such a case, although composed before the music, are only like defining forces that are applied to the musical expression to give it a more distinct and more intelligible meaning. It is from this point of view that the poetry of Quinault should be judged; and if he is severely censured for the weakness of his verses, it is up to Lully to justify him in that regard. It is not at all the most beautiful verses that best support music, but the most touching. (pp. 303–4)

Unlike Rémond, Batteux views opera in the light of a generalized theory of the combination of the arts, yet he shares with Rémond the belief that opera must be governed by musical considerations as well as the belief that the feelings to be expressed should not exceed a certain limit of intensity.

Additional evidence of a generally favorable attitude toward opera in the 1740s can be found in the writings of Voltaire, who wrote several librettos for Rameau. Voltaire carefully examined the claim of opera to be a descendent of ancient tragedy, and he found much to admire in both Italian and French opera. Many of his ideas are put forward in the preface to his drama *Sémiramis* (1748).[22] Obviously, spoken drama in no way duplicates ancient tragedy, Voltaire points out, although this does not mean that it is inferior to it, but opera does indeed resemble Greek drama. It has an unfortunate defect, however, in the aria, which interrupts the action and sacrifices interest and common sense to musical charm. Voltaire's criticism is reminiscent of Saint-Evremond's view of when singing is appropriate and when it is ridiculous. "What would the Athenians have said," Voltaire asks, "if Oedipus and Orestes, at the moment of recognition, had sung little airs with grace notes and recited similes to Jocasta and Electra?" The arias of Metastasio, however, are often related to the action. They are impassioned "and sometimes compete with the most beautiful odes of Horace." Still they are out of place. But just as Voltaire does not hesitate to compare Metastasio with Horace, he finds two scenes of Metastasio's drama *La clemenza di Tito* to be comparable, if not superior, to anything found in Greek tragedy. These scenes "are not based on operatic love but on the noblest sentiments of the human heart" (p. 77).

Voltaire's view of French opera is much less favorable. French airs are less closely tied to the action, he says, and they employ effeminate words that are suited to the writing of melodies similar to Venetian barcaroles. As for the chorus, instead of teaching virtue, it utters tedious panegyrics on love. In spite of these defects, however, the best *tragédies lyriques* have some resemblance to Greek tragedy. Voltaire's critique is shaped fundamentally by his respect for the ethical import of ancient tragedy; therefore, like Saint-Evremond, he resents the intrusion of musical delight into the dramatic action, resents the domination of the action by amorous interests, resents "the pleasure we derive from this happy mixture of scenes, choruses, dances, orchestral music, as well as from the variety of settings." It is a question, ultimately, of the competition opera offers to spoken drama: "And the best comedies and tragedies are never as assiduously frequented by the same people as are mediocre operas. The regular, noble, and stern beauties are not the ones most eagerly sought out by the masses" (p. 78).

Voltaire reveals to us quite clearly the dilemma that spoken drama and opera presented to literary people. The alternative represented by the two types of theater was a problematic one because both were descended from the same impressive source—ancient tragedy. Opera possessed the musical features—the intoned recitation and the choruses—while spoken drama possessed high ethical content and aroused pity and fear. At the same time, however, opera contradicted the spirit of ancient tragedy in the use of love as subject matter, in the happy ending, in the use of arias that interrupt the action and are extrinsic to it, and generally in its devotion to the delights of melody and varied diversions instead of sustained, serious content. It elevated what Aristotle had considered to be embellishment to the status of central importance. Yet Voltaire, and even Saint-Evremond, points occasionally to a way out of the dilemma, namely, through the improvement of opera, although both are unquestionably aware that, as an art of delight, opera would certainly be resistant to reform.

In his *Connaissance des beautés et des défauts de la poésie et d'eloquence dans la langue française* (1749),[23] Voltaire takes a much more negative view of French opera in particular, for he finds its deficiencies to be intrinsic. Fundamental is the fact that opera requires a passionate action, but no tragedy, or libretto, can be passionate throughout. Reasoning, preparation, and details are also needed; indeed, these help make a play interesting. Thus, opera faces an insoluble problem, which Voltaire illustrates by the opera *Teseo*, by Metastasio and Caldara. At a critical point in the action, Theseus simply states that he is the king's son, without explaining the secret of his birth or adding the details that would make the revelation credible and surprising. But the inclusion of these details would be boring in music. Either alternative would therefore involve a serious defect. Another apparently insoluble problem is presented by the French language, for it contains only a few words that are suitable to be set to music. Voltaire accuses French composers, in any event, of sterility. They are unable to express all the words of their language the way Italian composers can—an objection that is inconsistent with the claim that French is intrinsically not amenable to musical setting. Perhaps Voltaire vaguely senses the possibility of a vocal style that could successfully render the French lines he cites as unsuitable for music. Ultimately, it was the galant restriction of musical feelings and thus the whole cast of eighteenth-century musical culture that denied to opera an impressive tragic impact. Voltaire himself maintains that "*since the days of Quinault* we have had almost no tragedies that are tolerable when set to music" (my italics).

Rousseau shares Voltaire's high opinion of Quinault. In a letter written to Friedrich Melchior Grimm in 1750,[24] he finds Quinault's librettos much superior to those of Metastasio. They have nobility and regularity, he asserts; they imitate nature more successfully and are more suitable to operatic conventions. Rousseau's letter is devoted primarily to the contrast between French and Italian opera, almost as a prelude to the War of the Buffoons. He finds that Italian music excels in sonority, in vocal and instrumental brilliance. Besides having superior librettos, however, French opera is moving and touching; it arouses the passions.

Grimm took the opposite point of view. On the eve of the Buffoon War, in 1752, he published a pamphlet, the *Lettre sur "Omphale,"*[25] occasioned by a revival of Destouches's opera of that title, originally produced in 1700. Grimm attacks the opera and, through it, the *tragédie lyrique* in general. Instead of delighting the ears like Italian opera, *Omphale* is dull and tedious. Worse still, it fails to express the text. There is an alternative to this tired, post-Lullyan drama in French opera itself, Grimm urges, namely, the new and expressive operas of Rameau.

The Parisian performance of Pergolesi's *La serva padrona* in 1752, however, set off once again a controversy over the relative merits of French and Italian opera, the War of the Buffoons. The almost numberless pamphlets and articles, most of them published anonymously, that document this quarrel are less concerned with operatic aesthetics than they are with quibbling and displays of wit. Many essays simply rehearse the known characteristics of Italian and French opera. But there are a few that exerted considerable influence, that possessed literary merit, and that dealt with matters of substance. One of the chief expressions of the anti-French position was Grimm's *Le Petit prophète de Boehmischbroda* (1753), a satire of French opera or, for the most part, of the *performance* of French opera, delivered in the diction of a biblical prophet by an impoverished hermetic violinist from a fictitious town in Bohemia. To the naive view of the strange visitor, the vaunted simplicity of the *tragédie lyrique* is really dreariness, while the performance is poor beyond belief and utterly unconvincing.

Mathieu François Mairobert de Pidansat defended French opera in his *Réponse du coin du roi au coin de la reine* (1753). While Italian opera is light and coquettish, he maintains, French opera presents a serious depiction of the passions. Diderot answered Pidansat in his *Arrêt-rendu à l'amphithéatre de l'opera*, refuting many of the arguments of Pidansat's *Réponse*. The encyclopedists in general were critical of French opera and favorably disposed toward the Italians.

Still in the same year, 1753, Pidansat published a parody of Grimm's widely read *Petit prophète* that is entitled *Les Prophéties du grand prophète Monet*. Diderot then proposed a thorough method of examining the issue in his *Au Petit prophète de Boehmischbroda et au grand prophète Monet*. Both factions were to compare the celebrated monologue of Lully's *Armide* with a similar section of Terradellas's opera seria *Nitocris*. The pro-Italian faction, Diderot says, will have advanced their cause decisively if they can show that the excerpt from *Armide*, compared to the one from *Nitocris*, is "only a languishing psalmody, a melody without fire, without soul, force, or genius; that the musician of France owes everything to his poet, and that to the contrary the poet of Italy owes everything to his musician."[26] Diderot calls for a close comparison of the music itself, not of the two texts, and he seems certain of what the outcome will be.

The most renowned document of the Buffoon War, again published in 1753, was Rousseau's *Lettre sur la musique française*. Rousseau, who no longer had anything favorable to say about French opera, did indeed subject the famous monologue of *Armide* to the close examination Diderot had recommended, and his conclusion was that the *tragédie lyrique* was woefully inexpressive. *Nitocris* was left unexamined, but Rousseau did not hesitate to assert that Italian opera met his criteria of possessing a flexible language, bold modulation, exact rhythm and tempo, and melodic unity, the last requirement ruling out both counterpoint and complex harmony in the interest of a single effect. The *Armide* monologue, on the other hand, illustrates individual words rather than the general sense of the text, and it is not responsive to the most striking contrasts of meaning and feeling. "If it is regarded as song," Rousseau writes, "there is no measure, no character, no melody; if as recitative, there is nothing natural or expressive."[27] Indeed, without the aid of the text, he maintains, and of gesture and acting, the music would be unbearably monotonous. Rousseau also undertakes a general demonstration that French opera, and indeed French music of any kind, is essentially impossible since the language itself is intrinsically unsuitable for music. The reliance on harmony to conceal the deficiencies of melody does not help matters; it only creates a learned music in which harmony and melody obstruct one another.

Early in the year, Rousseau's opera *Le Devin du village* had revealed an entirely different kind of response to opera buffa, namely, the creation of a French counterpart. The positive reaction to the opera included Diderot's *Les Trois chapitres, ou La Vision*, which described the return to Paris of the *petit prophète*, who witnessed a performance of *Le Devin du village* and was now totally captivated by the plight of the characters and the heartfelt musical expression of their feelings. At about the same time, early in 1753, the Italian cause was directly argued by the republication of Raguenet's *Parallèle* of 1702, but without attribution and under the title *La Paix de l'opéra, ou Parallèle impartial de la musique française et de la musique italienne.*

The largest volume of publication of the whole Buffoon War was elicited as a response to Rousseau's provocative *Lettre*, with its wholesale rejection of French music and the French language. One of the protests was included in the impressive harmonic conception of music that Rameau presented in his *Observations sur notre instinct pour la music, et sur son principe* (1754). In his detailed refutation of Rousseau, Rameau examined the *Armide* monologue in detail once again, demonstrating, as he maintained, that Rousseau was simply mistaken on a number of points and that the expressive force of the monologue was in fact considerable. The expressiveness derived from the harmony, however, not from the melody.

That Lully continued to represent an important standard for operatic aesthetics can be seen from another and more general discussion of his achievement that had been included in a larger work the preceding year: Pierre Estève's *L'Esprit des beaux-arts* (1753).[28] Typically, it is Lully's attention to dramatic declamation that Estève finds responsible for his success. Because of this foundation, Lully's music is natural. Furthermore, it is directed to the interpretation of a scene or a tableau as a whole; individual words are stressed only if they further this purpose. For the same reason, strength and abruptness of sound are avoided in the poetry, in favor of gentle sonorities and imagery, which foster the general mood.

Concerned still with the issues of the Buffoon War, but removed somewhat from the heat of the controversy, is the reasoned discussion of Italian and French opera presented by Charles H. Blainville in his *L'Esprit de l'art musical*,[29] which was published in Geneva in 1754. Blainville acknowledges the merits of Italian opera and the deficiencies of French opera, but he also finds much to commend in the latter, and his general position is that the differences in the two are due to the intrinsic difference of the languages. French music is monotonous, for example, because the French language is monotonous. But the language is not unsuitable for music, as Rousseau maintains. It has only to take theatrical declamation as its model, following the path of Lully, who produced a kind of speaking song and who also understood how to express the passions in music. French composers can also learn from the Italians, who excel not only in expression, Blainville asserts, but in purely musical attractiveness as well. Thus, the controversy gives way to an acceptance of different styles, each of them representing *bon goût* in its own way. This expansion of taste to encompass stylistic variety is accompanied in a number of tracts by suggestions for the mixture or interchange of features of style, a process that did in fact take place in music and in opera.

A view comparable in its synoptic character to that of Blainville appeared in Lausanne in the same year: the *Réflexions d'un patriote sur l'opéra français et sur l'opéra italien*, by an otherwise unknown de Rochemont.[30] Here it is Italy rather than France that is most liable to criticism. Even though Italian music is excellent, de Rochemont grants, the dramatic aspect of opera is neglected, for the recitative is cursory and the aria contains a da capo repetition. There is continual digression from the action, and the expression of emotion is exaggerated. French opera, in contrast, emphasizes the dramatic constituent. Music takes a subordinate position, but it only *seems* to be indifferent in quality; it is not really so.

Another judicious examination of the issues involved in the Buffoon War was presented after the strife had ended by Jean le Rond d'Alembert, in his extended tract *De la Liberté de la musique* (1759).[31] D'Alembert gives a dispassionate history of the conflict and proposes rather naively that French opera be improved and made superior to Italian opera by the adoption of many features of Italian style. To carry this out, he proceeds to examine the two types of opera in the greatest detail, discussing recitatives, airs, and orchestral pieces in turn and offering concrete suggestions for the improvement of each.

Diderot's interest in opera was not limited to his three brief essays of the Buffoon War in 1753. In the third of his *Entretiens sur "Le fils naturel": Dorval et moi* (1757), Diderot's negative view of the *tragédie lyrique* gives way to a constructive theory for its improvement that seems to presage the coming operatic achievement of Gluck. Citing a passage from Racine's *Iphigénie* that is clearly appropriate for an obbligato recitative followed by an air, he distinguishes two modes of setting, one preoccupied with the accents of Clytemnestra's grief, the other with thunder, earthquake, and commotion. Both cannot succeed simultaneously. Devotion to description will result in the neglect of pathos, and "the whole will affect the ears rather than the soul." But Diderot makes it clear where his sentiments lie. "Clytemnestra's state of mind must wrest from her inmost heart the cry of nature." And in "the simple style" the composer "will fill himself with the pain and despair of Clytemnestra. He will not start to compose until he himself is haunted by the ghastly images that obsess her":

> Let these lines be sung by Mlle Dumesnil: and, unless I am greatly mistaken, she will render the confusion in Clytemnestra's mind, the feelings which succeed each other in her soul. Her genius will provide her with the proper clues, and it is with her declamation in mind that the composer ought to approach his task. . . . But don't believe that it is these parasitic words of the lyric style, "*lancer . . . gronder . . . trembler,*" which constitute the pathos of the piece, which is engendered by passion. And if the composer, neglecting the cry of passion, takes pleasure in finding sounds exactly suited to these words, the poet has set a cruel trap for him.[32]

The cast of Diderot's ideas is evident. The musical imitation is based on the natural expression of passion in vocal cries and declamation, and it is created by the composer and singer when they are in the grip of very real emotion, which is thought of as duplicating the nature and intensity of the "original" expression. Diderot's discussion testifies also to his close understanding of the expressive functions and possibilities of accompanied recitative, or orchestral commentary, and of the air itself, in which the repetition of words provides an opportunity for a wealth of different melodic forms of expression. These comprise various *musical* aspects of the governing feeling. Ordinary recitative, unfortunately, is not considered since Diderot doubtless believes it to be less suited to the emotional agitation of the passage.

A comprehensive picture of Diderot's conception of opera is contained in his *Le Neveu de Rameau*, which, apart from later alterations, seems to have been written during the period 1760–64.[33] The basis of the whole, as we have seen in the preceding chapter, is the idea of verisimilitude. A melody is "an imitation . . . of the physical sounds or accents of passion. . . . It is the animal cry of passion that should dictate the melodic line." But these models for melodic imitation are evidently approximated by speech: "Speech should be thought of as a line, and the melody as another line winding in and out of the first. The more vigorous and true the speech . . . and the more closely the melody fits it and the more points of contact it has with it, the truer that melody will be and the more beautiful" (pp. 98, 105).

From this basis the remainder of the theory can be deduced. The Italian language and melody are close to these accents of passion, the French language and opera quite removed. Indeed, French poems are "cold, tired, and monotonous. There is nothing in them that can serve as a basis for song" (p. 105). Epigrams, parenthetical remarks, and well-turned thoughts are far too distant from nature. "And don't imagine that the technique of the stage actors and their declamation can serve as a model. Pooh! we want something more energetic, less stilted, truer to life" (p. 106). Rameau's nephew, who is Diderot's spokesman, finds more what he wants in *opéra comique*, but he echoes, significantly, what had earlier been said of Lully: "Don't you think . . . it is a very odd thing that a foreigner, an Italian, a Duni should come and teach us how to put stress into our own music, and adapt our vocal music to every speed, time, interval and kind of speech without upsetting prosody?" (p. 106). In general, of course, Diderot agrees with Rousseau, maintaining that French is intrinsically unsuited to music. Neither takes into account, of course, that changes in musical style might reveal greater expressive possibilities even in the French language, although fundamentally they may well have been correct in their characterization of the language and of its poetic traditions of expression.

The similarity of Rousseau and Diderot can be seen quite readily in the article "Opéra" of Rousseau's highly regarded *Dictionnaire de musique* (1767). The operatic aesthetics in this article is set into the framework of a historical account of opera that starts with ancient Greek drama. In Rousseau's view, the operatic genre is fraught with problems, which are rarely solved. Modern poetry is unsuited both to melody and to musical meter and rhythm. A suitable "lyrical" language must be formed by choosing proper words, lines, and phrases. But it is then difficult to understand the meaning of what is said, and musical pleasures become the alternative to the moving expression of feeling. Thus, the joining of music to poetry, which was natural in Greece, is unnatural today. Again, to avoid an unnatural imitation of human life, opera turned to heaven and hell, to gods and devils. But the marvelous, supplemented with spectacle and large musical resources, remained cold and lacked interest. Feeling was therefore replaced by amazement, just as it was by auditory pleasure.

Rousseau finally conquers his tendency to discover inherent incompatibilities in opera: "Soon one began to feel that independent of the musical declamation, which was often hampered by the language, the choice of tempo, harmony, and song had something to do with the feelings to be expressed and that, consequently, the effect of the music itself, which was hitherto limited to the senses, could also be extended to the heart."[34] These new expressive powers, to be sure, were due, not to a fusion of music and poetry, but really to the music alone: "Having thus become a third art of imitation, music soon had its own language and expression and its own situations—all independent of the poetry. Even the overture learned to speak without the aid of words, and often the orchestra rendered emotions that were no less vivid than those conveyed by the actors" (p. 344).

At the same time, the expressive power of music is the key to the true nature of opera:

> It was felt that there should be nothing cold and rational in opera, noth-ing that the audience could hear so calmly as to be able to reflect on the absurdity of what was presented to it. And this is the main difference between lyrical drama and tragedy proper. All political deliberations, all conspiracies, expositions, narrations, sententious maxims, in short: whatever speaks to the reason alone was banished from the language of the heart. (p. 345)

This had now become an accepted principle of operatic aesthetics, although agreement between Rousseau and Diderot is particularly evident: "The force of all the emotions and the violence of all the passions are, then, the principal object of the lyrical drama" (p. 345). The power of music is such that even historical figures could sing without seeming to be unnatural, for

> the spectators, most appalled by hearing such men sing, soon forgot that they were singing, stunned and enraptured as they were by the mag-nificence of a music that was as full of nobility and dignity as it was of fire and enthusiasm. One began to see why feelings so radically different from ours must be expressed in such a different manner. (p. 345)

After Vinci, Leo, and Pergolesi, however, there is a recurrence of the basic difficulty, and "the poet and the composer, divided in their work, pro-duce simultaneously two similar but different images that harm each other" (p. 346). Rousseau can thus conclude by returning to his notorious attack on the French language, for in French this difficulty cannot be overcome:

> When a language is neither sweet nor flexible, however, the harshness of its poetry keeps it from lending itself to song—just as the very sweet-ness of the melody prevents it from making the recitation of the poetry more effective—and one feels in the unnatural union of the two arts a perpetual constraint that offends the ear and destroys the charm of the melody as well as the effect of the declamation. (p. 347)

A much more extensive essay than Rousseau's was the one written by Grimm for the *Encyclopédie* ("Poème lyrique," 1767). Grimm's article is comprehensive, detailed, objective, and remarkably perceptive. It is in fact an outstanding study of operatic aesthetics. Grimm begins with a discussion of imitation, which had become the traditional foundation of dramatic aesthetics, in accordance with the organization of Aristotle's *Poetics*. But he emphasizes the crucial role of convention, the acceptance of the artistic postulate, for example, that song is speech. Instead of verisimilitude, we have a "lie." Each component of opera is examined carefully, with a fine understanding of its nature. Grimm treats recitative and aria, the character of the action and of the poetry, the idiosyncrasies of French and of Italian opera, the chorus, the ballet, and gesture and performance. He develops, in fact, a complete poetics of opera, including the specific functions and relationship of composer and poet. And he makes instructive reference continually to spoken tragedy, to how it differs from opera. Grimm's writing style also is fully equal to his thought in its clarity and forcefulness. In all, the essay belongs among the few finest discussions of operatic aesthetics in eighteenth-century France.

Grimm's discussion of the aria is particularly perceptive. It holds up to view the more detailed relation of music and poetry that represented the core of the operatic genre. Out of four simple lines of poetry the music creates a complex emotional world. Instead of a pointless repetition of words for the sake of melodic expansion, there is actually a large variety of emotions, each of which reveals a different facet of the profound experience that arises from the dramatic situation.

The more exact structural consideration of the aria, of the relation of its musical and poetic components, become the focus of attention in the *Essai sur l'union de la poésie et de la musique* (1765) of François Jean de Chastellux.[35] The fundamental alternative presented by vocal music is whether it derives from speech or whether it follows specifically musical principles. A derivation from speech, of course, is in keeping with the theory of imitation, while a specifically musical principle, in Chastellux's view, calls for a musical idea that gives rise to a musical period. Now this musical principle is doubtless in some form intrinsic to all music, but Chastellux believes that it originated in instrumental music, from which it was transferred to vocal and in particular to the form of the aria. There are striking instances, in fact, where such a transfer from instrumental to vocal form did occur, even though it is not a universal rule or a general law of music. In any event, Chastellux contradicts the prevailing theory of imitation in a double sense: not only in finding a source of vocal form other than speech but also in finding this source precisely in instrumental music while imitation argues the priority of vocal music over instrumental. As far as the aria text is concerned, Chastellux urges logically that it be composed with this musical form in view rather than according to any divergent principles of its own.

Some years later issue is taken with this thesis by a *Traité du mélodrame*, *ou Réflexions sur la musique dramatique* (1771), published anonymously but evidently written by Laurent Garcin. The libretto should not be subjected to music, the author urges, but should proceed according to the theatrical expression, "sans liaison, sans méthode, sans ordre encyclique."[36] This called forth a defense by Chastellux, who was then supported by Diderot. Shortly after the opening of his "Letter," Diderot presents the controversy in clear terms:

> The main bone of contention between the Chevalier [de Chastellux] and his antagonist concerns the question of whether the poem ought to be made for the music or whether the poet can give rein to his fantasy with the composer being fated to follow him servilely as his trainbearer. The latter is the opinion cherished by the author of the *Traité*, who accordingly is unable to make a real distinction between the Comédie Française and the Opéra. . . . The ridiculous contrast between our poetry and the increasingly popular Italian music, the discordance of these two arts, set the Chevalier to thinking; and he found that if music is essentially a kind of song, that song has to be rigidly constructed. He expanded this idea and came to a conclusion that, heretofore, seemed revolting to Marmontel, namely that verses intended to be set to music must be subjugated—as far as their movement is concerned—to the form of the song. I do not think one can say anything more to the point.[37]

In the interest of the argument, of course, Diderot has taken a position here that is at the opposite extreme to that of the "cry of animal passion" and that is equally distant from his judicious image of speech and melody as two intertwining lines.

The last of the great wars of words in French operatic aesthetics of the eighteenth century was occasioned by the introduction of Gluck to Paris. François Le Blond Du Roullet, the librettist of Gluck's *Iphigénie en Aulide*, wrote a letter from Vienna on 1 August 1772 (published in October of that year in the *Mercure de France*) to one of the directors of the Opéra, proposing a production of *Iphigénie*. He justifies his recommendation primarily by the characteristic consideration of the nature of the language, stating that Gluck believed "that the Italian language, better adapted by its frequent repetition of vowels to what the Italians call passages, lacks the clearness and the energy of French; that the advantage which we have been conceding to the former was even destructive of the true musical-dramatic style, in which every passage is an anomaly or at least weakens the expression." Du Roullet went on to state that Gluck "became indignant at the bold assertions of our French writers who have dared to calumniate the French language."[38] He also described Gluck's achievement in glowing terms.

There was evidently ample reason in this introduction for Gluck to modify and contradict it in his "Letter to the Editor of the *Mercure de France*" (February 1773).[39] Refusing to accept Du Roullet's praise, Gluck attributes the invention of the new style of Italian opera to his librettist Calzabigi, and he takes pains to compliment Rousseau. Indeed, he tactfully subordinates the question of language to the concern of expressing the passions. Italian has no advantage for him since he never uses "the trills, the passages, or the cadenzas" with which the Italians are lavish. As a foreigner he feels he cannot "appreciate the delicate distinction" between Italian and French; he thinks "every foreigner should abstain from judging between them. But what I believe it is permitted to me to say is that the one which will always suit me the best is the one in which the poet will furnish me with the greatest number of different means of expressing the passions." This central idea is also announced in Gluck's reference to Calzabigi's *Orfeo*, *Alceste*, and *Paride*: "These works are filled with those happy situations, those terrible and pathetic strokes, which furnish to the composer the means of expressing the great passions and of creating a music energetic and touching." He seeks to attain the imitation of nature: "Always simple and natural, so far as is within my power, my music is directed only to the greatest expression and to the reinforcement of the declamation of the poetry." Gluck's aesthetics largely retains galant ideals, but it combines them with the newer interest in strong feelings that characterized the last few decades of the century.

The controversy that Gluck and his *Iphigénie* provoked seems to center around the style of accompanied recitative that was taken over from Italian opera, in which sharply defined orchestral motives play a prominent role. This stands in sharp contrast to the rounded, periodic melody of Italian opera. Now Gluck was regarded as essentially irregular and as realistically imitative of strong emotions. He seemed to exclude or persistently to interrupt the symmetry of pleasing melody, of which Piccini was the delegated representative. This new battle of French and Italian style, as exemplified by Gluck and Piccini, was excellently characterized and set into a historical context by the noted librettist Jean François Marmontel in his important *Essai sur les révolutions de la musique en France* (1777).[40] Although Marmontel favors the Italians, he is not blind to their defects and will have nothing to do with vocal virtuosity and arias of display. On the other hand, he sees the contest between Italian opera and Gluck in terms of fundamental aesthetic issues:

> The object of the arts that move the soul is not only emotion but the pleasure that accompanies it. It is not sufficient then that the emotion be strong; it must also be pleasing. . . .
>
> Why then do we not do in music what we have done in poetry? With

cries, shrieks, heartrending, or terrible sounds one expresses the passions; but these accents, if they are not embellished in the imitation, will
produce, as in nature, only the impression of pain. If we wanted only
to be moved, we would go and hear among the people a mother who is
losing her son, children who are losing their mother: it is there without
doubt that the expression of grief is without art; it is there also that it
is very forceful. But what pleasure would these heartrending emotions
give us? . . . It is thus just as strange an idea to want to banish melodious song from the lyric theater as to want to prohibit beautiful verses
in tragedy. . . . In a word, melody without expression is very little; expression without melody is something, but it is not enough. Expression
and melody, both in the highest degree to which they can rise together:
there is the problem of art. (pp. 166–69)

The point that eluded Marmontel lies beyond the polarity he describes,
for what was really involved was not the alternative of formlessness and
symmetry, or of emotional truth and sensuous pleasure, but the possibility of
a new kind of form that could contain more powerful emotional expression.
The stronger subject to be imitated broke through the traditional lyrical expression of tender sentiments and demanded a more irregular embodiment.
But this had long since occurred, of course, in the *recitativo accompagnato*
of Italian opera, which Gluck merely turned into *recitatif obligé* and applied
more generally.

The other characteristic of Gluck that was found objectionable was the
flexibility of his arias, in which the course of the action was reflected by
interruptions and by changes of pace. "Why not finish a melody you begin?"
asks Marmontel in exasperation. "Or why begin a melody you do not want
to finish?" (p. 168). But his criticism goes deeper than this. He concedes
that Gluck's opera may have more interest than those of Metastasio or even
than those of Quinault, in which a quieter feeling is dominant. The violent
passions manifest themselves only by degrees and do not have the urgent,
tumultuous, and rapid movements of Gluck's operas, which are reduced
almost to pantomime: "But there still remains to be known if the music is
made only to accompany the pantomime of the action or if the action is
not intended to develop the treasures and the charms of the music" (p. 173).
Clearly, the conflict here is one between the older galant aesthetics and the
new intensity of a Sturm und Drang.

The controversy continued most conspicuously in a series of letters published in various journals during the course of 1777 by Jean François de la
Harpe, who attacked Gluck, and a certain "Vaugirard Anonymous," who
defended him.[41] The two opponents were also indefatigable in attacking each

other, often on matters of terminology and accuracy, and the unremitting quarrel drew others into the fray, including Gluck. It is Vaugirard Anonymous, progressive and more musical, who emerges as the victor, for while la Harpe was able to understand the orchestra, for example, only as an accompaniment, Gluck's champion perceived the more comprehensive sense of melody and form that the composer projected.

Gluck's letter to la Harpe (*Journal de Paris*, 12 October 1777) comes right to the heart of the matter. It is cast ironically as a conversion:

> Heretofore I have been foolish enough to believe that it was with music as with the other arts, namely that all the passions form its subject, and that it should please no less by expressing the outbursts of a furious man and the cry of pain than by painting the sighs of love. . . . I was persuaded that song, completely filled, as it were, with the tint of the feelings which it aims at expressing, ought to change along with them, and use as many different accents as they have different nuances. . . . This, Sir, was my notion when I chanced upon your observations. Immediately light pierced the darkness. I was stunned to see, that, in a few hours devoted to reflection, you have learned more about my art than I after having practiced it for over forty years. You show me, Sir, that it is sufficient to be a man of letters in order to be able to discuss everything. I am quite convinced now that the music of the Italian masters is music par excellence, that singing, in order to please, must be regular and periodic, and that even in those moments of confusion when the singer, driven by several passions, passes successively from one to the other, the composer ought to stick to one melody.[42]

The chief outcome of the advent of Gluck in the field of musical aesthetics appeared some years after he had completed his epochal series of French operas in 1779. It was a two-volume treatise by Bernard Germain Lacépède, *La Poétique de la musique* (1785), which was devoted largely to opera. Lacépède generalizes Gluck's achievement and presents a series of principles and precepts for the composition of opera that is remarkable both in its breadth and in its exhaustive detail. More than a rationalization and summary of Gluck's practice, it is a program for the future and indeed anticipates numerous features of the operas and ideas of Wagner. Before discussing each component of the opera in detail, Lacépède considers at length the general effect of an opera.[43] He is concerned above all with what proved unquestionably to be the two most powerful and influential properties of Gluck's tragedies: the unified atmosphere of each work and the strength of its emotional expression. To what are these due, and how can they be produced? The answer takes us into every feature of operatic structure, from the nature of the action and the relationship between poet and composer to the use of recurrent musical material and the types of connection between successive sections with respect to their different expressive values and the changes in key these require. Even the considerations forced on the composer by the realities of convincing acting and staging are included. And Lacépède follows an ideal of realism throughout, which governed not only the operas of the Revolutionary period but also the first music dramas of Wagner and his large treatises of 1850–51.

Germany [44]

In Hamburg, the city in which a continuous tradition of German opera reached an efflorescence in the early eighteenth century, operatic aesthetics was importantly shaped by the reaction to a tide of neoclassicism that had its source in seventeenth-century France. The authorities responsible for this neoclassicism were, among others, Boileau, Jean de la Bruyère, and especially Saint-Evremond, whose notorious letter to the duke of Buckingham was continually referred to. The French literary conception, which derived in turn from sixteenth-century Italian neoclassicism and from Castelvetro in particular, gave rise to a surprisingly small body of operatic comment, yet its impact on opera in Germany was comparable to its influence in France. Christian Wernicke was an early representative who attacked the librettist Postel in his *Ein Helden-Gedichte Hans Sachs genannt* (1702). But French neoclassicism and the dramatic unities had more opponents in Hamburg than they had exponents. Among them were the novelist Christian Friedrich Hunold, who wrote under the pen name Menantes, and the clergyman Erdmann Neumeister, who wrote a manual on poetics for which Hunold contributed a preface (1707). Both these writers took issue with the requirement of the dramatic unities and with the standard of verisimilitude, and both emphasized the importance of theatrical effectiveness. Neumeister also recommended short iambic verse as more suited to music than long alexandrines.

Chief among the early Hamburg proponents of opera was the librettist Barthold Feind, the author of *Gedancken von der Oper* (1708), who insisted that the nature of drama was relative to time and place and who suggested Shakespeare as a model for the Germans rather than the French neoclassical writers. Feind insisted that opera was not bound by traditional dramatic rules and that it was devoted to the pleasure of the audience. Yet he emphasized, as a librettist, that the drama was primary and that opera was a genre of significance. He also effectively combatted the requirement of verisimilitude, as it was expressed by Saint-Evremond, and repeatedly emphasized the fictional character of opera and the necessity of its artistic conventions.

A man critical of the Hamburg operatic tradition was the poet and librettist Johann Ulrich König, who was a member of the important Teutschübende Gesellschaft, a literary and historical society founded in 1715 by the Hamburg senator and poet Barthold Heinrich Brockes. Societies of this type were dedicated essentially to the documentation and development of local German literary traditions, which tended to be submerged or suppressed by the influence of Italy and France. König was really a dissident member, for his views of opera, which he presented notably in the introduction to his *Theatralische, geistliche/vermischte und galante Gedichte* (1713), were based on Horace and on French neoclassicism. He criticized the complex style of older Hamburg librettos and stressed the French ideas of clarity, elegance, and good taste. He viewed opera as the highest form of art because it encompassed many other arts and various genres of literature. As a type of drama, however, it was subject to the principles of antiquity and to the dramatic unities. Music was one of the supplemental arts, and the librettist was in command. Among the characteristically German aspects of his ideas was the belief in the instructive and moral aim of opera, although this view of drama in general was itself derived from Horace's *Ars poetica*. Perhaps partly to further this moral purpose, König preferred to have a dramatic event depicted on stage instead of narrated so that the opera would have a greater impact on the audience.

In the 1720s, Johann Philipp Praetorius, who was a librettist for Keiser, again expressed positive and more purely German views of opera in his prefaces. Praetorius was particularly concerned about the growing popularity of opera in Italian, which he combatted by arguing the virtues of German opera and the German language. Pleasure in opera, he felt, was due to the perception of the agreement of words and music, and this obviously depended on the use of German. He also advocated a "noble simplicity" of style, an ideal consonant with contemporaneous Italian reforms and of increasing importance throughout the century. Important in addition was his positive evaluation of supernatural and allegorical figures in opera. These give opera an advantage over tragedy, he maintained, for they are pleasing to the fantasy, and since they are outside the limits of nature and truth, they contain a poetic quality. Praetorius evidently saw an advantage to the renunciation of verisimilitude.

Johann Mattheson, who was connected with the Hamburg opera as a singer and composer, was its lifelong champion, continually examining its aesthetics and supporting it. There was in the local support of the opera a confluence of German and English advocacy. Indeed, Mattheson was the tutor and friend of Cyrill Wich, who became the English diplomat resident in Hamburg. Both Wich and his successor, Thomas Lediard, were enthusiastic defenders of the Hamburg opera. Wich rescued it from bankruptcy, and Lediard became one of its librettists and directors.

Opera is repeatedly discussed by Mattheson, notably in *Das Neu-Eröffnete Orchestre* (1713), *Der Musikalische Patriot* (1728), *Der vollkommene Capellmeister* (1739), and *Die neueste Untersuchung der Singspiele* (1744). One of the more important questions he examines is the matter of verisimilitude, or probability. In *Das Neu-Eröffnete Orchestre*, he combats Saint-Evremond's view that opera lacks verisimilitude by comparing it to painting. Just as a painter cannot copy nature too exactly, so the theater cannot present simple nature in itself. Both painting and theater not only tolerate but at certain times expressly demand the concealment of nature and ornamental additions to it. The truth depicted in opera is figurative, not literal, and the inclusion of beautiful and artificial things in any event needs no justification beyond the goal of pleasure.

In *Der Musikalische Patriot*, Mattheson again criticizes Saint-Evremond and the criterion of verisimilitude, maintaining that "the opera in itself is a little art world," constructed from a variety of materials. He thus introduces an alternative to verisimilitude, and in fact to artistic imitation in general, that was probably the most powerful conceptual image of the century. Theatrical means artificial, he writes, or artificially imitative of nature. It refers to something that is made—and in some degree made with effort. This should not *seem* to be made, however; and it should not reveal any effort. Artificial means are foreign to reality by definition, but some seem less so than others. Opera seems to be more like nature because it is a three-dimensional depiction by living performers.

In *Der vollkommene Capellmeister*, Mattheson describes opera as the presentation of a fictitious reality. Everyone knows that it is a fabrication, but for the sake of enjoyment, disbelief is automatically or willingly suspended. The most elaborate discussion of verisimilitude is found in *Die neueste Untersuchung der Singspiele*. In artistic imitation, Mattheson asserts, a particular material is always selected to be worked on. The sculptor uses stone or wood, the painter a panel or canvas or wall. Some imitate nature with colors, others only with light and shadow. Many work in life size, many in reduction, and so on. Who can forbid such things? And why cannot the composer and poet undertake an imitation with harmonious sounds, melodies, verses, and rhythms? If an imitation resembled its model in every respect, he continues, it would be identical with it. But this should not be the case, and in fact it cannot be, for nothing can be completely similar to anything else.

Mattheson points out that, in the theater, daytime actions are depicted in the evening with artificial illumination. Opera is intrinsically different from the real world, like any other play, because it is art, and as such it presents "a new kind of pleasing order." Indeed, people doubtless go to the opera because they derive pleasure from observing how the performers make the new order seem probable. Otherwise, they would stay home and simply read the libretto. But their pleasure is not the result of a process of comparison— of the artistically probable with the naturally true.

Another prominent conception of Matteson's is that opera consists of an impressive assemblage of diverse fields of expression and thought. It is not a strange or deviant form of drama but "a musical university." It is characteristic of German operatic aesthetics to take a positive view of the numerous and varied components of opera, sometimes as the basis of the values of pleasure and entertainment, sometimes as the foundation of moral and educative value and of the highest status among the arts. This latter conception then leads logically to a *Gesamtkunstwerk*—to an interest in the cooperation of the component arts rather than their competition. This tends also to restrain or suppress the belief that one art should dominate others or that some should be subordinate to others or to one in particular. The next question to be asked, then, is how cooperation may best take place. Thus, a positive approach to opera would seem to be more likely in Germany than in France or Italy.

In *Der vollkommene Capellmeister*, Matteson asserts that opera combines all the other beauties of the stage. He sees this fusion as underscoring and intensifying the drama and to this end calls on the composer to avoid ornamental forms and to seek "a noble simplicity in expression." Expression of this kind is unaffected and artless, he says, and has only a single aim. It is conceived without constraint, according to pure natural laws. Thus, Matteson's galant aesthetics appears as a logical consequence of operatic unity. The "noble simplicity" of music, at the same time, is not thought of as a subordination or restriction.

In *Die neueste Untersuchung der Singspiele*, Matteson maintains quite explicitly that poetry and music are equals and that their cooperation is essential to a well-unified opera. The operatic unity really encompasses architecture, scenography, painting, mechanics, dance, acting, moral philosophy, history, poetry, and above all music. The aim is edification as well as pleasure.

The most prominent purveyor of French neoclassical aesthetics in Germany was the famous playwright, translator, editor, and critic Johann Christoph Gottsched, who resided in Leipzig. Gottsched subscribed wholeheartedly to the views that Saint-Evremond expressed in his influential letter on opera, insisted on strict adherence to traditional literary genres, and held up to German poets the clarity and good taste of the French. Thus, he inevitably came into conflict with the Leipzig librettist and critic Johann König and with the Zürich critics Johann Bodmer and Johann Breitinger, who looked on French neoclassicism with disfavor and turned to Milton and to the Italian literary critics instead.

Gottsched's attacks on opera appeared in 1728 in the periodical *Der Biedermann* and in his major work, *Versuch einer Critischen Dichtkunst* (1730). Since opera was neither tragedy nor comedy, he urged, it had no place in the legitimate system of the arts. It was not only nonsensical, since it was improbable and unnatural, but also dangerously seductive, because of its sensuality and splendor and lack of decorum. It ignored reason in favor of what pleases the eyes and ears. Art must be a rational imitation of nature, and it therefore cannot be based on marvels, wonder, and magic. Complex machines and singing are similarly unacceptable. Furthermore, opera has no ancient precedent.

Gottsched remained an active opponent of opera for most of his life. He wrote a German adaptation in 1740 of Saint-Evremond's satirical play *Les Opéra*, criticized Voltaire's opera *Samson* in 1745 for its infractions of dramatic rules, and attacked Christian Weisse's singspiel *Der Teufel ist los* when it was produced in Leipzig in 1752, objecting to its distracting music, its formal irregularity, and its English origins. Two of Gottsched's students, Christian Gottlieb Ludwig and Jacob Friedrich Lamprecht, expressed views similar to his in the 1730s, Ludwig concerned in particular about opera's dedication to sensuous pleasure and its lack of moral purpose, Lamprecht maintaining that continuous singing was ridiculous and that it involved frightening facial contortions. It is especially clear in Ludwig's case that hostility to opera is often coupled with inability to enjoy music.

But Gottsched and his disciples did not have the field to themselves. Ludwig Friedrich Hudemann published an essay defending opera in 1732, "Gedanken von den Vorzügen der Oper vor Tragedien und Comedien," which appeared as a preface to his libretto *Constantinus der Grosse*. Hudemann attacked Gottsched's ideas in particular, as presented in the *Versuch einer Critischen Dichtkunst*, insisting that opera was superior to ancient drama because of the more musical rhythm of German. It was also superior to all other contemporary types of drama because it was neither pretentious like tragedy nor coarse like comedy. Instead, the music called forth "a noble simplicity" in the text. At the same time, the combination of the arts gave opera an interesting variety, manifested in ingenious action, changes of set, machines, dances, and music. Opera was also more probable than other types of drama because the characters belonged to a higher realm of being and could therefore never exceed the limits of possibility. Hudemann emphasized at length the necessity of artistic fiction and maintained that continuous singing was no more unnatural than the poetic verse of spoken drama; both could be made convincing and probable within the framework of a dramatic work of art. He also denied the value of the unities of time and place. These did not further verisimilitude, for time and place were imaginary anyway in a drama. Finally, he discounted the value of arousing pity and fear, although he did not reject the traditional demand that drama must have a moral basis. A severe public reprimand from Gottsched, however, caused Hudemann to renounce all these ideas, so characteristic of Hamburg, and to become a proponent of French neoclassicism.

Another important defender of opera, Johann Friedrich Uffenbach, did not alter his position under Gottsched's onslaught. Uffenbach's essay "Von der Würde derer Singe-Gedichte" (1733), just like Hudemann's, was a systematic rejection of Gottsched's ideas. The adverse criticism of opera, Uffenbach argued, was due to its relative novelty and lack of precedents. Thus, there seemed to be no means of evaluating it, while its virtues as a modern form of art were not considered. Uffenbach saw opera as a "masterpiece of human ingenuity," as a "fusion of all poetic and musical beauties." It was a synthesis based on cooperation and, if necessary, on compromise. There was no reason for opera to follow traditional dramatic rules, for these were not even valid, Uffenbach pointed out, for the older genres. It is as mistaken, in any event, to judge modern art by ancient standards as it would be to judge ancient by modern. As far as verisimilitude is concerned, Uffenbach held that all forms of theater are hypothetical. Opera is no more improbable and unnatural than ancient drama. Indeed, all the poetic arts are inventions, fabrications; and divergence from nature is more to be praised than blamed.

In the case of Johann Adolph Scheibe, Gottsched's views did not provoke opposition so much as they produced a prolonged effort to apply them to opera profitably. Scheibe was subjected to Gottsched's influence in Leipzig, where he had been a student before his removal to Hamburg. He published his operatic ideas in Hamburg in his journal *Der Critiche Musikus* (1737–40). He argued that foreign styles of opera be abandoned and native ones cultivated according to the principles of reason and good taste. In contrast to the ancient dramatists, he maintained, modern librettists were inferior talents who were artistically ignorant and morally indifferent. Their coarse texts had led to the decline of German opera. Egotistical performers and careless composers were also to blame. But earlier librettists did not use the spectacular components of opera naturally and reasonably because they lived in an era devoid of good taste and reason.

As a disciple of Gottsched, Scheibe saw art as a rational branch of knowledge governed by absolute rules. He sought to reform opera by applying neoclassical precepts as they were codified for spoken drama in the *Pratique du Théatre* (1657) of Francois Hédelin, Abbé d'Aubignac. Epics and novels were in the worst taste for opera, he insisted, for this was a dramatic genre. He decried the fashion in writing for the theater of ignoring rules and indulging in an arbitrary freedom. In one of his essays, Scheibe designated opera a separate genre rather than a subgenre of drama. And opera had its own subgenres: when it concerns great persons, it has a great similarity with regular tragedy, whether it has a tragic or a happy ending; when it concerns ordinary citizens, it has a great resemblance to regular comedy, which is either moral or satiric; and when it is a pastorale, it will be either playful or serious, and the persons will represent either real shepherds and shepherdesses or disguised ones.

Very much like Scheibe, and also subject to Gottsched's influence as a Leipzig student, Lorenz Christoph Mizler von Kolof strove to reform opera through the application of rationalistic ideas. Something of the same mentality is revealed by his general aim of giving music a basis in mathematics and thus of establishing it again as a scientific discipline with a place in the faculty of philosophy of the university. In his *Neu-Eröffnete musikalische Bibliothek*, which appeared irregularly from 1736 to 1754, he republished selected articles on opera—among them those of Hudemann and Uffenbach—adding annotations that presented his own opinions. The rationalistic reform of opera and the intrinsic resemblance of music and poetry were his two principal themes. If opera avoided artificial machines, observed dramatic rules, and reinforced a didactic purpose appropriately with music, he believed, it would be as great as tragedy and comedy. The abuses of opera should not be mistaken for intrinsic defects.

In his republication of the operatic section of Gottsched's *Versuch einer Critischen Dichtkunst*, Mizler objected to Gottsched's dependence on French authorities and on Saint-Evremond in particular. He also maintained that opera was condemned because it was a form of art unknown to antiquity. In the notes to his translation of Muratori's condemnation of opera, Mizler questioned the value of ancient drama as a modern standard for criticism. And he defended the continuous singing of opera by insisting that an imitation cannot be completely similar to nature and that there are many improbabilities even in the very best tragedies.

Particularly effective polemics against artistic imitation were advanced by Johann Elias Schlegel. Mattheson applied some of Schlegel's ideas to opera in 1744 in his *Die neueste Untersuchung der Singspiele*, and Schlegel also brought opera into his deliberations in 1745:

> If it has been said about opera that it is unnatural for heroes to sing their deeds, their anger, and their compassion, it has been protested against drama in verse that it is unnatural for ordinary people to rhyme their decisions and ideas. But if it is unnatural in the poetic arts to imitate the

actions of everyday life in verse and the emotion of heroes in verse and music together, then it is also unnatural in sculpture to imitate animate bodies with inanimate ones, and black-haired horses, for example, with white marble, which is smooth and not covered by any hair, or a horse's mane that consists of an endless number of little particles with a single solid body, namely with the marble which is carved like the external surface of a mane. And then it is also unnatural in painting to imitate bodies with surfaces, and it is also unnatural in engraving to imitate multicolored bodies with monochrome surfaces. Prose and verse are not even as different as bodies and surfaces. At least the difference between the first two is not greater than between the last two. If we reject rhyme and meter in drama and sung tones in opera because this property of the imitations contradicts the property that is intrinsic to what is imitated, namely, this: that the conversations of people in ordinary life are never measured and rhymed, and that the threats of kings are never sung by them, then we must also condemn all of these arts that have been cited.[45]

Instead of reproducing nature, Schlegel maintained, art sought to create a new, artificial order, the perception of which would arouse sensuous pleasure. This was an idea that had occasionally been adumbrated in the past and that was destined in various forms to become the successor of verisimilitude.

The refutation of Gottsched in particular was again an objective of the *Beurtheilung der Gottschedischen Dichtkunst* (1747–48) of Georg Friedrich Meier. Essential to operatic criticism, Meier held, in agreement with Hamburg tradition, was the actual experience of opera. Gottsched's incompetence and his extreme and unfounded views were due to the fact that he was simply unfamiliar with opera. His claim that opera lacked the potential to become good revealed that he was not conversant with Aristotle's ideas about undeveloped artistic genres and their capacity for progress. Meier saw opera as a literary form created and controlled by the poet. It was great because it combined the ode and the tragedy, the most sublime forms in their respective genres. Singing was the proper means of operatic expression because it enhanced and reinforced the emotional impact of the dramatic situation. In the case of intense emotional states, he pointed out, we do not reflect about probability. Operatic probability is in any event of a special kind because opera depicts heroic action that does not belong to the realm of ordinary reality. Meier subsequently rejected Batteux's aesthetics of imitation, although his own views of opera were not really so different from those of Batteux's *Cours de belles-lettres* of 1747–50.

Batteux's theory of imitation was also rejected by Johann Adolph Schlegel, the younger brother of Johann Elias and the father of the illustrious Friedrich and August Wilhelm. Johann Adolph Schlegel translated the original version of Batteux's treatise as *Einschränkung der schönen Künste auf Einen einzigen Grundsatz* (published anonymously in 1751), and he appended a series of essays to both the first and later editions of the translation. He saw no sense in setting up a closed system of rules for writers to follow or in judging a work according to rules that had nothing to do with its construction. If the ancients limited the time and place of their dramatic action, he said more specifically, they did so to suit their own tastes and the needs of their own types of drama. A work was justified not by historically irrelevant rules but simply if it gave pleasure by presenting the beautiful or the good or both. Beyond this, the artist's success must be judged by his own basic assumptions.

Schlegel compared the poetic arts to a tree; they could never be circumscribed or limited to a specific number. Opera in particular had had difficulty with the critics because it defied classification. Batteux incorrectly assigned opera to the supernatural realm since the operas of Quinault did not imitate any conceivable aspect of ordinary nature and had to be accommodated somehow to the idea of imitation. The marvelous provided a justification for continuous singing and a basis for some kind of probability. But Schlegel believed that operatic probability depended on internal structure. The artificiality of the medium had nothing to do with it. As his brother had done, he resorted to a telling comparison of the arts to reveal the absence of exact imitation in other media also:

Opera deviates from actual nature one degree further than tragedy does; but will that which is not wondrous in opera therefore stop being probable? The imitations of sculpture lack the colors of nature that are inherent to the imitations of painting. Would one therefore be able to conclude that sculpture must present nothing but higher beings, nothing but gods, because then the dissimilarity that immediately becomes evident in statues when contrasted with human beings would to some extent be hidden or made more credible? (my translation) [46]

Thus, one could justify opera without recourse to the condition that it take the marvelous as its subject matter. Indeed, this condition was ignored in practice, while the "justification" it provided was in any event a logically fallacious one, for the meaning of a "faithful imitation of the marvelous" cannot be made clear.

Schlegel's essays found appreciative readers for at least twenty years after the appearance of the first six in 1751. They came to be regarded as a decisive step in the battle against the theory of imitation and in its replacement by more adequate conceptions of art.

Unlike the commercial opera in Hamburg and Leipzig, opera in Berlin was an activity of the court. As such, it came under the control of Frederick the Great (Friedrich II) on his accession to the throne in 1740. Contradicting his father's will, Frederick decided to establish a prestigious court opera and participated avidly in operatic productions. This meant that opera in Berlin, as was the rule with court opera, was exclusively in Italian, for the king, who spoke and wrote in French, desired opera in Italian and had a poor opinion of German singers and of the musical capacities of the German language.

The exclusion of German opera, like its failure earlier in Hamburg and Leipzig, created a discontent that fostered an examination of its defects and its possibilities as well as those of Italian opera. The chief forum for such a discussion, aside from the informal literary *Montagsklub* (Monday club), was the journal *Der Critische Musicus an der Spree*, which was founded in 1749 by Friedrich Wilhelm Marpurg in emulation of Scheibe's earlier journal in Hamburg, *Der Critische Musikus*.

In the first volume of his journal, Marpurg attacked the poor dramatic quality and the artificiality of Italian opera. He also praised the musical and expressive capacities of the German language. When native composers employed German, he maintained, they did not recognize its beautiful qualities or at least did not make use of them. Germans were in the habit of preferring whatever was foreign, a habit they had learned from their rulers. But if German art was fostered and given proper models, it would soon cease to appear inferior. The models that Marpurg proposed were the operas of Rameau, in which he felt the drama was essential and the music subservient. Thus, the musical style should be simple and unadorned, a requirement that was in conformity with the ideal of antiquity, which Marpurg characterized in the same way Winkelmann did. Indeed, he helped the phrase "a noble simplicity of song" secure its wide currency by employing it in the preface to another journal he founded, the *Historisch-Kritische Beyträge zur Aufnahme der Musik*, which started publication in 1754. Quite consistently, he asserted often that the ornate and totally unnatural Italian style had stifled indigenous types of opera in other countries.

The chief product of Berlin operatic aesthetics was Krause's *Von der Musikalischen Poesie* (1752), which had been a center of discussion in the Montagsklub for years before it was published in final form and which was to exercise a wide influence for many years afterward. The treatise was directed to the interrelations and combination of the arts, particularly to the writing of poetry intended for musical setting. Krause was guided a great deal by Du Bos's *Réflexions critiques* (1719), which had become increasingly influential in Germany toward the middle of the century. Of particular importance was Du Bos's interest in the development of music since its participation in ancient tragedy. Krause's treatise is primarily a composite, summary view of previous ideas, but his positive view of the cooperation and fusion of the arts is detailed and persuasive. A distinctive feature of this union is that it does entail restrictions or compromise of the individual arts. The only other condition for their unity was the conformity of both poetry and music to the galant and neoclassical principle of simplicity and naturalness. The action must also be plain and simple.

Beyond this idea of an art that was a single unified totality, Krause maintained—influenced by both Du Bos and Baumgarten—that the purpose of opera was the nonrational pleasure that only an actual performance could provide by affecting the senses, the emotions, and the imagination. Thus, the reaction of the audience was primary, and rules were formulated from this. Krause's theories of probability were even more derivative. Yet he expanded previous ideas and expressed them well, as in his assertion that a work would be probable as long as it was well enough organized and motivated to be convincing, for then it would engross the imagination of the viewers so completely that they would never notice whether it deviated from actual reality. Opera could do this better than any spoken form of drama because its music in particular could imbue it with a different kind of life. In addition, "the soul and the fantasy of a person who enters the opera house are prepared to surrender themselves to the deception of the imagination and to the outbreaks of passion." [47]

In Hamburg, Krause was often echoed by Wilhelm Adolph Paulli, the city's poet laureate, in the journals he published. In Leipzig and Dresden, Johann Adam Hiller was impressed with Krause's discussion of the cooperation of the arts. In his essay "Abhandlung von der Nachahmung der Natur in der Musik" (1754), which we have considered in chapter 6, Hiller's discussion of the role of feeling in operatic criticism clearly derives from Krause. The idea of the immediate verdict of feeling as an alternative to reason also underlies his analysis of verisimilitude. Opera is enjoyed even though we know it would be nonsensical in the real world. Our enjoyment certainly does not derive from a comparison of opera with reality. Indeed, Hiller approves the use of the marvelous in opera. It has often been abused, he acknowledges, but can be employed in a sensible way, and it gives a great deal of pleasure. Music itself, in the hands of a genius who sets his own rules, can effect miracles.

The Hamburg critic Friedrich Nicolai was still another publisher of journals in which operatic aesthetics was a major concern. Nicolai was particularly influenced by Du Bos and by the English dramatists and found fault with Gottsched and Batteux. Music should not serve poetry in opera, he argued, in agreement on this point with Batteux. Indeed, it was the most important art in the operatic compound, for it made the strongest impression on the audience. Not only can music hide or ameliorate absurdity or weakness in the libretto, but it can also explain the action without the help of words. In appealing to the lower powers of the soul, Nicolai asserts, adopting Baumgarten's view of art, it affects the whole range of emotions. For this reason also, instrumental music is a legitimate independent art.

Carl Wilhelm Ramler, an associate of Nicolai's, took a more conservative and rational view of art. He was concerned with the theory of imitation and with artistic rules, following Horace and the philosophers Leibniz and Christian Wolff. Ramler had spent some years in Berlin, where he helped revise Krause's manuscript, and his ideas in general were derivative and eclectic. He translated Batteux's *Cours de belles-lettres* into German as *Einleitung in die Schönen Wissenschaften* (1756–58). But instead of confining opera, as Batteux did, to the actions of gods and to the wonderful, he found human actions perfectly satisfactory as subject matter. In his "Vertheidigung der Opern" (1756), which was published in Marpurg's *Historisch-Kritische Beyträge*, he maintained that opera was neither unnatural nor improbable. He viewed it as a kind of drama in which the poet used music as a decorative accessory but adhered to the three unities and to the Horatian rules. Yet he found artificiality to be acceptable in imitation; just as the fable introduced animals that spoke, so opera could employ men who sang. We have only to imagine that we are in another world where people speak and act more slowly.

A third member of the Montagsklub, Moses Mendelssohn, believed in a systematic description of the arts, as Ramler did, but rejected imitation as the basis for such a description, adopting instead the effect of art on an audience. He studied Du Bos's *Réflexions critique* and engaged in discussions with Nicolai and Lessing, who had also examined Du Bos. A key idea here was the recognition of different types of artistic signs.

In his *Betrachtungen über die Quellen und die Verbindungen der schönen Künste und Wissenschaften* (1757), Mendelssohn defined art as the sensuous expression of perfection. The work of art selects and assembles from a single viewpoint the most beautiful aspects of several parts of nature. But the arts can be synthesized only if one chosen art dominates the others. Music, sculpture, painting, and dance are composed of natural signs, which appeal to sight and hearing and are therefore limited. But poetry and rhetoric are composed of arbitrary signs, which appeal to the mind and can express everything. Signs also are either successive or simultaneous. Now natural and arbitrary signs can be combined if both types are successive. In music, the expression of feeling is strong, lively, and moving, but the feeling is indeterminate: it is obscure and general. The addition of such arbitrary signs as those of poetry, for example, can make the feeling an individual one. But the major art in opera is music, and its rules can call for the alteration, adjustment, or suppression of the rules of poetry or drama. Opera itself, as Mendelssohn viewed it in 1758 in his *Betrachtungen über das Erhaben und das Naive in den schönen Wissenschaften*, is an instance of the sublime—of the sensuous expression of perfection that arouses admiration.

The *Laokoon* (1766) of Gotthold Ephraim Lessing, which studied the distinctive differences between poetry and the plastic arts, was intended as the first part of a comprehensive, three-part work devoted to the individual limitations and distinguishing properties of all the arts. This would not only help the creative artist formulate appropriate goals and projects and avoid unsuitable ones but also point the way to successful syntheses of the arts, an achievement entailed in every form of theater. Thus, Lessing's investigation was a logical continuation of the ideas of Du Bos, Batteux, Krause, and Mendelssohn. Music and its relation to poetry belong to the uncompleted parts of Lessing's project, but we know something of his ideas in this area from his preserved notes.

He found music and poetry fundamentally akin, for they both appealed to hearing and they both progressed in time. Tones, however, which are natural signs, have meaning only in relations of succession, while words, which are arbitrary signs, have meaning individually. Thus, one word can express as much as a series of tones, and this difference, which amounts to a difference in the temporal extension demanded by each art, produces the chief difficulties in combining them.

Overcoming this difficulty, reconciling the basic conflicting demands of music and poetry, would produce a true unity and joint effect. In practice, however, one art is made to subserve the other. Poetry subserves music in Italian opera, while French opera seeks to emphasize poetry. Or perhaps we should say that recitative and aria in general reveal the alternative subservience of music and poetry, respectively. But is this natural in a single work of art? Will the sensuous relation in which music dominates not make the other art seem uninteresting? Also, why can there not be an art in which music subserves poetry throughout?

Lessing extended this searching examination of artistic combinations to the other arts as well, continuing his speculations in various issues of his *Hamburgische Dramaturgie* (1767–69) when he was the resident critic of the Hamburg National Theater. The use of instrumental music in drama is one of his recurrent themes. Among other things, we find a consideration of melodrama and also an idea usually connected with Wagner, that the orchestra can play a role in drama comparable to that of the ancient Greek chorus. Furthermore, instrumental music can enhance the enjoyment of drama; in particular, it can compensate for the weaknesses in the poetry or in the dramatic structure. Each drama, however, as Scheibe pointed out, calls for its own musical accompaniment that is directly related to the action.

In his discussion of Agricola's music for Voltaire's *Sémiramis*, Lessing finds that the introductory music presents the tone of the drama and prepares the audience by adumbrating its action while the entr'acte music sustains the suspense by summing up the past action. The music also supports sudden changes in emotional intensity and mood. It can even compensate for a lack of motivation in the text. But poetry can help music as well. Music alone leaves us uncertain and confused:

> We feel without perceiving a logical succession of our feelings; we feel as though in a dream; and all these disorderly feelings are more fatiguing than pleasing. Poetry, in contrast, never allows us to lose the thread of our feelings; here we know not only what we should feel but also why we should feel it; and it is this alone that makes the most sudden transitions not only bearable but also pleasing. In fact this motivation of sudden transitions is one of the greatest advantages that music derives from its connection with poetry; indeed, perhaps the greatest of all. (my translation) [48]

In connection with the musical plays of Charles Simon Favart, finally, Lessing writes about drama in general as an artistic world of its own. Although the characters (taken from a story of Jean Francois Marmontel)

> are not, to be sure, from this real world, they could nevertheless belong to another world; to a world whose contingencies are connected in a different order, but still connected just as precisely as in this; to a world in which causes and effects, it is true, follow one another in a different sequence, but yet aim equally at the general effect of the good; in short, to the world of a genius, who—(permit me to signify the nameless Creator by means of his noblest creature!) who, I say, in order to imitate the supreme genius in the small, transposes, interchanges, reduces, increases the parts of the present world, to make of them a whole of his own, with which he combines his own intentions. (p. 230; my translation)

Evaluation, obviously, will then be based on works of art themselves, not on abstract rules.

Art as an autonomous world of imagination becomes a dominant theme in the writings of Justus Möser, who connects this conception with native German forms of expression as contrasted with the rational French ideal of imitation and prescriptive unity. In his *Harlekin oder Vertheidigung des Groteske-Komischen* (1761, reprinted in 1777), Möser's views are presented by Harlequin, who effectively combats the ideal of a universal taste and urges the primacy of genius, original creation, living theater, and the infinite variety of art that is produced by the ceaseless and unpredictable evolution of nature. Nature has its own laws, its own kind of unity, and so does a great work of art, which similarly synthesizes divergent elements into an organic whole. Opera in particular becomes a symbol of nonimitative artistic expression. Operatic aesthetics becomes the battleground on which a new view of art triumphs over the forces of tradition, almost as though a new and aggressive German consciousness were destroying French order and regulation. Thus, reason, with its limitation, gives way in opera to the imagination, to the strange and the dreamlike.

Closely related to Möser's theories were the patriotic poems of Friedrich Gottlieb Klopstock. In *Hermanns Schlacht, Ein Bardiet für die Schaubühne* (1769), Klopstock created a type of theatrical work that incorporated bardic poems and that called for defined gestures, dances, and instrumental music as well as gradations of sound and intervals of silence. Gluck agreed to set the bardic songs, but never completed the task. Johann Georg Sulzer, in the article on opera for his *Allgemeine Theorie der Schönen Künste* (1771, 1774) found that the *Bardiet* invented for *Hermanns Schlacht* was completely new, yet closer to Greek tragedy than any other type of modern drama because it incorporated music in a way that was not only effective but also rationally comprehensible. What Germany required to produce a perfected tragedy, he maintained, was the kind of cultural unity that the ancient Greeks had enjoyed.

Heinrich Wilhelm von Gerstenberg was also enthusiastic about *Hermanns Schlacht*. Unlike Sulzer, who supported neoclassical principles, Gerstenberg found rationalism and imitation powerless to explain creative imagination and genius. He was unable to relegate music to a subservient role, as Sulzer did, and he held instrumental music to be an independent art fully capable of expressing the whole range of human feelings. In this he agreed with Nicolai, and he generally shared the views of Berlin aesthetics. Thus, he was concerned with the nature of opera as well as of tragedy, and he agreed with Mendelssohn that music had to be included in any general theory of aesthetics.

In *Hermanns Schlacht*, Gerstenberg wrote, Klopstock revealed the true nature of mimesis, for the ancients had not attempted a realistic imitation of nature, instead using choruses, dances, instrumental music, and other non-naturalistic elements in order to create "a second poetic nature." The most systematic statement of Gerstenberg's conception of opera can be found in his "Schlechte Einrichtung des Italienschen Singgedichts; Warum ahmen Deutsche sie nach?" (1770). He objected to Italian opera because of its

combination of recitative and aria. The two are so fundamentally different in nature that they are incompatible. Declamation conveys ideas, and
song depicts feelings. In addition, Gerstenberg maintained, coloratura and
the invention of new instruments have removed opera too far from natural
declamation. It really should be based not on song but on recitation. Italy
and France must be set aside in favor of a noble imagination.

As a poet, Gerstenberg contributed to the melodrama, at first indirectly,
rather than to the opera. One of his cantata texts, *Ariadne auf Naxos* (1767),
was made into the text of a melodrama by Johann Christian Brandes and
performed with music by Georg Benda in 1775. Gerstenberg also wrote
Minona, oder Die Angelsachsen, ein tragische Melodrama (1785), which
was influenced by the purported translations (published in 1762–63 by James
Macpherson) of the Celtic poems of Ossian.

As far as opera was concerned, however, alternatives to the war song
seemed to offer greater possibilities. These were discussed in 1767 by Daniel
Schiebeler, the librettist of Hiller's *Lisuart und Dariolette* (1766). Epics provided a wealth of subjects, as did novels and even parts of the Bible. Schiebeler tried to relate various types of epic to corresponding types of theater.
The serious epic gave rise to the heroic tragedy or the heroic opera, notably
that of Metastasio. Ovid's *Metamorphoses* led to operas about gods, like
many of Quinault's. The comic epic produced comedy and comic opera. Of
all the types of epic, the romantic appealed to innate human preferences.
Schiebeler traced out its history. Its chief subject matter is the experiences of
knights in search of adventure or on missions of chivalry, and it mixes the
serious with the comic, as we find in Ariosto. The serious aspect is the source
of romantic tragedies and romantic-tragic operas, while its playful side is
the source of romantic comedy and romantic-comic opera, although these
really do not conform to the system hypothesized, for they are derived from
the fairy tale. Schiebeler's operatic typology gave rise to the use of generic
subtitles, and his use of the fashionable epithet "romantic" gave impetus to
a central new conception of opera.

The poet and novelist Christoph Martin Wieland was also active in the
cause of native opera, particularly from the time of his arrival in Weimar in
1772, where he spent the remainder of his life. In his "Briefe an einem Freund
über das deutsche Singspiel, 'Alceste'" (1773), which was published in his
journal *Der Teutsche Merkur* for that year, Wieland discussed his alteration
of Euripides' tragedy for operatic purposes. He had reduced the number
of characters, shortened the long monologues, omitted the choruses, and
changed the role of the heroine, for the operatic stage—so he maintained—
called for simple plots, short songlike dialogue, convincing characters, and,
above all, diversity and change. Wieland claimed to have surpassed both

Euripides and Metastasio, in that his work had a high degree of internal truth, which did not allow the listener to entertain the sober thought that it was only a fairy tale. In addition, to suit the medium of opera, he had made the verse lyrical and poetic rather than rhetorical and philosophical. A lyrical play in particular, he wrote, calls for the difficult art of using few words: "How infinitely different is the language of feeling from the language of the schools of oratory! What unutterable things it can say with a glance, a gesture, a tone!" (p. 259). Wieland credited the composer, Anton Schweitzer, with intensifying the emotional impact of the opera, supplementing poetry when transitions were needed or when it reached its expressive limits. Schweitzer had also assumed a subservient role, which Wieland felt at the time to be the correct one. In any event, the performances of *Alceste* were so successful that Wieland was acclaimed by many as the regenerator of German opera.

Wieland's major essay on opera was "Versuch über das deutsche Singspiel und einige dahin einschlagende Gegenstände" (1775). In the first part of the essay, Wieland proposes a distinctly German form of opera that is to be called "singspiel." He argues in the second part that the defects of Italian opera—as discussed by Algarotti in 1755—would not exist in the new German type. The singspiel would not seek the sensuous appeal of elaborate costumes, complicated scenery, intricate choreography, and musical virtuosity. Instead, it would affect the emotions through simplicity of plot, poignancy of action, and poetic quality of text. It would deceive the imagination in order to touch the heart. Wieland also included a long and largely derivative defense of operatic verisimilitude.

The third part of the essay considers the subject matter suitable for opera. Instead of using the subjects of ancient tragedy, which would be senseless because society and culture had become so different, the singspiel should emphasize the lyrical rather than the dramatic, for music seems to contain certain intrinsic limitations. Wieland's thought indeed reveals the restrictive influence of the galant. Music beautifies whatever it imitates, and it provides emotional pleasure. Thus, it cannot imitate ugly things, tragic elements, or violent passions without contradicting its nature. Singspiele should be devoted to mood and sentiment; their plots should permit music to reveal psychological states and inner action and to intensify the effects of these on the feelings of the audience. Complicated intrigue, long dialogues, reasoning, and rhetoric are to be excluded, as well as divertissements, dances, and the wonderful. The pastorale provides the best subject matter of all and, after this, the divinities of myth, the heroic world, knightly adventure, and history, in that order of preference.

The fourth and last part of Wieland's essay considered the need for artistic cooperation. The domination of composers and singers had turned Italian opera into a sensuous spectacle. Poetry had achieved dignity, however, with Metastasio, and Gluck had pointed the way to operatic reform. What was also called for was a generous royal patron of the singspiel.

The novel was particularly congenial to Wieland, and it is not surprising that his operatic aesthetics secured a wide influence when incorporated in the highly successful novel *Die Abderiten*, which he published serially in *Der Teutsche Merkur* starting in 1774. In "Euripides unter den Abderiten" (1778), the section of the satirical novel that is devoted to opera, Wieland presents a criticism of every aspect of German operatic practice and operatic thought (the fictitious republic of Abdera in Thrace represents a characteristic German province). Included are not only satires of all eighteenth-century types of opera but also a description of the ideal proposed by Wieland himself, as realized in an exemplary production. Here Euripides stages his own *Andromeda* for the Abderites, who at first are bewildered by how different everything is from what they are used to but are soon completely won over by the experience:

> Since moreover the music was now in perfect conformity with the poet's purpose and thus was everything the music of Nomofylax Gryllus was not; since it always directly affected the heart and was always new and surprising in spite of the greatest simplicity and singability: so all this, united with the vivacity and truth of the declamation and pantomime and with the beauty of the voices and the delivery, produced a degree of deception among the good Abderites, such as they had never before experienced in a play. They forgot entirely that they were sitting in their national theater, believed themselves to be unobserved in the midst of the real scene of action, sympathized with the fortune and misfortune of the characters as if they had been their very closest friends. (pp. 277–78)

After the advent of Gluck's reform operas, starting with Calzabigi's *Orfeo* and *Alceste* in Vienna, German operatic aesthetics was concerned mostly with the properties of these works and with the issues that were made concrete by the contrast between Gluck's innovations and the more traditional features of Italian opera, especially of the operas of Hasse and Metastasio. The native Italian reform that occurred in the later operas of Jomelli and Traetta was not widely enough experienced to lessen Gluck's impact. Thus, a traditional Italian art of sensuous melody and soft sentiment stood in sharp contrast to an apparently unprecedented art of powerful emotions that was compounded of Italian, French, and German ingredients.

The competing aesthetic views that were produced by these two types of opera are in one instance elaborated in the writings of the same man—the Sturm und Drang novelist Wilhelm Heinse, who was highly sensitive to the visual art and music of Italy but also deeply impressed with the reform operas of Gluck. Discussions of opera are scattered through Heinse's large novel *Hildegard von Hohenthal* of 1795–96. The consideration of traditional Italian opera revolves largely around Pergolesi, who is accurately described as excelling in sensuous and pleasing expression, in soft and tender feelings such as those of unhappy love. Heinse perceives also that Pergolesi's restricted emotional range does not encompass more powerful types of expression and that he has no capacity for characterization. Here the practice of vocal ornamentation and the subordinate position of the orchestra are partly to blame. But Heinse is also aware of a native reform in Italian opera that was initiated by Jomelli. The reformers typically create a noble and facile melodic flow, clarity and purity, and appropriate and diversified harmony. They combine characterization, however, with this beauty, and it is a characterization that develops in time. Jomelli excels, Heinse finds, in grasping what is most essential in the action and representing it vividly, an accomplishment that is furthered by the elimination of melodic decoration and particularly by the greater participation of the orchestra in the expression of the affections.

Heinse's view of the role of instrumental music, however, is not a simple one. The orchestra "strengthens and defines the expression of the singing personae," he maintains. It "expresses their mute feelings and the feelings of the associated people and of the whole society and the whole life of nature."[49] Elsewhere he remarks that two feelings can be active in a person simultaneously, both of equal strength in cases of doubt or one subordinated to the other in decisions of passion. An instrument could thus give voice to one or the other since the singing persona cannot express both at the same time with one melody. But Heinse also writes, more generally: "What is our huge orchestra to represent and mean in a dramatic situation? The harmonic walls, so to speak, of the scene? or the associated feelings of the singing personae? or the feelings of the other participants? or the feelings of the listening public? or all these together?" He concludes, with a suggestion of sophistry, that "the orchestra, in the ordinary course of things, represents . . . the orchestra!" (p. 32). It is evident, at any rate, that Heinse was well aware of the importance of the orchestra and that he was interested in the crucial problem of its function. In this as in other matters, his concerns are characteristic of the end of the century.

Gluck is discussed repeatedly and in considerable detail. In his expression of the violent, the powerful, and the sorrowful, Heinse claims, he belongs with the finest masters of tragedy. "Gluck created a unique genre," Heinse also asserts, "between tragedy and opera" (p. 34). As an author, Heinse is sensitive to Gluck's treatment of verbal rhythms, to the compelling rhythm of his declamation. "In theory," he remarks, "Gluck gave by far the dominant position to poetry and followed it as an obedient servant. But he contradicts himself best: for precisely in his good operas music rules more than elsewhere, only it does not flutter about and engage in play but expresses the feelings given in the text with decisive power" (p. 31). Italian or French words are all iambs, Heinse points out subsequently, yet all the feet of Greece can be found in Gluck, although in an untamed and approximate form. "It is a joy to hear how Gluck transforms the iambs of the French poets into all the possible feet of Greek poetry" (p. 35).

In Gluck, and in opera in general, Heinse is particularly concerned with the newly prominent achievements of characterization. Melody must distinguish different types of personality and character, he urges; it must characterize powerful passions, compliant persons, coarse ones, those who are calm, and so forth. It is largely from the point of view of characterization that he rejects castrati. They represent a great impoverishment of vocal music, for they can produce no contrast between a man and a woman or between people of different ages. Comparable to characterization in its importance, and also novel in its strength, is the unified effect made by one of Gluck's operas as a whole. Gluck rarely equals the great Neapolitans in high beauty, Heinse feels, but in "the deep impression of the whole" (p. 34) he ranks with the greatest of dramatists.

With all his enthusiasm for the achievements of Gluck, however, Heinse also remains aware of the fundamental value that resides in Italian melody. The words of the aria must contain what is most beautiful, he writes, "because arias are the chief thing in music." The action seems to stand still during such lovely expressions of the feelings that gather during the raging course of events. "Too rapid a progress of the action robs music of its greatest beauties, opera of its foremost charm over the tragedy, which can express such places only by pantomime and silence, by far not so vividly seizing hold of heart and sense" (p. 32). Gluck's most valuable arias, however, are "truly German in melody and harmony," although his high points "are neither Italian or German . . . but the expression of universal, noble humanity" (p. 34). Indeed, the "Classical" features of Gluck, including his use of the chorus, seemed striking to the observers of the time.

Twenty years before *Hildegard von Hohenthal*, Heinse had treated musical matters at some length in his *Musikalische Dialogen*, which were written in 1776 or 1777 but not published until 1805. The second of the three dialogues is devoted to operatic aesthetics.[50] It consists essentially in a conversation between "The Princess" and "Metastasio," who is not an accurate depiction, however, of the historical Metastasio. "He who has seen an excellent opera performed in Naples," Metastasio says, "will not doubt the possibility that an opera can deceive and set the spectator into such a forgetfulness of the improbability that he believes he sees the real Alexander, the real Dido, the real Hercules." He cites the tears and violent emotions of the audiences:

> Even the often inappropriate figure of the castrati for the personae they represent does not interfere with the deception. When perhaps Faustinas, Luzzonis, Porporas have the roles suitable to them, when at the same time an Apostolo Zeno expresses the passion of the personae in the language of the Muses, and a Pergolesi has experienced in his soul the accents for that purpose—oh! how little must he then know Nature who can deem the song of these persons to be unnatural! (pp. 378–79)

But the Princess cannot understand how people of the best taste cannot keep the improbability in mind. "Where Nature is," Metastasio explains,

> the poet and the composer can easily charm the improbability out of the heads of the listeners. The improbability is not much greater than in tragedies and comedies. Caesar, Cato, Brutus, Alexander, Medea, and Lucretia speak in French, English, and Italian verses in the theater. When the poet has drawn their characters well and powerfully, when the actors and actresses are excellent, Nature banishes the improbability. (p. 379)

Thus, Metastasio replaces the probable with the natural. The new value is really an original musical experience rather than an imitation of anything else. He elaborates the point by appealing to the superiority of musical nature over nature as ordinarily understood:

> Thus an opera is nothing less than unnatural; much more is there an addition made here of that which natural beauty and perfection still lack. Thence it comes that an aria affects the heart a hundred times more strongly when it is sung than when it is only declaimed in a tragedy. I have seen the finest tragedies of Corneille and Racine performed, and the almost superhuman action and declamation of the most famous actresses have not lured forth so many tears by far from the spectators as an excellent cantatrice can pour out with the transporting song of an aria in which the most profound degree of a melancholy tenderness is expressed in the divine language of the Italians. Her tender, sighed accents sung by a mouth suffused with melancholy grace, the tears of her eyes looking up to heaven, her anxiously heaving breast with which

the heart can speak more than with the tongue! bound to the activity of a beautiful body—Who will feel nothing here? (p. 380)

Heinse's love of Italian sensuousness, which was to be so influential ten years later in his novel *Ardinghello*, is also enthusiastically expressed here.

The theory of the perfection of beauty also explains why song in opera is held to be natural for gods and unnatural for men, for the gods—as the Princess comes to perceive—were imagined as the most perfect men. In the course of the dialogue, the theory takes on a Platonic aspect: "Nature endows human beings in particular with this basic impulse to become always more perfect. From this there arises the love of supernal beauty" (p. 381).

In addition to the analysis of musical nature, Heinse discusses the basic features of operatic dramaturgy. The development of the action is described in a way that anticipates Wagner. As Metastasio explains, when a person in a violent passion only tells of the history of his passion, the tone of usual utterance will not change much:

But as soon as he expresses his feelings about it, as soon as he groans over his fate, or as soon as two persons are in a scene in which they no longer act, but can only feel, there the tone changes very noticeably, the accents become now faster, now slower; now words fail them for the expression of their feeling; it thus expresses itself simply in tones; now it can no longer do even this, and the all too violent feeling chokes off tone and words. The narration or the described history of the passion makes up the recitative, and the feelings expressed about it arias and choruses. This takes place with most of the passions: anger, love, fear, horror, jealousy mount up from their beginnings to their greatest height, and with their growth the accents of threats, tenderness, laments, sighs, rage, and horror continuously change. . . . Even behavior is more natural in the opera than in a tragedy; here it is often so rapid that it makes the whole action unnatural; the battle of the mind with the passions in their full strength is often not finished in as short a time as an actress in a tragedy allows it to last in order to avoid emptiness.

Poet and composer must both have one and the same final aim: the poet may put nothing into his action that the composer cannot treat, and the composer may not interrupt the action or diminish its interest through the pomp and the empty noise of his music.

Therefore the poet may do nothing more than gradually realize the passions in actions from their interesting beginnings up to their highest point. Their fire may not entirely die out, the flame must always grow little by little. Cold, deliberated sentences, thoughts without feelings, syllogisms, political subtleties, in short, witticism and understanding must not force their way into the language of feeling and the heart. The composer cannot express these. Music either expresses passions and feelings or it is nothing more than a pleasant noise for the ears. The spectator must feel continuously; as soon as the feeling is interrupted, as soon as the soul can think as it pleases, that soon is at least the interest in the action weakened, if it has not totally disappeared. Hence the first and the somewhat later operas were nothing more than a concert of recitative and arias intermixed. The music was a thing in itself, and the poetry also. At the most they set up an alliance, like a not too loving married couple. They should be connected, however, like the parts of a human being; one must be able to distinguish separately neither poetry nor melody; they must flow together, fuse together with one another. And then the deception will be produced with complete certainty, and the opera will always be with respect to tragedy and comedy what tragedy is with respect to the real actions of men. (pp. 379–81)

Much of this is astonishingly close to the ideas of Lacépède, and in Heinse apparently without the influence of Gluck's operas. Clearly, aesthetics was here well in advance of practice. And in both Heinse and Lacépède it is the conception of a self-contained artistic whole that underlies the conquest of imitation. In Heinse's words, "And then the deception will be produced with complete certainty. . . ."

It is finally this idea of a self-contained artistic whole that becomes the theme of Goethe's dialogue "Über Wahrheit und Wahrscheinlichkeit der Kunstwerke," which was published in 1798 in the first volume of *Die Propyläen*. Opera is characterized as "a little world of art" in which the audience participates. It possesses "an inner truth that arises from the consistency of a work of art" (p. 60). At the turn of the century, Goethe, and Schiller as well, viewed opera as the potential embodiment of an ideal type of tragedy. Largely because of music, it was able to create an engrossing unity and to free art from the requirements of imitation.

PART FOUR

THE NINETEENTH CENTURY

CHAPTER EIGHT

ROMANTIC AESTHETICS

Romantic conceptions of music can be found fully elaborated in 1799, in the *Phantasien über die Kunst für Freunde der Kunst* of Wilhelm Heinrich Wackenroder. The musician Joseph Berglinger, a character Wackenroder had created in his *Herzensergiessungen eines Kunstliebenden Klosterbruders* (1797), discusses music in some detail in a series of essays appended to the *Phantasien*. Thus, aesthetics, especially musical aesthetics, is embedded in a literary work—a practice that had occurred earlier in *Rameau's Nephew*, for example, or in *Hildegard von Hohenthal* but that became characteristic of Romanticism.

This literary context provides a kind of justification for the poetic style in which ideas about art are expressed, and, perhaps for this reason, the fusion of literature and aesthetics was fruitful as well as typical. Poetic criticism, as we find it in Hoffmann and Schumann, for example—which seeks to duplicate somehow the musical experience of an individual work in words—is clearly a related phenomenon. Thus, Romantic aesthetics—as a more specific outcome of its literary style—is generally infused with emotion: with enthusiasm and even ecstasy. Thought and rationality alone seem inadequate to serve as its vehicle.

A further characteristic of Romantic aesthetics is that the unique quality and status of music with respect to the other arts is always apparent. Comparisons of the arts, usually taken two at a time, were common from the Renaissance on, as we have seen. They go back to antiquity, and Horace in particular is often cited as a point of departure. But in the nineteenth century the arts are considered characteristically as a group of three: the "sister arts"—since the Muses were female—of music, poetry, and dance. More important and more general than this, however, is the preferred position of music as the highest, or ideal, art. As Joseph Berglinger asks himself: "But why do I, foolish one, strive to melt words into tones? It is never as I feel it. Come, Thou musical strains, draw near and rescue me from this painful earthly striving for words, envelop me in Thy shining clouds with Thy thousandfold beams, and raise me up into the old embrace of all-loving heaven." [1] In the primary matter of presenting feeling, at any rate, the other arts, and especially literature, must give way to music.

But beyond this, what is the actual nature of music or of the feeling with which it is connected? More than feeling is involved, or at least more than feeling as it is ordinarily understood. There are "shining clouds" and "thousandfold beams"—synesthetic qualities—and the "embrace of all-loving heaven." The feeling connected with music is in some way religious or metaphysical. It was a monk, in fact, that Wackenroder chose as his spokesman for art in his *Herzensergiessungen*. This spiritual property of music is revealed by the aerial transmission of sound, by the disappearance of music into the void: "Ethereal music floated up from the skiff into the open heavens; sweet bugles and I know not what other enchanting instruments brought forth a floating world of sounds" (p. 177). An outdoor setting will of course favor the identification of music with sound waves, and a description of cosmic harmony is only the logical consequence of the conception:

> The body of the saint had disappeared; an angelically beautiful phantom, woven of light vapors, floated out of the cave, stretched its slender arms longingly towards heaven, and ascended in a dancing movement from the ground into the sky, in rhythm with the sounds of the music. The luminous phantom floated higher and higher into the air, lifted up by the gently swelling sounds of the horns and the singing;—with heavenly gaiety the figure danced to and fro here and there on the white clouds which were floating in the heavens; with dancing feet it vaulted higher and higher into the sky and finally flew around between the stars in serpentine turns; then all the stars sounded and droned through the air an intensely radiating heavenly chord, until the spirit disappeared into the infinite firmament. (pp. 177–78)

As we might expect, however, the celestial character of music is sharply contrasted with the more grossly physical nature of musical instruments: "But from what sort of magic potion does the aroma of this brilliant apparition rise up?—I look,—and find nothing but a wretched web of numerical proportions, represented concretely on perforated wood, on constructions of gut strings and brass wire" (pp. 179–80). Mathematics, as we can see, shares the fate of instruments. The antithesis of language, expression, and imitation in the preceding epoch, as harmony was of melody, it continues, along with musical instruments, as the antithesis of Romantic feeling.

Yet the relation of mathematics and music is not a simple one. Intrinsically antithetical to feeling, mathematics is nevertheless mysteriously connected with it through the order and system of tones: "Between the individual, mathematical, tonal relationships and the individual fibers of the human heart an inexplicable sympathy has revealed itself, through which the musical art has become a comprehensive and flexible mechanism for the portrayal of human emotions" (p. 188).

But music fuses "qualities of profundity, of sensual power, and of dark significance" in an enigmatic way. And while the emotions it expresses and evokes are human, they are also divine, for they are experienced in the soul. Furthermore, they can only be felt, not understood or named:

> Whoever wants to discover with the divining-rod of the investigating intellect that which can only be felt from within will perpetually discover only thoughts about emotion and not emotion itself. An eternally hostile chasm is entrenched between the feeling heart and the investigations of research, and the former is an independent, tightly sealed, divine entity, which cannot be unlocked and opened up by the reason. (p. 190)

In spite of this cleavage between feeling and "research," Berglinger somewhat inconsistently proceeds to discuss certain features of musical feeling. Each musical work and each melody, he maintains, has its own feeling, just as each painting does. Furthermore, these feelings cannot be described or explained in words. We cannot resolve a richer language into a poorer one. Have those who make such a demand never felt without words? he asks. "Have they filled up their hollow hearts merely with descriptions of feeling?" (p. 191). But music is more than a particular language of feeling: it is *the* language of feeling, and it has a unique pedagogical function in this regard. The human heart becomes acquainted with itself, Berglinger says, in the mirror of musical sounds; we learn to feel emotion through them; they enrich our souls with entirely new, bewitching essences of feeling. It is part of Berglinger's conception also that art "does not know the relationship of its emotions to the real world" (p. 192). Thus, music reveals feeling to us, yet what it reveals cannot be stated in words and is not related to the world of reality. There is an evident paradox in the Romantic conception, for if we learn to feel emotion through music and the feelings we learn are unrelated to the real world, then how do we learn about the feelings that arise in the real world, and what is the nature of these "real" feelings? The lesson that music teaches must therefore have a value that is either limited to propaedeutics or unrelated altogether to the feeling that is encountered elsewhere.

Berglinger does provide a curious resolution of this difficulty—a resolution that reappears in the course of nineteenth-century aesthetics. It is important in the writings of Wagner, for example. Despite the innocence of art, Berglinger says, "nevertheless, through the overwhelming magic of its sensual force, it arouses all the wonderful, teeming hosts of the fantasy, which populate the musical strains with magical images and transform the formless excitations into the distinct shapes of human emotions, which draw past our senses like elusive pictures in a magical deception" (p. 192). In music, then, instead of known emotions, we have essences and nuances of emotions, innocent of cause and effect. The musical realm of emotional experience is related to reality only in the conjuring up of images by the fantasy; real emotions are only fortuitous associations. A stronger contrast to eighteenth-century theories of the imitation of language and of the affections can hardly be imagined.

If the development of instrumental music prepared the way for the Romantic conception of musical feeling, this conception seems to have produced in return a new awareness of the value of instrumental music. Wackenroder cannot refrain from extolling "the latest, highest triumph of musical instruments: I mean those divine, magnificent symphonic pieces . . . in which not one individual emotion is portrayed, but an entire world, an entire drama of human emotions, is poured fourth" (p. 193).

This high regard for instrumental music was shared by Ludwig Tieck, an intimate friend of Wackenroder's, in the reflections on art that he added to Wackenroder's writings when he published them in 1799. In instrumental music, Tieck finds, art is independent and free, it prescribes its own laws, and it fantasizes playfully and without purpose—a description that was doubtless prompted by Kant's characterization of music in the *Critik der Urteilskraft* (1790). "These symphonies," Tieck writes, "can represent a colorful, manifold, intricate, and beautifully developed drama such as the poet can never give us; for they envelop the greatest enigma in enigmatic language, they depend on no laws of probability, they remain in their purely poetic world."[2]

Closely connected with the evaluation of instrumental music is the idea of music as a separate world of its own:

But what can be more astonishing than that through human art and effort, suddenly in the silence invisible spirits arise which storm our heart with rapture and bliss, and conquer it? That when we gladly close our eyes on the arid present, which often oppresses us and hems us in like the walls of a prison,—then a new land stretches out over our heads, a paradisaic region of flowers and glorious trees and golden fountains?[3]

This echoes Wackenroder: "O, then I close my eyes to all the strife of the world—and withdraw quietly into the land of music, as into the land of belief."[4]

A final characteristic of Romantic aesthetics is the absence of social considerations: the musical experience is that of an individual who is alone or withdrawn, related only to music and to the world it reveals, which is typically one of vast spaces, the cosmos, or infinity and often inhabited by supernatural beings. Very much as a devout monk might experience the religious world of revelation, the reverent listener is put in touch with the metaphysical world of music. The religious and metaphysical experiences are often literally combined, but a symphony in itself represents a kind of religious experience; art becomes a religion.

The poetic descriptions of music that are so characteristic of early German Romanticism constituted the inception of an important literary tradition that persisted into the twentieth century. Music became a modern literary topos, and during the course of the nineteenth century, the views of the 1780s and 1790s, which we considered in part in chapter 6, recur essentially unchanged, along with related ideas. This is especially evident in the first half of the century, in the writings of Hoffmann, Tieck, Ludwig Börne, Achim von Arnim, Kleist, Eichendorff, Theodor Körner, Schumann, and Wagner. There is a representative example of such literary continuity in Tieck's *Musikalische Leiden und Freuden* (1822), in the narrative of an old composer and violin teacher:

> A tone if it is correctly produced must rise up like the sun, clear, majestic, becoming brighter and brighter, the listener must feel in it the infinitude of music, yes, the singer must not give the impression that he cannot sustain the tone to the end. Music, correctly executed, moves gently like the sky and looks down upon us from the pure atmosphere and draws our heart heavenward. And what I want to hear purely and simply in a musical sound is the rapture. Flowing out of every musical tone is a tragic and divine enthusiasm which redeems every listener from the limitations of earthly existence.[5]

Herder's discussion of music in the *Kalligone* (1800) is conceived as a refutation of Kant's thesis in the *Critik der Urteilskraft* that music is a play of sensations. It is Herder's contention that music is an art of humanity. He does not deny the existence of tonal stimulus and response, but he understands these in an internal sense. The inside of the source affects the inside of the receiver, whether animate or inanimate. Sound makes known the interior of an object, in the internal forces of displacement and restoration that give rise to it, and it sets every similarly constituted object into an equivalent vibration. In sensitive beings "it brings about an analogous sensation." The response is one of the recipient as a whole; it is not just a matter of auditory sensations. The auditory organ of man "is hidden most deeply from the outside, reaches most deeply into the interior of his head . . . and spreads out in such a way that . . . we hear almost with our whole body":

> The voice of the species communicates itself sympathetically to the species, especially when it lives socially, in herds. . . . An utterance of one in anxiety summons all together, allows them, as long as it sounds, no peace; anxiously they commiserate and hurry to help. The tones of joy, of longing, summon the one they apply to just as powerfully. . . . The power of tone, the cry of the passions, belongs sympathetically to the whole species, to its bodily and mental constitution. It is the voice of nature, the energy of one deeply moved, announcing himself to the whole species for sympathy.[6]

Thus, Herder takes sympathetic vibration as a point of departure—that mysterious action at a distance that has been endlessly suggestive for musical thought—and treats man as an integral part of the universe.

If the whole bodily and mental constitution of man is involved in the production of tone and in the response to it, music is inevitably bound up with dance, gesture, and facial expression. All these are intimately connected through a bond of nature. There is accordingly a natural bond between tone, gesture, and word that all peoples have recognized or felt.[7] Music provokes dance; feelingful language demands tone and gesture. Thus, music for a long time clung to dance and song.

There are three realms in particular, Herder continues, in which word, tone, and gesture, inwardly bound to one another, act most strongly: the realms of reverence, love, and powerful action. After describing these he considers the nature of tones in their own right, separated from word and gesture. Tones may pursue and overtake themselves, he says, contradict and repeat one another; the flight and return of these magical spirits of the air is precisely the essence of the art that acts through buoyancy.[8] In addition, we can see in the powers of Pan, Apollo, and Orpheus what music can accomplish with instruments alone.

It was difficult, however, for music to separate itself from its sisters, word and gesture:

> What helped it upward, that trusting its own strength, it lifted itself aloft on its own wings? What was the something that severed it from everything foreign, from sight, dance, gestures, even from the accompanying

voice? Reverence. It is reverence that raises men and a gathering of men above words and gestures, for then nothing remains to their feelings but—tones. . . .

Reverence does not want to see who sings; the tones come to it from heaven; they sing in the heart; the heart itself sings and plays. Just as the tune, then, freed from the struck string or from its narrow pipe, resounds freely in the heavens, certain that it is affecting every sympathetic being, and re-echoing everywhere, is born anew in the contest of the echo, is imparted anew: so reverence, borne aloft by tones, hovers pure and free above the earth, enjoying as one the universe, in one tone harmoniously all tones. (pp. 185–87)

To the harmony of the spheres, Herder then adds the conception of music as a microcosm, only to describe it finally as spirit. As reverence "senses in the narrow compass of our few tonal successions and keys all the vibrations, motions, and accentuations of the universe, is there still a question whether music will surpass in inner effect every art that clings to the visible? It must surpass them, as spirit does the body; for it is spirit, related to great nature's innermost force—motion" (p. 187).

Herder concludes his discussion with a consideration of transience and its relation to inner experience:

Transient, therefore, is every moment of this art and must be so: for precisely the briefer and longer, stronger and weaker, higher and lower, more and less is its meaning, its impression. In arrival and flight, in becoming and having been, lies the conquering force of tone and of sensation. Just as the one and the other fuse with many, rise, sink, and are submerged, and on the taut line of harmony, in accordance with eternal, indissoluble laws, again rise up and act anew, so my heart, my courage, my love and hope. . . . On fleet tones come and fly away, you wandering spirits of the air; stir my heart and leave behind in me, through you, for you, an endless longing. (p. 187)

Turning to Kant's assertion that music does not endure repetition without creating boredom, Herder maintains that this is contrary to all experience:

Precisely music conveys and demands repetition most among all the arts; in none other is *ancora* so often heard. A mere decomposition of the tones, that is, harmony, tires and must tire, because it always says the same thing, and in addition a very well known one; true music, however, namely, melody, the buoyant line of the whole course of the tones, becomes precisely through its repetition more enjoyable; its effect can become intensified in this way up to the point of rapture. Passages that move us inwardly we cannot hear enough. (pp. 188–89)

Although Herder's aesthetic outlook is definitively formulated in his "Viertes Wäldchen" of 1769, which we examined in chapter 6, *Kalligone* expands his view beyond the focus on sound and tone to encompass the sister arts, the development of independent music, and the larger significance of music as an expression and response of man as a whole and as a social being. Herder's criticism of Kant, however, is so concerned with depicting Kant's view as antithetical to his own that it fails to come to grips with the true meaning and importance of Kant's musical ideas.

From Herder's poetic philosophy we turn to the poetic essays of E. T. A. Hoffmann, whose views on instrumental music, opera, and sacred music were a definitive formulation of Romantic ideas that exerted an influence continuing far into the future. Many of Hoffmann's views appeared in the Leipzig *Allgemeine Musikalische Zeitung*, to which he was a contributor from 1809 to 1819 and in which his ideas had been anticipated to a considerable extent by the writers on musical aesthetics in the very first years (from 1798 to 1801) of the periodical, notably Franz Horn and Friedrich Rochlitz, who was its editor for its first twenty years (1798–1818).[9] The contributions of these authors, and especially those of Hoffmann, constitute the major formulation of the aesthetics of Romantic opera, including the vital role of instrumental music.

Hoffmann's essay "Beethovens Instrumentalmusik" (1813), which is derived from two reviews published anonymously in the *Allgemeine Musikalische Zeitung* (1810 and 1813), opens with a synoptic statement of what had become by then the established doctrine of Romantic musical aesthetics:

When we speak of music as an independent art, should we not always restrict our meaning to instrumental music, which, scorning every aid, every admixture of another art (the art of poetry), gives pure expression to music's specific nature, recognizable in this form alone? It is the most romantic of all the arts—one might almost say, the only genuinely romantic one—for its sole object is the infinite. The lyre of Orpheus opened the portals of Orcus—music discloses to man an unknown realm, a world that has nothing in common with the external sensual world that surrounds him, a world in which he leaves behind him all definite feelings to surrender himself to an inexpressible longing.[10]

To seek to represent definite emotions or definite events, Hoffmann maintains, is to treat music as a plastic art, although it is diametrically opposed in its nature to the plastic arts. In the case of opera, where definite emotions are suggested by the poetry, these emotions are "clothed by music with the purple luster of romanticism," and we are thus guided by the experiences of life into "the realm of the infinite" (p. 776).

After expressing his scorn for instrumental tone painting and its "laughable aberrations," Hoffmann launches into a description of the instrumental music of Haydn, Mozart, and Beethoven that apparently contradicts what he has just said, for it makes conspicuous use of concrete visual images and definite emotions:

> Thus Beethoven's instrumental music opens up to us also the realm of the monstrous and the immeasurable. Burning flashes of light shoot through the deep night of this realm, and we become aware of giant shadows that surge back and forth, driving us into narrower and narrower confines until they destroy us—but not the pain of that endless longing in which each joy that has climbed aloft in jubilant song sinks back and is swallowed up, and it is only in this pain, which consumes love, hope, and happiness but does not destroy them, which seeks to burst our breast with a many-voiced consonance of all the passions, that we live on, enchanted beholders of the supernatural! . . .

> Beethoven's music sets in motion that lever of fear, of awe, of horror, of suffering, and wakens just that infinite longing which is the essence of romanticism. He is accordingly a completely romantic composer, and is not this perhaps the reason why he has less success with vocal music, which excludes the character of indefinite longing, merely representing emotions defined by words as emotions experienced in the realm of the infinite? (p. 777)

How are we to reconcile Hoffmann's scorn for tone painting with his consistent use of visual images and designated emotions? For one thing, the images are evoked by the music; they do not represent the composer's aim. In addition, they are always qualified by Romantic properties that are intrinsically connected with them or that arise out of them. Haydn's symphonies, for example,

> lead us into vast green woodlands, into a merry, gaily colored throng of happy mortals. Youths and maidens float past in a circling dance; laughing children, peering out from behind the trees, from behind the rose bushes, pelt one another playfully with flowers. A life of love, of bliss like that before the Fall, of eternal youth; no sorrow, no suffering, only a sweet melancholy yearning for the beloved object that floats along, far away, in the glow of the sunset and comes no nearer and does not disappear—nor does night fall while it is there, for it is itself the sunset in which hill and valley are aglow. (pp. 776–77)

211

Apparently the concrete pictures are not the essential matter in themselves. They do occur, however, in Romantic descriptions of music, notably in poetic criticism, and seem to constitute an alternative to technical description. They direct us to what was felt to be important about music. But they are not simply pedagogical in intent; they are evidently a mode of response to music that was spontaneous and irrepressible, almost as a way of grasping and containing somehow the strange intoxication of a suddenly expanding new art. They also undoubtedly constitute a genuine poetry of their own— the contagion of creation passed from a poetic composer to a poetic listener.

Technical considerations appear also; most important is the discussion by Hoffmann and others of the unity of the musical work, a characteristic that became central around 1800 both in instrumental music and in opera. The organic inspiration of this unity is evident in Hoffmann's passing reference to Shakespeare: "In Shakespeare, our knights of the aesthetic measuring-rod have often bewailed the utter lack of inner unity and inner continuity, although for those who look more deeply there springs forth, issuing from a single bud, a beautiful tree, with leaves, flowers, and fruit" (p. 778). In Beethoven's Fifth Symphony, "The internal structure of the movements, their execution, their instrumentation, the way in which they follow one another—everything contributes to a single end; above all, it is the intimate interrelationship among the themes that engenders that unity which alone has the power to hold the listener firmly in a single mood" (p. 778). The unity of the musical work, however, is that of a cosmos as well as that of an organism; it is the unity of a "spirit realm," of a "magic world."

Finally, Hoffmann rejects harmony and mathematics in themselves. They are acceptable only as instruments of emotional and magical power: "That composer alone has truly mastered the secrets of harmony who knows how, by their means, to work upon the human soul; for him, numerical proportions, which to the dull grammarian are no more than cold, lifeless problems in arithmetic, become magical compounds from which to conjure up a magic world" (p. 779).

Hoffmann's dialogue on opera "Der Dichter und der Komponist" (1813) is concerned chiefly with the subject matter most appropriate for opera and with the nature of the poetry that is suitable. Considering the nature of artistic creation, the composer, Ludwig, maintains that music and poetry are fundamentally akin, "for the secret of word and tone is one and the same" (p. 787). Accordingly, the music of a true opera will arise directly from the poem as its inevitable offspring. But instrumental music is a "mysterious language of a faraway spirit world"; it cannot deal with the commonplace. The poet must therefore prepare himself for "a bold flight into the faraway land of romance." The romantic opera is the only genuine one, "for only in the land of romance is music at home." And only a gifted and inspired poet

> can bring to life the wondrous phenomena of the spirit world; on his wings we are lifted over the chasm which otherwise divides us from it, and, grown accustomed to the strange country, we believe in the marvels which, as inevitable effects of the action of higher natures on our being, take place visibly and bring about all the strong, powerfully affecting situations which fill us, now with awe and horror, now with the highest bliss. It is, in a word, the magic force of poetic truth which the poet representing the marvelous must have at his command, for only this can transport us. . . . So, my friend, in an opera the action of higher natures on our being must take place visibly, thus opening up before our eyes a romantic existence in which language, too, is raised to a higher power, or rather, is borrowed from that faraway country— from music, that is, from song—where action and situation themselves, vibrating in powerful harmonies, take hold of us and transport us the more forcefully. (pp. 788–89)

Ludwig finds a place for tragic opera and opera buffa also, if they are properly conceived. In the older, tragic operas, the true heroic element in the action, the inner strength of the characters and situations, takes powerful hold of the viewer: "The mysterious and somber force that governs gods and men stalks visibly before his eyes, and he hears revealed in strange, foreboding tones the eternal, unalterable decisions of fate which even rule the gods" (p. 790). A higher means of expression was needed than ordinary speech; this was true also of the tragedies of antiquity, which were declaimed musically.

Returning for a moment to the kinship of composer and poet, Ludwig maintains that the librettist must set everything to music inwardly, just as the musician does: "Only the clear consciousness of particular melodies, even of particular sounds of the instruments taking part, in a word, the ready control over the inner realm of sound, distinguishes the one from the other" (p. 791). He then turns to opera buffa, pointing to the features of the fantastic, of the reckless abandon of characters, of the bizarre play of chance: "Precisely in this intrusion of the adventurous into everyday life, and in the contradictions arising from it, lies in my opinion the nature of the true opera buffa" (p. 792).

It is obviously of the greatest importance, in Hoffmann's view, that the action of an opera display the conflict of two realms of being or the intrusion of one on the other. In Romantic opera the spirits stalk into human life, while in opera buffa the adventurous and the fantastic take over the role of the supernatural. There is a manifestation of this characteristic in musical tragedies also, for they "have inspired gifted composers to a sublime, shall I say, sacred style, and it is as though man were drifting, in a miraculous ecstasy, on sounds from the golden harps of cherubim and seraphim, into the realm of light, where is revealed to him the mystery of his own being" (pp. 791–92). It is clear, however, that Hoffmann's preference goes to Romantic opera. In addition to its intrinsic suitability to music, it also possesses a kind of universality: "Only in the genuinely romantic do the comic and tragic combine so naturally that they blend as one in the total effect, laying hold of the feelings of the audience in a wonderful way of their own" (p. 789).

As far as the requirements of operatic poetry are concerned, the poet, Ferdinand, complains about the "incredible brevity" that is demanded. Every situation or passion must be dispatched in a couple of lines, and these must permit "turning and twisting" in accordance with the composer's pleasure. Like the scene painter, Ludwig elucidates, the poet "must cover his whole canvas, after designing it properly, in bold, powerful strokes" (p. 794). It is the music that will place the whole in a correct light and in the proper perspective so that everything stands out as though alive and individual. The librettist must make a special effort

> to arrange the scenes in such a way that the story unfolds clearly and plainly before the beholder's eyes. Almost without understanding a word, the beholder must be in a position to form an idea of the plot from what he sees happening. No dramatic poem needs this to such an extreme degree as does the opera, for, aside from the fact that, even when the words are sung most clearly, one still understands them less than when they are spoken, the music too entices the audience all too easily into other regions, and it is only by constant firing at the point in which the dramatic effect is to concentrate that one succeeds in hitting it. (p. 794)

Ferdinand then asks a question that leads to a closer view of the interrelation of words and music:

> Are we then, not only to avoid poetic elegance, but to be barred also from every detailed delineation of interesting situations? For example, the young hero goes off to war and takes leave of his stricken father, the old king, whose kingdom a conquering tyrant is shaking at its foundations; or a cruel fate separates an adoring youth from his beloved; are then the two to say nothing but "farewell?" (p. 794)

Ludwig answers:

> Though the former may speak briefly of his courage, of his confidence in his just cause, though the latter may say to his beloved that life without her is but slow death, the composer, who is inspired, not by words, but by action and situation, will be satisfied if the inner state of the young hero's or parting lover's soul is depicted in bold strokes. To keep to your example, in what accents, penetrating deep into one's innermost self, have the Italians, countless times already, sung the little word "Addio"! Of what thousands and thousands of nuances musical expression is capable! Is not this precisely the secret of music's miraculous power, that, just where plain speech runs dry, it opens up an inexhaustible spring of means of expression? (p. 795)

He points out again that composers are stimulated by situation and subject matter, adding that, as a consequence, they "have often set poetry that is even downright bad quite magnificently to music. But in this case it was the genuinely operatic, romantic subject matter that inspired them" (pp. 795–96). The detailed emotional course of operatic song is thus shown to be the specific graduation of the feelings peculiar to music.

Hoffmann's view of opera is clearly the product of his view of instrumental music, for it is in the light of the Romantic conception of music, realized primarily by music in its highest form, that he understands the nature of operatic song and operatic dramaturgy. Much the same thing can be said about his aesthetics of church music, which can be found in a historical essay of 1814 entitled "Alte und neue Kirchenmusik." "Now we may speak of music," he says, "in the deepest meaning of its specific nature, namely, when it enters life as religious cult. . . . The intimation of the Highest and Most Holy . . . expresses itself audibly in tone":

> In its inner, true nature, therefore, music is—as has just been said—religious cult, is to be sought and to be found uniquely and alone in religion, in the church. Entering life increasingly rich and powerful, it poured its inexhaustible treasures out over mankind, and even the profane was then able to shine, as though with childlike joy, in the glow with which it now streamed through life itself in all its small and petty earthly connections; but even the profane appeared in this finery as though longing for the higher, divine kingdom and striving to enter into its manifestations.[11]

Because of its particular nature, Hoffmann continues, music in the proper sense could not exist in antiquity, where everything was manifested in corporeality, but had to unfold in the modern world. Here we have, then, the fundamental antithesis of ancient and modern—sculpture and music—that runs through the entire nineteenth century and into the twentieth. Needless to say, the basic determinant of the modern world is Christianity.

Even the rough beginnings of music in antiquity served religious cult, Hoffmann asserts, which is really what ancient drama was. In the course of history, the "wondrous sounds of the spirit world were awakened," and after a mistaken concern with harmonic artificialities had turned music into a speculative science for a time, Palestrina revealed "the holy wonder of music in its truest nature" (p. 121):

> Love, the accord of everything spiritual in nature, as it was promised to the Christian, expressed itself in the chord, which thus also awakened to life only in Christianity; and thus the chord, harmony, became the image and expression of the community of spirits, of union with the eternal, with the ideal, which reigns over us and yet encloses us. That music must therefore be the purest, holiest, and most churchly that rises from the soul only as an expression of that love, scorning and not heeding everything secular. (p. 122)

The growth of instrumental music also represents a kind of religious aspiration, a wondrous striving to perceive the animating spirit of nature. Our home in this spirit "was intimated by the foreboding tones of music, which spoke more and more abundantly and perfectly of the wonders of the distant realm" (p. 129). But as instrumental music developed, song was neglected, and there is still a question to what extent the new instrumental riches can be brought into the church without profane ostentation. Nor is it possible now to return to Palestrina's simplicity and greatness.

How, then, is the young composer to compose true church music? The spirit of truth and piety must drive him to praise God and to speak "of the wonders of the celestial realm in the wondrous tones of music." Indeed, his composing will be "only the writing down of the holy songs" that pour from his heart in "reverent ecstasy": "Only in the truly pious heart, ignited by religion, do holy songs reside that will kindle reverence in the congregation with irresistible power" (p. 130). But as we have seen in Wackenroder and Herder, it is reverence that the listener must bring to music of all types, for music is a celestial art. Hoffmann concludes with a wish for the future: "May the time of the fulfillment of our hopes be no longer distant, may a pious life in peace and joyfulness begin and music freely and powerfully stir its seraph wings to begin anew its flight to the Beyond, which is its home and from which consolation and salvation shine down into the restless breast of man!" (p. 134).

A conception of opera somewhat different from Hoffmann's, but one quite compatible with it, can be found in Carl Maria von Weber's review "Über die Oper *Undine*." Weber is concerned, not with the subject matter of Hoffmann's opera or with Fouqué's poetry, but with the unified nature of the work. It is clear that this has become a well-known criterion of value: "By opera I understand, of course, the opera which the German desires—an art work complete in itself, in which the partial contributions of the related and collaborating arts blend together, disappear, and, in disappearing, somehow form a new world." [12] This is not easily accomplished, however, for opera is a whole composed of wholes: "As a result of the form which is its right, each musical composition gives the impression of an independent, organic, self-contained unit. Yet, as a part of the whole, it must disappear when the whole is beheld" (p. 803).

The individual piece contains a similar problem, for it should be multiform as well as unified. These considerations lead Weber to a few observations on the nature of music and of musical emotion:

> In this lies the great, mysterious secret of music, a secret to be felt but not to be expressed; here are united the fluctuating and resisting natures of anger and of love, of ecstatic suffering; here sylph and salamander intermingle, embracing one another. In a word, what love is to man, music is to the arts and to mankind, for it is actually love itself, the purest, most ethereal language of the emotions, containing all their changing colors in every variety of shading and in thousands of aspects. (p. 804)

Love is not too different from endless longing, and it also contains all the more particular emotions. Endless longing, however, as Hoffmann describes it, is universal not in including all the other emotions as such but in somehow absorbing and superceding them. At the same time, Weber attributes to music, very much the way Wackenroder had, the power to contain, and thus to present, a unique and otherwise unknown world of emotional gradation and differentiation.

These theoretical considerations are really a preface to Weber's review of *Undine*. They are taken from an unfinished novel and introduced, as he says, in order to clarify his point of view. He then proceeds to discuss *Undine* itself, which, in spite of certain blemishes, corresponds closely to his general principles. The following comment, distinctly reminiscent of Lacépède, will provide an example:

> With unusual self-denial, the greatness of which can be fully appreciated only by him who knows what it means to sacrifice the glory of

momentary applause, Herr Hoffmann has disdained to enrich single numbers at the expense of the whole, so easy to do if one calls attention to them by broadening and enlarging their execution beyond that proper to them as members of the artistic body. He proceeds relentlessly, obviously led on by a desire to be always true and to intensify the life of the drama instead of retarding or arresting it in its rapid progress. Varied and strikingly portrayed as the many-sided characters of the persons of the action seem to be, they are all encircled by— or better, creatures of—that ghostly, fabulous world whose awesome stimulations are the peculiar property of the fairylike. (p. 805)

Here the wholeness becomes the result of a unifying atmosphere. But this is exactly the property that was so impressive in Gluck's operas, now achieved with Romantic subject matter rather than heroic. The unifying atmosphere and the wholeness are continuing ideals.

Philosophical Aesthetics

The philosophical aesthetics that developed in Germany during the first few decades of the nineteenth century seems to provide a metaphysical account of the imaginative and poetic descriptions of music found in German literature and criticism during the same period. What is felt, intimated, and intuited in the latter is elaborated and deepened by speculative thought in the former, which retains the poetic quality of literary aesthetics but subordinates it to explicitly philosophic purposes. Both types of aesthetics have their origins in the eighteenth century: literary aesthetics is fully in evidence in the novels of Jean Paul Richter in the 1790s and even foreshadowed in the writings of Karl Philipp Moritz in the 1770s and 1780s, while philosophical aesthetics has a remote ancestry in Baumgarten (1747, 1750) and its foundation in Kant (1790). In addition to these origins, the views of Schiller around the turn of the century, which were shared by Goethe, constitute an aesthetics of Classicism that synthesized or brought into balance the two major ideals and traditions of thought of the eighteenth century: reason and feeling. The synthesis was found in the realm of beauty, and it took the form of a harmonious unity of the faculties, much as it had in Kant with respect to cognition and volition. But this made aesthetics the culmination of philosophy. Furthermore, art accomplished what philosophy reasoned about: matter became informed with spirit as it did in the universe, and the work of art was an organic unity just as the universe was a unified organism.

Schelling's "Philosophie der Kunst" was presented as a course of lectures in 1802–3 in Jena and again in 1804–5 in Würzburg, but it was published, as a composite of the two presentations, only after his death, in 1859. It is clear in the lectures that what we have called "philosophical aesthetics" is more philosophy—that is, philosophy of art—than it is aesthetics. For aesthetics as traditionally defined is a philosophy of art in an empirical sense; it considers art as it is revealed in perception and in practice. But the philosophy of art, as Schelling understands it, is concerned with "art in itself," or the essential nature of art. He maintains in his *System der transzendentalen Idealismus* (1800) that philosophy, "which concerns itself solely with ideas, has to exhibit, with respect to the empirical in art, only the general laws of appearance and even these only in the form of *ideas*; for the forms of art are the forms of things in themselves and as they are in the archetypes."[13] Similarly, Schelling writes to August Wilhelm Schlegel (in a letter of 3 September 1803) that, "just as there are intellectual things, things in themselves, there is also an art in itself, of which the empirical is only the appearance, and it is this through which there is a bearing of philosophy on art."[14]

Fundamental to his methodology are "intellectual intuition" (*intellektuale Anschauung*) and "construction" (*Konstruktion*). Intellectual intuition, as conceived in his *System der transzendentalen Idealismus*, is a kind of mystical insight into one's self-consciousness that provides an immediate lived experience of productive nature (*natura naturans*) so that the external world can be produced from the ego. Similarly, things-in-themselves will be known only if they are intrinsically related to the forms of knowledge, only if the intuited objectivities are identical with the organ of intuition. Thus, the mind must produce what it intuits, and being is identical with knowledge, or essences with concepts.

Schelling also defines intellectual intuition, somewhat differently, as the capacity to see the general, or the infinite, united in a living unity with the particular, or the finite. He considers it otherwise, again, as the capacity to produce a mental action unconsciously and at the same time to contemplate it consciously. But in a single instant to be conscious of oneself as unconsciously productive is impossible, he continues; only for this reason does the self-produced world appear to be objectively given.

Construction is closely related to intellectual intuition. It depends on it and elaborates it. As conceived in the "Philosophie der Kunst," it demands a constant inner activity of producing the original actions of the Absolute and also a constant reflection on this producing that is really aesthetic. Thus, philosophy, like art, depends on creative power, special endowment, and genius, while the philosophy of art will be the true instrument of philosophy in general. Just as production in art is directed outward in order to reflect the unconscious in products, so philosophical production is directed inward in order to reflect the unconscious in intellectual intuition. Schelling's aesthetics in particular will be an aesthetics from inside, an aesthetics of artistic creation, as opposed to an aesthetics from outside, which is one of contemplation.

The principle of construction Schelling compares to the physical principle that nature abhors a vacuum: wherever there is an empty place in the universe, nature fills it in; no possibility is unfulfilled; everything possible is also actual. Only those objects are amendable to construction, then, that are capable of taking up the Absolute into themselves and representing it in their fashion, for such objects actualize the possible. To construct music, for example, is first to presuppose that it is capable of taking up the Absolute into itself and then to determine its place in the universe. This provides the only true explanation there is for the object. Subsequently, what has been constructed, or deduced with apodictic certainty, can never be contradicted by experience but will always be confirmed.

In the first half of his "Philosophy of Art," Schelling seeks to solve "the greatest mystery of the universe," the problem of individuation, as it is found in art: the concretion of absolute art in particular art, of the infinite in the finite. For the Absolute can be beautiful only when it is seen in the limited. But the Absolute can be brought together with the limited only through the Ideas, each of which possesses two unities, "one through which it is in itself and absolute, and through which the Absolute in its Particular is therefore constituted, and one through which it as Particular is taken up into the Absolute as its center." [15] This double unity of each Idea is the mystery through which we can apprehend the Particular in the Absolute and the Particular as such. The whole universe is in the Absolute as plant, as animal, as man: not as a particular unity, but as an absolute unity, as an Idea. Only in appearance, where it ceases to be the whole, does each thing become the particular and definite unity. For artistic representation in particular, Schelling demands that complete "indifference" hold true: that the general wholly be—not simply mean—the particular and the particular at the same time wholly be the general. The creative capacity, the imagination, or the "informing" power of genius is the power of individuation, through which an ideal is simultaneously also a real, the soul also a body. The work of art contains an "unconscious infinity." Clearly, form as such will have no value, nor will sensuous effect or the representation or expressions of real feelings.

In the second half of the "Philosophy of Art," in the construction of the forms of art, Schelling starts from the two unities according to which the Absolute can be considered and to some extent made susceptible of distinction and knowledge: reality and ideality. This universal law of the Absolute implies that everything included in the universe can be conceived only in the form of the general opposition of the real and the ideal. In the Absolute these unities or external ideas are absolute and therefore indistinguishable and not distinguished; the absolute real and the absolute ideal are identical. They can become truly objective only if they become symbols, or forms, through which appears the absolute unity, the idea in and for itself. The world of art, then, will take both unities as form and be either formative art or linguistic art. Within each of these groups, both unities will then be taken up again and expressed through the particular forms of art, but this time not with the alternative of the complete exclusion of the real or the ideal: instead there will be a predominance of one over the other so that formative art can be designated as a relatively real symbolization of the Absolute and linguistic art as a relatively ideal one. But besides these forms representing the real and ideal unities there will now be a third form, which is a symbol of the identity of the absolute real and the absolute ideal: a real-ideal form, which represents the unity of the real and the ideal fused in indifference. Thus, music and painting find their indifference in sculpture, while lyric and epic poetry find their indifference in drama.

The determinations thus applied to the Absolute to make diversity possible and comprehensible are called "powers" (*Potenzen*), and in each of the successive differentiations the new unities developed from each earlier unity are called the particularity or symbol of the earlier one. On the basis of this scheme of powers, Schelling brings the most heterogeneous realms of being and culture into relation, setting up parallels between things simply because in his system they stand in the same power. Thus, the form of music as the form of a first power of the real series of arts is connected not only with lyric poetry, the corresponding step of the ideal series, but also with the inorganic, the first dimension, the quantitative, the straight line, the celestial bodies, cohesion, magnetism, self-consciousness, and reflection (optics). These comparisons are even used in the construction of music. Furthermore, the same wealth of mutual relations is also set up between the various forms of art at each step of the scheme. Although the profusion of analogies both between the various arts and throughout the universe can only be called fantastic, each of the comparisons adds an appreciable degree of definiteness and clarity to Schelling's abstract discussion.

The first unity in the Absolute is the essence of material; all art that takes this as form is formative art. As the first, or "real," unity in formative art, music is a particularity or symbol of formative art as such, and it takes the implantation of multiplicity in unity as its form. Since it is the first unity of its power, Schelling is also able to assert that it has only one dimension (the first) and that its necessary form is succession:

For time is the general form of the informing of the finite by the infinite, insofar as it is regarded as form, abstracted from the real. The principle of time in the subject is consciousness of self, which is precisely the informing of multiplicity by the unity of consciousness in the ideal. From this we comprehend the close relation of the sense of hearing in general and of music and speech in particular with consciousness of self.—We can comprehend from this also . . . the arithmetic side of music. Music is a factual counting to itself of the soul. (p. 491)

Like formative art as a whole, music itself is differentiated into three unities, of which the first is rhythm. Rhythm is "nothing other than a periodic division of the similar, by which the uniform of the similar is connected with diversity, and therefore unity with multiplicity" (p. 492). Schelling proposes as the most elementary instance the equality of time intervals in succession, as found, for example, in the beat of a drum or in the repetition of a tone of a given duration. Rhythm, like music, is the informing of multiplicity by unity. But it is included within music, and is therefore "the music in music," and thus the ruling principle in it. The second unity in music is "modulation," which refers, in a general way, to differences in pitch; it is "the art of sustaining amid a *qualitative* difference the identity of that tone that is dominant in the whole musical work, just as the same identity is observed amid *quantitative* difference by rhythm" (p. 495).

"The third unity, in which the first two are equally posited, is melody." Schelling goes on to assert that rhythm is the first dimension, modulation the second, and melody the third: "By the first, music is defined for reflection and self-awareness, by the second for sensation and judgment, by the third for intuition and imagination. We can also foresee in advance that, if the three basic forms or categories of art are music, painting, and sculpture, then rhythm is the musical in music, modulation the painterly . . . and melody the sculpturesque" (p. 496).

When music is subordinated to rhythm, it becomes melody, as it was in ancient Greece, where the realistic, plastic heroic principle was the ruling one in general. When it is subordinated to modulation, it becomes harmony, which is the antithesis of melody. Melody elevates the identity in rhythm into difference. Harmony gives this identity breadth, extending it into the second dimension. It unites several melodies into a euphonious whole or unifies many tones into a single sonority: "In the one case we obviously have unity in multiplicity, in the other multiplicity in unity, in the one succession, in the other coexistence" (p. 498). Melody is related to harmony as ancient art is to modern. With respect to form, ancient art, like melody, represents only the factual, the essential, the necessary; modern art, like harmony, represents also the ideal, the unessential, the contingent, in their identity with the essential and necessary:

> Ancient art remains truer, as it were, to the natural determination of music, which is to be an art of succession; it is therefore realistic. Modern art would like to anticipate in the lower realm the higher ideal unity, to supercede succession ideally, as it were, and to represent multiplicity in the momentary as unity. Rhythmic music [i.e., melody], which represents the infinite in the finite, will be more the expression of satisfaction and of active emotion, harmonic music more that of striving and longing. (pp. 499–500)

Thus, the Greek state, Schelling maintains, where a purely general entity, the species, had molded itself completely into the particular, had to be rhythmic in art, while in the church, where the fundamental outlook rests on longing and the striving of difference to return to oneness, the common striving of each subject to look on himself as one with all in the Absolute had to express itself in harmonic music devoid of rhythm.

The final theorem of Schelling's discussion of music is that "the forms of music are the forms of eternal things in so far as they are considered in their real aspect": "Furthermore, then, insofar as the eternal things or the ideas in their real aspect are apparent in the heavenly bodies, the forms of music as forms of ideas considered materially are also the forms of the existence and life of the heavenly bodies as such and thus music nothing other than the perceived rhythm and harmony of the visible universe itself" (p. 501). Philosophy and art are not concerned with things, Schelling remarks, only with their forms or eternal essences. Plastic art does not strive to compete with products of nature, which deal with factual solidity. It seeks only the form, the ideal. And rhythm and harmony make manifest only the form of the motion of the heavenly bodies, "the pure form freed from the object or matter. Music is that art that most casts off the corporeal insofar as it presents pure motion itself as such, abstracted from the object, and it is borne by invisible, almost spiritual wings" (p. 502). We are reminded of the language of literary aesthetics and of the poetic conception that assimilates the physical transmission of music to the vision of a supernatural world. After a discussion of Pythagoras, Schelling again fuses his musical philosophy with literary poetry:

> We can now finally establish the deepest meaning of rhythm, harmony, and melody. They are the first and purest forms of motion in the universe and, factually considered, the way in which material things resemble the ideas. On the wings of harmony and rhythm the heavenly bodies

hover; what we have called centripetal and centrifugal force is nothing other than—the latter, rhythm, the former, harmony. Borne by the
same wings, music hovers in space, to weave an audible universe from
the transparent body of sound and tone. (p. 503)

Music expresses only the pure form of the general motion of the heavenly
bodies, severed from the corporeal; it takes up the character of reason lying
in these motions only as rhythm, harmony, and melody.

Some of the difficulty of Schelling's discussion of music is lessened by a
knowledge of the broader context of his thought, which we have considered
above. Particularly helpful, of course, are the preceding sections of his philosophy of art. Propositions 8 and 18 of the "General Part of the Philosophy
of Art" provide a fundamental orientation: "The infinite affirmation of God
in the universe, or the informing of reality by his infinite ideality as such,
is eternal nature" (p. 377); "the organic work of nature represents the same
identity [of ideal and real] still undivided that the work of art represents
after the division, but again as identity" (p. 384).

Schelling opens his discussion of music, by way of preface, with a consideration of sound as such, the material of music. Even here, in the realm of
natural processes rather than art, the same principles prevail: "In the informing of the finite by the infinite, identity [indifference] as such can manifest
itself only as tone" (p. 76). It could be expressed in matter, Schelling argues,
only as otherness, as difference, not as form in its own right, as absolute
form. Purely as such, as form, the indifference in the informing can be expressed only as tone, for tone is merely a dimension in time, not a dimension
in space. It is in fact a living unity of a multiplicity since what we hear in
tone is a whole group of tones as though veiled in one or borne by it. Tone is
the intuition of the very soul of the material object. But Schelling also anticipates Hegel in deriving tone as the indifference in the object at rest (identity)
and the object displaced from rest (difference); the indifference need only be
restated as a synthesis.

Karl Wilhelm Ferdinand Solger, a philosopher who received very little
public recognition in his time, published his major work in aesthetics—
Erwin: Vier Gespräche über das Schöne und die Kunst (1815)—in dialogue
form, with the specific intention of combining art and philosophy, for the
conception of the kinship of the two was fundamental to his philosophical outlook. The philosophical tendency of Romantic literature and poetry
accordingly found a counterpart in a poetic philosophy. Solger's aesthetic
ideas were strongly influenced by Schelling and were in their turn, along
with those of Schelling, an important influence on the aesthetics of Hegel.
Central to Solger's philosophy is the belief that art is a sensuous manifes-

tation of the Idea and thus accomplishes concretely what philosophy seeks to grasp by abstract thought. In philosophy itself, aesthetics was a culmination, an idea that extended the role given to it by Kant as a mediation between nature and mind. Indeed, the concern with system, in aesthetics as well as in philosophy as a whole, is another distinguishing feature of Solger's thought. His aesthetics doubtless integrates the arts for the first time in a comprehensive and systematic way.

The discussion of music in *Erwin* is preceded by a discussion of architecture.[16] The two arts are often connected in the nineteenth century, and Solger elaborates the relation in a systematic way that has no precedent. Included are the relation of architecture to the other spatial arts, the relation of music to the other temporal arts, and the foundation of architecture and music in the nature of space and time, respectively.

Toward the end of the third conversation, the participants become involved in the question of the relation between matter and knowledge, between the corporeal object and that which takes up the object. Matter or mass, it is maintained, can also become the existence of essence and Idea if it is known according to a general law that succeeds to actuality in it. The body would then become a complete expression of this knowledge and become one with it. There must therefore be something between the body and the general law that is also in both and filled with both, but in the one as appearance and the other as knowledge. That something is space. Space is the form subject to which matter is seen. In space, accordingly,

> there are present at the same time the whole matter in so far as it is perceived and also the knowledge in so far as it perceives, for it can perceive no matter outside of space. But space carries in itself as knowledge certain general laws, which in relationship to the particular in space are called measure and are the basis of the art of measurement. Matter must therefore be known according to these laws, if in it, as art demands, the appearance is to become one with the Idea. (p. 269)

Music, in contrast, is grounded in time. But time, like space, is also something in which the general in knowledge is fused with the individual and the particular. It is a form through which the particular is taken up into knowledge. What is taken up, however, is not the same external things that are found in space but the series of ideas of these things that continue our consciousness itself and repeat, as it were. This kind of material must itself be a knowledge that reveals itself simply as particular and temporal without any general concept. The soul also manifests itself in this way through sound as self-activating and yet perceptible.

Music is similar to architecture, for in both the material externally mani-

fested is a manifold existence stripped of all singleness and organic perfection—a material that also, precisely because it is completely in keeping with
and comprehended by the general law of knowledge, brings the unity of
the general and the particular, or the Idea, to the actual immediacy of life.
Architecture, however, is attached to the corporeal, or plastic, arts because
its particular is corporeal material, which is revealed to perception, while
music is attached to the spiritual, or poetic, arts because its particular, sound,
comes from inwardness and is the self-revelation of this inwardness, through
which alone it becomes perceptible. For sound must not be regarded as a
means of communication with others. From this slanted viewpoint there
often arises a misunderstanding of music, and much that as the utterance and
manifestation of the heart itself has the most glorious effect is distorted and
unintelligible when we try to grasp it from the standpoint of purpose. Even
in dramatic music, where several persons express themselves to one another,
the mutual communication still remains subordinated always to the sense
of the work of art as a whole, to the self-revelation of a context of ideas.
When the listener is drawn into the work of art with his whole soul, he can
no longer see himself in an external relation of comprehension to it, so the
purpose of communication disappears.

At this point, Adelbert, who has the role throughout the discussions of
guiding and directing as well as participating, undertakes a summary statement:

Through sound, we said, the soul itself comes to sensuous appearance
as an active life. Sound is its most external manifestation in manifold,
changing particularity. Thus it expresses first of all the momentary state
of the soul in its contact with the outer world, which we call feeling. But
a soul dwells not only in living being, but also in lifeless being. This is
the general soul of nature, which equally expresses itself in sound when
bodies are struck—sound that contains a dark allegorical relationship
to the meaning of the human voice. Now it is this meaning of sound that
produces the widely diffused delusion that music is destined only for the
arousal of feelings and passions, by which it is wholly degraded to sensual pleasure, since it much more should elevate the external existence
of the soul in feelings to lawfulness and order.

Just as architecture is connected with need without being derived
from it, so music is connected with the change of pleasure and displeasure, which have been completely transformed and conciliated, however, in the pure and general unity of knowledge, which subordinates
all particularity to the same perfect measure. But the means of connection between measure and the measured is time, which in general

makes possible the relationship of the concept to the purely particular and constantly changing multiple. In time, there comes into sound itself a regular graduation through which it becomes tone and also the law by which the changing tones are taken up into a completed whole. But when the highest law of unity is completely one with manifold existence, there divinity is, as we have always found. Thus this art dissolves our own existence, as a temporal and feeling creature, into divine being. (pp. 275–76)

The fourth conversation turns from the examination of the arts individually to their combination. This is a logical sequence of topics, for since every art is in some way the manifestation in external or tangible form of inner experience, which ultimately is the divine Idea, art must possess an essential unity in spite of the multiplicity of its forms of appearance. Indeed, it seems to strive in actuality for a unification of its various forms. In this unification music is of unique importance, and Solger takes considerable pains to deduce its efficacy from its very nature, as this has been revealed in the preceding conversation.

Ancient art found its unification in the drama, Adelbert says, which not only was the center of ancient poetic art but which also interpenetrated with music and gathered about it the corporeal arts. In modern drama, this is no longer the case: "Music is precisely the art which is most suited to tie the arts together for a common effect and to dissolve them in a common element" (p. 286).

Anselm offers confirmation. In beautiful churches the relations of the building and even the actions represented in the sacred paintings seem to come alive only through music, without which they seem to be only preparations for an actual religious service. Erwin agrees: "When we stroll through the pointed vaults and slender, bundled pillars of a beautiful church and contemplate the altar paintings, which are really true works of art, the prevailing mood we feel, no doubt, is usually one of a reflective longing" (pp. 286–87). It is not only that sometimes we wish the times would return when such beautiful works were created but mostly that we feel the need of music, which alone would make all these objects a possession of our soul: "For through none of the other arts is the world of outer perception so completely bound up with our most inward being" (p. 287).

Adelbert provides the explanation. Is this different from what time always does in binding the generality of the concept to the particular perception? The concept in its unity runs through all time, remaining totally unchanged and one and the same, while the changes of things in their particularity fall completely into the same time in which the concept persists unchanged. Now if there is a medium that represents time so that time in general, which is simple and contains the concept, and the momentary present time, in which a definite change of the particular takes place, are seen to be completely one, then this medium will bring about the unification of the general and the particular that the understanding can only try to account for. There can be no doubt that this is exactly the case in music, the effect of which is precisely that in the feeling of each present moment a whole eternity becomes evident to our heart. "Then music actually achieves," Erwin adds, "what to the usual activity of the understanding is unachievable."

"But now consider," Adelbert says, "how music attaches itself to poetry and the other arts, in which actual objects are already present. Must it not therein be the best bond between the general in knowledge and the particular external object? Therefore it seems to us often precisely in works of the corporeal arts that music must first generally dispose our inner being, open or soften it, so that these can press into it unhindered" (p. 288). Modern drama does not need music because it expresses the inner experience that is connected with the outer action in words. But musical drama connects the outer circumstance with the most inner "without diversion and directly." Thus, opera places everything it can in the external action, and it should also make full use of fantasy.

The true modern counterpart of ancient drama, however, is found not in art but in religion. Where is there any institution of the modern world, Adelbert says, that has such power to unite the arts into a magic

> as the complete musical divine service in the song of sacred hymns before the paintings of divine actions and surrounded by the bold structure, which uplifts the soul to the highest, of the house of God? Here indeed the soul draws all these various elements into the depth of its inner being and raises itself, as the expression rightly goes, through art into a dwelling of the presence of the Divinity. Thus if the most perfect connection of the arts in Antiquity was the greatest actuality of them, the drama, in the modern world, as we see clearly, it is in the purest inner being of the Idea, the divine service. (pp. 292–93)

Anselm finds this confirmed by the fact that ancient drama was itself an outgrowth of religious rite.

Thus, art and religion are closely connected in Solger's thought, as they are in Romantic literature and philosophy in general. He undertakes to solve the problem of their relation, which he regards as a central philosophical problem of his time. His aesthetics is systematic in its inclusion of this general philosophical problem but also in the deduction of the entire subject from general principles and—largely as a consequence—in the comprehensive relation it establishes between the various individual arts. Finally, aesthetics is shown to encompass the major problems of philosophy as a whole, for this is what is called for if the work of art is to be fully understood.

In Arthur Schopenhauer's *Die Welt als Wille und Vorstellung*, which was published in its initial form in 1819, music is identified again, as it was by Schelling, with the very being of the world. It is now not the Absolute that is fundamental, however, with its Ideas of the infinite and the finite, for Schopenhauer identifies the being of the world with the Will, and it is this that music copies. The other arts, like the world itself, are copies of the Ideas by way of the principle of individuation, but since the Ideas themselves are copies or objectifications of the Will, the other arts are only copies of copies. These arts, Schopenhauer says, "speak only of the shadow, but music of the essence." [17] Thus, music is removed entirely from the system of the arts and given a unique position in which it is equivalent to the Ideas rather than to their phenomena.

On this foundation Schopenhauer erects a metaphysics of music that does remarkable justice to the facts of musical experience as these were known to him. For one thing, the effect of music is understandably more powerful and penetrating than that of the other arts, for it addresses the Will itself, as the inner nature of the self. Also, it is completely understood as a universal language, the distinctness of which surpasses even that of external perception itself. With this observation, at any rate, Schopenhauer replaces the Romantic conception of undefined and nameless feeling with the conception of precision.

He goes on to compare in detail the bass, the soprano, and the intermediate voices of music with the various manifestations of nature in their general form, from the inorganic world to the human will:

> Now the nature of man consists in the fact that his will strives, is satisfied, strives anew, and so on and on; in fact his happiness and well-being consist only in the transition from desire to satisfaction, and from this to a fresh desire, such transition going forward rapidly. For the nonappearance of satisfaction is suffering; the empty longing for a new desire is languor, boredom. Thus, corresponding to this, the nature of melody is a constant digression and deviation from the tonic in a thousand ways, not only to the harmonious intervals, the third and dominant, but to every tone, to the dissonant seventh, and to the extreme intervals; yet there always follows a final return to the tonic. (p. 260)

But the invention of melody cannot be understood by conscious reflection and concepts: "The composer reveals the innermost nature of the world . . . in a language his reasoning faculty does not understand." Schopenhauer compares him to a clairvoyant sleepwalker, who imparts knowledge that disappears when he wakes. The discussion of melody continues with analogies between tempo, dance music, major and minor, and modulation, on the one hand, and properties of the will and feeling, on the other: "The inexhaustibleness of possible melodies corresponds to the inexhaustibleness of nature in the difference of individuals, physiognomies, and courses of life" (p. 261).

Schopenhauer resumes the consideration of the feelings connected with music, qualifying, in a memorable passage, his initial description of the distinctness of these feelings with deductions from the principle that music never expresses the phenomenon, but only the in-itself of the phenomenon—the Will:

> Therefore music does not express this or that particular and definite pleasure, this or that affliction, pain, sorrow, horror, gaiety, merriment, or peace of mind, but joy, pain, sorrow, horror, gaiety, merriment, peace of mind themselves, to a certain extent in the abstract, their essential nature, without any accessories, and so also without the motives for them. Nevertheless we understand them perfectly in this extracted quintessence. (p. 261)

In the nature of these feelings and in their perfect intelligibility Schopenhauer finds the origin of song and opera, reducing the words and events of these compound arts to an extrinsic and secondary status:

> For this reason they should never forsake that subordinate position in order to make themselves the chief thing, and the music a mere means of expressing the song, since this is a great misconception and an utter absurdity. Everywhere music expresses only the quintessence of life and of its events, never these themselves, and therefore their differences do not always influence it. It is just this universality that belongs uniquely to music, together with the most precise distinctness, that gives it that high value as the panacea of all our sorrows. Therefore, if music tries to stick too closely to the words, and to mold itself according to the events, it is endeavoring to speak a language not its own. (pp. 261–62)

Not only do the undefined feelings of Romanticism receive their explanation and their correction in this remarkable passage, but the "panacea" of Schopenhauer also appears to clarify both the traditional curative properties of music and the equally venerable connection between music and joyful feelings that was held to derive from the very nature of music as an expression of praise of God and thankfulness to him.

Schopenhauer proceeds to compare music with concepts by comparing the relation of each of these to phenomena. The universality of music "is by no means that empty universality of abstraction, but is of quite a different kind; it is united with thorough and unmistakable distinctness." Music is like numbers and geometrical figures, "which are the universal forms of all possible objects of experience and are a priori applicable to them all, and yet are not abstract, but perceptible and thoroughly definite" (p. 262). If the real world of particular things presents *universalia in re,* then music gives the *universalia ante rem* and concepts the *universalia post rem,* for concepts contain only the forms of things, the "stripped-off outer shell." They are literally *abstracta,* while music gives the "innermost kernel preceding all form" (p. 263). Yet melodies, like universal concepts, are to a certain extent an abstraction from reality, and they also present the universality of mere form, for reality furnishes the particular case to both the universality of concepts and the universality of melodies.

It is difficult to exaggerate the importance of this conception. Not only does it grasp the nature of instrumental music with remarkable accuracy, but at the same time it offers extraordinary insight into the nature of song, pantomime, and opera. Individual pictures of human life that are set to music "are never bound to it or correspond to it with absolute necessity, but stand to it only in the relation of an example, chosen at random, to a universal concept." The words and events are set to music, not music to them—a conception that is sometimes exemplified in compositional practice, particularly in the nineteenth century. In addition to this, the close relation that Schopenhauer finds between music and the in-itself of things can explain the fact that, "when music suitable to any scene, action, event, or environment is played, it seems to disclose to us its most secret meaning, and appears to be the most accurate and distinct commentary on it" (p. 262).

The analogy between the universal expressed in a poem and the general significance of a melody that is revealed by the composer comes "from the immediate knowledge of the inner nature of the world unknown to his faculty of reason; it cannot be an imitation brought about with conscious intention by means of concepts, otherwise the music does not express the inner nature of the will itself, but merely imitates its phenomenon inadequately" (p. 263). This again suggests that musical creation takes place in a special state of consciousness that is comparable to clairvoyance. Schopenhauer's metaphysical conception of music is made increasingly plausible by the range of musical experience he accounts for, by the ingenious parallels he provides between various aspects of music, on the one hand, and Ideas or concepts, on the other.

In volume 2 of *Die Welt als Wille und Vorstellung,* published in 1844, twenty-five years after the first version of the work, the discussion of music (chapter 39) consists essentially of details that are added to the parallel originally considered between various aspects of nature—of the world as Idea—and various aspects of music. The spacing of the four voices of music and their respective types of motion are connected with counterparts in nature, and instrumental music is exemplified by a Beethoven symphony, in which the interplay of confusion and order, of conflict and harmony, gives "a true and complete picture of the nature of the world, which rolls on in the boundless confusion of innumerable forms, and maintains itself by constant destruction" (p. 450). In what follows, dissonance is considered the natural image of what resists our will since it resists a unified apprehension, while consonance, by adapting itself to our apprehension, becomes the image of satisfaction. There is a trace of representation of the will in this, by which music partakes slightly of the nature of the other arts. Thus, music never causes us actual suffering, remaining pleasant even in its most painful discords, while in real life our will itself is tormented. Melody is then explained, not only as an alternation of harmonious and dissonant intervals, but also as an alternating discord and reconciliation of its two elements, the rhythmic and the harmonious. The dualism of major and minor is compared to the two fundamental moods of serenity and sadness.

Beyond this, Schopenhauer adds certain details to his analysis of vocal music and opera. He undertakes in particular to justify writing the music after the words:

> It might perhaps appear more suitable for the text to be written for the music than for the music to be composed for the text. With the usual method, however, the words and actions of the text lead the composer to the affections of the will that underlie them, and call up in him the feelings to be expressed; consequently they act as a means for exciting his musical imagination. Moreover, that the addition of poetry to music is so welcome, and a song with intelligible words gives such profound joy, is due to the fact that our most direct and most indirect methods of knowledge are here stimulated simultaneously and in union. Thus the most direct is that for which music expresses the stirrings of the will itself, but the most indirect that of the concepts denoted by words. With the language of the feelings, our faculty of reason does not willingly sit in complete idleness. (p. 449)

But the force of Schopenhauer's vision of music understandably leads him to overlook certain aspects of the interdependence of the various elements of opera, as in the following exaggeration: "The music of an opera, as presented in the score, has a wholly independent, separate, and as it were abstract existence by itself, to which the incidents and characters of the piece are foreign, and which follows its own unchangeable rules; it can therefore be completely effective even without the text" (p. 449).

The fascination of Schopenhauer's conception of music was such that, not only did he himself return to it after a lapse of twenty-five years, but it was also taken up again, after another lapse of twenty-five years, by Wagner (1870) and Nietzsche (1871), to become what is doubtless the major tradition of musical aesthetics in the century. The continuity and successive elaborations of the theory were accompanied and probably in some degree caused by historical changes in music that made this aesthetic conception increasingly appropriate. It was almost as though music evolved or transformed itself so as to fulfill what aesthetics had envisaged to be its true nature.

Hegel's monumental *Vorlesungen über die Ästhetik*, which in its posthumously published form is based on his lectures in Berlin of 1820, 1823, and 1826, is a remarkable synthesis of basic philosophical conceptions and concrete detail—a synthesis that is characteristic of his thought in general. Although he was at first regarded as a disciple of Schelling, he came to differ from him substantially, somewhat as Aristotle did from Plato. In comparison with Schelling, Hegel is rational rather than visionary. In his comprehensive view of the historical and logical unfolding of the world-spirit, the earthly form of the absolute Idea, music represents a particular phase in the series of the arts, preceded by architecture, sculpture, and painting, in that order, and followed by literature, while the arts as a whole are then succeeded by philosophy. The successive order of the arts represents the stages of the self-realization of the world-spirit, with the corresponding stages of the reduction of the weight of its material embodiment. In music, spatial objectivity is annihilated, and we apprehend, through the ear rather than eye, the ideal activity of the soul rather than a material object. Music gives "a resonant reflection, not to objectivity in its ordinary material sense, but to the mode and modifications under which the most intimate self of the soul, from the point of view of its subjective life and ideality, is essentially moved." [18] Similarly, music exists only for the inward realm of conscious life.

In its general character, music has an affinity with architecture. Both arts, in spite of their obvious contrast, do not adopt forms but invent their own according to intrinsic laws. The distinctive feature of music in relation to plastic art is that it lies close to the formal freedom of the life of the soul. Thus, musical works lack the unity and connection of parts that are found in fine works of plastic art: "No doubt the ideal articulation and rounding off in a whole, in which the one part follows inevitably from another, ought to be present in a musical composition. But in some measure the execution here is of a totally different type, and moreover we can only accept the unity in a restricted sense" (p. 349).

To be sure, Hegel admits, a musical composition, as opposed to improvisation, determines the freedom of the composer. It limits this freedom to a more self-contained execution and the observance of what we may describe as a more plastic unity. Or it fixes digressions and spontaneity. Yet the formal deficiency of the musical work cannot be removed, for it is an outcome of the intrinsic nature of music, which Hegel describes in very positive terms: "If we are in a general way permitted to regard human activity in the realm of the beautiful as a liberation of the soul, as a release from constraint and restriction . . . it is the art of music which conducts us to the final summit of that ascent to freedom" (p. 349). In addition to this, Hegel provides a foundation for the view that music, at least in its improvised form, can reveal the distinctive spirit of the composer: "The recollection of a theme proposed is likewise a self-revealment of the artist, in other words is an ideal realization, to the effect that this self is the artist, and he may progress just as he likes, and by what by-paths he likes" (pp. 350–51).

With respect to the relation of music and poetry, Hegel finds similarly that the two arts are closely affiliated, but also very different. What this amounts to essentially is that both arts employ tone, but use it quite differently. Clearly, the sensuous medium, or external objectivity, of music is further reduced in poetry and largely replaced by the ideal objectivity of images and ideas. From a different point of view, music is literally associated with poetry, which provides it with a definite content and of which it becomes an "accompaniment." In this association, however, one art will predominate at the expense of the other.

An important difference between music and the other arts is in the way in which it expresses a content. Music absorbs and takes as content everything that can enter the life of the soul and disclose itself under the veils of emotional movement. It does not matter whether this content receives an independent and more direct definition by means of words or is emotionally realized from the music itself and its harmonic relations and melodic animation. The inwardness of soul is in either case differentiated, in the mode in which music is related to it, by feeling, and this is the sphere that is claimed by music: "It is a province which unfolds in expanse the expression of every kind of emotion, and every shade of joyfulness, merriment, jest, caprice, jubilation and laughter of the soul, every gradation of anguish, trouble, melancholy, lament, sorrow, pain, longing and the like, no less than those of reverence, adoration, and love fall within the appropriate limits of its expression" (p. 359). Thus, Hegel at least suggests the Romantic tradition according to which music is not restricted to feelings that can be named or clearly defined.

The tonal medium, in addition, is peculiarly cognate with its content since, like feeling, it exists in time and also does not entail a distinction between the ego and an object of perception, conception, or thought. Finally, music exercises a direct and unrivaled power on the soul. Since it grasps the life of the soul, it can set the soul in motion. The musical work of art posits at least an incipient distinction between the work itself and the individual who enjoys it, between a sensuous existence and the soul of the listener. Yet the sensuous existence is wholly evanescent, and music seizes on consciousness so that it is no longer confronted with an object. Time coalesces with the ego, for just as each now annuls itself in the next and yet remains always the same, so the ego continually becomes its own object, which it annuls in order to enforce itself as a subjective unity. Although the ego is in time, time is the very being and unity of the conscious subject itself. But the time of the conscious subject is also the time of tone, and thus tone penetrates into the self of conscious life, seizes hold of the same by virtue of the most basic aspect of its existence, and places the ego in movement by means of the motion in time and its rhythm. In addition to this, the other configuration of tones, as the expression of emotions and the content of music, brings a more definite material to enrich the unity of consciousness, a wealth by which it is at once affected and carried forward. The transience of tones also makes necessary the repeated reproduction of music, which necessarily calls for the expression of a living person. In this way, the active effect of the musical work substantiates the subjective aspect of music.

Having discussed the general character of music—by examining its relation to the other arts—Hegel turns to the particular means of expression that are specific to music, considering first rhythm, then harmony, and finally melody as their synthetic unity. This section is of little interest. In the consideration of melody, Hegel maintains that there is a limit to the definition and detail of musical expression—a position that is clearly a consequence of his conception of musical content:

We may further observe that it lies in the nature of music itself that we should find the task of presenting and expounding particular detail in general terms a less easy matter than in the case of the other arts. For however much music also takes up into itself an intellectual content and makes the interior of this entity or the inward motions of feeling the object of its expression, this content yet remains—precisely because it is grasped according to its inwardness or reflected in sound as subjec-

tive feeling—more indistinct and vague, and the musical modifications
are not in every case also modifications of a feeling or idea, of a thought
or an individual form, but a purely musical progressive motion, which
consists in play and avails itself of artistic method for this purpose.
(p. 394 [3:168])

As the second part of Hegel's consideration of music is devoted to form, so
the third and final part is devoted to content. Music can be either an "accompaniment"—when it is subordinate to the significance given by words—or
absolutely independent. This distinction defines the difference between vocal
and instrumental music. Hegel divides music as accompaniment into three
types: melodic, declamatory, and a combination of the two. The melodic
type is simply the expression of emotion, but it is not a purely natural utterance of passion. Instead, tone that is elaborated under definite conditions of
progression is vitalized with emotional forces; the expression is resolved "in
a medium of sound wholly created by art and inseparable from the artistic
purpose, a medium in which the mere cry becomes a series of musical tones
with a definite progression, the transitions and course of which are subject to the laws of harmony and unfolded in the completeness of a melodic
phrase" (p. 405). Melodic music preserves a sensuous beauty, a spirit of reconciliation, assurance, and grace. Hegel refers to a series of composers who
represent truly ideal music: "Tranquillity of soul is never lost in the compositions of these masters. Grief is no doubt often expressed, but the resolution
is always there; the luminous sense of proportion never breaks down in ex-
tremes: everything finds its due place knit together in the whole; joy is never
suffered to degenerate into unseemly uproar and even lamentation carries
with it the most benign repose" (p. 406). Particularity of emotional expression is represented, but melody "should at the same time lift the soul that
is absorbed in such emotion over the same" (p. 407). Italian melody is exemplary, and it often parts company with the emotional stimulus and its
particular mode of expression.

In declamatory music, the expression should vary according to the changing nature of the content, as supplied by words. In recitative, the content of
the words is imprinted on the musical expression. Instrumental music can
be added as an accompaniment to support the general import and to depict
other aspects and movements of the situation.

The combination of melodic and declamatory expression attains a concrete unity. For this a good text is necessary. The content of the text should
ring true as a whole, avoiding what is commonplace, trivial, and barren. It
should not call for reflective thought and should not be absolutely complete

as poetry. The emotion should be true and spontaneous. What is needed is a certain intermediate type of poetry:

A poetry genuine in its lyricism, extremely simple, indicating the situation and feeling in few words; clear and vital in its dramatic aspect, avoiding too complex a development, and generally more concerned with giving outlines than works that are fully articulated poetically. Here the composer receives, as is necessary, only the general foundation upon which he can erect his building, according to his own invention and his own threshing out of all the motives and can in many ways become vitally engaged.

If the words depict the content in too much detail, the declamation will be fussy and pulled in different directions too much, with the result that "the unity is lost and the general effect is weakened" (p. 415 [3:207]).

The main requirement of the melodic-declamatory type of music is that the melodic expression, which is the factor of synthetic unity, must always win the day rather than any factor that "tends to distract and break up the whole into particular characterization." In general, the declamatory or characteristic component of the style must not become so prominent as to overstep "the finely drawn boundaries of musical beauty" (p. 417).

Independent music is foreshadowed by music as an accompaniment in the melodic style, which in opera, for example, almost emancipates music entirely from the libretto. It is instrumental music, however, that is the true province of musical independence. Such music, however, is "compelled to have recourse to emotions of a more indefinite character, emotions which in such music can only be expressed in general terms" (p. 424). What is important here is "the varied motion of the music simply, the ups and downs of the harmony or melody, the stream of sound through its degrees of opposition, preponderance, emphasis, acuteness, or velocity," and so on. These details are not content, the expression of which remains "necessarily less defined" than when a text is present. Yet Hegel is not entirely unequivocal on this point. "In respect of detail," he asserts,

there is an endless field in which subjectivity, provided it keeps within the boundaries that lie in the essential nature of tonal relationships, may otherwise disport itself at will. Indeed, in the course of the elaboration of these types of music also, subjective volition makes itself an unfettered master, with its sudden ideas, caprices, interruptions, ingenious bantering, deceptive tensions, surprising turns, leaps, and lightning flashes, eccentricities, and unheard-of effects. (pp. 425–26 [3:218])

Again, however, this does not seem to be emotional content, and there is still doubt that Hegel does full justice to instrumental music.

In line with the two kinds of music he has distinguished, music as accompaniment and independent music, Hegel finally distinguishes two kinds of executive art: purely reproductive and creative. Creative execution is particularly called for when the composer himself has made personal idiosyncrasy prominent. The performer may also add to the composition, as the singer does, for example, in Italian opera. Creative execution is especially remarkable in instrumental music, where the expression of the soul breaks through the alien crust of mechanism and the externality of the instrument vanishes.

As became evident in the subsequent course of history, the Romantic era was a time of intense creativity both in literature and in philosophy. The thought of the second half of the century, in contrast, is devoted in considerable measure to the reworking of Romantic ideas and to the eclectic combination of viewpoints. In this eclecticism, however, there participated the traditions of realism and formalism, which we shall examine in the next two chapters, along with a variety of new scientific trends.

CHAPTER NINE

EMOTIONAL REALISM

Although the ideas of Romantic aesthetics were active throughout the nineteenth century both in their original form and in a variety of transformations, other conceptions of music were created alongside them, gained currency as dominant new ideas, and were accompanied by their own manifestations in musical practice. Thus, after the efflorescence of Romanticism in music during the 1820s and 1830s, which expressed with such remarkable fidelity the conception of musical feeling that had been formulated decades before both in literature and in philosophy, a new and more vivid kind of music became prominent in the decades from 1840 to 1860 in which the veiled and suggestive feelings of Romanticism, nostalgic and unfulfilled, gave way before specific and clearly defined feelings along with representation of external scenes and events. There was a certain kinship in this art to the Baroque imitation of the affections. Indeed, a revival of a vocabulary of musical patterns again became an integral part of the musical language. This Neoromantic music had its conceptual complement—simultaneous with it in this case—in an aesthetics of emotional realism. Once again, the ideal was vocal music rather than instrumental, and in particular opera, in which the greatest realism and force could be achieved and the feelings in fact made coincident and apparently identical with those of experience outside music. Environmentally and psychologically realistic program music was also responsive to demands of this kind. The central subject matter was sensuous and erotic feeling, which found direct and forceful expression.

This aesthetic outlook was forecast by the writers of the Young Germany movement of the 1830s, the very time of the antithetical manifestations of Romantic music, and the authors of Young Germany in turn took for their model the enthusiastic adulation of Italian sensuality and art found in Heinse's novel *Ardinghello* (1787). It was also in the 1830s that Wagner rejected German Romanticism and, as part of the Young Germany movement, espoused the cause of erotic expression and turned to Italian music for his inspiration and model. Wagner converted Shakespeare's *Measure for Measure* to his own purposes in *Das Liebesverbot* by transferring the setting from Venice to Palermo, where the opposed forces of the action become precisely German hypocrisy and Italian sensual indulgence, which collide in the anguish of the novice, Isabella. There were elements in Herder as well as Heinse that became influential in this aesthetic so opposed to Romanticism, notably the natural coherence of the three sister arts of bodily expression that were allied in ancient Greek music. It was through this alliance, consciously constructed to that end, that Wagner achieved his goal of the maximum realism and force of emotional expression.

An enthusiastic testimonial to emotional realism in music is created by Søren Kierkegaard in the essay "The Musical Erotic," which is part of the first volume of his *Either/Or*, published in 1843. While Hoffmann saw Mozart's *Don Giovanni* in Romantic terms, as the intrusion of the supernatural world into the human, Kierkegaard (who speaks through a fictitious personality) sees it as the apotheosis of eroticism:

> The Middle Ages had much to say about a mountain, not found on any map, which is called the mountain of Venus. There the sensuous has its home, there it has its own wild pleasures, for it is a kingdom, a state. In this kingdom language has no place, nor sober-minded thought, nor the toilsome business of reflection. There sound only the voice of elemental passion, the play of appetites, the wild shouts of intoxication; it exists solely for pleasure in eternal tumult. The first-born of this kingdom is Don Juan.[1]

We are reminded by this passage that Wagner's *Tannhäuser* (1845), a musical document roughly contemporaneous with Kierkegaard's essay, contains evidence of the same glorification of eroticism. Essential for sensuous love, Kierkegaard maintains, is woman in the abstract:

> Psychical love does not exactly move in the rich manifold of the individual life, where the nuances are really significant. Sensuous love, on the other hand, can lump everything together. The essential for it is woman in the abstract, and at most is a more sensuous difference. Psychical love is a continuance in time, sensuous love a disappearance in time, but the medium which exactly expresses this is music. Music is excellently fitted to accomplish this, since it is far more abstract than language, and therefore does not express the individual but the general in all its generality, and yet it expresses the general not in reflective abstraction, but in the immediate concrete. (p. 94)

The "either/or" of Kierkegaard's title is an either/or of the aesthetic or the ethical life, which provides a context, as we can see in the following passage, that clarifies the significance of music. Speaking of Don Giovanni, Kierkegaard says, "But this energy, this power, cannot be expressed in words, only music can give us a conception of it. It is inexpressible for reflection and thought. The cunning of an ethically determined seducer I can clearly set forth in words, and music will try in vain to solve this problem" (p. 100). Similarly,

> this force in Don Giovanni, this omnipotence, this animation, only music can express, and I know no other predicate to describe it than this: it is exuberant joy of life. . . . By these considerations we are again brought to the main subject of this inquiry, that Don Giovanni is absolutely musical. He desires sensuously, he seduces with the daemonic power of sensuousness, he seduces everyone. Speech, dialogue, are not for him, for then he would be at once a reflective individual. Thus he does not have stable existence at all, but he hurries in a perpetual vanishing, precisely like music, about which it is true that it is over as soon as it has ceased to sound, and only comes into being again, when it again sounds. (pp. 100–101)

Kierkegaard's operatic aesthetics is concerned largely with the property of unity. It employs a comparison of opera with drama as a point of departure. Spoken drama is reflective, and the action is swift; the general impression it gives is that of an idea, a thought. But opera is concerned more with mood and lyricism. This difference creates a difference in the nature of the unity achieved by each:

> In drama I see factors which are external to each other together in the situation, a unity of action. The more, then, the discrete factors are separated and the more profoundly the dramatic situation is self-reflective, so much the less will the dramatic unity manifest itself as a mood and so much the more will it become a definite idea. . . . The musical situation has the contemporary quality like every dramatic situation, but the activity of the forces is a concord, a harmony, an agreement, and the impression made by the musical situation is the unity achieved by hearing together what sounds together. The more the drama is self-reflective, the more the mood is explained in the action. The less action, the more the lyrical element dominates. This is quite proper in opera. Opera does not so much have character delineation and action as its immanent goal; it is not reflective enough for that. On the other hand, passion, unreflective and substantial, finds its expression in opera. The musical situation depends on maintaining the unity of mood in the di-

verse plurality of voices. This is exactly the characteristic of music that it can preserve the diversity in the unity of mood.

The more reflection there is in drama, the faster the action. But this would be prejudiced by a lyric or an epic element, which would produce a kind of lethargy:

> This haste is not inherent in the nature of the opera, for this is characterized by a certain lingering movement, a certain diffusion of itself in time and space. The action has not the swiftness of the denouement or its direction, but it moves more horizontally. The mood is not sublimated in character and action. As a result, the action in an opera can only be immediate action. (pp. 117–18)

Similarly, "What one in a stricter sense calls action, a deed undertaken with consciousness of a purpose, cannot find its expression in music, but only what we might call immediate action" (p. 119).

The unity of opera is ensured by music, and in *Don Giovanni* this reaches its greatest strength, for Don Giovanni himself is intrinsically musical in nature, and the other characters become musical too because they are really posited by him as consequences; they are passions rather than characters. In turn, also, the unity of the opera is responsible for the illusion it creates, which is so convincing to Kierkegaard that he does not even consider the issue of verisimilitude:

> It is this musical life of Don Giovanni, absolutely centralized in the opera, which enables it to create a power of illusion such as no other is able to do, so that its life transports one into the life of the play. Because the musical is omnipresent in this music, one may enjoy any snatch of it, and immediately be transported by it. One may enter in the middle of the play and instantly be in the center of it, because this center, which is Don Giovanni's life, is everywhere. (pp. 118–19)

The emphasis on music as the basic determining feature of opera carries with it an important conception that found expression in Romantic literature and was often to influence the musical thought of the nineteenth century, namely, the idea of the antagonism of vision and hearing. However curious a component this may be of the aesthetics of opera in particular, it is nevertheless occasionally present as a decisive factor. "We know from experience," Kierkegaard says,

> that it is not pleasant to strain two senses at the same time, and it is often very confusing if we have to use our eyes hard when our ears are already occupied. Therefore we have a tendency to close our eyes

when hearing music. This is true of all music more or less, and of *Don Giovanni* in *sensu eminentiori*. As soon as the eyes are engaged, the impression becomes confused; for the dramatic unity which presents itself to the eye is always subordinate and imperfect in comparison with the musical unity which is heard at the same time. (p. 119)

Kierkegaard relates, as Wagner did, how he sat further and further back at performances of *Don Giovanni*, how he tried a corner of the theater "where I could completely lose myself in the music." Now he need not even spend a penny for a ticket: "I stand outside in the corridor; I lean up against the partition which divides me from the auditorium, and then the impression is most powerful; it is a world by itself, separated from me" (p. 199).[2]

Kierkegaard shows how several individual numbers of the opera bear out his general ideas. He also admires the character of the overture, which indeed perfectly exemplifies the criteria long accepted as desirable for the genre. The overture should not have the same content as the opera, he maintains, nor should it contain anything absolutely different. It should contain "the central idea, and grip the listener with the whole intensity of this central idea. . . . This overture is no interweaving of themes, it is not a labyrinthine hodge-podge of associated ideas; it is concise, definite, strongly constructed, and, above all, it is impregnated with the essence of the whole opera" (p. 126). The essay concludes with a discussion of the champagne aria:

> Here is the clear indication of what it means to say that the essence of Don Juan is music. He reveals himself to us in music, he expands in a world of sound. Someone has called this the champagne aria, and this is undeniably very descriptive. But that which especially needs to be noted is that it does not stand in an accidental relationship to Don Juan. His life is like this, effervescent as champagne. And just as the bubbles in this wine ascend and continue to ascend, while it seethes in its own heat, harmonious in its own melody, so the lust for enjoyment sounds through the primitive seething which is his life. Therefore, that which gives this aria dramatic significance is not the situation, but the fact that the keynote of the opera sounds and resounds in itself. (pp. 133–34)

With surprising regularity, Richard Wagner's treatises and essays in the field of aesthetics fall externally into five groups separated from one another by intervals of ten years, the dates in question running from 1840 to 1880. This body of writings contains a remarkable variety of aesthetic ideas, some of which contradict others, a circumstance that is not surprising in view of the span of time involved. The works that contain an aesthetic of emotional realism are those written at mid-century, from 1849 to 1851, during the first years of Wagner's exile in Switzerland. The most important of these works from an aesthetic point of view are *Die Kunst und die Revolution* (1849), *Das Kunstwerk der Zukunft* (1849), and *Oper und Drama* (1851). Together they represent a consistent and comprehensive aesthetics that reveals Wagner's thought at the most important turning point of his career, in his late thirties, about to begin the composition of the *Ring*, and in the process of formulating and clarifying the conceptions that were intended as a foundation for this gigantic work.

While Romantic aesthetics had entailed a metaphysical outlook, Wagner's realistic aesthetics entailed a social one: art is conceived as a manifestation of society—a perspective almost inevitable for a man of political mentality, shortly before engaged as an active revolutionist. It is no accident, of course, that the metaphysical aesthetics was concerned chiefly with instrumental music and the realistic with opera. In *Art and Revolution*, Wagner's approach is historical; he seeks to understand the art of his time by examining how it developed from its origin in ancient Greece. At the center of this historical view, however, is the traditional antithesis of ancient and modern: "Let us now compare the chief features of the public art of modern Europe with those of the public art of Greece, in order to set clearly before our eyes their characteristic points of difference."[3] The ensuing glowing description of Greek tragedy, against which is set the drastically negative account of modern theatrical art, is interrupted, however, by the fatal flaw of slavery:

> This *slave* thus became the fateful hinge of the whole destiny of the world. The slave, by sheer reason of the assumed necessity of his slavery, has exposed the null and fleeting nature of all the strength and beauty of exclusive Grecian manhood and has shown to all time *that beauty and strength, as attributes of public life, can then alone prove lasting blessings when they are the common gifts of all mankind.*
>
> Unhappily, things have not as yet advanced beyond the mere demonstration. In fact, the revolution of the human race, that has lasted now two thousand years, has been almost exclusively in the spirit of reaction. It has dragged down the fair, free man to itself, to slavery; the slave has not become a freeman, but the freeman a slave. (pp. 26–27)

Grecian art was conservative, Wagner continues, because it was a worthy expression of the public conscience. "With us, true art is revolutionary because its very existence is opposed to the ruling spirit of the community." It lives only in the conscience of the individual:

> With the Greeks the perfect work of art, the drama, was the abstract and epitome of all that was expressible in the Grecian nature. It was the

state itself—in intimate connection with its own history—that stood mirrored in its work of art, that communed with itself, and within the span of a few hours, feasted its eyes on its own noblest essence. All division of this enjoyment, all scattering of the forces concentrated on *one* point, all diversion of the elements into separate channels, must needs have been as hurtful to this *unique* and noble work of art as to the like-formed state itself. . . .

With the subsequent downfall of tragedy, art became less and less the expression of the public conscience. The drama separated into its component parts; rhetoric, sculpture, painting, music, etc., forsook the ranks in which they had moved in unison before; each one to take its own way and in lonely self-sufficiency pursue its own development. (pp. 28–29)

Each one of these separate arts, Wagner says, cultivated for the entertainment of the rich, has filled the world with its product, but the one true art, the perfect work of art, the great united utterance of a free public life, has not yet been born again, for "it cannot be *re*-born, but it must be *born* anew." Only the great revolution of mankind can win this work of art for us:

The task we have before us is immeasurably greater than that already accomplished in days of old. If the Grecian work of art embraced the spirit of a fair and noble nation, the work of art of the future must embrace the spirit of a free mankind, delivered from every shackle of hampering nationality; its racial imprint must be no more than an embellishment, the individual charm of manifold diversity, and not a cramping barrier. (pp. 29–30)

The revolution intended in the title of Wagner's essay has both a broader and a more specific meaning. In one sense, it is a revolution of mankind that started with the dissolution of the Athenian state and the disintegration of Greek tragedy; in another, it is the revolution of 1848, which is regarded by Wagner as a continuation of the French Revolution—a revolution that has not yet reached its ultimate goal.

The new work of art that Wagner envisages is intimately tied to revolution: it can be made possible only through revolution, and it will at the same time help this revolution to succeed. In this last function, art plays a role somewhat similar to the role assigned to it by Schiller, for as we have seen, the *Briefe über die ästhetische Erziehung des Menschen* (1795) carries Kant's connection between aesthetics and morality one step further, making aesthetic freedom a prerequisite of political freedom.

Where is the revolutionary force to be found that will oppose the crushing pressure of a civilization that uses man only as a tool? Wagner appeals to nature in the sense of human nature:

> If culture, starting from the Christian dogma of the worthlessness of human nature, disowns humanity, it creates for itself a foe who must inevitably destroy it, in so far as it no longer has a place for manhood....
>
> In the man-destroying march of culture, however, there looms before us this happy result: the heavy load with which it presses nature down will one day grow so ponderous that it will lend at last to downtrodden, never-dying nature the necessary impetus to hurl the whole cramping burden from her, with one sole thrust; and this heaping up of culture will thus have *taught* to nature her own gigantic force. The releasing of this force is—*revolution*. (p. 31)

Christianity does not fare well in Wagner's historical survey. Its dogmas cannot be realized: "How could those dogmas become really living, and pass over into actual life, when they were directed against life itself and denied and cursed the principle of living?" (p. 36). The Christian ideal was morbid, Wagner maintains, born of the enfeeblement of human nature and sinning against its intrinsic robust qualities. But if this physicalism, akin to Feuerbach and a continuation of the sensualism of the 1830s, rejects the Christian religion, it embraces Jesus along with Apollo and the ideal of love along with that of nature.

Wagner's plans for art become increasingly evident toward the end of his essay, as in the following statement of his ideals by way of peroration:

> When human fellowship has once developed its manly beauty and nobility—in such a way as we shall not attain, however, by the influence of our art alone but as we must hope and strive for by union with the great and inevitably approaching social revolution—then will theatrical performances be the first associate undertaking from which the idea of wage or gain shall disappear entirely....
>
> Art and its institutes, whose desired organization could here be only briefly touched on, would thus become the herald and the standard of all future communal institutions....
>
> Thus would *Jesus* have shown us that we all alike are men and brothers, while *Apollo* would have stamped this mighty bond of brotherhood with the seal of strength and beauty.... (pp. 40–41)

Wagner begins *The Art-Work of the Future* by grounding art in nature. From nature there develop in turn, by necessity and not by change, life, consciousness, and art:

> Man will not be that which he can and should be until his life is a faithful mirror of nature, a conscious pursuit of the only real necessity,

inner natural necessity, not a subordination of an *outer* imagined *force,* imitating imagination, and hence not necessary but *willful.* . . . In the same way, art too will not be that which it can and should be until it is or can be a faithful, manifestly conscious copy of genuine man and of the genuine, naturally necessary life of man, in other words, until it need no longer borrow from the errors, perversities, and unnatural distortions of our modern life the conditions of its being.

Genuine man, therefore, will not come into being until his life is shaped and ordered by true human nature and not by the willful law of state; genuine art will not live until its shapings need be subject only to the law of nature and not to the despotic caprice of fashion.[4]

Consonant with the foundation of art in nature is the transformation of the natural into the universal. Hellenic art, Wagner maintains, must be made into the altogether human art; the specifically Hellenic religious bond must become the bond of the religion of the future—that of universality—in order to arrive at a just conception of the work of art of the future: "Yet, unfortunate as we are, it is precisely the power to close this bond, this *religion of the future,* that we lack, for after all, no matter how many of us may feel this urge to the work of art of the future, we are *singular* and *individual.* A work of art is religion brought to life; religions, however, are created, not by the artist, but by the *folk*" (p. 880).

Proceeding to the more particular nature of the art of the future, Wagner proposes that man is the subject and material of his own art. Outer man is presented to the eye and inner man—through the tone of his voice—to the ear: "*Tone* is the direct expression of feeling, as it has its physical seat in the heart, the starting and returning point for the circulation of the blood. Through the sense of hearing, tone penetrates from heart to heart, from feeling to feeling; grief and joy communicate themselves directly, through the manifold tone of voice" (p. 881). Finally, in addition to corporeal man and the man of feeling, there is the man of understanding, whose medium is speech.

Parallel to these three human faculties are the three types of purely human art—of dance, of tone, and of poetry—which Wagner examines in turn. Each of them finds fulfillment, not in going its separate egoistic way, but only in loving union with its sisters. The discussion of the art of tone is dominated by the simile of the ocean, which is introduced at the outset:

The sea divides and connects the continents; thus the art of tone divides and connects the two extreme antitheses of human art, the arts of dancing and of poetry. . . .

If *rhythm* and *melody* are the shores at which the tonal art meets with and makes fruitful the two continents of the arts primevally related to it, then tone itself is the primeval fluid element, and the immeasurable expanse of this fluid is the sea of *harmony*. . . .

Into this sea man dives to yield himself again, radiant and refreshed, to the light of day; he feels his heart expand with wonder when he looks down into these depths, capable of unimaginable possibilities, whose bottom his eye is never to fathom, whose fathomlessness fills him accordingly with astonishment and forebodings of the infinite. This is the depth and infinity of nature itself, which veils from man's searching eye the impenetrable mystery of its budding, begetting, and longing, precisely because the eye can comprehend only what has become visible. (pp. 883–84)

In a remarkable passage that demands extended citation, Wagner takes the occasion to elaborate on the nature of harmony:

The nature of harmony corresponds to no other capacity of man as artist; it sees itself reflected, neither in the physically determined movements of the body, nor in the logical progression of thought; it can conceive its just measure, neither, as thought does, in the recognized necessity of the world of material phenomena, nor, as bodily movement does, in the presentation, as perceived in time, of its instinctive, richly conditioned character; it is like a natural force, apprehended, but not comprehended, by man. From out its own fathomless depths, from an outer—not inner—necessity to limit itself for positive finite manifestation, harmony must shape for itself the laws it will obey. These laws of harmonic succession, based on relation, just as the harmonic columns, or harmonies, were themselves formed from the relation of tonal materials, combine now as a just measure, which sets a beneficial limit to the monstrous range of willful possibilities. They permit the widest possible selection from out the sphere of harmonic families, expand to the point of free choice the possibility of connections through elective relation with members of distant families, demand above all, however, a strict conformity to the house rules of the family momentarily chosen and an implicit acceptance of them for the sake of a salutary end. To postulate or to define this end—in other words, the just measure of the expansion of the musical composition in time—lies beyond the power of the innumerable rules of harmonic decorum. (pp. 887–88)

In spite of the concrete nature of his aesthetic ideal, Wagner makes frequent use of the Romantic concept of endless longing, particularly in connection with Beethoven, who is compared to Columbus: "What inimitable art Beethoven employed in his C-Minor Symphony to guide his ship out of the ocean of <u>endless longing</u> into the harbor of fulfillment! He succeeded in intensifying the expression of his music almost to the point of moral resolve, yet was unable to proclaim this resolve itself" (p. 892). Wagner discusses the Sixth Symphony and then the Seventh. Finally, he turns to the Ninth, in which Beethoven discovers the new world:

> From the shores of dancing he plunged again into that endless sea from out whose depths he had once saved himself on these same shores, into the sea of insatiable heart's longing. . . .
>
> Thus the master forced his way through the most unheard-of possibilities of absolute tonal language—not by hurriedly stealing past them, but by proclaiming them completely, to their last sound, from his heart's fullest depths—until he reached that point at which the navigator begins to sound the sea's depths with his lead; at which he touches solid bottom at ever increasing heights as the strands of the new continent reach toward him from afar; at which he must decide whether to turn about into the fathomless ocean or whether to drop anchor in the new banks. But it was no rude hankering for the sea that had urged the master on to this long voyage; he wished and had to land in the new world, for it was to this end that the voyage had been undertaken. Resolutely he threw out his anchor, and this anchor was the *word*. . . .
>
> This *last symphony* of Beethoven's is the redemption of music out of its own element as a *universal art*. It is the *human* gospel of the art of the future. Beyond it there can be no *progress*, for there can follow on it immediately only the completed work of art of the future, *the universal drama*, to which Beethoven has forged for us the artistic key. (pp. 894–95)

After considering architecture, sculpture, and painting, particularly in relation to the drama, Wagner devotes his final two sections to the fundamentals of the work of art of the future and to the artist of the future. Man as artist can be fully satisfied, Wagner maintains, only "in the union of all the art varieties in the *collective* work of art." In every individual art, he is not wholly what he can be and therefore, in Wagner's view, not free. The highest collective work of art, furthermore, is the drama, which includes all the individual arts, each in its ultimate completeness: "True drama can be conceived only as resulting from the *collective impulse of all the arts* to communicate in the most immediate way with a *collective public;* each individual art variety can reveal itself as *fully understandable* to this collective public only through collective communication, together with the other art varieties, in the drama" (p. 900). Wagner develops his chief themes: the work of art of the future will employ all the arts, and each individual art will find its fulfillment in the combination of all. He considers the various constituent arts, turning finally to music:

> Not *one* of the richly developed capacities of the individual arts will remain unused in the collective work of art of the future; it is precisely in the collective work of art that these capacities will attain to full stature. Thus especially the art of tone, developed with such singular diversity in instrumental music, will realize in the collective work of art its richest potentialities—will indeed incite the pantomimic art of dancing in turn to wholly new discoveries and inspire the breath of poetry no less to an undreamed-of fullness. For in its isolation music has formed itself an organ capable of the most immeasurable expression—the *orchestra*. Beethoven's tonal language, introduced through the orchestra into the drama, is a force wholly new to the dramatic work of art. (p. 901)

In what follows, the nature of the combination of the arts is more closely considered:

> If architecture and, still more so, scenic landscape painting can place the dramatic actor in the natural environment of the physical world and give him, from the inexhaustible font of natural phenomena, a background constantly rich and relevant, the orchestra . . . offers the individual actor, as a support, what may be called a perpetual source of the natural element of man as artist. The orchestra is, so to speak, the soil of infinite universal feeling from which the individual feeling of the single actor springs into full bloom; it somehow dissolves the solid motionless floor of the actual scene into a fluid, pliant, yielding, impressionable, ethereal surface whose unfathomed bottom is the sea of feeling itself. (p. 901)

The orchestra is the perfect complement of the scenic environment, adding human emotions to the physical world and forming a composite that encircles the actor "with an atmospheric elemental ring of nature and art":

> Thus completing one another in their ever-changing round, the united sister arts will show themselves and bring their influence to bear, now collectively, now two at a time, now singly, as called for by the need of the dramatic action, the one determinant of aim and measure. At one moment plastic pantomime will listen to thought's dispassionate appraisal, at another the will of resolute thought will overflow into the immediate expression of gesture; at still another music will have to utter the flood of feeling, the awe of apprehension; finally, however, all three,

in mutual entwinement, will exalt the will of drama to immediate active deed. (pp. 901–2)

At the close of the section, Wagner describes the process through which, in the drama, the individual being of the creative artist is widened to become the being of the human species. The strongest and most necessary need of the perfect artist, he writes,

is to communicate himself in the ultimate completeness of his being to the ultimate community, and he attains this with the universal intelligibility necessary to it only in the *drama*. In the drama he expands his particular being to general being by representing an individual personality other than his own. He must wholly forget himself to comprehend another personality with the completeness necessary to representation; he attains this only when he explores this individuality with such precision in its contact, penetration, and completion with and by other individualities—hence also the being of these other individualities themselves—when he apprehends this individuality so accurately that it is possible for him to become conscious of this contact, penetration, and completion in his own being; the perfect representative artist is therefore the individual expanded to the *being of the species* in accordance with the ultimate completion of his own particular being. (pp. 902–3)

The last section of the tract is devoted to the artist of the future. Wagner's argument here is unusually diffuse and bombastic. The artist of the future will undoubtedly be the poet, he asserts, taking this to include both poetry and music. But the poet will undoubtedly be the actor, he says. And the actor will necessarily be the fellowship of all the artists. This fellowship, Wagner continues, is based on a single definite aim—the drama. But it is really made possible, and in fact necessary, by the dramatic action, which is borrowed from life—in particular, from a life in common. In addition, the episode from life must have had a definite conclusion, which means that the chief person who has brought it about must have died; he must have sacrificed himself to the inner necessity that ruled him: "*The celebration of such a death is the noblest thing that men can enter on.* It reveals to us in the nature of this *one* man, laid bare by death, the whole content of universal human nature."[5]

The member of the brotherhood of artists who most feels an affinity to a particular hero will seek to represent this hero and will make his project a common one by his enthusiasm. He will become a poet as well as an impersonator: "*The free artistic fellowship* is therefore the foundation and the first condition of the work of art itself. From it proceeds the *performer*, who in his enthusiasm for this one particular hero whose nature harmonizes with his own, now raises himself to the rank of *poet*, of artistic *lawgiver* to the fellowship" (p. 166). The ultimate basis of this guild of artists finally becomes the people (*das Volk*). Wagner does not succeed very well in defining this rather fuzzy conception. He addresses himself to anyone who is unable to remain in "cowardly indifference to the criminal assemblage of our social and political affairs," who,

> from the fullness and the depth of naked *human nature* and the irrefutable right of its absolute need, draws force for resistance, for revolt, for assault on the oppressor of this nature—he then who must withstand, revolt, and deal assault and openly avows this plain necessity in that he gladly suffers every other sorrow for its sake and, if need be, will offer up even his life—*he and he alone belongs to the folk,* for he and all his fellows feel a common *need.* (pp. 174–75)

In the utopian compound of revolution, communal ideals, and an all-encompassing art devoted to the commemoration of a hero and aiming at universal intelligibility, *Opera and Drama* tends to focus more narrowly on the details of theory and construction for the work of art of the future. The elaboration of the nature of Wagner's new art, however, is again set into a large context, for it is preceded by detailed critical and historical accounts of conventional opera and then of spoken drama. These accounts demonstrate—as Wagner believes—the dire consequences of artistic "egoism" and thus the need for the union of the arts that is to take place according to fundamentally sound principles.

In the first part of *Opera and Drama*—"Opera and the Nature of Music" —Wagner undertakes to demonstrate both the error of opera and the error of instrumental music. The error of opera was to treat music as an end and drama as a means; the error of instrumental music (with Beethoven again as the crucial instance) was to attempt to portray definite, individual feelings clearly and intelligibly. Stated in a more temperate manner, these contentions are not unreasonable. The musical component of the effect of opera has at times had considerable weight, while Neoromantic instrumental music frequently seeks a highly specific expression of feeling, although generally with the aid of a program or title. Indeed, both these "failings" are as evident in Wagner's musical dramas as they are elsewhere. But it is indisputable that the effect of opera is often theatrical and often dramatic, not to say spectacular and intense, and even that the presentation of a course of action, of intrigue, and of human relationships is in general the controlling purpose and effect. Wagner had a much more penetrating insight into opera many years before he wrote his monumental treatise, for in the essay "Bellini" (1837) he finds that a melodic line (one that is formally constructed) is capable of concentrating and expressing the whole character of a dramatic situation;[6] there is a fusion of musical and dramatic components that defies dissection.

Wagner opens the second part of *Opera and Drama*—"The Play and the Nature of Dramatic Poetry"—with one of the chief tenets of his aesthetic realism:

> Wherever Lessing sets up limits and boundaries for poetry, he does not mean the *dramatic work of art* directly brought before the senses by physical performance, that work of art that sums up in itself each factor of the plastic arts, in highest potency such as it alone can reach, and that by its power has first brought to these their higher potentiality of artistic life; but he means the exiguous phantom of this work of art, the narrating, depicting, literary poem, appealing to the imagination and not the senses—the form in which that force of imagination has been turned into the virtual performer, toward which the poem acts merely as stimulus.
>
> Such an *artificial* art, it is true, can produce an effect at all only by the most exact observance of boundaries and limits since it must ever be on its watch to guard the unlimited force of imagination—which has here to play the performer's role in place of it—from any bewildering digression and thus to guide it to the one fixed point at which it can display the purposed object as definitely and distinctly as possible. But it is to the force of imagination alone that all the egoistically severed arts address themselves—and especially plastic art, which can bring into play only the weightiest factor of art, namely motion, by appealing to the fantasy. All these arts merely suggest: an actual representation would be possible to them only if they could deal with the universality of man's artistic receptivity, if they could address his entire sentient organism, and not his force of imagination; for the true work of art can be engendered only by an advance from imagination into actuality, that is, physicality.[7]

In spite of his critique of Lessing, Wagner is really retracing in his own way the path of Moses Mendelssohn and Lessing, his eighteenth-century German predecessors in operatic theory, seeking in the nature of the individual arts, particularly in the case of language and music, the principles and method of their correct combination.

After developing the thesis, in his historical discussion of drama, that there is no drama in his own time, Wagner considers at length what subject matter is appropriate for drama.[8] Myth should be the material, he argues, and so far Greek myth has been the source of the only drama that can be called genuine. In the more recent world, on the other hand, we find the cycles of Christian myth and Germanic myth.

Feeling rather than understanding is to play the central role in the drama of the future; it is a factor coordinate in Wagner's aesthetics with full physical realization. Actions become intelligible through their emotional motivation, and it is through feeling that understanding is to be achieved. But feeling demands tonal speech. It is also to be grounded in the marvelous, and this in turn demands condensation of the action. Wagner presents a large complex of interrelated ideas, although they are far from clear either in their definition or in their interconnection:

> In presence of the dramatic work of art, nothing should remain for the combining intellect to search for. . . . Things that can be explained to us only by the infinite accommodations of the understanding embarrass and confound the feeling. In drama, therefore, an action can be explained only when it is completely vindicated by the feeling; and thus it is the dramatic poet's task not to invent actions but to make an action so intelligible through its emotional necessity that we may altogether dispense with the intellect's assistance in its vindication. The poet therefore has to make his main object *the choice of the action*, which he must so choose that both in its character and in its compass it makes possible to him its entire vindication from feeling, for in this vindication alone resides the achievement of his intention. (pp. 78–79)

An action that can be understood only on the basis of historic relations, Wagner continues, cannot be presented directly to feeling and the senses; it will contain a mass of connections that cannot be brought into physical view. Thus, the poetic intention came to be stated explicitly in a political-historical drama. In an action that is to be justified by feeling, however, the poetic intention is contained in the justification: the action is vindicated simply by the feeling from which it arises. The action must therefore proceed from relations that are closest to human emotions, are grasped most readily by feeling, and thus are the simplest—from relations that can proceed only from a society at one with itself and not influenced by any bases of right that come down from the past instead of belonging to the present.

No action stands alone, Wagner points out; it always has some connection with the actions of other men, who also condition it:

> But the greater and more decisive an action is, and the more it can be explained only from the strength of a necessary feeling, in so much the more definite and wider a connection does it also stand with the actions of others. A great action, one that the most demonstratively and

exhaustively displays the nature of man along any one particular line, issues only from the shock of manifold and mighty opposites. (p. 80)

A great action can be understood only in a large circle of relations, Wagner proceeds. The poet must gauge the compass of this circle and examine the relations it contains in detail. His understanding of these things will permit him to make them understandable as a drama, which he does by shrinking the circle, by condensing it to the circumference that conveys an understanding of the central hero. This condensation (*Verdichtung*) is the poet's proper work.

Wagner describes the poet as a receiver and an imparter. Appearances (or the phenomena of life) are grasped initially by feeling, then conveyed to the understanding by way of the imagination (or fantasy). To impart what it has recognized, the understanding reverses the process and reaches the feeling through the imagination. The image received by the understanding is broken up in the process of understanding but must be restored in order for it to be transformed into feeling once again: "This image of the phenomena, in which alone the feeling can comprehend them, and which the understanding, to make itself intelligible to the feeling, must model on that image that the latter originally brought it through the fantasy . . . this image is nothing other than *the wonderful [Das Wunder]*" (p. 81). The wonderful makes the nature of things comprehensible to the feeling.

In what follows, Wagner shows how condensation serves the purpose of strengthening the chief motives of the action. In the interest of intelligibility, the poet must limit the number of components of the action. But the motives contained in the components he eliminates must be fitted into the motives of the main action. They must be included in the chief motive in such a way that they strengthen it. The strengthening of a motive requires a strengthening of the component of action itself, which is nothing but the fitting utterance of that motive and which can be strengthened only by lifting it above ordinary human experience through the poetic creation of the wonderful. Wagner tries repeatedly—but without full success—to clarify the crucial process of strengthening a dramatic motive. The strengthening of a motive, he explains finally, is not the addition of lesser motives but the absorption of many motives into one. An interest common to various men at various times and under various circumstances is to be made the interest of one man at one given time and under given circumstances:

In the interest of this man, all outward differences are to be raised into one definite thing, in which, however, the interest must reveal itself according to its greatest, most exhaustive compass. But this is as good as saying that from this interest all that savors of the particularistic and accidental must be taken away, and it must be given in its full truth as a necessary, purely human *utterance of feeling.* (pp. 89–90)

Wagner has arrived at his goal; verbal speech must now become *tonal speech,* which is "the beginning and end of verbal speech, as *feeling* is the beginning and end of understanding, as *myth* is the beginning and end of history, the *lyric* the beginning and end of poetry" (p. 91).

The first human mode of expression, Wagner asserts as though it were established fact, was a succession of vowels, a melodic language of emotion, accompanied by gesture, from which it took its rhythm. It appeared "to be nothing but the simultaneous inner expression of an outer announcement through those gestures" (p. 92). To denote and distinguish between outer objects, the feeling cast about for distinctive garments to clothe the open tone and fitted dumb articulations onto the open sounds to initiate or terminate them so that they were enveloped and made definite just as the objects were—animals by their skin, trees by their bark, and so on. These roots of speech were set together according to likeness of sound to produce alliteration and assonance, and this also knit like objects into one collective image for the feeling.

The poet's intention is never realized, Wagner maintains, until it passes from the understanding to the feeling. At the same time, a concentration of the phenomena of human life produces a simplification of them, an intensification of the motives of action, and a consequent strengthening of the components of action: "But a motive can gain an accession of strength only through the ascension of the various intellectual factors contained in it into one decisive factor *of feeling;* while the poet in words can arrive at imparting this convincingly only through the primal organ of the soul's inner feeling— through *tonal speech*" (p. 99). This tonal speech must be employed from the beginning of the drama, for the strengthened motives and components of action—raised above those of ordinary life—demand a basis that is itself also raised above ordinary life and its habitual means of expression.

This expression is the prime condition for the realization of the poetic intention, without which it

> could never step from the realm of thought into that of actuality. But the sole effectual expression here is an *altogether different one* from that of the poetic understanding's own organ of speech. The understanding is therefore driven by necessity to wed itself with an element that shall be able to take up into it the poet's intention as a fertilizing seed and so to nourish and shape this seed by its own necessary essence that it may bring it forth as a realizing and redeeming utterance of feeling. (pp. 101–2)

A <u>sexual conception</u> of the relation of word and tone, which Wagner proceeds to elaborate, is the ultimate formulation of his insight into the nature of dramatic melody and into the nature of musical drama, insofar as this is represented by a sung text. His insight into the melody of Bellini has finally received an elaborate, theoretical parallel that leads to a freer and more flexible musical form.

In the third part of *Opera and Drama*—"The Arts of Poetry and Tone in the Drama of the Future"—Wagner turns first to the problem of the relation between poetic verse and melody. Three features of poetry are relevant to this consideration: meter (which is accentual rather than quantitative), end rhyme, and the rhetorical or prose accent that is evident in a spoken delivery and that expresses the meaning of the verse. Wagner's argument is well presented in a fairly long summary statement toward the end of the first section of his plan for the drama of the future. The whole dispute in the different conceptions of melody, Wagner asserts,

> has revolved around the question of whether, and how, the melody should be governed by the verse. The ready-made melody, essentially obtained from dance—the melody that alone represents the essence of melody as our modern ear can conceive it—will in no way accommodate itself to the speaking accent of the verse. This accent shows itself now in this, now in that member of the verse and never returns to the same position in the line because our poets have flattered their fancy with the will-o'-the-wisp of either a prosodically rhythmic verse or a verse become melodic through its end rhyme and for the sake of this phantom have forgotten to take the actual living accent of speech as the only factor of the verse that can determine the rhythm. (p. 114)

Poets have not even placed the speech accent on the end rhyme, Wagner says. In fact, the end rhyme often falls on a syllable that is entirely without emphasis. But a melody can impress itself on the ear, Wagner contends, and be apprehended by it only if there is a repetition of definite components of melody in a definite rhythm. If such components do not return at all or if they return on a part of the measure that does not correspond to their original position, the melody will lack the bond of unity that would make it a melody. If repeated melodic components do correspond, however, the melody will not fit the verse, for the only accent of the verse that is not merely imaginary is the speech accent, which conveys the meaning of the verse but does not coincide with the necessary recurrence of the melodic and rhythmic accents of the melody. The musician, however,

> who does not wish to sacrifice his melody, but to give it forth before all else—since in it alone can he address the feeling intelligibly—seems

himself therefore compelled to attend to the speech accent only where it *accidentally* coincides with the melody. But this is tantamount to giving up all cohesion of the melody with the verse: for once the musician leaves the speaking accent out of account, far less can he feel any compunction as to the imaginary prosodic rhythm. (p. 115)

Wagner then abandons verse (in the usual sense of the term) and takes the prose of ordinary speech as a basis for the heightened expression of music. This leads him—through a lengthy process of reasoning—to a particular kind of alliterative poetry that is free of meter and end rhyme (the line offered as an illustration of this *Stabreim* is "Die Liebe bringt Lust und— Leid"). "In frank emotion," Wagner says, "when we let go all conventional consideration for the spun-out modern phrase, we try to express ourselves as definitely as possible, briefly and to the point, *in one breath*":

> The harm of our complex modern phrase, as regards the expression of feeling, has consisted in its being overstocked with unemphatic accessory words, which have consumed the speaker's breath to such an extent that, already exhausted or for the sake of holding his breath in reserve, he could dwell only briefly on the main accent. Thus a comprehension of the hastily accented main word could be imparted only to the understanding, but not to the feeling, since it needs the *fullness* of a sensuous expression to rouse the interest of the feeling. (pp. 119, 120)

These requirements are met by eliminating from the poetry everything concerning historical and social relationships and religious dogma—everything that appeals to the understanding and cannot be imparted to feeling. What remains is the purely human content.

In the course of his discussion, Wagner identifies two different functions of consonants: outward and inward: "The first function of the *consonant* consists in this: that it raises the open sound of the root to a definite characteristic by firmly hedging in its infinitely fluid element and through the lines of this delimitation it brings to the vowel's color, in a sense, the drawing that makes of it an exactly distinguishable shape" (p. 129). This function is exercised mostly by an initial consonant; a terminal consonant usually conditions the vowel less than it is conditioned by it. Repetition of an initial consonant is necessary to arouse attentive interest, and in the alliteration of two root words their connection in a phrase is grasped by feeling as an utterance of feeling.

The second or inward function of a consonant determines the character of the vowel: "Just as the consonant hedges the vowel from without, so does it also bound the vowel within: that is, it determines the specific nature of the vowel's manifestation by the roughness or smoothness of its inward contact with it" (pp. 133–34). Here Wagner tries to elucidate his conception by means of an elaborate analogy which is so curious and so typical of his mode of thought that it deserves extended quotation:

> We have called the enclosing consonants the garment of the vowel, or, more precisely, its physiognomic exterior. In view of their inward agency, let us call them still more accurately the fleshy covering of the human body, organically ingrown with the interior. We thus shall gain a faithful image of the essence of both consonant and vowel as well as of their organic relations to one another. If we take the vowel for the whole inner organism of man's living body, which prescribes from itself the shaping of its outward manifestation as offered to the eye of the beholder, then we have to ascribe to the consonants—beyond the outward function of displaying themselves to the eye as that outward manifestation—the additional important function of bringing to the inner organism through the branching conduits of the sense organs those outward impressions that in turn determine this inner organism to a particular employment of its faculty of utterance. Just as the fleshy covering of the human body has a skin that hedges it outward from the eye, so has it also a skin turned inward to the inner vital organs. Yet through this inner skin it is nowise completely sundered from these organs but clings together with them in such a fashion as to win from them its nourishment and power of outward shaping. The blood, that bodily sap that in unbroken flow alone can mete out life, this blood drives onward from the heart, in virtue of that connection of the fleshy covering with the inner organs, and thrusts to the outermost skin of this flesh. From thence, leaving behind it the needed nourishment, it flows back to the heart again, and the heart, as though in an overfill of inner riches, now pours forth through the lungs—which had brought the outer stream of air for the blood's vitalization and freshening— this stream of air pregnant with its own impassioned content, this most direct outward manifestation of its inmost living warmth. This heart is the *open sound*, in its richest, least dependent energy. Its vitalizing blood, which it outwardly condensed into the consonant, it turns back from this consonant to its primal seat since its overfill could never be consumed in that condensation. And now, with its blood directly vitalized by the stream of air, the heart in utmost fullness breathes *itself* without. (pp. 134–35)

All the vowels are fundamentally akin to one another, Wagner maintains, as is suggested by the practice of alliterating different vowels ("Aug' und

Ohr"). But this kinship becomes unmistakable with the use of musical tone, which gives full value to the vowel's emotional content. The vowel is nothing but a "condensed tone," and the individuality it has acquired from an outer object through its initial consonant is expanded by tone into the universality of pure emotion.

Approaching his projected drama more closely, Wagner considers the nature of key and modulation, which he discusses in terms of human relationships:

> The *key* is the most tightly bound and most closely interrelated *family* of the entire *genus of tone;* it shows itself to be truly related to the whole genus of tone, however, where it progresses, through the inclination of the individual members of the tonal family, to an automatic connection with other keys. We can compare the key very fittingly here with the old patriarchal genealogical families of the human races: in these families the members were conceived in accordance with an involuntary error as special people, not as members of the whole human genus; it was the sexual love of the individual, however—which was kindled not by an accustomed but only by an unaccustomed appearance—that surmounted the confines of the patriarchal family and secured the connection to other families. (p. 148)

In a larger musical composition, Wagner continues, the underlying relation of all keys is brought before us in the light of a particular principal key. The "patriarchal" melody is illustrated by Beethoven's "Ode to Joy," which was not Beethoven's goal, Wagner says, but represented an intentional lowering of his inventive power in order that he might grasp the hand of the poet:

> As he feels the hand of the poet in his own with this simple, confined melody, he now strides forward on the poem and out of this poem, shaping in accordance with its spirit and its form, to ever bolder and more manifold tonal construction, so that finally marvels arise before us from the power of poetic tonal speech—marvels such as we previously never even suspected, marvels like "Seid umschlungen, Millionen!" "Ahnest du den Schöpfer, Welt?" and finally the securely intelligible concord of the "Seid umschlungen" with the "Freude, schöne Götterfunken!" If we now compare the broad melodic structure in the musical realization of the whole verse "Seid umschlungen" with the melody that the master only spread out, so to speak, from the means of absolute music over the verse "Freude, schöne Götterfunken," we will then obtain an exact understanding of the difference between the patriarchal melody—as I

called it—and the melody growing up over the linguistic verse out of the poetic intention. (pp. 150–51)

Wagner develops the relation between the poetic intention and modulation, taking as a basis the relation of different feelings:

The alliterative verse, as we saw, already connected speech roots of opposed emotional expression in sensuous hearing (like "Lust und Leid" [pleasure and pain], "Wohl und Weh" [weal and woe]) and presented them to the feeling as generically related. On a higher level of expression by far, musical modulation is now able to make such a connection intuitive to feeling. If we take, for example, an alliterative verse of completely unchanging emotional content, like "Liebe giebt Lust zum Leben" [Love gives light to life], the musician would also receive here, just as in the alliterative roots of the accents the same feeling revealed itself sensuously, no natural impulse to depart from the key originally chosen, but instead he would define the rise and fall of the tone for the feeling with complete sufficiency within the same key. If we contrast with this a verse of mixed feeling, like "Die Liebe bringt Lust und Leid" [Love brings pleasure and pain], the musician could feel impelled here, just as the alliterative verse connects two opposed feelings, also to change over from the key first sounded, that corresponds to the first feeling, to a second key corresponding to the second feeling, which is defined according to its relation to the feeling of the first key. The word *Lust*, which as the highest intensification of the first feeling seems to press toward the second, would have to receive a totally different emphasis in this phrase than in the former, "die Liebe giebt Lust zum Leben." (p. 152)

"Lust" would be sung to the leading tone of the second key, Wagner says, with the result that the phrase "Lust und Leid" discloses a resultant feeling that embodies the relation of the two opposed feelings. Furthermore, he continues, modulation can also lead back from the second feeling to the first:

If after "Die Liebe bringt Lust und Leid" we allow to follow as a second verse "Doch in ihr Weh auch webt sie Wonnen" [Yet in its plaint it also plaits pleasure], then *webt* would now become the leading tone to the first key, just as the second feeling returns from here to the first again, which is now enriched—a return that the poet could represent to the sensuous emotive perception by virtue of the alliterative verse only as a progress of the feeling of *Weh* into that of *Wonnen*, but not as a termination of the emotional genus *Liebe*, while the musician becomes perfectly understandable precisely through the fact that he quite noticeably goes back to the first key and therefore designates the generic feeling definitely as a unified one, which was not possible to the poet, who had to change the sound of the root in the alliterative verse. (p. 153)

But the poet indicated the generic feeling, Wagner points out, by the meaning of both verses and thus called on the musician to realize this meaning in terms of feeling. The scheme of modulation, then, which would appear arbitrary from the point of view of absolute music, is an outcome of the poetic intention. Wagner continues to elaborate the drama he envisages, imagining that the general meaning of the two verses is set forth

in such a manner that between the progression away from the one feeling and the soon consummated return to it in the second verse a quite lengthy series of verses expressed the most manifold intensification and mixture of feelings lying in between, in part strengthening and in part appeasing, up to the final return to the principal feeling. Here the musical modulation, in order to realize the poetic intention, would have to lead into and back from the most various keys; all the keys touched on, however, would appear in an exact familial relationship to the original key, by which the special light they cast on the expression is indeed qualified and the capacity for this illumination in a certain measure even first bestowed. The principal key, as the fundamental tone of the feeling that is sounded, would manifest in itself an original relatedness to all keys and consequently, by virtue of its expression, make the appointed feeling known during its utterance in an intensity and extension such that only what was related to it could specify our emotion, such that our general emotional capacity would be filled solely by this feeling by virtue of its increased extension, and such that this single feeling would accordingly be elevated to an all-encompassing, universally human, and infallibly intelligible one.

If the poetic-musical *period* has herewith been characterized as it is defined in accordance with a principal key, then we can provisionally characterize *that* work of art as the one most perfect for expression in which many such periods are represented in the greatest fullness in such a way that one is conditional on the other and they develop into a rich collective revelation in which the nature of man in a major decisive direction, that is, in a direction that is able to comprehend human nature in itself completely (just as a principal key is able to comprehend in itself all other keys), is presented to the feeling with the greatest certainty and tangibility. (pp. 153–54)

In spite of the originality of this important passage, which describes both the poetic-musical period and the entire drama based on it, we should not fail to observe that the fundamental idea of a relation of keys as the counterpart of a relation of feelings was clearly formulated by Lacépède in 1785 and that the conception also has a distant ancestry at the very beginning of the monodic style, for it is adumbrated, at any rate, in terms of consonances in Jacopo Peri's foreword to the score of his opera *Euridice* (1601).[9]

The fourth and fifth sections of the third part of *Opera and Drama* are devoted to the orchestra. In order for the melodic progression from one key to another to realize the poetic intention, Wagner argues, the help of harmony is essential. The conception is much like that of Rameau, who called for fullness of harmony so that the tendencies of harmonic progression would be unequivocal. Wagner likewise insists on full realization, "for only that is an organic work of art that encloses in itself and communicates to the most distinct perception the conditioning together with the condition."[10]

Harmony, or polyphony, however, cannot be presented by human voices that accompany the melody of the main character, for the drama of the future has no place for subordinate individualities:

> With the density and intensification of the motives as well as the actions, only participants in the action can be thought of who exert a decisive influence on this at every moment through the necessary, individual pronouncement. . . . Even the *chorus* used previously in the opera . . . will have to disappear in *our* drama. . . . A mass can never interest us, but instead simply disconcert us: only exactly distinguishable individualities can capture our sympathy. (p. 162)

In the drama of the future, Wagner further maintains, lyricism will grow out of the motives that are condensed before our eyes; it will not occur unmotivated at the outset.

It is only the orchestra, then, that can serve to make harmony perceptible. The orchestra is distinct from human voices both in its expressive capacities and in its tone color. The tone of a musical instrument, in its detachment from the word, "resembles that primeval tone of human speech that only with the consonant condensed itself into the actual vowel and in its connections—as opposed to today's speech in words—becomes a special language that still has only a relation of feeling, but not of understanding, to actual human speech." Now this pure tonal speech, Wagner continues, has secured in the individuality of the instruments

> a special individual peculiarity that is defined by the *consonant* character, so to speak, of the instrument much like speech in words is by

the consonantal articulations. We could designate a musical instrument in its defining influence on the peculiarity of the tone to be announced by it as the consonant *initial rootlike sound*, which represents itself for all the tones to be made possible on it as the *uniting alliteration*. The relatedness of instruments among themselves would very easily permit a definition in accordance with the similarity of the initial sound, which according to circumstances might reveal itself almost as a softer or harder pronunciation of the same consonant originally held in common. We possess in fact instrumental families to which an originally equivalent initial sound is proper, which is simply graduated according to the varied character of the family members. (pp. 165–66)

The ramified individuality of the powers of speech of the orchestra, however, will be recognized only when the orchestra participates more intimately in the drama than it has so far, "when it largely has been used only for luxurious decoration" (p. 166).

Because of the difference between the orchestra and the voice with respect to tone color, the human voice should not be used as an essential constituent of the instrumental harmony, but neither should the vocal melody be duplicated in the instrumental accompaniment, for this would make the voice superfluous. But this dilemma, Wagner argues, is the result of the vocal presentation of "absolute melody," that is, melody carried over to the voice from instruments. Melody of such a kind is only damaged by vowels and consonants. In contrast, vocal melody should proceed both intellectually and sensuously from the verse; it should be the offspring of poetry and music, the bond of connection and understanding between the verbal and tonal languages. Wagner discusses the relation of this "verse melody" to the orchestra in terms of the relation of a rowboat to a lake:

Yet the boat does not rove on top of the surface of the mirror of water: the lake can carry it in a sure direction only if the part of its body that is turned directly toward the water sinks into it. A thin board that touches only the upper surface of the lake is thrown hither and thither without direction by its waves according to whichever way they are running, while on the other hand a heavy stone necessarily sinks down into it. But not only the side of the boat's body that directly faces the lake sinks into it; the rudder also, with which its direction is determined, and the oars, which provide motion in this direction, receive this determining and impelling force only through their contact with the water, a contact that first makes possible the effective pressure of the guiding hand. With each forward-driving motion the oars cut deeply into the sounding surface of the water; raised out of it, they allow the liquid clinging to them to run back again in melodic drops. (p. 192)

The following section (the fifth) of the third part of *Opera and Drama* distinguishes three functions of the orchestra, which in general, Wagner maintains, has a capacity for "speech"—namely, a capacity for disclosing what is unutterable in words. The expression conveyed by corporeal gesture—which is the defining feature of the first orchestral function—is also unutterable in verbal language. But when feeling is concerned, the expression of words requires intensification by gesture:

> In its communication to the eye—which had become necessary—gesture here uttered precisely what verbal language was no longer able to express; if it could have, then the gesture would have been superfluous and disturbing. The eye was therefore excited by the gesture in a way still lacking the corresponding counterpart of the communication to hearing: this counterpart, however, is necessary for the completion of the impression so that it becomes one fully understandable to the feeling. The verse, which in its excitation has become melody, ultimately does dissolve the conceptual content of the original verbal communication into an emotive content: but the component of the communication to the ear that corresponds fully to gesture is still not contained in this melody. (p. 175)

The auditory counterpart of gesture is provided by the orchestra. The basis of this orchestral capacity can be found in dance "since the gesture of dance, like gesture in general, is related to orchestral melody almost as verse is to the vocal melody conditioned by it, so that gesture *and* orchestral melody really constitute just such a whole, understandable in itself, as the melody of tonal speech taken alone" (p. 176). But the gesture called for by the drama Wagner projects requires an intensification above the level of the ordinary gesture of speech and involving also the figure, countenance, attitude, motion, and dress of the individual character.

The inner state of a person, however, is not always truthfully revealed by gesture; it is revealed instead by the verse melody, which can actualize remembered feeling, for example, as present feeling. The words of the verse melody contain the past feeling as it is thought of and described; the melody itself contains the new, present feeling that arises from the absent feeling and that is experienced by the audience as well as by the dramatic character. When this character, in thinking of this manifestation of feeling, feels impelled again by his recollection to announce a new and once more present feeling, he only portrays this recollection to the understanding, just as he had revealed to us in the same verse melody, now familiar, the recollection of an earlier feeling as a thought creative of feeling:

> We, however—we who receive the new communication—are able to take hold of that feeling, now still only recollected, *in its purely melodic manifestation itself,* through the hearing: it has become the property of pure music and is brought to us as the *actualization,* the *presence,* of what has just now only been *thought.* Such a melody, just as it has been imparted to us by the actor as the outpouring of a feeling, makes actual to us the thought of this actor when it is performed expressively by the orchestra at the time when the actor still harbors that feeling only in his memory; indeed, even when the present informant appears no longer even aware of that feeling, the characteristic sounding of the melody in the orchestra can arouse in us a feeling that becomes a *thought*—for the completion of a context, for the highest intelligibility of a situation through the interpretation of motives that are indeed contained in this situation but cannot come into clear appearance in their representable components—but that in itself is *more* than the thought, namely the *emotive content* of the thought *made present.* . . .
>
> Music cannot think; it can, however, actualize thoughts, that is, reveal its emotive content as a no-longer-remembered one but as one made present: it can do this, however, only when its own message is qualified by the poetic intention, and this again reveals itself, not as something only thought, but first of all as clearly expounded through the organ of the understanding, spoken language. (pp. 184–85)

Thus, a motive connects a determining feeling not present with one determined by it and now appearing. We perceive the organic growth of one feeling from another, Wagner says, and "endow our feeling with the power of thinking, which here, however, is the involuntary knowledge, elevated above thinking, of the thought that is actualized in feeling" (p. 185). The adoption of the verse melody produces the second, or recollective, function of the orchestra.

The third function is that of foreboding, which is the conveying of a feeling that is still unutterable. The stirring of this feeling is the demand of the feeling for definition by an object:

> Such a foreboding mood the poet has to awaken in us *in order through its demand to make us ourselves joint creators of the work of art.* . . .
> In the production of such moods as the poet must awaken in us for the indispensable cooperation on our part, the absolute language of in-

struments has already shown itself to be all powerful, for precisely the arousal of undefined feelings was its most characteristic effect, which had to become a weakness everywhere that it also sought to define the aroused feelings clearly. . . .

What presents itself to our eye from a natural scene or from a silent, gestureless human appearance, and directs our feeling through the eye to calm contemplation, music is able to conduct to the feeling in such a way that, departing from the element of calmness, this feeling moves toward tension and expectation and thus awakens precisely the desire that the poet requires on our part as an aid making possible the revelation of his intention. This arousal of our feeling in the direction of a definite object the poet in fact requires even to prepare us for a defining appearance to the eye, that is, even so as not to present to us the appearance of the natural scene or of the human individualities until our aroused expectation of them qualifies them, in the way they are revealed, as necessary because they correspond to the expectation. (pp. 186–87, 189)

The experience of music in this respect will remain totally vague and undefined, Wagner takes the occasion to remark, as long as it does not take up into itself the poetic intention of the drama. With this intention, the expectation and foreboding will make the particular appearances of the drama present to the feeling as wonderful and standing out above ordinary life.

Wagner then considers (in the sixth section of the third part of *Opera and Drama*) the construction of the drama as a whole. There is to be a single unified expression that will have its focus in the verse melody and its uniting bond in the orchestra. The dramatic situation, like the verse melody, will be unintelligible if it is readymade. Instead, the drama must be led forth in continuous growth, and it must make the audience organic helpers in that growth:

Plastic art can display solely the finished, that is, the motionless, so that it can never make the beholder a confident witness to the becoming of a thing. In his furthest strayings, the absolute musician fell into the error of copying plastic art in this and presenting the finished in place of the becoming. The drama alone is the work of art that so addresses itself in space and time to our eye and ear that we take an active share in its becoming and therefore can grasp the become as a necessity, as a thing that our feeling clearly understands. (p. 192)

Like Lacépède in the eighteenth century, Wagner emphasizes the importance of not interrupting the continuity of this organic growth. The point of departure must be in predicaments that have a recognizable likeness to those of ordinary life. From the very beginning, the orchestra must arouse expectancy and foreboding. These can then find fulfillment only in tonal speech. The necessary conditions of the drama can be set forth only in words if they are to be understood, but this speech must already be wedded to tone and will grow into actual tonal speech as the dramatic wonder appears and then finally blossom into melody in expression of the purely human core of a sure and settled feeling. A situation arising and culminating in such a way will be a distinct section of the drama.

A unified artistic form in general, Wagner continues, will be the manifestation of a unified content. This content in turn can be made manifest only by a unified means of expression, and this means, finally, must contain the poet's intention in each of its components. The unified expression will then be sustained by the give and take of these components. Whenever the tonal speech is more verbal than tonal, for the sake of defining the dramatic situation or keeping in touch with the moods of ordinary life, the orchestra will compensate for this lowered expression by conveying a foreboding or remembrance. Such melodic orchestral components will become guides to feeling throughout the drama. They will withdraw into the background whenever the protagonist advances to the full expression of the verse melody, which the orchestra will then merely support, until the verse melody declines again to an essentially verbal speech in tones, at which time the orchestra will resume its compensatory function.

The melodic moments of foreboding and remembrance arise only from those important motives of the drama that correspond to the basic motives of the concentrated action, that are the pillars of the dramatic structure, and that are few enough to be easily surveyed. The necessary repetition of such musical motives will produce the highest unity of the musical form of the whole drama, in which the content can impart itself to the feeling in a completely intelligible expression and in such a way that the feeling is both stirred and satisfied: "*The content, then, has to be one that is ever present in the expression and therefore the expression one that ever presents the content in its fullest compass, for only thought can grasp the absent, but only the present can be grasped by feeling*" (p. 203). This unity of the expression, Wagner concludes, replaces the traditionally required unity of time and space with the unity of the dramatic action, for the continuous expression of this action keeps it continuously present.

In the seventh and last section of the third part of *Opera and Drama*, Wagner returns to a question that had been examined long before by E. T. A. Hoffmann. What should the relation be between the dramatic poet and the dramatic musician? They should not restrict one another, Wagner says, nor should each display his own talent independently or, on the other hand, practice self-restraint. Instead, each should arouse the other's highest powers through love. Every moment of the musical expression must contain the poetic intention, he insists, and the poetry must be realizable completely in the musical expression. "So let us finally denote the measure of poetic worth as follows: as Voltaire said of the opera, 'What is too silly to be said, one has sung,' then let us reverse that maxim for the drama that we have in view and say, *What is not worth singing neither is worth the poet's pains of telling*" (p. 208).

Poet and musician need not be combined in a single person, Wagner continues. In fact, the musician should be younger and instinctive rather than reflective. Much of this final section of the treatise is subsequently devoted to a description of the operatic situation that Wagner finds around him. There is an extended general discussion of language. Of the three operatic nations, Wagner maintains—the Italian, French, and German—"the *German* alone possesses a language whose daily usage still hangs directly and conspicuously together with its roots. Italians and Frenchmen speak a tongue whose radical meaning can be brought home to them only by a study of older, so-called dead languages: one might say that their language . . . speaks for them, but not that they themselves speak in their language" (p. 211).

German is closer to nature than French and Italian, and only German is suited to revitalize the expression of art, for it is the only language "that in daily life has retained the accent on the root syllable" (pp. 211–12). In Wagner's view, the indispensable basis of a perfect artistic expression is provided by ordinary speech. The discussion proceeds to the failings of German operatic singers and to the evils of texts that are translated into German from Italian and French. As he does throughout the treatise, Wagner continually contrasts the failings of operatic practice with the virtues of the musical drama he is designing for the future. This drama is obstructed by every aspect of conventional operatic life. Finally, he turns on the public: "Let us suppose for an instant that in some way or other we acquired the power of so working on performers and performance, from the standpoint of artistic intelligence, that a highest dramatic intention should be fully carried out. Then for the first time we should grow actively aware that we lacked the real enabler of the work of art, a public to feel the need of it" (p. 225). The public wants simply to distract itself, Wagner complains. It seeks artificial detail, not an artistic unity. The nobility had fine taste and feeling, but taste is now ruled by the Philistine, who orders the work of art and pays for it and who opposes innovation: "As this Philistine is the most heartless and the basest offspring of our civilization, so is he the most domineering, the cruelest and foulest of art's bread givers" (p. 226). Wagner can find no hope in the statesman, politician, socialist, or philosopher—only in the artist, who "longs for the only truth—*the human being*" and who has the power "of seeing beforehand a yet unshapen world, of tasting beforehand the joys of a world as yet unborn" (p. 227).

With Herbert Spencer, the realistic conception of musical feeling assumed a more specifically biological character, and this ostensibly scientific context became a feature of English musical thought that persisted into the early twentieth century. Spencer was concerned with the origin of music and with its function in human life. Insofar as the "origin" and "function" of music refer to its first appearance in evolutionary development and its first function—and it is this that Spencer evidently has in mind—any descriptive process we envisage will have its justification solely in its explanatory power, for clearly no evidence on the matter is available. While the value that resides in Wagner's ideas will have its measure in the value of the drama based on them, the worth of Spencer's theory will have its measure in its ability to account for the properties of music in general. Thus, although an evolutionary conception of music plays an important role in Wagner's aesthetics, the ultimate significance and value of this aesthetic rests not on its evolutionary basis but on its artistic outcome.

Spencer opens his controversial essay "The Origin and Function of Music" (1857) with what he evidently considers to be "evidence" in some sense of the term: the behavior of animals. Dogs, cats, and so on display muscular excitement when they experience joy or rage or pain, and humans do the same: "In ourselves, distinguished from lower creatures by feelings alike more powerful and more varied, parallel facts are at once more conspicuous and more numerous. We may conveniently look at them in groups. We shall find that pleasurable sensations and painful sensations, pleasurable emotions and painful emotions, all tend to produce active demonstrations in proportion to their intensity." [11] After citing numerous examples in illustration of this idea, Spencer continues, "All feelings, then—sensations or emotions, pleasurable or painful—have this common characteristic that they are muscular stimuli." He states as a general law that "alike in man and animals there is a direct connection between feeling and movement, the last growing more vehement as the first grows more intense" (p. 397). In fact, Spencer claims, this law depends on the physiological principle of reflex action: These initial considerations are then applied to music. "All music is originally vocal. All vocal sounds are produced by the agency of certain muscles. These muscles, in common with those of the body at large, are excited to contraction by pleasurable and painful feelings. And therefore it is that feelings demonstrate themselves in sounds as well as in movements" (p. 397).

Spencer proceeds, however, with more questionable deductions. The muscles that move the chest, larynx, and vocal chords contract in proportion to the intensity of the feelings, he argues, and every different contraction of these muscles will involve a different adjustment of the vocal organs, which differences in turn will cause changes in the sound emitted. It follows, Spencer claims, that "variations of voice are the physiological results of variations of feeling." Each inflection or modulation, he asserts, "is the natural outcome of some passing emotion or sensation; and it follows that the explanation of all kinds of vocal expression must be sought in this general relation between mental and muscular excitements" (pp. 397–98). But even if emotional experiences caused vocal expressions that corresponded to them, which is certainly not the case all the time, we cannot go on to say that "all kinds of vocal expression" have such an origin. Step by step we are being led to conclusions that are less and less justified, for Spencer conveniently overlooks the fact that not all emotions and sensations produce overt muscular contractions as well as the fact that not all vocal expression arises from real emotional experience. He goes on, nevertheless, to try to account for the chief characteristics of vocal utterance in terms of his theory.

Loudness presents no difficulty, for it reflects the strength of the air expelled, which in turn, Spencer says, is caused by the force of the contraction of certain muscles of the chest and abdomen. These in turn are proportionate to the intensity of the feeling experienced. Vocal quality or timbre is similarly explained, for in states of excitement "the tones are more sonorous than usual," in ill temper the voice "acquires a metallic ring" (p. 398), and the voice of an eloquent speaker becomes more resonant in emotional passages. With respect to pitch, ordinary and calm speaking will use medium tones, while those used in excited states will be higher or lower and rise or fall increasingly as the feelings grow stronger. Intervals of pitch show a similar variability: calm speech is comparatively monotonous, while emotion employs wide intervals. The variations of pitch, finally, become increasingly rapid under the influence of emotion.

Thus, vocal phenomena have a physiological basis, Spencer maintains; they manifest the general law that feeling is a stimulus to muscular action:

The expressiveness of these various modifications of voice is therefore innate. Each of us, from babyhood upwards, has been spontaneously making them, when under the various sensations and emotions by which they are produced. Having been conscious of each feeling at the same time that we heard ourselves make the consequent sound, we have acquired an established association of ideas between such sound and the feeling which caused it. When the like sound is made by another, we ascribe the like feeling to him; and by a further consequence we not only ascribe to him that feeling, but have a certain degree of it aroused in ourselves. Thus these various modifications of voice become not only a language through which we understand the emotions of others, but also the means of exciting our sympathy with such emotions.

Spencer then applies these general considerations to music: "These vocal peculiarities which indicate excited feeling, *are those which especially distinguish song from ordinary speech*. Every one of the alterations of voice which we have found to be a physiological result of pain or pleasure, *is carried to its greatest extreme in vocal music*" (p. 400). Just as impassioned utterance is loud, so is song as compared to speech. Just as emotional tones are sonorous, so the singing tone is the most resonant we can produce. Just as mental excitement gives rise to the higher and lower notes of the vocal register, so does vocal music habitually employ tones above and below those of speech, especially—for its most passionate effects—the tones at the upper extremity of the vocal range. Just as strong feeling makes use of larger intervals than those of ordinary conversation, so is this trait systematically elaborated in every ballad and aria, while the directions of these intervals have similar meanings in music, diverging from or converging toward the medium tones to express increasing or decreasing emotion. Rapid variations of pitch, finally, are characteristic of mental excitement in speech and are at least as evident in vocal melody. "Thus in respect alike of *loudness, timbre, pitch, intervals,* and *rate of variation,* song employs and exaggerates the natural language of the emotions—it arises from a systematic combination of those vocal peculiarities which are the physiological effects of acute pleasure and pain" (p. 401).

Spencer also cites various minor features found in both speech and song: trembling of the voice in extreme anger, fear, hope, or joy; staccato execution in energetic passages that express exhilaration, resolution, or confidence; slurred intervals to express gentler and less active feelings; and slow changes of pitch in largo and adagio movements to express grief or reverence or faster changes to express various degrees of mental vivacity. Rhythm is similarly an expression of strong feeling, Spencer maintains, and he cites not only music but also dance, oratory, and poetry. Although he will not undertake to explain definitely "the more special peculiarities of musical expression," Spencer states, they probably "all in some way conform to the principle that has been worked out." Indeed, it is impracticable to trace the principle in its more ramified applications, he says, and it is not necessary to his argument to do so: "The foregoing facts sufficiently prove that what we regard as the distinctive traits of song are simply the traits of emotional speech intensified and systematized. In respect of its general characteristics, we think it has been made clear that vocal music, and by consequence all music, is an idealization of the natural language of passion" (p. 402).

This permits him to infer that vocal music diverged from emotional speech in a gradual manner. Just as recitative, for example, arose by degrees from emotional speech, so song arose from recitative by a continuation of the same process. In poetry, similarly, the lyric grew out of the epic as the appropriate vehicle to express the stronger passions. Spencer emphasizes the gradual nature of this developmental process. It proceeds by degrees from a monotonous, primitive state to the highest form of vocal music, which has great complexity and range. There was a gradual accumulation of changes, in response to increasing strength of feeling:

> Not only may we so understand how more sonorous tones, greater extremes of pitch, and wider intervals were gradually introduced, but also how there arose a greater variety and complexity of musical expression. For this same more passionate, enthusiastic temperament which naturally leads the musical composer to express the feelings possessed by others as well as himself, in extreme intervals and more marked cadences than they would use, also leads him to give musical utterance to feelings which they either do not experience, or experience in but slight degrees. . . . And thus we may in some measure understand how it happens that music not only so strongly excites our more familiar feelings, but also produces feelings we never had before—arouses dormant sentiments of which we had not conceived the possibility and do not know the meaning; or, as Richter says—tells us of things we have not seen and shall not see (p. 404).

Thus, differentiation joins development, leading finally to the production of feelings that are unknown in previous experience. This exploratory or inventive capacity of music was described again by Susanne Langer in 1942 (in *Philosophy in a New Key*), although she conceived it in respect of feeling that was "symbolic" rather than real.

In further support of his theory, Spencer now presents various kinds of "indirect evidence." It is impossible to account for the expressiveness of music in any other way, he argues. Do special combinations of notes have special effects on our emotions because they have intrinsic meanings apart from human constitution, or are their meanings conventional, learned like those of words? Rejecting these conceptions, Spencer characterizes music as "an idealized language of emotion," departing somewhat from a more strictly realistic theory, as he did in the idea of feelings that were previously unknown.

Again, the tones of the human voice are more pleasing than any others, and this will naturally be the case if music originates in the modulations of the voice under the influence of emotion. Furthermore, the genesis of music cannot be accounted for in any other way. Music is clearly the product of civilization; savages have only "the vaguest rudiment of music properly so called" (p. 405), and there is nothing from which it could have developed other than the modulations of the voice in states of emotion. Negative evidence confirms the positive.

Spencer finally considers the function of music. Does music have any effect beyond immediate pleasure? Generally, he argues, in fulfilling one desire, we facilitate the fulfillment of the others. Indeed, there is a general law of progress to the effect that human pursuits having a common root have gradually diverged to become distinct. They do not become truly independent, however, "but severally act and react on one another to their mutual advancement." This can be seen in the relation of speech and music. There are two elements in speech: words and tones, signs of ideas and signs of feelings. These have undergone a simultaneous development. Having its root in the feelingful component of speech, music "has all along been reacting upon speech, and increasing its power of rendering emotion":

> The use in recitative and song of inflections more expressive than ordinary ones, must from the beginning have tended to develop the ordinary ones. . . . The complex musical phrases by which composers have conveyed complex emotions, may rationally be supposed to have influenced us in making those involved cadences of conversation by which we convey our subtler thoughts and feelings. That the cultivation of music has no effect on the mind, few will be absurd enough to contend. And if it has an effect, what more natural effect is there than this of developing our perception of the meanings of inflections, qualities, and modulations of sound, and giving us a correspondingly increased power of using them? (p. 406)

Thus, the Italians, who excel in melody, also speak in more varied and expressive inflections and cadences than any other people. The Scots, in contrast, have a limited range of musical expression and are also unusually monotonous in the intervals and modulations of their speech.

Because of its function of facilitating the development of emotional speech, Spencer claims, music must assume the highest rank among the fine arts. It is the art that most ministers to human welfare, for the feelingful modifications of the voice in speech excite like feelings in others; they are the chief media of sympathy. It is by fellow feeling that men are led to behave justly and kindly to one another, that civilized humanity replaces barbarous cruelty:

Just as there has silently grown up a language of ideas, which, rude as it first was, now enables us to convey with precision the most subtle and complicated thoughts; so there is still silently growing up a language of feelings, which, notwithstanding its present imperfection, we may expect will ultimately enable men vividly and completely to impress on each other all the emotions which they experience from moment to moment. (p. 408)

A number of years after the publication of Spencer's essay, Charles Darwin's *The Descent of Man and Selection in Relation to Sex* (1871) presented a theory of the origin of music that differs significantly from that of Spencer. In discussing the secondary sexual characteristics of man, Darwin comes to speak of the voice and of human musical capacity. "Although the sounds emitted by animals of all kinds serve many purposes," he states, "a strong case can be made out, that the vocal organs were primarily used and perfected in relation to the propagation of the species." [12] The males of nearly every species of mammals use their voices much more during the breeding season than at any other time, and the male vocal organs of some quadrupeds become larger than those of the female during this season.

Concerning the human ear, Darwin cites the question of a critic as to how it could have been adapted by selection to distinguish musical notes. An ear that can distinguish noises, he points out—which is a capacity obviously of great importance—must also be sensitive to musical tones:

If it be further asked why musical tones in a certain order and rhythm give man and other animals pleasure, we can no more give the reason than for the pleasantness of certain tastes and smells. That they do give pleasure of some kind to animals we may infer from their being produced during the season of courtship by many insects, spiders, fishes, amphibians and birds; for unless the females were able to appreciate such sounds and were excited or charmed by them, the persevering efforts of the males, and the complex structures often possessed by them alone, would be useless; and this it is impossible to believe. (pp. 280–81)

Music does not arouse horror, fear, and rage, Darwin states, but the gentler feelings of tenderness and love. It also arouses the sense of triumph and the ardor for war. We can concentrate greater intensity of feeling in a single musical tone than in pages of writing:

It is probable that nearly the same emotions, but much weaker and far less complex, are felt by birds when the male pours forth his full volume of song, in rivalry with other males, to captivate the female. Love is still the commonest theme of our songs. . . . The sensations and ideas thus excited in us by music, or expressed by the cadences of oratory, appear from their vagueness, yet depth, like mental reversions to the emotions and thoughts of a long-past age.

All these facts with respect to music and impassioned speech become intelligible to a certain extent, if we may assume that musical tones and rhythm were used by our half-human ancestors, during the season of courtship, when animals of all kinds are excited not only by love, but by the strong passions of jealousy, rivalry, and triumph. From the deeply laid principle of inherited associations, musical tones in this case would be likely to call up vaguely and indefinitely the strong emotions of a long-past age. As we have every reason to suppose that articulate speech is one of the latest, as it certainly is the highest, of the arts acquired by man, and as the instinctive power of producing musical notes and rhythms is developed low down in the animal series, it would be altogether opposed to the principle of evolution, if we were to admit that man's musical capacity has been developed from the tones used in impassioned speech. We must suppose that the rhythms and cadences of oratory are derived from previously developed musical powers. (pp. 283–84)

We may go even further than this, Darwin claims, and believe that musical sounds were one of the bases for the development of language. He cites Spencer to the opposite effect:

He concludes, as did Diderot formerly, that the cadences used in emotional speech afford the foundation from which music has been developed; while I conclude that musical notes and rhythms were first acquired by the male or female progenitors of mankind for the sake of charming the opposite sex. Thus musical tones became firmly associated with some of the strongest passions an animal is capable of feeling, and are consequently used instinctively, or through association when strong emotions are expressed in speech. (p. 284n)

It appears probable, Darwin says by way of summary, that the progenitors of man, either the males or the females or both sexes, before acquiring the power of expressing their mutual love in articulate language, endeavored to charm each other with musical notes and rhythm: "The impassioned orator, bard, or musician, when with his varied tones and cadences he excites the strongest emotions in his hearers, little suspects that he uses the same means by which his half-human ancestors long ago aroused each other's ardent passions, during their courtship and rivalry" (p. 284).

Darwin returned to his musical theory the following year, in *The Expression of the Emotions in Man and Animal* (1872). Chapter 4 of this work, "Means of Expressions in Animals," deals first with the emission of sounds. "We have seen, in the last chapter," Darwin says, "that when the sensorium is strongly excited, the muscles of the body are generally thrown into violent action; and as a consequence, loud sounds are uttered, however silent the animal may generally be, and although the sounds may be of no use." Having been used habitually as a serviceable aid under conditions inducing pleasure, pain, rage, and so on, the voice "is commonly used whenever the same sensations of emotions are excited, under quite different conditions, or in a lesser degree":

> The sexes of many animals incessantly call for each other during the breeding season; and in not a few cases, the male endeavours thus to charm or excite the female. This, indeed, seems to have been the primeval use and means of development of the voice, as I have attempted to show in my *Descent of Man*. Thus the use of the vocal organs will have become associated with the anticipation of the strongest pleasure which animals are capable of feeling. Animals which live in society often call to each other when separated, and evidently feel much joy at meeting. . . . Woe betide the man who meddles with the young of the larger and fiercer quadrupeds, if they hear the cry of distress from their young. Rage leads to the violent exertion of all the muscles, including those of the voice; and some animals, when enraged, endeavour to strike terror into their enemies by its power and harshness, as the lion does by roaring, and the dog by growling. . . . Rival males try to excel and challenge each other by their voices, and this leads to deadly contests. Thus the use of the voice will have become associated with the emotion of anger, however it may be aroused.[13]

But why different emotions cause different sounds to be uttered Darwin calls "a very obscure subject." "It is not probable," he says, "that any precise explanation of the cause or source of each particular sound, under different states of the mind, will ever be given." Referring to Spencer's "general law that a feeling is a stimulus to muscular action," he admits that the voice is affected in accordance with such a principle,

> but the explanation appears to me too general and vague to throw much light on the various differences, with the exception of that of loudness, between ordinary speech and emotional speech, or singing.

This remark holds good, whether we believe that the various qualities of the voice originated in speaking under the excitement of strong
feelings, and that these qualities have subsequently been transferred to
vocal music; or whether we believe, as I maintain, that the habit of
uttering musical sounds was first developed, as a means of courtship,
in the early progenitors of man, and thus became associated with the
strongest emotions of which they were capable,—namely, ardent love,
rivalry and triumph. (pp. 85–87)

Pursuing the subject, Darwin accepts as fact that animals utter musical tones,
and this leads him to infer

> that the progenitors of man probably uttered musical tones, before they
> had acquired the power of articulate speech; and that consequently,
> when the voice is used under any strong emotion, it tends to assume,
> through the principle of association, a musical character. We can plainly
> perceive, with some of the lower animals, that the males employ their
> voices to please the females, and that they themselves take pleasure in
> their own vocal utterances; but why particular sounds are uttered, and
> why these give pleasure cannot at present be explained. (pp. 87–88)

It seems clear, he continues, that the pitch of the voice bears some relation
to certain states of feeling, but the relation is far from being unequivocal.
When dogs are impatient, they emit tones that strike us as plaintive, "but
how difficult it is to know whether the sound is essentially plaintive, or only
appears so in this particular case, from our having learnt by experience what
it means!" In man, deep groans and piercing screams both express an agony
of pain, and laughter may be high or low and still equally express enjoyment
or amusement.

When it comes to expression in music, as we might predict, Darwin finds
that a biological explanation is seriously deficient. He appeals to a Mr. Lichtfield, a man he considers to be knowledgeable about music. "Up to a certain
point," Lichtfield says,

> any law which is found to hold as to the expression of the emotions by
> simple sounds must apply to the more developed mode of expression
> in song, which may be taken as the primary type of all music. A great
> part of the emotional effect of a song depends on the character of the
> action by which the sounds are produced. In songs, for instance, which
> express great vehemence of passion, the effect often chiefly depends
> on the forcible utterance of some one or two characteristic passages
> which demand great exertion of vocal force; and it will be frequently
> noticed that a song of this character fails of its proper effect when sung

by a voice of sufficient power and range to give the characteristic passages without much exertion. That is, no doubt, the secret of the loss
of effect so often produced by the transposition of a song from one key
to another. The effect is thus seen to depend not merely on the actual
sounds, but also in part on the nature of the action which produces the
sounds. (pp. 88–89)

When we feel that the expression of a song is due to its tempo, for example,
or to its fluidity or loudness, Lichtfield continues, we are really interpreting
the muscular actions that produce these qualities.

Lichtfield does not carry this questionable realism any further, however,
for he is well aware of its inadequacy as an explanation of musical expression:

But this leaves unexplained the more subtle and more specific effect
which we call the musical expression of the song—the delight given by
its melody, or even by the separate sounds which make up the melody.
This is an effect indefinable in language—one which, so far as I am
aware, no one has been able to analyze, and which the ingenious speculation of Mr. Herbert Spencer as to the origin of music leaves quite
unexplained. For it is certain that the melodic effect of a series of sounds
does not depend in the least on the loudness or softness, or on their
absolute pitch. A tune is always the same tune, whether it is sung loudly
or softly, by a child or a man; whether it is played on a flute or on a
trombone. The purely musical effect of any sound depends on its place
in what is technically called a "scale"; the same sound producing absolutely different effects on the ear, according as it is heard in connection
with one or another series of sounds.

It is on this relative association of the sounds that all the essentially
characteristic effects which are summed up in the phrase "musical expression," depend. But why certain associations of sounds have such-
and-such effects, is a problem which yet remains to be solved. (pp.
89–90)

As a consequence of this conception, Darwin confines himself to the association of certain kinds of simple sounds with certain states of mind. A scream
for help, he points out, "will naturally be loud, prolonged, and high." Sounds
uttered by males to please females will naturally be those that are sweet to
the ears of the species, while sounds produced to strike terror into an enemy
will naturally be harsh or displeasing.

In chapter 7 of *The Expression of Emotions*, in connection with the discussion of love and tender feelings, Darwin returns to the ideas on music
that he had expressed in the *Descent of Man*:

Music has a wonderful power, as I have elsewhere attempted to show, of recalling in a vague and indefinite manner, those strong emotions which were felt during long-past ages, when, as is probable, our early progenitors courted each other by the aid of vocal tones. And as several of our strongest emotions—grief, great joy, love, and sympathy—lead to the free secretion of tears, it is not surprising that music should be apt to cause our eyes to become suffused with tears, especially when we are already softened by any of the tenderer feelings. Music often produces another peculiar effect. We know that every strong sensation, emotion, or excitement—extreme pain, rage, terror, joy, or the passion of love—all have a special tendency to cause the muscles to tremble; and the thrill or slight shiver which runs down the backbone and limbs of many persons when they are powerfully affected by music, seems to bear the same relation to the above trembling of the body, as a slight suffusion of tears from the power of music does to weeping from any strong and real emotion. (p. 270)

Spencer's theory was examined at length in 1876 by Edmund Gurney, in his essay "On Some Disputed Points in Music." After mentioning both Darwin's and Spencer's ideas concerning the origin of music, Gurney devotes his criticism to Spencer, who has failed to demonstrate, Gurney says, that song arose by intensifying the characteristics of emotional speech. Even loudness, which is the most plausible property to have provided a basis for song, "is by no means a universal or essential element, either of song or of emotional speech." [14]

As far as pleasing tone color or quality is concerned, Gurney finds Darwin's supposition as probable as Spencer's: it is just as probable to suppose that the power of producing pleasing tones was first acquired for making love and then applied to emotional speech as it is to suppose that such tones were first acquired to make speech pleasingly emphatic and then utilized for independent musical purposes. In respect of pitch, intervals, and rate of variation, finally, Gurney finds song to be more restrained than emotional speech rather than more extreme.

There are effects in emotional speech that do play an important part in many musical effects, Gurney admits, but they depend on pace and motion, and these in turn on an elementary sense of force or effort. In this connection, Gurney cites Helmholtz's opinion that music can adumbrate the forces underlying motion in space because it resembles such motion. From this in turn derives the power of music to represent emotion. Rhythm, on the other hand, Gurney argues, is the all-important element of melody that distinguishes it from both emotional and unemotional speech: "No one can suppose that the sense of rhythm can be derived from emotional speech" (p. 110). Music also makes use of fixed degrees of pitch, while the changes in pitch of emotional speech have a gliding character. Proportion is Gurney's chief principle, for it lies at the root of rhythm, of timbre, and of harmony. Tonality and modulation again have nothing to do with speech, which suggests that rudimentary music was similarly ruled by rudimentary musical sensibilities.

Finally, in Gurney's opinion, Spencer's theory of the function of music is even more unsatisfactory than his account of its origins. The complex musical phrases that convey complex emotion are supposed to influence us in formulating the complex cadences of speech that convey subtler thoughts and emotions. But the cadences of conversation are infinite with respect to variation of pitch, and musical phrases are also practically infinite; thus, "it would be a fruitless task to search for definite melodic resemblances" (p. 116). Gurney points to the contradiction between Spencer and Wagner in this regard, for Wagner maintains that speech, far from showing the increasing influence of music, had at first a great resemblance to music and then gradually became less and less musical: "I feel that my apprehension of music must differ so totally from Mr. Spencer's, that I perhaps fail fairly to catch his point of view. To me a melody has a certain musical meaning which is its real essence: it may be pitched high or low, played on a whistle or a double-bass, played within certain limits at different paces, and this essence will remain absolutely constant" (p. 117).

Spencer considers music to be an idealized language of passion and emotion, while Wagner holds it to be the expression of poetical ideas. The truth is, Gurney says, that musical emotions "are now so differentiated and ultimate that they can in no way be said to depend even on an imaginative realisation" of other emotions:

> Every bit of music that I care much about conveys to me an impression peculiar to itself; and just as only a few chords—minor thirds and sixths for instance as compared with major—have a definite emotional character, so not one in ten of these impressions can I docket off under the most general heads. We find as a pure matter of experience . . . that just as we cannot express the effect on us of a beautiful face or landscape in terms of definite emotions, so musical works may be throughout independent of any emotion now conceivable outside the musical sphere. (pp. 118–19)

In chapter 21 ("The Speech Theory") of *The Power of Sound* (1880), Gurney returns to Spencer's essay. He repeats his objections, expanding them and adding examples that compare speech intonations with melodic phrases.[15] Detached successions of notes are neutral, he maintains; they assume all sorts of character in their various melodic contexts. Configurations in melody have a distinct and indescribable musical individuality and frequently lack any expressive quality that can be described in terms of emotional categories. Even when such terms are applicable, their generality prevents them from being specific to the individuality of the melodic configurations. Furthermore, there really are no separable units of "cadence" or melody in speech, each with its known definite expression, while in music, melodies are not compounded of simpler emotions that are contained in a stock of intervals and cadences.

Gurney's discussion gradually becomes a more general one. He takes issue with Du Bos and with Rousseau, with the theory of music as imitation, and with the idea that primitive speech contained the essential germs of music. Instead, he urges, "the primary and essential function of Music is to create beautiful objective forms, and to impress us with otherwise unknown things, instead of to induce and support particular subjective moods and to express for us known things" (pp. 485–86).

Music is presentative, not representative, Gurney insists, announcing a conception that is strikingly similar to that of Susanne Langer: "It is primarily bound, by presenting its own things . . . to stir up its own indescribable emotions" (pp. 437–38). The musical faculty and pleasure,

> which have to do with music and nothing else, are the representatives and linear descendants of a faculty and pleasure which were musical and nothing else. . . . Music was a separate order, an adjustment of proportional elements of which speech knows nothing, introduced in conformance with the instincts of a pleasure to which the organism had been through long ages more and more adapted; a pleasure greatly associated with speech, because the voice was the naturally available instrument, but which would have been in essence the same had words had no existence. (pp. 492–93)

Gurney finally deals with the relations between speech and music that he considers to be factual, discussing the general character or utterance, found even in instrumental music, and then such things as the play of energy and the factors of continuity, repetition, climax, and rhetorical emphasis, all of which testify to some "faint resemblance" of music to the phenomena of speech, some "dim affinities" between them. But Gurney's conception of music, which will concern us again in the following chapter, is clearly dominated by his remarkable insight into the specific nature of music as an independent manifestation.

Spencer's "The Origin and Function of Music" was reprinted in his *Es-*

says: Scientific, Political, and Speculative and in the "Library Edition" of this collection, which was published in 1891, but with a postscript added to the essay that replied to the objections of Darwin and Gurney. He finds Darwin's observations inadequate and his reasoning inconclusive. The song of birds is by no means peculiar to the mating season, Spencer has discovered, but rather results, like the whistling and humming of people, from high spirits and an overflow of energy. Furthermore, as Darwin admits, there is no evidence that supports his theory in the higher vertebrates. Nor is there, Spencer adds, in the human race itself, where song is prompted by a variety of feelings and incidents of the moment, as is suggested by a derivation from emotional speech in general.

Addressing the criticism presented by Gurney, who adopts Darwin's theory, Spencer adds to his preceding remarks an argument based on "one of the fundamental laws of evolution":

> All development proceeds from the general to the special. First there appear those traits which a thing has in common with many other things; then those traits which it has in common with a smaller class of things; and so on until there eventually arise those traits which distinguish it from everything else. The genesis which I have described conforms to this fundamental law. It posits the antecedent fact that feeling in general produces muscular contraction in general; and the less general fact that feeling in general produces, among other muscular contractions, those which move the respiratory and vocal apparatus. Within these it joins the still less general fact that sounds indicative of feelings vary in sundry respects according to the intensity of the feelings; and then enumerates the still less general facts which show us the kinship between the vocal manifestations of feeling and the characters of vocal music: the implication being that there has gone on a progressive specialization. But the view which Mr. Gurney adopts from Mr. Darwin is that from the special actions producing the special sounds accompanying sexual excitement, were evolved those various actions producing the various sounds which accompany all other feelings. Vocal expression of a particular emotion came first, and from this proceeded vocal expressions of emotions in general: the order of evolution was reversed.[16]

Also, Gurney does not realize that a higher degree of evolution in some or most respects is generally accompanied by an equal or lower degree in other respects. Thus, loudness, for example, can occasionally be absent if the other features of emotional utterance are present. The same is true of the absence of variations of pitch in recitative, for two of the features of emotional utterance are present: resonance of tone and relative elevation of pitch.

Furthermore, according to Gurney, "no one can suppose the sense of rhythm can be derived from emotional speech":

Had he referred to the chapter on "The Rhythm of Motion" in *First Principles*, he would have seen that, in common with inorganic actions, all organic actions are completely or partially rhythmical—from appetite and sleep to inspirations and heart-beats; from the winking of the eyes to the contractions of the intestines; from the motions of the legs to discharges through the nerves. Having contemplated such facts he would have seen that the rhythmical tendency which is perfectly displayed in musical utterance, is imperfectly displayed in emotional speech. (pp. 438–40)

In connection with the purported dichotomy between the transitions of pitch in speech and the fixed scalar degrees of music, Spencer replies:

Had Mr. Gurney known that evolution in all cases is from the indefinite to the definite, he would have seen that as a matter of course the gradations of emotional speech must be indefinite in comparison with the gradations of developed music. Progress from the one to the other is in part constituted by increasing definiteness in the time-intervals and increasing definiteness in the tone-intervals. (p. 440)

Spencer turns to *The Power of Sound*, taking up Gurney's claim that the germs of music are related to developed music as the acorn is to the oak:

Now suppose we ask—How many traits of the oak are to be found in the acorn? Next to none. And then suppose we ask—How many traits of music are to be found in the tones of emotional speech? Very many. Yet while Mr. Gurney thinks that music had its origin in something which might have been as unlike it as the acorn is unlike the oak, he rejects the theory that it had its origin in something as much like it as the cadences of emotional speech; and he does this because there are sundry differences between the characters of speech-cadences and the characters of music. In the one case he tacitly assumes a great unlikeness between germ and product; while in the other case he objects because germ and product are not in all respects similar! (p. 443)

Finally, in his postscript, Spencer seeks to forestall all inapplicable criticism by pointing out that his theory of the origin of music is not intended to be a complete theory of music. Even apart from harmony, in fact, there are really three types of musical effect: sensational, perceptual, and emotional. It is only to the last of these that his theory of origin pertains.

To the history of Spencer's hotly debated essay there belong the later synoptic discussions of Carl Stumpf ("Musikpsychologie in England," 1885) and

Ernest Newman (in *A Study of Wagner*, 1899, and *Musical Studies*, 1905). Stumpf deals in turn with Spencer, James Sully (*Sensation and Intuition: Studies in Psychology and Aesthetics*, 1874), Darwin, and Gurney, discussing the ideas of each in considerable detail. He also includes a discussion of the numerous writers before Spencer who expounded a speech theory of music, mostly notably Rousseau and Herder in the eighteenth century and Villoteau (*Recherches sur l'analogie de la musique avec les arts qui ont pour objet l'imitation du langage*, 1807) and Wagner in the nineteenth.

Newman is concerned with the subject because of his interest in Wagner. In *A Study of Wagner* (1899), he turns briefly to Spencer, discerning at once the logical fallacy in Spencer's theory:

> It errs in supposing that because song exhibits some of the character-istics of speech, the one has necessarily taken its rise in the other. The resemblance between the external characteristics of speech and those of song are only what might be expected, seeing that both are phenomena of sound, and sound can only vary in the ways indicated by Mr. Spencer. There is no necessity, however, to assume, merely on the basis of these resemblances, that song is only an intensification of speech; any more than when a man has a headache and looks pale, we need assume that the paleness is due to the headache—the truth being that both head-ache and paleness are due to some underlying common cause. The mere resemblance of song and speech in their most external characteristics is not a proof that one is the outcome of the other, but simply that they have certain causal phenomena in common; while the internal differences between them are greater than their resemblances.

The speech-theory leaves unexplained "precisely those elements in music that *make* it music." Newman calls on Jules Combarieu to expand the point:

> Mr. Spencer neglects or ignores everything that gives to the art he is studying its special and unique character; he does not appear to have realised what a musical composition is, what are the rules it obeys, what is the nature of the charm and the beauty we find in it. In short, we can bring against him a fundamental fact, in comparison with which everything else has only a quite secondary value: that is, the existence of a *musical manner of thinking*. The musician thinks with sounds, as the *littérateur* thinks with words.[17]

It is physiology that provides the final sanction of Newman's critique. Music and speech, he argues, "proceed from distinct cerebral centers." A "faculty psychology" was a logical part of the constellation of biological sciences that became increasingly influential during the latter half of the century.

Finally, in "Herbert Spencer and the Origin of Music," one of the essays of his *Musical Studies* (1905), Newman defines his position once again with his customary precision: "Could not, and would not, song have had all these peculiarities even if speech had never been invented? Given, that is, the capacity of men to feel emotion in varying degrees, would not a strong emotion naturally express itself in louder, more varied, more resonant tones than a weak emotion—and this even if man had as yet no language?"[18]

Biological ideas—among them those of Darwin and Spencer—play a significant role in *Die Musik als Ausdruck* (1885), a judicious and well-thought-out treatise by Friedrich von Hausegger, who was a teacher at the University of Graz. After explaining in detail how expressive gestures and sounds irresistibly arouse sympathy and are instinctively understood, Hausegger continues, "We must be careful not to think that we have penetrated with these things even one step into the temple of art." Yet he concedes that, in the application of such a mechanism of understanding, "we find all the factors that we shall come on again in art in a state of higher clarity and finer development."[19] The distinction is a subtle one. If the machinery of expression and comprehension is preliminary to art, how can we find it in art again in higher clarity and finer development? How can we speak of "music as expression?"

In his journey from automatic expression and response to art, Hausegger turns first to the play impulse (sec. 2). This also is placed in a biological context. It is common to animals and man. It is the enjoyment of certain motions, the manifestation of vitality, the enjoyment of existing. This is also a type of "expression," but it is expression without any specific emotional excitation. In man it is intensified by a social factor, a "feeling of belonging together."

In an argument fundamental to his treatise but unfortunately quite convoluted, Hausegger undertakes to show how states of emotional excitement can come to resemble the activation of the play impulse. Such states would then produce pleasure regardless of the character of the emotion they involved. For this to take place a crucial requirement must be fulfilled: our sympathetic response to the emotional states of others must be detached from any desire to eliminate the factual causes of these states or to achieve other external practical goals. But this is what happens in art:

> In such states of excitation our basic nature becomes awake in an intensified way. They flash through us like a storm, cleansing and clearing, in that they lead us back to the source of our nature and of all existence; in such circumstances we feel as though our sensibility suddenly secured a deeper insight into the process of all becoming, we feel lifted above ourselves, the creative force that resides in us becomes perceptible to

a degree that gives us a presentiment that its fecundity extends far beyond our individual existence: we become aware of our identity with the whole remaining sphere of life.

Aristotle called purging of the passions the aim of tragedy. What moves us in art as feeling or passion, however, is only the intensified awareness of existence that is conveyed to us, arising from sympathy. . . . To the capacity for this intensified sympathy man owes his capacity to experience inner states of excitement readily merely through imagination. (p. 47)

Hausegger's next concern is the perfecting of our means of expression, which he takes to be gesture and audible utterance. In the process of perfecting these, gesture will become pantomime and dance and audible utterance song. The demands of the eye and ear will play an important role, with the result that the requirement of beauty will now become prominent. At the same time, the veiling of the body by clothing will necessitate the emphasis not only of gesture but in particular of audible utterance, which will come to reveal a threefold nature: that of a means of expression, of a means of understanding (as speech), and—in its perfection as tone—of a phenomenon that has its own special effects.

The section of Hausegger's work that follows these considerations (sec. 3) is devoted, in a fashion characteristic of the second half of the century, to an "evolutionary" account of the origin, separation, development, and mutual influence of language and music, which indiscriminately combines the observation of animal behavior and speculation about prehistory with specifically historical material that purports to be factual. For the fateful separation of the unity of the three media of expression, speech, song, and gesture, the invention of written language and the draping of the body by clothing are held to be of critical importance. Both manifestations indirectly furthered the independence of art—of song and of dance—by emphasizing practical function, for this entailed the neglect of expressive properties and forced these to find a more adequate embodiment. In the musical development that ensued, a decisive event was the new meaning secured by tone as such. No longer conveying simply the effect of a state of excitement, it also conveyed other properties that produce pleasure. Tone was no longer merely a human expression; it was also an object of nature; in consequence, the tonal use of the voice was followed by the invention of tone-producing instruments.

Here again, with this second musical source, we seem to be deserting the thesis of "music as expression," but Hausegger is not ready to abandon his conception. What gave meaning to tone as an object of nature, he asserts, "are the specific seductive and provocative peculiarities that it manifested in itself and that belong to it as a phenomenon, apart from its mission of being a human expression." But, he continues, "We shall see in what follows that these peculiarities also, more precisely examined and correctly applied, are serviceable to the task of tone we affirmed originally—to be human expression—and that they may claim significance for artistic life only in such subordination" (p. 90).

Hausegger then examines (in sec. 4) the transition from antiquity to the Middle Ages, when the two aspects of tone separated, that of expression, in which tone was attached to the other media of expression, and that of natural object, in which tone was the province of scholars and became an object of speculation, experiment, and combination. The history of Western music, Hausegger maintains, is distinguished by an effort to unite these two domains, which can be characterized as the domains of folksong and art music, respectively. There follows an examination of musical history from this point of view, including the history of opera and the history of instrumental music.

The most extended section of Hausegger's treatise (sec. 5) undertakes to show that, in its fully developed state and in all its major aspects, music remains expression. The very nature of the enjoyment we expect from music, Hausegger maintains, is such that "we demand, more or less consciously, that the music our ear receives present itself as human expression" (p. 128). This is most obvious in the case of song, but it is present also in connection with musical instruments and the orchestra. The musical work in general is perceived as an expressive form because we are able to grasp it as song. Thus, *melody* is the primary demand on a work. Similarly, rhythm, tonality, measure, tempo, and form are dependent on the organization of the active organs of human beings—on the length of the breath and on the apparatus through which vocal sound is produced, with its succession and grouping of tones with respect to pitch. "*Inviolable laws of the conduct of melody,*" Hausegger maintains, "*or absolute unacceptability in this regard, can be traced back to laws or limits of sonorous expression in the human organism*" (p. 133). This applies, he states, to both the productive and the receptive organs for tonal patterns.

After considering opera at length, Hausegger proceeds to instrumental music, program music, and melodrama. Instrumental music obviously presents a crucial test of his theory—and a difficult one: "The difference between a purely instrumental work and dramatic music consists simply in the fact that the stimulus to production in the latter is generated by the vivid idea of the dramatic event, while in the former the cause of the impulse remains hidden and is often not clear to the composer himself." This becomes more convincing, or at least more positive, in what follows: "The expressive means that are active in an instrumental work, since they are derived from the expressive capacity of the human organism and set into operation under its influence, are able to impart themselves as expression directly to the listener and to affect him as such and in the manner of such" (pp. 155–56).

It is therefore a mistake, Hausegger continues, "to believe that instrumental music is exclusively a play of tones, however inventive or delightful to the ear." It testifies to the expressive need from which it arose. More specific arguments are also advanced.

> The laws of tonal and rhythmic arrangement manifested in a purely instrumental work correspond in a surprising way with the demands that the human organism must meet in expressive behavior. Indeed, we find the laws of this arrangement in a remarkable way—the sections conformable to the length of the breath, for example, sharp, symmetrical division according to intensified gestural motions, regular beat corresponding to the beat of the heart, strictly rounded-off melodic groups analogous to the play of muscles in unitary impulses—much muscles in unitary impulses—much more strictly adhered to in pure music than in music tied to the word. (pp. 158–59)

Continuing these considerations with tempo and form, Hausegger comes finally to speak of the performer and the conductor. These are naturally seen as a decisive demonstration of his conception: "*We demand from the reproductive artist nothing other than that he grasp the work of art as an expressive manifestation and endow it accordingly with the appropriate beat in gratification of our sympathetic response*" (p. 172). The work of art must live again in *him* and seem to be his own expression.

The result of his deliberations, as Hausegger states it, is the following: "The nature of music is *expression,* clarified expression intensified to its noblest effect" (p. 173). In this he finds the high value of the art, not in sensory delight or in tonal or rhythmic relations. Of fundamental importance also is the revelation by tones of properties of the world of nature, which are manifested in tone color. In tonal structures, however, the unconscious "Will" of nature is superceded by chance, by intention, and by historical changes of taste. Even the depiction of nature in music is heard through the feelings of man. And human expressive utterance, as we know, is the form in which nature commands our highest attention and sympathy. The same state of feeling is aroused in us, and we are impelled to a similar expression of it. But our freedom from external factors of cause and effect here reveals that we have the power to experience and express states of feeling independently, merely through imagination. Such states can then be described as play. Hausegger finds himself in the aesthetic sphere of Kant and Schiller. "Our art originated in play," he affirms, "and it preserves the character of play where it is not untrue to its nature" (p. 185).

But since the artist creates not simply from his own life of feeling but also from the feeling of others, what he expresses belongs not only to him but to all. He is the organ of expression of all those who are bound together by the same sympathetic feeling: "It is given to him to find an adequate expression through which anyone impelled to the same expressive utterance can satisfy his own need, can find a liberation, as in the activation of play. Thus the artist succeeds in granting expression to those sharing his feeling" (p. 186). There develops from this a productive interaction of artist and public that heightens, clarifies, and refines the expressive possibilities of art as such. What art reveals, ultimately, is the ideal worth of humanity. Hausegger cites Schopenhauer: "While listening to great music, everyone feels distinctly what his ultimate worth is, or, much more, what his worth could be" (p. 190). Art owes its existence and its development, Hausegger concludes, "to that power that in relation to a definite object we call love. Born from communal feeling, art keeps this alive, for souls are united in art into a community of feeling. This feeling manifests itself in the most distilled expressive forms, which in imparting themselves become an assuaging, ennobling, purifying force" (p. 195). Music is expression, but the expression is intrinsically ethical in nature, an outcome that is characteristic of the Germanic view of art.

CHAPTER TEN

FORMALISM AND AUTONOMY

T he division of ideas between this chapter and the next proceeds not from a modern perspective but from the perspective of the Germanic nineteenth century, for which the entire life of the soul was regarded as a manifestation of the Absolute, even by authors who do not make this conception explicit. In its simplest terms, a duality of "objective" and "subjective" was taken to be self-evident, in the prephenomenological sense of these designations, the one being the province of material and formed material, the other the province of mind, of ideas, of feeling—of "the ideal." If the feelings connected with music, however, are in no way thought of as a manifestation of the Absolute or as a manifestation of the realm of subjectivity or of "the ideal," they have been assigned to the present "objectivity" chapter, whether they are considered to be peculiar to music or to be feelings also known elsewhere. (Feelings met with both in music and outside it, of course, must necessarily be of a special or somehow restricted kind, and their existence, paradoxically, is not incompatible with a belief in either the formalist or the autonomous nature of music.) Whether an author belongs in this chapter or the next, then, depends on a crucial matter that defines the basic character of his thought: whether his emphasis falls on feelings as incidental manifestations that are secondary to musical form and autonomy or on feelings as primary constituents of musical experience that belong to the ideal world of subjectivity. Thus, "moods," to take the most important equivocal conception, are in some cases part of a basically formalist view of music and in other cases part of an idealist view. Whether they are considered autonomous or specific to music is not a decisive issue.

The types of musical aesthetics that have been considered to represent formalism constitute a wide range of conceptions, many of which could be described, with equal or greater accuracy, as conceptions of musical autonomy or musical specificity. For formalism often carries with it views of musical content or expression or effect that are conceived as peculiar to music rather than as alternative presentations by music of things also known elsewhere or independently. It is hardly possible to maintain that music is nothing *but* form since, if the form in question is to be realized, it cannot remain entirely abstract but must be incorporated in some perceptible medium, which is then, strictly speaking, not identical with the form as such.

What is intended here by *formalism*, then, is a view of music that finds the distinguishing or most significant aspect of the art to be its form, the property, in fact, that defines its essential nature. Nineteenth-century formalism in aesthetics doubtless has its chief source in Kant's *Critique of Judgment* (1790). As our examination of this work in chapter 6 revealed, Kant considers art in the light of cognition, for it is cognition that he takes as the province of philosophy in general. But it is *form* that we know, not the material that is formed. And aesthetics, which is concerned with nature as well as art, deals with judgment and with the pleasure that is attached to the apprehension of form. This pleasure expresses the formal purposiveness of an object in its appearance as perceived. It is form, therefore, that is judged to be the ground of aesthetic pleasure, not sensation or the material in which the aesthetic object is realized; the object is then called beautiful.

Although aesthetic judgment is not based on any present concept of the object, and the beautiful is the object of a necessary satisfaction without any concept, in art there is a preconceived concept that is a purpose, and art thus entails the property of perfection in its conformity to this purpose. There is a type of beauty, however, that Kant calls "free beauty," as opposed to "adherent beauty" (sec. 16). He regards this as a pure judgment of taste and therefore as independent of charm and emotion, of the concept of perfection, and of any concept of what the object ought to be. Now it is not only nature that manifests free beauty; decorative visual designs, musical fantasies, and instrumental music do so also. They are evidently devoid of the preconceived concept that otherwise prevails in art. The question arises, then, of whether (instrumental) music is really a fine art, which is a matter of judgment and in which our representations are regarded as modes of cognition, or whether it is a pleasant art instead, which is a matter of enjoyment and in which our representations are regarded merely as sensations.

This alternative, however, presents a problem. Pleasant art would seem to be excluded from aesthetics entirely, yet it is art and as such must possess form and be susceptible of judgment. It is open to cognition and to beauty, then, in contradiction to the demand made by its classification. Kant is thus able to conclude that music is either a fine art (a beautiful play of sensations) or a pleasant art (a beautiful play of *pleasant* sensations), although perhaps only in part (sec. 51). This would seem to represent the alternative of form in which the formed material in itself possesses no enjoyable sensuous properties or form that is entirely or partly obscured by such properties.

In addition to this concept of artistic beauty, Kant maintains that beauty—considered now from the standpoint of creation rather than apprehension—is the expression of aesthetic ideas. An aesthetic idea is a representation of the imagination that is associated with a concept but to which no concept is adequate (sec. 49). What is in question here is doubtless the preconceived concept that is a purpose, of which Kant spoke initially, so that there intervenes in the creative process the elaborating action of the imagination. There can accordingly be no "present" concept in the finished work or its apprehension, for the beautiful cannot be reduced to concepts: it is judged by the purposive attuning of the imagination to agreement with the conceptual faculty in general.

In the section of the *Critique* that deals with aesthetic value (sec. 53), Kant defines music as a language of the affections (derived from the tonal inflection of speech) that communicates the aesthetic ideas naturally associated with these affections. In a given instance, then, harmony and melody—the form of the composition of the musical sensations—will express the aesthetic idea of a connected whole that corresponds to the dominating affection of the piece. (The "dominating affection," however, cannot be a "presupposed concept," for then whatever beauty may be involved would be adherent.) The form of the composition of the sensations—the harmony and melody—is mathematical, Kant tells us; it rests on the proportional relations between the successive and simultaneous vibrations of the tones, and it is the source of aesthetic satisfaction or pleasure. But when music is devoted to enjoyment, to the production of charm and mental movement by means of affections, its mathematical form is no longer part of our experience.

It is clear, then, that the *Critique of Judgment* provides a substantial foundation for the development of aesthetic formalism, and Kant's influence is often quite conspicuous in the authors who followed him. The *Critique* presents a formal aesthetics that denies the relevance of feeling to beauty, for example, just as Hanslick does, and that seeks to suppress sensuous qualities as well. Pleasant sensations are a liability, and sensations themselves are admitted only as a minimal concession to the necessity of some material in which musical form is realized.

The first significant proponent of formalism in nineteenth-century aesthetics is the philosopher and psychologist Johann Friedrich Herbart, whose aesthetic views are included in his *Schriften zur Einleitung in die Philosophie* (1813) and his *Kurze Enzyklopädie der Philosophie aus praktischen Gesichtspunkten* (1831). The theory of art, he maintains in the earlier work, is concerned with how the aesthetic elements of an art can be combined into a pleasing whole. In music, for example, the elements are tones, or really relations of tones, and the objectively beautiful arises from their combination. As an outcome of such a conception, aesthetic judgment will be permanently associated with its object: "He who really wishes to learn by analysis of works of art, that is to learn about aesthetics, is neither admirer nor critic, but permits analysis to reveal separately each and every fibre of the fabric of art, to throw light on all, often very different, relationships wherein beauty dwells and in the confluence of which there resides the power of a work of art." [1]

There are two main types of relation, which are distinguished clearly in music:

> The elementary aesthetic relations can be divided into two main classes, according to whether their members appear simultaneously or successively. This is most readily perceived in the difference between harmony and melody. Music also clearly demonstrates the possibility of the most artful interlacings being produced by several series of the successively beautiful (several melodic voices) developing simultaneously in such a way as, at the same time, continuously to meet the demands of harmony. (p. 371)

No pleasing aesthetic relations can be formed between close neighbors, Herbart continues, a principle that applies both to colors and to tones that are nearly the same. But symmetry in space, he observes, "curiously differs from rhythmical symmetry" (p. 378). In the one, the central member tends to become prominent, while in the other (pentametric rhythm in music) it does so only with difficulty. Also, spatial succession is easily reversed, while temporal succession is not. But there is a parallel again, finally, between the temporal perception of the spatial and the spatial perception of the temporal. At the end of a successive work of art "there appears the notion of a whole, the parts of which are bound to possess a sort of spatial proportion, although knowledge of these parts has come to us only gradually" (p. 374).

It is the unity of the elements of art to which Herbart returns repeatedly and that is clearly the central concern of his formalism: "As the ideal of virtue is based on the unity of the person, so is the concept of a work of art based on the unity of effect, to which all of its parts are supposed to contribute, albeit with a great difference as concerns application" (p. 375). Again, "With all works of art the question arises as to the rigorousness of their claim to unity. It is after all clear that for them to have a great effect they must not dilute the conception, nor divide judgment" (pp. 378–79).

It is characteristic of formalism in the nineteenth century that it deals more with what aesthetics is not than with what it is. Herbart's opening chapter is devoted to the "difficulties" of aesthetics, and his efforts thereafter to identify and separate out the associated factors and conceptions that confuse the field are exhaustive and unremitting. In the interest of clarifying the true nature of aesthetics, he conducts a logical analysis and classification of ideas that seems to emulate scientific precision.

Since the beautiful is objective, it must be separated from various subjective states of mind, particularly from emotions and from general attributes such as "lovely." Musical beauty, for example, has to do specifically with the relations of tones. What the observer contributes, in contrast—which Herbart calls the *apperception* of the aesthetic object—produces a great variety of judgments. But enthusiasm and criticism are equally beside the point; they are not properly involved in aesthetic judgment or in aesthetic perception.

The determination of the nature of the various types of apperceived elements and of their relation to the properly aesthetic elements is a complex enterprise that calls for considerable thought. The similar effort of Hanslick later on not simply to eliminate feeling from aesthetics but to determine its factual place in musical experience is largely a polemic and not comparably searching and ramified. The relation of ethics and volition to aesthetics is particularly complex in Herbart's view. It is at least as important, therefore, for an understanding of Herbart's thought as it is for an understanding of Hanslick's to keep in mind the range and the various kinds of relevance of these larger considerations in the overall conception of art and artistic activity:

The abstract attitude demanded so far, according to which only aesthetic elements should be accepted, and even these separately from one another, is opposed by a more pluralistic attitude. Such an attitude is already present when the beautiful or the ugly is at the same time also thought of as an object of preference or rejection; as useful, or amusing, or pleasant, or as harmful, dangerous, strenuous, as producing pain and grief, as transient, seductive, etc. Many of the common-sense axioms of everyday life refer to this.

The concept of an aesthetic object which, in addition to a *single* aesthetic relation, is also the subject of other thoughts, is in itself already a theoretical concept, since what distinguishes the object from its aesthetic attributes as a subject of the same is precisely the fact that it is *not exclusively* determined by this attribute. The other characteristics can either be aesthetic themselves, or such as express other kinds of preferences or rejection, or, finally, theoretical (merely pertaining to the perception of the object itself). In the latter case they would refer either to what the object already is, or to what it can become. (p. 374)

Like formalism itself, of course, the related factors to which Herbart here refers had also been examined in Kant's *Critique of Judgment*, which remains the definitive foundation of the whole circle of nineteenth-century formalist conceptions.

In his *Kurze Enzyklopädie der Philosophie*, Herbart returns to the consideration of apperception in art. It is difficult, he acknowledges, to escape the demand that the work of art represent, depict, or mean something:

> Thus even true connoisseurs of music repeat the statement, right up to the present day, that music expresses feelings, as though the feeling that in some way is excited by it, and for the expression of which it therefore precisely—*if we wish*—permits itself to be used, is the foundation of the general rules of simple or double counterpoint on which its true nature rests. But what did the old artists who developed the various forms of the fugue . . . want *to express*?[2]

The affection that a work can excite through its own inner aesthetic conditions, Herbart concedes, is not to be denied it. He is critical, however, of any affection that is strongly aroused, for then we cease to be aware of what it was that aroused it: "It is easy to cry or to laugh; for this no art is needed" (p. 405).

Unfortunately, Herbart's desire to exclude apperception occasionally becomes overzealous: not only is the libretto an extrinsic addition to an opera, but even the auditory realization of music becomes unessential: "In strict composition (e.g., in the fugue), music does not even depend on *forte* and *piano*, which the performer or the instrument (say, the organ) can dispense with; the tones need simply to be heard, indeed the notes only to be read, and yet they please" (p. 403). It is the fantasy, not the ear, that perceives music. The aesthetic experience, however, excludes personal additions to the work by the percipient that have no intrinsic connection to it. Essentially, the beauty of music rests on tonal relations, which are numerical. It can be grasped most directly by a technical and psychological analysis of the score and of its perception.

Another early proponent of musical formalism was Hans-Georg Nägeli, a native of Zurich who was a composer, music teacher, and music publisher. Nägeli's aesthetic views are contained in his *Vorlesungen über Musik mit Berücksichtigung der Dilettanten* (1826), which presents the substance of lectures delivered on a succession of tours in Germany. Nägeli sees art as rooted in the three basic contents of our mind: feelings, perceptions, and ideas, which are developed respectively by music, visual art, and poetry. Music is thus primarily, although not exclusively, the art of feelings. Musical dilettantes, however, are attracted mostly by "musical painting." Furthermore, our aesthetic nature in general has its origin in the power of perception, and tone itself can be perceived in its externality, as emanating from an external source. For this reason even a slight and unintentional resemblance of music to the rippling of a brook, for example, will provoke a corresponding image.

Similarly, plastic art can have a musical effect, as we can see in the arabesque and in Gothic architecture. In both cases, there is a temporal effect of succession, of motion from one partial form to another, that creates a playful movement of the mind, a musical mood. Our spatial aesthetic sense, by which affection is caught and held still, is transformed into a temporal experience in which we are led on from feeling to feeling. Thus, the arabesque and Gothic architecture are anticipations of instrumental music, which was to be devised long afterward. Music itself is a play of anticipation, transition, and deception, an interweaving and undulation of feeling and of fantasy that belies its numerical basis in measure and order.

Nägeli finds fault with the new science of aesthetics; the actuality of art has become lost in philosophic idealism, for which art is essentially one. Thus, the arts are connected instead of distinguished. In addition, aesthetics is based on visual art, as the earliest art developed, and visual principles are mistakenly applied to music, with the result that its specific nature is overlooked. But Nägeli insists on the difference between music and the visual arts, a distinction characteristic of formalism. Unlike the other arts, music does not produce a specific affection; it has no defined character. It sets up movements in us; it does not generate static moods or states of mind. Its play of movement is inconsistent with anything that might be termed a lasting temperamental disposition. Its theory can and should be grasped through the fundamental concept of *play*, which has always been of the highest importance in its descriptive language. "Its *essence* is *play*, through and through; nothing else." There is no content that can be imputed to it:

> It possesses only *forms*, regulated combinations of tones and series of tones into a whole. . . .
>
> By its play of forms, music counteracts any possible tendency of contemplation that through attraction to color, figure, and shape might in any way impel the mind to emotion. Music strives to *play away* emotion.
>
> The richer a musical work is in form, the more playful it is, the more comprehensively and unfailingly will it accomplish this, and the more

striking and excellent it is. It must exercise its effect everywhere, on the most various individuals and on their most various kinds of emotion. It must dispel from the mind every particular affection, every mixture of affections, must overcome, as it were, any random perception. In this way it makes the soul receptive, makes it truly *receptive* to the *pleasures* of its free play of forms.[3]

This leaves no doubt that music is simply a play of forms; it is not even a play of sensations or sensational forms; the forms, at most, are composed of "tones and series of tones." Apart from the ideas of Zimmermann, which we shall consider below, it is difficult to find a more extreme version of formalism. Nägeli's view initially, we will recall, was that the province of music is feeling. But he so qualifies and modifies this view that what he presents finally is "pleasure" rather than feeling.

The kinship of Nägeli's ideas with those of Romantic aesthetics, however, is occasionally evident, for formalism does not take a position contrary to Romanticism in any rigorous way. The total absence of content in music and especially the undulating effect of feeling and fantasy it tends to produce are not diametrically opposed to the generalized feeling of longing in which all particular emotions are submerged, as described in Romantic literature. For the effect of Nägeli's view varies only in magnitude, not in quality, and the involvement of feeling and fantasy is not intrinsic, but only a tendency. Fundamentally, an intrinsic role of feeling is impossible because the temporal fluctuation of music does not permit the deployment of cognition, which demands a static environment and which is the essential prerequisite of the generation of any affection or mood or of any designated feeling. Also reminiscent of Romanticism is Nägeli's ascription of a magical and mystical quality to music that connects it with religion.

The most impressive and influential expression of formalism in music is Eduard Hanslick's *Vom Musikalisch-Schönen* (1854). But the form that he regards as the essential manifestation of musical beauty, or aesthetic value, is not simply abstract—it is neither empty nor purely mathematical but imprinted with the spirit of the composer, with his personal style of formulation. Thus, Hanslick is concerned with the specific nature of music rather than with form in itself, and it is this more adequate conception of the art that has given his work its lasting value.

The treatise takes the general form of a polemic against feeling in music, and feeling is indeed the appropriate object of a formalist critique since in some form or other it is the chief representative of musical content. But Hanslick's polemic involves distinctions of considerable importance. Real feelings, as known outside music, are by no means absent from musical experience, and Hanslick fully acknowledges their presence both as unavoidable and as desirable. He refuses to admit them, however, as aesthetically relevant; they have nothing to do with musical beauty. They would in fact—if they were intrinsic to music—destroy the semblance that is an essential feature of art. Instead, they should be considered "pathological." They belong to the realm of subjectivity, which is extra-aesthetic, while aesthetics is a science that is objective and specific to art itself. Real feelings are at most the causes or effects of art, but not the intrinsic force of artistic production or the intrinsic object of artistic perception.

As far as music in particular is concerned, individual feelings can be neither represented nor expressed, for they are necessarily defined by ideas, and these cannot be conveyed by music. Here Hanslick echoes Nägeli, and it is evident in other respects also that he draws both on Nägeli and on Herbart. Music is restricted by Hanslick, then, to the dynamics of feeling. The organ of musical production, contemplation, and judgment is the fantasy, a specifically musical and artistically trained endowment. Real feeling plays a part only when it is a contemplative delight in the specific beauty of a musical work, not a pathological subjection to the natural power of tonal sensation. Sensuous feeling, however, which Hanslick does not consider, is actually the precondition of aesthetic comprehension, for musical beauty, and the musical idea presented by the composer, exist uniquely in the tonal formations.

Musical forms, then, are not simply sound and motion. They are animated with the formative activity of mind, they are thought in tones, and they reflect the individuality of the composer. As far as mathematics is concerned, it merely regulates the elementary tonal material.

Hanslick fails to give an account, however, of this formative musical activity, perhaps because he is so intent on destroying the pretensions of feeling in music. The strongest impression made by his treatise is a negative one, for the negative ideas are the ones he emphasizes. His sounding forms in motion (*tönend bewegte Formen*) steal attention away from the formative activity of mind (*sich heraus gestaltender Geist*). Like Nägeli, Hanslick confines music to the dynamics of feeling, to patterns of motion; it is a moving arabesque. This bloodless theory was anticipated by Nägeli and formulated even before him by Daniel Webb and also by Schopenhauer, who discusses the abstract nature of musical feelings.

In contradiction with himself, then, Hanslick excludes any trace or aspect of feeling itself from music, even indistinct or undefined feeling and the essence of feeling; nothing is left for music to express or contain. He maintains that music expresses musical ideas; these are its content, but since no further description of musical ideas is provided, they reduce themselves to sounding forms in motion. He also indulges in other circular reasoning and sophistry, stating that the content of music is the theme, the part thus becoming the content of the whole, or that music consists of successions of notes, of tonal forms, which have no content other than themselves. In short, Hanslick is seduced by the attractiveness of a negative argument and the easy opportunity it offers for a display of cleverness. He does insist correctly that form and content are inseparable in music, but this thesis cannot be supported or confirmed by contending that form and content are both form since this makes them identical and indistinguishable.

In his search for content, Hanslick dissects the theme of Beethoven's *Prometheus* Overture, but the only content he finds is the component motives. To demonstrate that music expresses only the dynamics and motion of feelings, he employs the device—borrowed from Boyé—of replacing Orpheus's words "J'ai perdu mon Euridice" with "J'ai trouvé mon Euridice," maintaining that the music serves equally well to express both feelings, in spite of their diametrical opposition. His explanation, of course, is not the only possible one, and certainly not a very convincing one. Indeed, in the later editions of his treatise, Hanslick suppressed a contention to the same effect, namely, that Beethoven's "O namenlose Freude" would serve equally well to express Pizarro's rage. He doubtless had come to realize that this is obviously not the case. Other proposed demonstrations are also fallacious, and the general formalist claim, in fact, that music has no emotional expression or content will not stand the test of closer examination.

As though to cover up the incorrectness of his central thesis, Hanslick is zealous in finding various aspects of music in which actual feeling does play a part—as a motivation of the composer, as a subjective response of the listener, and as the expressive content of a performance and especially of an improvisation. The various feelings, significantly, are all real feelings. Hanslick nowhere acknowledges the existence of aesthetic feelings. And the participation of the feelings that he does appeal to—certainly incorrectly, in the case of performance and improvisation—cannot remove the weakness of his central argument.

Both the use of music as an unspecific stimulus to feeling and the elemental effect of tone and rhythm as such are of particular concern to Hanslick. Here we are not dealing with art, he contends; nor can effects of this kind—even the most immediate and most powerful—be explained by science: "The power which music possesses of profoundly affecting the nervous system cannot be ascribed so much to the artistic forms created by and appealing to the mind as to the material with which music works and which Nature has endowed with certain inscrutable affinities of a physiological order." Again,

The form (the musical structure) is the real substance (subject) of music —in fact, is the music itself, in antithesis to the feeling, its alleged subject, which can be called neither its subject nor its form, but simply the effect produced. In like manner, that which is regarded as purely material, as the transmitting medium, is the product of a thinking mind, whereas that which is presumed to be the subject—the emotional effect—belongs to the physical properties of sound, the greater part of which is governed by physiological laws.[4]

As far as aesthetics is concerned, of course, these laws—which Hanslick believes can never be determined—are of no importance whatsoever; they are simply irrelevant.

Hanslick's tract gave rise to a flood of commentary that reaches into the twentieth century. Of the early reviews, one of the most discerning was that of the philosopher Hermann Lotze. Always aware of the limitations of both formalism and science, Lotze easily sees beyond Hanslick's rejection of feeling and points the way to a more adequate conception of the nature of music:

> Since music is not a product of nature which we must take as it is, what is it that drives man to produce it continuously if its content is nothing besides that *dynamics* and the infinitely manifold variations of its elements? Where else can this drive lie than precisely in the fact that all these forms of connection and development in which music binds its tones are not merely possible matters of fact but formulations in which our heart finds a peculiar value of which the enjoyment satisfies it? If it must be admitted that music represents none of those feelings that are comprehensible in their full extent only through the knowledge of the empirical causes from which they proceed, why cannot other feelings be connected to the patterns of music that are not necessarily indistinct simply because they must for the most part remain nameless on account of the lack of definite objects to which they are related? The argument of the author leads us only to the necessity of setting other feelings against empirical ones.[5]

Das Leben der Seele (1857, 2d. ed. 1882), the major work of Moritz Lazarus, develops a view of music that rests on a formalist foundation (see vol. 2 of the 1st ed. and vol. 3 of the 2d). Lazarus was a professor in Bern and subsequently in Berlin. He was one of the founders of comparative psychology, and he pursued a psychological method in philosophy, but one concerned with society rather than with the isolated individual consciousness.

The most important discussion of music in *Das Leben der Seele* takes place in the framework of a comparison of music and painting. This naturally serves to emphasize Lazarus's musical formalism:

If we start with what is given to us, we must affirm first of all that a musical work consists of measured tones with definite tonal relations; these tones—and nothing more—are contained in it, or, conversely, they alone contain what is musical and what is aesthetic in the work. There is no other content to be discovered, and with every postulation of such, the danger is immanent of deception or of transgression beyond what is musical.[6]

Music cannot represent a conceptual content, Lazarus continues. Nor is it an imitative art since it cannot properly be directed to the imitation of natural sounds. Even definite feelings and affections, which are so often held to be the content of music and to be contained in tones as meaning is in words, cannot really be represented by it. In short, music can represent nothing other than itself, that is, measured tones in relations that are beautiful:

> These relations, from which melody, harmony, and rhythm are formed, alone make up the content and the form of music; they are the content of musical beauty or the musical form of the beautiful. These pure relations without any content other than tone constitute a musical beauty just as much as pure logical laws without application to a concrete content constitute a real and lofty truth. (p. 445)

Having insisted on his formalist conception in terms quite similar to those of Hanslick, Lazarus proceeds to offer a supplement to this conception that has a certain resemblance to Hanslick's positive view of form as the manifestation of formative personality. But the elaboration and variety of Lazarus's idea testify to his dominant psychological interest and insight. His objective consideration of music gives way, it would seem, to a detailed examination of the effects of music. While the beauty and actual content of music consist merely in tones and their relations, he argues, we cannot deny the connection of music with the entire sphere of mental life. For one thing, the various epochs of the history of music correspond closely with those of the other arts and of culture in general. Can this be purely coincidental, Lazarus asks? He appeals to the various musical genres also, with their completely different effects on the mind of the listener, taking these as further evidence—perhaps because they have counterparts in the other arts—that music is not isolated from other manifestations of intellectual life: "Finally, even the most rigorous defender of the absence of content or the purely formal beauty of music must acknowledge a 'mental content' [*geistigen Gehalt*] in its masterworks that so little consists in a mere adroitness of tonal composition that it can arise only from the abundance of cultural life as a whole" (p. 446). Here Lazarus cites Hanslick: "Thoughts and feelings run like blood in the veins of the symmetrically beautiful body: they are not *it*, and they are not *visible*, but they animate it" (p. 446). There remains the mystery, of course, unexamined by either Hanslick or Lazarus, of the meaning and result of this process of animation.

A central task of Lazarus's is to clarify the relation of music to the general life of the soul. Like all beauty, he asserts, the beauty of tonal successions and tonal forms rests on general and formal laws of the beautiful. The identity of these laws and ideas in various fields produces an almost automatic transfer of their effects. Thus, tonal successions appear to be certain activities and to have certain properties that they represent and also produce in the listener's mind. They rustle, billow, rise, fall, hurry, obstruct, yearn, caress, or banter, or they are strong, gentle, severe, delicate, sudden, or gradual.

Lazarus now invokes a basic principle of his psychological thought: Herbartian "apperception." The relation of tonal successions to any definite content of ideas, he maintains, is possible only because their constitution provides the basis for apperception. Thus, when the undefined expression of longing is created by a musical phrase, it is perceived, according to the apperception of the listener, as the longing of love, or for home, or for freedom. Lazarus has not really explained, of course, how a given phrase can appear as, possess, represent, or produce "longing," for this is not accounted for by "general and formal laws of beauty"; nor has it been shown to result from the transfer of properties from some other field. He insists, however, that tonal successions have an individual form and that they create various moods in the soul of the listener that correspond to the nature and constitution of the successions. Since all beauty derives from the form of beautiful motions of the soul, music has a unique power to relate itself to other manifestations of beauty.

Having concluded his central argument, Lazarus proceeds to distinguish, as Hanslick did, the sensuous effect and the feelings aroused by the elements of music from the aesthetic effect—the mental or artistic one—produced by the musical work as a whole. The one is a physiological effect to which various recollections are joined, the other a contemplation of beauty in which enjoyment derives from the inner musical relations, from the musical-mental content (*musikalisch-geistige Gehalt*). In the latter reside the artistic content of a work and its aesthetic value, which is a matter of *knowledge,* while the sensuous effect arises from the aesthetic *quality,* but not from the knowledge of this quality.

This distinction is expanded in the second edition into an elaborate discussion of five types of effect: aesthetic (the feeling attached to judgment); pathetic (feelings and moods created by musical contemplation); symbolic (based on analogy); subjective (based on personal recollections); and general (deriving from an idealized atmosphere of nature, environment, celebration, and so on). Basically, however, as we see clearly in the first edition, Lazarus arrives at Hanslick's distinction between musical aesthetics, which establishes principles, and musical effect, which belongs to psychology and deals with feeling. His conclusion returns to his point of departure, but it is hardly consistent with his argument, for in discussing apperception he had separated, not feeling from principles, but rather concrete feeling from undefined feeling—a distinction that is doubtless closer to musical experience.

Die Lehre von den Tonempfindungen (1862) of the great scientist Hermann Helmholtz seeks to provide "a physiological basis for the theory of music." In spite of its range of ideas, which extend to aesthetics as well as to musical scales and consonance, it is concerned chiefly with "tonal sensations." But sensations are of exceptional importance in music, Helmholtz maintains: "It is clear that music has a more immediate connection with pure sensation than any other of the fine arts, and, consequently, that the theory of the sensations of hearing is destined to play a much more important part in musical aesthetics, than, for example, the theory of *chiaroscuro* or of perspective in painting."[7] Part 1 of the treatise is in fact devoted to the relation between partial vibrations and tonal qualities, while part 2 is given over to the influence of combination tones and beats on consonance and dissonance, an investigation that includes chords as well as intervals.

It is only in the third and final part of the treatise that Helmholtz turns to "the relationship of tones": to scales and tonality, which bear more directly on matters of aesthetics. He leaves no doubt as to the distinction:

> We pass on to a problem which by its very nature belongs to the domain of aesthetics. When we spoke previously, in the theory of consonance, of agreeable and disagreeable, we referred solely to the immediate impression made on the senses when an isolated combination of sounds strikes the ear, and paid no attention at all to artistic contrasts and means of expression; we thought only of sensuous pleasure, not of aesthetic beauty. The two must be kept strictly apart, although the first is an important means for attaining the second.
>
> The altered nature of the matters now to be treated betrays itself by a purely external characteristic. At every step we encounter historical and national differences of taste. Whether one combination is rougher or smoother than another, depends solely on the anatomical structure of the ear, and has nothing to do with psychological motives. But what degree of roughness a hearer is inclined to endure as a means of musical expression depends on taste and habit; hence the boundary between consonance and dissonance has been frequently changed. (p. 234)

Architecture is used to clarify the point:

> Although the gothic style has developed the richest, the most consis-
> tent, the mightiest and most imposing of architectural forms, just as
> modern music among other musical styles, no one would certainly for
> a moment think of asserting that the pointed arch is nature's original
> form of all architectural beauty, and must consequently be introduced
> everywhere. . . . Just as little as the gothic pointed arch, should our dia-
> tonic scale or major scale be regarded as a *natural product*. At least such
> an expression is quite inapplicable, except insofar as both are necessary
> and *natural* consequences of the principle of style selected. (p. 236)

This principle of style, for Western music, Helmholtz states as follows:

> As the fundamental principle for the development of the European tonal
> system, we shall assume *that the whole mass of tones and the connection
> of harmonies must stand in a close and always distinctly perceptible
> relationship to some arbitrarily selected tonic, and that the mass of tone
> which forms the whole composition, must be developed from this tonic,
> and must finally return to it.* The ancient world developed this principle
> in homophonic i.e., monophonic music, the modern world in harmonic
> music. But it is evident that this is merely an aesthetical principle, not a
> natural law. (p. 349)

The principle is clearly formal in nature, but it is stated as the principle of
a tonal system rather than of a work of art. Shortly before this, however,
Helmholtz expresses a somewhat different attitude: "In reality the mode in
which the materials of music are now worked up for artistic use, is in itself a
wondrous work of art, at which the experience, ingenuity, and aesthetic feeling of European nations has laboured for between two and three thousand
years, since the days of Terpander and Pythagoras" (p. 249). In addition to
this, of course, the principle of the tonal system may at the same time also
govern the individual musical work. Perhaps it will necessarily do so and,
among the aesthetic principles that underlie a musical work, actually be the
most fundamental of all.

In the following chapter (chap. 14), the formal basis of music is more
definitely outlined:

> Music was forced first to select artistically, and then to shape for itself,
> the material on which it works. Painting and sculpture find the funda-
> mental character of their materials, form and colour, in nature itself,
> which they strive to imitate. Poetry finds its material ready formed
> in the words of language. Architecture has, indeed, also to create its

own forms; but they are partly forced upon it by technical and not by purely artistic considerations. Music alone finds an infinitely rich but totally shapeless plastic material in the tones of the human voice and artificial musical instruments, which must be shaped on purely artistic principles, unfettered by any reference to utility as in architecture, or to the imitation of nature as in the fine arts, or to the existing symbolical meaning of sounds as in poetry. There is a greater and more absolute freedom in the use of the material for music than for any other of the arts. (p. 250)

Specifically, Helmholtz singles out as the first fact in all music that *"alterations of pitch in melodies take place by intervals, and not by continuous transitions."* The psychological reason for this is the same, he believes, as that "which led to rhythmic subdivision periodically repeated." Thus, the same formal principle applies to both pitch and rhythm:

As we have seen, then, melody has to express a motion, in such a manner that the hearer may easily, clearly, and certainly appreciate the character of that motion by *immediate perception*. This is only possible when the steps of this motion, their rapidity and their amount are also exactly *measurable* by immediate sensible perception. Melodic motion is change of pitch in time. To measure it perfectly, the length of time elapsed, and the distance between the pitches, must be measurable. This is possible for immediate audition only on condition that the alterations both in time and pitch should proceed by regular and determinate degrees. This is immediately clear for time, for even the scientific, as well as all other measurement of time, depends on the rhythmical recurrence of similar events, the revolution of the earth or moon, or the swings of a pendulum. . . . It was also necessary that the alteration of pitch should proceed by intervals, because motion is not measurable by immediate perception unless the amount of space to be measured is divided off into degrees. . . .

The individual parts of a melody reach the ear in succession. We cannot perceive them all at once. We cannot observe backwards and forwards at pleasure. Hence for a clear and sure measurement of the change of pitch, no means was left but progression by determinate degrees. This series of degrees is laid down in the musical scale. . . . The musical scale is as it were the divided rod, by which we measure progression in pitch, as rhythm measures progression in time. Hence the analogy between the scale of tones and rhythm naturally occurred to musical theoreticians of ancient as well as modern times. (pp. 252–53)

Helmholtz proceeds to consider how tones are selected for the various scales of the world. Since it seems that the octave, the fifth, and the fourth are found universally, he tries to explain that the reason for this lies in the partial structure of tones. In discussing smaller intervals, Helmholtz refers to the principle of determining differences in pitch by ear that seem to be equal. This principle, however, "has never prevailed over the feeling of tonal relationship for the division of the fourth, at least in artistically developed music." Helmholtz defines the natural relation of tones in terms of coincidence in their partial structure:

> We shall consider musical tones to be related in the first degree which have two identical partial tones; and related in the second degree, when they are both related in the first degree to some third musical tone. The louder the coincident in proportion to the non-coincident partials of compound tones related in the first degree, the closer is their relationship and the more easily will both singers and hearers feel the common character of both the tones. (p. 256)

This relation, however, has its basis in mathematics, and it is obviously formal.

In connection with the consideration of dissonance and discord, Helmholtz once again distinguishes between sensation and aesthetics: "That which is physically agreeable is an important adjunct and support to aesthetic beauty, but it is certainly not identical with it. On the contrary, in all the arts we frequently employ its opposite, that which is physically disagreeable, partly to bring the beauty of the first into relief, by contrast, and partly to gain a more powerful means for the expression of passion" (pp. 330–31). But it is the formal relations of a musical work that provide the essential government of the whole:

> Up to this point we have considered only the relations of the tones in a piece of music with its tonic, and of its chords with its tonic chord. On these relations depends the connection of the parts of a mass of tone into one coherent whole. But besides this the succession of the tones and chords must be regulated by natural relations. The mass of sound thus becomes more intimately bound up together, and, as a general rule, we must aim at producing such a connection, although, exceptionally, peculiar expression may necessitate the selection of a more violent and less obvious path of progression. (p. 350)

Helmholtz's final chapter is devoted to aesthetic matters. In it, he again considers the relation between rational form and diversity of style. Since the principle of tonal relation does not always or everywhere "exclusively" determine the construction of the scale, he argues, this principle must be regarded "to some extent as a *freely selected principle of style*. . . . But, on the other hand, the art of music in Europe was historically developed from that principle, and on this fact depends the main proof that it was really as important as we have assumed it to be. The preference first given to the *diatonic scale,* and finally the exclusive use of that scale, introduced the principle of tonal relationship in all its integrity into the musical scale" (p. 364). This principle, he then shows, penetrated far deeper in its harmonic form than in its melodic one. As we can see, however, by the qualifications "exclusively" and "to some extent" in the argument presented above, Helmholtz is nowhere willing to relinquish his formal principle altogether.

He treats the ear much as he does the external world, for the two are closely related, in his conception, in their mathematical-physical nature and thus in their intrinsic formal characteristics. He has tried to show, he says,

> that the construction of scales and of harmonic tissue is a product of artistic invention, and by no means furnished by the natural formation or natural function of our ear, as it has been hitherto most generally asserted. Of course the laws of the natural function of our ear play a great and influential part in this result; these laws are, as it were, the building stones with which the edifice of our musical system has been erected, and the necessity of accurately understanding the nature of these materials in order to understand the construction of the edifice itself, has been clearly shown by the course of our investigations upon this very subject. But just as people with differently directed tastes can erect extremely different kinds of buildings with the same stones, so also the history of music shows us that the same properties of the human ear could serve as the foundation of very different musical systems. Consequently it seems to me that we cannot doubt, that not merely the composition of perfect musical works of art, but even the construction of our system of scales, keys, chords, in short of all that is usually comprehended in a treatise of Thorough Bass, is the work of artistic invention, and hence must be subject to the laws of artistic beauty. (pp. 365–66)

Thus, the musical system and the formulated elements of music apart from tone as such become matters of beauty fundamentally comparable to the musical work itself. There is an essential equation between the product of culture and the product of the individual. As the argument advances, the formal basis weakens, but it persists, even if only as a belief:

The aesthetic analysis of complete musical works of art, and the comprehension of the reasons of their beauty, encounter apparently invincible obstacles at almost every point. But in the field of elementary musical art we have now gained so much insight into its internal connection that we are able to bring the results of our investigations to bear on the views which have been formed and in modern times nearly universally accepted respecting the cause and character of artistic beauty in general. It is, in fact, not difficult to discover a close connection and agreement between them. . . .

No doubt is now entertained that beauty is subject to laws and rules dependent on the nature of human intelligence. The difficulty consists in the fact that these laws and rules, on whose fulfillment beauty depends and by which it must be judged, are not consciously present to the mind, either of the artist who creates the work, or the observer who contemplates it. Art works with design, but the work of art ought to have the appearance of being undesigned, and must be judged on that ground. Art creates as imagination pictures, regularly without conscious law, designedly without conscious aim. (p. 366)

With this, mathematical relation has become "law" and "rules." But these can no longer be identified; the regularity and the design are unconscious and should be so. At most, Helmholtz argues, we can single out particular connections, but not all, and even these are in general not mathematical relations. A work of art must be "reasonable," Helmholtz urges, but our critical examination, our effort to make its harmony and beauty clear, can be only partly successful. But a conscious understanding of the adaptation of a work to reason is not really necessary either for the creator or for the percipient: "What is aesthetically beautiful is recognized by the immediate judgment of a cultivated taste, which declares it pleasing or displeasing, without any comparison whatever with law or conception" (pp. 366–67). Artistic form is thus unperceived as such. It is essential to art, but so is its imperceptibility. The paradox can be solved only if we divine its presence, or if art presents an unmistakable quality or feeling of form, or if aesthetic experience can be accounted for in no other way. Delight in beauty, Helmholtz says, coming now fully into Kant's territory, we hold to be "in regular accordance with the nature of mind in general":

The principal difficulty in pursuing this object, is to understand how regularity can be apprehended by intuition without being consciously felt to exist. And this unconsciousness of regularity is not a mere accident in the effect of the beautiful on our mind, which may indifferently exist or not; it is, on the contrary, most clearly, prominently, and essentially important. For through apprehending everywhere traces of regularity, connection, and order, without being able to grasp the law and plan of the whole, there arises in our mind a feeling that the work of art which we are contemplating is the product of a design which far exceeds anything we can conceive at the moment, and which hence partakes of the character of the illimitable. (p. 367)

Although the term does not appear, what Helmholtz conveys in this passage is nothing other than Kant's "aesthetic idea."

The properties of the work of art testify to the mental powers of the artist and therefore give rise, in Helmholtz's view, to a feeling of moral elevation. In the contemplation of works of art, he believes, we learn to feel

that even in the obscure depths of a healthy and harmoniously developed human mind, which are at least for the present inaccessible to analysis by conscious thought, there slumbers a germ of order that is capable of rich intellectual cultivation, and we learn to recognize and admire in the work of art, though draughted in unimportant material, the picture of a similar arrangement of the universe, governed by law and reason in all its parts. The contemplation of a real work of art awakens our confidence in the originally healthy nature of the human mind, when uncribbed, unharassed, unobscured, and unfalsified.

But for all this it is an essential condition that the whole extent of the regularity and design of a work of art should *not* be apprehended consciously. It is precisely from that part of its regular subjection to reason, which escapes our conscious apprehension, that a work of art exalts and delights us, and that the chief effects of the artistically beautiful proceed, *not* from the part which we are able fully to analyse. (p. 367)

Thus, as he emphasizes, Helmholtz has found, in the musical system and harmony themselves, "a comparatively simple and transparent solution of that fundamental enigma of aesthetics." In the course of his investigation, he claims, he has also deduced the whole theoretical system of European music. Just as Rameau believed that he had developed the modern harmonic system and the foundation of aesthetics as well from mathematical and physical "science," so Helmholtz presents a still more sweeping expression of the same visionary project, extending his scheme into aesthetics even more generally than Rameau did. But aesthetics, as Descartes had conceded long before, contains problems for which the powers of science are insufficient.

A totally abstract kind of formalism can be found in the *Allgemeine Aesthetik als Formwissenschaft* (1865) of Robert Zimmermann, a professor of philosophy at the University of Vienna. As Kant had done, Zimmermann attributes aesthetic pleasure solely to form, but the form he has in mind can be apprehended only by thought, not by sense perception. There are elementary forms—correctness, perfection, agreement, balance, closure, the characteristic. And there are derived forms—the application of these to more than two members. What appears in these forms—the content—and the material through which this content becomes manifest are extrinsic matters that cannot affect the nature of the beautiful or the pleasure it gives, for these are due only to the forms, which remain the same eternally. The development of art concerns only the material, while aesthetics has the task of seeking out the forms. Which tonal connections are pleasing, for example, is decided by the ear, but the forms by means of which they please can be determined only by thought. Ideas themselves and their attributes are sufficient. And the a priori nature of the forms enables them to serve as norms for the evaluation of musical experience.

Whatever music as perceived may seem to possess in addition to form Zimmermann must account for as a contribution of the listener, as subjective rather than objective. Thus, what appears as a dissonance in music is taken to be a consonance; or, otherwise expressed, the nature of a dissonance is to represent itself to be a consonance. In this way, dissonance is transcended, and the form of "correctness" arises. The idea (consonance) takes the place of the actual (dissonance) and passes for it. But this artifice is not pleasing and must be suppressed, with the result that now the form of balance arises, and this produces the appearance of vitality, which is transformed into soul. Then, with the occurrence of actual consonance at the end of the music, the form of closure arises, and the whole motion reveals itself as a work of harmonious intelligence.

Thus, by substituting an elaborate fiction for the properties of music that are evident in ordinary experience, Zimmermann seeks to explain the life and soul that these properties irresistibly imply in music but that *cannot* be accounted for by forms alone as products arising from a complex psychological process of the listener. An aesthetic that argues away the clearly perceived properties and qualities of music instead of taking them as a point of departure is, however, forced to add excessive ingenuity to excessive abstraction and is too far removed from the reality of experience to possess much interest or value.[8]

"Vom Musikalisch-Schönen" (1854), Zimmermann's lengthy review of Hanslick's treatise, is largely an enthusiastic presentation and endorsement of Hanslick's ideas. It has the value, in addition, of calling attention to the undeveloped positive aspects of the treatise, although without fully elucidating Hanslick's conception. While music does not represent feelings, Zimmermann says, it does represent ideas. But these are musical ideas—ideas such as "dying away" or "hurrying"—and are expressed in tonal relations. The *Geist* (spirit or mind) that we demand of all art manifests itself in music purely in tonal relations. It is essentially invention—of new motives and tonal combinations. But aesthetics can investigate this only in the musical work, not in the psychology of the composer. Nevertheless, the participation of the composer's personality is not excluded by the strictly objective character of music:

> On the contrary, where the *Geist* of music resides in invention, but only in musical invention, the subjectivity of the artist has more than sufficient scope in the idiosyncrasy of this invention. But what makes Halévy's music bizarre, Auber's graceful, what brings about the peculiarity by which we at once recognize Mendelssohn, Spohr, Schumann, all this can be traced back to purely musical specifications, without an appeal to the enigma of feeling. Why the frequent six-five chords, the narrow diatonic themes in Mendelssohn, the chromaticism and enharmonics in Spohr, the short, two-part rhythms in Auber, produce just this definite ineradicable impression, that, to be sure, neither psychology nor physiology can answer.[9]

The content or import of music (its *Gehalt*), Zimmermann concludes, lies in its definite tonal configuration as the free creation of the mind in material that is devoid of any concept but receptive to mental formulation.

In addition to this, Zimmermann elaborates in his own way Hanslick's conception of opera as a ceaseless battle between musical and dramatic principles. In fact, Zimmermann says, opera simply is not part of the aesthetics of pure music. The demand for a dramatic music represents a confusion of concepts, a belief that all the arts are basically the same, whereas they are all completely disparate in their nature: "The true root of the error resides in the effort to trace everything beautiful to one principle.—But what is beautiful in tones has no application to colors at all. . . . Thus either we explain the opera as a purely musical work and thereby explicitly renounce its dramatic nature as not belonging to music, or we save its dramatic character in that we cease to consider it as a pure work of music. There is no third way. The opera is precisely not a work of a *single* art but of a joint action *of all* the arts."[10] In a compound work of art, then, all we can do is to see that the musical part does not contradict the text too blatantly. Such is the inevitable outcome of a formalist view of opera.

Hermann Siebeck, a university professor in Basel and in Giessen, adopts the characteristic formalist conception of music as an art of motion in his work *Das Wesen der ästhetischen Anschauung* (1875). Tones enable us to convey the character of motion, whether of the external world or of the heart. But as far as inner motion is concerned, only its most general property can be reproduced: differences of speed and of intensity. The true content of music, then, very much as Hanslick maintained, is forms of tonal motion. Like Hanslick also, Siebeck presents a supplementary "positive" conception, for he describes the motions reproduced by music as feelingful and individually defined. But this gives the motions a content—namely, mood—and they cease to be mere succession. It is mood that shapes the various forms of motion, and mood dwells in them as the soul does in the body, becoming the law of the whole that underlies each particular feature. Thus, content, again, is inconsistently characterized both as mood and as sounding forms in motion.[11]

The formalist view of music presented by Gustav Theodor Fechner in his *Vorschule der Ästhetik* (1876) is characterized by a basic distinction between direct and associative factors in aesthetic impressions. No one doubts, he maintains, that tones and tonal relations can please or displease to some degree apart from any meaning or purpose that may be connected with them and without recollection of any previous external or inner experience of them. A pure, full tone, for example, is more pleasing than an impure one or a shriek. But when association plays a role, it can disturb as well as increase the pleasure. In music, however, as opposed to visual art, the direct factor rather than the associative one plays the chief role in impressions.

There are, then, essential and unessential effects of music, and the essential ones are independent of association. These include musical moods, which depend merely on modifications of tempo, beat, rhythm, direction and change of ascent or descent in pitch, and strength and register of the tones. These moods are not "feelings," for feelings have a greater definiteness owing to the qualities of association. Thus, Hanslick is indisputably right "when he denies music the power to call forth or, as we say, to express such feelings with definiteness. It is not able to because it cannot call forth the associative ideas of these feelings with definiteness. It is different with those general moods. It requires in fact no association to be gently moved by gentle music, aroused by lively music, tragically disposed by sad music."[12] Similarly, the development and refinement of this sensitivity to musical relations are due, not to associations that accrue to them, but simply to the ability to grasp more complex tonal relations.

To be sure, the various features of music can bring to mind many things outside music so that along with music associative ideas may exist. These are only secondary, however, and the imitation or recollection of other things should certainly not be considered the chief impression made by musical configurations. Musical representation is in fact far from perfect; conversely, what is represented can in no way reproduce the magic of music or account for it.

Fechner acknowledges that music has much in common with the outside world and that it can suggest relations and events of all kinds, but he does not believe that the composer's experience of life and thought outside music will enhance the intrinsic value of his compositions. Because of its relation to the external world, however, music can serve to characterize extramusical occurrences, as represented on the stage or in poetry. Similarly, independent musical compositions can be given verbal interpretations that may even agree with the music in general character and certain central features but will certainly not agree with it in detail. But such interpretations, Fechner points out, are neither equivalent to musical enjoyment nor necessary to it. Indeed, they have nothing to do with the specifically musical enjoyment, which remains the core of the whole experience.

If we exclude the associative factors of musical experience, however, we are still left with more than tonal relations, for the evocation and expression of moods by these relations, are, in Fechner's view, characteristic if not intrinsic parts of music as such. It is difficult to see why *mood* is not simply another term for feeling that is defined only in its general character. The conception can apparently be described as one of autonomy, therefore, but not very well as one that is formalist.

In his important treatise *Das Musikalisch-Schöne und das Gesamtkunstwerk vom Standpunkt der formalen Aesthetik* (1877), Ottokar Hostinsky, a professor at the Czech University of Prague, sought to reconcile the views of Hanslick with those of Wagner. The means at the disposal of an art, he announces, following Hanslick,

> define and delimit also the compass of its territory. If it desired to extend its rule beyond these natural boundaries, desired to venture on tasks that only another art, with other means, would be equal to, it would obviously have to deal with a rival whose capacities in this respect would be far superior to its own. Thus every art, in spite of elements it has in common with other arts, has a certain field of specific beauty.[13]

Above all, Hostinsky maintains, every art must preserve its own nature strictly and in a pure state. Its specific beauty will always be its highest goal. In support of this idea, he cites not only Hanslick but also Aristotle, Lessing, and Herbart.

A vital part of Hostinsky's formalist position is the distinction he makes between "feelings" and "moods" since he accepts the thesis that music arouses moods but not feelings. A definite ideational content is implied by the term *feeling,* while *mood* designates only a certain inner condition that is determined by the rest or motion, by the demeanor or comport, of whatever is progressively presented:

> The mood is thus more the how, the formal side of our feeling, opposed as such to the ideational content that underlies the feeling, the what of the feeling. Now it is clear that this ideational content can belong to the most various fields: feelings can be produced by thoughts, by tones, by colors and shapes, by corporeal sensations, and many other things, or, respectively, by certain motions and interactions of these ideas—in the various categories, to be sure, to very various extents. It lies in the nature of the matter that of the feeling belonging to a certain category of ideas, for example, the realm of concepts and thoughts, not the "content" at all, but at most the "mood," that is, not the what, but only the how of the feeling, can be reproduced by another category of ideas, for example, by the world of tone; in the case, namely, that the latter category of ideas calls forth through its progress an internal state of motion similar to what the former did. (pp. 464–65)

When a musical work puts us in a certain mood or changes our mood, it creates the mood in us—with extreme rapidity—as the result of a psychic process that starts with the entrance of tonal sensations into consciousness. But to arouse a mood is not to "express" one and still less to "represent" or to "describe" one. Now the poet or painter or sculptor presents a definite content of thought that calls forth a mood, as a cause does an effect. But the musician puts us in a mood from which we infer a cause—not the true cause, the tonal sensations, but an entirely different one, which could have called forth that kind of mood under different circumstances. This happens often enough, if not invariably. The mood that music puts us into reproduces ideas that elsewhere precede it as a basis and then generally accompany it. But these ideas are our subjective addition to the music; they do not belong to the musical work the way the mood that a poem necessarily creates does to the poem. The objectivity of the work of art has ended and the subjectivity of the listener begun.

Hostinsky undertakes next to consider the content of the beautiful in music, and he eliminates five classes of object as possible contents. Spatial objects cannot be represented musically, nor can objects in motion, or natural sounds, or the sound of speech, or the content of speech. It is therefore generally said that music addresses not the understanding but the heart, that its content is not thoughts but feelings, affections, and passions. Even so, the emotions excited in us by musical works "*are only the effect, the subjective impression of the objective work of art as such, not, however, its 'object,' its 'content,' or even its 'purpose,'* even when it has demonstrably been the *cause of their excitation"* (p. 470).

Thus, the aesthetic pleasure or displeasure in certain forms in any area of experience is an original or direct one. It is not due to the fact that these forms "recall" analogous relations of motion in the world of feelings and thoughts, in the microcosm or macrocosm, in the realm of the good and the true, and so on or that they "adumbrate" such relations or mirror them in any way: "In a musical work of art—even when it actually purports to be the 'image' of an emotion—there are only forms and relations that are borne by tones; they also can be judged, therefore, only as *tonal forms, tonal relations"* (p. 471).

Having considered the general nature of music, Hostinsky turns his attention to opera. If the intrinsic limits of music cannot be widened by its union with poetry, as Hanslick maintained, then the connection of music and poetry must give rise to a new art, and song and opera are not a subdivision of "music." The postulate of "purity of style" requires a strict separation of vocal music and instrumental music. Indeed, the judgment of song and opera in terms of instrumental music is the central defect of Hanslick's treatise. Hanslick is fundamentally inconsistent. He maintains, on the one hand, that the ideal of opera is to satisfy the dramatic and musical demands equally, that opera is therefore a constant battle between the principles of dramatic accuracy and musical beauty. There must be a constant mediation between the two, but never a predominance of one over the other. But he also insists, on the other hand, that, before all else, opera is music, not drama. Wagner, of course, expresses the opposite point of view.

The key to the problem of opera, in Hostinsky's opinion, lies in the excitation of moods. Now musical moods do not belong to aesthetics, but they cease to be irrelevant to beauty when they become a disturbance, and this happens when they conflict with other moods that are excited at the same time. Such a situation would arise, for example, if dance music were used to accompany a graveyard scene in a drama. It follows, then, that subjective impressions are of the greatest importance, that they are in fact of decisive significance, in the organization of every composite work of art. The agreement of word and tone in this respect may be termed a psychological rule of art. It is not an aesthetic rule, but it is of vital importance nevertheless.

From an objective point of view, Hostinsky continues, taking up basic arguments of German operatic aesthetics that reach back well into the eighteenth century, an agreement or harmony in the union of two arts concerns their content or material and the form of their manifestation. In their content, poetry and scenery can agree, but poetry and music have no point of contact. Since the material of music is completely different from that of the other two arts, there can be no contradiction in this respect with either of the others. Formally, all three arts agree in the fact that they are temporal manifestations, so there can be an organic union of the three. But with respect to the subjective impression of the artistic union, a third factor appears: the unity of mood of the arts. Since this involves not aesthetics but the subjectivity of the perceiver, we must distinguish two viewpoints applicable to the mutual relations of the arts in a *Gesamtkunstwerk:* that of aesthetics and that of the theory of art.

In the creation of a work of art, which belongs to the theory of art, the material determines the form; in a union of the arts, the material and form of the whole will be determined by the art whose forms are tied to a material existing outside its own sphere. Poetry, reinforced by scenery, thus gives drama its material and its form. Pantomime and gesture follow poetry, and music follows gesture. All the component arts have equal rights, however, from the point of view of aesthetics; the loss in beauty of one cannot be justified by the gain of another. But the intention of the dramatic poet is decisive in the acceptance or rejection of any particular contribution of a component art. Relatively speaking, then, the text of an opera is the most independent component because its form proceeds from its specific content, while music is in some degree dependent:

> From the standpoint of aesthetics, namely, the judgment of the beauty of the objective work of art, anyone is at all events wrong who will in any way subordinate music to poetry or place a lower value on it; here the pronouncement of Hanslick cited above is much more valid: "The equal satisfaction of the musical and the dramatic demands passes correctly for the ideal of opera." From the standpoint of the theory of art, however, that is, of the creative artist, Wagner's axiom, that the opera is first of all drama, and only then music, is in principle perfectly justified. (p. 480)

That opera is first of all music, and only then drama, cannot be endorsed from either standpoint. In sum, then, Hostinsky makes use of Hanslick's formalism to reinforce Wagner's theory of opera, thus producing an impressive synthesis of a powerful thesis and an equally powerful antithesis. He even advocates an important supplementary thesis: "There is no formally satisfying poetic creation the compositional schema of which cannot be used successfully for music" (p. 482).

In our discussion of Edmund Gurney as an opponent of Spencer (chapter 9), it was evident that his rejection of the speech theory of music was really a consequence of a larger conception of musical autonomy. *The Power of Sound* (1880) presents this conception of music in detail, together with its ramifications, and the central idea appears also in the essay "On Some Disputed Points in Music" (1876).

Gurney finds support for his theory of a special musical faculty in the views of Darwin, who maintained, as we have seen (chapter 9), that, "although the sounds emitted by animals of all kinds serve many purposes, a strong case can be made out that the vocal organs were primarily used and perfected ₁in relation to the propagation of the species." [14] Of the sounds produced by animals in general Darwin states, "Their chief, and in some cases exclusive, use appears to be either to call or to charm the opposite sex." The facts he adduces, many of which Spencer contests, lead to a hypothesis that Darwin expresses as follows: "The impassioned orator, bard, or musician, when with his varied tones and cadences he excites the strongest emotions in his hearers, little suspects that he uses the same means by which, at an extremely remote period, his half-human ancestors aroused each other's ardent passions during their mutual courtship and rivalry" (p. 119). Gurney continues:

These ideas may seem at first sight somewhat startling; but when we realize the extraordinary depth and indescribability of the emotions of music, the very remoteness and far-reachingness of the explanation is in favour of its validity. Till we come to examine the actual phenomena of musical emotion, I cannot hope to show how admirably Mr. Darwin's theory fits in with them; and how it not only stands alone, among theories as yet suggested, in resting on a broad ground of evidence, but is apparently the only possible one which will the least account for present facts. It must suffice here to mention in the briefest way the prime characteristic of Music, the alpha and omega of its essential effect: namely, its perpetual production in us of an emotional excitement of a very intense kind, which yet cannot be defined under any known head of emotion. So far as it can be described, it seems like a fusion of strong emotions transfigured into a wholly new experience, whereof if we seek to bring out the separate threads we are hopelessly baulked; for triumph and tenderness, desire and satisfaction, yielding and insistence, may seem to be all there at once, yet without any dubiousness or confusion in the result; or rather elements seem there which we struggle dimly to adumbrate by such words, thus making the experience seem vague only by our own attempt to analyse it, while really the beauty has the unity and individuality pertaining to clear and definite form. Even when the emotion takes on a definable hue, a kinship it may be to laughter or to tears, it still has the character of directing down these special channels a high-pitched excitement having its independent source at the general watershed of unique musical impression. And it is just this characteristic of fused and indescribable emotion which seems explicable on Mr. Darwin's view: for a pleasure which was associated with the most exciting passions, would have correspondingly large opportunities not only for increase but for differentiation. (pp. 119–20)

It cannot escape our notice that this theory, in spite of its claim to generality and its attachment to form and beauty, is cast essentially in terms of the emotional effect of music and that it also bears marks of the Romantic conception of the all-inclusive character of musical emotion. Similarly, there is a characteristic nineteenth-century perspective in the conception of the universality of music, which appears, somewhat paradoxically, in a discussion that reveals the social position of music as a consequence of its nature:

Our whole argument as to the nature of musical impressions and the roots of musical pleasure, with their deep and separate place in the human organisation, our whole survey of that independence of intellectual, moral, and external conditions which specially characterises Music, tend to the same result, a unique width and depth of popular instinct for it. In its peculiar isolation lies its peculiar strength: in the fact that its utterances pass direct to the consciousness, without the chance of obscuration or distortion from vulgarity, ignorance, or prejudice, lies its power to awaken in thousands who are inaccessible to any other form of high emotion a mighty sense of beauty, order, and perfection. (p. 399)

In the final analysis, the preconceptions of Gurney's thought cannot obscure the profundity and range of his conception. His treatise remains one of the most impressive in the field of musical aesthetics. Of particular value is the painstaking effort, in the context of a theory of autonomy, to analyze the relations that music bears to experience of all kinds and to the human condition. The specific nature of music cannot be questioned, but music is nevertheless not a sealed-off department of human experience. What are the ways, Gurney asks, that it is penetrated by properties found also in the external world, how extensively do such properties determine its nature, and how importantly or intrinsically do they connect it with other manifestations of human intelligence and creativity? These are obviously large, significant, and difficult questions, and their detailed investigation in the framework of a treatise devoted to the specific nature of music is one of the most valuable features of Gurney's voluminous work.

CHAPTER ELEVEN

THE IDEALIST TRADITION

T he course of idealism after Hegel is characterized chiefly by a secularization in which the Absolute recedes in importance or plays no easily discernible role. At the same time, the other major foundation of idealist views that is represented by Kant's conception of the aesthetic idea increases in importance. But this changed field of force, so to speak, prompts a consideration of what "idealism" can be taken to mean in general. If we regard music as an objectivity that is produced and perceived by human agency, the alternative presents itself in aesthetics of considering either the music itself to be the essential matter in the whole of the interrelation or, on the contrary, the activity and experience of the composer and listener. This alternative is thus manifested in the contrast of formalism and subjectivity. But if inner experience is taken to be the essential matter, it is possible to conceive its nature not only as a manifestation of the Absolute but also as an aspect of human experience in its own terms, as simply given empirically. In the latter case, we can further believe that this musical experience is essentially or most importantly emotive and proceed to view it either in a realistic light, as containing feelings or feelings basically the same as those occurring outside music and therefore in some degree open to scientific examination, or in an idealistic light, as belonging to a realm of mind distinctly separate from material reality and therefore to be described or known, if at all, through its own special methodology, be it intuitive or philosophical.

Unfortunately, however, these various alternatives are not neatly distinct from one another. In the present chapter in particular, the Absolute often leads a shadowy existence behind an apparently nonmetaphysical examination of inner experience, and a consideration of feeling or musical feeling as entirely separate from the material world often turns to scientific psychology. Just as formalism does not deny the existence of feeling but only its relevance, so idealism can include formalism, especially as manifested by mathematics, and an ostensibly idealist consideration of the special realm of feeling often produces a highly realistic picture of musical feeling that closely connects it with the feelings known in the concrete contexts of life. We can speak then of a tendency during the course of the nineteenth century to eclecticism and syncretism in musical aesthetics and set this tendency against an earlier phase of the century in which ideas were presented in more definite or more striking form—a classical phase, as it were, that was then subjected to elaboration.

Idealism, of course, was not inaugurated by Schelling and Hegel; as a perennial philosophic type it presents a wide variety of forms and is hardly confined to the philosophy of Absolute idealism. Idealist aesthetics is represented, for example, in A. W. Schlegel's lectures on fine art and literature (pt. 1, 1801–2), and it was an established feature of Romantic literature at the beginning of the century. There is no doubt, however, that it was given a new impetus in music as a reaction to Hanslick's treatise of 1854.

Kant's conception of the aesthetic idea has a persuasive exponent in the Danish scientist Hans Christian Oersted, whose essay "Ueber die Gründe des Vergnügens, welches die Töne hervorbringen" was published in 1851 but had been written in 1808.[1] Musical pleasure depends on reason, Oersted maintains, as well as on the senses—a thesis that has antecedents as far back as antiquity and is discussed in some detail, for example, at the beginning of Ptolemy's *Harmonics*. We are not conscious of the rational basis of this pleasure, Oersted continues, for the rationality contained in tones and their relations is a hidden one, which unconsciously penetrates our soul. (Leibnitz's unconscious counting of the soul has clearly become a modern topos.)

In his discussion of the idea in aesthetics Oersted takes the geometric figure of the circle as an example. The concept of a circle, he says, is constructed by abstract thought: the circle is analyzed into characteristics that are then added together. In contrast, the circle can be contemplated as a whole, and this contemplated whole will contain properties intrinsic to its nature that are not included in its concept. The contemplation is of a multiplicity that is fused into a unity, and the beauty we perceive in this way is not dependent on our recognition of the properties.

The circle is beautiful, Oersted maintains, as the representation of an idea that is one with its nature; it is beautiful as a consequence of its nature or its idea. But its nature remains, for us, tied to its sensuousness; space cannot be excluded from it. This leads back to Oersted's point of departure: the beauty of forms is a union of reason and sense. The source of this beauty is solely in the idea that is expressed, but this idea acts unconsciously on the outer and inner sense: the recognition of it is not necessary to the impression of beauty.

Turning to music, Oersted finds convincing evidence of this theory in the famous acoustic demonstration of Chladni, who produced a tone by bowing a metal disc that was covered with powder. The vibration produces a striking symmetrical pattern of hills and nodes, which leaves no doubt, Oersted feels, of the operation of a hidden reason even in what we perceive as a single tone. But this secret reason is clearly operative also in the octave, the fifth, and the triad, and it is operative as well—without being known to the listener or even to the composer—in a musical work of art. The activity of the musician is thus a manifestation of divinity; it rests on the activation of eternal reason, which also contains an infinite mathematics. Since works of art harmonize with the highest reason, they fire our soul with enthusiasm, carry it away, and fill it with a nameless bliss. Art is therefore to be honored, as are nature and reason.

If Romantic literature is often devoted to aesthetic ideas, the aesthetics of Oersted, like that of Herder, reveals a reverse kind of conjunction, for it often assumes a poetic expressiveness. It is thus evident once again that there is a close kinship between literature and aesthetics in the first half of the nineteenth century. Paradoxically, the soberly scientific idealism of Oersted is also poetic. Still more surprisingly, however, it appeals to a divine principle and thus contains an eighteenth-century predecessor, which in turn has its own long history, of the subsequent idealism of the Absolute.

Writers critical of Hanslick predictably turn to some form of idealism. *Die Grenzen der Musik und Poesie* (1856), of Wilhelm August Ambros, clearly has an explicit thesis deriving from Lessing's *Laokoon*, but the definition of the boundary between the arts of music and poetry is necessarily based to an important extent on considerations of idealism. Ambros by no means, however, conceives music as purely or essentially formal and poetry as purely idealist. His remarkable artistic sensitivity—which in this early work already extends to the visual arts—leads to a more complex conception, in which idealism in some fashion enters music as well as poetry. Both a formal and an ideal aspect of music are presented almost at once, by an appeal to Bernhard Adolph Marx, who "lays hold . . . of the full life" of music:

> The process of the historical development of music . . . is traced back by him to definite fundamental features, and divided into grand periods, in which one develops itself out of the other, so to speak, with natural necessity. The first period of development he regards as that in which the formalism of melody, of harmony, of counterpoint was germinating,

grew and perfected itself, as it were the body of music, the "crystalline tone-growth," as he calls it. . . . The transition to the following period is brought about by Sebastian Bach . . . "the marble begins, through the fervor of the new Pygmalion, to be warmed from within, and to take on a glimmer of life-color." The complete life-color is given to it by the school of Haydn and Mozart, the "art of the soul," which has to do with moods of the soul; whence the art of the intellect (Beethoven) then develops, which poetizes in tones, and no more excites feelings as though incidentally, but develops them in an orderly sequence, justified in itself.[2]

This process of development, however, produces the problematic situation that Ambros seeks to resolve:

Music, ever striving conformably to its nature after more definite expression and more distinctly stamped individuality, has at length attained a standpoint which, in itself belonging to the art of the intellect, seems to push to its outermost boundary, because it tries to represent, on the stage of inner soul-life, what speech alone can illustrate perfectly—some external event, some object to be grasped by the senses—thus trespassing upon another domain. (p. 311)

"In short," Ambros concludes, "music acts toward the adherents of mere play with forms, pretty much as Diogenes did to the philosopher who denied motion, in that he, when the latter was proving that there was and could be no motion, arose and actually walked to and fro" (p. 311).

It is only because music is more than form, of course, that it is able to intrude into the domain of poetry, thus giving rise to the attempt to define the line of division between the two arts. More specifically, as Ambros argues, there is an area of overlap between music and poetry, which consists in the "excitement of moods." This is true not only of lyric poetry but even of didactic, epic, epigrammatic, and satirical poetry. In the epigram, for example, the point "unexpectedly springing forth, can express the effect of the humorous up to the provocation to laughter," while in the satire Horace fills us "with his graceful waggishness" and Juvenal "with his profoundly moral indignation": "The effect of music likewise consists essentially in this, that it awakens moods in the hearer, and, indeed, moods of very determinate coloring. Mozart's 'Figaro' has, as yet, hardly disposed anyone to solemn seriousness, his 'Requiem' hardly anyone to a cheerful love of life" (p. 313). Ambros pursues his argument:

Now, music conveys moods of finished expression; it, as it were, forces them upon the hearer. It conveys them in finished form, because it possesses no means for expressing the previous series of ideas which speech can clearly and definitely express. The charm of music, which one is so very much inclined to ascribe to sensuous euphony alone, lies, in a great measure, if not for the most part, in this contrasting of finished states of mind, concerning whose previous series of ideas it gives us no account; for we speak of charm when we see powerful results produced whose causes remain enveloped, as far as we can see, in mysterious obscurity. Now, the state of mind which the hearer receives from music he trans- fers back to it; he says: "It expresses this or that mood." . . . With the expression "music awakens moods," there is no infringement of it, nor is the matter pushed too far into the subjectivity of the hearer, for the resources of the real poetry of sentiment, of lyric poetry, also extend no further. It is only in the same improper sense as of music that we can say of lyric poetry that "it expresses feelings." A versified dry statement of joy or sorrow excites no mood at all, therefore bears none in itself, and cannot lay claim to the name of a lyric poem, for the reason that it is no poetry at all. (p. 314)

Poetry either mentions the ideas that have a certain mood as their result or presents images that evoke a mood:

Thus, we infer, from the given conception, the sentiment conjecturable from it, but not named. In the case of music, just the opposite way is to be taken. From the given feeling we infer the idea conjecturable from it, but not expressly mentioned to us. . . . Now, if certain chains of ideas usually call forth moods of a decidedly individual coloring, and if music succeeds in calling forth precisely these moods, we infer these definite chains of ideas from the mood in question; we go so far (for the same reason for which we carried our feeling over into music) as even to transfer to music these definite chains of ideas. . . .

The circumstance is not to be overlooked, however, that there are moods for whose designation the ordinary terminology possesses no names. To these belongs directly that state of mind which might be called "well-tempered," "good-natured," a result of several heteroge- neous states, which hold each other reciprocally within bounds. . . .

It would be wrong to think that this or that music "says nothing" be- cause it does not point to any one nominally defined point of division on the scale of feeling; just as a human countenance is not to be denied all character and expression because at a given instant it does not bear the expression of a casual, transitory emotion, but exhibits only its usual collective expression as the corporeal reflection of its combined mental and moral endowment. Indeed, the portrait-painter can make no use at all of such transient traits of special emotion, he must conceive the personality which is to be represented, as a whole, in its normal intermediate state, and endeavor thereby to exhibit through his art simply a faithful characteristic picture of that personality, without painting, for example, a choleric man actually with the facial distortions generally caused by anger. (pp. 314–16)

"Poetry, as well as music," Ambros urges, "is also able to express moods for which it would be fairly impossible to find a fitting specific designation." Pauses in drama in particular are often filled with feelings that can be expressed only by music, a point Ambros supports with telling examples of "the unspeakable" from Beethoven, Wagner, and Shakespeare.

Toward the end of his tract, which is really of interest more for varied and apt descriptions of works of art than for profundity or detail in its philosophical argument, Ambros is explicit and emphatic in stating his underlying idealist conception:

For the artist embodies his ideas in the art-work in order that they, through the medium of the latter, may become the ideas of other men also. The painter counts upon a spectator, the musician upon a hearer, the poet likewise upon a hearer or at least a reader. That which is to bring the three into relation with one another is something spiritual, something incorporeal, the idea. The art-work forms, in this connection, the conducting, sensuous medium. To the man that is intellectually blind, a picture is present in hardly any other sense than it is to one physically sightless. If a composition is not understood, it is the same as if it were not played. (p. 352)

In his comprehensive *Ästhetik, oder Wissenschaft des Schönen* (1846–57), Friedrich Theodor Vischer deals with music in the fourth and last volume. The treatise in general was influenced by Hegel, and beauty is defined as the Idea in the form of limited appearance, but this metaphysical conception is no longer evident in the discussion of music. The concern with dialectic remains important, however, and so does the decisive notion of music as an art of subjectivity and feeling. Like Hegel, Vischer had misgivings about his technical knowledge of music. He wrote only the short general part of the music discussion; the more detailed and much longer following sections were written by his friend Karl Köstlin, who was to publish his own treatise on aesthetics in 1869.

Vischer considers feeling to be the center of mental life; he undertakes to characterize it by reference to consciousness, on the one hand, and self-consciousness, on the other. But it has an essentially undefinable subjectivity.

Any attempt to hold it fast, to fix its vacillating nature, almost unavoidably invokes its relation to an object, with the result that consciousness is involved. Thus, on the horizon of fear, for example, the object that has caused this fear hovers like a tenuous cloud that seems to be in the process of condensation. Feeling is devoid of an object and yet always in the process of becoming objective.

Now the language of feeling, Vischer believes, is the art of music, and just as the conscious and objective world is always near in the instance of feeling, so music excites the outwardly directed mental activity of the listener, and vague, dreamlike forms move before his fantasy. Correspondingly, music will seek the support of another species of art that can light its darkness and give it a definite content by specifying an object. Vischer's ensuing discussion of the role of the word in vocal music cannot fail to remind us of the operatic aesthetics of Wagner in the early 1850s. We have a troublesome choice to make in connection with feeling, Vischer says in more general terms: "Either pure feeling, but always afflicted with the need for supplementation that interprets it, remedies its lack of an object—or feeling that is interpreted, referred to an object, but no longer present in its pure form."[3]

Turning from consciousness to self-consciousness, Vischer derives his conception of feeling, as Hegel did, from a vibrating object. The logic of his thought, however, is rather obscure. In drawing tone from such a source, Vischer says, the composer dissolves the world of forms into tones, and this very process expresses the nature of feeling. Feeling is the world as dissolved into the inner life of the subject. Tone, filled with feeling, transmits the composer's life of feeling to the listener, in whom the same mood is to be aroused. This is accomplished through the medium of hearing, which stands in the deepest relation to feeling by the very fact that it occupies the same intermediate position between sense and mind.

Vischer continues with a synoptic glance back to his previous discussion:

> From the totality of these fundamental determinants we obtain the essentially amphibolic character that is peculiar to music in comparison to the other arts. Music is the ideal itself, the soul of all the arts laid bare, the mystery of all form, an intimation of the structural laws of the world and equally the fleeting, still enfolded ideal; it possesses everything and nothing, is sensuous and not sensuous, a source of high and pure enjoyment that yet is completely sealed off to many, tiring all when it exceeds a modest duration, driven by its inner deficiency to an annexation with the world and then dependent, but in its independence accompanied by a feeling like an unanswered riddle. (p. 222)

The most important aspect of the amphibolic, or ambiguous, character of music Vischer finds in the relations between instrumental and vocal music.

Vocal music is not pure music because there is a dependence on natural circumstance in the use of the human voice. The material of art, Vischer believes, is properly inert—a passive object separated from personality. But vocal music is also impure for the deeper reason that it presents feeling accompanied by consciousness. In the connection of music and word, the word says more than the music in that it points to a definite object, but it says less than the music with respect to feeling. For the expression of the life of feeling music is needed precisely because words are insufficient. But the absolute inwardness of feeling dissolves the object and flows beyond this limitation in every direction. Thus, in the pairing of tone and word, Vischer maintains, there is never complete congruity. Tone cannot be contained: "The stricter the bond to the text—the more declamatory—the less the true musical beauty; the more purely developed the music, the less the bond to the text" (pp. 223–24).

Purely instrumental music, on the other hand, gives us feeling in all its purity, in its unconsciousness, but it suffers from the deficiency of feeling with respect to clarity and determinate content. In his search for a solution to the problems of instrumental and vocal music, Vischer considers the combination of the two. We are reminded once again of the ideas of Wagner, which now clearly become the basis of the discussion:

> If we seek respite from this hither and thither between independent and dependent music in the thought that a union of the two would bring fulfillment, we would have in this, to be sure, the richest form of music. The concrete fullness and many-sidedness of feeling could not find a richer realization: song would now be the core of the feeling, itself already possessing tonal multiplicity and representing a wealth of distinguishable forms in the one feeling; instrumental music would be its still richer reverberation, seeming now like a resonance of our feeling in the environment, in the unbounded universe, and now like an endlessly repeating echo in the human breast. But this, in actuality, represents no solution to that incongruent relation of word and tone that confronted us first in song alone, but instead, only aggravating the difficulty by its doubled power, music threatens to flood over the text, to sweep it away, and if here again there seems to be an opportunity for music to be bound even more tightly to the words, this meets the obstacle that, chained in this way, music could not bring its increased wealth of means to full deployment. (p. 224)

The psychological ideas that in Vischer's musical aesthetics of 1857 are fused with metaphysical conceptions later become explicit. Vischer was fifty years old when he completed his large *Ästhetik* (1857); he was in his seventies when he gave his lectures on aesthetics of 1876–77 and 1882–83, which were published in 1897, ten years after his death, as *Das Schöne und die Kunst; Zur Einführung in die Ästhetik*. His thought here has turned from metaphysics to a sensuous conception of beauty and to psychological principles. In distinction to a symbolism of conceptions, such as is typified by the blindfolded figure of justice with a balance in her hand, he describes a dark type of symbolism of the soul as the essential concern of aesthetics: "It is the nature of our soul that it plants itself deeply into manifestations of the external natural world or into forms that man has produced and, by an involuntary and unconscious act, attributes moods to these manifestations, totally abstract in themselves, which really have nothing to do with expression—that it transplants itself with its mood into the object."[4]

This *Einfühlen* into inanimate forms, this dark symbolism, is nevertheless, in its own way, completely definite. In music, relations of pitch, meter, and rhythm can be measured numerically, but music rests on the impressions that the relations make on the soul and on the symbolism connected with these impressions. The discussion of relations of pitch will serve as an example:

> How totally different from the outspoken major, reminiscent of bright day, is the effect of the veiled minor, suggestive of moonlight! The difference between the major and minor thirds takes on the meaning of a difference in the disposition of the soul. And then the earnest restfulness and somber strength of a low tone, the impassioned, hot energy of a high one! Language cannot easily follow along here. The formalists will say, A chord rests on a coincidence of vibration numbers; a tone returns to its original unity; there we have it: all beauty is proportion. But I say, The first shepherd who by chance discovered a concord, an arithmetically representable consonance, on his simple pipe or with a few strings that he stretched over a large shell did not simply hear something pleasing to his ear but rather felt as though he was perceiving a unity of different moods of the soul—precisely because of the symbolism that is peculiar to man as man. (p. 200)

In his tract *Das Musikalisch-Schöne* (1858),[5] the Berlin critic Adolf Kullak seeks to clarify the nature of musical idealism largely by considering the relation of music to poetry and to the world of nature. He thus deals with the problems that were prominent in the music of his era, just as Ambros had done, but Kullak's study is more intensive; his ideas are particularly close to those of Vischer and Lazarus, his immediate predecessors. Of central importance again is the nature of feeling.

Tone and feeling are intimately related, Kullak maintains. There is an enigmatic charm in tonal connections, a strange sympathy with the primordial capacity of feeling. But music shapes feeling in a material that is really independent and that expresses its own nature according to specific laws. On the other hand, feeling in general seeks to attach its inwardness to actuality, to definite objects, such as a flower or a dark cloud. Thus, music contradicts the outward impulse of feeling by engaging and shaping its innermost nature. Indeed, feeling as it is expressed in music is changed to a certain extent; drawn back from the external world, it secures a new depth and inwardness, and its primordial capacities are elaborated into an infinitely refined differentiation that constitutes a strange, immense, and independent world. This process of the definite, individualized idealizations of feeling finds a striking manifestation in instrumental music, as it continuously strives toward inward expressiveness. Objective and conceptual content cannot be acquired in this way, however, so that instrumental music has a certain character of unfulfillment or, as Kullak sees it, of longing and infinity.

As far as the external world is concerned, it can enter music in two ways, subjectively and objectively. These are manifested in two different types of program music. A Sunday morning, for example, can be treated as a specifically musical formulation of feelings of quiet piety, or it can contain chorale-like sections or the sounds of bells. But the objective world can express itself in music only to the extent that it is accessible to feeling, to the extent that its various objectivities can be reached and touched by the inwardness of feeling.

In this way, music can succeed to an additional realm of ideas and can enhance its artistic value and force. And the object that has broadened the range of music is reciprocally affected. Taken up into the sphere of tones, the definite outlines of its objectivity are obscured in favor of that inner spiritual something that brings it into contact with the life of feeling. The connection with nature remains, but the object now appears in a magical light; it has cast off actuality and entered the realm of imagination. What poetry can only describe in words music makes sensible. Kullak cites a variety of examples from the program music of Haydn, Beethoven, Mendelssohn, Schumann, and a number of other composers. In all tone painting of value, he maintains, it is always the heart, transfigured in longing, sorrow, and the expiation of infinite love, that descends from its world to the finite object and draws this up into its higher sphere.

But program music and music making use of words are really no more than mixed genres, Kullak claims by way of conclusion. The core of music remains independent instrumental music, and with respect to fervor in taking hold of primordial feelings, modernity recedes far behind Classicism. No composer up to the present, he insists, has expressed more reverence than Bach, more bliss than Mozart, more longing and power than Beethoven.

Moritz Carriere's consideration of music in his *Ästhetik* (1859)[6] compares music repeatedly to the other arts to help define its nature. We clarify our thoughts in words, he concedes, but all mental life is by no means consummated in language. Plastic art and music exist precisely because much that cannot be said can nevertheless be shaped and sung. The Idea is not only conceptual thought but also the formative force of life, the principle of becoming that is never fixed in form or free activity, and it is this aspect of the Idea that is revealed in music.

Carriere complements this fundamental notion with the metaphysical conception of the relation of music to individual thoughts and objects that is found in various forms in a number of philosophers: music expresses the archetypal form of appearances, the inner core of things from which particular forms arise, the resonance of feeling that thoughts and objects produce in the soul. Now these conceptions rest on the further idea of the generality of music and the relation of this generality to the particularity of individual entities. Carriere seeks to explain this relation by appealing to an algebraic equation and its realization in various particular numerical values: music is the algebraic form for emotional experience and leaves to the listener the substitution of individual numbers for the letters. But, like an equation, music has a specificity of its own. Music is specific as well as general—a problematic state of affairs that Carriere does not subject to analysis—while the comparison between music and algebra correspondingly overlooks the difference between concrete experience and abstraction.

Also unresolved is the related problem of the nature of the feeling or feelings connected with music. Taking issue with Hanslick, Carriere maintains that form is always the shaping of content and that only when this content is fully revealed by its form will it result in musical beauty. The feelingful content, however, is not consistently characterized. Music presents definite feelings and moods, Carriere says, even though these can be further specified by relating them to various objects or ideas. Not only does music express these feelings; it also permits us to experience them. Yet Carriere believes also that feelings are not really aroused by music. Music is a creation of the fantasy, he maintains; song is not a cry of pain or joy—a sound of nature—but an ideal image of the motion of feeling and the state of the soul. Thus, idealism and reality are intermingled in Carriere's discussion, somewhat as they had been by Hanslick, but Carriere is not sufficiently careful to separate the ideal feelings of fantasy and contemplation from the real ones of emotional arousal, neural excitation, and performance.

In addition to idealism and realism, finally, Carriere also presents certain formalist conceptions, for he sees music as duplicating the rhythm of emotional states, the specific motion of love, hate, hope, and longing, the general form of the rise and fall of feelings, even as revealing the general laws of the universe. But Hanslick, at the end of the original edition of his treatise, had also connected music with the macrocosm. In any event, we can take a certain unreconciled eclecticism and lack of clarity to be characteristic of Carriere's discussion as a whole.

Karl Köstlin, the Tübingen scholar responsible for most of the musical part of Vischer's *Ästhetik*, published his own *Ästhetik* in 1869.[7] Although Köstlin is concerned in some detail with how tone and music reflect the physical and natural world and the numerical properties of vibration, he regards music primarily as a reflection of inner emotional life—of the moods and excitations of the heart. Even the elemental sounds of the wind or a storm, he remarks, remind us at once of gentle or agitated emotional expression, and this will obviously be much more the case with the conscious and complex tonal relations of music. Tone comes from the inside of objects and is thus diametrically opposed to color and light; it does not present the tangible world of vision but reveals the world of spirit and of mental life. Tone is in this sense ideal; it expresses the soul of a living being and makes feeling audible to others.

The beautiful in music secures meaning, Köstlin further maintains, only in that it is permeated by the tonal pulse of feeling and thereby given the energy and warmth of life. This tone becomes the symbol of inner life; it is heard as the expression of a soul. Hanslick was certainly right, Köstlin continues, when he insisted that music strive primarily for full and independent musical beauty, and he was also right when he insisted that music could not separate individual feelings such as love, hate, or longing from one another in their full definition. Yet the representation of the moods and emotions, Köstlin reaffirms, remains its chief task since musical beauty as such inevitably contains a more or less distinct relation to feeling as part of its nature. Thus, Köstlin radically revises Hanslick's conception of the relation of feeling to musical beauty: instead of being rejected as an extraneous factor, it is incorporated as an essential ingredient.

Most of the self-contained critics of Hanslick, a line that extends into the twentieth century, took over the title of his treatise either literally or approximately. In 1870, the organist and conductor Friedrich Stade published a short but painstaking refutation of Hanslick's theories, *Vom Musikalisch-Schönen*. Stade begins by examining the question of the content of music, and he maintains that the basis for answering this question is to be found in the statement that "every work of art, in correspondence with the human personality, represents a unification, an organic interpenetration of sensuousness and spirit [*Sinnlichkeit und Geist*]."[8] He finds in addition that feeling is the aspect of subjective life for which "the audible motions of time" are

331

the corresponding, necessary form of expression. In thinking, on the other hand, the motion of time recedes and is entirely generalized without being experienced as a necessary intrinsic form of consciousness.

Stade undertakes a close examination of the nature of feeling. In the case of feeling provoked by an external cause, he argues, the process is accompanied by ideas whose content determines the feeling, and thus the "psychic mode of incarnation and appearance" (p. 5) of this feeling, and also impresses itself sharply on the vibrations of the nerves. Since music represents these vibrations in an audible form, it does not express the ideational content directly. Nevertheless, this content is contained as a potentiality in the particular psychic excitation and thus also in the tonal forms.

Now since the psychic potentiality of the ideational content is immanent to the feeling that has been aroused, it is impossible to separate the feeling from the ideational content so that, after freeing the distinct apparatus of thought from an undefined dynamics, there remains "an undefined motion common to various feelings, a motion that is always the unessential element of the character of the definite feeling" (p. 5). This would contradict the organic solidarity of mental life, Stade maintains, which does not permit such mechanical separation of content and form, of mind and soul.

The detailed critique of Hanslick that follows can be derived almost in its entirety from these initial considerations. Thus, abstracted or general patterns of motion, for example, which manifest the dimensions fast-slow, strong-weak, rising-falling, and are common to feelings having different verbal designations, would still have a feeling character of their own; we could not therefore connect any idea we wish with the music expressing a feeling of this kind, but only those ideas that have an inner relation to the feeling. Such a generalized feeling, however, would also be unable to account for the numberless gradations and contrasts in a musical work of art:

> Music represents not a pure dynamics of feeling—there is none such in Hanslick's sense—but rather the feeling with the ideational content spiritualized into a pure dynamics in the more pregnant and vital sense of "potentiality." This ideational content is dissolved in the psychic excitation into pure potentiality, to the "Idea," and has indeed sacrificed in this form its concrete, fortuitous definition, without, however, evaporating into an abstraction. The individual Idea, the valuable ideal substance of the mental content, has entered into the psychic excitation and into the musical representation of this substance. (pp. 8–9)

To this rather complex conception, Stade adds the following: "Insofar as music casts off from the concrete material it draws into its domain all absolutely fortuitous characteristics up to the pure individual core, the artistic ideal appears in it in the purest, most ethereal form; it makes sensible the soul of concrete reality in the mirror of subjective inwardness" (p. 9).

When conscious ideas are not tied to feeling, the laws that underlie the relation of the life of feeling to the life of ideas are present to the fantasy in its formative activity so that the course of the psychic motions has the same necessity and inner consequence that would have been brought about by corresponding ideas actually present in consciousness. Stade is thus able to speak of ideas that "are latent" in the feeling process, of the immanence of unconscious ideas in inner experience, and he finds support for this view both in Kant and in the *Philosophie des Unbewussten* of Eduard von Hartmann.

Stade proceeds to what is doubtless Hanslick's most well-known proposition: the peculiar and sole content and object of music are tonal forms in motion. The principal error contained in this statement, Stade asserts, arises from a logical fallacy:

> Because the content in music is inseparably bound to the tonal forms, these tonal forms are the content itself. Thus Hanslick allows himself to be misled by the immediate immanence of the content in the tonal forms, and he takes these forms as a justification for denying any content that goes beyond the purely tonal as such. He could not take his stand more decisively on the ground of materialism. (pp. 11–12)

While the real feelings of the composer or the listener, with or without their specific objects and causal contexts, are unequivocally evicted from aesthetics by Hanslick, who calls them "pathological," Stade believes that they are closely related to musical content. This positive view of feeling is made possible through the conception of apparency. The composer represents his feelings not in their empirical materiality, Stade argues, "but objectivized, transfigured, idealized through the action of the fantasy":

> The listener is described in a similar way. Like musical production, the reception of the musical creation on the part of the listener is also a feeling through the medium of the fantasy or a contemplation of feelings in the fantasy. Since we stress the cooperation of the fantasy, the objection that Hanslick raises against the participation of the life of feeling in the enjoyment of musical art is removed. (p. 32)

Because there is no factual object that arouses it, Stade says subsequently, the effect of music with respect to feeling remains only "apparent," "illusory"; it is only a shadow, as it were, a reflex of reality. Every aspect of Hanslick's ideas about the relation of music and feeling is examined and refuted, from the significance of the immediate effect of the elements of music to the nature of the larger reactions connected with a musical work. Stade believes that the course of music is reflected in detail in the course of the apparent feeling of the listener and that, because of their relation to feeling, both nature and poetry are similarly reflected in detail in music. In the overture of the *Midsummer Night's Dream*, for example, although the poetic content cannot be recovered from the music alone, the character of the themes and the very details of the musical forms are decisively determined by the poetic material.

Not only is Stade's tract a thorough and persuasive revision of Hanslick's "revision of musical aesthetics"; it is also a valuable contribution to the field in its own right, exceeding Hanslick's contribution in its anticipation of future conceptions, although not approaching it, of course, in fame and direct influence.

Gustav Engel, a teacher of singing at the Königliche Hochschule für Musik in Berlin and a music critic for the *Vossiche Zeitung*, published his *Ästhetik der Tonkunst* in 1884. He undertook in this work to show how the fundamental concepts of metaphysics manifest themselves in music—how metaphysical ideas are connected with musical laws. In his foreword, Engel points out that both Moritz Hauptmann and Helmholtz, the one a speculative thinker and the other a scientist, agree that the only true basis of music is pure tuning rather than temperament. With respect to the aesthetic writings of his time, he cites Hanslick and Wagner as the most important. Although he is in agreement with Hanslick, he says, on the central point that music must first of all be considered formally, Engel believes he is able to avoid the one-sidedness of this view and to bind purely musical beauty closely to living expression.

"The path we will take," Engel states in his introduction,

> will lead us from the concept to the Idea, from the formalistic to the idealistic comprehension of music, insofar as under the concept of a thing we understand what is more delimited and empirical, which is indispensable in order to constitute this thing altogether, and under the Idea the complete realization of this very concept, which without its relations to other concepts, however, is simply not thinkable and necessitates a more universal mode of conception.[9]

Music grasped abstractly, he continues, really has to do only with rhythmic relations since even differences in pitch, Engel states, have a basis in unconscious rhythms and differences in loudness (as grounded in distinctions of arsis and thesis) also have a rhythmic foundation. But to realize the concept of music completely, he believes, we must see how motion in time is related to more concrete types of motion, such as the motions of the soul. Thus, in general, the abstraction of the concept will lead beyond itself, first to the factual and the poetic, then, through art, to the striving of the mind in general toward the reconciliation of the objective and the subjective.

The first of the six sections into which Engel's treatise is divided is entitled "The Concept of Music." The condition for music is not simply attractive sonority, he argues, but the presence of a mental factor as well: "Music is thus the penetration of the purely sensuous element of the audible with the specifically intellectual impulse to grasp the multiple as a unity—an interpenetration of sensuous apparency and determinative thought" (p. 5). The mind first introduces distinctions and divisions into the sensible and then introduces coherence into what has been divided. Engel examines this formative process first of all in rhythm. He then turns to distinctions in loudness, to relations of pitch, and to melody. Although rationality enters into even a single sustained tone since there is an equality of duration between any two cycles of vibration, the consonances are not clearly defined in melody alone, apart from the octave. The accurate determination of the others proceeds with certainty only for simultaneous perception. But after a beginning has been made with a single tone, the unification in all that follows of euphony, on the one hand, and rational and conceptual formulation, on the other, is inevitable.

In discussing the nature of the triad and the development of the diatonic and chromatic scales, Engel follows Moritz Hauptmann. Here, however, and in rhythm also, he is faced with the contradiction between the idea of music and its factual realization, between mathematical exactitude and practical execution. This disparity is due not only to the intrinsic structure of arithmetic and to the inherent imprecision of human sensory experience but, more important, to the force of passion and of characteristic expression— even to the interaction between rhythm and intonation.

In summarizing section 1 of the treatise, Engel writes,

Music even in its *first* principles rests not on caprice or blind natural necessity but on the unconscious operation of the same laws of reason that are active in its later course. . . . But as far as the concrete matters of chord progression and modulation are concerned, of voice leading and polyphonic texture, of thematic processes and similar things, the combining and evaluating understanding is often active even for musicians without any sensible stimulus: in creating, in teaching and studying, in analysis, in reading a score, and so on. This standpoint, however, is equally not the highest and final one but only the necessary transitional stage leading to something higher: to the ability to contemplate the rational and, while giving ourselves over to the full sensuous effect, to have a clear insight into the inner web, into its coherence, and into all its ramifications and diversifications, which escape the perception of an untrained observer. Knowledge does not destroy illusion but heightens enjoyment and brings about in the listener the quiet equilibrium of mind that should rule between the objective knowledge of things and the feeling they evoke. (p. 37)

The second and third sections of Engel's treatise are concerned, respectively, with "The Complementation of Music by Poetry" and "The Complementation of Poetry by Music." Pure music, Engel states in beginning the second section, is rationally articulated pure time. It is the most perfect imaginable pastime, in the literal sense of the word. Yet if music were nothing more than the most perfect formulation of rhythm, the amount of time we must spend to enjoy it intelligently would hardly be justified:

> But let us not forget that, as soon as we say that it can pass for a reflection of life or—in the strict regularity of its order—for a model of other human activities, or that it can awaken the most noble, most solemn feelings, we at once, according to our discussion above, go beyond what was supposed to be its sole content. For this life it is to mirror, this other for which it is to be the model, this solemn feeling it is to awaken— these do not actually reside in itself as long as it is considered to be the mere formulation of time. (pp. 40–41)

In this guarded and somewhat equivocal statement, Engel does provide, in any event, a moral obligation to proceed with his investigation. He demonstrates first of all that the beautiful in music is always definite and individual in nature, that it is "characteristic." Then he turns again to the question of

> whether it is possible and advisable to connect a further content to it. The content that music possesses is time in itself. It is this that is divided rhythmically into equal parts, a division that is pursued, in the difference of high and low tones measured according to mathematical relations, into the unconscious. But time has a concrete content in real occurrences, and there is a question whether this concrete content may be connected with the process of musical formulation, which bears on the mere *form* of time. (pp. 50–51)

This is the opening of a discussion so long and so detailed that it would be inappropriate for us to examine it here. What Engel presents, starting with the elementary features of music such as duple and triple meter, high and low pitch, consonance and dissonance, major and minor, and so on, is a comprehensive development of the thesis that "the beautiful in music is always at the same time the characteristic" (p. 50). There is little limit, he believes, to the capacity of music for definite expression. Since music as such is always more or less characteristic, he argues, it is possible to regard it as a mirror of inner life. Furthermore, in the irregularities of music, its departure from purely thematic principles of continuation, we can even find an objective insistence that it be regarded in this way. Careful qualifications undermine the pretensions of Engel's conclusions, of which the last is typically vague and far from momentous: "We can no longer doubt that music has the capacity to combine with poetry in an organic fashion" (p. 148).

The following part of Engel's treatise, "The Complementation of Poetry by Music," presents a counterpart to the preceding argument that is equally lengthy and detailed. Epic, lyric, and dramatic poetry, which Engel takes to correspond to the three basic activities of the soul—conception, feeling, and volition—are considered in turn with respect to how music is to be made use of in their various forms of realization. Engel objects in general to the idea that one type of poetry attracts music and another repels it. It is rather the case, he maintains, that, just as music seeks on the one hand to absorb poetic content and on the other to develop freely in its own right and to be a self-contained whole, so poetry seeks at one time to breathe itself forth in music and at another to sustain itself purely in its own sphere. Engel goes on to apply this basic conception to each art and to their combinations in order to describe a general scheme of the various dual possibilities with respect to inwardness and to form. Understandably, most of the subsequent discussion is devoted to the different types of opera.

Engel's point of view is grounded in the threefold division of poetry:

> Now if the drama is the actual synthesis of the epic and the lyric and music stands in a closer connection with the lyric and in a more distant connection with the epic, it follows that drama and music will attract one another in accordance with their epic side. The more the lyric element predominates in a drama, the more it will be suited to musical representation; the more the factual and the reasonable or cerebral predominate, the more decisively it will repel music. (p. 174)

The detailed examination of opera that follows this has recourse continually to a duality of types: "It all depends, then, on whether an opera text is presented as a colorful succession of scenes or as the logical, subjectively coherent, poetical representation of an action. That only the last method affords the possibility of a good drama hardly needs demonstration" (p. 250). As it turns out in the ensuing discussion, however, this good drama ideally calls not simply for a unified musical form for the whole but for a unified total form whose parts are also formally rounded:

> For the individual sections of an opera text the forms of unified structure had been found well before Wagner. He was not the first who with

conscious intention subordinated these individual sections to the higher idea of the whole. But he did it with that blind one-sidedness that destroyed the old forms instead of reshaping them. It will be reserved for the future to mediate the new and the old and to produce the true totality that preserves the individual forms it encompasses. With this as a point of departure it will no longer be possible to achieve a higher totality, but only to retreat again. (p. 257)

This composite totality, however, still contains a contradiction, just as the monolithic whole does: the composite type, designated as the most perfect, "the contradiction that two opposed principles are to be reconciled with one another—that of unity with that of multiplicity; the second the contradiction that it contents itself with one principle where the nature of the thing demands two principles" (p. 258).

In the fourth section of Engel's work, "The Composite Work of Art [*Gesammt-Kunstwerk*] and the Individual Arts," the comparison between these two types of art is really the point of departure for an examination of the nature of art in general: of the concept of art, of the concept of the beautiful, and of the interpenetration of concept and contemplation (or of concept and appearance). In the formative or visual arts and in music, Engel believes, sensuousness is overt, and the concept is the "immanent principle"; in poetry, however, the concept is overt, and sensuousness is the immanent principle. As a consequence, he argues, the full concept of art can be realized only by the union of the arts, and poetry is therefore complemented by scenic representation and tone. Since this union—the musical drama in performance—contains the whole concept of art, it has a higher status than any individual art. But because each of the individual arts in the combination must give up a part of its own perfection, there is also a justification, although a lesser one, for each art to exist independently.[10] Thus, the highest beauty open to art calls for both the individual arts and the collective art, the arts at one time separating and at another uniting in mutual complementation:

> But this beauty is purely intellectual and is not experienced in a single moment, or may be just conceived; but beauty can be constituted by the whole life of a human being who possesses sensitivity and understanding for all the arts in both their connection and their separation. This intellectual beauty will be objected to mostly by those who find beauty solely in the momentary sensuous impression as it is imparted by the particular sense organ that stands closest to the corresponding concept of the beautiful. But even here it is easy to demonstrate to them how the beautiful gradually transforms itself from the sensuous into the intellectual. (p. 285)

Here Engel provides examples of such a demonstration, which is based on the fact of relation: there is always a relation of parts in art and therefore something mental or ideal: "In music it is perhaps for the wholly inexperienced person at first only a single beautiful tone—of the horn, say—that delights him. But the beauty of the sound rests, as recent physics has taught us, essentially on a harmonic relation of overtones to a fundamental tone; we have accordingly here also not something simple, as immediate perception tells us, but a relation" (p. 285). This is again true with respect to duration, for the shortest tone we can perceive is made up of a succession of vibrations that are all in the same relation of equality of duration. Engel proceeds,

> The higher we rise in the consideration of a musical work of art, the more the beautiful, which at first seemed to be a simple sensuous perception, converts itself into a relation. In the melody it is the relation that exists between the successive tones of a succession in which we find beauty: without the recollection of tones that have already vanished, and without the attentive expectation of tones that are still to come, neither the understanding of a melody nor the enjoyment of it and therefore also not the sense of beauty for it is possible. (p. 286)

This provides Engel with a basis for explaining musical repetition: "For this reason also the repetition of one and the same melody in music is something long established, to help the memory and in this way partly to strengthen understanding and enjoyment and partly even to create them." The same process continues with more complex techniques: "With the addition of harmony or even of accompaniment of any kind the demand on the mind to grasp more distant relations is further increased. And this is the case to a still greater extent with larger musical works, which rest on the artful development of one or two basic ideas and demand a continuous and lasting comparison of the present with the past to be grasped in their full value" (p. 286). Finally, there is the additional complexity introduced by vocal music, in which Engel perceptively finds a comparison between a state of the soul that is produced by poetry and the musical forms of expression that are given to this state.

In this fashion, then, music depends on relations between the momentary sensible present and the mental retention of what has passed, a situation that in Engel's view is of central importance in making music an idealistic rather than a materialistic art.

The fifth section of Engel's treatise, "The Objective Judgment of Art," takes the characteristic individuality, correctness, and interest of a musical work as the properties that provide a basis for the evaluation of its beauty. Most of the section, however, is devoted to the question of correctness and, in particular, to the fact that the numerical or systematic foundation of music cannot be perfectly realized in its tonal material and can therefore achieve only a symbolic level of truth. What is theoretically false, however, can be empirically satisfactory.[11]

Engel's investigation of musical value again involves a search for the highest and most perfect beauty, which again involves the transcendence of sensuousness. This time the solution is found in history: "The full beauty of art is contained not in an individual art, or in a large work of art that includes many shorter works of the most varied character, or even in the entirety of the works of a single great composer, but only in the history of the art. It encompasses all the works that have brought into existence some kind of distinctive qualitative property in a distinctive way" (pp. 357–58).

The last section of the treatise, "Music as Part of the World of the Mind," completes Engel's planned progression from the concept of music to the Idea of music. In explicit dependence on Hegel, Engel concerns himself with evolutionary processes: in particular with the interconnected origins of music, language, and society, with the subject-object orientation of consciousness, and with the development of religion, morality, and art. A conception of the total interrelatedness of every aspect of mentality pervades the whole, together with an effort to show how each major area of experience and thought differentiated itself from the totality. In discussing the sense of beauty, for example, Engel says that finding joy in seeing, hearing, and verbal communication as such and making a choice between what is seen, heard, and perceived through spoken language are the first steps toward art:

> In the choice it is already apparent that the impression on the eye and the ear and so on is desired in a certain abstraction. Nature, for example, produces ugly and attractive people. An ugly person can be good, which an attractive person not always is, or his ugliness is unmerited, brought about with causal necessity and to this extent, considered with respect to truth, entirely understandable; but in certain circumstances we demand exactly this abstraction from the whole causal connection of things; we want only what is pleasing for the eye, for surface appearance in space; and in this sense we prefer one thing to another, in this sense we move toward art, in order to bring this abstraction as completely as possible to realization. (pp. 387–88)

Inevitably, however, as Engel maintains, the beauty that is desired, because of its intrinsically dialectical nature, breaks apart and becomes individualized into some particular characteristic kind of beauty.

The general process of differentiation is considered again with reference to art rather than to the sense of beauty. An intermediate stage concerns the composite of art and religion:

Thus we accepted the fact that art as well as religion proceeded from the public togetherness of people and from the development of speech and consciousness connected with this; if we saw that religion was only able to call art into life without exclusively ruling over it, then it is probable on the other hand that art exerted its influence on religion to the same extent—or, better, the original ideal creation of the human mind was a common product of his artistic and religious spirit, and it was only out of this unclear, confused interpenetration that art and religion separated from one another in the course of development. (pp. 389–90)

The differentiation that Engel describes in evolution and human history, however, is antecedent to the process of abstraction and idealization that becomes increasingly conspicuous in his treatise. In the discussion that concludes the fourth section we have considered what is doubtless the most elaborate example of Engel's characteristic type of idealism. There is a similar synoptic statement in the fifth section: "Generally speaking, the insight into the harmony of relations that is revealed in the history of an art produces more an intelligible satisfaction, which is related to the sensuous feeling of beauty and in certain circumstances is converted into this, but is not itself sensuous" (p. 359). There is a hierarchy of levels of beauty such that, in a particular art, "over the beauty of an individual work, of an individual master, of an individual period or nation, there stands the Idea of beauty in the historical development of the art; over the beauty of an individual art the beauty of composite art; and finally over the beauty of the composite work of art the Idea arising from the history of art in general of the combining and separating of the arts" (p. 360).

The abstract beauty that Engel sets at the summit of aesthetic idealization cannot fail to evoke its great Platonic ancestry. Nor does it lack the corresponding constituent of a kind of sensuousness, poetic in Plato but simply figurative in his distant descendant. The "idea" that Engel sees in music, however, is described in various other ways that do not seem mutually compatible. He discusses rationality, concept, numerical relations, logic, and dialectic as well as idea. Rationality itself comprises confusing variety; not only does it range from the ratios of intervals and rhythms to the proportions of a musical work, but it is also based essentially on the "unconscious counting" of Leibnitz—a paradoxical notion of rationality that cannot be perceived. It is the elementary constituents of music, unfortunately, that receive most of Engel's attention; he deals more with the acoustic accuracy of intervals, for example, than with the larger formal aspects of a composition and, correspondingly, more with correctness than with value.

Another questionable concern is the intensive examination of characteristic qualities, again with an unexpected amount of attention to elemental musical phenomena such as meter, dynamics, and register. More serious is a lack of clarity in relating character to musical beauty and value. Musical character is important for Engel, of course, because it is taken to demonstrate the inevitability of the limitation of beauty in any of its sensuous manifestations. It is therefore the basic motivation for the progression toward ideal beauty, which transcends this limitation. But the detail and the length of the analysis of characteristic beauty obscures its role in Engel's argument.

Musical character is important in another respect also, for it is intrinsic to the vital question of the supplementation of music by poetry and the other arts. Is it possible for music to be self-sufficient and at the same time demand complementation? Wagner's answer was a historical one. Engel too provides an affirmative answer, but from a historical perspective that differs from that of Wagner. Yet in the discussion of the characteristic qualities of music, notably of the introduction to Florestan's impressive aria in *Fidelio*, Engel seems to make complementation superfluous. From the orchestral introduction alone and without knowledge of the dramatic action, he claims, the listener knows that Florestan will make his initial appearance (the curtain has not yet risen). Engel cites the harsh, shrill dissonances, the gloomy sounds, the imploring motive that reveals "the purest innocence of heart." The music points to the speech and feelings of a man, not a woman, and to deep, physical suffering and the night of a lonely dungeon. In this remarkable discussion, which Engel pursues for pages on end, all the details of the situation are revealed, although Engel concedes that this degree of specificity is exceptionally achieved only by the music alone. There is little doubt, however, that his claims even for the piece he examines are exaggerated. Yet to the extent that they are well founded they do detract from the justification of musical drama, which must rest its case that much more heavily on its ability to realize the full concept of art.

It may finally be mentioned that, although Engel carefully examines the moral character of art, his analysis of the apparency of art—its source in imagination, its fictional character and separation from everyday reality—is not adequate. A foundation is laid for such an analysis, however, in his discussion of the possible and the actual, of the philosophical or conceptual as opposed to the real and the factual.[12] Art has an intermediate or transitional place, Engel states; it is a realization of the conceptual, but only in contemplative form. The elaboration of this Kantian basis into a full analysis of aesthetic apparency is nevertheless not contained in the treatise.

Many years after *Die Philosophie des Unbewussten* (1869), Eduard von Hartmann published his comprehensive aesthetics: *Die deutsche Aesthetik seit Kant* (1886) and *Philosophie des Schönen* (1887). Hartmann had a synthetic and scientific mentality; one of his fundamental projects was to combine the views of Hegel and Schopenhauer by means of the theory that Idea and Will are two aspects of a single ultimate principle. The *Philosophie des Schönen* (the "second systematic part of the aesthetics") has a distinctly Hegelian basis.

This work adopts the established division into "the concept of the beautiful" (bk. 1) and "the existence of the beautiful" (bk. 2). Of the six chapters of book 1, the first deals with aesthetic apparency and its ingredients. Hartmann considers first where the beautiful may be said to reside. The view that suggests itself at once is that it resides in external things, as they exist independently of being perceived: "This view corresponds to naive realism, which believes that in its perceptual objects it grasps things in themselves." [13] But no extensive consideration is needed, Hartmann points out, to convince oneself that this opinion is untenable.

If we eliminate this naive-realistic error, however, it is easy to fall into the opposite, subjective-idealistic error and adopt the view that the beautiful is purely subjective, "an exclusive product of the subject and his mental endowments and capacities" (p. 3). After discussing the difficulties entailed by these views and their one-sidedness, Hartmann turns to a third view, according to which

> only the artist produces the work of art, not its viewers also, but the latter receive the perceptual image to which the beauty adheres through the effective action of the objective-real work of art on their sense organs. The objective-real work of art in which the artist has objectified his fantasy-image is not beautiful, but only the subjective appearance that the artist or some other person carries in his consciousness in contemplating this. (p. 4)

To this Hartmann subsequently adds,

> Therefore in the perception of the beautiful the cause of the beauty of the perceptual image lies solely in the thing in itself, which is not beautiful, and in all production of the beautiful the artist is concerned with creating things in themselves that, although not beautiful, must yet be causes of beautiful perceptual images in normally constituted people.

This conception is that of *transcendental realism*. According to such a view, the beautiful adheres exclusively to the subjective appearance as the content of consciousness, but that the perceived subjective appearance is beautiful in contrast to other subjective appearances depends not on the preconscious activity of the subject who directly produces it but on the character and mode of constitution of the thing in itself of the work of art. The beautiful as subjective appearance is thus no longer a one-sided product of either the thing in itself or the viewer but the product of two factors acting together. (p. 5)

Although it is the indirect cause of the aesthetic product, Hartmann points out, the work of art is the more important of these two factors for aesthetic contemplation since a given work will give rise to the same subjective appearance in all subjects, and the normal unconscious reactions of these subjects, which directly produce the subjective appearance, can safely be left to psychology.

Hartmann elaborates this fundamental principle and returns to it more than once: "The beautiful thus always lies in appearance, whether in sensuous appearance or in the appearance of fantasy; always, that is, in subjective appearance as the content of consciousness and neither in the real motions of the air or the ether or in any kind of thing in itself. The beautiful is as such *purely ideal,* and its reality is only the ideal reality of an actually perceived content of consciousness." "We must therefore insist," he emphasizes again, "that only the subjective appearance can be called 'beautiful' in the true sense, which as purely subjective is called 'aesthetic appearance' " (pp. 11–12).

After the discussion of aesthetic apparency, chapter 1 is devoted in turn to the apparent feelings of aesthetics (which Hartmann considers particularly in their interaction with real feelings) and to real aesthetic pleasure. The apparent feelings and the real pleasure are of course the "ingredients" of aesthetic apparency. The succeeding chapters of book 1 deal, respectively, with the levels of concretion of the beautiful (essentially types of formal organization), the opposites of the beautiful (the ugly, the unpleasant, etc.), the modifications of the beautiful (chaps. 4 and 5; the sublime, the graceful, etc.), and the place of the beautiful in the world of mind and in the cosmos (which includes "the beautiful as the appearance of the unconscious Idea" [p. 463]).

Book 2, "The Existence of the Beautiful," comprises chapters on natural beauty and historical beauty, the origin of artistic beauty (both historically and psychologically), the dependent formally beautiful arts and the illiberal arts, the simple free arts, and the composite arts. The last two of these, which conclude the work, contain discussions of instrumental music (chap. 10) and of dance, vocal music, ballet, and opera (chap. 11). Our present purpose is best served by a consideration of the ideas on instrumental music.

The significance of formal beauty is greater in music than in the other fine arts, Hartmann maintains, and this is true of sensuous pleasure also. Thus, aestheticians who look primarily to music are inclined more than others to formalism and sensualism: "In contrast, ideal content in music takes a place that is less clearly illuminated by the light of consciousness than in the other arts; it can be neither pointed to nor put into words but must be felt and cannot be demonstrated to anyone who asserts that he can find no sign of it" (p. 634). As far as the sensuous effect of music is concerned, it makes music the most popular of the arts. But the real feelings that are aroused by sound as a physiological stimulus remain outside art. Their meaning for art "lies only in the possibility of suppressing these real excitations through reflexive inhibition and of reevaluating merely the felt tendency to them as a connecting link in the genesis of aesthetic apparent feelings of the same or similar kind" (p. 659). As a work of art, in Hartmann's view, music must be abstracted from all objective and subjective reality and regarded purely aesthetically, something that is already entailed by the apprehension of formal beauty. But the pleasure in a purely aesthetic comprehension of musical form is also the product of an ideal content that is implicit in the concrete appearance. This content is comprehended unconsciously along with the expressive concrete appearance; it is the immanent principle of the appearance. Thus, the appearance is shaped by the content, and its appropriateness is measured by the resulting aesthetic pleasure.

How this takes place, however, is difficult if not impossible to explain: "The natural process of mediation through which definite tonal connections become the correct and generally intelligible expression of a definite ideal content is nevertheless more difficult to discover and demonstrate in music than in other arts" (p. 661). But our relative lack of insight must not obstruct our recognition of the basic fact:

An inwardly directed attentiveness shows us that, in music as in all other arts, the implicit unconscious grasp of the ideal content occurs on the basis of feeling but also that, objectively regarded, the idea of music consists exclusively of emotive states and agitations of the soul, while in the other arts it is only partly of this kind. . . .

Music is therefore in an eminent sense an art of feeling because it can express only the emotive side of mental content, while other arts can also, along with feeling, draw intellectual things into their realm. Music can express the Idea only insofar as this has taken the form, in feeling, of inwardness or subjectivity. Music is therefore also in an eminent sense the art of subjectivity, while other arts, alongside the Idea in the form of subjectivity, are open also to the Idea in the form of objectivity. (p. 661)

Each art, Hartmann maintains, can reveal an aspect of the Idea that is closed to the other arts—or at least reveal this aspect in a more complete way. And each art expresses the content it represents in a completely definite fashion for the aspect accessible to this art—and for the aspect not accessible only indistinctly and by way of indication, provided its expressive means are equal even to this. The aesthetic apparency of a given art, therefore, is in one respect a definite representation of the ideal content, in another respect an indefinite indication, and in still other respects an idle stammering and fruitless effort to say what in this language is unsayable. Precisely those aspects of the ideal content that for one art are completely unsayable or remain only an indefinite indication are expressed in another art with the greatest definiteness. To this Hartmann adds the important remark, "If we understand under 'definiteness' simply conceptual definiteness, musical content, to be sure, is wholly indefinite; but conceptual definiteness is precisely that kind of definiteness that falls outside the province of aesthetics and can never yield a measure for the concrete definiteness of the beautiful" (p. 662).

Hartmann concludes the section on instrumental music with a discussion of tone painting and symbolism. While tone painting is conventional and culturally-historically determined, natural tonal symbolism rests on intrinsic connections of the physical and the psychological, the sensuous and the inner. Thus, musical transitions and contrasts, dissonances and resolutions, changes in register and mode, and so on come to represent

alterations of the course of feeling, and themes and voices struggling with one another become symbols on the one hand of feelings and strivings battling with one another in the same soul and, on the other hand, of the competition of impassioned individuals or groups of individuals.

What the language of tone reveals in this way of the more or less dark content of the life of feeling it reveals like all art not for the understanding but again for the feeling and its obscure weaving, turned away from the light of understanding; the organ of comprehension is the same as the organ in which the ideal content secured its subjective concrete definiteness. But that which in this way succeeds to definite if one-sided representation as immanent ideal content in the musically beautiful is nothing other than the Idea at the stage of individuality; for the inner life of feeling, in particular that of man, is only one side of the concrete individual Idea, which as such includes the Idea at the stages of inner activity and of the laws of feeling of the species. The tone poet reveals to us first of all his own subjectivity, but only as subjectively potentiated and transfigured in the aesthetic apparency; but then he becomes also, through the power of his divinitory fantasy, an interpreter of the life of feeling of all other human individuals, indeed even of the animals and plants and the inner side of the cosmic life of nature. (p. 664)

Thus, the discussion of instrumental music leads to a synoptic view of idealism and also, as it often does in the nineteenth century, to a cosmic conception of music.

The various kinds of idealism that can be surveyed at the end of the century are described in Hartmann's history *Die deutsche Aesthetik seit Kant* (1886). The interrelation of these different idealistic types bears a certain similarity to the interrelation of the general types of aesthetics that are represented in the topical chapters of part IV of our history. For the types of idealism cannot be totally separated from one another, just as there is an overlap, as we have seen at the beginning of this chapter, between Romantic aesthetics, idealism, emotional realism, and formalism. In the second half of the century in particular, writers on musical aesthetics possess a large heritage of aesthetic thought and often display an encompassing understanding of the nature of art and music. The result can be internal contradiction in their argument, or at any rate an inclusiveness that cannot be compressed into an aesthetic category without demanding qualification because of what is outside this category. Difficulty of this kind is certainly common in efforts to schematize the historical course of complex thought, and it is quite evident in the aesthetics of the twentieth century.

PART FIVE

THE TWENTIETH
CENTURY

CHAPTER TWELVE

THEORIES OF MEANING

M usical aesthetics in this century—like music itself—is distinguished primarily by its concern with specifically musical forms and principles: with the interrelations and transformations of motives, with the permutations of sets of tones, with the characteristics of forms such as the fugue or the sonata, and with underlying or background structures that are not really audible themselves but that nevertheless are important determinants of the form and sense of the music. The twentieth-century conception of form generally contains dynamic features. Music is understood as an interplay of forces, as a manifestation of energy, but the forces and the energy are an intrinsic part of the music; they are neither physical nor psychological in nature. Whatever the forms or formal laws may be, they are investigated and revealed by the analysis of compositions. If the present century is in general one of analysis, as the eighteenth was one of criticism, then musical thought is a highly characteristic department of human expression. For the various theories of form are dwarfed by the huge mass of application and practice to which they give rise: analysis and more analysis, in an unremitting and apparently endless activity.

This emphasis on objectivity and form is accompanied, naturally enough, by a neglect and even a rejection of feelings and moods, as of something irrelevant or fortuitous and therefore symptomatic of an inappropriate attitude on the part of the performer or listener. Even in program music, ballet, and vocal music, it has often been contended that the only matter of importance is the form of the music in its own right. Thus, music and musical thought in this century have been determined in important ways by a reaction, notably in the 1920s, against the predominating qualities and values of the nineteenth century. Largely for this reason, the term *aesthetics*—which was also rejected, like the music with which it was connected—is less applicable to twentieth-century musical thought than to that of the preceding century, or even to that of the eighteenth century, when the field of aesthetics, strictly speaking, had hardly come into existence. For emotion, as attached to musical experience, is one of the principal areas of interest to the aesthetician, the other one, still more directly connected with aesthetics, being auditory qualities themselves. Interest in these, of course, has been intense in the present century, but auditory qualities, whether of instruments, intervals, or chords, have rarely given rise to explicit or extended discussion. Yet we cannot really take issue with the retention of the term *musical aesthetics*. Its meaning has expanded, for one thing, well beyond the sphere of actual auditory impressions and their effects, and although *philosophy of music* is doubtless a more accurate designation for our increasingly diversified world of musical thought, *musical aesthetics* has the advantage of an established use that will probably overcome its disrepute. In spite of this new generality of meaning, however, musical aesthetics can still be distinguished from musical theory, although it must be admitted that the concern of both fields with form has brought them unusually close together.

Related to the fascination with form is the twentieth-century interest in meaning, which has doubtless been the chief object of musical speculation in our century. For good or for ill, it has largely replaced older philosophical and aesthetic concepts such as beauty, imitation, expression, and content. The replacement seems very much to the good as far as content is concerned, for it is not at all clear that music "contains" anything, but there seems little doubt that it has meaning of some kind, if only because the music of distant times or cultures does not always make sense.

The question of meaning, then, has superceded the traditional problem of emotional content (which had derived in turn from conceptions of emotional expression and emotional effects). The step from content to meaning seems to have taken place as a kind of formalization. Meaning reduces the problematic vagueness of "content" to a matter of relations that can be specified. It replaces a subjective notion with an objective one. For forms to have a meaning is a much more operational conception than for them to have a content. Indeed, in the final version of the quest for meaning—"musical semiotics (or semiology)"—meaning has been abandoned in favor of syntax; form finds its explanation in form or in laws of form. The only added factor is the appeal to language for procedures and principles, and this is certainly not a new occurrence in musical thought, although the model is now linguistics rather than rhetoric. If the meaning of music is included, somewhat paradoxically, in music itself, as seems to be the case, then not much is lost—or so it might be argued—if we overlook it entirely and deal with form alone. Perhaps sufficient meaning will be found, unexpectedly, in form itself.

The predominance of meaning in musical thought is a reflection, as we might expect, of its importance to twentieth-century philosophy, which brought about a deeper understanding of logic, mathematics, and language. The problem of knowledge became a problem of the symbolic formulation of knowledge. The domain of meaning was expanded by anthropology and by the psychology of childhood. But the conception of meaning, ramified and complex in general, was peculiarly intractable in its application to music, for even if music is unquestionably meaningful, it rarely possesses meaning in the most obvious sense—that of referring to or representing extramusical objects or occurrences. Nevertheless, considerations of musical meaning proliferated, starting with the overview in Max Dessoir's *Aesthetics and Theory of Art* (first published in German in 1906) and Carroll Pratt's *The Meaning of Music* (1933), which echoes Schopenhauer's volitional theory, and extending through Leonard Meyer's widely circulated *Emotion and Meaning in Music* (1956), which elaborates the commonplace of tension and release, to Peter Kivy's *The Corded Shell* (1980), which rediscovers the tired topic of "expression." But many American works in particular are of little value; those making use of linguistic analysis often painstakingly point out meanings that are quite obvious. The works of importance that remain, how-ever, constitute a large and diversified body of material. This understandably produces a rather complex task of selection and classification.

Apart from the interest shown recently in musical "understanding," the emergence of meaning as a central concern of philosophical thought has been attested to by three types of investigation: hermeneutics, symbolism, and semiology. However diverse their original fields of application may have been, these approaches to meaning are alike in claiming applicability to every area of human expression. This generality was attributed to hermeneutics by Dilthey and Gadamer, to symbolism by Cassirer, and to semiology by Peirce and Saussure. In each case, nothing less than the distinguishing feature of human mentality was at stake, an attribute that was to succeed reason and language as the defining characteristic of intelligence. As a logi-cal consequence of their generality, then, the three modes of understanding were applied successively to the question of meaning in music, only to be fol-lowed, at the end, by a close examination of the conception of understanding itself.

Hermeneutics

The term *hermeneutics* was applied originally to the interpretation of the spiritual truth of the Bible, but it was adopted by Wilhelm Dilthey to des-ignate a general theory and practice of interpretation or explanation that was applicable to speech, art, and, indeed, every area of human expression and behavior, on the ground that the products of human endeavor are intrinsically intentional and can therefore be elucidated. With Dilthey, writing in the late nineteenth and early twentieth centuries, hermeneutics became a foundational science for the achievement of understanding; it was a discipline that underlay every investigation of literary and artistic history and of cultural and intellectual history in general. It thus represented the basic methodology of what we now often call the "human sciences," which Dilthey sought to establish, starting with *Einleitung in die Geisteswissenschaften* (1883), as an independent domain of knowledge, different from but coordinate with the domain of the natural sciences. In emulation of Kant, he undertook a "critique of historical reason," which had its basis in the fundamental epistemological advantage of the historical or cultural sciences over the natural sciences: the basic similarity in nature between the investigator and his object of study.

Dilthey's influence was profound and ramified. Particularly influential was his fundamental concept of a "cultural system"—a context such as religion, for example, that coheres on the basis of a persisting purpose or intention and that to some extent also is connected with the external organization of society. Since cultural systems unite individuals on the basis of general human needs and these are realized in turn through certain psychophysical acts, Dilthey initially regarded psychology as the foundation of the cultural sciences. Important for literary theory was *Die Einbildungskraft des Dichters: Bausteine zu einer Poetik* (1887), in which Dilthey sought to provide a psychological basis for the creative process by analyzing the "poetic mood" into six elementary types of feeling. These six types arose respectively from physiological activity (pain and pleasure); sensory impressions; relations of these (or perceptions, such as tonal intervals or visual symmetry); connections of ideas (which can produce a feeling of logicality, say, or surprise); basic drives and passions; and the personal mode of expression of the artist or composer.

Fifteen years after this, Hermann Kretzschmar undertook to provide a specification of elementary feelings in the field of music—not as a psychology of the creative process, however, but as a psychology of the work of art, which he described as a progression of feelings. In two articles published in the 1902 and 1905 issues of the *Jahrbuch Peters*,[1] Kretzschmar advanced a detailed plan of musical hermeneutics. He provided a verbal interpretation first of intervals, rhythmic patterns, chords, and themes and then of the first fugue of the *Well-Tempered Clavier*. He used a conventional vocabulary of types of feeling: "joyous," "defiant," "elegiac," "energetic," "triumphant," and so on. The interpretation that he presents, however, still seems to deal with content rather than meaning. Its goal is "to penetrate the sense and ideational content that the forms enclose, to search out everywhere the soul under the body, to reveal in every part of a work of art the pure kernel of thought, to explain and interpret the whole" (p. 6). Most listeners, he asserts, remain caught in "sensible impressions," which involve "pleasure and admiration" or "astonishment and displeasure," while the gifted listener will be affected deeply on occasion by melodies that are both powerful and simple. But these responses are apparently of no importance to Kretzschmar, who calls for the understanding of content: "Instrumental music uninterruptedly demands the capacity to see ideas behind the signs and forms." As a result, both composing and listening "demand the highest clarity of mind" (pp. 7–8).

The content of untitled instrumental music is restricted to "the properties of character in feelings, images, and ideas," which Kretzschmar designates as "the affections," for he maintains that they are the same properties that were known by this term in the eighteenth century:

Now it is these affections that are embodied in motifs, themes, and tonal figures in general, either simply or, by contrast, in interconnections and mixtures that are impossible outside of music. The task of hermeneutics consists then in the following: to extract the affections from the tones and to give the framework of their development in words. Apparently a poor outcome, a shadow play, but in fact a valuable accomplishment! For he who penetrates through the tones and tonal forms to the affections elevates sensuous pleasure and formal workmanship to the level of a mental activity; he is protected from the dangers and the shame of a purely physical, animalistic reception of music. (p. 11)

Examining the subject of the first fugue of the *Well-Tempered Clavier*, Kretzschmar tells us that

it does not contain an unconditioned energy, a force or even a cheerfulness that is unrestrained. . . . As Bach has shaped it, with the descending close, with the considered rise to the main motif, the impulse of unmistakable energy that comprises its center is enclosed on both sides by expressions of melancholy. The theme accordingly expresses a serious mood that strives to rise up in order to gain control over an oppression. (pp. 33–34)

Occasionally, Kretzschmar's interpretation calls on visual imagery and external events. There is an example of this when he turns briefly to the prelude that precedes the fugue: "The prelude with its melody concealed in delicate broken chords and veiled by chains of dissonance is like a dream

355

image woven of distant little clouds of anxiety, of quiet lament and dark foreboding. In the fugue the composer raises his eyes and says to himself proudly and resolutely: Let come what may!" (p. 34). Basically, however, Kretzschmar is concerned with "the special virtue of instrumental music: that it represents the inner, spiritual kernel of important or interesting events without the fortuitous shell" (p. 40).

It is clear that the conception of music presented in these two articles takes up older ideas of musical content and its description. There is less a conception of meaning, with its defined relations and its concern with the specific properties of music, than there is of states of feeling and the progress of feeling as ways of pointing to the musical content; the description is essentially a guide. The affections are dynamically conceived; they present the course of feeling rather than aspects of feeling. But they are regarded as beyond history and culture; their applicability to music of whatever type, both in the past and in the future, is assumed. The poetic parallels to music, whether thought of as a point of departure or as an interpretation, are a repetition of the ideas of Schumann; the belief that music gives the metaphysical core of events is a revival just as clearly of the conceptions of German idealism. Thus, musical hermeneutics, as Kretzschmar conceives it, belongs less to the twentieth-century sphere of meaning than to older ideas of emotional content, which the interpretive technique purports to designate.

Kretzschmar has nothing but scorn for musical interpretations that consist of wild visions and anecdotes or of dry technical and statistical tabulations, and he is certainly entitled to demand that hermeneutic description proceed only with careful attention to the detailed course of the music. But his most fundamental criticism is directed against the very notion of "absolute music," of a "play of forms": against Kant and Nägeli and Hanslick. "In the sense of a solely *musical* content," he insists, "*there is no absolute music!*" (p. 13). Beethoven's sketchbooks reveal painstaking efforts to arrive at definitive tonal formulations, a demonstration, Kretzschmar contends, that the composer seeks to express a specific content. It does not follow, of course, that his hermeneutics succeeds in describing this content accurately. Although many persuasive arguments are produced, the impression of the whole discourse is one of traditional conceptions and terminology, for the feelings and moods that Kretzschmar makes use of in his hermeneutics are known independently of the music through outside experience.

The ideas of Dilthey himself extended well beyond the confines and limitations of psychological hermeneutics, particularly when such a hermeneutics appeals to a changeless stock of various kinds of feeling. For one thing, as we have seen, Dilthey thought in terms of "cultural systems": natural coherences of different fields of expression that were based on a community of purpose and related to the organization of society. While the analysis of "poetic mood" may reveal the basis for coherences of this kind, the broad significance of cultural systems as such can be studied without any appeal to their genesis. What is plain is that they are historical variables; thus, any field of expression will have a different constellation of relations to other fields at different times. Dilthey interpreted German music, for example, from the seventeenth century to the early nineteenth, in conjunction with the development of religious consciousness (*Von deutscher Dichtung und Musik*, 1933; written 1906–7).

In *Die Entstehung der Hermeneutik* (1900), Dilthey supplemented the conception of cultural systems by suggesting the development of a theory of interpretation that could be derived from the history of historiography. Such a history, he believed, would reveal a succession of different interpretations of a given field of expression and thus the different possibilities available to interpretation. It would also reveal the changing coherences between this field and others. Linguistic documents, however, were the basis of understanding throughout, for these were already clear objectifications of mutual understanding.

What this implies in the case of music, as Hermann Zenck makes clear in "Musikgeschichtliche Wirklichkeit" (1932), is that, in the cultural system of music (composition, performance, reception, conception, and theory), the conception and theory of music, since they are embodied in verbal documents, are the essential mediators of historical understanding.

In Dilthey's later writings, notably in the "Fragments for a Poetics" of 1907–8 and *Das Erlebnis und die Dichtung* (1910), the understanding of a work of art is no longer so heavily dependent on the psychic constitution of the creative artist. The work and the historical world have direct connections, and the meaning of the work can be shaped by sociohistorical contexts that are not operative at all in the mind of the artist. "Lived experience" is conceived differently: not simply as grounded in a subjectivity already largely preformed by previous experience, but as interacting with and shaped by its own objective expression, and also, in this process, as articulating large sociohistorical contexts. Thus, almost in contradiction to the psychological analysis of the creative mood into constituent basic feelings, which leads to the conception of an emotional content or meaning that has an existence distinct from the musical work, Dilthey stressed a hermeneutics "from without" rather than "from within" and considered the creative experience to be accessible only through the artistic product itself, with which it formed an indissoluble unity. The inner was to be read only through the outer. Motions of the soul give rise in music to schemata— relations of loudness, pitch, tempo, and rhythm to emotions—which have their source in speech and in dance. The expression of individual experience can be understood as a characteristic modification of such schemata, and fixation in objective form permits the application of hermeneutics. An interpretation of general validity, however, remains possible only for verbal documents.

Related to the idea of hermeneutics as a derivative of history is Dilthey's notion of types, which became most influential through his *Die Typen der Weltanschauungen* (1911). Types are to be found throughout the animate and inanimate worlds. Individuation is conceived as a variation of basic types, and it is type that permits the comparison of manifestations that are distant from one another in time and culture. Herman Nohl, a student of Dilthey's, found musical styles to be characterized by three different types of motion: flowing and effortless, struggling and pressing forward, and lingering and self-controlled. These were seen as the expressions of different attitudes and the attitudes in turn as related to different world outlooks. Nohl's typology, in his *Typische Kunststile in Dichtung und Musik* (1915), was extended by Gustav Becking, in *Der musikalische Rhythmus als Erkenntnisquelle* (1928), to include national types of motion and historical types of attitude. The types of motion distinguished by Nohl and Becking were thought of concretely, as a bodily participation of the musical listener that could be described in graphic form. Typology, in any event, can help account for the individuality of a musical work, but, if used incorrectly, it contains the danger of neglecting this basic task of hermeneutics in favor of the mere identification of type.

The epistemological advantage of the human sciences over the natural sciences is that the investigator has the same nature as the object he is investigating: he is able to understand human life and experience because he understands his own life and experience. This was a thesis underlying not only the thought of Dilthey but also the humanistic ideas of Giambattista Vico two hundred years earlier. The investigator in natural science, of course, also has the same basic physical and chemical nature as the object of his investigation, and the equivalence here may be even more exact than it is in hermeneutics. For the experience of another person, especially one of a distant time or culture, is to some extent different in nature from our own, and understanding it will call for an imaginative effort. Whatever text or evidence we start with will suggest a hypothetical view that will imply the relevance of an additional type of evidence, and this in turn will inevitably call for a modification of our hypothesis with new implications of relevant evidence. The result will be a back-and-forth process that produces increasingly accurate approximations of the experience we are seeking to understand, and this understanding will then provide the best basis we can find for the understanding of all the manifestations of that foreign culture, from texts and institutions to works of art.

Two articles of Arnold Schering's are concerned with the theory of hermeneutics: "Zur Grundlegung der musikalischen Hermeneutik" (1914) and "Die Erkenntnis des Tonwerks" (1933). In a conception that recalls Dilthey's theory of "cultural systems," Schering maintains that a musical work testifies to a larger historical consciousness, as this is constituted by biographical, historical, literary, and philosophic knowledge. His interpretations of instrumental works of Beethoven, however, which are found in *Beethoven in neuer Deutung* (1934) and *Beethoven und die Dichtung* (1936), deal essentially with literature. Schering finds the "poetic idea" of a composition in a particular literary work. The meaning that this provides for the music, however, is supposedly only a key to the actual content, while, in spite of his pedagogical purpose, Kretzschmar seems to believe that his system of hermeneutics produces an account close or identical to the true meaning of the music. Neither aesthetician, however, realizes Dilthey's ideal of a musical meaning that cannot be separated from the detailed perceptual configuration of the music.

A step toward such an immanent meaning can be found in the phenomenological aesthetics of Kurt Huber (*Der Ausdruck musikalischer Elementarmotive*, 1923). Huber finds that expressive values are not referred to or represented by elementary tonal configurations but are objectively present in the motives as such. Theodor Adorno is of the same mind when he writes, in 1930, that the contents of music are "continuously tied to its inner material-technical constitution."[2] They are by that token historical in nature, for they reveal the composer's treatment of the techniques and genres he adopts, his confrontation, in terms of specifically musical problems, with tradition and with his world. For later generations, the changing interpretation of a work similarly reveals the changing historical consciousness with which it is regarded.

Symbolism

The conception of symbolism has governed a large number of studies of musical meaning. While hermeneutics tends to suggest the interpretation of a musical work as a whole, symbolism suggests the interpretation of individual elements of a work, for the various meanings of individual symbols need not constitute a continuous or comprehensive meaning. The notion of symbolism also seems to entail some reference to an object symbolized and to a concept of this object that the symbol evokes. Yet the distinction between hermeneutics and symbolism is not a firm one; there are conceptions of musical symbolism, for example, that regard music as intrinsically and continuously symbolic and therefore have the interpretive scope, if not the interpretive power, that is normally expected of hermeneutics.

Arnold Schering is primarily responsible for introducing symbolism into musical aesthetics. Studies of symbolism play a major role in his work; they represented an area in which he attempted to combine the history of music, treated objectively and externally, with an investigation of the meaning of music, which was the concern of aesthetics. In the work of Theodor Lipps and Johannes Volkelt, aesthetics had found its most recent influential formulation, centered in the notion of *Einfühlung*. This kind of psychological aesthetics appealed to subjective data that were considered independent of culture. Psychological aesthetics had already been combined with historical considerations in the hermeneutics of Kretzschmar, who was Schering's teacher, and the problems and lack of clarity evident in Kretzschmar's essays became even more conspicuous in Schering's thought. There is a positive side to the continuity also, for Kretzschmar also foreshadowed Schering's remarkable musical insight. In any event, the Baroque affections that would be the historically appropriate explanatory basis for an interpretation of a musical work of Bach nevertheless have the character of timeless significance in Kretzschmar's hermeneutics. Schering's impressive studies of Bach's symbolism are much more concretely historical and are of course much more than a guide to the true meaning. His studies of Beethoven, on the other hand, are rendered unacceptable in their methodological confusion: lacking the public language of the Baroque, Beethoven's music is not easily interpreted in terms of a historical type of symbolism, and Schering returns to the nonhistorical aesthetics of subjective response, which he tries to legitimate by laying claim to a musical sensitivity and cultivation that gives his interpretations a normative value. But in spite of the ingenious network of circumstantial evidence he adduces, his theory that individual literary works were the bases of various instrumental compositions of Beethoven—and that they are therefore symbolized by these compositions—remains a brilliant but unconfirmed speculation.

In "Symbol in der Musik" (1927), Schering distinguishes four large categories of symbolism: (1) the sensuous tonal progression, which is at first not symbolic but becomes an image of inner motion, a symbolism of affection and mood; (2) elementary musical manifestations that are emphasized; (3) musical forms or techniques, such as the fugue or the ostinato; and (4) melodies or musical configurations with associations outside the work. The second of these calls for considerable elaboration. It applies to the whole field of tone painting and program music and acts by relations to our bodily or mental constitution: to corporeal motion, sensations of space, sense perceptions, logical relations, and so on. Such symbols may be rising and falling pitch, tone color, crescendos, rhythms, tempo, harmonic progressions, and so on. Even the representational symbolism of the horn, oboe, and trumpet is included: the relation of these instruments to the hunt, to pastoral scenes, and to war or majesty, respectively.

Schering calls attention to the fact that these types can come into play simultaneously, which he regards as a peculiarity of musical symbolism. He also suggests a generation or evolution of the types. They represent an order of increasing fullness of meaning, or mental character. Each element of music *can become* symbolic; each is *accessible* to meaning. The first type of symbolism "at first" has no symbolic meaning. This evolutionary notion is complemented by a more concretely historical one: "That music is *not* understandable beyond all time boundaries rests precisely on the circumstance that, with the change of the tonal system, that is, with the change of the basic laws according to which the musically usable tones are ordered in a rational context, the key for at least a very great part of the time-bound symbolism is also lost.[3]

The ideas expressed in "Symbol in der Musik" are elaborated in "Musikalische Symbolkunde" (1935).[4] Schering here deals at length with his project of constructing a history of musical symbolism. This would have its place between music history and musical aesthetics or, more specifically, between the history of style—an objective but external study of music—and a supposedly transtemporal aesthetics, which rests on invariant subjective data: "We will keep philosophical aesthetics and the study of style at our side as true helpers, but for the rest we seek to find a new path" (p. 188). In considering his project from the standpoint of style, he makes use of Husserl's conception of *Wesensschau:*

> There seems to be a limit beyond which the concept of style, as we conceive it today, does not lead us. Behind it something further opens up. I mean the intuition of the actual essence of the artistic. Under this there is understood the search for the roots of the musical work in an intellectual world, in a world that lies *behind* the tangibility of sense impression and in which there is unveiled what must pass as the true inner nature of sonorous objectification. (p. 186)

Thus, Schering combines Husserl and Kretzschmar in his effort to specify the nature and locus of musical significance.

In considering his project from the standpoint of aesthetics, which he criticizes for its lack of historical awareness, he naturally seizes on the nineteenth-century dispute between "idealists" and "formalists," stating the issue at stake in his own terms:

> Have the musical creations of all periods arisen from an urge that is not further explainable towards the mere forming of sound and are they thus creations of an absolute tonal fantasy that is sufficient unto itself, or do they have as a basis at the same time demands from the extra-musical side? This leads to the concept of the intuition of essence that has already been mentioned above. Here is the point, I believe, at which the *study of symbolism* must come into its own. (p. 188)

It is the idealist side of the aesthetic controversy that is identified with the essence of music, and this is revealed in what follows to be historical in nature. The essence of music is to be given by historical aesthetics—by the history of musical symbolism.

Schering begins a long and resourceful argument that seeks to character-ize and to show the necessity of a historical study of symbolism, such as is familiar in visual art: "For wherever and however music appears—even on lower levels of culture—we cannot do otherwise than receive it as an 'em-blem' of something, as a sounding 'image' or as a 'mirror' of some kind of sense. . . . Considered in its historical course, music simply cannot be com-prehended except on the basis of an unquenchable impulse to achieve new formulations of meaning" (pp. 188–89). He defines *symbol* unequivocally: "We can speak of a symbol only when and only where it is also actually recognized or *known* as such" (p. 189). Schering also maintains, however, that a symbol always contains the element of irrationality or mystery. What he means by this is not altogether clear. "Everything meaningful occupies us reflectively," he asserts, "even if only for a few seconds" (p. 190). But what a symbol means can never be completely known. What concepts such as "sin," for example, or "peace" "conceal in meaningful relationships can never be fully exhausted; something irrational always remains attached to them. This is also transferred to the symbol, the image of these meaningful contents" (p. 190). Now we can hardly know all the instances of sin or of peace, but that does not seem to make the concepts irrational or mysterious. The symbol is the image not of the contents but of the concepts themselves.

What seems to make most sense in Schering's confusing discussion of the mystery or irrationality of symbolism is the idea that the connection between the symbol—a tonal formulation or the auditory mental image of such a formulation—and the concept it symbolizes is mysterious and that the sym-bol itself is for that reason also mysterious. This idea enters into the history of symbolism that Schering projects, for the first type of symbolism he describes is to be known as "magical symbolism," a type that runs through history, from the most ancient times to the present. The only fundamental change in the type is a recent one, of which Schering disapproves: "In place of the mystical wonder at the secret symbolic forces of music there has entered a similar wonder at the artist" (p. 192).

Another type of symbolism is "elementary," or "original," symbolism—of high and low, loud and soft, and so on—which is based on transtemporal features of our biological nature. Such symbolism is unchanging, at least within an entire cultural sphere. Growing out of elementary symbolism is composite symbolism, which "sets the elementary symbols into higher relationships of meaning and thus achieves an increased spirituality" (p. 194).

Symbols come into being and change or lose their meaning with changes in style: "Not only each epoch, but also each generation, each significant personality, knew and knows how to create its own symbolic world. This process comprises a ceaseless becoming, persisting, and passing away of symbolic forms" (p. 194). Schering's discussion becomes unclear again, however, when he turns to the historical development of individual symbols. There are themes, he points out,

> that descended through generations, conveyed therefore always the same symbolism, and nevertheless are continuously subordinated to a new, comprehensive symbolism.
>
> In many symbols there is actually an organic growth to be observed, for we see that a formerly stronger and unambiguously imprinted meaning is gradually connected with new components of meaning and consequently grows out beyond its original symbolic significance. In instances that have been preserved in an especially fortunate way, like the one presented in what follows, a formal genealogical tree of the symbolic core can be demonstrated. The ten stages that the simple phrygian faux-bourdon cadence of the 15th century runs through up to the opening of Wagner's *Tristan* are equivalent to just that many stages of symbolic thought. At each step only insignificant changes are made, but they designate important deepenings of meaning, which, if we so desired, could be partitioned successively over the four centuries lying between. (pp. 195–96)

But what meaning and what deepenings of meaning does Schering have in mind here? We can define the meaning of the opening of *Tristan*, but are the meanings of the earlier cadences supposed to be anticipations in some way of the final meaning? If they have no discernible meaning at all, it is difficult to see why they are symbols.

In the final part of his study, Schering distinguishes two large types of symbolism, which seem to bear some relation both to the earlier typology of elementary and composite symbolism and to the fourfold typology of "Symbol in der Musik." The new types are the symbolism of feeling and the symbolism of idea, of which the latter is divided into depictive (objectifying) and conceptual (intellectual). The symbolism of feeling presupposes "the capability of higher ego-analysis, that is, a capacity to evaluate the inner life of others on the basis of one's own experience" (p. 197). It is not clear that this capacity underlies every instance of the symbolism of feeling, and in the further discussion of this type of symbolism, we are again led to the question, When is a symbol not a symbol? Schering cites examples of music to which our inner experience

> answers at once with the thought of a definite mood or inner state. The inner resonance aroused by the music is so strong and specific that it provokes the listener to a symbolic interpretation. Whether this permits sharp linguistic formulation or not makes no difference. Conceptual indefiniteness does not exclude, as everyone knows, the certain feeling of inner definition. Only this may not be lacking altogether, since when the sense of the inner facts is not in any way "conscious" or consciously known at all, symbolism, as we have seen, cannot be spoken of. (p. 198)

Does the listener have the thought of an inner state, or does he just have the inner state? If just the inner state, where is the symbolism?

Schering proceeds to the symbolism of ideas and to its objectifying and conceptual types, which present relatively little difficulty. He proposes finally a study of general intellectual history in order to discover how the symbolic thought of each era was constituted in music. This information is then to be applied to the interpretation of the individual musical work. The basis of the whole project is given as follows: "What magical, religious, philosophical, spiritual, sociological and other meanings an era found worthy of perpetuation was the result of a common disposition of mind and spirit to which its total artistic impulse can be related and thus its musical impulse also" (p. 202).

In conclusion, Schering criticizes the neglect of the symbolism of idea, which he attributes to the layman's aesthetics of music—starting around 1750—as purely an art of feeling and to the more recent conception of "the purely musical."

In "Das Entstehen der instrumentalen Symbolwelt" (1936), Schering considers musical symbolism in connection with the basic duality of voice and instrument. He distinguishes first, with respect to the comprehension of music, between "natural" man and "influenced" man, the one listening naively and the other sentimentally, the one accepting music on its own terms, the other filtering it through reflection—as mentally shaped will, for example, or a mirror of the self. To the natural man, song is simply speech, and what is sung is what is factually intended; nothing is symbolic. The sense lies in the text and in gesture, and the singing takes place in the real world, not in an aesthetic world of apparency. Any symbolism derives from instrumental music, which is the true sphere of the symbolic. "Natural" instrumental music is determined by the character of the instrument. It is play and favors improvisation and virtuosity. Its resemblance to dance is unmistakable. It "represents" only itself.

But instrumental music seeks to raise itself to a higher state through a relation to vocal music, which has a basis at once in the tonal resemblance of many instruments to the voice. An instrument may take up a vocal melody, or it may imitate the rhetorical characteristics of affective speech and song, becoming in the latter case definitely symbolic. It may also take up simply an idea as such, without relation to any presentation of it in speech or song, and seek to present its meaning, usually in conjunction with other instruments. This is symbolism in the fullest sense.

With respect to symbolism, then, Schering divides instrumental music into four types: playful, adopting vocal melodies, imitating vocal formulations, and representing ideas. He discusses each of these in turn, maintaining that the third type can be interpreted only through singable linguistic contents of some kind. This conception underlies Schering's Beethoven studies.

The fourth type of symbolism involves the history of symbolism once again. Until about 1740, Schering maintains, music manifests essentially the symbolism of ideas. Between this and the symbolism of feeling, which characterizes the music of Romanticism, there is the high Baroque symbolism derived from visual impressions:

> The feeling that flows in the unconscious, difficult to take hold of, is still not the goal of reproduction, but rather the stationary, visible affect. Its nature resides in the impassioned gesture, the visible motion. In it is disclosed everything that man and living creatures experience inwardly; in it is reflected also the activity of nature. There arises a music of almost palpable distinctness, loaded with symbols of affect of the utmost boldness (Schein, Schütz, Bach).

Toward the end of Schering's historical sketch, there appears the conception that his work on Beethoven was intended to exemplify:

> A new openness to the world that today is still not describable more closely seems, since 1760, to have sharpened the insight of the creative musician into the connections between the world of tone and the world

of lived experience. The great era of instrumental music—of the piano sonata, the string quartet, the symphony, the overture—began, fed by a fantasy that to a totally different degree than earlier was borne by *poetry*. Song and opera, both now growing into everyday bourgeois life, remain for a long time afterward the inexhaustible source of stimulation for the instrumental musician. But since his power of symbolic interpretation has increased endlessly, poetry becomes his guide in wordless music also. Without it and without its images that stir up the fantasy, the great instrumental music of the following Romantic era cannot even be imagined. Its nature rests directly on a new connection with poetry, whose wonders in the description of characters and situations inspire the musician to the creation of tonal worlds of equal rank. It does not matter to him where the visions come from—whether from lyric, epic, novel, or drama. He seizes them and conjures them up in tones. There arise creations that for the first time truly deserve the name *tone poems* and that no longer make their originators comparable to word poets only figuratively but in the true sense.[5]

The idea that musical symbolism is indigenous to instrumental music is capable of accounting for a large range of symbolic manifestations, but not for all. Schering mentions, for example, that, just as instruments become more serious or noble the closer they come to the voice, so the voice becomes more comic or playful the closer it comes to an instrument. But this alteration of the character of the voice is not considered to be symbolic.

Susanne Langer first presented a symbolic philosophy of music in *Philosophy in a New Key* (1942). The basis of her conception of symbolism, however, was established by Ernst Cassirer, in his monumental *Die Philosophie der symbolischen Formen* (1923–29). Cassirer considered symbolism to be a fundamental manifestation of human mentality, and the broad context of his thought can be seen in Langer's subtitle: *A Study in the Symbolism of Reason, Rite, and Art*. Langer considers symbolization to be a basic need of man. The symbol-making function, she maintains, is one of man's primary activities, like eating, looking, or moving about. It is in fact the fundamental process of his mind, she believes, and goes on constantly. The material furnished by the senses is wrought into symbols; these are our elementary ideas, of which some can be combined and manipulated to produce a process of reasoning. Thus, symbolization is "the starting-point of all intellection": "The fact that the human brain is constantly carrying on a process of symbolic transformation of the experiential data that come to it causes it to be a veritable fountain of more or less spontaneous ideas."[6]

Langer distinguishes two basic kinds of symbolism: discursive, the type found in language, and presentational, the type found in art. The meanings given through language are successively understood; the meanings of presentational symbols are understood only through the meaning of the whole: the symbolic elements are understood only through the relations within the total structure. But no symbolism is exempt, Langer points out, from the office of logical formulation, of conceptualizing what it conveys, and the conveyed import is always a meaning and therefore addressed to the understanding. Clearly, the symbolic view of art, as Langer conceives it, makes the understanding of art comparable to the conceptual understanding of language. The two types of understanding are seen as basically similar rather than as sharply contrasted.

As far as music is concerned, Langer regards it as a formulation and representation of emotions, moods, and mental tensions and resolutions—a "logical picture" of sentient, responsive life and a source of insight into it. The feelings revealed in music are presented directly to our understanding, she maintains, that we may grasp, realize, and comprehend them: "Just as words can describe events we have not witnessed, places and things we have not seen, so music can present emotions and moods we have not felt, passions we did not know before" (p. 180). Although the subject matter of music is the same as that of self-expression, the borrowed, suggestive elements are formalized and the subject matter "distanced." The "distance"

> does not make the emotive contents typical, general, impersonal, or "static"; but it makes them conceivable, so that we can envisage and understand them without verbal helps, and without the scaffolding of an occasion wherein they figure. . . . A composer not only indicates, but articulates subtle complexes of feeling that language cannot even name, let alone set forth; he knows the forms of emotion and can handle them, "compose" them. (p. 180)

Thus, the content of music is symbolized, and what it invites is not emotional response but insight. "Psychical distance," in Langer's interpretation of Edward Bullough's term, is simply the experience of apprehending through a symbol what was not articulated before. The symbols that reveal the life of feeling, impulse, and passion will not be the sounds or actions that normally would express this life; not associated signs but symbolic forms must convey it to our understanding. The explanation given by Langer of how this can happen is that there are certain aspects of inner life, whether physical or mental, that have formal properties similar to those of music: patterns of motion and rest, tension and release, agreement and disagreement, preparation, fulfillment, excitation, sudden change, and so on:

> So the first requirement for a connotative relationship between music and subjective experience, a certain similarity of form, is certainly sat-

isfied. Furthermore, there is no doubt that musical forms have certain properties to recommend them for symbolic use: they are composed of many separable items, easily produced, and easily combined in a great variety of ways; in themselves they play no important practical role which would overshadow their semantic function; they are readily distinguished, remembered, and repeated; and finally, they have a remarkable tendency to modify each other's characters in combination, as words do, by all serving each as a context. (p. 185)

Music presents emotive experience, then, through global forms that are indivisible. But it seems peculiarly difficult, Langer remarks, for our literal minds to grasp the idea "that anything can be known which cannot be named" (p. 189). Why does some music seem to bear a sad and a happy interpretation equally well? Langer asks. Perhaps what music actually reflects is only the morphology of feeling, for some sad and some happy feelings may have a very similar morphology. The idea that music conveys only the general forms of feeling, however, makes music an abstraction and musical experience a purely logical revelation. It does not do justice to the sensuous value of tone. Yet music does not have an assigned connotation. It is a form capable of connotation, but its import is never fixed. At the same time, music harbors a principle of development in its own elementary forms, which is characteristic of a good symbolism. It cannot be pretended that Langer makes sense from all this. Music is clearly a symbolic form, she decides, but it is an unconsummated symbol. The actual function of meaning, which calls for permanent contents, is not fulfilled; the assignment of one rather than another possible meaning to each form is never explicitly made. Yet it can correctly be called, in the phrase of Clive Bell, "significant form."

It turns out in the ensuing discussion that this ambivalence of content is a virtue. Music is revealing because it can have a transient play of contents and articulate feelings without becoming wedded to them. The assignment of meanings is a shifting, kaleidoscopic play, probably below the threshold of consciousness, certainly outside the pale of discursive thinking. Music gives us knowledge of "how feelings go." At the same time, however, Langer believes that certain effects of music are so much like feelings that we mistake them for feelings. Her explanation is that music is a young, or mythical, symbolism: "Until symbolic forms are consciously abstracted, they are regularly confused with the things they symbolize" (p. 199). What are these things in the case of music? Are they feelings, or forms of feeling, or "certain effects" that are like feelings? What is an "unconsummated symbol?" Langer may raise more questions than she answers. The most insistent criticism of her theory, however, was directed against the idea of a symbol without a specific meaning. In the controversy that arose over this issue, the underlying disagreement was between a Germanic and an Anglo-American conception of symbolism.

Nelson Goodman's study of symbolism, *Languages of Art: An Approach to a Theory of Symbols* (1976), is a revision and elaboration of a series of lectures given in 1962. In spite of its title, it is not restricted to the province of art but has the scope of a general theory of the subject, comparable to the works of Cassirer and Langer. It differs from these, however, because it is concerned not so much with the fundamental nature of symbolism and its role in human mentality as with a close comparison of the various types of symbol, which it develops as a matter of course in terms of linguistic analysis. Typologies of symbolism have been a traditional part of studies of musical symbolism, but they have been established on the basis of rational principles rather than linguistic distinctions. For this reason, Goodman's investigation has an Anglo-American character in contrast to a Germanic one.

As far as music is concerned, Goodman has been most influential in calling attention to the idea of "exemplification." From his point of view of the relations and distinctions between different types of symbol, he examines the relations, for example, between exemplification, denotation, representation, expression, and possession. The following will serve as an illustration of his concerns:

> Before me is a picture of trees and cliffs by the sea, painted in dull grays, and expressing great sadness. This description gives information of three kinds, saying something about (1) what things the picture represents, (2) what properties it possesses, and (3) what feelings it expresses. The logical nature of the underlying relationships in the first two cases is plain: the picture denotes a certain scene and is a concrete instance of certain shades of gray. But what is the logical character of the relationship the picture bears to what it is said to express?

Exemplification, Goodman asserts, is an important mode of symbolization both in the arts and outside them. He illustrates it by the function of a swatch of cloth as a tailor's sample. The swatch exemplifies certain of its properties—its color, weave, texture, and pattern—but not its size or shape, for example: "Exemplification is possession plus reference. To have without symbolizing is merely to possess, while to symbolize without having is to refer in some other way than by exemplifying. The swatch exemplifies only those properties that it both has and refers to."[7]

In the essay "Understanding Music" (1981), Monroe Beardsley applies the concept of exemplification to music. He starts with the idea that the properties or qualities of a musical work are exemplified when they are displayed or exhibited. Exemplification is a kind of reference of a work to its own properties: "The semantic understanding of a sonata, then, involves discerning which of its heard qualities are thus exemplified." Beardsley goes on to distinguish two kinds of displaying—of an object itself and of the properties of this object. The second is dependent on the first: a property can be displayed only when the object that possesses this property is itself displayed. In a performance of Beethoven's Piano Sonata in A Major, op. 101, for example, "the pianist displays that work and thereby enables the sonata to display some of its qualities; so by our principles, since there is object-displaying, the sonata's own property-displaying amounts to reference (and hence to exemplification)." But which properties of the sonata are displayed, and which are not? Beardsley asks. The properties that are displayed and thus exemplified, he maintains,

> are just those properties which are worthy of note in the context of concert-giving and concert-going (and recording, too): that is, they are those properties whose presence or absence, or degree of presence, have a direct bearing on the sonata's capacity to interest us aesthetically. They may or may not be of special concern to musicologists or music analysts, but they are qualities to attend to if you are taking the aesthetic point of view. The first movement of opus 101 is in the key of A, with few and restricted modulations; that is a property, but, by itself, it neither enhances nor inhibits the aesthetic satisfactoriness of the sonata. Therefore it is not exemplified. On the other hand, the first movement is unusually hesitant, diffident, indecisive in character; this is a quality that can be enjoyed in it, and . . . it is a feature that plays an essential role in the marvelous course of the whole sonata. Therefore, it is exemplified.[8]

This "Goodman-Beardsley theory" of semantic understanding is the most important outcome for music of Goodman's *Languages of Art*. The idea of "representation as," however, has also found musical application, in the aesthetics of Roger Scruton, which is discussed below under the head "Understanding."

Semiotics

Just as the modern development of hermeneutics was grounded in the work of Dilthey and the modern interest in symbolism had an important point of departure in the work of Cassirer, so the modern development of the field of semiotics had its foundation in the work of Charles Peirce and Ferdinand de Saussure. In this case, there were two independent and rather different origins: Peirce saw the study of signs as a philosophical undertaking, while Saussure conceived of such a field as closely related to linguistics. The two traditions—Anglo-American and French—even made use of separate designations for their field of study—*semiotics* and *semiology*.

Peirce was responsible for a highly elaborate classification of types of signs and also for the fundamental triadic relation of representation (the sign itself), interpretant (an interpretation referring the sign to some "object"), and this designated "object" to which both the sign and the interpretant referred. Since the interpretant was a second "sign" that again called for an interpretant (which would refer again to the same "object"), a process of continual regress arose. Deriving from this relational triad were the three dimensions that were defined for semiotic analysis by Charles Morris: syntax, semantics, and pragmatics.

Saussure believed that language could be studied only after it was shown to comprise a semiological system. This made linguistics part of semiology and linguistic laws applications of the general laws of semiology. But language occupied a privileged position: it is the most characteristic system of signs, for it has a conventional character and a conspicuous regularity; its systematic nature is not obscured because its individual elements lack distinctive meanings of their own. In the wake of Saussure, consequently, investigations of other fields of expression looked for guidance to the structure of language and to the terminology and procedures of linguistics. Following the descriptive procedure of distributional linguistics, then, and the theory of generative grammar, music was directed to analysis and classification, which would establish the elements or units in a given work or body of music, and then to the laws of generation for such a style, which would permit the construction, for example, of characteristic, or "correct," melodies.

Art presents its own problems to semiotics. Although even aesthetic qualities must be conveyed to a percipient, art is certainly not restricted to the function of communication, nor is it even primarily communication. Instead, it is most essentially the creation of certain kinds of meaning, and it has been increasingly recognized that this meaning is self-referential. Acknowledging then also its communicative function, we can call the work of art a message that has a reflexive meaning. The status of meaning in semiotics is in general a curious one. Far from being central or prominent either in linguistics or semiotics, it is frequently not considered at all and even explicitly held to be unessential. In Morris's behavioral conception, "semantic rules" are simply part of the rules of use for a sign; that is, they give the conditions under which a sign is applicable to an object or a state of affairs. Such a formal conception of meaning has a counterpart in the thesis that meaning is added to syntax by the reaction of the percipient; the reaction becomes the meaning. In either case, it is syntax that is the fundamental aspect of semiotics; meaning is secondary and dispensable, somewhat as communication is in the field of art. There is the alternative, however, particularly in music, of integrating semantics into syntax, for self-referential expression actually does contain the meaning as well as the order of what is presented; syntax and semantics may in fact coincide.

Before any semiotic investigation of music is begun, however, there are two questions that must be answered. If a linguistic treatment is in question, we must ask whether and in what sense music is a language. But even more fundamental to any type of semiotic examination of music is the question whether music is a sign or a system of signs. As far as the similarity between music and language is concerned, the distinction between an individual musical work (or an improvisation) and the musical system in which it is grounded does indeed mirror the distinction between an individual literary work (or an improvised discourse) and the systematic structure of the language it employs. Tones can be compared, with some degree of accuracy, to phonemes, just as successive musical motives, themes, phrases, and so on (in an articulated style) can be compared to morphemes, words, linguistic phrases, and so on. Cadences are comparable to junctures, the scalar system to the phonological system, melodic grammars to linguistic grammars.

Resemblances such as these, however, do not appear to advance our understanding and analysis of music in any significant way; they seem simply to provide fashionable rubrics for problems that can be handled just as well with traditional terminology. Even worse, they pretend to be sufficient in themselves and thus succeed in eliminating the historical study of style, which is their true competitor in defining musical meaning. It is also doubtful how thoroughgoing the similarities are. Double articulation in music, for example—if it exists at all—is certainly different from double articulation in language, for the relation of tones to themes is really not the same as the relation of phonemes to words, which differ from one another much more sharply. But even the comparable aspects of music and language belong almost entirely to the province of structure; a comparative consideration of meaning yields a completely different and much more negative result. In the end, *semantics* may be no more than a new word for the familiar referential aspects of musical meaning and *syntax* a new word for form or for structure.

The value of replacing *form* and *meaning* with *syntax* and *semantics* may be simply that our attention will be directed to aspects of music that would otherwise not be considered, to the detailed course of meaning, for example, through whole musical statements or sections, which would be analogous to sentences or paragraphs. The intimate connection of syntax and semantics, which is more striking in music than it is in language, is a relevant circumstance here. While it may seem to prevent or obstruct the separate study of syntax, it suggests at the same time that we may be able to get at musical semantics through musical syntax—to get at the invisible, as it were, by means of the visible. Certainly, the types of repetition, recurrence, and equivalence in musical syntax, which play so prominent a role, are responsible for conspicuous aspects of musical meaning. They are also an example of the character of the relation between music and language, for syntax in language is based on principles that are entirely different from repetition and equivalence; music would therefore seem to be closer to poetry and rhetoric in particular—as indeed it has been historically—than to language in general. On the other hand, syntax is responsible for meaning in language also, even if this kind of "structural meaning" is relatively inconspicuous.

If music is thought of as a system of signs rather than more specifically as a kind of language, it becomes comparable to any semiotic system, not necessarily to language in particular. Thus, Claude Lévi-Strauss, in the "Ouverture" of his *Le Cru et le cuit* (1964)—*The Raw and the Cooked*—has examined the resemblance of music to myth, considering them both, however, to be "languages" that transcend articulate expression. They are also both obviously temporal, he points out, but in the act of listening they transform their diachronic nature into a synchronic totality on the basis of the internal organization of the individual myth or of the musical work.

In myth, Lévi-Strauss continues, each society selects a limited number of relevant incidents from the theoretically infinite historical series of events. In music, similarly, each musical system selects a scale from the theoretically infinite series of tones that can be produced. The scale provides music with an initial level of articulation, which is a function of the hierarchical relations among the tones—their division, for example, into fundamental, dominant, leading tone, and so on. The composer modifies this discontinuity: his melodic inventiveness either creates temporary lacunae in the scalar grid or fills in the intervals (which in some scales are really gaps). His rhythmic inventiveness similarly modifies the physiological grid of respiration, which is natural rather than cultural.

As far as painting is concerned, colors are a material only because of the prior existence of colored objects, from which they are abstracted. Colors are natural rather than cultural; their true counterpart in sound would be noises, not tones. The "congenital subjection of the plastic arts to objects" results from the fact that the organization of forms and colors within sense experience acts as an initial level of articulation of reality. Only because of this is it possible to introduce a secondary articulation, which consists of the choice and arrangements of the units in accordance with a given technique or style. In language, the two levels of the double articulation are phonemes (elements of articulation without significance) and morphemes (significant elements composed of phonemes): "Consequently, in articulate speech the primary nonsignifying code is a means and condition of significance in the secondary code: in this way, significance itself is restricted to one level." In poetry, however, the significance of words and syntactic configurations on the second level is combined with the aesthetic properties of sonority, which were adumbrated on the phoneme level.

> It is the same thing in painting, where contrasts of form and color are perceived as distinctive features simultaneously dependent on two systems: first, a system of intellectual significances, the heritage of common experience and the result of the subdivision and organization of sense experience into objects; second, a system of plastic values which only becomes significant through modulating the other and becoming incorporated with it. Two articulated mechanisms mesh to form a third, which combines the properties of both.[9]

Lévi-Strauss believes that the power to signify in any code depends on double articulation—on the existence of a primary code whose units are combined to make up the units of the secondary code. Thus, abstract painting loses the power to signify because it abandons the primary level of articulation and makes use of the secondary level alone. The same is true of *musique concrète*, in Lévi-Strauss's view:

> Before using the noises it has collected, *musique concrète* takes care to make them unrecognizable, so that the listener cannot yield to the natural tendency to relate them to sense images: the breaking of china, a train whistle, a fit of coughing, or the snapping off of a tree branch. It thus wipes out a first level of articulation. . . .
>
> If such music used noises while retaining their representative value, it would have at its disposal a first articulation which would allow it to set up a system of signs through the bringing into articulation of a second articulation. But this system would allow almost nothing to be said. To be convinced of this, one has only to imagine what kind of stories could be told by means of noises, with reasonable assurance that such stories would be both intelligible and moving. Hence the solution that has been adopted—the alteration of noises to turn them into pseudo-sounds; but it is then impossible to define simple relations among the latter, such as would form an already significant system on another level and would be capable of providing the basis for a second articulation. *Music concrète* may be intoxicated with the illusion that it is saying something; in fact, it is floundering in non-significance. (p. 23)

Serial music shares the same defect. The primary level of articulation, which Lévi-Strauss believes to be indispensable in any language, has been abandoned or at least reduced to discrete tones that are equally spaced and have no intrinsic functional distinctions (aside from pitch difference itself). But this fails to meet the specified criterion: "The elements raised to the level of a meaningful function of a new order by the second articulation must arrive at this point already endowed with the required properties: that is, they must already be stamped with, and for, meaning" (p. 24). Whether the system of the primary level is natural or cultural evidently makes no difference: it can in either event create "a priori conditions of communication among beings similar in nature" (p. 24).

A few years after the appearance of this attack on serialism, Umberto Eco undertook a systematic refutation in his *La struttura assente* (1968). Eco begins by defining a distinction in the nature of a structural model: is it an operative procedure that enables us to regard various phenomena from a single point of view and thus a metalinguistic element that permits us to speak of these different classes of phenomenon as sign systems? Or does it represent an ontological reality? Certainly, there is a strong tendency to regard structures that are found in different factual circumstances as fixed and "objective" and to feel convinced that we have come on repeated manifestations of an intrinsic structure of the human mind. Eco takes systems of kinship as an example. A family is a "message" in the code represented by the kinship system of a society, he says, but his code becomes a message in the more general code that represents the kinship systems of all societies. Similarly, this general code becomes in turn a particular manifestation of that underlying code, or metacode, on the basis of which various general codes—of kinship, of language, of cooking, of myth, and so on—can be regarded as homologous. Stating the matter in a slightly different way, if we have determined a number of different but homologous structures in a community—of the language, of the kinship system, of the spatial organization of the village, and so on—their homologous form can be regarded as the result of a deeper structure that is basic to all of them. Similarly, if additional phenomena are discovered that are different in structure but homologous to each other, this new group must be derived from a second basic structure. The two deep structures arrived at, however, will in turn be the superficial manifestations of a still deeper structure that underlies both.

The question then arises of whether this metacode is the end point in the construction of an operational model or, alternatively, whether it is the discovery of a basic principle of organization, of a fundamental mechanism that is intrinsic to the functioning of the human mind, in which case a law of nature will be constitutive for laws of culture. In the one case structure is an operational model, in the other an ontological reality. Lévi-Strauss starts with the one, Eco maintains, and shifts to the other. But while the advent of serialism and modern art is compatible with functional structuralism since it merely calls for a new structure of increased depth and generality, it is not compatible with ontological structuralism, and this is the reason for Lévi-Strauss's rejection of "serialist thinking." It is understandable, Eco argues, that structuralist thought favors "universals" while serialist thought seeks to destroy any supposed universal that is recognized as historical rather than eternal:

> Let us say that the concept of a universal structure of communication, of an archetypal code, constitutes simply a hypothesis of research . . . in such a case it is natural that serial thought, insofar as it is an activity of the production of forms and not of research into their ultimate characteristics, would not be called into question by structural research— which it implies but which it is not called on to develop. It may be that under every modality of communication there are constant structures, but serial technique . . . aims at constructing new structural realities, not at discovering eternal structural principles.[10]

If we subscribe to ontological structuralism, Eco continues, then the structures of communication brought to light by linguistic and ethnological research *really exist;* they are operations inherent to the human mind, perhaps modes of functioning of a cerebral apparatus whose structures are isomorphic with those of physical reality. In such a case, however, structural research would tend to reveal the deep structures, the deepest, "the structure *cujus nihil majus cogitari possit*" (p. 314). But why should these structures be those of tonal music rather than much more general structures that encompass and explain, along with other types of musical logic, tonal music also? Why would they not be generative structures, through which every grammar (like the tonal one) and every negation of grammar (like the atonal one) and indeed every constitution of sound selected from the whole continuum running from tone to noise will be revealed as distinctive products of culture? There would then be no primary system of tones but simply a generative mechanism of every possible tonal opposition, in the sense of a Chomskian generative grammar. Instead of this, however, it appears from Levi-Strauss's discussion

> that the chief aim of structural thought is that of opposing to a serial technique—directed to *the creation of history,* to the production of varieties of communication—preestablished and preexisting structures in order to judge, in reference to these assumptions as parameters, the validity of new types of communication that arise precisely in oppo-

sition to the parameters called into question. It would be like judging a revolutionary act that opposed a given constitution, by an appeal to the rejected constitution; formally the procedure is perfect . . . but historically it is laughable. (p. 315)

Yet there is value, Eco maintains, in transforming serial technique into a way of thought—into serial "thinking," namely,

the recognition of the social and historical foundation of codes, the persuasion that a suprastructural action may contribute to transform these codes and that every change of codes of communicative behavior permits the formation of new cultural contexts, the organization of new codes, the continued restructuring of these, the historical evolution of the modalities of communication, following the dialectical interrelations between the system of communication and the social context. It is sufficient to think of the correlations looked for by Henri Pousseur between the world of tonal music and an aesthetic of repetition, of the equal, of the eternal return, of a periodic and closed conception of time, which comprehends and mirrors a conservative ideology and pedagogy proper to a committed society, to a fixed political and social structure. (pp. 316–17)

In closing his discussion of the duality of structural and serial, Eco presents a clear juxtaposition of "structure as constant and history as process." "If structure is identified with the mechanisms of the mind," he states, "historical knowledge is no longer possible. The idea of a structural unconscious that is found not only in all human beings but in every historical epoch (and that simultaneously preserves the characteristics of historicity and of universal validity) is destined to generate contradictory explanations" (p. 319).

The assumption that music is a semiotic system is the foundation of the discussion of musical analysis in Nicholas Ruwet's essay "Méthodes d'analyse en musicologie" (1966). Accordingly, music is considered to possess a syntax and to be subject to the basic dichotomy of code and message, which is derived from the theory of communication. Analysis in this context consists of manipulating a message or body of messages "in order to extract the unities, the classes of unities, and the rules of their combination that constitute the code."[11] The crucial problem in analysis, Ruwet maintains, is determining a method or a procedure. When the code has been extracted, a procedure that is the inverse of the analytic one will permit the generation of messages: "Given an analytic model, then, we set up a synthetic model, which starts with the most abstract and the most general elements and arrives at concrete messages. . . . If the analytic model is good, its synthetic transformation will generate messages that would not appear in the initial corpus (limited by definition) but that subjects will recognize as equally well formed" (p. 484).

The most obvious problem in analysis is to determine the process of division—of a melody, let us say—that will result in the various basic units that make up the melody. It is taken as a matter of course that a melody will have a hierarchical plan, that is, will be divided into parts of different levels. According to Ferretti, for example, as Ruwet points out, Gregorian melodies are divided into periods, these in turn into phrases, the phrases into members, and these into incises. Division according to this scheme, however, apart from implying that a taxonomy of the parts of a melody can be a valid conception, at least for some melodies, brings up the crucial question of what the criteria are that have governed the division. This question entails a series of others: "If I divide a section A into two segments a and b, do I take pauses as a basis, differences in tone color, contrasts of register, melodic and/or harmonic cadences, identity or contrast of rhythms, the equal or unequal duration of the segments, etc.? Or does a combination of these criteria come into play? Do the divisions rest on the identities or on the differences between the segments?" (p. 489). The list Ruwet gives is actually very much longer than this, and it is still only a partial one.

Ruwet bases his division of melody chiefly on the criterion of repetition, which he explains before beginning his analysis as signifying the identity of segments distributed in different places in the syntagmatic chain. But this involves the question of which of the musical dimensions—pitch, duration, intensity, tone color, and so on—will determine when two different segments will be considered repetitions of one another: "Here, it being understood that the examples will be taken from Occidental written tradition and will be monodic, we shall retain only pitch and duration. But we must remember that segments with varying pitches and durations can be considered as repetitions only if they are identical from other points of view" (pp. 494–95). In many instances, a unity will not be a literal repetition of another but a transformation of it—a variant, either melodic or rhythmic or both. When the longest repetitions (or variants) have been extracted, the procedure is repeated for these, and so on, until the elementary unities and their variants are obtained. These become the paradigms of the musical code of the melody and are written below one another in the same column.

Ruwet then applies this analytic procedure to a number of melodies, after which his conclusions are far from encouraging: "Precisely because it attempts to define levels and unities rigorously, the procedure followed has led us . . . to call into question a purely taxonomic conception of musical structure." It is impossible even in a simple case, Ruwet continues, to picture the structure completely so that the large unities of the first level decompose integrally into the unities of the second level, and so on:

> The principal reason for this state of affairs is evidently connected with the fact that musical syntax is a syntax of equivalences: the diverse unities have among themselves relations of equivalence of all kinds, relations that can unite segments, for example, of unequal length—one segment will appear as an expansion or as a contraction of another—and also segments encroaching on one another. The consequence of all this is, as we have been able to confirm, that it is impossible to represent the structure of a musical piece by a unique schema. (pp. 507–8)

Since Ruwet's "Méthodes d'analyse" is a representative study by one of the most respected semiologists of music, these results have important implications, which Ruwet himself has made explicit elsewhere. In his *Langage, musique, poésie* (1972)—a collection of his essays—the opinion he expresses in the "Avant-propos" is a mixed one. Most of the essays, he tells us, are centered on the fundamental property that is common to musical language and poetical language, namely, repetition or, in the words of Roman Jakobson, the "projection of the principle of equivalence of the axis of selection on the axis of combination." But Ruwet makes it clear that he has never tried to apply the concepts, rules, and results that are specific to natural languages directly to music in particular. Only the large general principles of linguistics can be applied in that way, such as the distinction between language and speech (between competence and performance), not such specific concepts as that of "morpheme."

As far as "musical semantics" is concerned, it has little to gain by turning to linguistics. Since "the sense of a musical work is an immanent one, it can appear only in the description of the work. If we absolutely insist on speaking of *signifiant* and *signifié* in music, we will say that the signifié (the 'intelligible' or 'translatable' aspect, as Jakobson says) is given in music in the description of the *signifiant* (the perceptible aspect)." In concrete terms, it is in the homology between musical structure and the structure of reality or lived experience that Ruwet finds the key to the sense, or meaning, of music. He considers the simple example of a fragment of tonal music that is composed of two parts, of which the first ends on a half cadence and the second, otherwise identical, ends on a full cadence. This will be interpreted as a movement that is interrupted or suspended but then repeated and carried to a conclusion—a structure that is homologous to a great many others outside music: "It is in this relation of homology that I would see what may be called the (partial) meaning of the fragment in question, and it is evident that only internal formal analysis will permit us to extract it." [12]

The nature and value of musical semiotics were matters that concerned Ruwet as early as 1959, in his "Contradictions du langage sériel." If music is a language, he affirms in that essay, it must obey the rules of a system of communication. Now there are modes of relation of human beings, he continues, that fall short of language, such as cries and caresses. These manifest a wealth of resources and an infinite variety, but the richness is confused, undifferentiated, and ineffable. On the other hand, there are articulated and differentiated systems, such as myth, arts, languages, and systems of kinship or economics, in which the totality of articulated significations is expressed in a complex manner but which at the same time involve certain limitations. When Henri Pousseur speaks of the infinite riches of noises in relation to the relative poverty of the musical tones selected by traditional kinds of music, it is like preferring the riches of infantile babbling to the phonological system of French or Chinese.

But the question remains what the rules are that govern articulated systems. Ruwet pursues his theme. From linguistics we obtain the distinction between the level of language and the level of speech, he points out, the first corresponding to reversible time and the second to irreversible. We also learn that language is a whole that is made up of several systems in reciprocal relations—phonological systems, a grammatical system, and various semantic systems. It is a system of systems. The phonological system constitutes the infrastructure of a language, and it is based on distinctive binary oppositions between elements that are called "phonemes"—between *i* and *a*, for example, as in the words *it* and *at*.

Applying linguistic principles in some detail, Ruwet cites a number of instances of serial music that fail to meet the requirements of a system of communication, anticipating by some years Lévi-Strauss's unqualified indictment of serialism. As Ruwet indicates, the shortcomings of serialism as a "language" could easily be matched by the more obvious deficiencies of noise in the same capacity. Yet serialism, at any rate, can be redeemed by combining it with traditional factors of music, as Ruwet suggests and Schönberg, Berg, and Webern actually demonstrate. The negative verdict delivered by linguistic structuralism in the case of serial music was in any event set aside shortly afterward, as we have seen, in favor of the incontrovertible argument of historical novelty. But even if traditional varieties of music conform to linguistic principles, it does not follow that we shall learn anything about music from them beyond what we already know without an appeal to semiotics. Still worse, such an appeal, in fact, since it is grounded in the concept of "communication," excludes the possibility of understanding what there may be in the nature of music that altogether eludes this concept.

The case for musical meaning in the field of semiotics, finally, is not made

out most convincingly in terms of Ruwet's conception of a homology between musical structure and external structures. Syntactic meaning provides
a much more satisfactory argument, even though meaning of this kind is not
exactly what meaning is generally considered to be. It is precisely defined,
however, in contrast to the meaning only vaguely suggested by homology.
There is an excellent discussion of syntactic musical meaning in Peter Faltin's
essay "Musikalische Bedeutung: Grenzen und Möglichkeiten einer semiotischen Ästhetik" (1978). The context and the various aspects of this conception are treated in detail, but the central notion will be conveyed quite
well by the following excerpt:

> It is not feelings, changing scenes, or verbal ideas that lend music
> its meaning but primarily the syntactic intentions through which the
> compositional-constructive will to shape a dynamic form is realized.
> These intentions constitute the essence of the musical meanings and are
> audible as the structure and form of the music.
>
> A thematic unfolding, a succession of chords, a syncopation that
> interrupts a prevailing rhythm, an ostinato, a dynamic gradation, a false
> cadence, or a sequence, all these are specifically musical ideas. As struc-
> tural intentions they are not a sign for the contents of ideas standing
> outside them but results of specific mental activity of the individual;
> Hanslick spoke metaphorically of the "working of the mind on material
> capable of receiving the forms the mind imparts." Such ideas can be
> articulated only by a sounding construction. The sounding in which the
> musical idea realizes itself is the manifestation of its own and not of
> a foreign substance. It is the product of an intention that is primarily
> directed to the forming.[13]

Faltin's essay is characteristic of musical aesthetics, however, in that it is devoted more to the description of what musical meaning is not than to what
it is.

Understanding

During the 1970s and 1980s there appeared another group of ideas bearing on the question of musical meaning. The central concept now was that
of "understanding." This development was to some extent a revival of the
tradition of hermeneutics, for which understanding was a fundamental concept, but linguistics and semiotics had intervened, and they seem to have
been responsible for the more specific way in which musical understanding
was conceived and examined.

Hans Eggebrecht undertakes a basic definition of understanding in his densely written and intensively thought-out essay "On the Conceptual and Nonconceptual Understanding of Music" (1973). He conceives these two types of understanding, reversing the order of his own title, as directed respectively to the *Sinn* and the *Gehalt* of music, its sense and its import ("content"). The nonconceptual understanding of music is the grasp of its musical sense, which resides purely in the structured sound. The musical material is formulated in such a way that it makes sense in its own right, and as far as this type of understanding is concerned, any reference of music to objects that can be grasped in words is extramusical, for it goes beyond the nature of the art.

Eggebrecht does not treat the distinction between two types of understanding, or what we may call two types of meaning or two different objects of musical understanding (sense and import), simply as an analytic or systematic distinction. He examines it in detail as a historical manifestation as well and connects it with the idea of musical autonomy that appeared at the end of the eighteenth century. The idea of "pure" music, he argues, produced the controversial status of "program music" along with the duality of "form and content" (*Inhalt*). The very nature of aesthetics, however, led inevitably to a resolution of this issue in favor of sounding and moving form:

> In "aesthetics," namely, in its origin and prevalence, the division of musical meaning into the inner- and the extramusical (which implied an evaluation) as well as the idea—closely associated with this—of the autonomy of music, the emphasis on the absence of concepts as its specific feature and together with this the dominance of the formalistic comprehension of music, found its philosophically established basis, which was scientific and at the same time fundamentally historical.[14]

In its very name, Eggebrecht points out, *aesthetics* attests that the sense of an artistic formulation exists essentially for sensuous comprehension and is grounded in and understandable through the specific sensuousness of the artistic material. It is a separate world that contains its own sense and can be approached verbally only as form or "structure." The ultimate historical basis of this isolation of art, furthermore, is not simply aesthetics but the social cause of aesthetics, namely, the specific artistic need of the bourgeois consciousness, "which sought the emancipation denied to it by the real world in a fictive world, particularly in music. . . . Aesthetics is the theory of art as an antiworld, art as an autonomous manifestation whose lack of function it establishes so that art can fill the function of an antiworld" (p. 117). But in this, Eggebrecht remarks tellingly, the nonconceptual nature of music becomes conceptual, just as its lack of function becomes functional.

The "era of aesthetics" produced a number of important developments in musical thought. The idea of an intrinsic musical sense, for one thing, gave rise to the "scientific" method of "analysis," which was of course also a historical manifestation, however much it may not have been regarded as such. Analysis conveys the nonconceptual sense of music conceptually by describing its detailed course in the technical terminology of the organization of musical form. But this description can also be reduced to the mathematical theory of information, which really represents an effort to purify the language of analysis from conceptuality altogether.

Because of its historical nature, as Eggebrecht further argues, the conception of music is social as well as historical: it is the expression of a collective consciousness that is both temporally and spatially specific. Thus, musical sense is a social sense, the product of a collective intention and the object of a collective understanding.

The historical process through which this sense is transmitted is described by Eggebrecht in terms of the categories "norm," "concretion," and "innovation." Norms are abstract rules that are interdependent and that form a system. The prohibition of more than three successive imperfect consonances in the fourteenth century, for example, is necessary to secure the general sound of "perfection" created by the periodic recurrence of the perfect consonances as points of reference and articulation. But the dominance of sounding perfection can be understood and explained only as an integral part of a total system of norms that also includes, for example, the rule of contrary motion.

Norms are realized in concretions or, more specifically, in the structure of individual musical works, while innovation represents the appearance of a new system of norms, which is heralded, for example, by the regular succession of as many as six parallel imperfect consonances in Dufay's chanson style. Eggebrecht wishes essentially to make the point, however, that all these aspects of the transmission of musical sense, although historical, remain completely within the sphere of the nonconceptuality of music and are open to the specifically aesthetic and formalistic techniques of musical analysis.

The conceptual understanding of music, to which Eggebrecht now gives his attention, has an encompassing nature that extends well beyond the particular intended meanings of older traditions, such as the pastoral significance of F major:

What music presents for conceptual understanding is that which in or by means of its inner organization, of the interfunctionality of its specifically musical kind of sense, it "designates," "means," or "expresses," that is, that which is designated, or—as I call it—its *"Gehalt"* [content, or import]. The import has as its peculiarity that it appears musically (i.e., in a conceptless materiality) but is itself conceptual. It is the content enclosed in the sense of music, the "sense-content" [*Sinngehalt*], and we can say of it that it is as total, as concerned with the whole of a musical work as is the musical sense and that it is just as involved in the thought process of musical production, just as much involved in the hearing process of musical reception, and just as much to be scientifically determined unambiguously and concretely as is the musical sense.

Now if it remains undisputed that the musical sense exists (it is a scientific object, e.g., in aesthetically conceived musical analysis), and if it is said here that a conceptually comprehensible musical import also exists in the degree of totality and unambiguousness of the musical sense, then the problem lies first of all in the separation of sense and import, a separation that is not transcended even in the concept of "sense-content." Although there is no musical sense without content [import] and the content of music appears as musical sense, the separation is nevertheless methodologically possible and necessary. The sense and content [*Sinn und Gehalt*] of music are as different as tone and concept. They are as a duality, however, not something mutually contradictory, but two sides of the same thing: the conceptual appears in the conceptless. (pp. 120–21)

Thus, a particular import, as Eggebrecht adds by way of elucidation, can appear only in a particular organization of musical sense.

But if we seek to determine the import of music through its sense—in effect, through its organization, its "form"—we have recourse to structural analysis, which will be a science of musical sense to the extent that music proceeds from an aesthetic intention. Even music purely aesthetic in conception, however—music of the most "artificial" kind—has an import, which structural analysis leaves out of account. This can be seen even in our linguistic response—what we may almost call our "linguistic reflex." Eggebrecht cites a description by Kretzschmar of the first movement of Beethoven's Fifth Symphony. The language lacks precision and fails to meet what Eggebrecht sees as the basic requirement of the definition of musical import, namely, the binding of the import closely to the musical sense. Nevertheless the vocabulary of the description defines a "semantic field," he maintains, in the center of which stands the designation "struggle." (Another similar description, of Mahler by Schönberg, is cited subsequently.) While other words may be used equally well instead, the semantic field itself is determined and circumscribed by the specific import of the musical sense of the concrete tonal complex. Conceptual fields are revealed by the history of the reception of music, Eggebrecht adds, and can be defined by uniting research in the interpretation of import with the analytic examination of musical sense.

Ultimately, as Eggebrecht points out, conceptual fields are yielded not only by particular aspects of the organization of music, such as those Kretzschmar cites in Beethoven as a depiction of an intense struggle, but by the totality of the form of any piece of music that possesses intrinsic sense. Thus, the formulation of musical sense is a process that simultaneously formulates musical import:

> The collective consciousness for music, with its models of expectation and tendencies of innovation, is a predetermined consciousness not only for the sense of music but also for its import. This consciousness thinks in traditions of musical sense as well as in traditions of the conceptual understanding, of the emotional appeal and verbal designation, of that which is nonconceptually manifested. And just as the musical sense not only pertains to the concrete musical formulation but is also to be traced through the system of norms all the way back to the elements of the musical material (which is in every case historically and intersubjectively prepared), so also is the import of music already attached to its material elements, already inherent in them. (p. 125)

Eggebrecht proceeds with an example. Only a musical system containing chords of the dominant could permit such conceptuality to appear in musical concretions as that revealed in the reception of Beethoven and Mahler. The areas of overlap of the two conceptual fields in question have their basis in the areas of overlap of the musical material.

There are a few final observations. What the import of music loses in concreteness as an individualized, distinct concept it more than wins back as a conceptual field, for music designates conceptual fields so concretely, with so much intensive exactitude and fine nuance, that words cannot even approach it. Eggebrecht comments also on the reception of music in changed circumstances—in later times or other social contexts. The musical sense and import originally objectified in tone must then be understood again or reinterpreted. This task, he affirms, will exist equally for both sense and import.

Finally, the conceptual understanding of music must be given particular attention, for the discovery and definition of musical import needs to be brought to the same level of methodical and scientific security that musical analysis already possesses. The full range of the "linguistic reflex" to music must be taken into consideration: first, the intentional significations of older traditions as well as all depictive, imitative, expressive, and programmatic factors, including tone painting; then vocal texts, superscripts, verbal mottoes, titles, performance indications, and so on; further, composer's statements, the language of analysis, and so forth; finally, musical terminology in particular, "which in its principle *names* the conceptless: for just as even to the elements of musical material there adheres the musical sense-content that is organized (and also organizable) from them, so also can musical terms (for example, *perfectio* or *dominant*) designate the elements with respect to their import" (p. 127).

A view of musical understanding that is very different from Eggebrecht's has been developed by Roger Scruton, an English philosopher at the University of London. Where Eggebrecht's perspective is that of a historian, Scruton's is essentially that of an analytic philosopher. Scruton is an empiricist with little use for idealism and phenomenology. His interest is directed specifically to the meaning that is intrinsic to music, without regard to the distinction—produced by a particular historical configuration of forces—between sense and import. If Eggebrecht has revealed a distinction that logically may someday become inapplicable in other cultural contexts, Scruton's analysis is of course subject to the same condition, even though it is presented as independent of history.

Scruton's conception of musical understanding is developed in *Art and Imagination* (1974), which deals with a large variety of aesthetic problems. In this comprehensive setting (the subtitle is *A Study in the Philosophy of Mind*), the discussion of imagination occupies a central position. Imagination involves thought that is unasserted, Scruton states; it is a species of thought. In imagination, we are engaging in speculation, not asserting how things are. Also, imagination is a special case of "thinking of *x* as *y*," but since *y* must be appropriate to *x*, imagination is a rational activity. The events in Lewis Carroll's *Through the Looking-Glass* (*y*), for example, are appropriate to life behind a mirror (*x*). There is a similar analysis of "imagery," which Scruton also places in the category of thought, for, like thought, an image has intentionality, is the object of immediate knowledge, is subject to the will, and must be evinced by verbal description.

Of particular importance in the discussion of imagination is the notion of "seeing as," for which Scruton also uses the term *aspect perception*. A well-known example of this is an ambiguous figure that can be seen as a duck. Here imagination becomes part of seeing; thus, thought is incorporated into sense experience. The parallel auditory manifestation, "hearing as," which is fundamental to the experience of music, enables Scruton to regard "understanding" as the fundamental category of musical aesthetics. Tones are heard as connected with one another in various ways: we hear a series of tones as a melodic phrase or a melody, the second phrase of a melody as a natural continuation of the first, or one melody as a variation of another. Tones themselves are heard as tones rather than simply as "notes" because of their implicit connections with the other tones of the tonal system. The capacity to understand music in this sense of the term *understand,* then, is clearly an auditory capacity that contains thought intrinsically: " 'Hearing as' is an interesting concept from our point of view, partly through its close relation to 'seeing as,' and partly through the light that it casts on the understanding of art in general. First of all, we find that we cannot analyse 'hearing as' in terms of hearing." [15]

Hearing a series of "notes" is no different from hearing them as a melody with respect to hearing alone:

> The case of hearing notes as a melody is unlike the case of seeing a group of coloured patches as a man, in that we do not have independent access to the concept of a melody. All we know of melodies is derived from our capacity to have *this* kind of experience (if "experience" is the proper word). Hearing a sequence as a melody is more like seeing a group of lines as a pattern or figure than it is like seeing a pattern of lines as a face. Here the "organisation" of experience cannot be described in terms of some independently specifiable concept. (p. 176)

Even though hearing a melody differs in some respects from "seeing as," Scruton adds, it possesses formal properties of the same order as those of aspect perception generally. We hear a process begin in the first tone and carry through to the last, and the process can be divided into definite episodes, of which the second seems to answer the first, and so on. We hear a melody begin, the beginning has a precise location in time, and the melody has a precise duration. These are characteristics, furthermore, that are found in experience in general—in sensory experience and in bodily sensations, for example. Also, " 'Hearing as' shares with 'seeing as' a formal relation to the concept of (unasserted) thought. For example, it is to some extent within voluntary control. I can sometimes stop myself from hearing a sequence series of notes as a melody; or I may voluntarily group notes together in contrasting or conflicting ways" (p. 178).

Beyond this, we do not hear a melody instead of just a series of tones unless we can say something at any point about what has gone before— whether the melody was moving upward or downward to the point in question, whether the phrase now being completed corresponds to the previous one, and so on: "The intuitive connection with thought is exemplified in the rationality of musical understanding: my knowledge of a piece of music may influence the way I hear it, by providing reasons (and not just causes) for my hearing it in a certain way" (p. 179). Our knowledge of a melody, for example, may enable us to hear it as a variation of another melody, of a theme. We do not have to remember the theme while hearing the variation; we recognize the theme in the variation; we hear the variation as the theme. Similarly, if a relation we do not hear between one melody and another is pointed out to us, it can become part of our auditory experience of these melodies. Thus, in general, a knowledge of musical structure based on our examination of a score, for example, can radically alter the way we hear a given piece of music.

Scruton returns to a point made in connection with "seeing as": if we conceive aspect perception as the sensory "embodiment" of a thought,

> we must recognize that the thought itself can never be fully specified independently of the "perception" in which it is embodied. We can now see that there are cases—the hearing of melodies, and the seeing of patterns—where the element of thought has been reduced to something entirely formal. There is no way of achieving even a partial description of the *content* of the musical thought: we can only point once more to the experience in which it is "embodied." (pp. 180–81)

Thought-impregnated perceptions of this kind, Scruton believes, are crucial to the understanding of art; they are the basis, he maintains, of seeing representation in painting and hearing expression in music. The very media of painting and music, then, are subject to the imaginative interpretation of experience, which Scruton places "at the heart of the aesthetic attitude."

In what follows, Scruton turns his attention to representation and expression. He believes, as he says in a previous chapter, that the experiences of representation and expression form part of our experience of art and that the appreciation of them is simply a special case of aesthetic interest. Now the experience of art and aesthetic interest are broader conceptions than understanding, but they are closely related to it, for they are also instances of imaginative perception. In Debussy's *La Mer*, for example, we can hear a certain passage as a representation of the slow, silent swell of the sea, and if we do so, we then hear an enormous power and tension in the musical line. Even if we do not *hear* the music *as* the slow swell of the sea, we *are* led to grasp an aspect of the music. The important point, however, is that we could hear the tension in the musical line without being aware that it represents the sea: "Representation does not determine our understanding of music the way that it determines our understanding of painting or prose" (p. 210).

Scruton seems to have arrived at a distinction here that is similar to Eggebrecht's distinction between sense and import, for the music he is discussing is composed of tones that are *heard as* a melodic line but that simultaneously can be heard as a representation of the sea. Indeed, in the case of an acoustic object of representation, music can be *heard as* both a melodic line and the bubbling of a brook, for example, and these different meanings certainly exemplify two different modes of understanding close to Eggebrecht's sense and import.

For expression in aesthetics Scruton prefers the term *expressiveness*, which may be loosely defined, he says, as the power to recall, evoke, or "symbolize" objects, such as emotions and states of mind. Expression in art, Scruton believes, is primarily affective, but if intentionality is less important than the affective object, the recognition of intention is by no means irrelevant to our interest in art. There is not even a clear contrast between an affective and an intentional approach to the concept of expression, for a sense of intention will determine our experience of art. Indeed, it is also difficult to distinguish between expression and representation, as in the example of mimicry; intentionality, which is a property of both, will then enable us to separate the two aspects of the object. We may simply recognize a mime's gestures as those of a public figure, but if we learn that this is the mime's intention, the aspect we see will become more stable and more immediate.

Not all artistic expression, however, is elucidated by the notion of an aspect. In fact, the most important artistic expressiveness is the phenomenon of "atmosphere," in which the work of art seems to be suffused with emotion. Such works are prime examples of artistic "symbolism" and are regarded as perfect expressions of a state of mind. Scruton seeks to describe the subtle relation between art and emotion in this phenomenon. It possesses the same double intentionality that exists in "seeing as" and "hearing as." In a painting or poem that expresses an attitude toward the transience of happiness, for example, we feel or imagine an emotion that has as its object the state of mind expressed in the work of art and is also directed toward the work of art itself. We must refer to features of the work in order to describe our emotion and in order to give a complete account of the thought on which our feeling is founded. But if our thought depends so closely on the appearance of a painting, for example, we will tend to see it "embodied" in the appearance. It may transform the appearance and make us want to describe it differently. Now the experience of an appearance so transformed by thought is analogous to the experience of seeing an aspect and also resembles understanding in that we cannot say in words how the details of the painting must be seen. The recognition of expression and representation, then, has the same experiential dimension as understanding has. It is an instance of knowledge by acquaintance and demands the experience of the work itself. Thus, Scruton can say that he has extended the analysis of understanding "until it covers the dimensions of reference that until now have seemed inexplicable" (p. 239). Representation and expression become kinds of understanding, which remains the central concept of musical aesthetics.

Scruton examines understanding in his subsequent writings also, notably in "Understanding Music" (1983) and in "Analytic Philosophy and the Meaning of Music" (1987). In the first of these, understanding that is derived from appearance is opposed to scientific understanding, which seeks out the causal connections that underlie and explain appearance. Musical understanding, Scruton argues, is based on our capacity, as language users, for metaphoric transfer, through which concepts are extended. Thus, we hear movement and space in music, but these are facts about our experience that have no correspondence to actual movement and actual space. They cannot be eliminated, however, from musical experience:

> If we take away the metaphors of movement, of space, of chords as objects, of melodies as advancing and retreating, as moving up and down—if we take those metaphors away, nothing of music remains, but only sound.
>
> It seems then that in our most basic apprehension of music there lies a complex system of metaphor, which is the true description of no material fact. And the metaphor cannot be eliminated from the description of music, because it is integral to the intentional object of musical experience. Take this metaphor away and you cease to describe the experience of music.[16]

Scruton accounts for this situation in terms of his fundamental notion of imagination. A face in a cloud can be seen only when we also see that it is not really there. A transfer is involved: an intentional object must be described using a concept that is known not to apply to the material object.

The perception of rhythm may not be based on metaphoric transfer, Scruton admits, but it does involve imaginative transfer. The sounds are not simply heard as a temporal pattern but are instead subject to peculiar forces and connected in ways that go well beyond the simple perception of succession in time. Rhythm displays the peculiarly "active" character of imaginative perception, and it has no counterpart in the material realm of sound.

Harmony, the third fundamental category of musical experience, again must be described in metaphoric terms. The tones in a chord are perceived not simply as simultaneous tones but as one thing. Chords are "spaced," "open," or "hollow," and harmonic progression involves ideas of "tension," "transition," and "resolution."

Musical perception, then, is intentional understanding that, as imaginative understanding, is "active" and also essentially dependent on metaphor. Scruton seeks finally to show how this conception can cast light on the nature of musical expression. If music can be described as motion, he argues, then it can also be "melancholy" or "passionate." Now in observing a gesture of expression—in a dramatic performance, for example—we can have the experience of knowing what it is like; the gesture becomes, in imagination, our own, and we feel it not from the observer's point of view but from the subject's: "It is as though we have been granted a first-person perspective on a world that we know is not ours. Neither is it anyone else's. It is a creation of the imagination, and retains the impersonality of the imaginative act." This is a sense of "what it is like" from which all intentionality has been extruded. When we see a gesture from the first-person point of view, we not only see it as an expression but grasp the whole state of mind that is intimated by it. Musical gestures are of the same nature, and musical expression is as much part of musical understanding as is the ability to hear a melody: "Understanding music involves the active creation of an intentional world, in which inert sounds are transfigured into movements, harmonies, rhythms— metaphorical gestures in a metaphorical space. And into these metaphorical gestures a metaphorical soul is breathed by the sympathetic listener. At a certain point, he has the experience of a first-person perspective on gestures that are no-one's" (p. 98).

In "Analytic Philosophy and the Meaning of Music" (1987), Scruton explicitly acknowledges that we must go beyond the bounds of analytic philosophy in order to reach a full account of *musical meaning,* a term that Scruton employs to designate an enlarged conception of musical understanding. Musical understanding must connect, he now insists, with our social faculties and our lives. If our response to music is to have the depth and sensuousness that "will give cogency" to the composer's labors, we must distinguish in music the varied aspects of our own spiritual existence. We must be able to hear musical relations and musical development in terms of values and interests that govern our life as a whole. All our varied experiences of this kind are united by a common basic characteristic. In each "we discern a peculiar operation of the imagination," which has been referred to by the term "hearing as": "By virtue of the auditory imagination, the excitement of music can become, in an immediate way, the excitement of life itself." Underlying this considerable demand, Scruton advances a still more unexpected thesis of historical development: "It is custom, habit, the intertwining of music with everyday life, which generate the basic discriminations to which I referred, and which therefore permit the more refined and adventurous musical enterprises that are the prerogative of high art." "To understand musical meaning, therefore," he says by way of summary, "is to understand how the cultivated ear can discern, in what it hears, the occasions for sympathy."[17] How to find an explanation of this—a method that will guide us forward into these "obscure regions"—Scruton is unable to say, thus modestly discounting the explanations he has offered in his previous work.

It would appear, then, that the investigation of musical meaning in the sphere of Anglo-American analytic philosophy has arrived at a stage that seems to typify the state of philosophical analysis in general. Comparisons of the perspectives and outcomes of Continental philosophy, particularly phenomenology and idealism, with those of empiricism and analysis have become increasingly common, and the awareness of an unexpected parallelism, if not a potential combination, has in some measure replaced the unmediated antithesis that was manifest earlier. Even the realization that philosophical problems are intrinsically historical and cultural has invaded areas of Anglo-American philosophy and thought that were traditionally sealed off from such conceptions. We have seen an instance of this when Scruton comes to affirm that musical understanding has its foundation in the larger context of culture and seems to suggest the need, as a consequence, for an explanation of how understanding arises from such a foundation. But a theoretical investigation of this genetic process would again produce theories of musical understanding of the same general kind as those of Dilthey. Eggebrecht's concept of the conceptual understanding of music is, of course, thoroughly historical, not to mention that both conceptless and conceptual understanding are products, in his view, of a conjunction of forces specific to a particular time and place.

Nevertheless, what is most important about the conception of musical understanding in the 1970s and 1980s is the emphasis on a type of understanding that is intrinsic to music, an understanding that cannot be achieved except in terms of tonal configurations themselves, whether or not it is also amenable to other kinds of understanding or also connected with other kinds of experience. This peculiar type of understanding is at the same time subject to description in terms of the properties and perception of music itself. Both Eggebrecht and Scruton have proposed such a description and have arrived—each in his own way—at a close and detailed characterization of a kind of musical meaning that is of crucial importance in the aesthetics of music of the twentieth century.

CHAPTER THIRTEEN

CONCEPTIONS OF
OBJECTIVITY

A longside the investigation of musical meaning, which sought to find an explanation of music in terms of its relation to feelings or to other external objects, there was a contrasting aesthetic that examined music in its own right, seeking a rationale for the musical work without looking beyond the music into any attendant circumstances or extramusical influences. These two contrasting and mutually antagonistic trends are twentieth-century descendants of idealism and formalism, respectively, of the theories of content and idea, on the one hand, and of musical autonomy, on the other. If the replacement of content by meaning and the growing realization that meaning lay chiefly within music itself represent a fundamental trend toward understanding music in its own specific terms, theories of objectivity and autonomy took this position from the outset and set about discovering the properties and laws of music that were peculiar to it and that defined its form and value. Needless to say, analysis, or the explication of structure, was the central activity of aestheticians of this type. It dominated their writings and gave them a status as "theorists" as well as aestheticians.

Theories of Inherent Musical Law

Perhaps the most influential of all the writers presenting a theory of intrinsic law in music was the Viennese Heinrich Schenker, who advanced a specifically musical theory of the "organic coherence" of musical masterworks. This coherence was manifested by a stratified structure, not audible as such in itself, but revealed by a special type of analysis of what was directly audible. The analysis established a basic underlying "layer"—the *Ursatz*—that was essentially the same for every composition of value and that consisted of a basic descending melodic line (the *Urlinie*), accompanied by a pendular bass that sounded the fundamental pitches of the primary triads. This *Ursatz* was elaborated to yield an intermediate stratum (the *Mittelgrund*), and this in turn was elaborated to yield the foreground (*Vordegrund*), which was the score itself.

Schenker's polemical stance against all types of "meaning" in music is clearly seen in his *Kontrapunkt* (1910), which is included in his *Neue musikalische Theorien und Phantasien* (1906–35): "With the absolute character of the life of tone, as it is confirmed for the first time precisely by counterpoint, there is also given at the same time the emancipation of the life of tone from every external purpose, whether it be the word, the stage, or, in general, the anecdotal of any kind of program."[1]

This rejection also extends to the philosophy of music. Schenker takes issue in particular with Schopenhauer's claim that the composer reveals the innermost core of the world. What he really reveals is the organic and absolute nature of the life of tone. The intrinsic laws of tone are like the laws of the cosmos: they rest on only a few fundamental forces. "Consonance is the unique law of everything harmonic, or vertical," Schenker writes in *Der Tonwille* (1921–24):

> It belongs to Nature. Dissonance belongs to voice leading, to the horizontal, and is thus art. . . . Consonance lives in the triad, dissonance in passage. . . . More laws than consonance and dissonance do not exist, or more basic derivations. We must even comprehend dissonance merely as determined by consonance and thus recognize the consonance of Nature alone as the ultimate ground and at the same time the final goal of everything transitional and striving.[2]

Schenker's basic conception of the musical work as organic is an expression of a literal vitalism in his thought, as we can see from a passage of his *Meisterwerk in der Musik* (1925–30): "Music is the animated motion of tones in naturally given space, the composing-out (melodizing, horizontalizing) of the chord given in Nature. The law of all life—motion—which as a creation continues active beyond the bounds of the existence of the individual, man also carries into the chord that Nature has prefigured in his ear."[3]

Another influential aesthetician of the absolute character of music was August Halm. In *Von zwei Kulturen der Musik* (1913), Halm discusses and compares the fugue and the sonata in a way that is specific to music itself. He is explicitly antagonistic to any connection of music with external experience, finding the essence of music in form, which triumphs over chaos and which he identifies with the Platonic Forms:

We have indeed weaned ourselves long since from the coarse Philistin-
ism that made use of music as entertainment for the enjoyment of tea
and dinner. Let us guard ourselves now from being refined Philistines
who use it for nervous shocks, for "inner experience," that is to say,
for higher or concealed animalistic experiences, basically for a surro-
gate of emotional life, or who in the best case lower it to the status
of background music for poetic pleasures, and thus to the status of a
servant to a subordinate art. Let us strive on the contrary to regain respect for its autonomy. In this respectful frame of mind we will also
regard the course of musical history from unclear to clear forms quite
differently again. . . . We will then, in the victory of forms over the manifold world of the distorting, the confusing, and the miscarried, perceive
the steadily growing idea, the *always more excellent incorporation* (as
command, as need) *of preexisting form*, and finally it will no longer
seem to us as though there were merely fugues and sonatas, but we will
surmise that in the final analysis and from the beginning the *fugue and
the sonata exist*.

In the face of this absolute conception of music, even the organic conception
of music becomes analogical: "The fugue has more a structure than a construction; it resembles more a separated existence, a living being, a tree, say,
if we wish to venture concrete representations; *it is the formula of individuality*. The sonata by contrast is the collective activity of many individuals; it
is an organism in the large: *it is equivalent to the state*.[4]

Halm's distaste for the connection of images and feelings with music finds
pointed expression in *Die Symphonie Anton Bruckners* (1914):

We have only to hear something of slow, burdened motion: immediately
the image of a funeral march occupies our visual field; we hear a tender
melody of sweet euphony: at once we think of the sorrow and longing
of love; we hear music in the process of a dynamic crisis or ebb; at once
we feel sadness, renunciation, departure from an ideal desired in vain—
and we see this as living in the music itself or "expressed" through it
as though in the name and commission of its author, who tells in it of
his own wishing, struggling, and renouncing. In short . . . we resemble
primitive men, who import human feelings into natural events.

The Adagios of Beethoven and of Bruckner were victims of such a process,
and Halm writes of getting to know them more properly, "according to their
immanent will,"[5] of freeing and purifying them of all images and feeling
carried into them from a lower world. Echoes of the Romantic view of Beethoven are unmistakable, for "infinite" feelings do not conflict noticeably

with musical purity and autonomy or with specifically musical laws. But Halm's polemic against feeling echoes Hanslick most of all.

In his *Beethoven* (1927), Halm understandably espouses the ideals of rationality, perfectly organic structure, tonal logic, and large form, which is made possible by instrumental music. Indeed, Schenker and Halm are alike in endorsing a defined body of music that exemplifies their values. The belief in intrinsic laws of music leads in both cases, but especially in Schenker's theories, to the selection of a traditional repertory in which these laws prevail. The tone of their writings, however, is the one most typical of aesthetics but increasingly out of place in a context of historical and cultural relativism, for they consider the properties they value in music to be absolute; they show little or no awareness that music exists outside their cultural horizons.

The influential theorist Ernst Kurth also subscribes to a conception of intrinsic law in music, but he does not succeed in clearly defining the nature of such a law. In spite of their value and the insight they provide, his theories are expressed more in terms that are essentially qualitative, and in an almost poetic description of music, than in terms that are unequivocally defined and precisely used. As a result, his work is in some sense a fusion of nineteenth- and twentieth-century modes of thought. In his *Die romantische Harmonik* (1919), for example, Kurth sees music as the sensuous expression of underlying psychic energy, and he directs attention to the crucial event in which the energy gives rise to tone. How and why this happens he is evidently unable to make clear, and the heart of his theory remains a mystery. The inner dynamism itself, however, is characterized repeatedly. Music arises from powerful unconscious forces, which Kurth regards as much more important than the total expression itself, for the psychic energies are the "supporting and formative contents" of music:

> Considered in itself, harmony represents empty material, and all lawfulness, forms, and formulas exhibited by the organization of the tonal image only touch the torpid surface of music and glide over it without leading to its core. But the vital basic events of harmony consist in letting us feel always the upward forces that are translated from the unconscious underground of formativity into sensuously perceptible tonal forms. The nature of harmony is thus its continuous upwelling, the overflowing of force into appearance.[6]

Kurth consequently directs theory to the nature and expressive urge of this peculiar play of psychic forces. Music will be a "symphony of flowing energies" instead of a symphony of tones. The conception seems to combine psychology with metaphysics: "Music is a natural power in us, a dynamic of the excitations of the will." Although this dynamic of tensions is specific to music, Kurth still expects it to provide "unexpected insights into psychological phenomena in general" (p. 359). It is even identified with a universal cosmic process: "The feelings of tension within us are the characterized traces of similar vital forces as they are manifested in the archetypal origin of all physical and organic life" (p. 360).

Melody is the objectification of the duality in music of spiritual and sensuous content; it is the first projection of the will into material, into the temporal and spatial form of appearance. Melody, and the flow of harmony and counterpoint in general, is the "kinetic energy" of psychic tension; the chord is "potential energy," which demands resolution in motion. "Every chord is only an auditory image of certain tendencies of energy" (p. 362).

In spite of his emphasis on psychic force and energy, however, Kurth insists that the sensuous aspect of music must also be considered. But we must view this "from beneath and within, not from without." Finally, the relative weight of the sensuous element depends on style and is thus a historical variable: "The different historical epochs reveal vast differences also in the significance and independent effect they permit to the tonally sensuous component of music as opposed to its inner dynamic component" (p. 362).

What can be said of this conception, which Kurth claims to be fundamental to musical theory, musical aesthetics, and "the psychology of musical style"? It is somewhat puzzling in its terminology, which is composed principally of the words *force, tension, energy* (potential and kinetic), *will, unconscious,* and *inner.* These belong to psychology, to physics, or to both fields, even to metaphysics. Yet Kurth is thinking largely in psychological terms; the physics is really figurative and the metaphysics parenthetical. Still, the nature of the theory is difficult to specify. While Kurth acknowledges that the relative prominence of the sensuous changes historically, it is basically regarded as a superficial manifestation, almost dispensable, as it is in Saint Augustine, for example, although never morally reprehensible, as it can be in Platonic or patristic writings. But if music can be understood only in terms of an underlying psychology, does the music produce the inner events or do these events produce the music? Are the inner events specifically musical, or are they forces of general occurrence? The events seem to produce the music, and they seem also to occur generally. Kurth is not precise in these issues. It is thus not clear whether music is autonomous or whether it is a reflection, at least to some extent, of inner life in general. It is certainly not objective in the sense of a self-contained and opaque auditory experience. It is, however, governed by or subject to general principles, even if we cannot be certain, once again, that these principles are valid only in music.

Objectivity

In contrast to the reflective aesthetic conceptions of intrinsic musical law, which are theoretical and analytic and directed to existing bodies of music, there is also an active aesthetic of musical objectivity that is directed to the future rather than retrospective—an aesthetic that is closely allied to composition rather than to the understanding and analysis of established styles. The conceptions of objectivity that arose in this area are thus accompanied by the appearance of qualities of objectivity in music itself, particularly in the crucial decade of the 1920s. But this aspect of music and this type of aesthetic value are characteristic of the twentieth century and occur repeatedly, under a variety of names and in connection with various related manifestations such as comprehensibility and simplicity. It is also characteristic that they are not purely aesthetic in the traditional sense but rather socioaesthetic, for the social component of aesthetic ideas, when it was present at all in the preceding century, had been prominent only in France and in the writings of Wagner. In the twentieth century, however, as a consequence of abstruse musical techniques and styles and of radical changes in the nature of music and of musical audiences, compositional aesthetics has been typically concerned with social values. Doubtless in part for the same reasons, a discipline of musical sociology was gradually elaborated that addressed this concern and reinforced the growing social and cultural orientation of musicology itself.

There has thus been a recurrent interest on the part of aestheticians and serious composers in musical accessibility. Along with simplicity there has often been a return to forms, styles, and stylistic features of the past, which seems to ensure a kind of objectivity. Simplicity in itself somehow fosters musical objectivity, which is thus connected with both historicism and the social motive of accessibility. Associated with these movements, finally, there has often been a polemical attitude not only toward complexity but also toward the emotionalism and realism of the nineteenth century—especially toward Neoromanticism and Postromanticism. It was the twentieth-century intensification of these trends in Expressionism that provoked the objectivist reactions of the 1920s.

Among the objectivist ideas of the 1920s were those of Busoni's "Young Classicism." In a letter of January 1920 to Paul Bekker, Busoni discusses the attitude of the creative artist toward tradition. He distinguishes artists who cling to the tradition that is currently in favor and those who seek to free themselves from it. He also mentions isolated experimenters who represent defiance, rebellion, satire, or just foolishness. This type has appeared frequently during the last fifteen years, he observes, and after the unprecedented standstill of the 1880s it strikes one all the more forcibly.

> Exaggeration . . . is becoming general and portends the end of such a period; and the next step is that which inclines towards Young Classicism (which opposition is bound to stimulate).
>
> By "Young Classicism," I mean the mastery, the sifting and the turning to account of all the gains of previous experiments and their inclusion in strong and beautiful forms.[7]

At first, Busoni believes, this art will be old and new at the same time. But one of its most important foundations, he maintains, will be the idea of oneness in music—the idea "that music is music, in and for itself, and nothing else, and that it is not split into classes" (p. 21). Thus, no music is church music, for example, in and of itself; "church" music is really absolute music to which words are added or that is simply performed in church. If the text is changed, the music seems to change also:

> With "Young Classicism" I include the definite departure from what is thematic and the return to melody again as the ruler of all voices and all emotions (not in the sense of a pleasing motive) and as the bearer of the idea and the begetter of harmony, in short, the most highly developed (not the most complicated) polyphony.
>
> A third point not less important is the casting off of what is "sensuous" and the renunciation of subjectivity (the road to objectivity, which means the author standing back from his work, a purifying road, a hard way, a trial of fire and water) and the re-conquest of serenity (*serenitas*). Neither Beethoven's wry smile nor Zarathustra's liberating laugh but the smile of wisdom, of divinity and absolute music. Not profundity and personal feeling and metaphysics, but Music which is absolute, distilled, and never under a mask of figures and ideas which are borrowed from other spheres.
>
> Human sentiments, but not human affairs, and this too, expressed within the limits of what is artistic.
>
> The measurements of what is artistic do not refer only to proportions, to the boundaries of what is beautiful and the preservation of taste, they mean above all not assigning to art tasks which lie outside its nature. Description in music, for instance. (pp. 21–22)

What Busoni describes is multifaceted. It is not so much the rejection of emotion but its containment. It excludes "personal feeling" but not "human sentiment." Somewhat later, in a letter of June 1921 to his son, Busoni returns to his idea. There is something strange about the expression "Young Classicism," he writes, for today it is circulated and nobody knows who coined it. So it is said at times that Busoni also follows the Young Classicism:

It is not necessary to be a prophet to imagine it. After a seriously large number of experiments from the original "Secessionists" to the "Anti-Secessionists" and finally, after the manner of crowds, to separate groups getting further apart, the necessity for a comprehensive certainty in style must be met.

But, as with everything else, I was misunderstood about this also, for the masses look upon Classicism as upon something turning back. . . .

My idea is (this is feeling, personal necessity rather than constructed principle) that Young Classicism signifies completion in a double sense; completion as perfection and completion as a close. The conclusion of previous experiments. (pp. 22–23)

There is a further clarification of Busoni's view in 1922, in *Von der Einheit der Musik*:

In the editions I possess of Poe, there are many carefully arranged, good, and characteristic portraits of the poet to be found. But a picture by Manet, etched with a few strokes, sums up all the other pictures and is exhaustive. Should not music also try to express only what is most important with a few notes, set down in a masterly fashion? Does my *Brautwahl* with its full score of seven hundred pages achieve more than *Figaro* with its six accompanying wind instruments? It seems to me that the refinement of economy is the next aim after the refinement of prodigality has been learnt.[8]

Among the roots of musical objectivism, then, is certainly dissatisfaction with experimentation and the need, which became pressing in the 1920s, for some kind of stability of style.

In 1926, some years after Busoni had introduced the concept of Young Classicism in music, the stylistic term *Neue Sachlichkeit* (new objectivity, new matter-of-factness) was taken over from painting, where it had appeared a few years before, and applied to music. Heinrich Strobel's article " 'Neue Sachlichkeit' in der Musik" (1926) seems to be the first application of the term to music. "In its striving for absolute clarity of form," Strobel wrote, "the most recent music again coincides with plastic art and indeed with the newest movement, for which, since the Mannheim Exhibition, the general concept *Neue Sachlichkeit* is current."[9]

A general view of the artistic situation at that time is provided by Heinrich

Besseler in his "Grundfragen der Musikästhetik," an essay of 1926 (published the following year):

> Although the concepts Expressionism and *Neue Sachlichkeit* were coined first in painting, there is no reason not to carry them over into music, where they are grounded in forces at least as decisive. It is not necessary to go into details: it is enough to affirm that both concepts belong essentially to the present and are directed to the phenomenon of expression. Relations to the expressive romantic art of the nineteenth century thus reveal themselves at once.[10]

For Besseler, the *Neue Sachlichkeit* that succeeded Romanticism was an instance of a recurrent type of reaction in the history of music. It was the embodiment of an underlying stylistic duality that manifested itself in different historical contexts. He also described it unequivocally as a counterpart of Expressionism, and the two tendencies were indeed a preliminary form of the polarity of Schönberg and Stravinsky that became so prominent in the next decades. The initial representative of *Neue Sachlichkeit*, however, was Hindemith.

Erich Doflein was a sympathetic and penetrating critic of the music of his own time, and his writings reveal an unusual degree of insight into the aesthetic character of that music. As the editor of numerous collections of instrumental music, both new and old, for pedagogical use in music making, he was also really a participant in the *Neue Sachlichkeit* movement. In "Die neue Musik des Jahres," a retrospective survey of the new music of 1926, he finds that the important change in music is due to its new objective basis. It is not so much that the style of the music is "objective," he believes, but that there is an objective attitude that underlies the composer's work and that determines how he conceives the possibilities of his work:

> Discoveries in the audible, the new experience of unexpected sonorous possibilities, no longer play any role in the determination of form; form is oriented to itself, which makes possible precisely the recognition of an objective task; sound for its own sake recedes before form; a self-evident expressive basis is obtained. Yet at the same time the expressive world itself has also radically changed; and it had to change. The disclosure of the new possibilities of sound was given in and with the huge intensification of expression that we experienced right up to those works we can call, in music also, expressionistic. In that music so intensified in its expression, one could speak of an isolation of expression, often even of an empty course of intensity, although such a formulation is paradoxical. This was the "modern" music of the years before the war.[11]

The intensification, or overintensification, of expression, Doflein continues, which probably was the source of the new conjunctions of sound
as well as making them possible and justifying them, has itself now almost
completely receded. A considerable range of dissonance received the function of consonance, was divested of its function of resolution or leading tone,
and lost its expressive intensity: "Thus there was given the objective ground
for the expressive world of that playfulness—joyful in making music, cheerful, and formally organized—that today is so prominent in the most diverse
national variants and in whose realm that factor of 'objectivity' that I called
the clear recognition of the 'task' is present most palpably." With the advent
of *Neue Sachlichkeit*, as Doflein now points out, there was also a change in
the social situation of music:

> Along with this acquisition of a self-evident quality and a relaxation
> into objectivity and playfulness, the public of modern music has fun-
> damentally changed. Many of those disinclined by temperament and in
> principle suddenly feel interested and won over. This observation could
> be made in many localities. The belligerent loneliness of the above-
> mentioned first modern music from which the new bases of style devel-
> oped was really necessarily bound up with its nature and its intensely
> expressive stylistic character . . . a stylistic character that indeed was
> still in great measure tied to the spirit of the Romantic, to the subjective
> in principle. (p. 334)

Doflein considers the function of style. In Romanticism, he states, style
was attached to continual novelty. Each personality and even each work in-
tentionally realized a new style, but this arose from the unconscious; it was
often an unfilled intimation and a striving rather than a finished achievement. But in *Neue Sachlichkeit* style became a defined consciousness that
was clearly distinguished from the unconscious of Romanticism; it created
a community, not an isolation and separateness. The consciousness of style
produces a corresponding expressive world:

> The not seeking, the inner arrived at, must manifest itself in play-
> ful cheerfulness, while along with the playfulness, contrapuntal-formal
> problems at the same time move to the foreground of consciousness.
> The tangibility of style thus comprises distinct kinds of characteristic
> features, is the product of a specific constitution, of its "objectivity."
> The style arising today is tangible in its actuality, in the doing itself, in
> and during its being made in the individual works.

It is naturally no service, Doflein adds, to speak "like all the feuilletons of
objectivity, of objective style in music, of the end of the expressive, of the

overcoming of the Romantic" (p. 337). But it did seem important, he says, to question popular rubrics in order to dissolve hasty formulations and interpret the essential content of the new situation. Of principal importance is that we are dealing not with a new nuance or phase of progress in the framework of the increasingly novel, but with an alteration of fundamental attitude that is basically different from the new that has appeared repeatedly up to the present.

By 1928 it had become obvious that *Neue Sachlichkeit* represented a manifestation of considerable importance in the 1920s, even though the significance of the decade as a whole could be grasped only with the elapse of time. Hanns Eisler characteristically sees the developments of the 1920s as socially motivated. The musician of today, he asserts in "On the Situation of Modern Music" (1928), cannot be deluded about the fact that his art is frightfully isolated. He gets no satisfaction from writing one work after another merely for the sake of writing; he aspires to something vital, vital "because it concerns everyone, and consequently is a vital part of everyone, and he is fed up with helping a few gourmets to procure increasingly esoteric pleasures." All the styles of the past few years, Eisler believes, are a result of this knowledge: "The departure from the Romantics can also be traced to these facts. It was felt that the emotions of one individual were no longer adequate to express something of general validity and so what was wanted was pure music-making, without feeling, without expression, simply a play on tones." [12]

It is not the social aspect of the expressive-objective duality that interests the composer Heinz Tiessen but rather the different creative motivations of the two styles. In his *Zur Geschichte der jüngsten Musik*, published in 1928, the elements of the new expressionistic language had been felt as a need of the time, while the new "music-making impulse" was accompanied by the effort "to unburden itself from the pressure of the all-too-artful cerebral, differentiated, and purely personal—in short: to overcome decadence": "Once we . . . formulate and accept an antithesis of personal 'I-music' and objective 'It-music,' the 'object' to which 'objectivity' is oriented lies in the pure creative function, in the formative occurrence, and this objectivity can purport first of all: organic growth from pure material. 'It' makes music in me." The same antithesis enters into Tiessen's discussion of Busoni: "His aversion to the 'feeling-pathos' of the German 'Romanticism,' his veneration of Bach and Mozart, his will to art attuned to a fresh cheerfulness, had a marked effect on the spirit of the time and on his followers and on the certainly one-track mentality of the 'neusachlichen' development." [13]

Writing in *Melos* again, a periodical of central importance in the evaluation of new styles of the 1920s, Eric Doflein thoughtfully considers the value and the sense of new music ("Über Grundlagen der Beurteilung gegenwärtiger Musik," 1928). There is no longer a single idea of music as self-sufficient, he maintains, an unchanging expectation that is the basis of evaluation, but a splitting up and transformation of this idea in accordance with a multiplicity of use and purpose:

> This orientation to use and the style connected with the use is the real outcome of the *Neue Sachlichkeit,* an outcome that rises above popular rubrics. Thus a closer tie of music to the human being and to human beings among one another in their relation to music, a *human* resolution, was yielded by the idea of objectivity. There are various degrees of "communality" that work themselves out in this resolution and determine with their various forms the no longer "societal" basis of musical life. The most extreme degree of these various forms of the tying together of music and man is represented by communal music, which as a controlling idea makes independent what in the other cited areas only cooperates as a motivating factor in the forces affecting style. On the other hand, an elementary degree of such working out of the drive toward the communal would have to be recognized in, say, the demand for "active" hearing in the grasp of the polyrhythmic structure of modern chamber music.

Doflein reveals the importance of the social component of new music with particular clarity. All the tendencies of renewal, he states, that are directed against the stylistic stance of the societal music of the previous century are encompassed by the working out of the communal idea. The experience of the isolated individual loses its positive evaluation, and this defines the general direction of the goal: "Whether it be the masses, the community, or the parishioners who strive for a new tradition, all are various forms of a new togetherness of people that are set in opposition to the societal." [14]

We can turn finally to Theodor Adorno's pronouncements in 1928 on New Objectivity, expressed with his characteristic bitter sarcasm:

> They speak so much now of serenitas, which comes marching along arm in arm with the new objectivity. If we only know why we suddenly are to be so happy. Have we abandoned the sick Tristan merely to correct his painfully drawn mouth with the attitude of keep smiling? And if expression in music had already become questionable, why must this expressionlessness, whose intention is still enshrouded in darkness, accommodate itself immediately to the joyfulness of bright emptiness? Is it not far more difficult to achieve the expressionless? Has serenitas

not been hurriedly devised in the final analysis only to deceive people about the emptiness and to persuade them that emptiness is the holy of holies of their community? Is not serenitas even intended to prevent them from inquiring into that community all too searchingly? There is an authentic Serenade in these days: of Schönberg. So joyful it is not.[15]

Social influence and social explanation are replaced here by social interpretation and by an incisive criticism of the social order. Rather unexpectedly, we have come on the relation of sociology and style that will be the subject of our final chapter.

A later number of *Anbruch* in the same year carries another polemic by Adorno directed this time against the conspicuous mechanical activity of the style. Many contemporary composers are praised for their "will to motion," he writes, "as though it was a question of motion without any concern for what is moved. In the world of the machine, which one insults when one compares that kind of music with it, there are masses of material that are moved, or men, and for a purpose. And in the static undialectic structure of motion music," Adorno adds, in which there is no compulsion for anything to change, "motion soon enough turns out to be apparent motion. It marks time like soldiers on drill."[16]

This "powerfully awakened will to new objectivity" in Germany (*Objektivität*, as opposed to *Sachlichkeit*, "matter-of-factness"), Adorno traces to France—to Stravinsky and Cocteau, the advanced representatives of the grand bourgeoisie, "to whom the sphere of the individual-particular no longer offered any sensation, whose purposes it doubtless even contradicted still to be an individual at all, and who for the sake of sensation now made use of the role of a ready collectivity as an attraction—a collectivity undecided, to be sure, between sports and Neothomism, but inclined without condition to every excitement." Thus, Adorno moves from the mechanical motion of New Objectivity to its social foundation in the economic order, "which alone makes it possible for the snobs to be snobs"[17] and which they therefore have every interest in talking others into as divinely ordained *Objectivität* and true reality. Adorno also seems to be distinguishing between German *Sachlichkeit* and its origin in French *Ojektivität* or, more specifically, between Hindemith and Stravinsky.

In the following year, 1929, still another careful examination of New Objectivity by Erich Doflein appeared in *Melos* ("Gegenwart, Gebrauch, Kitsch und Stil"). Strict polyphonic form in general, he argues, demands "complete realization." It cannot simply "be enjoyed." We must take our place in the midst of it; it demands music making. A strict fugue or an invention or a through-imitative chorus are not concert music but rather the truest amateur art, performing music. The exclusion of the spirit of the sonata development, Doflein maintains,

> of the dialectical in music, of the outright symphonic, of the epic and psychological, in favor of simple presentation, of the concertante, of the successive, of strophic form, and especially of the dancelike—this overrides all the features of music that are specific to the work as such, to its "language," its style, its individuality. The personal, the flexible, and the deliberative recede. A work of this kind, however, which is to be evaluated not because of its unique, personal meaning but rather because of its completed sense, demands a situation in which it is listened to, a basis for its sense, a place in which its value is a value; it demands a purpose. Thus the path through Objectivity compels the search for purpose and the affirmation of utility. The exclusivity of concert hall and opera is transcended. A new multiplicity of values is produced. The *one* sense of music has split up into many, from the most serious to the lightest: into some kind of scale from the deep "sense" in pedagogical music to the least compelling "purpose" in entertainment music.

It may be rather modest, Doflein concedes, to content ourselves with a music of purposes, but it is called for after the excessive immodesty of the preceding generation. Those who are saddened by the necessary sacrifice of Romantic values may be consoled by the prospect "that on the 'craft-art' of this decade there will perhaps once again be erected an 'art.' " [18]

It was inevitable that New Objectivity would be connected with a materialist philosophy, and we find the polyhistorian Richard Benz, writing in *Die Musik* in 1929, contrasting it with music as divinely inspired. To the extent that the present-day musician feels himself bound to the ideal of unconditional progress, Benz says, which represents the dethroning of the spiritual and the victory of matter, "the rubric *Sachlichkeit* makes it a duty for him also to regard and to treat tone as something thinglike-given-actual, as a pure object, and to express nothing with it that could be felt as a spiritual value, but rather to carry on an autonomous play of form with its perceptible material as with something objective." [19]

Examining the widespread change in concert programs, Erik Reger makes explicit the important relation of New Objectivity to the revival of the music of the eighteenth century and thus to neoclassicism and to smaller performing forces. The huge orchestral apparatus attached to the Romantic weltanschauung has given way before music of the eighteenth century, he points out, and this has been indirectly fruitful for the work of young composers and has indirectly smoothed the way for them: "On the one hand, the ears of the public are sharpened by our transparent compositions for what is called 'objective' music. And on the other hand, understanding for contemporary composers increases because the public learns to know the great models on which the objective music of today is based." [20]

The cheerfulness that Adorno found so inane and so irritating in New Objectivity, or, in Busoni's phrase, the *serenitas*, is the subject of a letter of Adorno's written in 1930 in reply to Hans Heinz Stuckenschmidt. Typically, Adorno deals both with the cheerfulness and with its social interpretation:

> It is much more a matter of the consciousness of reality: *serenitas* seeks to counterfeit and to persuade its hearers of a condition of objectively settled society, or secure ontological orientation, and of a just social order, which does not exist, and to represent which aesthetically is nothing other than to divert attention from the misery of society. I oppose the new *serenitas* as an ideology, as an attitude that is grounded not in the objective state of reality but in the quite transparent interests of production. I oppose it as the music of false stabilization. Objectively there is no reason for joyfulness, and that today joyfulness is announced as such (which never happened to it in the prized eighteenth century) shows its questionableness; that is burying your head in the sand and kicking motorically with your feet in addition—as long as you can. . . . The inhuman cheerfulness of bright emptiness, which consists in nothing other than its own tempo, in which nothing at all beyond is moved—this will only drive back the improvement of the here and now and must for the sake of improvement finally be seen through.[21]

Alongside Adorno and influenced by him, the other important critic of New Objectivity was Ernst Krenek. In his *Ueber neue Musik* of 1937, Krenek formulated a comprehensive and definitive characterization of the style that became well known and was repeatedly cited. *Neue Sachlichkeit* was a conformist movement, Krenek observes; it was exemplified in many works of Hindemith, but especially in the music of his numerous followers:

> It has in common with neoclassicism the anti-espressivo tendency and began equally with the intention of expressively neutralizing the material newly formed by Expressionism under the compulsion of its expressive will, of freeing it from its freight of emotion, and of regarding it in itself as given, indifferent. The lack of passion and absence of emotion in which extraordinary pride was taken was due to a certain demonic possession by the spirit of craft, and the essential characteristic of this music became a motoric quality of which the less apt examples are often reminiscent of a water wheel or a sewing machine. Here the shock proceeded from the never before so coldly produced display of inhuman aridity of spirit and emptiness of ideas, but it was soon para-

lyzed and stilled through the fact that such music, because it did not busy the mind of the interpreters, was that much the more enjoyable for their fingers. The concept of *Spielfreudigkeit* [playing joy] soon compensated for everything else, while the factor of feeling, although in the long run much too neglected, found itself satisfied by the renascence of the "performer."

This ghost or shade of vital music making is most vulnerable from a sociological point of view, in Krenek's opinion; nevertheless, he contents himself with stating that under the music-making idea, which seems to be so harmless and conciliatory, "there hides everything that is lazy, dull, boring, and musty and that without it would long since have been recognized and seen through. . . . Not in vain have the merciless motorists, when their spinning along began to contrast all too sharply with the reviving appreciation of emotional values, discovered their elective affinity to the bird of passage." From then on the recorder culture expanded, Krenek continues, and this "permitted every fool to march ahead in the latest fashion because he also performed a poor composition of an acknowledged master in a still poorer manner." [22]

In spite of the fact that the term *neoclassicism* was sometimes applied to Hindemith and that it was even interchangeable for a time with the term *Neue Sachlichkeit,* it came to be used most often for the music of Stravinsky. Objectivity is considered to be a characteristic of neoclassicism as well as of *Neue Sachlichkeit,* although the term has a number of meanings in this sphere, many of which are different from its meaning in reference to Hindemith. What seems to be the earliest use of the term *neoclassicism* in connection with Stravinsky occurs in an essay on the composer by Boris de Schloezer in 1925; the concepts "neoclassicism" and "*Neue Sachlichkeit*" are essentially contemporaneous in origin. The views of Stravinsky are absolutely not in agreement with those of Impressionism, Neoromanticism, and Expressionism, Schloezer maintains. His art is a reaction against these that might be called "neoclassic," except that this designation provokes academic and scholastic associations, so that it should really be called "classic." It is in fact comparable to the work of a great mathematician or logician, Schloezer continues. It may call for the joint action of numerous psychological factors, but the final result of this complex process "will be a series of theorems that constitute a closed, self-contained system and possess a definite objective meaning":

The classicism of Stravinsky consists precisely in this: since Bach and Mozart there has been no music that is purer, more unobscured by extramusical elements. Psychologism, which makes our musical art impure just as it corrodes our logical thought, is completely absent in Stravinsky's production, which appears just as impersonal, just as objective, as the great creations of Classicism in painting, sculpture, and poetry.[23]

When Schloezer comes to discuss Stravinsky's treatment of the orchestra from *Les Noces* to the *Octet*, he cites a remark of Stravinsky's that curiously anticipates Krenek's characterization of *Neue Sachlichkeit* and thus unwittingly points to the objectivity that is common to Stravinsky and Hindemith alike: "The orchestra must function like a carefully regulated motor. 'It was a real sewing machine,' Stravinsky said enthusiastically when he spoke of the performance of the 'Concertino' by the Belgian 'Pro Arte' Quartet."[24]

An entirely different kind of objectivity is found to be characteristic of Stravinsky by Adorno in his important essay of 1932, "Zur gesellschaftlichen Lage der Musik." Adorno is discussing composition that does not subordinate itself unconditionally to the law of the market. This "serious" music expresses alienation, he maintains; he proceeds to distinguish four types, of which the second is exemplified by Stravinsky:

> The second type includes music which recognizes the fact of alienation as its own isolation and as "individualism" and further raises this fact to the level of consciousness; it does so, however, only within itself, only in aesthetic and form-immanent terms. It thus attempts to annul this insight without respect for actual society. For the most part, it would achieve this through recourse to stylistic forms of the past, which it views as immune to alienation, without seeing that such forms cannot be reconstituted within a completely changed society and through completely changed musical material. This music can be called objectivism, insofar as it—without becoming involved in any social dialectic—would like to evoke the image of a non-existent "objective" society or—in terms of its intentions—of a "fellowship." In the highly capitalistic-industrial nations, neo-classicism is a major component of objectivism; in the underdeveloped, agrarian countries, it is folklore. The most effective author of objectivism who in a highly revealing manner manifests each of these major directions—one after the other, but never simultaneously—is Igor Stravinsky.[25]

According to Adorno, then, music exemplifies objectivism when it seeks to evoke the image of an "objective" society that no longer exists. But if objectivism is the act of objectifying, what is being objectified by Stravinsky's music? Apparently a society is being objectified, evidently because music represents the society in which it arises. This society is being objectified, in the case of neoclassicism, because it is no longer existent, no longer in its natural historical context; separated from this it becomes an object instead of a vital manifestation. Stravinsky's music represents societies, then, in that it objectifies them. Yet any neoclassic composition of Stravinsky really acts in two or more different ways at the same time: it objectifies or represents one or more older cultures by presenting or suggesting their musical styles, and simultaneously, it objectifies or expresses the culture of its own time in its caustic quality—its mordant tonal and harmonic ideal—and even in its recourse to the past.

Neoclassicism is not objective in the sense of being totally abstract or devoid of all relation to anything outside itself, for this is impossible as well as contradictory to the meaning of *neoclassic,* but it is weakened in the normal musical property of expressing its culture and to that extent becomes "objective." This objectivity that arises from objectivism, however, clearly differs from the objectivity of *Neue Sachlichkeit* as well as from the objectivity achieved by the use of nonexpressive media of performance. There are evidently a number of different conceptions of objectivity or, if we wish, a number of ways to achieve it, although they may of course act simultaneously.

Another conception of neoclassicism in which the conception of objectivity plays a role can be found in the 1935 lectures delivered by the composer Gerhard Frommel, which were published in 1937 as *Neue Klassik in der Musik: Zwei Vorträge.*[26] To Frommel, classicism is the highest manifestation of art, for it alone is the perfect self-fulfillment of the idea of art in sensuous appearance. Classicism is always constructive, however, and Frommel treats constructivism as part of it. On this point he cites a remark of Stravinsky's: "My work is an architectonic and not an anecdotal construction, an objective and not an anecdotal one" (p. 165). Yet for the most part, Frommel maintains, Stravinsky's music is grounded in a human realm of being, such as ritual:

> In and for themselves, rites are already objectivities in the highest sense. In exactly the same sense, the music that authentically summons up these pagan cults is objective. But this is something basically different from a musical constructivism that is merely an objectification of form. Perhaps to a still greater extent than in *Petrouchka* and *Sacre* is folklore solidified to constructive objectivity in *Les Noces villageoises,* a vocal work to Stravinsky's words. (p. 166)

Similarly, when Stravinsky expands his scope from Russian folklore to European style as a whole, constructivism remains an intrinsic feature of his art: "Stravinsky aims at a classical, comprehensive style. The constructivism of the second epoch gives him mastery of the whole of the European musical language. What already distinguished the first epoch in Stravinsky's production, precision in expression, mastery of form, and objectivity in the representation of content, now becomes the most essential task" (p. 166–67).

Frommel subsequently characterizes Stravinsky as always concrete, never abstract. His melody is clearly articulated and singable, his polyphony not excessively complex. His music "is visual in the highest degree; Stravinsky is an objective musician, but not an absolute one" (p. 167). Thus, even in Frommel's relatively brief lectures, "objectivity" again takes on a variety of meanings.

We can finally consider the kinds of objectivity that appear in Adorno's *Philosophie der neuen Music* (1949). In this work, objectivity is not simply a reaction to Expressionism or an alternative to it as an opposite kind of consequence of Romanticism; rather the antithesis of objectivity and Expressionism is an instance of Adorno's negative dialectic: Expressionism becomes its opposite. In the duality of Schönberg and Stravinsky on which the study is based, therefore, this dialectic appears clearly even in the first part of the book, the essay devoted to Schönberg (which was written in 1941):

If the drive towards well-integrated construction is to be called objectivity, then objectivity is not simply a counter-movement to Expressionism. It is the other side of the Expressionistic coin. Expressionistic music had interpreted so literally the principle of expression contained in traditionally Romantic music that it assumed the character of a case study. In the process, a sudden change takes place. Music, as a case study in expression, is no longer "expressive." . . . As soon as music has clearly and sharply defined what it wishes to express—its subjective content—this content becomes rigid under the force of the composition, manifesting precisely that objective quality the existence of which is denied by the purely expressive character of music. In its case-study disposition towards its object, music itself becomes "matter-of-fact." With its expressive outbursts the dream of subjectivity explodes, and along with it all conventions. These chords—reflecting the character of the case study—blast the subjective illusion. Thereby, however, these chords invalidate their unique expressive function. What they portray as their object—no matter how precisely this might be done—becomes a matter of indifference: it is, after all, the same subjectivity, whose magic dissolves before the exactness of the penetrating eye cast upon it by the work. Thus the case-study chords become the material of construction. This happens in *Die glückliche Hand.*[27]

Since objectivity is a central characteristic of Stravinsky's music, it figures prominently in the second part of Adorno's book—the essay on Stravinsky (which was written in 1948). In general, Adorno derives objectivity from the absence of expression or meaning. Discussing the cabaret element in *Petrouchka*, for example, he writes of a tendency that leads from commercial art—"which readied the soul for sale as a commercial good—to the negation of the soul in protest against the character of consumer goods: to music's declaration of loyalty to its physical basis, to its reduction to the phenomenon, which assumes objective meaning in that it renounces, of its own accord, any claim to meaning" (p. 142).

A more extreme conception of objectivity, as devoid of meaning altogether, is connected with the aim of totally detaching reality from the individual. For Adorno this is "illusory realism":

> On the one hand, the principle of reality alone is decisive; on the other, this reality grows empty for him who unconditionally follows it. In terms of its own substance, such reality is unattainable and removed from the striving individual through an abyss of meaning. Stravinsky's objectivity rings with such illusory realism. The totally shrewd and illusionless ego elevates the non-ego to the level of an idol, but in its eagerness it severs the threads that connect subject and object. The shell of the objective—now abandoned with no relationship whatsoever—is now offered as truth, as a super-subjective objectivity, all for the sake of such externalization. (pp. 170–71)

Stravinsky's music does not make its appearance as a direct life process, Adorno maintains subsequently, but as indirectness. It registers the disintegration of life in its own material and the alienated state of the consciousness of the subject as well: "Compositional spontaneity itself is overwhelmed by the prohibition placed upon pathos in expression: the subject, which is no longer permitted to state anything about itself, thus actually ceases to engage in 'production' and must content itself with the hollow echo of objective musical language, which is no longer its own" (pp. 181–82).

This absence of life is further emphasized in Adorno's view of musical time in Stravinsky, which he describes as a pseudomorphism of spatial dimension. In this pseudomorphism, music establishes itself as an arbiter of time, "causing the listener to forget the subjective and psychological experience of time in music and to abandon himself to its spatialized dimension. It proclaims, as its unique achievement, the fact that there is no longer any life— as though it had achieved the objectification of life" (p. 195). The weakness of Stravinsky's production during the last twenty-five years, Adorno asserts, arises from a chain of events that makes music a parasite of painting. That weakness is the price he has paid for his restriction to the dance, "although this limitation once seemed to him a guarantee of order and objectivity" (p. 196).

Adorno then distinguishes two types of listening (which have their coun-terparts in two types of time)—the expressive-dynamic and the rhythmic-spatial: "The two types are separated by force of that social alienation which separates subject and object. Musically, everything subjective is threatened by coincidence; everything which appears as collective objectivity is under the threat of externalization, of the repressive hardness of mere existence. The idea of great music lay in a mutual penetration of both modes of lis-tening." The unity of discipline and freedom was conceived in the sonata, in which objective pseudo-spatial time coincides with the psychological time of experience in the happy balance of the moment: "This conception of a musical subject-object was forcibly extracted from the realistic dissociation of subject and object" (p. 198). By the time of Stravinsky, of course, the two types of musical experience have diverged, and both in the Viennese school and in Stravinsky, only subtypes of spatial time are evident. Subjective time has disappeared: "The dying out of subjective time in music seems totally unavoidable in the midst of a humanity which had made itself into a thing—into an object of its own organization" (p. 194).

Adorno sees Schönberg as achieving a kind of objectivity that is superior to that of Stravinsky, whose objectivism in the meantime "has degenerated to everyday jargon." Schönberg relies step by step on the concrete demands of the encounter "between the compositional subject which is conscious of itself, and the socially established material. In so doing he preserves with par-ticular objectivity the greater philosophical truth as the open attempt at the reconstruction of responsibility" (p. 213). In the authenticity of its approach, the Schönberg school endangers almost every one of its own structures, but at the same time it gains

> not only a more cohesive and instinctive artistic view, but also a higher objectivity than Stravinsky's objectivism—an objectivity, namely, of immanent correctness, and further, of undisguised appropriateness to the historical condition. It is forced to go above and beyond this to a manifest objectivity which is sui generis—to twelve-tone constructiv-ism—without total illumination by the subject of the animation of the material. (pp. 214–15)

Stravinsky, on the other hand, forcibly demands of the recalcitrant material "a contrived style of objectivity":

> The will to style replaces style itself and therewith sabotages it. No ob-jectivity of that which the structure wills from within itself is present in objectivism. It establishes itself by eradicating the traces of subjectivity; the hollows are proclaimed as the cells of a true brotherhood. The de-cay of the subject—which the Schönberg school bitterly defends itself

against—is directly interpreted by Stravinsky's music as that higher form in which the subject is to be preserved. . . . Therewith objectivism designates itself as that which it fears and the proclamation of which constitutes its entire content. It defines itself as the vain private concern of the aesthetic subject—as a trick of the isolated individual—who poses as though he were the objective spirit. If this were today of the same essence, then such art would still not be validated by it; for the objective spirit of a society, integrated by its presumed domination over its subjects, has become transparent as false in itself. (pp. 215–16)

But if the objective spirit of the time does not conform to Hegel's conception, it is also not a travesty of Hegel to cast Stravinsky in the role of objective spirit.

Order and Organization

During the second half of the century the concept of "order" is of central importance. "Objectivity" is no longer considered explicitly, but it does not really disappear. Rather, it is assumed, or taken for granted; it becomes a presupposition of musical thought that underlies not only the practice of analysis, which remains stubbornly objective, but also the conception of what music is. "Order" is understood to have an objective nature and is spoken of in these terms; it is the chief representative of conceptions of objectivity, but it need no longer be described as such. Thus, the antiexpressive stance of musical thought remains characteristic of the century throughout, even when music itself becomes highly expressive, as it does particularly toward the end of the century. The expressive qualities that appear are new, of course, but they are unmistakable, and they have their own kinds of intensity. They simply lack theoretical recognition and description.

The importance of the principle of order can be seen as early as Stravinsky's 1939–40 lectures *Poétique musicale sous forme de six leçons*. Here music is described as "a phenomenon of speculation": "The elements at which this speculation aims are those of sound and time. . . . Music presupposes before all else a certain organization in time."[28] Following Pierre Souvtchinsky (*Revue musicale*, 1939), Stravinsky distinguishes two kinds of music: one parallel to the course of ontological time, the other following psychological time. In the first type, which Souvtchinsky calls "chronometric music," the musical process is in equilibrium with ontological time, and the music induces in the mind of the listener a feeling of euphoria, of "dynamic calm." In the second type, the musical centers of attraction and gravity are dislocated, and the music is subject to the composer's emotive impulses. In this type, which is best exemplified by Wagner, the will to expression is dominant. "Music that is based on ontological time," Stravinsky states, "is generally dominated by the principle of similarity. The music that adheres to psychological time likes to proceed by contrast" (p. 31). It is similarity that Stravinsky prefers, for he believes it gives music more strength and solidity. He therefore favors the first, or objective, type of temporality. In Souvtchinsky's view, Stravinsky belongs to the great classical tradition of music: "In the course of the two decades of his musical life, Stravinsky has given back to music its laws of composition and its immanent experience. This interior and formal reestablishment of laws and order in the art of music was accomplished little by little and was perhaps begun by Stravinsky almost unconsciously."[29]

In more concrete terms, Stravinsky believes that musical form depends on tonal attraction. The centers of this attraction may be defined by the relation of the tones that are involved in the composition, or it may be given by the underlying tonal system:

> Composing, for me, is putting into an order a certain number of these sounds according to certain interval-relationships. This activity leads to a search for the center upon which the series of sounds involved in my undertaking should converge. Thus, if a center is given, I shall have to find a combination that converges upon it. If, on the other hand, an as yet unoriented combination has been found, I shall have to determine the center towards which it should lead. The discovery of this center suggests to me the solution of my problem. It is thus that I satisfy my very marked taste for such a kind of musical topography. . . .
>
> A system of tonal or polar centers is given to us solely for the purpose of achieving a certain order, that is to say more definitively, form, the form in which the creative effort culminates. (pp. 37, 41)

But form is not only shaped by these specific centers of attraction; it is also furthered in general by the deliberate limitation of means. For Stravinsky, a mode of composition that does not assign itself limits becomes pure fantasy or the caprice of the imagination. But imagination is also the handmaiden of the creative will, he affirms, and the composer must make a selection from the elements his imagination provides, for human activity must impose limits on itself. In fact, the more art is controlled and limited and worked over, the more it is free: "As for myself, I experience a sort of terror when, at the moment of setting to work and finding myself before the infinitude of possibilities that present themselves, I have the feeling that everything is permissible to me" (p. 63).

It is this fear that lies at the root of Stravinsky's search for order. His mentality is such that he must find salvation and support in the external materials of his art and in the manipulation and organization of these materials. The process—one is tempted to say, the technique—of composition produces structures of convincing power because of the total dedication to construction and the grounding of this construction in the inherent relations of the tonal material, which really represent its intrinsic potentialities for order. Expressive and emotional forces, the whole sphere of subjectivity and inspiration, are entirely absent. Stravinsky sits at his composing desk with the attitude of an engineer:

> Will I then have to lose myself in this abyss of freedom? To what shall I cling in order to escape the dizziness that seizes me before the virtuality of this infinitude? However, I shall not succumb. I shall overcome my terror and shall be reassured by the thought that I have the seven notes of the scale and its chromatic intervals at my disposal, that strong and weak accents are within my reach, and that in all of these I possess solid and concrete elements which offer me a field of experience just as vast as the upsetting and dizzy infinitude that had just frightened me. (p. 64)

"Let me have something finite, definite," he asks, "matter that can lend itself to my operation only insofar as it is commensurate with my possibilities." He seeks to surround himself with obstacles and believes, rather surprisingly, that "the arbitrariness of the constraint serves only to obtain precision of execution" (p. 65). Stravinsky's perfect awareness of how he operates suggests that objectivity and order are characteristic of his life as well as of his music. He believes, in fact, that we have an innate preference for unity and order, that "we instinctively prefer coherence and its quiet strength to the restless powers of dispersion—that is, we prefer the realm of order to the realm of dissimilarity" (p. 69). The fugue becomes a paragon of order. It is "a pure form in which the music means nothing outside of itself. Doesn't the fugue imply the composer's submission to the rules? And is it not within those strictures that he finds the full flowering of his freedom as a creator?" (p. 76).

Stravinsky's aesthetic is finally set into relief by a polemic against any type of expression or extramusical meaning:

> Do we not, in truth, ask the impossible of music when we expect it to express feelings, to translate dramatic situations, even to imitate nature? And, as if it were not enough to condemn music to the job of being an illustrator, the century to which we owe what is called "progress through enlightenment" invented for good measure the monumental absurdity which consists of bestowing on every accessory, as well as on

every feeling and every character of the lyrical drama, a sort of check-room number called a Leitmotiv—a system that led Debussy to say that the Ring struck him as a sort of vast musical city directory. (p. 77)

Order demands, in fact, that contrary impulses be subdued and controlled: "What is important for the lucid ordering of the work—for its crystalliza-tion—is that all the Dionysian elements which set the imagination of the artist in motion and make the life-sap rise must be properly subjugated be-fore they intoxicate us, and must finally be made to submit to the law: Apollo demands it" (p. 80–81).

Since serialism is grounded in tonal order, we might expect that an aes-thetics of order would grow out of serial practice; it is therefore rather surprising to meet first with the explicit concept of order in the writings of Stravinsky rather than in those of Schönberg or Webern. But it is not until an essay by Karlheinz Stockhausen on the craft of composition in "punc-tile" music, "Situation des Handwerks (Kriterien der punktuellen Musik)," which was written in 1952 but not published until 1963, that serial technique gave rise to a conception of music as tonal order. It was only in the 1950s, however—coincidentally with its aesthetic—that an adequate theory of seri-alism also was developed; Schönberg's essay of 1941, "Composition with Twelve Tones," did little more than lay down the axiom of the equivalence of inverted, reversed, and transposed tonal patterns to an original one. The power and importance of this axiom cannot be exaggerated, but although it provides a broad if questionable foundation for radically new kinds of ordered music, it simply takes tonal order itself as a given.

The conception of music that is put forth by Stockhausen is unequivocally governed by the idea of order. Although the craft of musical composition is no longer being imparted by teachers, Stockhausen affirms, independent endeavors have nevertheless led to a common "style"—one that is "totally organized" and that is based on the music of Anton Webern:

Music as *tonal order* is directed to the human capacity of perceiving order in tones. Perceiving is understood here as: existing and remaining in existence without further intention. In this way musical thinking-along-with is provoked. With "order" there is meant: the disappearance of the individual in the whole, of the various in the unified. The crite-ria of order are richness of relation and absence of contradiction. The goal of ordering is the approach to an imaginable perfection of order in general and in particular.[30]

Principles of order arise from an idea (or representation) of order, Stock-hausen continues. This re-presentation presupposes a unity that is able to relate different particulars to itself. Total representation, according to this, is the presupposition that a single whole will result from an ordered totality. Stockhausen specifies the basic properties of such a whole: "In a total order every particular is of equal status. The sense made by an order is grounded in the lack of contradiction between the particular and the whole. Tonal order, therefore, means the *subordination of tones to a unifying principle* that is conceived—and *lack of contradiction* between particular and whole" (p. 18). The conception of tonal order, Stockhausen observes, is also called a "musical idea." Especially in the perspective of Webernian serialization, of course, this musical idea can designate an entire composition as properly as an initial abstract series on which the composition is based.

Stockhausen turns to the concept of "craftsmanship" in its relation to order. Craft, he states, is concerned with the imparting and development of the ability to translate an idea into an actual tonal order. The criterion for judging this ability is the degree of contradiction, if any, between the idea and the ordering of the tonal material. The imparting of craftsmanship, therefore, will make sense in teaching how to order particulars into a whole, but not how particulars can be ordered in their own right. On the other hand, it is obvious that musical craft has nothing to do with the "power of invention."

The idea of music as a representation of order, Stockhausen specifies, contains the implication that this idea be unique and thus that the resultant ordering of tonal material also be unique. Furthermore, composition should no longer be thought of as merely "placing together," for, in ordering the material, the idea does not simply place it together but, more accurately, "organizes" it. Finally, Stockhausen maintains, if a unique individuality is to emerge from a whole, the choice of material that is already preformed must be excluded. Since a tone has the four dimensions of duration, loudness, pitch, and tone color, tonal ordering, in Stockhausen's opinion, would logically begin with these dimensions: the subordinate principles of order should also be derived from the idea. "The ability to do this I called craftsmanship. The inability to do it I will call dilettantism" (p. 19). With this strict, objective, and rather terse prescription, Stockhausen opens his discussion of order in punctile music.

He examines next the question of preformed material. Traditional kinds of music, he points out, accept the preformation of the smallest units—of the motive, the theme, and the series: "But the insight today into the inner relations of tones uncovers the contradiction between the individual ordering of preformation and the necessity of deriving integral order from a unified idea" (p. 20). It follows that the idea of a work cannot be preceded without contradiction by the choice of preformations that are to embody this idea.

Stockhausen's position is evidently a radical one that rejects even traditional serialism; punctile music may have its point of departure in Webern, but although it depends on the order of individual tones, it is altogether uncompromising in the application of its principles. Thus, Stockhausen asserts specifically that the reduction of music to an ordering of tones without intention, as this is understood with respect to some idea, is tied to the necessity of recognizing and no longer accepting the contradictory character of preformation:

> The ordering mind thus begins with the individual tone; that is, it orders tones in accordance with a unified total conception of tonal order because it allows tones to proceed from the idea. Tones therefore exist in a "total" music as a necessary consequence of the immanent principle of order that is derived from the idea. *The ordering principles of traditional craft* are now to be examined, then, to determine the extent to which they are still usable today. (p. 20)

The fact alone that for several centuries music was composed in the same "preformed" tonal system shows clearly enough, in Stockhausen's opinion, how much the ordering of tones in the craftsmanship of our time differs from traditional craftsmanship. It is not only the major-minor system, for example, or the modal system that preceded this, that comes into question here but also the twelve-tone chromatic system. It is even conceivable that the complete idea of a tonal order that is contained in the idea of a given work will call for an organization of tones, both individually and in relation to each other, suitable to this work alone and realizing its sense only here and nowhere else.

But Stockhausen's conception of order has a generality that is not restricted by the consideration of musical use. Ideas of order seem to exist in an abstract universe of their own and are thus to be examined after they have been conceived to determine whether they have musical utility. Tones, arise, for example, only as a result of the collective action of the principles of order for duration, pitch, loudness, and tone color, and it is clear in this regard, Stockhausen argues, that the idea of order originally has nothing to do with an idea of the sonority of "finished" tones. In Stockhausen's view, then, it would seem that the process of composition encompasses even the genesis of music. But it does not follow, of course, that every conception or type of order will have some relevance to music: "The extent to which an idea of order can be transferred to music must be tested by the craftsman for each idea occurring to him. Through this it will be decided whether he can accept the idea in question or not" (p. 22). Carrying ordered thinking into the tonal material itself, in Stockhausen's opinion, will be made possible in the future by the electronic creation of sound; the composer will no longer have to work with the repertory of sounds that can be produced by available musical instruments.

The nature of musical order is examined more closely in the article "... wie die Zeit vergeht ...," which Stockhausen wrote in 1956 and which appeared in *Reihe* in 1957: "Music consists of relations of order in time; this presupposes that one has a conception of such time. We hear alterations in an acoustic field: silence–tone–silence, or tone–tone; and between the alterations we can distinguish time intervals of varying magnitude. The time intervals are called *phases*."[31] (By *phase* Stockhausen evidently means the interval of time between the onset of one tone and the onset of the succeeding tone, e.g., or between the onset of one tone and the onset of the succeeding silence. But he also uses the term in the usual sense to mean the interval of time between any two successive vibrations—i.e., between a point on one sine wave and the corresponding point on the succeeding wave.) Stockhausen proceeds to consider the relations between phases. To distinguish different phases, he points out, we compare the duration of one with the duration of another. Our sense perception measures shorter or longer phases, and proportions make possible an exact determination: one phase is two or three times as long, say, as another. To make the proportions definite, also, we need a unit quantity of time so that we can say that the phase lengths in question, for example, are one second and two seconds. These basic facts of perception apply to pitch as well as to duration.

Conceptions of order are literally the foundation of *Klavierstück X*, and they dominate the description of the work that Stockhausen wrote for its premiere in 1962:

> In the *Klavierstück X* I have made the attempt to mediate between relative disorder and order. With the help of a scale of disorder-order relations I have composed structures in series of different degrees of order. Higher degrees of order are marked by greater unequivocality (lack of contingency), lesser degrees of order by the greater probability and evenness of differences (increasing exchangeability, decreasing transparency). Greater order is connected with lesser density and greater individualization of the events. In the course of the piece extremes are reached: structures are crystallized to unique individual shapes (highest degree of order), or structures are leveled to masslike complexes. In the course of the process of mediation between disorder and order, increasingly more shapes and more concentrated shapes are unfolded from an undifferentiated initial state of great disorder (evenness).[32]

A general tendency can be observed in the whole course of Stockhausen's musical thought as it is revealed by the successive volumes of his *Texte*, and this tendency can manifest itself even in the course of a single essay.

". . . wie die Zeit vergeht . . . ," for example, moves as though inevitably in an analytic direction. It starts with considerations of comparison that have a certain aesthetic interest and goes on to increasingly specific descriptions of tonal perception that are connected with the characteristics of audition and the properties of the musical system. Indeed, there is an increasing interest in the second half of the century in unrelieved analysis and in the detailed arrangements for performance. Certainly, the equipment and the physical arrangements needed for performance no longer go without saying and demand careful specification simply because the composer's conception is not fully evident from the score alone.

This change has important implications for the character of musical thought. Just as the concept of objectivity became implicit as a presupposition of the discussion of order, so order as well as objectivity become implicit as presuppositions of the exclusive concern with analysis. But with the resulting forest of analytic detail any further aesthetic significance disappears; it simply gives way to a mass of data, while ideas and even words themselves are replaced by numbers. There is considerable aesthetic interest, however, simply in the remarkable fact that Stockhausen translates the increasing abstraction of his ideas of order into music, for these abstract ideas are treated as a foundation for composition. It would seem that whatever can be thought of can be realized in sound and thus secures musical status and value—an example, perhaps, of the general and still more astonishing thesis that whatever is conceivable will be found to exist.

What is most striking and significant about Stockhausen's ideas of order and organization is their logical progression and their generality. This can readily be seen in the overview of his thought that he presented in lectures in 1971:

> I use the words "point," "group," and "mass" in order to generalize what is happening in music, and to make it clear that each is a particular manifestation of a larger trend. . . .
> The drawback of point music is that if one wants the music to be different all the time, it becomes very monotonous because trying to be different from element to element becomes something they all have in common.[33]

Inevitably, it would seem, Stockhausen was led to another compositional idea—a second stage of development in a continuing process of thought—and individual tones or formulations of two successive tones gave way to groups:

> By group I mean the number of tones that can be separately distinguished at any one time, which is up to seven or eight. And they have

to have at least one characteristic in common. A group with only one characteristic in common would have a fairly weak group character. It could be the timbre, it could be the dynamic: let's say for example you have a group of eight notes which are all different in duration, pitch and timbre, but they are all soft. That common characteristic makes them a group. Naturally, if all the characteristics are in common, if all of the notes are loud, high, all played with trumpets, all periodic, all in the same tempo, and all accented, then the group is extremely strong, because the individual character of each of the eight elements is lost.

So what is happening now is that more and more groups are combining with individual notes, and from that time on the point doesn't exist as a separate category anymore, because it becomes one of the definitions of the group: if I have three notes, four notes, two notes, one note, five notes, six notes, then the one note is the smallest group. It's a question of context. (p. 40)

Stockhausen then explains what he finds to be the rationale of this developmental process: "The notion of groups is transcended in *Gruppen*, just as in *Kontra-Punkte* the notion of point was transcended by introducing groups. This is always happening, and is always very interesting. If one concentrates on something, or on a certain aspect, then one transcends it, because one cannot be content to remain permanently in a closed system" (p. 41). The importance of types of organization was a result, in Stockhausen's opinion, of the avoidance both of formulated tonal patterns and of repetition:

What seems to be interesting in this context is this: whereas all music up to that historical moment, even the music of Webern, had been made by using certain *Gestalten* (figures), objects like a theme or a motif, and then transforming this object, varying it, transposing it, putting it into sequences, even destroying it or developing it further, in the music written since 1951 there was an explicit spirit of non-figurative composition. We tried to avoid all repetition of figures, and through this it became very clear to us that the way sounds were organized was the most important aspect, and not the particular *Gestalt* that occurred in a given moment. (pp. 41–42)

The generality of the process is its most significant characteristic:

The fact that certain groups were composed as points, and others as groups, that was what mattered: being recognizably points, or being groups, or a mixture of both. The groups could be completely different in their intervals or in their shape, and the points could be in different regions and of different overall quality, generally shorter or longer or higher or lower. . . .

There is a unity underlying all the different events which occur. That is why, when we listen to this music, we shouldn't become caught up too much with their differences, but try to sense and discover the underlying proportioning principle—the genetic principle—that gives birth to them all. (p. 42)

Stockhausen proceeds to explain the transition from groups to masses: "When we cannot count the individual notes in a group anymore, they surpass the group" (p. 43). In a succession of tones, of course, this depends on speed. But generally, if there are too many events, even simultaneously, as in a swarm of bees, we perceive a shape; the swarm becomes a single entity: "If we see a tree, we don't count the leaves, but are still able to tell a pine tree from a beech" (p. 43). There is an effect of the elements, but the mass is characterized also by the shape, the overall form. In this the similarity to visual form plays an important role, and Stockhausen tells of basing musical masses on the shape of mountains and of describing tonal masses in terms of density but also of textures being perforated, of rising or drifting shapes, or even of tonal masses that are dark or bright or muted in color.

An important concept introduced in connection with the description of tonal masses is that of "statistical form." This has another illustration in the electronic generation of sounds based on curves that are drawn on a sheet of paper. Stockhausen gave different individual curves to three collaborators, each of whom was instructed to follow his own curve by varying his one dimension of the sound output. One control varied the frequency of the pulses produced, another their loudness, and a third the frequency level of their frequency band. Eight different sets of specifications of the ranges of frequency and loudness were given in order to produce eight successive results, the taped recordings of which were then superimposed. The overall result is a certain mass, Stockhausen says, a mass "with a very distinct shape and a very precise tendency compared to another mass" (p. 46).

Besides music in points, in groups, or in masses, Stockhausen distinguishes three additional types of composition: determinate, variable, and statistical. In determinate composition, "one can hear very clearly the intervals which make the proportions, the durations of the individual points, the shapes of the individual groups and masses" (p. 48). To explain variable composition, Stockhausen turns to his work *Zeitmasse*:

Five woodwinds: oboe, flute, cor anglais, clarinet, bassoon—is a traditional ensemble, but in this work you hear determinate structures alternating and mixed very clearly with variable structures. For example, there is a point where all five instruments start together. They have been playing chords. Everything organized in the vertical, such as chords, is clearly determinate because you would never find notes falling by accident together in a series of chords. . . . In this example, however, the starting-point is a point of departure where every instrument starts playing at a different speed.

So the oboe, for instance, is playing a given number of notes as fast as possible, the bassoon is playing as slow as possible, in an unrelated tempo; the English horn is playing an accelerando from as slow as possible to as fast as possible. . . . Another player starts as fast as possible and slows down in turn until he reaches a speed four times as slow. Then, after a longer time which is a time value within which everybody can finish playing their written notes, they wait for each other and come together again in the same metronomic tempo. . . .

Sometimes one instrument is out of time with the others; there are sections where all five have individual tempos. There is a continuum between complete determination and extreme variability. And when we listen, we can feel when the music is very determinate because we know exactly where we are . . . but when we are in a region of high variability, the music is floating. (pp. 48–50)

In statistical composition, Stockhausen continues, you can permutate or change the order of events without it really making any difference. Statistical methods are introduced into music by the use of bands of frequency, duration, and tone color. Every aspect of music is considered to fall between a minimum or a maximum value: in pitch between a highest and a lowest, in rhythm between a shortest and a longest duration, in tone color between, say, dark and bright. If bandwidths are specified for a given work, statistical composition will allow the use of any pitch, duration, and tone color whatsoever, provided that whatever is used falls within the bandwidth established for that particular musical aspect.

Three final types of composition are distinguished by Stockhausen: developmental, or dramatic, form, which has a strong directional orientation; sequential and variation forms, which can also be called epic; and lyric form, in which moments are found without regard to any past or future. "This order of three-times-three terms," Stockhausen says in summarizing all the compositional types he has defined, "is an order in which every term can be combined with every other term." Points, groups, and masses, for example, can all be either determinate, variable, or statistical. And determinate, variable, and statistical points or groups or masses can all be in either a developmental or a sequential or a moment form:

What this is ultimately leading to is not that one way of forming is avoiding other ways of organization, but can be combined with all the other methods. As I said, once we reach statistical ways of controlling it does not mean we forget about determinacy or directionality or variability, just as once we attain the lyric, we don't ignore the dramatic. Rather, what we are striving to reach is a universal conception, within which we may move in different directions from work to work and within individual works, but having all the possibilities of organization available to us in every composition. (p. 61)

In explaining moment form, Stockhausen refers to his work *Momente*. This composition employs three principal types of moments, which are determined, respectively, by the predominance of melody, the succession of chords or tone colors, and the juxtaposition of different durations. The third type of moment is described in some detail:

Moments based primarily on principles of measured durations, of different lengths, give rise to two important characteristics of any musical construction. One is silence; the other is polyphony, the superposition of more or less independent layers which are sounding at the same time. . . . When I am working with a continuous melodic line of a particular shape, then the duration question does not arise. However, as soon as I start cutting the line into smaller sections, then I have to deal with different durations, and with the inevitable possibility that the fragments of melody may become separated, producing silence. Silence is the result of the concept of duration: to deal with durations means to break the flow of time, and that produces silence.

Secondly, once something is cut, the pieces cannot only be separated but also superimposed, since they become independent of one another. And that superimposition produces polyphony. So the principle of polyphony and the principle of silence are both based on the concept of duration and the differentiation of durations. (p. 66)

In the composition of *Momente*, Stockhausen proceeds, having distinguished the three types of moments possible,

by composing a purely melodic moment, a purely verticalized Klangmoment, and a purely durational polyphonic moment, I am able to derive further moments from these centres which have elements more or less in common with the others. . . . I can now build up a whole tree of different generations of inter-relating moments, and I can control very carefully how much they have in common. This is quite opposed to the traditional concept of building a musical continuum into which you then have to insert breaks, producing sudden changes, in order to sustain momentum. Instead of starting with something very homogeneous and then breaking the homogeneity, we start with completely separate instants: Now! Now! Now! Now! Now!—and then begin to determine how much memory or hope each Now may have—how much it may be related to what happened before or will happen next. (pp. 66–67)

In addition, *Momente* is a variable work; the conductor is free to decide on the order of the moments for a particular performance. Also, the sonorous material of the work is extremely diversified in character, extending from the sound of applause to nonsense syllables, speech exclamations, and the Song of Songs. In the systematic progression of types of order and organization, Stockhausen would seem to have arrived at the possibilities of lack of organization and of disorder—possibilities that in the works that follow are combined in various ways with types of order. As a whole, then, Stockhausen's works can be said to represent a comprehensive inventory of types of organization of sound. There is a lawfulness or logic even in their encompassing diversity and their apparent willfulness. A logic of progress is the implicit law of change in this series of types of musical order. The progress eventually calls forth a reaction—total serialization leads to chance and increasing order to disorder—so that progress and reaction represent a dynamic or intrinsically historical version of the thesis and antithesis of a Hegelian triad. In itself, however, the progress of order is an example of a general conception of the historical evolution of music—an "intrinsic law" that was increasingly believed in and obeyed in the nineteenth and twentieth centuries and that leads through Schönberg and Webern to Stockhausen.

A striking example of ordered progress with respect to types of order is the change from instrumental to electronic music during the 1950s, which was essentially a change from the organization of tone to the organization of sound in general. This is clearly a central feature of electronic music, and Stockhausen connects it with the analysis and synthesis of individual sounds:

Until around 1950 the idea of music as sound was largely ignored. That composing with sounds could also involve the composition of sounds themselves, was no longer self-evident. It was revived as a result, we might say, of a historical development. The Viennese School of Schönberg, Berg and Webern had reduced their musical themes and motifs to entities of only two sounds, to intervals. Webern in particular, Anton von Webern. And when I started to compose music, I was certainly a child of the first half of the century, continuing and expanding what the composers of the first half had prepared. It took a little leap forward to reach the idea of composing, or synthesizing, the individual sound. (pp. 88–89)

Stockhausen's search for order has led him to what can be described as the unified structuring of time: patterns of variation and intermittence can be compressed and expanded in duration so that tone color, rhythm, and form are determined by the same patterns run off at very different speeds. If we were to take any sound, he says, and stretch it out so that it lasted twenty minutes instead of one second, we would have a musical piece whose form is the expansion of the time structure of the original sound:

> What we perceive as rhythm from a certain perspective, is perceived at a faster time of perception as pitch, with its melodic implications. . . . If now we slow down the speed of a given rhythm we come into the realm of form. What is form in music? Well, we usually say a musical structure of between the one or two minutes of a piece of entertainment music, and the hour and a half of a Mahler symphony, which is about the longest we encounter in music of the western tradition. . . . So, according to the fixed perspective of our tradition form varies between dimensions of around one minute and ninety minutes. This corresponds to 1, 2, 4, 8, 16, 32, 64, 128—a range of around seven octaves. Amazingly enough, we find a similar seven-octave range within the traditional formal subdivisions of music, from the length of a phrase, the smallest formal subdivision, say eight seconds, to the largest complete section, or "movement," of about sixteen to seventeen minutes duration. . . . So there is a range of about seven octaves for durations from eight seconds up to seventeen minutes. (pp. 92–94)

Similar considerations are applied to rhythm and meter, with similar results, and Stockhausen then presents a summary view:

> The ranges of perception are ranges of time, and the time is subdivided by us, by the construction of our bodies and by our organs of perception. And since these modern means have become available, to change the time of perception continuously, from one range to another, from a rhythm into a pitch, or a tone or noise into a formal structure, the composer can now work within a unified time domain. And that completely changes the traditional concept of how to compose and think music, because previously they were all in separate boxes: harmony and melody in one box, rhythm and metre in another, then periods, phrasing, larger formal entities in another, while in the timbre field we had only names of instruments, no unity of reference at all. (p. 95)

In these techniques of unifying the levels of temporal structure, the desire for order would seem to have gone its own way, in total disregard not only of feeling but also of any perceptual significance altogether. Stockhausen addresses this point, however, in terms of a musical illustration, a crucial moment in his work *Kontakte*:

> The moment begins with a tone of about 169 cycles per second, approximately F below middle C. Many of the various sounds in *Kontakte* have been composed by determining specific rhythms and speeding them up several hundred or a thousand times or more, thereby obtaining distinctive timbres. What is interesting about this moment is that if I were to play little bits of the passage one after another, like notes on the piano, nobody would be able to hear the transition that takes place from one field of time perception to another. The fact that I make the transition continuously makes us conscious of it, and this effort of consciousness changes our whole attitude towards our acoustic environment. Every sound becomes a very mysterious thing, it has its own time. (p. 96)

Stockhausen turns to the decomposition of a sound, which can be accomplished by stretching out its duration:

> You hear this sound gradually revealing itself to be made up of a number of components which one by one, very slowly leave the original frequency and glissando up and down: the order is down, up, down, up, up, down. The original sound is literally taken apart into its six components, and each component in turn is decomposing before our ears, into its individual rhythm of pulses. In the background one component of the original sound continues to the end of the section. And whenever a component leaves the original pitch, naturally the timbre of the sound changes. (p. 97)

The significance of this process, as Stockhausen describes it, entails conceptions of the nature of music:

> This is the point: whereas it is true that traditionally in music, and in art in general, the context, the ideas or themes, were more or less descriptive of inter-human relationships, or descriptive of certain phenomena in the world, we now have a situation where the composition or decomposition of a sound, or the passing of a sound through several time layers, may be the theme itself, granted that by theme we mean the behaviour or life of the sound. . . . So there you have it: the theme of the music, of *Kontakte* itself, is the revealing of such processes, and their composition. . . .
>
> There are many visual artists today who are mainly concerned with the exploration of new ways of seeing. Seeing itself is the theme: how

to look at things and what we can see, the widening of our perception. (pp. 98–99)

In addition to the continuum of temporal manifestations, Stockhausen is concerned with the continuum of tone and noise. Both are of fundamental importance in the larger realm of order that is made accessible by electronic music. If I change the periodicity of a sound, Stockhausen says,

> a little faster, a little slower, or to be more precise, make the duration of each period a little shorter or a little longer, then the sound starts oscillating around a certain middle frequency, and all the half vowel or half consonant components, which are already fairly broad-band, begin to break up. So the continuum between sound of fixed pitch and noise is nothing more than that between a more and a less stable periodicity: the noisiest noise being the most aperiodic. This discovery of a continuum between sound and noise . . . was extremely important, because once such a continuum becomes available, you can control it, you can compose it, you can organize it. . . . If now we slow down the speed of a given rhythm we come into the realm of form. (pp. 92–93)

Stockhausen subsequently discusses the equality of tone and noise in more general terms. A tone can be transformed into a noise, he points out, if it is made more and more aperiodic, and the resultant noise will be determined by its bandwidth or band of frequencies. The integration into music of noises of all kinds has taken place only since the middle of the century, largely through the discovery of new methods of composing the continuum between tones and noises. In this connection, Stockhausen mentions an important principle: since noises tend to mask tones, a proper balance between the two can be established only if the number of noises is very much smaller than the number of tones. In addition to this, Stockhausen has uncovered a relation between the bandwidth of sounds and the size of the scale steps that are appropriate for a scale of these sounds:

> Put at its simplest, the noisier the sound, the larger the interval, the bigger the step size. The noisiest sounds in *Kontakte* are two octaves in width, and the scale for these noises is the largest and most simple scale in the whole work: a scale of perfect fifths. . . . The narrower the band-width, on the other hand, and the more the sound approached a pure tone, the finer the scale: this is the principle I have applied. With the purest tones you can make the most subtle melodic gestures, much, much more refined than what the textbooks say is the smallest interval we can hear. (pp. 110–11)

This consideration leads Stockhausen to the conclusion that the traditional duality of material and form is no longer valid in music:

> We have discovered a new law of relationship between the nature of sound and the scale on which it may be composed. Harmony and melody are no longer abstract systems to be filled with any given sounds we may choose as material. There is a very subtle relationship nowadays between form and material. I would even go so far as to say that form and material have to be considered as one and the same. I think it is perhaps the most important fact to come out in the twentieth century that in several fields material and form are no longer regarded as separate, in the sense that I take this material and put it into that form. Rather, a given material determines its own best form according to its inner nature. The old dialectic based on the antinomy—or dichotomy— of form and matter has really vanished since we have begun to produce electronic music, and have come to understand the nature and relativity of sound. (p. 111)

Electronic music has at its disposal, finally, the literally spatial resources of producing an apparent motion of sound and of permitting the combination of sounds that come from different directions or from different apparent distances. This last possibility is of interest in producing a kind of multilayered spatial composition. Stockhausen illustrates such stratification in his work *Kontakte,* in which

> there are dense, noisy sounds in the forefront, covering the whole range of audibility. Nothing can pierce this wall of sound, so to speak. Then all of a sudden . . . I stop the sound and you hear a second layer of sound behind it. You realize it was already there but you couldn't hear it. I cut it again, like with a knife, and you hear another layer behind that one, then again. Building spatial depth by superimposition of layers enables us to compose perspectives in sound from close up to far away, analogous to the way we compose layers of melody and harmony in the two-dimensional plane of traditional music. (pp. 105–6)

This effect is occasionally found in conventional music also, when it is sometimes a result of distinctly different distances of the sources of sound. But it can be produced as well by the abrupt silencing of part of the orchestra, when the remaining sounds appear to originate from a more distant place.

Stockhausen's pursuit of musical order clearly encompasses every aspect of music that is amenable to organization. In contrast, Stravinsky preferred to achieve order by working within a restricted range of variability or a limited number of tonal dimensions. The first is a progressive or expanding technique, the second a classical one.

Of the many kinds of musical order that Stockhausen has investigated and made use of, some involve the combination of distinct constituents. The spatial stratification we have just considered provides an excellent example, in which the constituents are distinguished at least in part by differences in apparent distance. But composite structure is such a characteristic feature of music that it is manifested in a great number of different forms. Indeed, the structural constituents of music often have no objective tonal existence but are essentially theoretical constructs that belong to musical thought rather than to music in any literal sense. In the case of Schenker, for example, the conception of stratification was part of a theory of the intrinsic order of music—a conception very much like the linguistic theory of deep structure.

An objective and concrete theory of composite structure in music is presented by Charles Lalo, in the preface of his *Eléments d'une esthétique musicale scientifique* (1939).[34] Lalo introduces the conception of a "polyharmonic aesthetics," which is based on the theory that art is always a combination of different kinds of structure—of chords, melody, rhythm, and tone color in music, for example—into a suprastructure or trans-structure. The play of structures, then, is what constitutes the source of aesthetic value and the object of aesthetic investigation. All the constituent structures are audible parts of the music, unlike the structures or strata of other conceptions, in which some strata may be inaudible or theoretical. Lalo's component structures are objectively present in the music; indeed, he sees each of them as the object of a special branch of study. The structures are heterogeneous in nature, not all of the same kind. The work of art has the unity of an artificial suprastructure that is "superadded to structures that exist separately in our consciousness in the anesthetic state, the whole acquiring a new quality or value by virtue of the mutual actions and reactions that that specific structuralization produces in each technique" (p. 444). In every artistic domain, then, the work of art is "a play of technical combinations," of structure against structure. The structures may be compared "to the *cells* that live their own life by and for themselves in an organism that also lives another life by and for itself as much as by and for them. *Art is not a transcendence, but a transstructure*" (p. 445).

Lalo is quite scornful of supernatural or metaphysical "explanations" of musical beauty. Analysis of the triad will produce no evaluation of triadic leitmotiv in Wagner, he insists, nor will analysis of the diatonic tetrachord explain the Lento of Beethoven's Sixteenth Quartet or his "Ode to Joy": "We glimpse at least in what direction the realist or positivist exploration of aesthetic systems must be oriented: every masterpiece is assuredly a miracle, but once again, miracle of transstructure, and not of transcendence" (p. 448).

With the influence of structuralism and of linguistics in particular, there was a proliferation of analyses of music, or even of one element of music—rhythm or melody, for example—into strata or components. The components were sometimes theoretical rather than audible, but the conception of music that was implicit in such studies was nevertheless one of musical objectivity and autonomy, as it is in the various branches of musical theory. In their specific structural focus, however, these studies are no longer part of the history of aesthetics; they belong instead to the history of theory.

Something similar can be said about the tendency of objectivism toward the detailed analysis of individual compositions. For just as a conception of musical objectivity, in opposing or ignoring any relation music may have to human experience and feeling, permits the ordering and organization of musical material on the basis of purely abstract principles, so it also leads to an aesthetic that contains no explicit reference to feelings and that tends to deal either with analysis or with detailed technical instructions for performance with respect to the physical arrangements of instruments, singers, and electronic equipment. Even with the broadest construal of the term *aesthetics*, however, descriptive detail of these kinds can hardly be considered to belong to the field; rather, they belong to the field of *theory* in some sense of the word.

A broad conception of musical stratification can be found in the *Aesthetik* (1953) of Nicolai Hartmann. This conception is probably best considered here since it belongs both to the sphere of musical objectivity and to the sphere of "meaning," in the inclusive sense given to this concept in the preceding chapter. Hartmann divides music primarily into a foreground and a background. The foreground is "real"; it is the sensuously audible, the perceived tonal succession as far as retention holds it together, and what is "heard together" in this way is a tonal configuration of only a few seconds in duration. The background, in contrast, is "unreal" and consists of several strata. Of these the first is what is musically rather than sensuously audible. It rests on a complex process of synthesis that is totally different from the synthesis that takes place in purely acoustic hearing, for a musical piece or movement cannot really be heard together in a sensuous-acoustic way; at any instant, only a fragment of it is actually present to hearing. Yet the whole is grasped as a unity, and only on the basis of this whole does each detail acquire its sense. A musical work is the unreal "musical background" that is heard "through" the sensible sounding succession. In the work of the composer, this changing foreground is actually determined by the background, just as it is in the other arts.

The status of the musical background, however, is itself split into a number of strata that are composed first of phrases and then of larger unities created by the recurrence, variation, or development of themes. These strata are followed by the stratum of "movements" and finally by the whole multimovement work. Beyond these lie the inner strata of music—those of subjective, emotive, or extramural "content." Hartmann stresses the peculiar relation of the inner strata to the inner experience of the listener:

> Of course every work of art demands from the perceiver an inner accompaniment or a joint consummation: painting and sculpture a joint viewing as the artist "views," poetry a joint imagining as the poet imagines. This can be intensified in these also to the state of being swept along. But in music this assumes an altogether different essential form: being taken hold of and carried away is here from the outset the central matter: seen subjectively, one can describe it by saying that one's own inner life is totally taken up by the motion of the tonal work and drawn into its mode of movement; this communicates itself to the soul and in the joint consummation becomes its own. By this the object relation is actually suspended and transformed into something different: the music penetrates into the listener, as it were, and in the listening becomes his.

He subsequently adds to this:

> Yet music remains objective. How is that possible? Here lies an antinomy that must be resolved. For with the entrance of the listening ego into the music the "across from" indeed disappears. Thus how can it sustain itself? And how can the inner strata into which we feel ourselves removed remain equally well objects of our contemplation that also continuously preserve the required aesthetic distance? [35]

Hartmann distinguishes three inner strata: that of the direct sympathetic vibration of the listener, with the feeling of being led along or even carried away; that in which the listener is affected to the depths of his soul; and that of the ultimate or the metaphysical. The various strata of music, or of art in general, are connected by Hartmann with his general ontology. Basically, he maintains, the aesthetic object contains the same ontic strata that make up the structure of the real world: thing, life, soul, and mind. But in art each of these is further split up, "and indeed very differently split up in the various arts" (p. 458).

This elaborate theory of musical stratification, however, with all its discernment and detail, has been criticized by Ingarden as fundamentally misconceived. The basis of Ingarden's criticism is a strict definition of stratified structure as calling for diverse elements, a continuous texture of constructs of each element (a stratum) that remains a distinguishable member of the totality of the work, and an organic connection among the diverse elements that binds them into the totality. "But a work of pure music," Ingarden argues, "is not characterized by a stratified structure: it has only one stratum. Although a musical work is not homogeneous, nevertheless its diverse elements are not related into strata in the sense in question. Ingarden believes that there are various nonsounding elements in musical works and that such elements in fact play the chief role in musical "beauty." But he insists that they "do not form separate strata in the work, nor in particular do they constitute a distinct stratum in relation to what constitutes sound, or a certain clustered structure of sounds. They are so closely tied to sounds and sound-constructs that the musical work forms an extremely compact and cohesive whole and in this respect outshines work in the other arts, especially literature." [36]

In Ingarden's opinion, Hartmann operates with a different and unclear conception of stratum in art and confuses it in addition with the concept of stratum that Ingarden has defined for a literary work. For Hartmann, it would seem, objects constitute a stratum if they constitute an ontic base for objects of a different kind and if they designate objects of this different kind. Thus, the acoustic foreground of a musical work, for example, would fulfill the functions of an ontic base and an intentional designation of the background. It is not a stratum in Ingarden's sense, however, for—again in Ingarden's sense—it is not even an element of the work. It would appear, then, that Ingarden's argument with Hartmann rests on both a different concept of *stratum* and a different concept of *musical work*.

The objectivity of music, finally, is an implicit foundation of the ideas of John Cage, who, very much like Stockhausen, is as well known for his aesthetics as for his music. Indeed, in challenging basic conceptions of music, his compositions themselves often compel aesthetic speculation about what music essentially is. Cage is also reminiscent of Charles Ives in that his ideas were to a great extent not derived from or influenced by European thought; in comparison with the ideas of Stockhausen, for example, they represent more an experimental mentality than a systematic one.

Cage's central belief is that music will not continue to be constituted almost entirely of tones but will be made up of sound in general, including even environmental sound. Thus, noise and electronically produced sound will play a part in music, which will then consist of organized sound, or really of sound and silence, whether this material is selected and arranged consciously in every respect or distributed entirely or partially by chance. Ideas of this kind were formulated by Cage in a talk delivered in 1937 and eventually found their way into his *Silence* (1961):

Wherever we are, what we hear is mostly noise. When we ignore it, it disturbs us. When we listen to it, we find it fascinating. The sound of a truck at fifty miles per hour. Static between the stations. Rain. We want to capture and control these sounds, to use them not as sound effects but as musical instruments. Every film studio has a library of "sound effects" records on film. With a film phonograph it is now possible to control the amplitude and frequency of any one of these sounds and to give to it rhythms within or beyond the reach of the imagination. Given four film phonographs, we can compose and perform a quartet for explosive motor, wind, heartbeat, and landslide.[37]

Just as the duality of consonance and dissonance was transformed into a graduation of tension in atonality and serialism, so Cage's projection of a universal employment of types of sound will replace the consonance-dissonance duality with a new one: "Whereas, in the past, the point of disagreement has been between dissonance and consonance, it will be, in the immediate future, between noise and so-called musical sounds" (p. 4). Conventional musical notation will also require replacement by a more general notational system:

The present methods of writing music, principally those which employ harmony and its reference to particular steps in the field of sound, will be inadequate for the composer, who will be faced with the entire field of sound. The composer (organizer of sound) will be faced not only with the entire field of sound but also with the entire field of time. The "frame" or fraction of a second, following established film technique, will probably be the basic unit in the measurement of time. No rhythm will be beyond the composer's reach. (pp. 4–5)

The principle of form, Cage concludes, will be our only connection with the past. Particularly interesting to Cage—doubtless as a confirmation of his ideal of generalization—is his discovery that sounds can be detected even in what seem at first to be intervals of silence:

For in this new music nothing takes place but sounds: those that are notated and those that are not. Those that are not notated appear in the written music as silences, opening the doors of the music to the sounds that happen to be in the environment. This openness exists in the fields of modern sculpture and architecture. The glass houses of Mies van der Rohe reflect their environment, presenting to the eye images of clouds, trees, or grass, according to the situation. And while looking at the constructions in wire of the sculptor Richard Lippold, it is inevitable that one will see other things, and people too, if they happen to be there at the same time, through the network of wires. There is no such thing as an empty space or an empty time. There is always something to see, something to hear. In fact, try as we may to make a silence, we cannot. (pp. 7–8)

Cage tells of his experience in an anechoic room. When he entered, he heard two sounds, one high and one low: "When I described them to the engineer in charge, he informed me that the high one was my nervous system in operation, the low one my blood in circulation. Until I die there will be sounds. And they will continue following my death. One need not fear about the future of music" (pp. 7–8). What clearly is at stake here is the elimination of any distinction between art and nature (or between artistic experience and ordinary experience): "Any sounds may occur in any combination and in any continuity. And it is a striking coincidence that just now the technical means to produce such a free-ranging music are available." But one may also give up the desire to control sound and "let sounds be themselves rather than vehicles for man-made theories or expressions of human sentiments" (p. 8). One implication of this approach is that synchronization becomes artificial, for if we allow sounds to be themselves and accept the sounds we do not intend, the synchronization called for in a conventional score will not be an accurate representation of how things are. Thus, we may compose parts but not scores and then combine these parts in a variety of random ways: "This means that each performance of such a piece of music is unique, as interesting to its composer as to others listening" (p. 11).

The only relation Cage accepts between sound and human feeling is the automatic one of stimulus and response, for the emotions of human beings "are continually aroused by encounters with nature" (p. 10). As a mountain evokes a sense of wonder or night in the forest a sense of fear, so sounds in themselves evoke feelingful responses. But this is the objectivity of normal experience, and it can be increased only by explicitly invoking an artificial attitude of detachment or adhering to a musical style that is consciously made uneventful.

CHAPTER FOURTEEN

THE PHENOMENOLOGY
OF MUSIC

T he modern discipline of phenomenology had its beginning in the late nineteenth century, in the work of Edmund Husserl. Types of investigation that can be considered phenomenological, however, can be found much earlier. Hegel used the designation *phenomenology* in a sense not entirely different from the modern one, and we can with considerable justice call the musical theory of Aristoxenos phenomenological in fact if not in name. The same is true of book 6 of Augustine's *De musica* and of the philosophy of time in book 11 of his *Confessions*. Yet the concentration on methodology, together with the continuous development of the field, is sufficient to distinguish twentieth-century phenomenology from any earlier manifestations.

One of Husserl's investigations, in fact, the "Lectures on the Phenomenology of the Inner Consciousness of Time," which deals with a matter of central importance to phenomenology in general, is so fundamental to the phenomenological examination of music that it can be considered to represent the inception of this specialized field. As an instrument of peculiar appropriateness to the study of consciousness, tonal experience plays an important part in the investigation, just as it did in Augustine's studies of memory.

Husserl's work on the consciousness of time (1905–10) deals with one of the most fundamental processes of consciousness: the temporal constitution of a pure datum of sensation:

> The question still remains how the apprehension of transcendent temporal objects which extend over a duration of time is to be understood. . . . Objects of this kind are constituted in a multiplicity of immanent data and apprehensions which themselves run off as a succession. Is it possible to combine these successive expiring, representa-

tive data in one now-moment? In that case a completely new question arises, namely, how, in addition to "temporal objects," both immanent and transcendent, is time itself, the duration and succession of objects, constituted? . . .

It is indeed evident that the perception of a temporal object itself has temporality, that perception of duration itself presupposes duration of perception, and that perception of any temporal configuration what- soever has its temporal form. And, disregarding all transcendencies, the phenomenological temporality which belongs to the indispensable essence of perception according to all its phenomenological constitu- ents still remains. Since objective temporality is always phenomeno- logically constituted and is present for us as objectivity and moment of an objectivity according to the mode of appearance only through this constitution, a phenomenological analysis of time cannot explain the constitution of time without reference to the constitution of the tempo- ral object. . . . When a tone sounds, my objectifying apprehension can make the tone which endures and sounds into an object, but not the duration of the tone or the tone in its duration.[1]

In examining immanent, or internal, perception more closely, Husserl em- phasizes the certainty and self-evidence of temporal extension. Perceptions that are purely intuitive, he affirms, are truly constitutive of enduring (or of changing) objects as such; they contain in themselves nothing further that is questionable. It is a continuous tone, as usual, that provides Husserl's example:

Let us now consider the self-evident consciousness of duration and ana- lyze this consciousness itself. If the note C is perceived (and not merely the quality C, but the entire tonal content, which must remain abso- lutely unaltered) and given as enduring, then the note C is extended over an interval of the immediate temporal field, i.e., another note does not appear in each now but always and continually the same note. That the same note always appears, that there is this continuity of identity, is an internal characteristic of consciousness. The temporal positions are not separated from one another through divisive acts. The unity of per- ception is here a breachless unity which dispenses with all interrupting internal differences. On the other hand, differences do exist as far as every temporal point is distinct from every other—only distinct, how- ever, not separated. The indistinguishable likeness of temporal matter and the constancy of the modification of the time-positing conscious- ness essentially establish the coalescence into unity of the breachless extension, and therewith a concrete unity first comes into being. Only as temporally extended is the note C a concrete individual. . . . The breachless unity of the note C, which is the primary given, proves to be a divisible unity, a coalescence of moments ideally to be distinguishable therein. (p. 112)

But the flux of consciousness that constitutes temporal objects is itself subject to investigation, although not to constitution as an object. This flux Husserl takes to represent absolute subjectivity. An examination of the temporal constitution of melody as well as tone enters subsequently into a consideration of the absolute flux of consciousness:

Subjective time is constituted in absolute, timeless consciousness, which is not an Object. Let us reflect now as to how this absolute consciousness attains givenness. We have a tonal appearance; we pay attention to the appearance as such. In such a thing as the sound of a violin (materially considered) the tonal appearance has its duration, and in this duration its constancy or alteration. I can pay attention to any phase of this appearance whatsoever (appearance is here the immanent tonal stimulus, apart from its "significance"). This, however, is not the final consciousness. This immanent sound is "constituted," i.e., continuous with the actual tonal now; we also have tonal shadings. In fact, exhibiting itself in these is the interval of tonal pasts which belong to this now. We can in some degree attend to this series. With a melody, for example, we can arrest a moment, as it were, and discover therein shadings of memory of the past notes. It is obvious that the same holds true for every individual note. We have, then, the immanent tonal now and the immanent tonal pasts in their series or continuity. In addition, however, we must have the following continuity: perception of the now and memory of the past; and this entire continuity must itself be a now. In fact, in the living consciousness of an object, I look back into the past from the now point out. On the other hand, I can grasp the entire consciousness of an object as a now and say: now I seize the moment and grasp the entire consciousness as an all-together, as an all-at-once. (pp. 150–51)

Analysis of this kind is clearly fundamental to the whole phenomenology of music and to the psychology of musical perception as well. It also provides a basis for the explanation of many fundamental issues in musical aesthetics— the relevance of the concept of "form," for example, to an art of "temporal succession."

Husserl's investigation of the consciousness of time was directed more specifically to music by the social philosopher Alfred Schutz, in his "Fragments on the Phenomenology of Music," which dates from 1944 but was not published until 1976. Basic to Schutz's conception of the musical work, which he recognizes as an "ideal object," is his contention that it must be grasped "polythetically" rather than "monothetically": "The work of music itself . . . can only be recollected and grasped by reconstituting the polythetic steps in which it has been built up, by reproducing mentally or actually its development from the first to the last bar as it goes on in time.[2] But this conception leads to problems, and Schutz questions whether the antithesis "polythetic-monothetic" is not applicable only to "operational processes of the mind within a conceptual scheme of reference" (p. 32). If music exists in inner time, why is it not experienced as a unit, the way the flight of an arrow is? Schutz wonders if the phenomenological method can really account for musical experience or if music may not expand phenomenological theory.

Since music takes place in inner time, Schutz reviews the properties of retentions and reproductions and of protentions and anticipations, presenting a compact restatement of Husserl's analysis. He feels that this analysis gives a wrong impression, however, because language is atomistic: "It dissects the continuity into pieces; it creates the impression of parts and pieces, where a single indivisible unit should be depicted" (p. 41). Schutz is strongly influenced by the *durée* of Bergson, and he is led to the specious present:

> The vivid present encompasses everything that is actually lived through, it includes elements of the past retained or recollected in the Now and elements of the future entering the Now by way of protention or anticipation. . . . It may include very unequal elements of the past and the future. Its shape will depend upon what Bergson calls the tension of our consciousness, and this tension itself is merely a function of our attention toward life. (p. 42)

Members of the musical audience, then, "are no longer engaged in the dimension of space and spatial time" (p. 43). They surrender to the flux of music, which is that of their stream of consciousness in inner time.

A phenomenological analysis of music, Schutz continues, must take into account the existence of some frame of reference at the disposal of the listener, for only this will permit protentions (anticipations). But there are also certain elements found in all musical experience, for this always takes place in the flux of inner time; it is based on the faculty of recollection and anticipation, and it contains a theme, which may recur, be modified, or be combined with other themes. (The presence of a theme, of course, cannot be regarded as an indispensable feature of music.)

Schutz then presents a phenomenological analysis of a sequence of tones (C-D-E-C-D-D), pointing out instances of retention, passive recognition, and protention. He proceeds to a discussion of certain basic categories of all musical experience. The first of these is continuance-repetition (in the case of a single tone) or continuance-intermittence (in the case of a succession of different tones). Continuance-repetition is applicable to themes as well as to tones, for what follows a theme can be anticipated as a continuation, or a theme can be repeated. Another category is sameness, which again applies to a single tone or to a theme. Sameness in music, or in inner time, however, is actually recurrent likeness rather than numerical unity.

The difference between listening and reflection is considered at length by Schutz. While listening is directed toward music as its object, reflection is directed toward the act of listening as its object. In listening, the theme is an indivisible unit. This unity is produced by the interplay of the retentional and protentional mechanism of consciousness, but this mechanism becomes sensible only on reflection. To the listener, in any event, the unity of a theme or motive implies that his experience has phases of flight alternating with phases of rest. Schutz connects meaning with the phases of rest, when the mind adopts a reflective attitude toward its own experiences: "An experience while occurring, that is, while we are living in it, does not have any meaning; only the past experiences toward which we may turn back, are meaningful" (p. 61). Meaning is explicitly defined as "the attitude of the experiencing mind towards its past experiences" (p. 62).

More generally, reflection retains or reproduces certain past experiences, bringing them into our specious present, and this selection from the past is different for each successive act of reflection. Some recollections are imposed on us by similarity, for example, to the present experience; others are selected by the direction of our interest and attention. Besides recollection, which is involved in reflection, we "remember" a stock of continuously available knowledge that acts as a determinant of our anticipation.

After the constitution of a theme, Schutz remarks, it can be recollected as an entity with a particular meaning and recognized even when modified. "Finally, it may become entirely familiar, it will be known in such a way that no recollection will be necessary. It has been remembered and is now at hand" (p. 67). This final familiarity of the thematic entity, however, contradicts Schutz's previous insistence that music must always be constituted polythetically. It would seem to suggest also that an entire musical work might become very much like a concept, thus amenable to monothetic constitution.

Husserl conceived phenomenology as a universal instrument of investigation, as much applicable to concepts, for example, as to sense experience. In the writings of Roman Ingarden, the Polish phenomenologist who was a student of Husserl's, the object of study is not the perceptual experience of art but the work of art, which Ingarden calls "a purely intentional object." An initial version of this type of investigation in music—"Das Musikwerk"—was written in 1928, translated in large part into Polish in 1933 and published in that year as "The Problem of the Identity of the Musical Work." It was rewritten in German in 1957 and published in 1962 in Ingarden's volume *Untersuchungen zur Ontologie der Kunst*.

Ingarden devotes himself first to the distinction between the musical work and the performances of this work. The work does not possess all the properties of its performances. It persists in time; it is not determined by actual physical processes; it is not definitely localized in space; it does not become perceptible in various aspects; it is a unique individuality as opposed to the multiplicity of its performances; as the entity defined by the score, it is not uniquely determined in all possible respects, although this may not be true of it as the correlate of an aesthetic conception.

It is shown next that the musical work is not identical with mental experiences. The auditory data of sensation that we experience in hearing are radically different from the tones and tonal images that we perceive. The tonal images are objects of perception; the sensible auditory data are merely experienced in the consummation of this perception. It requires a peculiar reflection for them to be raised to full consciousness. A tone that lasts for several seconds is perceived as one and the same; the simultaneously experienced sensational data, in contrast, form a continuous multiplicity and are continually new. On the basis of the data, the tone is *intended;* it is an objectivation, an object perceived through an interpretation belonging to the nature of perception. Since all the components of a performance are thus objects "to which we have reference in the consummation of acts of perception," the performances of a work are definite objectivities. The work itself is different from these: "The musical work, with respect to the perceptual experiences in which the individual performances are given and through the assistance of which and so to speak on the basis of which the work is intended and in its true selfness grasped, is transcendent in a still higher degree than its performances. It forms so to speak a transcendence of the second order." Musical works are therefore not mental experiences "but only objectivities of an entirely special kind and manner of being."[3]

Ingarden demonstrates next that the musical work cannot be identified with the score. For one thing, not every work is written down. Beyond this, the score is a system of symbols on paper, with properties that the represented work does not have, and vice versa. Symbols are different from what they represent.

It is then shown that the musical work is not a real object, for it does not exist or take place in a here and now. Further, the work possesses both acoustic and nonacoustic components. It has a tonal foundation (tones, phrases, sections, and so on, with melodic, harmonic, rhythmic, and other properties), and various extra-acoustic components: rhythm and tempo, motion, forms, emotional qualities, "expressed" feelings, representational motives, and aesthetic values.

The mode of being of the musical work is then defined as that of a purely intentional object. Ingarden closes his discussion with the problem of the unity (or wholeness) of the musical work and with the problem of its identity. The wholeness is a gestalt of higher order that encompasses or arises from smaller gestalten, ultimately melodies and motives. Pauses in a work are not interruptions; they belong to the immanent time of the work. The identity of a musical work cannot be questioned if the work is defined as the intentional counterpart of the score, for then it has a schematic foundation that remains unchanged in the course of history. If the work is defined as the counterpart of an ideal aesthetic object, we will be faced with the insoluble problem of finding a perfect, ideal performance. Instead, we will be able to find only an intersubjective aesthetic object that is relative to a specific musical community and that changes historically. An appeal to the score, however, can justify the conception of the musical work as a transhistorical image, for the supposed historical change in the work will then appear to be only "*a process of the discovery and actualization of continually new possibilities of the potential forms of the work that belong to its schema*" (p. 134). The limits of this process, however, are set by the score, and a different work will result if they are exceeded.

Ingarden's effort to develop a rigorous determination of the musical work is perhaps overly painstaking, and his discussion encompasses digressions into matters that do not always seem connected with his theme. But the redundancy and the scope of his tract are doubtless due to his desire to elaborate the consideration of the musical work into a comprehensive philosophy of music and to relate it in addition to corresponding theories in the other arts.

A remarkably detailed and concrete investigation of the temporal nature of music, but one that does not represent itself as phenomenological, is contained in Gisèle Brelet's monumental work *Le Temps musical: Essai d'une esthétique nouvelle de la musique* (1949). Like Ingarden's treatise, but more explicitly, this massive work seeks to present a complete musical aesthetics under the head of a specific theme. The treatise is divided into three parts, dealing with, respectively, "sonorous form," "rhythmic form," and "musical form." These are preceded by a lengthy introduction that deals with the different temporal properties of the various arts and with the contrast between the transcendental aesthetics of music as found in Schopenhauer and Bergson and the immanent metaphysics that Brelet will present. Needless to say, it is impossible to represent the contents of so voluminous a work (753 pages of text) or even to characterize the contents adequately on the basis of a few selected passages. We can expect only that our brief discussion will convey a general idea of the nature of the treatise.

After a general consideration of the relation of sonority to time and to space, the first part, "La Forme sonore," examines in turn the temporal course of melody, the nature of melodic expression, the nontemporal character of harmony, and the connection between harmony and thought. Brelet finds the foundation of "sonorous form" in the interplay of melody and harmony: of expression and thought. This fundamental polarity appears in a variety of forms. It exists in harmony itself, in which Brelet, taking issue with Bergson, finds a distinction that is not spatial:

> The primary fact of music—the significance of which is immense for the problem of musical time—is that there exists a nonspatial distinction, but one purely interior and qualitative: that of harmony. The "interval" (intermediary space) seems to be an essentially spatial notion, but it applies equally to time and to sound, and the question is to know if it then does not shed its spatiality. If it is true, as Bergson thought, that *durée* [inner duration] is continuity and fusion, every distinction effected in it would then appear as the expression of an intrusion of space; but there exists precisely a qualitative distinction that is properly temporal, which it is the very character of the harmonic interval to incarnate.[4]

The significance of this becomes clear in what follows, when Brelet begins to define the fundamental duality in music on the twofold basis of proximity of pitch and harmonic partials:

> We have distinguished two series that are necessary and sufficient for the definition of sonority as well as for the constitution of music: the series of pitches and the series of tonal qualities; these are really derivatives of the so-called two components of pitch: "height" and "tonicity." Now the series of tonal qualities, as we shall see, is founded on the harmonic relations that fix the tones of the scale, that is to say, on the perpetual return of analogous and related sonorities. Thus harmony, in melodizing itself in the scale, by no means loses its internal unity but transmits it to time itself and continues to unite, in time and in spite of time, the sonorities that there are successive, by a qualitative relatedness. Harmony unites in succession what space separates, just as it separates what space unites. (p. 106)

Brelet refers to the spatial representation of the two series, which is given by a spiral that rises vertically from low to high pitch. On this there can be shown clearly the separation and individuality of "tonicity" and "height." The tones of the scale, she points out, are united by two types of relation: spatial proximity and tonal kinship or consonance. Thus, the shortest interval harmonically is the fifth, but spatially the second, while the octave is harmonically almost one and the same tone, but spatially a considerable distance. The second, on the other hand, is the shortest interval spatially, but an extreme leap harmonically. Spatial and harmonic relations are the inverse of one another.

This duality is ubiquitous in music. One of its most prominent manifestations can be seen in tendency tones and their resolution:

> Attraction and consonance, these are the two fundamental principles of music and almost the very essence of melody and harmony: on the one hand there is *tendency*, virtual and temporal, on the other *possession*, actual and sufficient. And these two principles symbolize the underlying character of time itself and that ambiguity in it of an *élan* always unsatisfied and unconsummated and of a present always consummated and sufficient, both the one and the other simultaneously repulsing and summoning each other.
>
> Harmony, immobile form, delimits the frame and the structure of melodic succession; and the pure movement of melody tends toward harmonic repose, the virtuality of becoming toward sonorous actuality. What the ear accepts as pure passage it will not accept as repose; the melodic tone is essentially a "passing note," and it is in this way that its indetermination assumes sense and value. (p. 116)

The basic duality is not confined to the traditional Western tonal system but extends, in Brelet's conception, to all music. This is made quite explicit, for example, in her discussion of the tendency tone: "Indetermination is almost the fruit and the very mark of the becoming that inheres in tendency, and the *universality of the notion of leading tone* in the most diverse musics attests that the expression of this becoming in melody is one of the fundamental and permanent aspects of musical time" (p. 117). To be sure, Brelet's study is concentrated essentially on Western tonality and Western music, but it is not restricted to these. In considering melodic closure, for example—the departure from and return to the tonic, which is a larger instance of the underlying duality of motion and rest—Brelet draws atonality into her discussion. The tonic "is only the provisional messenger of the nontemporality of an act," she maintains. "And one can imagine that this nontemporality may be otherwise expressed, that the return of the melody to its origin may be conveyed in a less brutal, less obvious, more subtle manner than by a return to the tonic" (p. 177).

The second and least novel part of Brelet's treatise, "La Forme rhythmique," treats of the general character of musical rhythm, the interaction of rhythm and meter, the temporal structure of rhythm as experienced, the relation of rhythm to musical time, and the relation of musical time to tempo. An important feature of her discussion, once again, is a reliance on basic dualities that underlie and account for the audible manifestations. Also of considerable interest is a reliance on parallels between rhythmic form and sonorous form; the second sphere is presented as a counterpart of the first.

Brelet's conception of musical rhythm is readily grasped in her discussion of the relation between rhythm and musical time. Rhythm reveals musical time more clearly than tone does, she maintains, for it abstracts the essence of musical time. The rhythmic figure is like the melodic figure: it is a synthesis of the flow of time, the theme of the rhythm, which is thus constructed by the repetition and variation of a nontemporal theme, by the introduction of permanences, recurrences, into process. In all this, rhythm is obviously conceived as a counterpart of melody.

But rhythm has sense, Brelet continues, only if it is inserted into subjectivity, where the theme and variation become a dialectic of expectations and surprise. Also, the rhythmic theme is like the musical theme in that it sets up a future and creates a desire for its return: "The law of rhythm, in primitive music just as in Occidental music, is *variation within repetition*: for rhythmic time, like musical time, is simultaneously rational time, subjected to the principle of identity, and inner time, in which the creative heterogeneity of duration is respected, the acceptance and refusal of time" (p. 361).

The third and most extended part of the treatise, "La Forme musicale," examines in turn musical expression, the relation between psychological duration and musical time, the relation between form and expression, the nature of musical thought and musical concepts, the character and types of temporal feeling, and the basic temporal types of music, particularly, the music of becoming and the music of rational time. There is also a concluding discussion of musical time and the philosophy of time.

The discussion of psychological duration and musical time is of critical importance for Brelet's whole conception of musical form. Musical time is aesthetic, Brelet argues, because it is contemplated time, not immediate psychological duration. It is not abstract, however, but fully alive as well as fully intelligible. It reconciles life and intellectuality, which reveal themselves in it as intimately related rather than opposed. The musical work, therefore, like sonority itself, makes us experience the intelligibility of time, so that we live and think in the same act. And it can do this only because musical creation is a reconquest of the musical time intrinsic to sonority itself; it is "*the ascent* of the creator *from psychological duration to musical time*" (p. 424). Far from being a pure negation of psychological duration, musical time is the ascent of this duration to its highest powers, where it discovers the secret essence of itself, casts off its inertia and inefficacy, and secures plenitude and creative dynamism.

A paradox is contained in musical time, Brelet continues, for it is intelligible and lived, a stable structure and a moving duration, an eternal form and a flowing dynamism. The ultimate qualitative immediacy of musical time is mediately obtained; it arises in us from the comprehension of a form that would seem to be its negation. This form, which is responsible for the objectivity of musical time, can recreate a singular duration indefinitely, a duration that can live again without doubt, in its eternal freshness, only because it is sustained by the essence of time appearing through it.

Brelet returns to the musical time that is immanent in sonority or tone. Tone cuts off a portion of time, which it organizes, in her conception, since in unfolding it unifies its diverse moments. As the union of permanence and change, tone determines unaided the fundamental law of all musical form, for this also "develops" in time and also associates a principle of permanence with a principle of change. More specifically, the time immanent in tone is both form and experienced duration, for tone incarnates the fundamental action of psychological duration: it effects a union between remembrance and expectation; "it makes us live in that metaphysical time in which evolution is the captive of the eternal present":

> But is it not precisely in this metaphysical time that the antinomy of psychological duration and musical time is resolved? Tone is simultaneously form and duration, but is it not because it is true duration that its temporal form is a living one, and is it not because true duration is close to the nontemporal that the duration in it does not contradict the form? In the eternal present of tone, form and duration join, for it is in the present that becoming collects and realizes itself and that temporal form, accompanying the becoming, can thus be born. And tone, which is at once psychological duration and musical time, and which subordinates the one to the other, . . . prefigures the very ascent toward temporal wisdom that constitutes the inmost process of musical creation. (pp. 428–29)

The relation between psychological duration and musical time subsequently becomes the basis of a typology of musical styles according to the nature of their temporal constitution—a typology that comprises the major subject matter of the third part of the treatise. Musical creation, Brelet reminds us, is the ascent of psychological duration toward musical time, for the nontemporal time of the musical work arises from the demise of spontaneous duration. In this ascent, however, the creator stops sometimes further from and sometimes closer to psychological duration: "It may be that he wishes to preserve this at any price, that he forces musical time to gather it up in its fragility and its very imperfection: alongside of musics that have ascended fully to musical time there are those that have remained close to pure duration and that have attempted to inscribe it on sonorous form" (p. 592). The result, Brelet continues, is that spontaneous duration is subjected to form and thought, and music expresses not only this duration but also the manner in which it is conceived. Even the music of becoming—in fact, especially the music of becoming—shows us more than any other that all music realizes a certain conception of time. Whether it is a question of Classical music or Romantic music—of that which chooses being or that which chooses becoming—their particular techniques are always the expression of a certain fundamental option, a certain will to form, from which the coherence of the musical work arises.

The formal types Brelet distinguishes are essentially those of the polarity Classical-Romantic, but to each of these there is attached a subtype. Thus, two additional styles are considered, typified, respectively, by the music of Stravinsky and Bach. In fact, the styles described are really those of individual composers: Romanticism is represented by Wagner, as its subtype is by Bach and the Classical subtype by Stravinsky. Only Classicism in its basic eighteenth-century form does without a particular representation by an individual composer. The whole schematic duality is quite symmetrical and clearly more systematic than historical in nature.

It is obviously a paradox, Brelet begins, to express the immediate process of consciousness in the eternality of form, yet we can see in the music of Wagner, for example, an expression in sound of temporal conceptions of duration that are the same as those of Schopenhauer or Nietzsche. Classical music expresses a rationalism of time, which is manifested in square rhythm, tonality, and thematism, all of which permit musical form to close on itself harmoniously outside everyday time. This music fulfills itself in the actuality of sonority. In contrast to the Classicist, who accepts only a duration that is transparent to intelligence, the Romanticist rejects clear intelligibility: having chosen a desire that cannot be appeased, he is cut off from the serene enjoyment of sonority and from its perfect repose: "*Pure becoming destroys the intelligibility of sonority.* What connects chords is no longer the necessity of their relations but the contingency of dynamic relations freely instituted in them by the expressive will of the musician" (p. 595). Sound itself is transformed in Romanticism, for musical time cedes to vital becoming. Sound is no longer essence, in Brelet's phrase, but phenomenon; deprived of its autonomous reality, it remains only a symbol. The contrast can be put in more concrete terms also: "All music of pure becoming is atonal in essence since each tone, instead of being a stable element, becomes only a leading tone aspiring to move out of itself, the tone becoming only an imaginary pole and the instrument of a perpetual postponement" (p. 600).

Many of the concrete and technical features of music encompassed in Brelet's description are of fundamental importance. A characteristic example is the contrast between the role of the fifth in Classicism and the role of the third in Romanticism. Of equal importance is the discussion of repetition in the two styles—that is, of repetition and sequence, respectively:

> There is, we may say, a Classical repetition and a Romantic repetition, animated by two opposed feelings and conceptions of time. Now precisely what distinguishes the Classical theme from the Romantic theme is that, on being repeated, the one gathers up the work toward its origin while the other distances it from that origin, confirms becoming instead of surmounting it. *Classical repetition is permanence; Romantic repetition is growth.* (p. 613)

To some extent, in Brelet's broad view, the Classical-Romantic duality is generally supported by the equally familiar duality of harmony and melody:

> In a general way, *the music of becoming is characterized by the prevalence of melody, the incarnation of becoming.* While in the music of rational time it is harmony, the rationalizing element of musical becoming, that governs melody, in the music of becoming it is the emotivity of the melody, an expression of vital energy, that governs harmony, coming thus to introduce disturbance into its rational essence. (pp. 613–14)

Brelet is tireless in setting forth the technical and qualitative details of her central Classical-Romantic duality; indeed, the elaboration and length of her account inevitably entail repeated statements of many characteristic features.

The music of becoming is also manifested in polyphony, specifically, in the polyphony of Bach, which is thus coupled with the music of Wagner as a subtype or even a second type of "Romantic" style. (This pairing had already appeared, of course, in dualistic stylistic theories of the continual alternation of opposed styles throughout the history of Western music and of the Western visual arts as well. Curt Sachs's *Commonwealth of Art*, 1946, provides an elaborate example.) For Brelet, both Bach and Wagner stand opposed to Classical music; they are founded on a process of growth and decrease, and to this process all the aspects of polyphonic style are submitted. The curve of the contrapuntal line is an ascending one: "Like the becoming of a living being, the becoming of the contrapuntal curve expresses first of all its growth" (p. 647). The summits of successive curves, she maintains, often form between them an ascending or descending line, a curve of growth spread out in the large, in a long breath. Brelet finds other aspects of the phenomenon of growth in the progressive rhythmic animation of the melodic flow, in the transition to chromaticism, and even in the increasing amplitude of the successive smaller curves and of the intervals that compose them. To these various kinds of growth she then adds the fugue and the stretto.

The same conception of time, Brelet therefore argues, can unite differences as great as those between the Wagnerian harmonic style and the polyphonic style of Bach. Clearly, a systematic perspective has here superseded a historical one. Brelet proceeds, however, to the differences between the two styles. Each incarnates becoming with its own means. This is done in Bach in a less immediate way, for polyphonic rigor must consciously conquer the spontaneity of temporal experience. Ultimately, this devolves for Brelet into the fundamental difference between "lived time" and "thought time":

> In the final analysis, however, an irreducible difference separates musical becoming in Bach from that in Wagner: polyphony, a music of becoming, is faithful, in the heart of becoming itself, to the eternal present; and the lived time in which it has its source finds itself raised up and drawn along with it toward intelligible time, where finally there is accomplished and achieved the transparent and rigorous universe of its forms. (p. 653)

But it is a mistake on Brelet's part, certainly, to look for "formal rigor" where form is a joint product of music, text, and dramatic action. In any event, she traces the stability and calm majesty of becoming in Bach's polyphony to the prevalence in it of "thought time," without which it could not be constructed.

In a chapter on Classicism, or what Brelet calls "the music of rational time" or, alternatively, "the music of the eternal present," the characteristics of the two types of Classical style—eighteenth-century Classicism and the Classicism of Stravinsky—are discussed in detail. After characterizing the rhythm, harmony, and thematism of the earlier style, "the music of rational time," Brelet turns to the style of Stravinsky, "the music of concrete rational time."

The rational time of Classical form arrives at musical time only incompletely, Brelet explains, for it is always in some measure abstract and subservient to preliminary schemata:

It expresses understanding rather than creative thought; it is an "I think" turned toward its categories and unconscious of their source and of itself. And if Classical form unfolds most often in a spatialized time, it is because the Kantian "I think" of the Classical, forgetful of itself, depends more willingly on the object than on its act. Now living rational time can be the expression only of an act heedless of its effects and seeking form only in the depths of its spontaneity, and it is this concrete rational time that Stravinskian music presents to us. In it the "I think" of musical thought is no longer that imaginary pole, that empty form, that it is in Kant but *the living me of Fichte,* which is conscious of uniting in itself supreme intelligibility and supreme reality. (p. 678)

Stravinsky is a *classic* in the strongest sense of the term, Brelet affirms, for more than those so called, he has attained the very heart of Classicism: the experience of a time essentially submissive to the acts of reason.

Brelet further maintains that, while the music of rational time in general is ruled by the category of necessity, in eighteenth-century Classicism necessity never ruled with the authority and force that it has in Stravinsky, for here it is no longer imposed in any way from outside the creative act, which finds its liberty and the basis of its activity in the categories of musical thought and in the immanent laws of the sonorous material. For the musician of concrete rational time, the category of necessity not only rules over the completed objective work but also inspires the creative activity that produces it, which can proceed in Stravinsky's case only after he has chosen his own necessities, imposed his own limits on his material.

A discussion not easily understood, of "the eternal present," concludes the chapter. Brelet compares Stravinsky's music and primitive music, a comparison that is suggested particularly by the repetition that is so conspicuous in both. In primitive music, she states, the completely pure and spontaneous life of the musical time leads to an implicit knowledge of the primacy of the eternal, while in Stravinsky the explicit knowledge of this primacy leads immediately to the most intensely living musical time there is. The overflowing life that animates the pure and austere forms in both musics is the expression of the total victory of musical time over psychological duration. The musical time of Stravinsky actually ignores psychological duration and situates itself in vital and elementary duration or in spiritual duration:

In the musical time of Stravinsky, life seizes its own eternity and discovers its kinship with spirit. But inversely, the pure and wholly spiritual form of this musical time creates by itself alone and its devotion to the eternal an intense and superabundant life: for if it is an eternity of vital duration (since this is always chained to the eternal instant), it is also an eternity of spiritual duration, which is both similar and contrary, is chosen and imposed by will on the psychological duration in which the eternity of life had broken, and is more intensely living than the duration of ordinary life.

In musical time, as in real time, just as life is the source of the eternal present, the eternal present of activity is the source of life. For to live and to exist, for the musical work as for ourselves, is to surmount time. (pp. 689–90)

Brelet's treatise is both poetic and repetitious, but the repetition is justified to some extent by its contribution to the poetic quality. Of more importance is the question of whether her investigation of time is phenomenological. As we know from the work of Husserl, the phenomenology of time, or, more specifically, the phenomenology of the consciousness of time, is an established and critically important area of phenomenology, in which most of the essential features and methods of the subject were first elaborated and clearly revealed. Husserl's work, however, was evidently unknown to Brelet, and her study of musical time is in any event not really *phenomenological* in the strict sense of the term. She does not show systematically, for example, as Alfred Schutz and Roman Ingarden do, how the phenomenological objects of music—notably, tones, melodies, and the musical work—come into existence; nor does she discuss in detail, if at all, intentionality, the bracketing of reality, the relation of essence and history, or the perspectives and modes of existence of phenomenological objects. She does provide close and sensitive descriptions of the synthesis of past, present, and future in melody and of fundamental types of rhythmic, melodic, and harmonic style and form, all of which are indeed phenomenological in a general rather than technical sense of the term, but without any discussion—even without showing any awareness—of the phenomenological character of these aspects of music or of music as a whole. The interest, novelty, and value of Brelet's treatise are nevertheless considerable, for she has elaborated a convincing systematic picture of musical time that appears to extract the essence of music from the various forms of it found in history. In this procedure at least, her "immanent metaphysics" or "new aesthetics" bears a certain resemblance to Husserl's technique of free imaginative variation that is used to achieve insight into the essence of the phenomenological object.

Again in the work of Jeanne Vial, *De l'être musical* (1952), we are confronted with a mixture of ontology and phenomenology rather than with a strictly phenomenological investigation. Vial is a disciple of Gabriel Marcel, and the philosophical questions she finds in music are treated not as objective problems that can be analyzed and solved but as mysteries that must be participated in and understood as lived experience. Yet this conception is combined, paradoxically, with unusual clarity and accuracy of expression.

Vial's study of music is devoted largely to the nature and role of the concept, starting with the elementary concept of a note, such as is represented by the syllable "do," which she defines provisionally as "the possibility, founded on a resemblance, of evoking an infinitude of signs and of images and of classifying an infinitude of concrete tones."[5] All resemblance, she points out, implies reference to dissimilarities. It turns out that the concept of a note permits it to be situated, not only in relation to the infinite dyad of high and low, but also in relation to a scale, so that the concept implies a structure.

But how do we arrive at the concept of "do" from the tonal perception? Vial asks, and she proceeds to describe the process in close detail. It implies primarily a passage from presence to absence: "The concept of 'do' is in effect the thought of a tone that I am not hearing, that is not present, and this is why I evoke it, for if we were able to perceive the totality of the universe, to be present at every point in space, conceptual thought would become useless" (p. 71). The existence of the concept also implies a relation between the thought of absence and the immediate perception. The concept of a note, however, is defined by reference to a whole structural system, to a conceptual network, which exists because the concrete musical configuration is organic. Thus, it can be decomposed into phrases, intervals, and tones that take their sense only as a function of the whole:

These remarks trace the path to be followed in response to the questions that we have posed: we shall be able to define the *ontological* status of the concept only when we shall have specified the characteristics of concrete musical consciousness, shown the possibility of conceiving music that we are not hearing, and examined thoroughly the nature of this thought of absence. It is only then that we shall be able to comprehend the relation that exists between the organicity of the concrete and the abstract system of the scales. (p. 73)

Vial turns to what she calls "the hypothesis of the Ideas." "When I think of the concept of the octave," she affirms, appealing to the psychology of Laporte, "or of the resemblance of the octaves do^3-do^4, re^3-re^4, etc., the feeling that the constitutive tendencies of the memory and of the concept may be confounded, substitutes for the organic structure that is lived through in the concrete experience" (p. 87). But as such, Vial maintains, these tendencies are not sufficient to give an account of the quod of the concept, which also implies a determined Being. This Being,

far from identifying itself with singular fragmentary experiences, permits us on the contrary to adjudge these limited. It implies finally a conceptual network that has reference also to the abstract notion of the Universe. Of such a kind that everything takes place as if, between the rupture with total Being—a rupture that engenders a completely indeterminate knowledge, that is to say, an ignorance—and the singular memory—that is to say, the rupture with such and such a known concrete experience, but of which the memory gives to the concept its sense—a rupture is situated with the beings of which we do not have temporal experience but of which the memory gives to the concept its sense: everything takes place as if there was a Being or an *Idea* of "do." (p. 88)

To help justify the hypothesis of musical Ideas, Vial refers to an experience related by Étienne Souriau, which took place when he was striking a piano key for an orchestra to use as a standard pitch in tuning up. While he was mechanically striking the key, Souriau occupied himself in separating the tone from the multitude of jarring approximations that seemed somehow to imprison it:

> At this moment a sort of bizarre amaurosis hid from me at this point all that surrounded me so that I was barely conscious only of the swarming of phosphemes in my retinal field, a swarming that I thought I felt in my entire body. At the instant at which this fervid mist became almost opaque, I suddenly had a strange impression, that of seeing gleam in some way across the chaos the *tone itself,* my soul finding itself wholly impregnated with its pure truth; and just as in bathing at high tide one feels oneself rolling entirely dazed by too powerful a wave, I felt as in a shock the tone sound out, entirely abstract, with the nearly insupportable acuity of its perfection. (pp. 91–92)

Vial finds "a mysterious richness" in this experience: a thought that combines and surpasses the two habitual forms of knowledge—reflection and attention to the sensible present. For what is reflected on is not absent, and the attention to the sensible is not restricted. Like the remembrance feeling of Proust, the experience "transcends the opposition of temporal ecstasies, for it is the unveiling of an Idea, of a perfect presence" (p. 92). Every unison, Vial continues, seems to contain the promise of such an experience: "In the unison, concrete beings (of voices and of different tone colors) in effect are unified into a unique being, which appears from that time as a common act in relation to the parceled acts that compose it. The unison thus possesses a capacity of unifying concrete notes, a capacity weaker but analogous to that which the Idea possesses, to which the whole mass of real and possible concrete experiences refers" (p. 92).

The concept, it turns out, is an incomplete activity that refers, on the one hand, to sensible experience and, on the other, to the nontemporal Idea. We can comprehend how the child learns to speak, Vial points out, only through the relation of concept and idea. "It is in effect a mystery," she affirms, "that the child is capable of detaching the sign from the precise and unique experience to which it was first tied. There suffices in effect a single experience to release in him knowledge that overflows infinitely" (p. 96). The absent Idea must clarify the *hic et nunc* experience and then tie the sign to the concept, not to the *hic et nunc*.

In her "ontological conclusions," Vial situates the singular incarnations of the Idea (its sonorous executions or performances) between the concept and the Idea: "The clarification of the relations between the Idea and the sensible presence will permit us to accomplish the description of the ontological structure of musical being and of the three levels of thought that apprehend it: sensation, concept, idea" (pp. 125–26). Just as there is a concept of the note and an idea of the note, so there is a concept and an idea of the Ninth Symphony of Beethoven.

What characterizes conceptual thought, Vial tells us, is not the absence of incarnation but the imperfection of the acts serving as analogues. Music remains absent, she maintains, as long as we are conscious that the sensible is helping us evoke it. It is truly present only if the incarnation attains a certain degree of perfection.

Vial's view of the musical work as a concrete Idea is close to the conception of Schloezer. Both are rather unexpected in the context of twentieth-century thought, and in Vial's case idealism is combined with a phenomenology that can easily turn into the metaphysics of the "presence," or incarnation, of the musical work. But perhaps we should regard phenomenology itself as a strangely objectivized conception of subjectivity. In any event, the Idea of Beethoven's Ninth Symphony, along with its various incarnations, can serve the same explanatory purposes as Ingarden's purely intentional object, the musical work, and its various performances.

The tendency to turn phenomenology into metaphysics is one of the central characteristics of Victor Zuckerkandl's two-volume *Sound and Symbol* (1956–73). The first volume, which was evidently completed in 1948, bears the subtitle *Music and the External World*. It deals successively with tone, motion, time, and space, giving in fact but not in name a phenomenology of these four manifestations. In addition to taking a metaphysical view of phenomenological objects by locating them in the "external world," Zuckerkandl's work is unfortunately marred by an obtrusive pedagogical tone that suggests the schoolroom rather than the undiluted investigative interest of the scholar or the philosopher.

Tones have a dynamic quality, Zuckerkandl affirms; *re* is in a state of tension, which is a relation of *re* to *do,* specifically a striving of *re* toward *do.* This is the musical "meaning" of the tone, and it is impossible to imagine it without the tone: "What tones mean musically is completely one with them, can only be represented through them, exists only in them." [6] In the context of a diatonic melody or scale, then, tones assume dynamic meanings, which Zuckerkandl maintains are in the tones. How they get there, however, is a matter for which Zuckerkandl apparently believes no explanation can or need be offered.

Much the same position is taken for musical motion, space, and time. Zuckerkandl solves the problem of motion in which nothing is moving by the notion of a "third stage." He insists that music "comes from without," that it is "a phenomenon of the outer world." This is taken as a matter of fact, without any appeal to evidence or to perception. Yet music belongs neither to the physical world nor the world of the psyche, Zuckerkandl insists; rather, it

> makes us aware, unmistakably and inescapably, that "beyond the world of things and places" is *not,* as common belief has it, identical with the world of the psyche; nor is "beyond the world of the psyche" identical with the world of things and places. A *third stage* must exist which is neither the world of the psyche nor the world of bodies nor yet a mixture of both, and which stands to the two others in the relation of the general to the particular, of the primary to the derivative. Motion that takes place entirely on this stage is "pure" in the twofold sense that it is bound neither to things and places nor to a stream of consciousness. Such is the motion of tones—motion that has not yet been wedded to a body or a psyche, the purest, most primal form of motion that we know. (p. 145)

Again in connection with time, Zuckerkandl distinguishes musical time from physical time; musical time possesses intrinsic dynamic properties or forces. Meter and rhythm are not the causes of these forces but the result of them. The cycles of meter exist, he maintains, even when there are rests and syncopations in the music. Thus, music is not a temporal art only in the banal sense that its tones are given in succession, for temporal succession always occurs as a wave, and "the phenomena of meter and rhythm are productions of the forces active in the wave":

> The question arises, what is it that beats here as wave, what moves here? It is not the tones; it is not the hearer; what remains to be said except that it is time? The forces of the wave are forces of time—or better, are time as force. Hence the second formula runs: Music is temporal art in

the more exact sense that, for its ends, it enlists time as force. If, accordingly, meter and rhythm are cleared of the suspicion of owing their existence to a mere illusion, if the feeling of rhythm must be granted the status of a genuine experience, perhaps even of a cognition, then what is experienced or cognized in rhythm can be only time itself. A third formula follows: Music is temporal art in the special sense that in it time reveals itself to experience. (p. 200)

Zuckerkandl's conception of space is the most equivocal and the least convincing part of his theory. One of his characterizations of tone appears in a section with the puzzling title "Is Space Audible?" "Hearing a tone includes a sensation of 'without'; it is not a wholly unspatial experience. The listener is aware of space" (p. 274). Shortly after this, Zuckerkandl takes a somewhat different position:

We appear to be dealing with two space experiences that differ in essential points. The space experience of eye and hand is basically an experience of places and distinctions between places; and the space we see and touch, in which we also move, and which, finally, serves our science of space, our geometry, as starting point, has been defined as the *aggregate of all places*. The ear, on the other hand, knows space only as an undivided whole; of places and distinctions between places it knows nothing. The space we hear is a space without places. (p. 276)

Zuckerkandl then adopts the view that there is an auditory space and that it is always in motion:

As a creature who sees, I know space as something that is without and remains without, that confronts me—here I am, there it is, two worlds rigidly and permanently separated; as hearer, hearer of tone, who has no conception of a *"being* without," I know space as something *coming from* without, as something that is always directed toward me, that is always in motion toward me. According to this, the step from visual to auditory space would be like a transition from a static to a fluid medium. . . .

We see—and touch—a space in which things move; the statement that space itself moves is, for the eye and the hand, meaningless. But not for the ear. We hear a space that itself is in a sort of motion; we hear—to try another formulation—*"flowing space."* (pp. 277–78)

Still another notion of auditory space is the following: "At best it would have to be regarded as a sort of rudimentary spatiality, as something out of which genuine space may one day develop—if, that is, eye and hand lend their aid" (p. 279). In a subsequent discussion, Zuckerkandl offers a more detailed description:

> The space of tones, then, is a placeless depth surrounding the hearer or, more properly, directed toward him, moving toward him, from all about. The depth of this space is not the depth that, together with height and width, makes up the three dimensions of visual space. Height, width, depth—there are no such distinctions in auditory space. Here there is only the one "from . . ."—which, if we like, we may call the one dimension of auditory space. Here "from . . ." does not mean "from there or from elsewhere" but "out of the depth from all sides." . . . For him who hears, to perceive space means to be at the point toward which space as a whole is directed, toward which it flows together from all sides. The space experience of him who hears is an experience of space streaming in toward him from all sides. (pp. 290–91)

Zuckerkandl's confusion becomes most conspicuous in his chapter "The Order of Auditory Space." He cites an idea of Ernst Mach's: "From the fact that different tones can sound together, as different colors can appear together, Ernst Mach has drawn the conclusion that the realm of tone has an order *analogous to that of space*" (p. 300). From this perfectly unobjectionable notion, much that is unacceptable arises. It is not clear, for one thing, whether order implies space or space necessarily entails order or whether for Zuckerkandl they are not actually equivalent; the same questions are attached to "relations:" "For space—we now enlarge our earlier definition—is not only that whence something encounters me; space is also that in which what encounters me is mutually related; space is the whence of the encounter and the where of the relation. In the encounter, space reveals itself as 'without'; in the mutual relations of what is encountered, space reveals itself as order" (p. 302). But we promptly meet with another condition for audible order, namely, the different dynamic states of the related tones. Differences in pitch will not suffice: "Tones of different pitch are simply present simultaneously, just like noises" (p. 302). This new requirement, however, leads to a more or less unintelligible complexity:

> The concept of placeless, flowing auditory space has already familiarized us with the idea that space is of the nature of a state rather than of a place; so it should not cause a shock if we now think of audibly spatial differences as differences in state. Thus place differences in visual space would be matched by differences in dynamic state in auditory space. "State" is here taken in the particular sense in which equilibrium or disturbed equilibrium are states: a condition that wants itself per-

petuated or wants to get away from itself, that points toward itself or points beyond itself, tendency, directed tension. But "direction" here must not again be misunderstood in the sense of visual space, must not in any way be interpreted locally, as "from somewhere to somewhere"; it is direction from one state to another state, from an "everywhere" to another "everywhere": direction, then, in a purely dynamic sense. (p. 303)

Zuckerkandl's difficulty is due in part to his failure to distinguish the spatial qualities specific to music from space as normally understood. "Compared with the individual tone," he observes,

> the chord seems to give us a greater sense of the presence of space, as if the chord occupied more space than the individual tone. . . . We know that it would be wrong to interpret the phenomenon in this manner; sounds do not occupy more or less space, and auditory space is not first empty, then filled. Auditory space is always "full," even when only one tone sounds. A chord does not occupy more space than a single tone; or tone occupies *all* available space; the whole of space is affected by the individual tone as by the chord. (p. 307)

Without further pursuing Zuckerkandl's confusion of phenomenal objects and reality, we can see that this confusion is most clearly revealed—predictably—in his consideration of the difficult problem of musical space.

Zuckerkandl's *Man the Musician* (published in 1973 but completed about ten years earlier), subtitled *Sound and Symbol, Volume 2*, consists of sections on musicality, the musical ear, and musical thought. It is more successful than its earlier companion volume because equivocal notions of the "external world" are not involved. The synoptic view it presents belongs essentially to the psychology of music, but the substance of the book is philosophical rather than experimental psychology, therefore hospitable to gestalt conceptions and to phenomenology.

Zuckerkandl approaches musicality not as the special gift of an individual but as an essential attribute of the human species. Singing represents togetherness with the group and also with the things to which the sung words refer. People sing in order to be aware of their existence on a plane where distinction and separation of man and man and of man and thing give way to unity and authentic togetherness. Thus, one and the same melody can express diverse and even opposite meanings with equal truth. Not only singing man, but music-making man in general, enters this deeper stratum of reality. Zuckerkandl has obviously retained the metaphysical aesthetics of nineteenth-century Germany. Yet he rejects any idea that music and words are radically different and that words supersede music. Music is rational, he insists, just as the depth opened by tones is not inaccessible to words.

In his discussion of "the musical ear," Zuckerkandl starts with the difference between hearing physical events and hearing music. He then distinguishes four layers in hearing music: we hear tones, dynamic qualities, motion, and organic structure. Hearing tones does not really belong to the field of musical perception, but the other "layers" of hearing do. They are not simply compounds of tonal sensations and mental associations; they belong properly to hearing itself in the broad sense in which Zuckerkandl understands this term. In discussing musical motion, Zuckerkandl rejects the duality of feeling and form in music, taking Susanne Langer as an example. "The emotion audible in music," he insists, "is that of the tones which communicate it to the listener."[7] Or, putting the matter in a slightly different way, "The inner life which music reveals behind the external tones is the inner life of the tones themselves, not that of a psyche" (pp. 153–54). This is the meaning of Zuckerkandl's title *Sound and Symbol*, as opposed to Langer's concept of symbolism: "The musical tone is symbolic not because it helps us to perceive something that is in principle unperceivable, but primarily because its pure dynamism is directly apprehended by the ear" (p. 154). What the ear perceives finally is "organic structure"—in the form of the strata of Schenker. This is purely a matter of "hearing" (!):

> Just as musical hearing first penetrates the acoustical surface of sound, apprehends the dynamic tone qualities, and rises to the level of comprehension, so now the process is repeated on a higher level: the dynamic/ motor phenomenon becomes a surface, a foreground, which is nourished and articulated by forces from deeper layers. Once again hearing must penetrate it and rise to the level of comprehension, perceive and interpret the background meaning of the tonal pattern. (p. 164)

The examination of "musical thought," which makes up the third part of the book, is concerned first with controverting the belief in two creative sources—inspiration and thought, the first supposedly producing the musical theme and the second the treatment or elaboration of the theme. But the hand of the plastic artist is not simply the instrument of the mind or the imagination: it is educated to cooperate closely with the intellect; it is involved in the conception of the work. It is Zuckerkandl's contention that this is true of music also—in musical instruments and in writing the musical score. Like the painter, he maintains, the composer has a "thinking hand." Thinking is really indistinguishable from doing, a conclusion that Zuckerkandl takes as an argument against the duality of inspiration and intellect. He finally casts doubt on the notion of inspiration by showing that what seems like a flash of melodic illumination can actually be the product of an extended process of growth and alteration. Where we cannot observe this process, he suggests, it may very well be because the stages of growth succeed one another too rapidly or because they take place in the unconscious. There is a single source of musical creativity, Zuckerkandl concludes, and that is "musical thinking." Whereas cognitive thinking is determined by the opposition between subject and object and thinker and thought are separated by an unbridgeable gulf, creative thinking does not think anything outside itself; it is itself motion, and it thinks motion; and the thinking subject is also the hearing subject. Also, where conceptual thinking leads to judgment, musical thinking leads to tonal patterns.

In *Music as Heard: A Study in Applied Phenomenology* (1983), Thomas Clifton discusses four phenomena that he takes to be essential constituents of music and musical experience: time, space, play, and feeling. Clifton is influenced primarily by Husserl and Merleau-Ponty, but he also deals with the ideas of Heidegger and Dufrenne. In connection with time, he elucidates the important concepts of horizon, retention, and protention. A horizon in music he takes to extend to the limits of whatever temporal object we are listening to—a melody, for example, or a musical work. Retention he distinguishes clearly from recollection, the first being "primary remembrance," which clings to events happening now and interacts with them, and the second being "secondary memory," which is cut off from the felt present and is re-presentative rather than presentative. Protention refers not to a future we merely await but to a future we anticipate or intend: "If we just expect this future to occur, we diminish the possibility of establishing a relation of possession between us and the composition. . . . We shall have to speak instead of an open future, meaning one whose content is intended as neither exclusively determinate nor indeterminate, but rather as vital and indispensable, and hence just as real as present and past." [8]

In connection with space, Clifton uses the term *musical space,* regarding it as a manifestation of synesthesia. He also takes *texture* to be a manifestation of musical space or even to be identical with it. Changes in pitch produce the phenomenon of line, and texture is taken to include not only line but surface and mass as well. Finally, texture is taken also to have a tactile quality. In Clifton's presentation, at any rate, this whole characterization of musical space is unfortunately not clear, and the difficulty of comprehending it is further increased by the inclusion of the contribution of the experiencing subject as well as the musical object, with the result that we must think of "space and spatial relations not as properties of objects, but as fields of action for a subject" (p. 70). At the root of the trouble is the intrinsic complexity of the spatial aspect of music and of the connection between music and space in general.

As far as play is concerned, Clifton takes the position that it is part of reality, not the antithesis of it. Music, he proposes, includes aspects of controlled play that are experienced in ritual and in problem solving as well as aspects of the contest, of chance, and of the comic. Finally, Clifton addresses the phenomenon of feeling and understanding, two necessary constituents that he regards as distinct but not separable. A person always has feelings, he maintains, and they are prior to cognition and volition, yet they should not submerge understanding, or musical expression will be confused with the spontaneity of our own responses. On the other hand, the reflective attitude should not ignore the felt presence of music as an aesthetic object. Feeling is the capacity to throw oneself into something that matters, he argues; it is essentially a movement toward something, and it is immediate, that is, direct and spontaneous. It must also be authentic, however, and the dialectic between feeling and understanding can guide us in this respect:

> One feature of this dialectic is the constant interplay between the synthetic activity of feeling and the analytic activity of reflection. I am talking about a kind of musical analysis which seeks to answer the question, How is the work expressive? rather than, What are the theoretical techniques and historical forces which can explain how the work was made? This is analysis from the inside, not the outside, and what we can hope to gain is not how gaiety or expansiveness can constitute the meaning of a piece of music, but how the music constitutes the meaning of gaiety or expansiveness. In this way, feelings are discovered through, or by means of, the music, which is perhaps different from saying that feelings are discovered *in* the music. But it is because of this discovery that we can speak of a *musical* gaiety, expansiveness, etc., as something distinct from the gaiety of a political convention. (pp. 76–77)

After this survey of the four phenomena he identifies in music, Clifton presents a detailed discussion of each of them in turn. The examination of time in motion is divided into sections on beginning, ending, continuity, contrast and interruption, temporal intercut, and time strata. The term *temporal intercut* is used to designate a section of music that interrupts the established flow of the piece by a section that is clearly of a different character, after which the normal course of the piece resumes.

The chapter on space in motion comprises discussions of the foundation of space as value, the notion of musical line, the varieties of surface (undifferentiated and those with low, middle, and high relief), and depth (with sections on distance and penetration and on multidimensional linear forms). Although the first discussion is particularly opaque, some idea of what it presents may be derived from the following statement: "Ultimately, musical space has significance because a person finds himself there, as a place to take up a temporary habitation" (p. 141). The ensuing details make the conception still more obscure, although it is clear that Clifton's view is very different from that of Zuckerkandl's. The other discussions are often not much more satisfactory. The section on undifferentiated surfaces, for example, starts as follows: "The most elemental kinds of surface occur under three conditions: the first requires the absence of movement; the second, the absence of any contrast in dynamics; and the third, an absence of timbral complexity" (p. 155). Surfaces with high relief, however, are clearly described: "Simply stated, a surface with high relief implies the presence of a more or less stable ground from which is projected a figure of doubtless individuality which, nevertheless, is still fastened to its ground" (p. 172). "Faceting" is again elusive, but the examples given involve primarily abrupt shifts in key.

The chapter on the play element has a section on the ludic, which is divided into ritual and heuristic behavior. There follows a section on other play forms, which has divisions devoted to the aleatoric, the agonic, and the comic. Some idea of what Clifton means by music as ritual and both as play is conveyed by the following passage:

> There seems to be general agreement that one essence of play is a ritualized kind of movement. It is musical motion as ritualized motion which provides the experience of an ordered process whose outcome is nevertheless unknown, but not unknowable. That is, in a game such as chess, you know that you will either win, lose, or draw, but it is your overall strategy, the way you live through the game, which is going to lead you in one of these three directions. Similarly, in music, no composition is ever so thoroughly ordered that we know in advance the precise route that it will take, and . . . even if we are thoroughly familiar with the piece, we tend to suspend the knowledge in order to live through it again and to keep the experience as fresh as possible. (pp. 207–8)

Heuristic behavior, similarly, is connected with music insofar as the outcome of musical experience is unknown but not unknowable: "To a greater or lesser degree, the listening experience raises questions, and arouses, in a twofold way, the sense of wonder: the 'How wonderful!' is coupled with 'What is going to happen?'" (p. 221). Actually, heuristic behavior straddles both the ludic and the comic aspects of play, Clifton maintains; it partakes of both "the problem" and "the riddle." In addition, there is more than a trace of the aleatoric, since a certain amount of indeterminacy is involved in problem solving, and the agonic, since the action of putting a riddle to someone is suggestive of a contest or competition. Thus, heuristic behavior is implicated in four major forms of play.

The final chapter, "The Stratum of Feeling," has six divisions: "Belief as a Component of Possession," "Possession and Freedom" (with sections on the moment of willing, the voluntary-involuntary liaison, and consent as an aspect of possession), "The Eradication of Boundary" (with sections on genetic epistemology, psychology, and aesthetics), "Possession and Language" (with sections on etymological associations and on Vorhanden and Zuhanden), "Possession and Culture," and "Possessing and the Possessed." Possession, Clifton maintains, is a feeling that underlies and prepares for more recognizable feelings. He describes the contents of possession as follows: "(1) Acts of belief, which underlie all cognitive and affective acts; (2) freedom, which provides the possibility for either possessing or not possessing; (3) caring, a fundamental feeling stemming from an attitude of concern for the object of possession; and (4) willing, which urges the continuity of the possessed object and the act of possession" (p. 281). Under the head "The Eradication of Boundary," Clifton undertakes to describe possession as the reduction, in Husserl's terms, of "naive exteriorization":

> There is no music without the presence of a "music-ing" self. In each other's presence, each subtracts something from the other. The self enters the phenomenal world of the music by neutralizing all references to its purely physical qualities. The music enters the self, subtracting self-consciousness. But there remains consciousness of music which now can be more accurately rendered as consciousness *in* music. The self-sphere extends its perimeter to include music. If I become tender and dignified, it is because the music is tender and dignified; if I am tonal, the music exhibits the pull and tension of tonality. In the presence of music, I qualify my own ontology. I *am* tender and dignified; I *am* tonal. But I am not just this corporeal shell occupying a few cubic feet of space. I am one with the melody, such that the terms "tender, dignified, and tonal" are meant as requirements for the Being of that melody, as long as there is an I who is tender, dignified, and tonal when that melody is heard. (pp. 281–82)

Although Clifton maintains that his book is not intended to present a complete description of the phenomenon of music, I have cited the whole arrangement of the book because it does seem to represent the first effort we have to lay out a complete scheme, at any rate, of the application of phenomenology to music. Sometimes the meaning of a passage is obscure or there is no clear line of argument, but there is little doubt about the originality and depth of Clifton's thought and about his knowledge of Husserl, Heidegger, and Merleau-Ponty.

David B. Greene's *Mahler, Consciousness and Temporality* (1984) is devoted essentially to the "phenomenological analysis" of four symphonies of Mahler: the Fifth, Third, Eighth, and Ninth. It is based on the view that Mahler's music violates the standards of coherence and continuity that seem to be implicit in consciousness and its temporality. We expect future perceptions to be coherent with remembered and present perceptions, and this expectation is controlled by limits that derive ultimately from our sense of a universe, of a single inclusive totality, and from our preconceptions about the nature and limitations of reality: "We must assume that there is some sort of coherence between what is and what will be."[9] With this as a foundation, Greene continues, two different kinds of explanation for events can be identified: explanations based on mechanical causation and those based on the decisions of a free, self-reflective individual.

Difficulty in synthesizing what is expected to happen with what actually happens—which we meet with in the case of Mahler—will upset this normal structure of presuppositions and cause us to consider the possibility, for example, of an ungrounded event or to search for some previously unexpected basis of explanation. Sometimes Mahler begins a passage that promises to conform to our usual notions of continuity

> and whose process closely resembles that of an event causing a subsequent event or of a decision, made by a free agent, shaping a future; but then the passage subverts this continuity and leaves us feeling at the end that what has transpired has simply happened, its process resembling that of events like nuclear decay, beauty and accidents for which no ground may be determined. Sometimes he blurs the distinction between an event that, like an event shaped by a free decision, seems to mark a new beginning, as though it were responsive to the preceding music but not determined by it. He begins ideas that fizzle out; new ideas enter from nowhere; the banal is harshly juxtaposed to the sublime; interruptions and interpolations upset the continuity. (pp. 13–14)

Some principle of continuity may be operative, Greene concedes, but the principle of one section may be different from or even contradictory to that of the preceding section, and sometimes two contradictory principles operate at the same time: "Things happen that respond to no actual past; events that are evoked are sometimes not even partly actualized. The more ungrounded events take place and grounded ones fail to materialize, the more listeners feel not so much that expectations are frustrated as that expecting anything at all is sometimes inappropriate to this music" (p. 14). Sometimes the future becomes so indeterminate and the past so irrelevant, Greene feels, that both future and past disappear even as possibilities, and the temporality becomes essentially futureless and pastless.

Yet Mahler's symphonies also project temporal processes that cohere with one another and thereby respond to this confusion. The responses are of two types:

> First, some of his movements appeal both to our common-sense presuppositions about temporality and also to our sense that some kinds of events are groundless. They do justice to both of these by creating a kind of continuity that is fundamentally different from what our usual reflection on consciousness seems of necessity to ascribe to the temporal process. These movements imply an understanding of consciousness that accordingly is basically different. Perhaps they understand consciousness as it actually is, not as we would like to think that it is.
>
> Second, some of his movements suggest a totally unfamiliar temporal process that differs from the temporality of groundless events as much as the latter differs from a world in which events are assumed always to have a ground. These movements lead us into transformed temporalities that are different from those of causation, decision-making and ungrounded events, all three. Perhaps they understand consciousness as it might be, not as it actually is. (pp. 14–15)

Mahler responds in the first way in the Fifth Symphony and in much of the Third, according to Greene. He responds in the second way in the Finale of the Third, all the Eighth, and the first and last movements of the Ninth. What Greene proposes to do is to identify the assumptions about temporality that the music embodies and that the listener must share, at least provisionally, if it is to make sense. It is equally possible to say, however, or perhaps more accurate to say, that the consciousness of the listener will necessarily conform to the temporality of the music, for it is shaped by music even more compellingly than by other kinds of experience, and there is no need for explicit assumptions. But the course of the listener's experience will include elements of surprise, disappointment, shock, and even puzzlement and wonder, all tempered by their detachment from realistic concerns of personal harm and gain and caused by features of the musical occurrences that differ from what is expected on the basis of the normal course of events with their usual kinds and degrees of predictability.

Greene's discussion of the first movement of Mahler's Ninth Symphony (1909–10) can be taken as an illustration of his approach. He considers the symphony's treatment of finality to be its central theme throughout the four movements. "In one way or another," he believes, "a sense of being near the end or an attempt to dismiss or accept or transmute this feeling makes itself continuously present" (p. 263). The basis of the first movement is the descent of two whole steps from F♯ to E and from E to D, the motive that opens

Beethoven's *Les Adieux* Sonata, op. 81a, and above which Beethoven had written "Lebewohl." But even apart from this familiar conventional meaning, the motive can be regarded as a natural symbol or appropriate metaphor for a final farewell. An awareness of the tonal context of D major gives the first note a downward tendency toward the final D, but as the third of the scale it presents a degree of stability and is not drawn strongly downward.

This tonal situation is compared by Greene to the difficulty in departing that is experienced in leaving a person to whom we feel attached. When the motive advances to E, the downward tendency becomes very strong, and the sense of departure dominates the sense of attachment. With the final note, the departure clearly has been completed. Toward the end of the movement, the motive is transformed into a new motive consisting only of the descent from F♯ to E, a motive to which the word "ewig" was set the year before, at the end of the song "Der Abschied," which closes Mahler's *Das Lied von der Erde* (1908). In the "ewig" motive, there is no tendency toward closure on D, but E is not heard as a closure either:

> To say that there is no closure on the second note is to say that there is not a sense of having arrived at a point toward which the past has been moving, and to say that there is no drive to closure is to say that working toward a future in no way affects the content of the present.
>
> These aspects of Mahler's "ewig" motif—that it is neither complete nor incomplete, that it neither has nor seeks closure, and that the sense of movement from past to future is weakened—lead us into a new kind of temporal process. (pp. 265–66)

The movement suggests, according to Greene, what it is like to be eternally conscious—not simply to be unendingly conscious in the ordinary way, but to be conscious in a fundamentally new way. Ordinarily, Greene expects closure in that what he expects to see of an object will harmonize with what he now sees and remembers of it and in the sense that the self he sees himself becoming is the completion of the self he now is. But if he did not sense or expect closure in these ways, it would be impossible to say what consciousness would be like except to say that it would be very different. What Greene asserts, however, is that Mahler's movement suggests what it would be like actually to experience such an eternal temporality.

This is more graphically depicted in "Der Abschied," the last song of *Das Lied von der Erde*, in which the "ewig" motive acts as a "resolution" of the fundamental tension between celebration of the endless renewal of life and resignation to the transitory character of human existence, terminated in a final departure. A new kind of temporality is created in the song that is neither incomplete nor complete—that transcends both natural self-renewal and human self-awareness. And at the end of the first movement of the Ninth Symphony, the "ewig" motive is repeated slowly several times and then sounded even more slowly by the oboe, which holds the final E for four slow measures. Before it fades away, the final D is sounded, but two octaves higher, so that it does not really affect the evocation of a perpetual absence of closure: "One is simultaneously aware of 'Lebewohl' and its finality and of 'ewig' and its uncanny openness" (p. 267).

During the course of the movement, a series of changes occur that eliminate the descending force possessed by the E in its "Lebewohl" context:

> Primarily responsible for this transformation are the way Mahler gradually pulls the background into the foreground, making the background into a void, and the way he gradually drains the movement of a sense of moving toward a goal, making the future into a void. . . .
>
> Mahler does not go directly from a texture consisting of melody with accompaniment to a backgroundless foreground. Rather, each of the five statements of the melody pulls another piece out of the background into itself. (pp. 268–69)

By the final section (the sixth restatement of the theme), the background has nearly become a void; everything is foreground. Greene describes all these changes in detail and then provides an explanation of the result:

> The function of a background is to define the musical space in which the foreground melody will sound closed. One of the most important differences between the beginning and the ending of the movement is that at the beginning the descending whole-step motif takes place in front of a backdrop that makes an expected D function as its goal, and we associate the motif with the word "Lebewohl." Partly because at the end the sense of a background is severely attenuated, we no longer hear the F-sharp—E as pushing on to D, and we associate the descending whole step that neither has nor seeks closure with the word "ewig." (p. 271)

Not only is musical space emptied; the musical future is emptied also. There is less and less sense of purpose in the movement. Between the appearances of the main theme there are angry protests, but after the climax reached in the first of these subsequent protests simply spend themselves. They are the kind of climax that occurs when excitement or energy begins to decrease, or to increase more slowly, before a goal or resolution is reached or when a frenzy dies away before its goal takes shape. Greene provides a picture of the first movement as a whole:

The movement is structured by the alternation between the main theme, built out of the "Lebewohl" motive, and the anguished sections struggling toward a goal. At each successive climax of these struggles, the sense of moving toward a goal is increasingly attenuated. Such a background structure not only does not give the movement a sense of direction, but in fact sucks it away. At the beginning of the movement, the main theme is heard in a world where goals are reached; then goals are expected but not reached, then they become impossible to reach, and finally impossible to imagine. At the end, the future has become empty in the sense that the present is utterly independent of the future. . . .

Just as sucking the background into the foreground creates a musical space that is a void, so sucking the very possibility of coming events into the present creates a musical future that is a void. . . .

As the movement runs its course, it transforms the consciousness of final separation into the kind of consciousness which knows no finality and in which one's sense of self is radically altered because one no longer closes the present self with the remembered or the possible self. (pp. 274–75)

CHAPTER FIFTEEN

THE SOCIOLOGY
OF MUSIC

T he sociology of music has been distinguished from the social history of music on the grounds that it deals with the effects on music of social forces in general, while the social history of music studies the place of music in society, apart from any influence that musical life may exert on music itself. Thus, social history looks objectively at music and musical institutions in their social context, while sociology searches for relations between society and music that affect the very style, structure, and nature of music. The distinction is a fundamental one, although it is not always observed in practice. There is also a tendency for sociology to deal with the present and social history with the past, but this distinction is also not always observed.

As far as the aesthetics of music is concerned, or its philosophy, social history is essentially irrelevant, while sociology is clearly entitled to an important place, for a sociological aesthetics, in accounting for the intrinsic properties of music, has a contribution to make, in principle, to many aesthetic investigations—perhaps to all. At first glance, the sociology of music seems the very antithesis of aesthetics, for the horizon of aesthetic thought has traditionally been a limited one. During the nineteenth century, it was often restricted to the work as a self-contained entity. The personality and experiences of the composer were often considered relevant, and so, on occasion, was metaphysics. The one thing conspicuously absent was social context, whether as social history or as sociology. But this exclusion could not be maintained if it could be shown that intrinsic and significant properties of the work had their most convincing explanation in social forces, if the work was a mirror of society rather than a microcosm of the universe. The composer also, as a creature of society, would then become an instrument by means of which social forces would produce their imprint on the musical work, and this view of the composer could easily coexist with the view that his importance was that of a distinctive individuality.

Interest in a musical sociology was doubtless fostered by the development of ethnomusicology in this century and by the adoption of social history as part of the history of music, which in this way took on something of the nature of cultural history. It is interesting that both the social history and the sociology of music would not come into existence in the study of the music of tribal societies, for the integration of all the facets of culture is so complete that the study of any one automatically involves a study of the whole. There can hardly be an investigation of music at all because it makes no sense to ask about the influence of society on music if the two are not separate but fused in rite or ceremony. For the same reason, there can be no separate investigation of musical aesthetics.

In any event, the neglect of society by the aestheticians of Western civilization came to be not a defect—an exclusion of something irrelevant—but an omission that called for an additional field of study. Sociology took its logical place: it would be not the antithesis of aesthetics but the complement of those approaches already available. For the study of meaning in music was in some measure directed outward, while both the study of musical objectivity and the study of phenomenology were focused on music itself, the one regarding it as an external object, the other considering its properties as these appeared to consciousness and were products of intentionality. The forces shaping music, insofar as these were social, awaited investigation. This would complete the circle of discernible possibilities, for the outward influences of music, as opposed to its outward relations, belonged to social psychology and to therapy rather than to aesthetics.

Although the relations between music and society have been thought about and discussed since antiquity, the modern discipline of musical sociology was inaugurated by the sociologist Max Weber's *The Rational and Social Foundations of Music*, which was written in 1911 and published in 1921, the year after Weber's death. What Weber means by a rational social action is one in which the means are appropriate to the ends, and *rationality* in this sense is also applicable to social relations and social structures since these are based on social actions. That Western history is characterized by the growth and increasing predominance of rational social action is one of Weber's most basic principles. This growth of rationality, of the consistent and increasing application of principles and rules, is evident in art as well as in other spheres of life. In music, it does battle with the forces of expression and tradition and is for the most part victorious.

Weber examines a wide range of factors in which the rationalization of music becomes manifest, considering in turn the roles of harmony and melody, of the scale system, of tonality, of notation and of the various types of polyphony, including counterpoint and homophony, of fifths and fourths, of the tonal system and temperament, and of musical instruments. Ancient and Oriental music are sometimes referred to for purposes of comparison. The scope and detail of Weber's knowledge of music and his insight into its nature assured this densely written essay a continuing influence in the field of musical sociology. One of the many influential aspects of the tract, for example, was Weber's conception of the interaction of harmony and melody: "Without the tensions motivated by the irrationality of melody, no modern music could exist. They are among its most effective means of expression. The manner in which such expressiveness is achieved falls outside this discussion. Here it should be remembered only as demonstrating an elemental fact of music, that chordal rationalization lives only in continuous tension with melodicism which it can never completely devour."[1]

Theodor W. Adorno

Many years after the pioneering study of Max Weber was published, musical sociology was provided with a second foundation in an article entitled "On the Social Situation of Music" (1932) by Theodor Adorno, who also developed the field considerably in numerous writings. Adorno was a prominent member and later the director of the Institute of Social Research in Frankfurt. The institute was transferred to the United States in 1934 and was affiliated with Columbia University, returning to Frankfurt in 1949–50. Part of what may be called Western Marxism, it subsisted in a capitalist world that provided little significant opportunity for effective political action. An alternative was found in the production of a large body of theoretical work that was deeply critical of the existing social order and often pessimistic in tone. Marxist theory in the West, unable to forge a union with practice, naturally turned from economics and politics to philosophy, thus reversing the route traveled by Marx himself. It also turned from a straightforward style to verbal complexity and from proletarian practice to bourgeois theory. Bourgeois culture and thought, in fact, manifested an unexpected vitality and interest when compared with the Stalinist reality of Communism.

The superstructures of society became the center of interest, especially the individual arts and aesthetics in general. As early as 1936, Walter Benjamin wrote an important article on "The Work of Art in the Age of Mechanical Reproduction," and after mid-century most Marxists in the West published works on artistic theory. Comprehensive treatises on aesthetics were the final works of Georg Lukács (1963) and of Adorno (1970).

With astonishing accuracy, Adorno's early "On the Social Situation of Music" mapped out the field that his succeeding writings were to explore. Some basic conceptions are presented at the outset. Adorno believes that music has become a commodity. He outlines a fateful historical course: starting with a "simple immediacy of use," music was first objectified and rationalized; then its alienation from man became complete through the total absorption of both production and consumption by the capitalistic process. The situation cannot be corrected by music itself, but only by changing society. All music can do now is to "portray within its own structure the social antinomies which are also responsible for its own isolation. Music will be better . . . the more purely it is able to express—in the antinomies of its own formal language—the exigency of the social condition and to call for change through the coded language of suffering."[2]

The belief that music reflects society is fundamental to Adorno's ideas. Another aspect of this principle appears shortly afterward: "Through its material, music must give clear form to the problems assigned it by this material, which is itself never purely natural material, but rather a social and historical product; solutions offered by music in this process stand equal to theories" (p. 130). In a still more positive passage, Adorno finds that music may actually intervene in the social process: "It might be possible for the most advanced compositional production of the present—solely under the pressure of the immanent development of its problems—to invalidate basic bourgeois categories such as the creative personality and expression of the soul of this personality, the world of private feelings and its transfigured inwardness, setting in their place highly rational and transparent principles of construction" (p. 131). In the dialectical interaction of music and society, there are in fact different roles that music can play, and these represent the most basic determinations of its nature.

The body of the essay is divided into two large parts dealing, respectively, with the "production" of music and with its "reproduction and consumption." With reference to production, Adorno establishes four types of music. The first type, "without consciousness of its social location or out of indifference toward it, presents and crystallizes its problems and the solutions thereto in a merely immanent manner." This type is represented by Schönberg and his school. Music of the second type "recognizes the fact of alienation as its own isolation and as 'individualism' and further raises this fact to the level of consciousness; it does so, however, only within itself, only in aesthetic and form-immanent terms" (p. 132). Disregarding the society of its own times, then, this music has "recourse to stylistic forms of the past, which it views as immune to alienation" (p. 133). The main representative of this neoclassicism, or "objectivism," is Stravinsky. The third type of music is represented by Kurt Weill. It is a hybrid type that can be called surrealist music and that combines the formal language of the nineteenth century with that of present-day consumer music. Aware of alienation, it recognizes objectivism as an illusion. It is partly objectivist, but it permits social flaws to manifest themselves. The fourth type attempts to break through alienation as "communal music." This is represented by Hindemith and by the proletarian choral works of Hanns Eisler.

In the consumption of music, alienation is made tangible by the very existence of reproduction as a mediation between music and its public. Logically, then, the first topic of this part of the essay is the nature of interpretation, and how it changes "with the victory of the bourgeois class" (p. 147). Adorno then discusses opera, concerts, musical life, and "light" music, showing how the nature of each of these reflects its place and function in society. The essay is nothing less than "the outline of a detailed sociology of music," as Adorno stated in his *Introduction to the Sociology of Music* of 1962 (which derives from lectures given in 1960). It is, in addition, more literally and actively Marxist than Adorno's later writings. The central concept of alienation, for example, is taken directly from Marx. One basic idea of the essay was explicitly modified in the later *Introduction*, where Adorno no longer maintains that the processes of musical production and economic production are identical, but only that they are similar.

Another important early article of Adorno's is "On the Fetish-Character of Music and the Regression of Listening" (1938), which identifies a whole series of manifestations of inadequate listening. Most of these are instances of response to parts of a work rather than to the whole. One of the descriptions of such listening is as follows:

> The works which are the basis of the fetishization and become cultural goods experience constitutional changes as a result. They become vulgarized. Irrelevant consumption destroys them. Not merely do the few things played again and again wear out, like the Sistine Madonna in the bedroom, but reification affects their internal structure. They are transformed into a conglomeration of irruptions which are impressed on the listeners by climax and repetition, while the organization of the whole makes no impression whatsoever.[3]

As this passage reveals, musical fetishism and regressive listening go hand in hand.

Another of the numerous manifestations of fetishism is found in the official ideal of performance, "the purity of service to the cause": "The new fetish is the flawlessly functioning, metallically brilliant apparatus as such, in which all the cogwheels mesh so perfectly that not the slightest hole remains open for the meaning of the whole. Perfect, immaculate performance in the latest style preserves the work at the price of its definitive reification. The performance sounds like its own phonograph record." Adorno also discusses the basic of musical fetishism:

> The consumer is really worshipping the money that he himself has paid for the ticket to the Toscanini concert. He has literally "made" the success which he reifies and accepts as an objective criterion, without recognizing himself in it. But he has not "made" it by liking the concert, but rather by buying the ticket. . . . The more inexorably the principle of exchange-value destroys use-values for human beings, the more deeply does exchange-value disguise itself as the object of enjoyment.[4]

The concept of reification is adopted from Lukács, and the concept of fetishism, like that of alienation, is taken from Marx. Adorno explicitly cites Marx's definition of the fetish character of the commodity.

One of Adorno's major works, *Philosophie der neuen Musik*, was published in 1949. The work is composed of two essentially independent monographs: a study of Schönberg written in 1940–41 and somewhat expanded, and a later study of Stravinsky written in 1948 as a complement of the first so that "new music" would be represented as a whole by the combination of the two. The relation of the two composers is dialectical. Schönberg is the progressive: he develops the historical tendencies inherent in the musical material of his time; Stravinsky is the reactionary: he returns to the musical language and forms of the past. The one follows historical necessity; the other capitulates to popular recognition. Where Schönberg is expressive, Stravinsky is antipsychological.

The Hegelian basis of Adorno's thought may underlie his concern with German music in particular. Indeed, nearly all the impressive series of monographs and essays on individual composers are devoted to Germans and Austrians—to Brahms, Wagner, Mahler, Schönberg, Berg, and Webern. The only conspicuous exception is the study of Stravinsky included in *Philosophie der neuen Musik*. It is also the case, of course, that Adorno's view of Schönberg is extremely positive and his view of Stravinsky sharply negative. Objectivity and neoclassicism, for example, are exposed as symptoms of fundamental deficiencies: "Compositional spontaneity itself is overwhelmed by the prohibition placed upon pathos in expression: the subject, which is no longer permitted to state anything about itself, thus actually ceases to engage in "production" and must content itself with the hollow echo of objective musical language, which is no longer its own. In the words of Rudolf Kolish, Stravinsky's work is music about music."[5] All of Stravinsky's works since *L'Histoire*, Adorno continues, are based more or less on the concept of "mutilated tonality":

Such material exists outside the immanent formal validity of the work and it is determined through a consciousness which exerts itself also from outside the work. The composition concerns itself with such subject matter. The composition feeds upon the difference between its models and the use which it makes of them. The concept of a musical material contained within the work itself—a central idea for Schönberg's school—can hardly be applied to Stravinsky in any narrow sense. His music continually directs its gaze towards other materials, which it then "consumes" through the over-exposure of its rigid and mechanical characteristics. (p. 183)

Musical time provides a particularly powerful instrument of explanation:

The remnants of memory are joined together; direct musical material is not developed out of its own driving force. The composition is realized not through development, but through the faults which permeate its structure. These assume the role which earlier was the province of expression: this recalls the statement which Eisenstein once made about film montage; he explained that the "general concept"—the meaning, that is, or the synthesis of partial elements of the theme—proceeded precisely out of their juxtaposition as separated, isolated elements. This results, however, in the dissociation of the musical time continuum itself. (p. 187)

Stravinsky's music avoids the dialectical confrontation with the musical progress of time that is the basis of all great music since Bach: "Stravinsky and his school bring about the end of musical Bergsonianism. They play off *le temps espace* against *le temps durée*" (p. 193).

This abandonment of temporal dialectic, which is connected with Stravinsky's dependence on dance, has a generality of entailment that encompasses Schönberg also:

Today there is no music showing any trace of the power of the historical hour that has remained totally unaffected by the decline of experience—by the substitution, for "life," of a process of economic adjustment dictated by concentrated economic forces of domination. The dying out of subjective time in music seems totally unavoidable in the midst of a humanity which had made itself into a thing—into an object of its own organization. The result is that similar aspects can be observed at the extreme poles of composition. The Expressionistic miniature of the new Viennese School contracts the time dimension by expressing—in Schönberg's words—"an entire novel through a single gesture." Furthermore, in the most convincing twelve-tone compositions, time plays a role through an integral procedure seemingly without development, because it tolerates nothing outside itself upon which development could experiment. (p. 194)

Adorno goes on, however, to distinguish such change in time consciousness in the inner organization of music from the "pseudomorphism of the spatial dimension within musical time," which disrupts the temporal continuity with abrupt shocks and sharp blows. In the pseudomorphism, music "establishes itself as an arbiter of time, causing the listener to forget the subjective and psychological experience of time in music and to abandon itself to its spatialized dimension. It proclaims, as its unique achievement, the fact that there is no longer any life—as though it had achieved the objectification of life" (p. 195). The weakness of Stravinsky—the nonintrinsic element in his general compositional makeup—

> is the price he has had to pay for his restriction to the dance; although this limitation once seemed to him a guarantee of order and objectivity. From the beginning it imposed upon his music an aspect of servitude which required the renunciation of autonomy. True dance—in contrast to mature music—is an art of static time, a turning in a circle, movement without progress. It was in this consciousness that sonata form came to replace dance form: throughout the entire history of modern music—with the exception of Beethoven—minuettes and scherzi have always been a matter of convenience and of secondary importance; this is particularly true when they are compared to serious sonata form and to the adagio. Music for the dance lies on this side of—and not beyond—subjective dynamics; to this extent, it contains an anachronistic element, which in Stravinsky stands in highly peculiar contrast to the literary-modish success of his hostility towards expression. (p. 196)

Another expression of this duality of sonata and dance can be found in the mode of listening to music, which is either expressive-dynamic or rhythmic-spatial, the first derived from singing and the second from the regular beat of rhythm, the first transforming "the heterogeneous course of time into the force of the musical process" (p. 197), the second articulating a spatializing time by dividing it into equal measures. There is a mutual penetration of the two modes in great music, Adorno maintains, and the sonata unites freedom and discipline—the *Lied* and the dance. But the conflict between the two cannot be resolved after Beethoven; this is evidently the reason, in Adorno's view, for a decline of music that parallels the decline of the bourgeoisie. The two types of music, he says, torn from each other, "have today diverged without mediation and must pay with untruth" (p. 199).

Schönberg does not conceal his entanglement in the decline of traditional society, Adorno maintains in concluding his study, but simply relies step by step on the concrete demands of "the encounter between the compositional subject which is conscious of itself and the socially established material":

> The obscure driving force within him is nourished by the certainty that nothing in art is successfully binding except that which can be totally filled by the historical state of consciousness which determines its own substance—by its "experience" in the emphatic sense. . . . The absolute renunciation of the gesture of authenticity becomes the only indication of the authenticity of the structure. This school, which has been re-proached for its intellectualism, is in such a venture naive compared to the pretentious manipulation of authenticity, as it thrives in Stravinsky and his total circle. (pp. 213–14)

The Schönberg school, Adorno continues, achieves not only the more cohesive and instinctive artistic view but also a higher objectivity—an objectivity of immanent correctness and of undisguised appropriateness to the historical situation. It produces, in twelve-tone constructivism, a manifest objectivity that is sui generis. Stravinsky's language, on the other hand,

> is as close to the language of communication as it is to the language of the practical joke: non-seriousness itself, play—from which the subject remains aloof, abdication to the aesthetic "development of truth," con-siders itself the guarantee of authenticity and therewith of truth as well. This contradiction destroys his music: the contrived style of objectivity is demanded of the recalcitrant material as forcefully and irresponsibly as art nouveau was formulated fifty years ago. . . . The will to style replaces style itself and therewith sabotages it. No objectivity of that which the structure wills from within itself is present in objectivism. It establishes itself by eradicating the traces of subjectivity. (p. 215)

The two monographic studies of which the *Philosophy of Modern Music* is composed are not so much investigations that belong to musical sociology in a strict sense as they are stylistic studies that are illuminated by a sociological viewpoint. There can be no question, however, that the styles of Schönberg and Stravinsky are conceived as shaped in general and in detail by social forces. These features continue to characterize all the later studies of individual composers, in which explicit sociological discussion is subordinate to specifically stylistic analysis, although social forces are always regarded as determinative even where they are not made explicit by Adorno. Often, there is a shift in Adorno's argument from specifically stylistic matters to specifically social ones. He moves back and forth between the two

with what seems to be an inconsequent abruptness. This is not a sign of incoherence, however, or of a failure in logic, but rather of a universe of thought
in which social and stylistic features have become closely identified. In the
consideration of musical genre, which is to begin with usually a product of
social forces, Adorno is more explicitly sociological. This is especially the
case in the treatment of popular genres of music and of mass media, where
complexity of style gives way to simplicity and the stylistic properties of
music have little interest of their own and thus become transparent to the
social forces that form them.

In the writings that are specifically sociological by intention, which we
can take to include the numerous articles on popular genres, the systematic
character of the early "On the Social Situation of Music" is taken up again
by the *Einleitung in die Musiksoziologie* (1962). Three of the chapters of this
work—which retains its original informal character as a series of lectures—
are devoted to musical genres: to popular music, opera, and chamber music.
Others are devoted to more general manifestations that are literally social in
nature: to social classes and strata, to the conductor and his relation to his
orchestra and his audience, to musical life, and to public opinion and critics.
A third, intermediate group of chapters can finally be distinguished, devoted
to topics that are more general than individual genres but essentially rather
than literally social: types of listener, the function of music, national style,
the avant-garde, and the interrelation of music and society.

The first chapter, appropriately, discusses characteristic types of listener,
of which Adorno identifies eight: the expert, the good listener, the culture
consumer, the emotional listener, the resentment listener, the jazz listener, the
entertainment listener, and the listener who is indifferent, unmusical, or antimusical. Each of these is trenchantly characterized. Not all of them can be
defined socially or in terms of class membership, yet Adorno always characterizes the types psychologically and usually sociopsychologically. The true
basis of the typology, however, is the degree to which listening is adequate
to the musical work.

The second chapter, on popular music, is of course explicitly social in
orientation, and the stylistic discussion has a clear sociological foundation throughout. The course of operetta and musical comedy receives a due
amount of attention. A characteristic perception is the following:

> The true reasons for the demise of revue and European-style operetta
> are difficult to find out, but a trend, at least, may be shown by general
> sociological reflections. Those types of music were closely connected
> with the economic sphere of distribution—more specifically, with the
> garment business. A revue was not only an undress show; it was also a

dress show. One of the biggest hit operettas of the Viennese-Hungarian type, the *Autumn Maneuvers* that made Kálman famous, came directly from the associative field of clothing manufacture, and even in the age of musicals this link remained perceptible in shows like *Pins and Needles* and *Pajama Game.* Just as the operetta's staff, mode of production, and jargon suggested the apparel business, it could regard people in that line as its ideal audience. In Berlin, the man whom the sight of a sumptuously bedecked and simultaneously bared star moved to exclaim "Simply fabulous!" was the archetypical coat-and-suiter. And since in Europe, at least, for reasons ranging from economic concentration to totalitarian terrorism, the relevance of this and other distributive trades declined decisively in the past thirty years, those genera of the allegedly buoyant Muse have lost some of their real basis.[6]

The discussion of the function of music (chap. 3) reveals the remarkable depth of Adorno's insight. It is also an excellent example of the anthropological-historical scope of his thought, which encompasses preliterate society as easily as it does the sociology of the present. Adorno's view of function becomes evident early in the discussion:

> In a society that has been functionalized virtually through and through, totally ruled by the exchange principle, lack of function comes to be a secondary function . . . in the context of social effects, the man-made in-itself of a work that will not sell out to that context promises something that would exist without defacement by the universal profit. . . . At the same time, however, profit takes the functionless into its service and thereby degrades it to meaninglessness and irrelevancy. The exploitation of something useless in itself, something sealed and superfluous to the people on whom it is foisted—this is the ground of the fetishism that covers all cultural commodities, and the musical ones in particular. . . . If something simply exists, without a raison d'être, and that is enough to console us for the fact that everything else exists for something else, the comfort, function, the anonymous solace to the congregation of the lonely, ranks surely not lowest among the functions of music today. (pp. 41, 42–43)

This conception is extended by the description of "entertainment music":

> But the merriment switched on by music is not simply the merriment of individuals at large. It is that of several, or of many, who substitute for the voice of the whole society by which the individual is outcast and yet gripped. The source of the sound, the font of the music, evokes preconscious reactions: that is where things are happening; that's where life

goes on. The feebler the subjects' own sense of living, the stronger their happy illusion of attending what they tell themselves is other people's life. The din and to-do of entertainment music feigns exceptional gala states; the "We" that is set in all polyphonic music as the a priori of its meaning, the collective objectivity of the thing itself, turns into customer bait. (p. 45)

Again the consideration of temporal properties has unusual explanatory value. It arises out of a discussion of film music and of "consumers' music" in general. Music colors the desolation of the inner sense, Adorno proposes:

It is the decoration of empty time. The more the emphatic concept of experience, the sense of a temporal continuum, dissolves under the conditions of industrial production, and the more time decomposes into discontinuous, shocklike moments, the more nakedly and menacingly will the subjective consciousness come to feel itself at the mercy of the course of abstract, physical time. Even in the life of the individual this time has inexorably separated from that *temps durée* which Bergson still viewed as rescuing the living experience of time. Music calms the sense of it. Bergson knew why he contrasted his *temps espace* with permanence. Abstract time is really not time any more when it confronts the content of experience as something mechanical divided into static, immutable units; and its gloomy, unstructured character becomes the opposite of permanence, something spatial and narrow at the same time, like an infinitely long, dark hallway. . . .

But people dread time, and so they invent compensatory metaphysics of time because they no longer feel really alive. This is what music talks them out of. It confirms the society it entertains. (pp. 47, 48)

These observations are complemented by a passage that still more explicitly couples musical style with industrial production:

The function of music in the time-consciousness of a mankind in the clutches of concretism cannot be conceived abstractly enough. The form of labor in industrial mass production is virtually that of always repeating the same; ideally, nothing new occurs at all. But the modes of behavior that have evolved in the sphere of production, on the conveyor belt, are potentially . . . spreading over all of society, including sectors where no work is performed directly in line with those schemata. With respect to a time thus choked off by iteration, the function of music is reduced to making believe that—as Beckett put it in Endgame— something is happening at all, that anything changes. (p. 49)

The same stylistic implication of production appears finally in connection with corporeal motions: "It is true that some of the bodily functions which the individual has really lost are imaginatively returned to him by music. Yet this is but half the truth: in the mechanical rigor of their repetition, the functions copied by the rhythm are themselves identical with those of the production processes which robbed the individual of his original bodily functions" (p. 52). It is precisely these features of industrial production, of course, that are now being replaced in the United States by the team assembly of complete units, by the operations of robots, and by the shift to a managerial and service economy.

This valuable and characteristic chapter is followed by one devoted to social classes and strata (chap. 4). Here Adorno is unable to make much headway. The relation of music to social classes is peculiarly elusive and seems largely to permit negative conclusions. Neither the preferences of musical consumers nor the social origin of composers tells us anything cogent about the class import of music. In any event, as Adorno points out, there was no great variety of social origin among composers; nearly all of them seemed to come from the petty bourgeois middle class or from their own guild:

> A marginal existence of protracted waiting for crumbs from the seignorial table, with no place in the regular bourgeois labor process—this was the specific social destiny of music under the aspect of its producers. Until far into the nineteenth century—in other words, in a fully developed capitalist society—composers were anachronistically kept in this situation. Their work had long been marketed as a commodity, but under backward copyright laws it did not provide them with an adequate living even if the theaters got rich on it.

Adorno remarks tellingly, "Society controlled music by holding its composers on a tight and not so very hidden golden leash; potential petitioner status never favors social opposition. That's why there is so much merry music" (p. 58).

Adorno then turns from the production of music to its reception, where the outcome of his examination is no more positive. Recourse to listening habits is fruitless for the relation of music and classes, he maintains; he proceeds to explain, "The reception of music can turn it into something altogether different; indeed, it will presumably and regularly become different from what is currently believed to be its inalienable content. The musical effect comes to diverge from, if not to conflict with, the character of what has been consumed: this is what makes the analysis of effects so unfit to yield insights into the specific social sense of music" (p. 61). Chopin's music provides an example. Its aristocratic bearing is conspicuous:

Yet this music, exclusive in both origin and attitude, has within a hundred years become exceedingly popular and ultimately, by way of one or two Hollywood hits, a mass item. Chopin's aristocratic side was the very one to invite socialization. Countless millions hum the melody of the Polonaise in A Flat Major, and when they strike a pose of a chosen one at the piano to tinkle out some of the less demanding Préludes or Nocturnes, we may assume that they are vaguely counting themselves with the elite. . . . This is how much, and with respect to class relations in particular, a music's social function may diverge from the social meaning it embodies, even when the embodiment is as obvious as Chopin. (pp. 61–62)

Yet Adorno will not renounce his purpose; he continues to seek ways of realizing it. If we do not hear anything of the revolutionary bourgeoisie in Beethoven, he insists, we understand him no better than someone who cannot follow the purely musical content of his pieces. If the social element in music is thought to be simply an extraneous sociological interpretation, it is because "the musical experience has been insulated from the experience of the reality in which it finds itself—however polemically—and to which it responds." While musical analysis and the study of the circumstances of the composer and his work were carefully developed, "the method of deciphering the specific social characteristics of music has lagged pitifully and must be largely content with improvisations" (p. 62).

As an approach to such a method of decipherment Adorno considers the music of several composers, pointing to the difficulties and pitfalls that continually present themselves. He finds that searching for the musical expression of class interests is not the correct way to proceed, suggesting instead the principle that any music will present the picture of antagonistic society as a whole. Intramusical tensions, he urges, are the unconscious phenomena of social tensions. Music has something to do with classes insofar as it reflects the class relation in toto. The more purely it grasps the social antagonisms and the more profoundly it represents them, the less ideological music will be and the more correctly it will represent objective rather than false consciousness. Still more optimistically, Adorno suggests the possibility, reminiscent of Ernst Bloch, that representation might itself be reconciliation already and that music also attests that, through all sacrifice and all distress, the life of mankind goes on. The chapter as a whole, however, presents us with a rather disheartening picture of the difficulties of musical sociology.

By way of contrast, the chapters on opera and chamber music (chaps. 5 and 6) provide a definite picture of the social nature and present social situation of these two genres. In connection with opera, Adorno undertakes to demonstrate that the reception of musical genres will not always harmonize with their original social function, that their reception, in fact, can depart entirely from their social origin and meaning. "The social conditions," he maintains, "and thus the style and content, of traditional opera were so far removed from the theatergoers' consciousness that there is every reason to doubt the continued existence of any such thing as an operatic experience" (p. 80). The picture of the self-emancipating bourgeoisie in opera, Adorno argues, and the glorification of the individual rising against the restrictions of the social order or against oppression find no echo among those who have foresworn individuality or no longer have any idea of it.

In the excellent chapter on chamber music, Adorno depicts in detail the social and stylistic properties of the genre in the time of its efflorescence and then proceeds to trace its history in similar detail, showing clearly how the divergence arose between its original significance and its present social status. The discussion explains and analyzes the situation that exists today, as sociology typically does, and it accounts for this situation in terms of how it came about.

Chapter 7, on the conductor and the orchestra, has the appropriate subtitle "Aspects of Social Psychology." Adorno in fact states at the outset that the main reason for examining the conductor and the orchestra is that they are a kind of microcosm in which social tensions recur and can be concretely studied. In considering the conductor, Adorno discusses his resemblance to the medicine man, to the political dictator, and to the actor. He seems to be committed to the cause alone, unconcerned with the audience and indeed turning his back on it; he thus acquires that loveless detachment that according to Freud is a constituent of the figure of the leader: "The exaggeration, the fanaticism that bursts forth as needed, the exhibition of an allegedly purely introverted passion—all of this recalls the demeanor of leaders trumpeting their own unselfishness. The histrionics at the podium are easy to credit with the dictatorial capacity for frothing at the mouth at will" (p. 106).

The orchestra's attitude toward the conductor is characterized by ambivalence, Adorno maintains. In performance its members want him to hold them on a tight rein, but they also distrust him as a parasite who does not play an instrument and gives himself airs at the expense of those who do. Adorno compares the relationship to the dialectic of master and servant. "A description of the conduct of orchestra musicians," he says subsequently, "would amount to a phenomenology of recalcitrance. The primary factor is unwillingness to submit" (p. 111). No orchestral ill is left out of account, and toward the end of this discourse Adorno understandably admits that "the musical result of the relation between conductor and orchestra is an antimusical compromise" (p. 116).

In the examination of "musical life" (chap. 8), Adorno takes as a basic tenet that musical life is tied to the capitalist marketplace and to its under-lying social structure. He announces also as a central thesis: "Music is real-ized in musical life, but that life conflicts with music" (p. 119). After this negative beginning, Adorno goes on to discuss all the ills of official musical life, particularly those of concert and opera, with their ceaseless repetition of a restricted repertory. The "sleek, glossy quality" of performances expunges the freshness of becoming. Works miss their meaning as a process, Adorno points out, if they are presented as pure results. In musical life as a whole, however, there is astonishing diversity, but this, too, has a negative signifi-cance. "The mutual hostility and irrelation of the branches of musical life is an index of social antagonism" (p. 135), Adorno maintains. "Embodied in the plurality of the musical languages that exist today and in the types of musical life, especially in its calcified educational levels, are different his-toric stages, one of which excludes the other while the antagonistic society compels them to be simultaneous" (p. 137).

Chapter 9 is devoted to "public opinion and critics." For the reified con-sciousness, Adorno says, music is to be approved simply because it exists. Yet this contradicts the essence of music, which is something literally rising above existence. Thus, public opinion reveals an antinomy: music is accepted and tolerated noncommittally but also regarded with hostility as a waste of time or as something pointing beyond the established social order. Music contains a complex relation of rationality and irrationality, Adorno states; he continues, "The irrational moments of the process of living are not re-moved without trouble by the advance of bourgeois rationality" (p. 140). Beyond these basic attitudes, opinion is shot through with clichés, with the automatic repetition of abstract verbalizations.

Musical criticism, as Adorno states, is the institutional organ of public opinion. It is an essential activity, in his view, because the historic unfold-ing of works and of their truth content occurs in the critical medium: "A history of Beethoven critique might show how each new layer of the critics' consciousness of Beethoven unveiled new layers of his work, layers which in a certain sense were not even constituted prior to that process" (p. 149). It is only criticism, also, that enables music to be taken in by the public con-sciousness. On the other hand, it is tied to such institutions of social control and economic interest as the press. The critic's problem is to maintain his own opinion of the truth against the public opinion. He must also discern what is specific and new in a musical work. But largely because of the need for promptness, criticism tends to become merely reporting: "The best part of musical cognition slips between the institutions of public life" (p. 152).

In discussing national style (chap. 10), Adorno starts with the problem that the concept of the nation contradicts the universal concept of the human being, from which the bourgeois principle of equality is derived. On the other hand, nationality was the premise of realizing that principle. Similarly, music has both universal characteristics and national ones, and it really does not become universal, as Adorno shows, except through its national concretion—not by abstraction from its spatial-temporal context: "It is that national element, that rejection of the German spirit, which essentially constitutes Debussy's spirit. To feel him without it would not only strip the fiber of that music of the very thing it is; it would also diminish it" (p. 157). Thus, access to the universality of music is only granted to those who perceive its definite social nature.

From this general perspective, Adorno proceeds to discuss concrete instances of musical nationalism as it is connected with various bourgeois, or urban, centers. "From the early days of the bourgeois era," he observes, "the interaction of music and nation involved not only the productive aspect of the nationality principle but its destructive one" (p. 159). What Adorno thereupon presents in considerable detail is nothing less than a history of the interrelation of nationalism and internationalism in European music.

The chapter on the avant-garde (chap. 11), like the chapter on public opinion and critics, must be read with its date of publication in mind (1962). What Adorno understandably has in mind is the development of total organization and of chance as compositional principles. The constituents of the latest music he finds to be "totality, atomization, and the opaquely subjective act of uniting antitheses," of which antitheses totality and atomization would seem to be typical. Integration comes to be one with disintegration, Adorno says; there is a remnant of chance in the universal necessity, "a remnant that is essentially the same as the irrationality of rationalized society": "The complete accident that shows its detachment from the senses and promises something like statistical legality, and the equally unsensual integration that has ceased to be anything but its own literalness . . . arrive at the point of their identity" (p. 181). Adorno writes of the demolition of subjective meaning, of the abdication of the subject: "Compositions from which the subject withdraws as though ashamed of its own survival, compositions left to the automatisms of construction or chance—these get to the borderline of an unleashed technology that is superfluous beyond the utilitarian world" (pp. 181–82).

Ultimately, Adorno finds the problem of the avant-garde in its lack of support by the "World Spirit." The generation of Schönberg and his disciples were sustained by a boundless need to express themselves, for they knew that what was in them "was one with the World Spirit":

This concordance with the historic trend that helped artists to bear subjective isolation, poverty, slander, and ridicule is now lacking. In reality the individual is impotent, and nothing he accomplishes by himself and defines as his own can any longer be viewed as so substantial and important. And yet the seriousness of art requires an unquestioned conviction of its relevance. At the same time the element of subjective constraint, the expressive urge, decreases due to the constructivism in production. (p. 186)

There is little or nothing Adorno can say that is positive about the avant-garde or about the music of his time in general. It distances itself from empirical reality—from both the reality of reception and the reality of expression—and thus tends to become its own fetish: "That is the ideological aspect of the radically technological, anti-ideological work of art." And it is undermined by still another factor: "Its fully achieved autonomy schools it for heteronomy; the procedural freedom, the knowledge of being no longer bound to anything extraneous, permits it, as a method, to adjust to extraneous ends" (p. 187).

The final chapter of Adorno's work is devoted to "mediation"—that is, the mediation between music and society. The aspect of this Adorno considers first is the mediation by sociology, with its alternative procedures of empiricism and theory. The difficulty presented by the sociology of music is described by Adorno in an example: we are hardly able to deduce from our abundant knowledge of late capitalist and imperialist society the specific traits of the contemporaneous composers Debussy, Mahler, Strauss, and Puccini. Either the music or the sociology seems to receive inadequate treatment in this field. To decide that sociology should deal with the social effects of music is no solution for Adorno: "The social distribution and reception of music is a mere epiphenomenon; the essence is the objective social constitution of music in itself" (p. 197).

Yet Adorno moves on to discuss the distribution and consumption of music, in which the question of the mediation between music and society exists in concrete form. Here he proposes the method of the descriptive analysis of institutions and in the sociology of listeners the method of statistical inquiry. Musical production is considered also, but musical composition cannot be equated to material production, for society is not directly visible in art. It enters generally as hidden formal constituents that have a dialectic of their own that only reflects the real one. Thus, Adorno is led to consider the theory of the superstructure and the infrastructure of society and to the idea that "the mediation of music and society is apt to be taking place in the substructure of the labor processes underlying both realms" (p. 206). After discussing the galant style and the style of Beethoven in their relation to the bourgeoisie, Adorno concludes his lengthy and complex chapter with a consideration of technology, which embodies the state of the productive forces in an epoch and thus reveals the interrelation of superstructure and infrastructure or, specifically, of music and society.

In a postscript added to the English translation of his *Einleitung*, Adorno considers what a complete sociology of music would call for, as distinguished from an introduction. He discusses first the relation and the interaction between the productive forces of society and the circumstances of production. Productive forces include composing and reproduction (whether as interpretation or as automatic reproduction), while the circumstances of production are "the economic and ideological conditions to which each tone, and the reaction to each tone, is tied" (p. 219) as well as the musical mentality and taste of audiences. Clearly, the circumstances of production will involve "musical life."

Adorno turns to the matter of ideology, discussing when music is ideological and when we can speak of ideology *about* music. In considering the ideological content and the ideological effect of music, he then points out, sociology becomes part of a theoretical critique of society and examines whether music represents a socially right or wrong consciousness. This leads Adorno to the duality of serious music and light music, which he connects with the antithesis of productive forces and circumstances of production: "The productive forces are pushed into the upper, quasi-privileged sphere, are isolated, and are thus a piece of the wrong consciousness even where they represent the right one. The lower sphere obeys the predominant circumstances of production" (p. 225). The postscript concludes with a few suggestions for empirical research, which will clarify such matters as when the reception of music can properly be called "consumption."

Zofia Lissa

The most prominent theorist of musical aesthetics in the Communist sphere of influence and certainly the best known is the Polish Marxist Zofia Lissa. Aesthetics in general in the Soviet Union and Eastern Europe took on a sudden prominence around mid-century largely as a result of the publication of certain works of Stalin and the republication of Marx, Engels, and Lenin, whose ideas Stalin extended and developed. The chief impetus was provided by Stalin's *Der Marxismus und die Fragen der Sprachwissenschaft* (2d ed., 1951). This work, along with Stalin's *Ökonomische Probleme des Sozialismus in der UdSSR*, gave rise to a great number of aesthetic studies, among them Lissa's three volumes published in German in the 1950s: *Fragen der Musikästhetik* (1952 in Polish), *Über das Spezifische der Musik* (1954 in Polish), and *Die objektive Gesetzmässigkeit in der Musik* (1954 in Polish). The first of these is the most important for our present purpose.

Fundamental in Marxist aesthetics are the concepts of materialism and reality: "Today we see in dialectical and historical materialism the only scientific *Weltanschauung* that leads to the true knowledge of reality."[7] The methods of materialism, Lissa maintains, are applicable both to nature and to society, and they have produced a revolution in the scientific conception of the order of the world. But this transformation is not purely of theoretical interest; Marxist aesthetics, for example, in changing the attitude of composers and the nature of their creative activity, contributes to changes in the actual state of affairs.

The presupposition of materialism, Lissa argues, is that "the objective world is situated outside our ego and exists independently of our knowledge and that objectively existing actuality is reflected in our knowledge" (p. 11). Connected with this presupposition is the basic thesis that all manifestations of mentality are reflections of the real world and that the basic problem in musical aesthetics, therefore, is of the reflection of reality in music (*Widerspiegelung der Wirklichkeit*).

Axiomatic in Marxism is a fundamental duality that divides all manifestations of society and culture into two basic categories—infrastructure (or base) and superstructure. With this as a point of departure, the entire edifice of Marxist thought is concerned with how the two phases of this duality are interrelated. Lissa cites Stalin's pronouncement on the historical principle of this interrelation: the superstructure does not reflect changes in the level of development of the forces of production directly; rather, it reflects those forces after the changes in the base. Thus, the task of Marxist aesthetics and criticism, Lissa continues, is to narrow this gap consciously and actively.

Lissa then lists the problems for musicology that are raised, in her opinion, by Stalin's *Fragen der Sprachwissenschaft*:

> First of all there appears in a new light the problem of music as an area of ideology and in particular the problem of music as an element of the superstructure. With this there are bound up many other problems: the problem of the class-bound character of music, the problem of the permanence of values in music, the problem of the relation of music to language, the problem of the national character of musical culture, the problem of the class-bound character of institutions that belong to this culture, as well as many other problems. (p. 13)

Lissa concludes her introduction with certain general characterizations of Marxist aesthetics. Works of art are the result of a distinct type of human activity that we call "production" (*Schaffen*). Production is occupational *work* and has a definite goal. It serves the alteration of reality and the utilization of nature, in order to prepare useful products or instruments for further work. Artistic activity was originally no different. The specific attitude toward the conscious production of aesthetic values and the aesthetic "utilization" of works of art evolved only slowly and in a society at first not split into classes. As part of this evolution toward a specific productive process, we can even speak of instruments of music: "Like all work, artistic production was also subordinated to class interests. Not only *creations* of this activity, that is, works of art, had a class-bound character but also the type of this activity itself, that is, the productive processes whose result is works of art" (p. 15).

Lissa then proceeds to the questions that are implied for music in particular by Stalin's writings on linguistics. All such questions can be derived from the basic problem, which is whether music is an element of the superstructure. In this connection Lissa again cites Stalin:

> The base is the economic structure of society in the given stage of its development. The superstructure—this is the political, juristic, religious, artistic, and philosophic views of society and the political, juristic, and other institutions corresponding to them. . . . Every base has its own, corresponding superstructure. . . . The superstructure is brought forth by the base, but that in no way means that it merely mirrors the base. . . . On the contrary, once come into the world, it becomes a powerful, active force. . . . Indeed, the superstructure is produced by the base precisely to serve it, to help it actively to assume its definite form and solidify itself, to struggle actively to discard the old superceded base together with its old superstructure. (pp. 17–18)

Since Stalin's pronouncements have reference to the artistic or aesthetic views of society, Lissa considers the relation of these views to art itself. On the one hand, she argues, the views or ideas depend on art and are derived from it, but on the other hand they are realized in works of art and determine their character: "A change in aesthetic views depends on changes in art and philosophy, and both together depend on changes in society and its ideology. In times of highly developed and definitely crystallized and clearly formulated aesthetic views, the influence of these views on art also increases" (p. 19). There is, however, an important difference between the two, for "aesthetic views of a given type disappear completely and make way for other views, while works of art that depended on those views can also continue to be active, although the actual production of art is already operating with totally different norms and incorporates new aesthetic views." From this organic connection of art and views of art, Lissa concludes that art is an element of the superstructure. More specifically, "Art, insofar as it represents the expression of the views of the ruling class of its epoch, is bound up with the superstructure; it belongs to the superstructure." For music in particular, she affirms, this is true in a special way. Lissa takes this occasion to draw an important distinction between superstructure, ideology, and social consciousness: the concept of social consciousness has the largest range, ideology constitutes a part of this, and certain forms of ideology become the superstructure: "The relation of these three realms is changeable in the various historical epochs. It is important to emphasize at once that certain ideological manifestations not yet belonging to the superstructure can in another epoch become elements of the superstructure, or the reverse, that elements of the superstructure of a definite epoch can lose their superstructure character in a later epoch" (p. 21). Thus, the ideology of a given period can have a complex constitution, containing not only the ideology and superstructure of that period but also elements of a past superstructure that have become purely ideological. The life of a musical work, then, will not necessarily end with the demise of the social formation that has produced it.

When the base of society consists of economic relations that reflect the opposition of antagonistic classes, Lissa continues, the work of art can support only one of these classes and its ideology, but never the whole base. This view constitutes a striking contrast to Adorno's thesis that in its inner structure music reflects the class conflicts of society as a whole. In keeping with the social and cultural context of her thought, therefore, Lissa sees music as a medium suitable for political purposes, while Adorno, in keeping with the capitalist context of *his* thought, gives music the role of revealing the nature of society or, at best, of holding up an ideal or promise for the future, as it does in the writings of Ernst Bloch.

An important corollary of the Stalin-Lissa conception of the superstructure is the changing role of musical works and genres in successive cultural epochs. Thus, Palestrina's masses, for example—as Lissa points out—were part of the superstructure of their time, contributing to the solidification of their base by reinforcing religious ideas that were bound up with the feudal order of society. Today they no longer reinforce religious feelings, but they continue to act as works of art that express an inner experience that remains human and artistic to the highest degree. They do not belong to our superstructure, but they do belong to our cultural tradition—to our social consciousness—and, as part of our *Weltanschauung*, to our ideology. Revolutionary works, on the other hand, which are directed against the ruling class and the base of society, can, with the victory of revolution, enter the superstructure and buttress the new social order.

At any given time, in addition, there will be different tendencies or directions in music, which will be manifested in music of different kinds, or perhaps in the works of a single composer, or even within a single work. Even in the music of the superstructure, Lissa maintains, elements of past superstructures will be contained as well as those of future superstructures. Precisely this is the basis of continuity and also of dialectical development through the struggle of opposites. Thus, it is not only the superstructure that confirms the social base but also certain elements of the social consciousness, of the cultural tradition—elements that are seen to be appropriate in the light of the superstructure. Music of the past will remain part of our tradition or be revived in accordance with its relevance to the present. This process is further complicated, as Lissa points out, by the complex constitution of music, for music, and to a lesser extent all the arts, not only expresses ideas but also arouses feelings on the basis of these ideas and provides aesthetic satisfaction. It is these last constituents in particular that ensure its longevity while the relevance of the ideas may easily disappear:

> Seen from the perspective of the development of humanity, it is evident that emotional manifestations are less changeable than ideas, representations, concepts, and judgments. Art, which brings feelings to expression, lives longer than the actual ideas that have aroused those feelings, and this is so because people in different epochs in fact subordinate changing ideas to the works of art they experience, but the kind of feelings brought to expression in these works is conceived with the same categories. (p. 74)

Lissa gives the example of the grief that is brought to expression in Bach's Passions. Originally, this was grief over the suffering of Christ, but for us it has become grief that we feel over the fate of tortured humanity. Yet in contrast to the continuing understandability and strength of the feeling it expresses, music changes more rapidly than the other arts in its expressive medium and is in addition more closely dependent than they are on its material. Its durability is therefore subject to two opposed forces. The various arts, in any event, and even various types of music, will clearly differ in their tempo of historical change, and this will be one of the countless factors that are responsible for the complexity of the superstructure as a whole.

One of the basic tenets of Marxist aesthetics is that all the manifestations of culture in any historical period are determined by social class. This principle, however, like the determinative force of the economic foundation of the superstructure, is essentially axiomatic. Explanations have a spongy character and merely a reiterative force. "The work of art is the outcome and the reflection of the action of various forces," Lissa writes,

> which are impressed on the economic life, the order of society, and the consciousness of the artist. The work of art can thus not be considered as separated from social life. Both the content as well as the form of a

work of art are the result of those forces and of the way in which they are grasped and interpreted by the artist; that is, in the work of art there is mirrored not only *what* the artist sees in his environment but also the way *in which* he sees it and the way *in which* he reacts emotively to it. Now the artist is never only an individual; he is always a person of his class, in whose categories he thinks and whose criteria of value are his own. He represents what he regards to be of value and to be worthy of representation. (p. 88)

This is as definite as Lissa can manage to be, and it is followed by concrete examples of musical works, but it rests on the tenuous foundation of "various forces" that are totally unspecified.

It is further the case, Lissa continues, that musical works are not only *genetically* but also *functionally* class bound. Not only are they determined in their peculiarities of content and form by definite conditions of class, but they also stand *actively* in the service of these conditions. They serve in themselves a definite class ideology, and they are at the same time determined by it. Adjunctive to this conception is the belief in the existence of some central social conflict that takes a different form in each epoch, with the result that the ideological struggle takes place on a different plane in each. In the Middle Ages, for example, it took place around the axis "secular elements–sacred elements"; later, in the secular field of opera, it took place between court opera and opera buffa.

In spite of the class-bound character of musical works, Lissa is able to distinguish a number of elements in music that stand outside this determination and that are indifferent with respect to the fact of the social base. The tonal material of music, the tonal system, monody, various techniques of construction such as linear independence of voices or homophony, the system that sets rhythm against a repeated scheme of meter, and the basic organizational principles of repetition, variation, and recurrence as well as types of musical form such as the symphony—all are such elements or factors of music that persist through a variety of social structures or that are common to various classes in the same historical period.

Of considerable importance in Marxist aesthetics is the question of the relation of melody to the intonations of speech, or so-called speech-melody. In support of this relation, Lissa maintains that various types of recitative result from transporting speech-melody into music. In this category she places, perhaps incorrectly, the melody of ancient Greek drama, the melody of epic folk legends, and opera recitative. Behind this theory there is the thesis we have come on so often of the original unity of melody, word, and dance, the differentiation of which was finally completed by the recognition of instrumental music as an independent species of the art. Folk music provides Lissa with a direct demonstration of the organic coherence of speech and melody, for the melodic styles of music in different ethnic milieus are exactly as distinct as the peculiarities of intonation of speech. This shows, she argues, that it is exactly the character of intonation of speech that exercises an influence on the specific character of folk melody, for precisely here, in the folk song, has the coherence between music and speech been preserved to an extent no longer found in professional music. Lissa adduces several instances in professional music also, however, in which the melody of speech has influenced the melody of music to a high degree.

These considerations are preliminary to the discussion of the important but elusive concept of "intonation" in Soviet aesthetics. Lissa turns to Boris Assafjew, who first introduced the concept. The basis of Assafjew's conception is the continuous processes of thought and emotive experience that take place in the inner life of a human being. He holds that "the changes of vocal tensions in the linguistic expression of a human being are the mirroring of this continuity of thinking and feeling. . . . This variation of vocal tension, which determines the spoken word and the 'musical speech,' we call 'intonation' " (p. 234). Assafjew also projects a development in which intervallically indefinite speech gave rise to musical intervals, which were more exact determinants of emotive-intelligible meaning. Intonations are thus a melodic whole or a melodic idea or image that is made up of two or more tones and that has a definite character and expression. But Assafjew used the term in different ways, and its meaning became ambiguous and seemed at times to encompass all the expressive means of music. A motive or expressive melodic turn, in particular, could be used throughout a musical work, varying in its harmonization, in its tone color, and in the techniques of continuation, variation, or development applied to it. But, clearly, an intonation in this sense would take on a range of expressive value and significance that no longer conforms to the concept of intonation as a purely melodic turn with a specific expressiveness.

A major question in connection with intonation is whether music essentially reproduces the intonation of speech or whether it creates musical images in its own sonorous medium that are merely similar to the expression of feeling and thought in speech. In a given case, however, either one of these possibilities may be realized; a composer may have as a goal, for example, in vocal music in particular, the duplication of speech intonations. Lissa emphasizes, however, that the folk languages of the various ethnic and national milieus do indeed have their typical melodic intonations, which are the foundations of the national character of the folk music in each case. It is not the tonality of the music that creates the character but precisely the peculiar melodic turns—the intonations. The longevity of these intonations does not imply that, like words, they have a fixed semantic meaning, but it does ensure the continuity of musical tradition, even when the intonations are consciously taken up into sophisticated national styles. As she does to some extent throughout her book, Lissa here acts as an obvious apologist for the stylistic principle that was prescribed officially by Soviet aesthetics. She goes on, however, to apply this principle generally to any type of national stylization: "The concept of intonation accordingly can also explain the principle of so-called stylization in music. The basis of a stylization must be the taking over of an existing stock of intonations from a specific national milieu" (p. 249).

In the brief discussion Lissa devotes explicitly to style, her central point is the factual determination of style—its context, its form, and its technical components—by "social reality." She compares Haydn and Beethoven as an illustration: "Their production does not differ too much as far as typical musical norms of construction are concerned. But the world picture and the attitude toward this world that comes to expression in the creation of the two composers determines that each of them uses the same norms in a very different way, transforms the meaning of the individual elements of construction in his work, and achieves a totally different kind of *individual* style" (pp. 269–70). Here Lissa briefly outlines the social basis of this difference. The same social perspective informs the interaction of musical form and content:

> The form is determined by the content, like the superstructure by the base, and in return actively affects the content: it furthers or prejudices the content. Thus every new style in art can be traced back not only to new content but also to the new way in which the creative artist sees and grasps reality, to the new way in which his feeling reacts to the manifestations of reality and thus in consequence to the new way of expressing his inner experience of reality; but this *must* come about through complexes of new expressive means. All these factors are conditioned with respect to their quality by the given epoch (i.e., by the social order), by the social class, by the national milieu, and by the individual endowment of the creative artist. (pp. 270–71)

Lissa concludes her work with a consideration of Stalin's remark about the active role of the superstructure with respect to the base. "Naturally no one demands," she writes,

> that we set up the thesis that music influences economic relations directly; but because it influences the social consciousness of people who

by their attitude and their relation to a particular social reality can ac-
celerate or obstruct its development, it nevertheless influences economic
relations indirectly. Thus the art of social realism, for example, participates consciously in the struggle for the solidification of the socialist
order of society. (pp. 338–39)

The strength of Lissa's treatise as a whole derives from her detailed knowledge of musical history and musical style and especially of the changing
significance that musical works and genres undergo with time. This makes it
possible for her to appeal to a wide range of pertinent examples and makes it
impossible for her to content herself with ill-founded generalities. The result
is that she must do justice to the full complexity of stylistic phenomena and
strike some sort of compromise with the overriding themes of Communist
sociology. For this reason she must acknowledge throughout the aspects of
musical style that escape explanation in terms of Communist theory or even
in terms of social forces altogether. She does this quite freely, while Western Marxists, paradoxically, are much more orthodox and characteristically
allow no aspect of music to escape from social and sociological explanation.

Lissa, however, speaks of music that is part of the superstructure and
music that is not, of class-bound elements of music and of elements that
belong to all social classes or that transcend class altogether. Her conception of musical aesthetics, theory, and criticism conforms much more closely
to the Marxist tenets of the superstructure and of the class determination
of philosophic ideas. This is clearly what she finds to be the case. Lissa's
awareness of the complex relation of musical thought to music itself and
of its independent historical course are obviously quite consistent with the
finding that music and musical aesthetics follow different principles. While
philosophical thought can readily be interpreted as a reflection of social
reality, music is at once seen to be recalcitrant to such an interpretation.
Lissa in fact finds her results compatible with Stalin's view that the peculiarity of each manifestation of reality is important, not only what unites
them all. And Lenin, she points out, mocked philosophers who brought the
most various manifestations of reality under universal laws. "Now music
is precisely one of the arts," Lissa affirms, "that most of all escapes such
superficial 'universal laws' " (p. 329). At the same time, of course, this apparent flexibility of the pronouncements of Stalin and Lenin is set into the
rigid framework of "manifestations of reality." To some extent Lissa breaks
through this framework, and in her subsequent writings, as the political climate became less severe, her thought became much more objective. She also
examined many issues to which sociological considerations were irrelevant
or not significantly applicable.

Although the second and third treatises of the three Lissa wrote in the early 1950s have much less relevance than *Fragen der Musikästhetik* (1954) to the chief concerns of musical sociology, some attention should be given to the discussion in the second treatise (*Über das Spezifische der Musik*, 1957) of the basic Marxist principle of the "reflection of reality" in art. The treatise as a whole examines the various arts with respect to their similarities and differences in order to determine what is peculiar to music in particular or "specific" to it. Among these specific properties of music is a property basic to all the others, namely, the way in which music reflects reality.

Music can reflect two types of real manifestations, Lissa states—physical motions and human feelings—but feelings can be reflected only through the mediation of the expressive corporeal motions that accompany them and, in particular, through the motions of speech, with its intonations. Motions, however, are only one characteristic of a represented object of any kind; they are general rather than concrete and can be made to represent a definite object only with the help of a text or a program or the help of vision, as in dance or in the theater. Thus, music is often tied to other species of art, and the importance of the resulting composite musical arts is also peculiar to music.

What music alone can show us, Lissa maintains, is either the form of motion of a moving object or the form of something that the composer has experienced or that is called forth in him by some concrete object. It cannot represent feelings or objects fully or directly except in the special case in which they produce a characteristic sound that can be imitated. In music, therefore, the reflection of reality is almost exclusively indirect, or secondary, whether the reality is taken to be some concrete object, the feeling provoked by this object, or simply some state of feeling not connected with any concrete object.

Georg Lukács

The Marxist philosopher Georg Lukács was a political militant in the earlier part of his life and a leading member of the Hungarian Communist party, but the independence of his political views was incompatible with his official responsibilities in the Communist party, and from 1929 on he confined himself to literary criticism and philosophy. Although he was born and died in Budapest, he studied in Heidelberg, spent much of his life outside Hungary, and was really more German than Hungarian in culture. His *Die Eigenart des Ästhetischen* (1963) was conceived as part 1 of a large, three-part *Ästhetik* but was the only part that appeared. In it, Lukács undertakes to determine the place of aesthetic behavior in the whole of human activity, tracing its social-historical development from its origins both in magic and in everyday life. Within this ambitious framework he then focuses almost exclusively on a surprisingly traditional concept, namely, mimesis, which he understands in Marxist terms as "the reflection of reality." This characteristically Marxist viewpoint is derived philosophically, for the most part, from Aristotle and Hegel. It is also combined with the apparently antithetical conception of the work of art as a self-contained world of its own. In addition to this, the traditional notion of catharsis plays an important role, for in the experience of art, it is catharsis that brings the practical man of everyday life to the consciousness of his humanity.

Lukács starts with the fact that the mimetic character of music is now often disputed, and he sees the basis of this rejection in the denial of the objectivity of the external world and therefore of the fact that the effects of this world are the basis of human feelings. Yet the conception of music as a type of mimesis was in the past taken to be self-evident. Lukács cites the myth of Athena, who represented the cries of grief of Euryale, Medusa's sister, as an aulos melody. Pindar distinguishes between the grief and the mental contemplation of this grief. The one is a living human expression of feeling. The other, which gives objective form to the grief, is a mental accomplishment and divine. Lukács also cites Aristotle's opinion in book 8 of the *Politics* to the effect that rhythms and melodies provide imitations of feelings that hardly fall short of the actual affections and that the habit of feeling pleasure or pain at mere representations is not far removed from the same feeling about realities.

The sphere of inwardness, however—the inner life of human feelings—which is the object of musical imitation, is a product of the social-historical development of mankind. Furthermore, its unfolding, Lukács maintains, reveals an exact parallelism to the rise and efflorescence of music as an independent art. It was originally the facilitating effect of rhythm on work, he argues, and the consequent greater productivity and available leisure, that made possible the expansion of the feelings that accompanied work and with these the whole life of human feeling.

It was mimesis, on the other hand—in conjunction with words, gesture, and dance—that broadened music from rhythmic repetition to a highly varied temporal, melodic, and dynamic imitation. The originally magical purpose of mimesis, of influencing hidden powers and forces, entailed the production of a variety of aesthetic effects, which then gradually succeeded to attention—so Lukács argues—and acquired an independent interest. From this larger mimetic composite formulation, music then evolved as a mimesis of feeling in particular. Lukács finds it evident, in addition, that every process of feeling is bound to the external world that gives rise to it, that reactions of feeling are originally concrete in nature, inseparably tied to their cause. He treats in some detail the relation of three apparently un-related conceptions—the facilitation of work, the reaction to the external world, and mimesis—laying out a hypothetical course of evolution in which music evolved from the rhythm of work by the addition of melody and words and musical mimesis evolved from the mimesis of dance. Reaction to the external world, finally, became the essentially self-governing play of feelings in connection with purely instrumental music. These prolonged evolution-ary processes, of course, are not open to investigation and remain almost entirely a matter of speculation.

The recognition of the mimetic character of music from antiquity to the Enlightenment leads Lukács to the question of why it is denied today. He finds an explanation in the assumption that mimesis must be exact (which indeed the words *Widerspiegelung,* "mirroring," and *Abbild,* "image," sug-gest). Now there is an obvious dissimilarity between the original and its image in the case of music—between vibrations that can be exactly deter-mined numerically and auditory perceptions with their accompanying sen-sations or feelings. But some difference between the original and its copy is the basis of any theory of an image, whether the image is of a material mani-festation or of an idea. What is the color green, Lukács asks, as a reaction to a definite number of vibrations per second, if not an image of the physical situation in the human soul?

The unfounded expectation of similarity is further illuminated by a sec-ond prejudice of our epoch, Lukács continues: the Kantian conception of time as entirely separate from space, time as the form of our insight into our self and our inner state. Object and subject no longer exist in this "puri-fied" inwardness; the objectivity of objects must derive only from an a priori space. In Hegel's dialectical conception of time, by way of contrast, time is treated in natural philosophy rather than epistemology, and it cannot be separated from space or from material and its motion. Only from this point of view, Lukács maintains, can the peculiarity of music be grasped. Music is not a subjective, purely auditory play of sensations; rather, it implies the interaction of time, space, material, and motion, or, as in dance, it literally involves this interaction. The effect of the musical work as a unity, for ex-ample, depends on a quasi space: on the togetherness of temporally separated objectivities and thus on the subjective transcendence of the flow of time. But in this subjective constitution of quasi space in music the past and future are transformed into presentness only as a for-us, not as an in-itself. This subjective simultaneity, however, is a reflection of objective spatiotemporal reality, which similarly contains a necessary reference to the observer.

Lukács goes to considerable length to show how feeling differs from other modes of reaction in its relation to its object. In simple perception and in clear thought, for example, there is an active intentionality directed to a definite object as well as a tendency to grasp the true constitution of this object and to transform its in-itself into a for-us. With feelings, this relation is loose and indefinite. Feelings are always a reaction to the external world, but they remain subjective. They determine not so much the objective for-us of the object as a purely personal attitude toward it. They also have a considerable independence of the object.

In the course of distinguishing feelings from practical modes of behavior with respect to their different relations to reality, Lukács lays the foundation for his important conception of the mimesis of mimesis:

> It is therefore quite possible that feelings or sentiments are released by a definite circumstance of the external world but can also free themselves from its further effects on the subject and lead their own life in the subject independent of other impressions of the external world. . . . All this can then have as a consequence that the external stimulus takes on more and more definitely the character of a simple cause, that the adequation between what excites the feelings and these themselves seems largely to fade, indeed to be extinguished. At the same time, feelings and sentiments are much more subjective, so far as they are reflections of reality, much more removed from an approach to their true nature than are all other human reactions. The component of the subjectivity of reaction, the needs and peculiarities of the receptive subject, predominates in them; they lead even in life to a doubling of the process of reflection. It is less the object that is directly effective and more its transforming mirroring in the emotional life of the subject.[8]

Even though the full expression of the feelings in terms of their own logic and dynamics conflicts with the practical demands of life, Lukács argues, there is a need for such a fulfillment, which represents in fact an enrichment and deepening of life. Just as this need can be seen in the myth of Euryale, it can be seen in the once widespread custom of the prolonged weeping and lamentation of women as a mimesis of the expression of grief, indeed, one in which "the release of the imitated feelings was disturbed by neither external nor inner restraints": "The complete unfolding of the feelings accordingly proceeded here not directly in life itself, as an inner reaction to its events, but rather as one reduced to a mimetic representation, which—excluding everything heterogeneous—concentrated itself solely and uniquely on this sphere of feeling and thus released cathartic emotions in human beings who had through life itself become the actual subjects of these emotions" (pp. 363–64). Lukács now adds music to his argument:

The homogeneous medium of music can bring the feelings and sentiments of human beings to fulfillment in completely unclouded purity that has no obstruction precisely because, above all, it radically frees the mimesis of reality often spontaneously occurring in it from its twofold tie to an object. Because in doubled mimesis—in the homogeneous medium of tones that arise in this way—where the represented feelings and sentiments lose every external tie to an object through the indefinite objectivity and can expand completely in accordance with their own logic and dynamics, the truth of the reflected life model not only remains perfectly preserved in the mimetic image but also acquires possibilities of fulfillment that necessarily must remain closed to it in life. . . . Music constitutes itself as an independent art when this mimesis of the sentiments released in life, this image of an image, is put in a position to shape its true object in its innermost particular nature—set free, that is, from its direct tie to the cause summoning it forth in life. (pp. 366–67)

As the objective world disappears from music or, rather, is retained only as indefinite objectivity, music becomes a "language" of its own, and the musical work becomes a separate "world." This is the central process that Lukács seeks repeatedly to elucidate in all its aspects. The mission of inwardness in the life of the human species, he insists, is to develop its potentialities of feeling into a complete "world" without regard to their practical realization—something that is possible only in music. Only in the musical mimesis of inner mimesis does the otherwise suppressed logic of the feelings develop into its fulfillment—as the response to objective reality and the mediated reflection of it. Lukács stresses the fact that not only modern instrumental music but also the relatively rich and independent life of feeling that is the basis of this music are the products of a long historical development. He also emphasizes that music, conceived as the mimesis of feelings, "at first accompanied the primary mimesis, that of the factual situations of life that release the feelings, to some extent commented on this mimesis in terms of feeling, and ordered and stylized its directly understandable representation—in dance and song—according to its own needs" (p. 382).

Lukács undertakes to account for the nature of the composite musical arts. The connection of music with dance and poetry is the most intimate there is in the realm of aesthetics, he affirms. Unlike poetry, dance never frees itself from it, and music remains tied to dance and song in the earlier stages of its movement toward independence. That this is not simply a matter of its social commission, whether in opera and ballet or in church music, can be seen in the nineteenth and twentieth centuries, when these social functions receded and *Lied*, opera, and ballet continued to be of great importance:

This attraction of the best and highest music—not affected even by such radical changes in social function with respect to content and form—an attraction by the word in its revelation of the spiritually concrete or by the expressive gesture, points to layers of compatibility that to be sure can be set in motion by concrete social situations and interests but that at the same time are anchored deep in the nature of musical mimesis. We mean the specific form of the indefinite objectivity in it, which encompasses exactly what word and gesture are able to express, namely, those circumstances of the external world that have released the feelings depicted in music. (p. 383)

Such fundamental compatibility and complementation of the musical arts with one another stand in contrast to an important difference between poetry and music that Lukács takes as the central problem of all types of vocal music, namely, the difference in "artistic logic" between words and music: "Music must be grounded in the full living out of feelings, while in poetry feelings constitute only one element among others and thus time and again must subordinate themselves to the course of the whole, of the action and its dialectical unfolding. In the drama, therefore, naturally with a qualitative increase in intensity, feelings assume the same proportion as in life, while in music, on the contrary, they need not tolerate any obstruction in their immanent unfolding" (p. 386).

Lukács examines the clarification of the indefinite objectivity of music that is achieved by the addition of word and gesture. This clarification is never complete, but any kind of clarification would be aesthetically impossible, Lukács holds, if it represented an unmediated leap from purely instrumental music. The various kinds of concrete content that are at times suggested by an instrumental work, however, are more than a matter of personal associations and chance. There are great differences, Lukács argues, even in the interpretations given to a work in its various performances. Differences of this kind, furthermore, are also to be found in the various conceptions of the work of a painter or the various interpretations of a literary work. The different exegeses of *Hamlet* or *Faust* are certainly not more unequivocal or convergent in meaning than those of the works of Bach, Mozart, or Beethoven. In fact, "a change in the content of the testimony of reception belongs to the nature of every aesthetic effect" (p. 391). Deviations in the receptive formulation of content are in principle unavoidable and constitute an important criterion of the continued vitality of a work of art.

On the other hand, the degree of distinctness that can be achieved in the indefinite objectivity of a given work certainly varies with the work, and every authentic indication of a compositional intention or a program, of an external influence, or of an informed response must be evaluated with this in mind so that the appropriate degree of definition of the indefinite objectivity can be arrived at. In this consideration, Lukács sees the key to the problem of realism in music. As possible and even necessary as it is, he affirms,

> to formulate the content of the indefinite objectivity conceptually, so certainly does even this generalization, if it is to remain true to its object, have a definite limit; this is the case in every art, but above all in music, where, as was shown, even in its definite objectivity a greater fading takes place, a far more complete cancellation of the general, than, say, in the formative mode of verbal art. Supplemental conceptual generalization can therefore very easily stray into fields that have hardly any connection or even none at all with the concrete music that they seek to explain; naturally the more so, the more the generalization is not even based on the work itself but finds support in isolated statements of the composer. (p. 393)

In the relation of its definite to its indefinite objectivity—of its defined initial source, external or psychological, to its indefinable but more immediate inner object of imitation—music bears a fundamental resemblance to all the other arts. In an obscure passage, Lukács connects these two objectivities in music with the momentary personal and historical motivation of a work and its lasting meaning in the development of mankind. The realism of a work will then depend on how clearly the momentary constituent is seen in the perspective of the larger meaning. Realism in this sense is especially important in the effect of a work, in particular in its cathartic effect, which both Plato and Aristotle emphasized in connection with the ethical and social-pedagogical significance of music.

Music differs from the other arts, Lukács continues, because its mimesis of mimesis makes possible the otherwise impossible subjective living out of feelings. Inwardness is remarkably intensified and brought to fulfillment. After the liberation, the transport produced by the new world, the transition to life afterward, and the carryover of the aesthetic catharsis to its ethical consequences in the conduct of life are much more difficult than in the other arts: "It is not opposing obstructions that cause this equivocality of the catharsis but rather a distinct lack of direction of the feelings themselves, without an unequivocal foundation in the world of objects and with their intention directed toward indefinite objects only" (p. 397).

Lukács refers to the concern of Plato and Aristotle about the approval or rejection of music: about which music reflects which ethical feelings and which moral qualities and thus awakens them in the listener. This question is much more pressing for modern music, Lukács maintains, with its immeasurably intensive and extensive expansion of the sphere of feeling, which is clearly the artistic expression of a development in social life. To a formerly unimaginable extent feelings have been made into an instrument of private life. The individual, however, has a double physiognomy: "On the one hand the fate of the epoch is expressed in his fate—the disintegration of the old, directly effective communities, by which the individual person formerly participated as a member in the life of society. On the other hand the person now becomes private, apparently independent of the general destiny, lives his life for himself: his thoughts, actions, and feelings seem not to raise themselves over the level of this existence, not to leave his sphere behind" (p. 398).

The freeing of the world of feeling in music, accordingly, expresses itself in two ways. These feelings can be carried to their last consequences, which flow from the deep and tragic problems of life in capitalist society but which are blocked and distorted by life itself in this social context. The feelings in their musically purified fulfillment will then provide an experience of the hidden tie of these feelings with life, with the struggles and hopes, despairs and perspectives, of the human species: "This is the peculiar catharsis, never before available in such intensity, that modern music is capable of disseminating. But from the same social situation and its ramifications in music there can also follow a completely opposite kind of setting free of the feelings" (p. 399). Since the individual is thrown back purely into his own inwardness, the freedom of inner life can evoke simply the resultant mere particularity and its self-satisfaction. In this way there arises the exact opposite of catharsis: there is a reconciliation of the particular individuality with itself by means of a disappearance of any disturbing external world and by means of setting feelings in music on the level of a low, average particularity.

A final consideration is the connection of the "world"-constituting character of art with the overcoming of the particularity of the subject:

> The indisputable fact that every genuine musical work creates a "world" is the deeper aesthetic ground both for the rejection of every formalist consideration and for the rejection of those theories that see in the experience of the work a quasi-mystical fusion of the hearer and the heard. The deep effect of music consists precisely in leading the receptive person into its "world," from which the I of the receptive person stands separate as one different from him and, precisely in this specific difference, as one important for him. The musical work acquires the character of a self-subsistent "world" from the sources of its content: from the sterling totality of the feelings it evokes. (pp. 400–401)

Only when these are essential from the point of view of humanity, Lukács maintains, can a "world" in the sense of art arise:

> Which feelings are demanded and tolerated for a "world" to be unfolded from them is above all a social-historical question. The old folksongs, folk dances, etc., which reflect and bring to expression an extremely limited world of feeling, can mold musically genuine totalities because the reality they depict—in its tendency—was with all its narrowness still a human community in which essential problems of human life were fought out. Where on the contrary the "model" of the musically depicted feelings remains caught in the particularity of the man of every-day life and the music conducts merely its inner poverty and brittleness to an apparent, formal, and "reconciling" rounding, the mimesis of this mimesis can never acquire a truly artistic form. (p. 401)

What Lukács has done in this extended discussion of music is to take the notion of "imitation" as a central principle and carry it through the full range of its implications and significance. Starting with its ancient ancestry and winding up with its modern application to instrumental music, he has explored its connections with the various musical arts both individually and in their combinations, encompassing at the same time the putative historical and prehistorical evolution of music, its interrelation with society, its relation to feelings, its cathartic effects and their ethical value, and the nature of the musical work of art. There is in fact hardly a major aesthetic aspect of music that Lukács is unable to examine from the vantage point of imitation, although much of the historical and factual support he adduces in the process is both familiar and speculative.

It can be said also of the very revival of the apparently superseded conception of musical imitation that it is really due not to Lukács but to Marxism. What Lukács unquestionably has accomplished, however, is to reveal the flexibility and explanatory power of the idea of imitation. And he has done this largely on the basis of his theory of the imitation of imitation, which compactly provides an explanation for both the autonomous character of music and its obvious involvement with feeling but does not entirely sever its required connection to the external world and the emotional experience of people in general, whether actual or fictional.

As far as the idea of imitation itself is concerned, we have seen in the case of music, at any rate, that it has appeared in the most varied guises and been subjected to an even still more varied aesthetic and scholarly analysis. Of this history Lukács displays little awareness. Instead of tracing it out, however, he does add to it a new and distinctive contribution. This contribution is so imaginative and so well worked out that it lends philosophical tradition and dignity to Marxist thought and at the same time is of value for aesthetic philosophy in general. The sociological constituent does not control or prejudice the whole but acts as a significant dimension that expands modern aesthetic thought.

Blaukopf, Silbermann, Kneif, and Others

The first several decades of musical sociology have seen the publication of a number of general introductions to the field, and while a new area of investigation will always call for a definition of the field, an explanation of how it differs from its related predecessors, and a map of its contents, there seem to have been special reasons for the continuing interest in such activities in the case of musical sociology. During these decades musicology itself was growing, and as this growth accelerated, musicology was subjected to a series of fads; the increasing number of people seeking admission to the discipline inevitably produced an interest in any area of study that was not overcrowded and that offered a chance of securing attention immediately. In addition, there was intrinsic difficulty in the task of determining the proper concerns of the sociology of music. For one thing, sociology has always been directed to the present rather than the past, and this has increasingly incurred ever-new problems. The field is a dynamic one that is rapidly expanding. Beyond this, its value was emphasized by the important place it had in Communist thought.

After a series of programmatic essays by Theodor Adorno, Walter Serauky, Hans Mersmann, Hans Engel, Paul Honigsheim, Alphons Silbermann, Tibor Kneif, and others had started to appear, a series of introductory handbooks repeatedly addressed basic questions of method, purpose, and scope. One of the earliest of these was the *Musiksoziologie* (1951) of Kurt Blaukopf, which bears the characteristic subtitle *Eine Einführung in die Grundbegriffe mit besonderer Berücksichtigung der Soziologie der Tonsysteme*. From this it is evident that Blaukopf's perspective derives from that of Max Weber, from whom he also took his interest in ideal types. Both these interests are revealed in Blaukopf's dependence on Joseph Yasser's theory of evolving tonality. From the preface to the essentially unchanged second edition of the *Musiksoziologie* of 1972, we learn that Blaukopf came to broaden his view of the field so that it was no longer restricted to a concern with tonal systems. The sociology of tonal systems is only one aspect of musical sociology, he now insists, but it remains a decisive aspect and an approach that is no less important than it was decades ago. The same preface also modifies his original belief that musical sociology is an auxiliary science of musicology that has a transitional character and that will last only until musicology itself assumes sociological tasks. But it has proved itself, he now admits, to be an independent discipline with its own methods of research.

Another noteworthy introduction to musical sociology is Alphons Silbermann's *Wovon lebt die Musik: die Prinzipien der Musiksoziologie* (1957). Silbermann seeks to end the confusion surrounding the nature of the field by proposing a general systematization. In three introductory chapters, he discards a variety of incorrect ways of approaching music, draws endless distinctions between related types and fields of social study, and examines the aspects of musical experience and how it is determined socially. He then introduces what he takes to be the correct foundational concept of the field: the sociomusical group. In the three chapters that constitute the main body of his book, he examines in turn the structure of such groups, their function, and their behavior. In connection with both structure and behavior, the groups involved in musical production are considered first and those involved in musical consumption second. In connection with the function of groups, Silbermann considers their leadership and their interaction, their types of activity, and their relation to musical taste, institutions, economics, and culture. The result is a well-organized scheme for a complete science of sociomusical groups. The work concludes with a short chapter on sociomusical planning and value.

By far the most important of the introductions is Adorno's epochal *Einleitung* of 1962, which we have considered above. This is the opposite of the abstract framework that Silbermann presents as a guide for future types of research, for Adorno's introduction is a series of vital engagements with concrete sociological problems, each containing its distinctive contribution to a sharply defined view of what musical sociology should be.

The *Musiksoziologie* (1971) of Tibor Kneif is a valuable critical study that subjects the views of others, notably those of Silbermann, Blaukopf, and Adorno, to severe criticism. In examining the assumptions, claims, methods, and results of empirical sociology, metaphysical sociology, and Marxist sociology, Kneif is merciless in exposing the failings of each school of thought. As the most important and most vulnerable of the writers, Adorno receives the most attention. Kneif cites two pronouncements: "The fewer demands of its own music makes, the more it is prepared as a social consumer commodity, that much the more directly can it be thought of in sociological categories." And, "The sociological interpretation of music is possible that much the more adequately, the higher the music ranks. With simpler, more regressive, worthless music the interpretation is questionable." [9] A discipline has little to recommend it, he comments, if in it someone can write twice on the same theme, but in diametrically opposed senses.

Kneif subsequently considers Adorno's view that music reflects society as a totality rather than merely one or another contending class or faction. This question can be answered neither empirically nor logically, Kneif points out: "A musical sociology seems completely arbitrary when we come on the assertion that one piece of music is better than another because the contradictions of society in the first case are expressed more clearly." Kneif finally extends his condemnation to the discipline itself—to musical sociology as a whole. "The value of any intellectual perception can be measured by the consequences that follow from it," he maintains. "Granted that the demonstration that all music is determined and caused by social relations was completely successful: what we were then to deduce from this would represent a considerable problem. With a fine sense of the uselessness of their labors, sociologists of music have until now restrained themselves from proposing conclusive proofs of the causal connection of society and the musical work." [10]

In his *Einführung in die Musiksoziologie* (1978), Peter Rummenhöller was guided by Blaukopf's postulate that the true task of musical sociology is the sociological grounding of music history and by Adorno's principle of inquiring into the various details of the structure of musical works, especially with respect to their social content. He was also guided by his intention to write about music itself, to make it the point of departure for all his reflections. As a result, the varied studies in musical sociology that make up his introduction leave little to be desired. Music provides an understanding of society that would be less complete without it, and society complements our understanding of music to make it more comprehensive. That musical sociology will eliminate itself, as Rummenhöller believes, after it has provided musicology with a foundation hardly seems inevitable, for new aspects of the relation between society and music will doubtless continue to be uncovered indefinitely, and, certainly, since music will continue to be created and society will continue to change, the relation between music and society will continue to change as well.

With Kurt Blaukopf's second introduction, *Musik im Wandel der Gesellschaft: Grundzüge der Musiksoziologie* (1984), we reach another kind of definitive work in the field, here with respect to comprehensiveness. Blaukopf has clearly given up his overriding interest in tonal systems, which are dealt with in a few pages, and has transformed the idea of musical sociology as an auxiliary science, producing a careful combination of the field with musicology. He uses the two disciplines in close conjunction in a general investigation of all the varied relations between music and society. The generality is conceived historically as well as analytically; it is the changing nature of society that is the explicit principle of the book, although the history is largely one of sociological thought itself. Thus, after an initial chapter on the goals of musical sociology, Blaukopf takes all the different aspects of his subject in chronological order.

In the earlier chapters of this series, the conjunction of sociology and history is not really in evidence; the two disciplines simply alternate from chapter to chapter. But gradually the conjunction becomes so intimate that it is impossible to disentangle the two, especially because music history itself becomes sociological and musical sociology itself is presented historically. There are chapters devoted, respectively, to the origin of music, the beginnings of general sociology, Taine's concept of a sociology of art, changes in the concept of the historical development of music, the influence of acoustical, sociological, and ethnological ideas, art and the materialistic concept of history, the influence on music of the mechanical characteristics of the piano, the work of art as a product and a factor of social activity, the issues of the sociology of art according to Marx, economics, leisure, and life-style, the contribution of Simmel to musical sociology, Combarieu and French sociology, the sociological analysis and the reception of the musical work, music in Max Weber's sociology, the development of the harmonic perception of music, Riegl's "will to art" as a sociological concept, Christianity and sensuousness, mutations in musical behavior, mutation due to technical media, the relation of architecture and music, the acoustic effects of the environment, the study of the musical public, the cultural influence of scientific discovery and technical invention, the economic dilemma of the performance arts, the contributions of Adorno, the relation between artistic change and social change, the new tasks of musical sociology, and the universal history of music.

Each of these topics is examined historically, and each is based on literal citations of authorities. The result is a copiously documented history of musical and sociological thought that taken as a whole gives a rather diffuse picture of a large field that somehow seems to contain the discipline of musical sociology, which is thus generally localized but not sharply defined.

As far as musical aesthetics is concerned, the value of sociology clearly resides in its enlargement and enhancement of our understanding of music through the revelation of new facets of musical meaning. Our present subject matter, in spite of the novel features of its concentrated view of the social aspect of music, is thus obviously related to the basic problems we dealt with in chapter 12, at the beginning of the twentieth-century part of this history. It also provides another instance, therefore, of the interconnections we have repeatedly observed among the different areas of aesthetic thought in music. These different areas themselves are simply an instance, in the twentieth century, of a systematic and exhaustive group of viewpoints from which the art of music can be regarded. Each viewpoint illuminates a corresponding aspect of music, which in spite of an appearance that is specific to its historical time, may represent an underlying possibility of music that is always available. For it would seem that music can always be examined with respect to its peculiar constitution or structure, with respect to its human significance—whether it is found to exert magical or emotional influence, to embody speculative thought, or to possess social or historical properties— or with respect to its relation to other areas of expression or its combination with other arts. The views of a given century, then, would seem to represent in some way all these diverse possibilities along with their intrinsic relation to one another.

CHAPTER ONE

1. Plato, *Dialogues*, 1:874–75.

2. Cicero, *Republic*, bk. 6, chap. 5. The translation can be found in Macrobius, *Commentary*, 73–74.

3. Spitzer, "World Harmony."

4. Milton, *Complete Works*, 52, 66.

5. Plato, *Dialogues*, 1:665, 675.

6. Ibid., 2:474–75.

7. *Riverside Shakespeare*, 280–81.

CHAPTER TWO

1. Listenius, *Musica*, chap. 1.

CHAPTER THREE

1. Strunk, *Readings*, 220, 256–57.

2. Vicentino, *L'antica musica*, bk. 4, chap. 29. When a quotation is referred to a foreign language source (or to Lippman, *Aesthetics*), the translation is by the author.

3. Strunk, *Readings*, 394, 396.

4. Ibid., 406–12.

5. Ibid., 406–10.

6. See Lippman, *Aesthetics*, 1:91–92.

7. See Strunk, *Readings*, 290, 301.

8. Ibid., 294, 299.

9. A partial translation can be found in ibid., 302–22.

10. Zarlino, *Sopplimenti*, 317.

11. Strunk, *Readings*, 367–69.

12. Ibid., 370–72.

13. Ibid., 371–72.

14. Ibid., 374–75.

15. Ibid., 377, 380, 381.

16. Ibid., 378, 391, 379.

17. See Lowinsky, *Secret Chromatic Art*.

18. Solerti, *Le origini*, 112–13.

CHAPTER FOUR

1. See Solerti, *Le origini*, 195–228.

2. Both quotations from Freeman, *Opera*, 258, n. 12.

3. Ibid., 2–4.

4. Ibid., 6–9.

5. Ibid., 32–33.

6. Ibid., 9–11.

7. See Cowart, *Origins*, 19–20.

8. Saint-Evremond, *Letters*, 206–10.

9. Ibid., 206–7, 215, 216–17.

10. Oliver, *Encyclopedists*, 5–6.

11. Flaherty, *Opera*, 13–14.

12. Ibid., 14–15.

13. Ibid., 15–16.

14. Ibid., 16–17.

15. Ibid., 17–18.

16. Weisstein, *Essence*, 39–42.

17. Ibid., 42–43.

CHAPTER FIVE

1. Mattheson, *Neu-Eröffnete Orchestre*, 126–27.

2. Ibid., 160–61.

3. Ibid., 231–53.

4. Buttstedt, *Ut, mi, sol*, 56–57.

5. See, e.g., Mattheson, *Forschende Orchestre*, 62–63.

6. Mattheson, *Capellmeister*, 17, 18.

7. Ibid., 19, 20.

8. Lippman, *Aesthetics*, 1:124, 125, 127. Page numbers of subsequent citations to Mattheson's *Capellmeister* are to this translation and are given in the text.

9. Lippman, *Aesthetics*, 1:164–65. Page numbers of subsequent citations of chap. 2 of Krause's *Poesié* are to this translation and are given in the text.

10. Krause, *Poesié*, 53. Subsequent citations of Krause's *Poesié* are from chaps. 3 and 4 and are the author's translations from the original. Page numbers are given in the text.

11. *Der Critische Musicus*, no. 8, pp. 46–47.

12. Strunk, *Readings*, 595, 594.

13. Ibid., 591.

14. Quantz, *Playing*, 254, 124–25, 133, 163.

15. Ibid., 126, 273.

16. Bach, *Essay*, 79, 81.

17. Ibid., 152, 153.

18. See, e.g., Lippman, *Aesthetics*, 1:138 (par. 64), 147 (par. 105).

CHAPTER SIX

1. Le Huray and Day, *Music*, 18. Page numbers of subsequent citations are given in the text.

2. Ibid., 28–29.

3. Ibid., 48–49. Page numbers of subsequent citations are given in the text.

4. Lippman, *Aesthetics*, 1:368.

5. Ibid., 328.

6. Ibid., 153–54.

7. Ibid., 282.

8. Ibid., 287. Page numbers of subsequent citations are given in the text.

9. Ibid., 300, 302. Page numbers of subsequent citations are given in the text.

10. Ibid., 179. Page numbers of subsequent citations are given in the text.

11. Ibid., 190. Page numbers of subsequent citations are given in the text.

12. Ibid., 202–3. Page numbers of subsequent citations are given in the text.

13. Le Huray and Day, *Music*, 140. Page numbers of subsequent citations are given in the text.

14. Lippman, *Aesthetics*, 1:216. Page numbers of subsequent citations are given in the text.

15. Ibid., 243. Page numbers of subsequent citations are given in the text.

16. Smith, "Imitative Arts," 205–6, 217. Page numbers of subsequent citations are given in the text.

17. Mattheson, *Capellmeister*, 15 (par. 49), 16.

18. Goldschmidt, *Musikästhetik*, 133–34.

19. Marpurg, *Beyträge*, 1:285, 292, 293.

20. Ibid., 523. Page numbers of subsequent citations are given in the text.

21. Marpurg, *Briefe*, 2:278.

22. See Goldschmidt, *Musikästhetik*, 139–42.

23. *Herders Werke*, 4:90. Page numbers of subsequent citations are given in the text.

24. Heinse, *Dialogen*, 47–49. Page numbers of subsequent citations are given in the text.

25. See, e.g., *Musikalisch-Kritische Bibliothek* 1 (1778): 53ff.; 2 (1779): 126ff.; see also 2 (1779): 348.

26. Goldschmidt, *Musikästhetik*, 203. Page numbers of subsequent citations are given in the text.

27. Kant, *Critique*, 12. Page numbers of subsequent citations are given in the text.

28. Goldschmidt, *Musikästhetik*, 225–27.

29. Schiller, *Aesthetic Education*, 105–6.

30. Seifert, *Körner*, 147. (*Körner* contains a reprint of the essay. See also Goldschmidt, *Musikästhetik*, 223–25.) Page numbers of subsequent citations are given in the text.

CHAPTER SEVEN

1. Freeman, *Opera*, 13. Page numbers of subsequent citations are given in the text.

2. Ibid., 15–16.

3. Ibid., 21.

4. The discussion of opera in the 1821 edition of Muratori's *Della perfetta poesia* occupies pp. 46–74 of vol. 3. Page numbers of subsequent citations are given in the text.

5. See Freeman, *Opera*, 32–35.

6. Ibid., 35–49. Page numbers of subsequent citations are given in the text. (There is also a more accurate English translation of the dialogue on opera in Weiss, "Pier Jacopo Martello.")

7. Weiss, "Pier Jacopo Martello," 403.

8. Page numbers of subsequent citations are to Pauly's translation and are given in the text.

9. Freeman, *Opera*, 52. Page numbers of subsequent citations are given in the text. My discussion of Maffei is based on pp. 51–54.

10. Strunk, *Readings*, 658. Page numbers of subsequent citations are given in the text.

11. Ibid., 670, n. e.

12. Goldschmidt, *Musikästhetik*, 321–24. Page numbers of subsequent citations are given in the text.

13. This controversy is considered in detail in Cowart, *Origins*, chap. 3, and it is reprinted in full in Bonnet, *Histoire*, vol. 3.

14. Strunk, *Readings*, 486.

15. Cowart, *Origins*, 56.

16. Strunk, *Readings*, 492.

17. See the discussion of Du Bos in chap. 6.

18. Weisstein, *Essence*, 66–67.

19. Goldschmidt, *Musikästhetik*, 290–91.

20. Ibid., 290.

21. Batteux, *Beaux-arts*, 267–68. Page numbers of subsequent citations are given in the text.

22. Weisstein, *Essence*, 75–78. Page numbers of subsequent citations are given in the text.

23. Ibid., 79–80.

24. Cowart, *Origins*, 106.

25. Facsimile included in Launay, ed., *Querelle*. This collection of French tracts contains facsimiles of all the letters and pamphlets of the Buffon War that are discussed below. There are English translations (or partial translations) of Grimm's *Petit prophète* and of Rousseau's *Lettre* in Strunk, *Readings*, and of Rameau's *Observations* in Lippman, *Aesthetics*, vol. 1.

26. Cowart, *Origins*, 108.

27. Rousseau, *Oeuvres*, 6:176.

28. Oliver, *Encyclopedists*, 16–17.

29. Goldschmidt, *Musikästhetik*, 122–25, 311–14; Cowart, *Origins*, 111–13.

30. Goldschmidt, *Musikästhetik*, 304–6.

31. Included in *Querelle*.

32. Weisstein, *Essence*, 94–95.

33. The discussion of music in Tancock's translation of Diderot's *Rameau's Nephew* is found largely on pp. 97–107. Page numbers of subsequent citations are given in the text.

34. Rousseau, "Opéra," 343–44. Page numbers of subsequent citations are given in the text.

35. Goldschmidt, *Musikästhetik*, 299–300.

36. Ibid., 300.

37. Diderot, *Oeuvres*, 8:505.

38. Strunk, *Readings*, 677.

39. Ibid., 681–83.

40. *Mémoires*, 153–90. Page numbers of subsequent citations are given in the text.

41. These letters are contained in ibid.

42. Weisstein, *Essence*, 110–11.

43. For an English translation of this section of the treatise, see Lippman, *Aesthetics*, vol. 1.

44. Much of the material of this section is derived from Flaherty, *Opera*.

45. Ibid., 139–40.

46. Ibid., 156.

47. Krause, *Musikalische Poesie*, 374.

48. Flaherty, *Opera*, 227–28. Page numbers for subsequent citations of Lessing and Wieland (also taken from Flaherty) are given in the text.

49. Moos, *Philosophie*, 33. Page numbers for subsequent citations are given in the text.

50. The passages cited below are taken from the English translation of the dialogue in Lippman, *Aesthetics*, vol. 1. Page numbers are given in the text.

CHAPTER EIGHT

1. Wackenroder, "*Confessions*," 194. Page numbers of subsequent citations are given in the text.

2. Gatz, *Musik-Ästhetik*, 353.

3. Ibid., 344.

4. Wackenroder, "*Confessions*," 179.

5. Siegel, *Music*, 131.

6. Herder, *Kalligone*, 179–81. Page numbers of subsequent citations are given in the text.

7. Ibid., 181, 183.

8. Ibid., 184–85.

9. See Rohr, *Hoffmanns Theorie*, pt. 1.

10. Strunk, *Readings*, 775–76. Page numbers of subsequent citations of Hoffmann's "Beethovens Instrumentalmusik" and "Der Dichter und der Komponist" are given in the text.

11. Hoffmann, *Novellen*, 119–20. Page numbers of subsequent citations are given in the text.

12. Strunk, *Readings*, 803. Page numbers of subsequent citations are given in the text.

13. Cited in Steinkruger, *Ästhetik*, 35.

14. Ibid.

15. *Schellings Werke*, pt. 1, vol. 5, 390. (Volume 5 of pt. 1 is Schelling's "Philosophy of Art.") Page numbers of subsequent citations are given in the text.

16. My consideration of Solger's *Erwin* is based on pp. 264–96 of the text, which is often presented with little change even when it is not given in the form of translated passages. Page numbers of citations are given in the text.

17. Schopenhauer, *World*, 1:257. Page numbers of subsequent citations are given in the text.

18. Hegel, *Fine Art*, 3:342. Page numbers of subsequent citations are given in the text. Osmaston's translation is widely available, but not always satisfactory. When necessary, I have made use of the *Vorlesungen*, which is cited in brackets by volume and page numbers.

CHAPTER NINE

1. Kierkegaard, *Either/Or*, 1:88. Page numbers of subsequent citations are given in the text.

2. Here the Classical aesthetics of the self-contained work of art becomes a Romantic aesthetics of a distant realm.

3. Wagner, *Schriften*, 3:23. Page numbers of subsequent citations are given in the text.

4. Strunk, *Readings*, 878. Page numbers of subsequent citations are given in the text.

5. Wagner, *Schriften*, 3:164. Page numbers of subsequent citations are given in the text.

6. Ibid., 12: 20.

7. Ibid., 4:1–2. Page numbers of subsequent citations are given in the text.

8. See ibid., 6–67 (secs. 1–3).

9. See Strunk, *Readings*, 374.

10. Wagner, *Schriften*, 4:158. Page numbers of subsequent citations are given in the text.

11. Spencer, "Origin," 396. Page numbers of subsequent citations are given in the text.

12. Darwin, *Descent*, 277. Page numbers of subsequent citations are given in the text.

13. Darwin, *Expression*, 83–85. Page numbers of subsequent citations are given in the text.

14. Gurney, "Disputed Points," 107. Page numbers of subsequent citations are given in the text.

15. Gurney, *Power*, 479–88. Page numbers of subsequent citations are given in the text.

16. Spencer, "Postscript," 437–38. Page numbers of subsequent citations are given in the text.

17. Newman, *Study of Wagner*, 163–64.

18. Newman, Musical Studies, 192.

19. Hausegger, *Ausdruck*, 33–34. Page numbers of subsequent citations are given in the text.

CHAPTER TEN

1. Katz and Dahlhaus, *Contemplating Music*, 368. Page numbers of subsequent citations are given in the text.

2. Gatz, *Musik-Ästhetik*, 404. Page numbers of subsequent citations are given in the text.

3. Nägeli, *Vorlesungen*, 105.

4. Hanslick, *Beautiful*, 89, 92.

5. Gatz, *Musik-Ästhetik*, 87.

6. Lazarus, *Leben*, 444. Page numbers of subsequent citations are given in the text.

7. Helmholtz, *Sensations*, 3. Page numbers of subsequent citations are given in the text.

8. See the discussion of Zimmermann in Moos, *Philosophie*, 254–61.

9. Gatz, *Musik-Ästhetik*, 435.

10. Ibid., 432.

11. See the discussion of Siebeck in Moos, *Philosophie*, 284–93.

12. Gatz, *Musik-Ästhetik*, 460.

13. Hostinsky, *Musikalische-Schöne*, 463. Page numbers of subsequent citations are given in the text.

14. Gurney, *Power*, 117. Page numbers of subsequent citations are given in the text.

CHAPTER ELEVEN

1. Oersted, *Schriften*, 3:17–38.

2. Lippman, *Aesthetics*, 2:310–11. Page numbers of subsequent citations are given in the text.

3. Gatz, *Musik-Ästhetik*, 221. Page numbers of subsequent citations are given in the text.

4. Gatz, *Musik-Ästhetik*, 198. Page numbers of subsequent citations are given in the text.

5. See the discussion of the work in Moos, *Philosophie*, 353–60.

6. See ibid., 307–13.

7. See ibid., 335–40.

8. Stade, *Musikalisch-Schönen*, 1–2. Page numbers of subsequent citations are given in the text.

9. Engel, *Musik*, 1–2. Page numbers of subsequent citations are given in the text.

10. A view that is of course in direct opposition to Wagner's realistic aesthetics of the 1850s.

11. See Engel, *Musik*, 302–11. The "immanent driving force" of music lies not in sensuousness but in the "logically rational," the "spiritual" (*Geistig*). Here arithmetic and physiology (Herbart, Euler, Helmholtz) serve a higher law— the simple logical law of thesis, antithesis, synthesis (Hauptmann).

12. See esp. pp. 266ff.

13. Hartmann, *Philosophie*, 1. Page numbers of subsequent citations are given in the text.

CHAPTER TWELVE

1. "Anregungen zur Förderung musikalischer Hermeneutik" (1902) and "Neue Anregungen zur Förderung musikalischer Hermeneutik: Satzästhetik" (1905). References are to the English translation of these essays in Lippman, *Aesthetics*, vol. 3. Page numbers of citations are given in the text.

2. Adorno, "Kontroverse," 20.

3. Schering, "Symbol," 380–81.

4. Page references are to the English translation of this essay in Lippman, *Aesthetics*, vol. 3, and are given in the text.

5. Schering, "Entstehen," 26–27, 28–29.

6. Langer, *New Key*, 34. Page numbers of subsequent citations are given in the text.

7. Goodman, *Languages*, 50, 53.

8. Beardsley, "Understanding Music," 65, 66, 67.

9. Lévi-Strauss, *The Raw and the Cooked*, 20. Page numbers of subsequent citations are given in the text.

10. Eco, *Struttura*, 313. Page numbers of subsequent citations are given in the text.

11. Ruwet, "Méthodes," 483. Page numbers of subsequent citations are given in the text.

12. Ruwet, *Langage*, 12, 14.

13. Faltin, "Musikalische Bedeutung," 16–17.

14. Eggebrecht, "Ueber begriffliches und begriffloses," 116. Page numbers of subsequent citations are given in the text.

15. Scruton, *Art and Imagination*, 174. Page numbers of subsequent citations are given in the text.

16. Scruton, "Understanding Music," 85. Page numbers of subsequent citations are given in the text.

17. Scruton, "Analytic Philosophy," 174.

CHAPTER THIRTEEN

1. Pfrogner, *Musik*, 352.

2. Schenker, *Der Tonwille*, no. 2, p. 3.

3. Schenker, *Meisterwerk*, 1:12.

4. Lippman, *Aesthetics*, 3:65–66.

5. Pfrogner, *Musik*, 346–47, 348.

6. Ibid., 358. Page numbers of subsequent citations are given in the text.

7. Busoni, *Essence*, 20. Page numbers of subsequent citations are given in the text.

8. Ibid., 23.

9. Strobel, "Neue Sachlichkeit," 256.

10. Besseler, "Musikästhetik," in his *Aufsätze*, 57–58.

11. Doflein, "Die neue Musik," 335. Page numbers of subsequent citations are given in the text.

12. Eisler, *Rebel*, 27–28.

13. Tiessen, *Jüngsten Musik*, 59, 70.

14. Doflein, "Beurteilung Gegenwärtiger Musik," 290.

15. Adorno, "Motive II," 200.

16. Adorno, "Motive III," 238.

17. Ibid., 238, 239.

18. Doflein, "Gegenwart," 299.

19. Benz, "Das Problem," 637.

20. Reger, "Bachs Funktion," 261.

21. Adorno, "Kontroverse," 21.

22. Krenek, *Neue Musik*, 12.

23. Schloezer, "Strawinsky," 132.

24. Ibid., 140.

25. Adorno, "Social Situation," 132–33.

26. See *Colloquium*, 151–72. Page numbers of subsequent citations are given in the text.

27. Adorno, *Philosophy*, 49–50. Page numbers of subsequent citations are given in the text.

28. Stravinsky, *Poetics*, 27–28. Page numbers of subsequent citations are given in the text.

29. Souvtchinsky, "La Notion," 317.

30. Stockhausen, *Texte*, 1:18. Page numbers of subsequent citations are given in the text.

31. Ibid., 99.

32. Ibid., 106.

33. *Stockhausen on Music*, 38–39. Page numbers of subsequent citations are given in the text.

34. Page references, given in the text, are to the English translation in Lippman, *Aesthetics*, vol. 3.

35. Hartmann, *Aesthetik*, 201–2.

36. Ingarden, *Work of Music*, 50, 51.

37. Cage, *Silence*, 3. Page numbers of subsequent citations are given in the text.

CHAPTER FOURTEEN

1. Husserl, *Phenomenology*, 42–43. Page numbers of subsequent citations are given in the text.

2. Schutz, "Fragments," 29. Page numbers of subsequent citations are given in the text.

3. Ingarden, *Ontologie*, 22–23. Page numbers of subsequent citations are given in the text.

4. Brelet, *Temps musical*, 104–5. Page numbers of subsequent citations are given in the text.

5. Vial, *Être musical*, 68. Page numbers of subsequent citations are given in the text.

6. Zuckerkandl, *Music and the External World*, 67. Page numbers of subsequent citations are given in the text.

7. Zuckerkandl, *Man the Musician*, 152. Page numbers of subsequent citations are given in the text.

8. Clifton, *Music as Heard*, 64. Page numbers of subsequent citations are given in the text.

9. Greene, *Mahler*, 6. Page numbers of subsequent citations are given in the text.

CHAPTER FIFTEEN

1. Weber, *Foundations of Music*, 10.

2. Adorno, "Social Situation," 130. Page numbers of subsequent citations are given in the text.

3. Adorno, "Fetish-Character," 281.

4. Ibid., 284, 278–79.

5. Adorno, *Philosophy*, 181–82. Page numbers of subsequent citations are given in the text.

6. Adorno, *Sociology*, 23. Page numbers of subsequent citations are given in the text.

7. Lissa, *Musikästhetik*, 8. Page numbers of subsequent citations are given in the text.

8. Lukács, *Eigenart*, 360. Page numbers of subsequent citations are given in the text.

9. Kneif, *Musiksoziologie*, 38.

10. Ibid., 96, 120.

Abegg, Werner. *Musikästhetik bei Eduard Hanslick.* Regensburg, 1974.
Abert, Hermann. *Die Lehre vom Ethos in der griechischen Musik.* Leipzig, 1899.
——. *Die Musikanschauung des Mittelalters.* Halle, 1905.
——. "Wort und Ton in der Musik des 18. Jahrhunderts." In his *Gesammelte Vorträge,* ed. Friedrich Blume. Halle, 1929.
Adorno, Theodor. "Motive II." *Anbruch* 10 (1928).
——. "Motive III." *Anbruch* 10 (1928).
——. "Kontroverse über die Heiterkeit." *Anbruch* 12 (1930).
——. *Aesthetische Theorie.* Edited by G. Adorno and R. Tiedemann. Frankfurt, 1970.
——. *Gesammelte Schriften.* Vol. 13, *Die musikalischen Monographien.* Frankfurt, 1971.
——. *Philosophy of Modern Music.* Translated by A. G. Mitchell and W. V. Blomster. New York, 1973.
——. *Introduction to the Sociology of Music.* Translated by E. V. Ashton. New York, 1976.
——. "On the Social Situation of Music." *Telos* 35 (1978).
——. "On the Fetish-Character of Music and the Regression of Listening." In *The Essential Frankfurt School Reader,* ed. A. Arato and E. Gebhardt. New York, 1985.
Ambros, W. A. *The Boundaries of Music and Poetry.* Translated by J. H. Cornell. New York, 1957.
Anderson, Perry. *Considerations on Western Marxism.* London, 1979.
Anderson, Warren. *Ethos and Education in Greek Music.* Cambridge, Mass., 1966.
Augustine, Saint. "On Music." Translated by R. C. Taliaferro. In *The Fathers of the Church,* vol. 4. New York, 1947.
——. *The Confessions of Saint Augustine.* Translated by E. B. Pusey. New York, 1952.
Avison, Charles. *An Essay on Musical Expression.* London, 1752.
Bach, C. P. E. *Versuch über die wahre Art das Clavier zu spielen.* Berlin, 1753.
——. *Essay on the True Art of Playing Keyboard Instruments.* Translated by W. Mitchell. New York, 1949.
Batteux, Charles. *Les Beaux-arts réduits à un même principe.* Paris, 1746; new ed., Paris, 1747; reprint, Paris, 1970.
——. *Cours de belles-lettres.* Paris, 1747–50.
Beardsley, Monroe. "Understanding Music." In *On Criticizing Music,* ed. K. Price. Baltimore, 1981.
Beattie, James. *Essays.* 3d ed. London, 1779.
Beaujean, Joseph. *Christian Gottfried Krause.* Dillingen, 1930.
Bekker, Paul. *Versuch einer soziologischen Musikbetrachtung.* Stuttgart, 1916.
Belvianes, Marcel. *Sociologie de la musique.* Paris, 1951.
Benjamin, Walter. "The Work of Art in the Age of Mechanical Reproduction." In his *Illuminations,* trans. H. Zohn. New York, 1969.
Benz, Richard. "Das Problem des Geistes in der Musik." *Die Musik* 21 (1929).
Besseler, Heinrich. "Grundfragen des musikalischen Hörens." *Jahrbuch der Musikbibliothek Peters für 1925.*
——. "Grundfragen der Musikästhetik." *Jahrbuch der Musikbibliothek Peters für 1926.*

————. *Aufsätze zur Musikästhetik und Musikgeschichte*. Leipzig, 1978.

Blaukopf, Kurt. *Musiksoziologie*. Cologne, 1951.

————. "Tonsysteme und ihre gesellschaftliche Geltung in Max Webers Musiksoziologie." *International Review of the Aesthetics and Sociology of Music* 1 (1970).

————. *Musik im Wandel der Gesellschaft*. Munich and Kassel, 1984.

Bonnet, Jacques. *Histoire de la musique*. Paris, 1715.

Boyé. *L'Expression musicale, mise au rang des chimères*. Amsterdam, 1779.

Brelet, Gisèle. *Le Temps musical: Essai d'une esthétique nouvelle de la musique*. Paris, 1949.

Brown, John. *A Dissertation on the Rise, Union and Power . . . of Poetry and Music*. Dublin, 1763.

Bruyne, Edgar de. *Etudes d'esthétique médiévale*. 3 vols. Bruges, 1946.

Bücken, Ernst. *Geist und Form im musikalischen Kunstwerk*. Potsdam, 1929.

Busoni, Ferruccio. *The Essence of Music and Other Papers*. Translated by R. Ley. New York, 1965.

Buttstedt, J. H. *Ut, mi, sol, re, fa, la, tota musica*. Erfurt, 1717.

Cage, John. *Silence*. Cambridge, Mass., 1961.

Cannon, Beekman. *Johann Mattheson, Spectator in Music*. New Haven, Conn., 1947.

Cassirer, Ernst. *Wesen und Wirkung des Symbolbegriffs*. Oxford, 1956.

Cecconi, A. "La dottrina della musica nella filosofia de Schopenhauer." *Rivista di filosofia neo-scolastica* 33 (1941).

Chabanon, Michel Paul Gui de. *Observations sur la musique*. Paris, 1779.

Chapman, Emmanuel. *Saint Augustine's Philosophy of Beauty*. New York, 1939.

Clifton, Thomas. "The Poetics of Musical Silence." *Musical Quarterly* 62 (1976).

————. *Music as Heard: A Study in Applied Phenomenology*. New Haven, Conn., 1983.

Colloquium Klassizität, Klassizismus, Klassik in der Musik, 1920–1950. Edited by W. Osthoff and R. Wiesend. Tutzing, 1988.

Cowart, Georgia. *The Origins of Modern Musical Criticism*. Ann Arbor, Mich., 1981.

Crescimbeni, Giovanni. *La bellezza della volgar poesia*. Rome, 1700.

————. *Comentarii intorno alla sua istoria della volgar poesia*. 5 vols. Rome, 1702–11.

Crousaz, Jean Pierre de. *Traité du beau*. Amsterdam, 1715.

Dahlhaus, Carl. "Wagners Begriff der 'dichterisch-musikalischen Periode.'" In *Beiträge zur Geschichte der Musikanschauung im 19. Jahrhundert*, ed. Walter Salmen. Regensburg, 1965.

————. "Eduard Hanslick und der musikalische Formbegriff." *Musikforschung* 20 (1967).

————. *Musikästhetik*. Cologne, 1967. Translated as *Esthetics of Music* by W. W. Austin. Cambridge, 1982.

————. "Soziologische Dechiffrierung von Musik: zu Theodor W. Adornos Wagnerkritik." *International Review of the Aesthetics and Sociology of Music* 1 (1970).

————. "Romantische Musikästhetik und Wiener Klassik." *Archiv für Musikwissenschaft* 29 (1972).

————. "Formästhetik und Nachahmungsprinzip." *IRASM* 4 (1973).

————. "Das musikalische Kunstwerk als Gegenstand der Soziologie." *IRASM* 5 (1974).

————, ed. *Beiträge zur musikalischen Hermeneutik*. Regensburg, 1975.

————. "Karl Philipp Moritz und das Problem einer klassischen Musikästhetik." *IRASM* 9 (1978).

Dahlhaus, Carl, and Michael Zimmermann, eds. *Musik—zur Sprache gebracht*. Munich, 1984.

Dalberg, Johann Friedrich. *Blicke eines Tonkünstlers in die Musik der Geister*. Mannheim, 1787.

Dammann, Rolf. *Der Musikbegriff im deutschen Barock*. Cologne, 1967.

Danz, Ernst-Joachim. *Die objektlose Kunst: Untersuchungen zur Musikästhetik Friedrich von Hauseggers*. Regensburg, 1981.

Darenberg, Karlheinz. *Studien zur englischen Musikästhetik des 18. Jahrhunderts.* Hamburg, 1960.

Darwin, Charles. *The Expression of the Emotions in Man and Animals.* New York, 1916.

——. *The Descent of Man and Selection in Relation to Sex.* New York, 1972.

Davenson, Henri [Henri Irénée Marrou]. *Traité de la musique selon l'esprit de Saint Augustin.* Neuchatel, 1944.

De Arce, David. "Contemporary Sociological Theories and the Sociology of Music." *International Review of the Aesthetics and Sociology of Music* 5 (1974).

Deditius, Annemarie. *Theorien über die Verbindung von Poesie und Musik: Moses Mendelssohn, Lessing.* Liegnitz, 1918.

Deliège, Celestin. "Indetermination et improvisation." *International Review of the Aesthetics and Sociology of Music* 2 (1971).

Dessoir, Max. *Aesthetics and Theory of Art.* Translated by S. A. Emory. Detroit, 1970.

Diderot, Denis. *Oeuvres complètes.* 20 vols. Paris, 1875–77.

——. *Rameau's Nephew and D'Alembert's Dream.* Translated by T. W. Tancock. Baltimore, 1966.

Dilthey, Wilhelm. *Die Entstehung der Hermeneutik.* In his *Philosophische Abhandlungen.* Tübingen, 1900.

Doflein, Erich. "Die neue Musik des Jahres." *Melos* 5 (1926).

——. "Über Grundlagen der Beurteilung gegenwärtiger Musik." *Melos* 7 (1928).

——. "Gegenwart, Gebrauch, Kitsch und Stil." *Melos* 8 (1929).

Du Bos, Jean Baptiste. *Réflexions critiques sur la poësie et sur la peinture.* Paris, 1719.

Dufrenne, Mikel. *The Phenomenology of Aesthetic Experience.* Translated by E. S. Casey et al. Evanston, Ill., 1973.

Echoreville, Jules. *De Lully à Rameau, 1690–1730: L'Esthétique musicale.* Paris, 1906.

Eco, Umberto. *La struttura assente.* Milan, 1968.

Edelstein, Heinz. *Die Musikanschauung Augustinus nach seiner Schrift "De musica."* Marburg, 1931.

Eggebrecht, Hans Heinrich. "Ueber begriffliches und begriffloses Verstehen von Musik." Reprinted in his *Musikalisches Denken.* Wilhelmshaven, 1977.

Ehrlich, Heinrich. *Die Musikästhetik in ihrer Entwicklung von Kant bis auf die Gegenwart.* Leipzig, 1882.

Eisler, Hanns. *A Rebel in Music.* New York, 1978.

Encyclopédie, ou Dictionnaire raisonné. . . . 35 vols. Paris, 1751–80.

Engel, Gustave. *Aesthetik der Tonkunst.* Berlin, 1884.

Engel, Hans. *Musik und Gesellschaft.* Berlin, 1960.

Engelke, Bernhard. "Neues zur Geschichte der Berliner Liederschule." In *Riemann-Festschrift.* Leipzig, 1909.

Faltin, Peter. "Musikalische Bedeutung: Grenzen und Möglichkeiten einer semiotischen Ästhetik." *International Review of the Aesthetics and Sociology of Music* 9 (1978).

Fauconnet, A. *L'Esthétique de Schopenhauer.* Paris, 1914.

Feuerbach, Ludwig. *The Essence of Christianity.* Translated by G. Eliot. New York, 1957.

Finscher, Ludwig. "Che farò senza Euridice? Ein Beitrag zur Gluck-Interpretation." In *Festschrift Hans Engel,* ed. H. Heussner. Kassel, 1964.

Flaherty, Gloria. *Opera in the Development of German Critical Thought.* Princeton, N.J., 1978.

Focht, Ivan. "Adornos gnoseologistische Einstellung zur Musik." *International Review of the Aesthetics and Sociology of Music* 5 (1974).

Förster-Nietzsche, Elisabeth. *Wagner und Nietzsche zur Zeit ihrer Freundschaft.* Munich, 1915.

Fowkes, William. "A Hegelian Critique of Found Art and Conceptual Art." *Journal of Aesthetics and Art Criticism* 37 (1977–78).

Frässdorf, W. "Der Begriff der Nachahmung in der Aesthetik J. J. Rousseaus." *Archiv für Geschichte der Philosophie* 35 (1923).

Freeman, Robert. *Opera without Drama: Currents of Change in Italian Opera, 1675–1725*. Ann Arbor, Mich., 1981.

Frommel, Gerhard. *Neue Klassik in der Musik: Zwei Vorträge*. Darmstadt, 1937.

Frotscher, Gotthold. "Die Aesthetik des Berliner Liedes in ihren Hauptproblemen." *Zeitschrift für Musikwissenschaft* 6 (1923–24).

Fubini, Enrico. *L'estetica musicale dal Settecento a oggi*. Enlarged ed. Turin, 1968.

———. *L'estetica musicale dall'antichità a Settecento*. Turin, 1976.

Galilei, Vincenzo. *Dialogo della musica antica e della moderna*. Florence, 1581.

Gatz, Felix. *Musik-Ästhetik in ihren Hauptrichtungen*. Stuttgart, 1919.

Geck, Martin. "E. T. A. Hoffmanns Anschauungen über Kirchenmusik." In *Beiträge zur Geschichte der Musikanschauung im 19. Jahrhundert*, ed. Walter Salmen. Regensburg, 1965.

Gérold, Theodor. *Les Pères de l'église et la musique*. Paris, 1931; reprint, Geneva, 1973.

Gilg-Ludwig, R. "Die Musikauffassung Wilhelm Heinses." *Schweizerische Musikzeitung* 91 (1951).

Glatt, Dorothea. *Zur geschichtlichen Bedeutung der Musikästhetik Eduard Hanslicks*. Munich, 1972.

Goldschmidt, Hugo. "Wilhelm Heinse als Musikästhetiker." In *Festschrift Hugo Riemann*. Leipzig, 1909.

———. "Die konkret-idealistiche Musikästhetik im 19. Jahrhundert." *Zeitschrift für Aesthetik* 6 (1911).

———. *Die Musikästhetik des 18. Jahrhunderts*. Zurich, 1915.

———. *Um die Sache der Musik*. Leipzig, 1970.

Goodman, Nelson. *Languages of Art: An Approach to a Theory of Symbols*. 2d ed. Indianapolis, 1976.

Graf, Max. *Composer and Critic: Two Hundred Years of Musical Criticism*. New York, 1946.

Greene, David. *Mahler, Consciousness and Temporality*. New York, 1984.

Griesser, Luitpold. *Nietzsche und Wagner*. Vienna, 1923.

Gross, Karl. *Sulzers allgemeine Theorie der schönen Künste*. Berlin, 1905.

Gurney, Edmund. "On Some Disputed Points in Music." *Fortnightly Review*, n.s., 20 (o.s., 26) (1876).

———. *The Power of Sound*. New York, 1966.

Halm, August. *Von zwei Kulturen der Musik*. Stuttgart, 1913.

———. *Die Symphonie Anton Bruckners*. Munich, 1914.

———. *Von Grenzen und Ländern der Musik*. Munich, 1916.

———. *Beethoven*. Berlin, 1927.

———. *Von Form und Sinn der Musik*. Edited by S. Schmalzriedt. Wiesbaden, 1978.

Hanslick, Eduard. *The Beautiful in Music*. Translated by G. Cohen, edited by M. Weitz. New York, 1957.

Harris, James. *Three Treatises Concerning Art*. 4th ed. London, 1783.

Hartmann, Eduard von. *Die deutsche Ästhetik seit Kant*. Berlin, 1886.

———. *Die Philosophie des Schönen*. Berlin, 1887.

Hartmann, Nicolai. *Ästhetik*. Berlin, 1953.

———. *New Ways of Ontology*. Translated by R. C. Kuhn. Chicago, 1953.

Hausegger, Friedrich von. *Die Musik als Ausdruck*. Vienna, 1885.

Hecht, H. *Daniel Webb*. Hamburg, 1920.

Hegel, G. W. F. *The Philosophy of Fine Art*. Translated by F. P. B. Osmaston. 4 vols. London, 1920.

———. *Vorlesungen über die Ästhetik*. 3 vols. Frankfurt, 1970.

Heimsoeth, H. "Hegels Philosophy der Musik." *Hegel-Studien* 2 (1963).

Heinse, J. J. W. *Hildegard von Hohenthal*. 3 vols. Berlin, 1795–96.

———. *Musikalische Dialogen.* Leipzig, 1805.

Helmholtz, Hermann L. F. *On the Sensations of Tone as a Physiological Basis for the Theory of Music.* 2d English ed. Translated by A. J. Ellis. New York, 1954.

Herder, J. G. "Viertes Wäldchen." In his *Kritische Wälder.* Vol. 4 of *Herders Sämmtliche Werke,* ed. B. Suphan. Berlin, 1880.

———. *Kalligone.* Vol. 22 of *Herders Sämmtliche Werke,* ed. B. Suphan. Berlin, 1880.

Hilbert, Werner. *Die Musikästhetik der Frühromantik.* Remscheidt, 1911.

Hildebrandt, Kurt. *Wagner und Nietzsche: Ihr Kampf gegen das neunzehnte Jahrhundert.* Breslau, 1924.

Hiller, Johann Adam. "Abhandlung von der Nachahmung der Natur in der Musik." In *Historisch-kritische Beyträge zur Aufnahme der Musik,* ed. Friedrich Wilhelm Marpurg, vol. 1. Berlin, 1754.

Hirschberg, Eugen. *Die Encyklopädisten und die französische Oper im 18. Jahrhundert.* Leipzig, 1903.

Hoffmann, E. T. A. *Musikalischen Novellen und Schriften.* Edited by P. F. Scherber. Munich, n.d.

Honigsheim, Paul. *Music and Society.* New York, 1973.

Hoogerwerf, Frank. "Cage contra Stravinsky, or Delineating the Aleatory Aesthetic." *International Review of the Aesthetics and Sociology of Music* 7 (1976).

Hostinsky, Ottokar. *Das Musikalisch-Schöne und das Gesamtkunstwerk vom Standpunkte der formalen Aesthetik.* Leipzig, 1877.

Huber, Kurt. *Der Ausdruck musikalischer Elementarmotive.* Leipzig, 1923.

———. "Herders Begründung der Musikästhetik." *Archiv für Musikforschung* 1 (1936).

———. *Musikästhetik.* Ettal, 1954.

Husserl, Edmund. *Zur Phänomenologie des inneren Zeitbewusstseins (1893–1917)* (vol. 10 of *Husserliana*). Edited by R. Boehm. Translated as *The Phenomenology of Internal Time-Consciousness* by J. S. Churchill. Bloomington, Ind., 1964.

Hutcheson, Francis. *An Inquiry Concerning Beauty, Order, Harmony, Design.* Edited by P. Kivy. The Hague, 1973.

Ingarden, Roman. *Untersuchungen zur Ontologie der Kunst.* Tübingen, 1962.

———. *The Work of Music and the Problem of Its Identity.* Translated by A. Czerniawsky. Berkeley and Los Angeles, 1986.

Jacoby, G. *Herders und Kants Aesthetik.* Leipzig, 1907.

Jaeger, Werner. *Paideia: The Ideals of Greek Culture.* 3 vols. New York, 1939–44.

Jansen, Albert. *Jean-Jacques Rousseau als Musiker.* Berlin, 1884.

Jarustowski, B. M. *Intonation und Gestalt in der Musik.* Moscow, 1965.

Jerger, Wilhelm. *Wagner-Nietzsches Briefwechsel während des Tribschener Idylls.* Bern, 1951.

Jones, William. *Poems . . . with Two Essays on the Poetry of the Eastern Nations and on the Arts commonly called Imitative.* Oxford, 1772.

Jullien, Adolphe. *La Musique et les philosophes au 18ᵉ siècle.* Paris, 1873.

Kahl, Willi. "Heimsoeth und Thibaut: Ein vergleichender Beitrag zur Geschichte der Renaissancebewegung des 19. Jahrhunderts." In *Festschrift Alfred Orel.* Vienna, 1960.

Kant, Immanuel. *Critik der Urtheilskraft.* Berlin, 1790; 2d ed., Berlin, 1793.

———. *Critique of Judgment.* Translated by J. H. Bernard. New York, 1951.

Katz, R., and C. Dahlhaus, eds. *Contemplating Music: Source Readings in the Aesthetics of Music.* Stuyvesant, N.Y., 1987.

Kierkegaard, Søren. *Either/Or.* Translated by D. F. Swenson and L. M. Swenson, revised by H. A. Johnson and Heinrich Besseler. Princeton, N.J., 1959.

Kindermann, Jürgen. "Romantische Aspekte in E. T. A. Hoffmanns Musikanschauung." In *Beiträge zur Geschichte der Musikanschauung im 19. Jahrhundert,* ed. Walter Salmen. Regensburg, 1965.

Kircher, Athanasius. *Musurgia universalis*. Rome, 1650.

Kneif, Tibor. *Musiksoziologie*. Cologne, 1971.

────, ed. *Texte zur Musiksoziologie*. Cologne, 1975.

Konold, Wulf. "Peter Cornelius und die Liedästhetik der Neudeutschen Schule." *International Review of the Aesthetics and Sociology of Music* 1 (1970).

Körner, Christian Gottfried. "Ueber Charakterdarstellung in der Musik." *Horen* 5 (1795).

Krause, Christian Gottfried. *Von der Musikalischen Poesie*. Berlin, 1752.

Krenek, Ernst. *Ueber neue Musik*. Vienna, 1937.

Kretzschmar, Hermann. *Musikalische Streitfragen*. Leipzig, 1903.

────. "Immanuel Kants Musikauffassung und ihr Einfluss auf die folgende Zeit." *Jahrbuch der Musikbibliothek Peters für 1904*.

Kristeller, Paul. "The Modern System of the Arts: A Study in the History of Aesthetics." *Journal of the History of Ideas* 12–13 (1951–52).

Kurth, Ernst. *Grundlagen des linearen Kontrapunkts*. 2d ed. Berlin, 1922.

────. *Die romantische Harmonik*. 2d ed. Berlin, 1923.

────. *Bruckner*. 2 vols. Berlin, 1926.

────. *Musikpsychologie*. Bern, 1930.

Lacépède, Bernard Germain. *La Poétique de la musique*. 2 vols. Paris, 1785.

Lalo, Charles. *Eléments d'une esthétique musicale scientifique*. 2d ed. Paris, 1939.

Langer, Susanne. *Philosophy in a New Key*. New York, 1942.

────. *Feeling and Form*. New York, 1953.

────. *Problems of Art*. New York, 1957.

Lasserre, Pierre. *Les Idées de Nietzsche sur la musique*. Paris, 1929.

Lauer, Quentin. *Phenomenology, Its Genesis and Prospect*. New York, 1965.

Launay, Denise, ed. *La Querelle des Bouffons*. Geneva, 1973.

Lazarus, Moritz. *Das Leben der Seele*. 1st ed., Berlin, 1855–57; 2d ed., 1882.

Le Huray, Peter, and James Day, eds. *Music and Aesthetics in the Eighteenth and Early Nineteenth Centuries*. Cambridge, 1981.

Lenoble, Robert. *Mersenne ou la naissance du mécanisme*. Paris, 1943.

Lessing, Theodor. *Schopenhauer, Wagner, Nietzsche*. Munich, 1906.

Lethen, Helmut. *Neue Sachlichkeit*. 2d ed. Stuttgart, 1975.

Lévi-Strauss, Claude. *The Raw and the Cooked*. New York, 1975.

Lichtenfeld, Monika. "Gesamtkunstwerk und allgemeine Kunst." In *Beiträge zur Geschichte der Musikanschauung im 19. Jahrhundert*, ed. Walter Salmen. Regensburg, 1965.

Lippman, Edward. "The Place of Music in the System of Liberal Arts." In *Aspects of Medieval and Renaissance Music*, ed. Jan LaRue. New York, 1946.

────. "Symbolism in Music." *Musical Quarterly* 39 (1953).

────. "The Esthetic Theories of Wagner." *Musical Quarterly* 44 (1958).

────. *Musical Thought in Ancient Greece*. New York, 1964.

────. "Theory and Practice in Schumann's Aesthetics." *Journal of the American Musicological Society* 17 (1964).

────. "Symbolik." *Musik in Geschichte und Gegenwart* 12 (1965).

────. "The Problem of Musical Hermeneutics: A Protest and Analysis." In *Art and Philosophy*, ed. S. Hook. New York, 1966.

────. "The Tonal Ideal of Romanticism." In *Festschrift Walter Wiora*. Saarbrücken, 1967.

────. *A Humanistic Philosophy of Music*. New York, 1977.

────. "The Dilemma of Musical Meaning." *International Review of the Aesthetics and Sociology of Music* 12 (1981).

────. "Progressive Temporality in Music." *Journal of Musicology* 3 (1984).

────. *Musical Aesthetics: A Historical Reader*. 3 vols. Stuyvesant, N. Y., 1986–90.

———. "Wagner's Conception of the Dream." *Journal of Musicology* 8 (1990).
Lissa, Zofia. *Fragen der Musikästhetik*. Berlin, 1954.
———. *Über das Spezifische der Musik*. Berlin, 1957.
———. "Einige kritische Bemerkungen zur Ingardenschen Theorie des musikalischen Werkes." *International Review of the Aesthetics and Sociology of Music* 3 (1972).
Listenius, Nicolas. *Musica*. Wittenberg, 1537; facsimile ed., Berlin, 1927.
Lodge, Rupert. *Plato's Theory of Art*. London, 1953.
Lowinsky, Edward. *Secret Chromatic Art in the Netherlands Motet*. Translated by C. Buchman. New York, 1946.
Ludwig, Hellmut. *Marin Mersenne und seine Musiklehre*. Berlin, 1935.
Lukács, Georg. *Beiträge zur Geschichte der Aesthetik*. Berlin, 1954.
———. *Die Eigenart des Ästhetischen*. Vols. 11–12 of *Werke*. Berlin, 1963.
———. *Probleme der Aesthetik*. Vol. 10 of *Werke*. Berlin, 1969.
———. *Ästhetik*. 4 parts. Darmstadt, 1972.
———. "The Philosophy of Art." *New Hungarian Quarterly* 13 (1972).
Macrobius. *Commentary on the Dream of Scipio*. Translated by W. H. Stahl. New York, 1952.
Maeklenburg, A. "Die Musikanschauung Kants." *Die Musik* 14 (1914–15).
Marcello, Benedetto. *Il teatro alla moda*. Translated by R. Pauly. *Musical Quarterly* 24–25 (1948–49).
Marks, Paul. "Aesthetics of Music in the Philosophy of 'Sturm und Drang': Gerstenberg, Hamann and Herder." *Music Review* 35 (1974).
Markus, Stanislaw. *Musikästhetik*. 2 vols. Leipzig, 1959–77.
Marpurg, Friedrich Wilhelm, ed. *Historisch-kritische Beyträge zur Aufnahme der Musik*. 5 vols. Berlin, 1754–62.
———, ed. *Kritische Briefe über die Tonkunst*. 3 vols. Berlin, 1760–64.
Masson, Paul. "Les Idées de J. J. Rousseau sur la musique." *Revue musicale de la Société Internationale de Musique* 8 (1912).
———. *L'Opéra de Rameau*. Paris, 1930.
Mattheson, Johann. *Das Neu-Eröffnete Orchestre*. Hamburg, 1713.
———. *Das Forschende Orchestre*. Hamburg, 1721.
———. *Der vollkommene Capellmeister*. Hamburg, 1739.
Mazzini, Giuseppe. *Filosofia della musica*. New ed. Milan, 1948.
Mei, Girolamo. *Letters on Ancient and Modern Music*. Edited by C. Palisca. American Institute of Musicology. Rome, 1960.
Mémoires pour servir a l'histoire de la révolution opérée dans la musique par . . . Gluck. [Edited by G. M. LeBlond.] Paris, 1781.
Mersenne, Marin. *Harmonie universelle*. Paris, 1636.
Mette, Alexander. *Die psychologischen Wurzeln des Dionysischen und Apollinischen*. Berlin, 1940.
Meyer, Kathi. "Kants Stellung zur Musikästhetik." *Zeitschrift für Musikwissenschaft* 3 (1920–21).
Milton, John. *The Complete Works of John Milton*. Edited by H. F. Fletcher. Boston, 1941.
Molino, Jean. "Fait musical et sémiologie de la musique." *Musique en jeu* 17 (1975).
Moos, Paul. *R. Wagner als Aesthetiker*. Berlin, 1906.
———. *Die Philosophie der Musik*. Stuttgart, 1922.
Morellet, André. *De l'expression en musique et de l'imitation dans les arts*. In his *Mélanges de littérature et de philosophie*, vol. 4. Paris, 1818.
Mornet, D. "La Véritable signification du 'Neveu de Rameau.'" *Revue des deux mondes*, 15 August 1927.
Moser, Hans Joachim. *Musikästhetik*. Berlin, 1953.

Müller, H. "Wilhelm Heinse als Musikschriftsteller." *Vierteljahrsschrift für Musikwissenschaft* 3 (1887).

Müller-Blattau, Josef. "Zur Musikübung und Musikauffassung der Goethezeit." *Euphorion* 31 (1930); *Musik und Kirche* 2 (1930).

Muratori, L. A. *Della perfetta poesia italiana.* 4 vols. Milan, 1821.

Die Musik in Geschichte und Gegenwart [articles on individual authors and subjects]. Edited by F. Blume. 17 vols. Kassel, 1949–86.

Nägeli, Hans Georg. *Vorlesungen über Musik mit Berücksichtigung der Dilettanten.* Stuttgart, 1826.

Nattiez, Jean-Jacques. "Sémiologie musicale: L'État de la question." *Acta musicologica* 46 (1974).

———. "Sur les relations entre sociologie et sémiologie musicales." *International Review of the Aesthetics and Sociology of Music* 5 (1974).

Newman, Ernest. *A Study of Wagner.* London, 1899.

———. *Musical Studies.* London, 1905.

Nichelmann, Christoph. *Die Melodie nach ihrem Wesen sowohl als nach ihren Eigenschaften.* Danzig, 1755.

Nietzsche, Friedrich. *Ecce Homo and The Birth of Tragedy.* Translated by C. P. Fadiman. New York, 1927.

Nowak, Adolf. *Hegels Musikästhetik.* Regensburg, 1971.

Nufer, W. *Herders Ideen zur Verbindung von Poesie, Musik und Tanz.* Berlin, 1929.

Oliver, Alfred. *The Encyclopedists as Critics of Music.* New York, 1947.

Oersted, Hans Christian. *Gesammelte Schriften.* 6 vols. Translated by K. L. Kannegiesser. Leipzig, 1850–51.

Otto, Irmgard. *Deutsche Musikauffassung im 17. Jahrhundert.* Berlin, 1937.

Palisca, Claude. "Girolamo Mei: Mentor to the Florentine Camerata." *Musical Quarterly* 40 (1954).

———. "Scientific Empiricism in Musical Thought." In *Seventeenth-Century Science and Art,* ed. H. H. Rhys. Princeton, N.J., 1961.

Patzer, Harald. *Die Anfänge der griechischen Tragödie.* Wiesbaden, 1962.

Pfrogner, Hermann. *Musik: Geschichte ihrer Deutung.* Freiburg, 1954.

Pietzsch, Gerhard. *Die Musik im Erziehungs- und Bildungsideal des ausgehenden Altertums und frühen Mittelalters.* Halle, 1932.

Pirotta, Nino. "Temperaments and Trends in the Florentine Camerata." *MQ* 40 (1954).

Plato. *The Dialogues of Plato.* Translated by B. Jowett. 4th ed. 4 vols. Oxford, 1953.

Preussner, Eberhard. *Die bürgerliche Musikkultur.* Hamburg, 1935.

Printz, Felix. "Zur Würdigung des Musikästhetischen Formalismus Eduard Hanslicks." Ph.D. diss., University of Munich, 1918.

Prodhomme, Jacques. "Diderot et la musique." *Zeitschrift der internationalen Musikgesellschaft* 15 (1914).

Proudhon, Pierre. *What Is Property?* Translated by B. R. Tucker. New York, 1966.

Quantz, Johann Joachim. *On Playing the Flute.* Translated by E. R. Reilly. New York, 1966.

Rameau, Jean Philippe. *Observations sur notre instinct pour la musique, et sur son principe.* Paris, 1754.

Reger, Erik. "Bachs aktuelle Funktion." *Die Musik* 22 (1930).

Riethmüller, Peter. *Die Musik als Abbild der Realität: Zur dialektischen Widerspiegelungstheorie in der Aesthetik.* Wiesbaden, 1976.

Rogerson, Brewster. "Ut musica poesis: The Parallel of Music and Poetry in Eighteenth-Century Criticism." Ph.D. diss., Princeton University, 1945.

Rohr, Judith. *E. T. A. Hoffmans Theorie des Musikalischen Drama.* Baden-Baden, 1985.

Rosenfeld, P. "Schelling als Musikphilosoph." *Allgemeine Musikzeitung* 40 (1913).

Roth, L., ed. *Correspondence of Descartes and Constantyn Huygens, 1635–1647.* Oxford, 1926.

Rothärmel, Marion. *Der musikalische Zeitbegriff seit Moritz Hauptmann.* Regensburg, 1963.

Rousseau, Jean-Jacques. "Opéra." In his *Dictionnaire de musique.* Geneva, 1767.

―――. *Oeuvres complètes.* 8 vols. Paris, 1839.

Rousseau, Jean-Jacques, and Johann Gottfried Herder. *On the Origin of Language.* Translated by J. H. Moran and A. Gode. New York, 1966.

Rummenhöller, Peter. "Romantik und Gesamtkunstwerk." In *Beiträge zur Geschichte der Musikanschauung im 19. Jahrhundert,* ed. Walter Salmen. Regensburg, 1965.

―――. *Einführung in die Musiksoziologie.* Wilhelmshaven, 1978.

Ruwet, Nicolas. "Contradictions du langage sériel." *Revue belge de musicologie* 13 (1959).

―――. "Méthodes d'analyse en musicologie." *Revue belge de musicologie* 20 (1966).

―――. *Langage, musique, poésie.* Paris, 1972.

Saint-Evremond, Charles de. *Letters.* Edited by J. Hayward. London, 1930.

Salmen, Walter, ed. *Beiträge zur Geschichte der Musikanschauung im 19. Jahrhundert.* Regensburg, 1965.

Schäfke, Rudolf. "Eduard Hanslick und die Musikästhetik." Ph.D. diss., University of Leipzig, 1922.

―――. "Quantz als Ästhetiker: Eine Einführung in die Musikästhetik des galanten Stils." *Archiv für Musikwissenschaft* 6 (1924).

―――. *Geschichte der Musikästhetik in Umrissen.* 2d ed. Tutzing, 1964.

Schelling, F. W. J. von. *Sämmtliche Werke.* 14 vols. Stuttgart, 1856–61.

―――. *Schriften zur Philosophie der Kunst.* Edited by O. Weiss. Leipzig, 1911.

Schenker, Heinrich. *Neue musikalische Theorien und Phantasien.* 3 vols. Vienna, 1906–35.

―――. *Der Tonwille.* 10 nos. Vienna, 1921–24.

―――. *Das Meisterwerk in der Musik.* 3 vols. Munich, 1925–30.

Schering, Arnold. "Die Musikästhetik der deutschen Aufklärung." *Zeitschrift der internationalen Musikgesellschaft* 8 (1906–7).

―――. "Christian Gottfried Krause." *Zeitschrift für Aesthetik* 2 (1907).

―――. "Zur Musikästhetik Kants." *Zeitschrift der internationalen Musikgesellschaft* 11 (1909–10).

―――. *Musikalische Bildung und Erziehung zum musikalischen Hören.* Leipzig, 1911.

―――. "Zur Grundlegung der musikalischen Hermeneutik." *Zeitschrift für Aesthetik* 9 (1914).

―――. "Symbol in der Musik." *Zeitschrift für Aesthetik* 21 (1927).

―――. "Das Entstehen der instrumentalen Symbolwelt." *Jahrbuch der Musikbibliothek Peters für 1935.*

―――. "Musikalische Symbolkunde." *Jahrbuch der Musikbibliothek Peters für 1935.*

Schibli, Siegfried. "Zum Begriff der Neuen Sachlichkeit in der Musik." *Hindemith-Jahrbuch* 9 (1980).

Schiller, Friedrich. *On the Aesthetic Education of Man.* Translated by R. Snell. New York, 1965.

Schloezer, Boris de. "Igor Strawinsky." In his *Von neuer Musik.* Cologne, 1925.

Schneider, Reinhard. *Semiotik der Musik.* Munich, 1980.

Schönberg, Arnold. *Style and Idea.* Edited by L. Stein. New York, 1975.

―――. *Theory of Harmony.* Translated by R. Carter. Berkeley, Calif., 1978.

Schopenhauer, Arthur. *The World as Will and Representation.* Translated by E. F. J. Payne. 2 vols. Indian Hills, Colo., 1958.

Schrade, Leo. "Music in the Philosophy of Boethius." *Musical Quarterly* 33 (1947).

Schubert, Giselher. "Aspekte der Bekkerschen Musiksoziologie." *International Review of the Aesthetics and Sociology of Music* 1 (1970).

————. "Zur Musikästhetik in Kants 'Kritik der Urteilskraft.' " *Archiv für Musikwissenschaft* 32 (1975).

Schueller, H. M. "Immanuel Kant and the Aesthetics of Music." *Journal of Aesthetics and Art Criticism* 14 (1955).

Schutz, Alfred. "Fragments on the Phenomenology of Music." In *In Search of Musical Method*, ed. F. J. Smith. New York, 1976.

Scruton, Roger. *Art and Imagination: A Study in the Philosophy of Mind*. London, 1974.

————. "Understanding Music." In his *The Aesthetic Understanding: Essays in the Philosophy of Art and Culture*. London, 1983.

————. "Analytic Philosophy and the Meaning of Music." *Journal of Aesthetics and Art Criticism* 46 (special issue) (1987).

Seidl, Arthur. *Vom Musikalisch-Erhabenen*. 2d ed. Leipzig, 1970.

Seifert, Wolfgang. *Christian Gottfried Körner: Ein Musikästhetiker der deutschen Klassik*. Regensburg, 1960.

Serauky, Walter. *Die musikalische Nachahmungsästhetik im Zeitraum vom 1700 bis 1850*. Münster, 1929.

Seydel, M. *Arthur Schopenhauers Metaphysik der Musik*. Leipzig, 1894.

Shakespeare, William. *The Riverside Shakespeare*. Edited by G. Blakemore Evans et al. Boston, 1974.

Siegel, Linda. *Music in German Literature*. Novato, Calif., 1983.

Silbermann, Alphons. *Wovon lebt die Musik*. Regensburg, 1957. Translated by C. Stewart as *The Sociology of Music*. Cologne, 1971.

Smith, Adam. "Of the Imitative Arts." In his *Essays on Philosophical Subjects*. Dublin, 1795.

Solerti, Angelo, ed. *Le origini del melodramma*. Turin, 1903.

Solger, K. W. F. *Erwin: Vier Gespräche über das Schöne und die Kunst*. Berlin, 1907.

Souvtchinsky, Pierre. "La Notion du temps et la musique." *Revue musicale* (May–June 1939).

Spencer, Herbert. "The Origin and Function of Music." *Fraser's Magazine*, October 1857.

————. "Postscript to 'The Origin and Function of Music.' " In his *Essays: Scientific, Political, and Speculative*, vol. 2. Library Edition. New York, 1907.

————. *Literary Style and Music*. New York, 1951. (Contains a later addition of Spencer's article, slightly altered, to which he has appended detailed replies to his chief opponents.)

Spitzer, Leo. "Classical and Christian Ideas of World Harmony." *Traditio* 2–3 (1944–45).

Springer, G.-P. "Language and Music: Parallels and Divergencies." In *For Roman Jakobson*. The Hague, 1956.

Stade, F. W. *Von Musikalisch-Schönen*. Leipzig, 1870.

Stege, Fritz. "Die deutsche Musikkritik des 18. Jahrhunderts unter dem Einfluss der Affektenlehre." *Zeitschrift für Musikwissenschaft* 10 (1927).

Steinkruger, August. *Die Ästhetik der Musik bei Schelling und Hegel*. Bonn, 1927.

Stockhausen, Karlheinz. *Texte zur elektronischen und instrumentalen Musik*. Vol. 1. Cologne, 1963.

Stockhausen on Music. Edited by Robin Maconie. London, 1989.

Strauss, A. *Zur Musikästhetik der deutschen Frühromantik*. Prague, 1935.

Stravinsky, Igor. *Poetics of Music*. Translated by A. Knodel and I. Dahl. Cambridge, Mass., 1947.

Strich, Fritz. *Deutsche Klassik und Romantik, oder Vollendung und Unendlichkeit*. Munich, 1922.

Striffling, Louis. *Esquisse d'une histoire du goût musical en France au 18ᵉ siècle*. Paris, 1912.

Strobel, Heinrich. " 'Neue Sachlichkeit' in der Musik." *Anbruch* 8 (1926).

Strunk, Oliver, ed. *Source Readings in Music History*. New York, 1950.

Stumpf, Karl. "Musikpsychologie in England." *Vierteljahrsschrift für Musikwissenschaft* I (1885); reprint, *Vierteljahrsschrift für Musikwissenschaft* 7 (1891).
Svoboda, K. *L'Esthétique de St. Augustin et ses sources.* Brno, 1933.
Terras, Rita. *Wilhelm Heinses Ästhetik.* Munich, 1972.
Thibaut, A. F. J. *On Purity in Musical Art.* Translated by W. H. Gladstone. London, 1877.
Tiessen, Heinz. *Zur Geschichte der Jüngsten Musik.* Mainz, 1928.
Twining, Thomas. *Aristotle's Treatise on Poetry, and Two Dissertations, on Poetical, and Musical, Imitation.* 2d ed. 2 vols. London, 1812.
Unger, Hans-Heinrich. *Die Beziehung zwischen Musik und Rhetorik im 16. Jahrhundert.* Würzburg, 1941.
Utitz, Emil. *Die Überwindung des Expressionismus.* Stuttgart, 1927.
Vexler, F. *Studies in Diderot's Aesthetic Naturalism.* New York, 1922.
Vial, Jeanne. *De l'être musical.* Neuchatel, 1952.
Vicentino, Don Nicola. *L'antica musica ridotta alla moderna prattica.* Rome, 1555.
Vogel, Martin. *Nietzsches Wettkampf mit Wagner.* In *Beiträge zur Geschichte der Musikanschauung im 19. Jahrhundert,* ed. Walter Salmen. Regensburg, 1965.
————. *Apollinisch und Dionysisch.* Regensburg, 1966.
Wackenroder, Wilhelm Heinrich. *"Confessions" and "Fantasies."* Translated by M. H. Schubert. University Park, Pa., 1971.
Wagner, Günther. "Exaktwissenschaftliche Musikanalyse und Informationsästhetik." *International Review of the Aesthetics and Sociology of Music* 7 (1976).
Wagner, Richard. *Sämtliche Schriften und Dichtungen.* 5th ed. 12 vols. Leipzig, 1911.
Webb, Daniel. *Observations on the Correspondence between Poetry and Music.* London, 1769.
Weber, Max. *The Rational and Social Foundations of Music.* Translated by D. Martindale et al. Carbondale, Ill., 1958.
Webern, Anton. *The Path to the New Music.* Translated by L. Black. Bryn Mawr, Pa., 1963.
Weiss, Piero. "Pier Jacopo Martello on Opera (1715): An Annotated Translation." *Musical Quarterly* 66 (1980).
Weisstein, Ulrich, ed. *The Essence of Opera.* New York, 1969.
Wieninger, Gustav. *Immanuel Kants Musikästhetik.* Munich, 1929.
Wiora, Walter. "Herders und Heinses Beitrag zum Thema 'Was ist Musik?'" *Musikforschung* 13 (1960).
————. *Komponist und Mitwelt.* Basle, 1964.
————. "Die Musik im Weltbild der deutschen Romantik." In *Beiträge zur Geschichte der Musikanschauung im 19. Jahrhundert,* ed. Walter Salmen. Regensburg, 1965.
Zarlino, Gioseffo. *Sopplimenti musicali.* Venice, 1588.
Zeitler, Julius. *Nietzsches Aesthetik.* Leipzig, 1900.
Zimmermann, Robert. "Vom Musikalisch-Schönen." In his *Kritiken und Studien zur Philosophie und Aesthetik,* vol. 2. Vienna, 1870.
————. "Zur Reform der Aesthetik als exakte Wissenschaft." In his *Kritiken und Studien zur Philosophie und Aesthetik,* vol. 2. Vienna, 1870.
Zoltai, Denes. *Ethos und Affekt: Geschichte der philosphischen Musikästhetik.* Translated by B. Weingarten. Budapest, 1970.
Zuckerkandl, Victor. *Sound and Symbol: Music and the External World.* Translated by W. R. Trask. New York, 1956.
————. *Man the Musician: Sound and Symbol, Volume 2.* Translated by N. Guterman. Princeton, N.J., 1973.

Abderiten, Die (Wieland), 194
"Abhandlung von der Nachahmung
    der Natur in der Musik" (Hiller),
    117–20, 187
Adorno, Theodor, 359, 472–88; on the
    avant-garde, 486–87; on chamber
    music, 483, 484; on the class import
    of music, 482–84; on the conductor
    and orchestra, 484; on consumption of
    music, 474; criticized by Kneif, 507–8;
    on the function of music, 480–82; on
    listening, 474, 477, 479, 482–84; and
    Marxism, 472, 474, 475; on music and
    ideology, 488; on music and society,
    473, 487–88, 491; on music as com-
    modity, 472–73; on musical criticism,
    485; on the musical life, 484–85; and
    musical sociology, 506, 507, 508, 509;
    on national style, 485–86; on New
    Objectivity, 404–5, 407; on opera,
    483–84; on popular music, 479–81; on
    production of types of music, 473–74;
    on Schönberg, 473, 475–78, 486; and
    Stravinsky, 405, 409–10, 411–14, 473,
    475–78
Aesthetics: and beauty, 98; definition of,
    19, 24, 219, 432; and morality, 98. *See
    also* Musical aesthetics
Aesthetics and Theory of Art (Des-
    soir), 353
Aesthetik (Hartmann), 432–34
Agricola, Johann Friedrich, 190
Agrippa of Nettesheim, 8
Alberti, Leon Battista, 8
Alceste (Calzabigi), 153, 174, 193, 194
Alembert, Jean le Rond d', 89, 91, 153, 168
Alessandro vincitor (Sbarra), 43
Alexander, 197
"Alexander's Feast" (Dryden), 13
Algarotti, Francesco, 149, 150–53, 193
*Allgemeine Aesthetik als Formwissen-
    schaft* (Zimmermann), 310–11

Allgemeine Musikalische Zeitung, 210
Allgemeine Theorie der Schönen Künste
    (Sulzer), 120, 191
"Alte und neue Kirchenmusik" (Hoff-
    mann), 215–16
Ambros, Wilhelm August, 322–25, 328
"Analytic Philosophy and the Meaning of
    Music" (Scruton), 390, 391–92
Anbruch, 405
André, Yves Marie, 87, 162
Andreas Hartknopf (Moritz), 126
Andromeda, 194
*Antica musica ridotta alla moderna
    prattica, L'* (Vicentino), 27
Anweisung zum Generalbass (Heinichen),
    74, 116
Apollo, 207, 246, 417
Arcadian Academies, 46, 137; members
    of, 45, 139, 140, 149
Architecture, 225, 249, 305–6; Gothic,
    297, 305
Ardinghello (Heinse), 198, 239
Aria, 45, 172, 175, 189, 192, 196
Ariadne auf Naxos (Gerstenberg), 192
Ariosto, Lodovico, 192
Aristotle, 23, 51, 498; on art and beauty,
    314; challenges to, 50; and effects
    of music, 503; on expression and
    imitation, 86, 107, 111, 162; and instru-
    mental performance, 21; and operative
    reform, 139, 140, 141, 145; and Plato,
    233; and undeveloped artistic genres,
    184; on tragedy, 31, 287. *See also
    Poetics; Politics*
*Aristotle's Treatise on Poetry Translated,
    with Notes* (Twining), 110
Aristoxenos, 437
Armide (Gluck), 94, 167
Armonia perfetta, 27
Arnim, Achim von, 207
Ars perfecta; challenges to, 26–41
Ars poetica (Horace), 22, 89, 178

Art, 20, 190; Hellenic, 247; philosophy of, 219; synthesis of, 188, 189. *See also* Fine arts; Liberal arts

Art and Imagination: A Study in the Philosophy of Mind (Scruton), 386

Art and Revolution (Wagner), 244–46

Arte rappresentativa premediatata ed all'improviso, Dell' (Perrucci), 46

Arteaga, 149

"Arts of Poetry and Tone in the Drama of the Future" (Wagner), 257–63

Artusi, Giovanni, 29–31

Artusi, ovvero, Delle imperfezioni della moderna musica, L' (Artusi), 29–30

Art-Work of the Future, The (Wagner), 244, 246–52

Assafjew, Boris, 494

Ästhetik (Carriere), 330

Ästhetik (Köstlin), 331

Ästhetik der Tonkunst (Engel), 334–42, 515n.10, 516n.11

Ästhetik, oder Wissenschaft des Schönen (Vischer), 325–28, 331

"At a Solemn Music" (Milton), 9–10

Auber, Daniel François, 312

Augustine, 14, 85, 87, 437

Aureli, Aurelio, 43

Ausdruck musikalischer Elementarmotive, Der (Huber), 359

Autonomy, 314, 319, 393; criteria for, 291–92; and feelings, 291

Autumn Maneuvers (Kálman), 480

Avison, Charles, 101–3, 115

Bach, C. P. E., 79–80, 121

Bach, Johann Sebastian, 125, 323, 403, 408, 476, 502; criticism of, 74–75; and feeling, 329; Passions of, 492; and phenomenology, 449–50; Romantic music of, 448, 449–50; studies on symbolism of, 360, 365; and Wagner, 449–50

Bardi, Giovanni de, 34–35

Bardiet, 191

Baroque, 15, 60, 77, 91, 239, 360

Batteux, Charles, 116, 189; criticism of, 117; on imitation and expression, 88–89, 95, 118, 161–63, 184–85; views on opera of, 187, 188

Baumgarten, Alexander, 19, 116, 187, 188, 218

Beardsley, Monroe, 369–70

Beattie, James, 106–10, 111

Beaux-arts réduits à un même principe, Les (Batteux), 88–89, 116, 161–63

Becking, Gustav, 358

Beethoven, Ludwig van, 323, 359, 477, 502; Adagios of, 395; *Les Adieux* Sonata of, 467; E-Minor Symphony of, 249; and feeling, 329, 395; Fifth Symphony of, 212, 384; Hanslick's discussion of, 300; history of criticism of, 485; instrumental music of, 211, 252; Kretzschmar's discussion of, 356, 384, 385; Ninth Symphony of, 249, 455; and objectivity, 399; "Ode to Joy" of, 260, 431; and opera, 55; Piano Sonata in A Major, op. 101 of, 370; *Prometheus* Overture of, 300; relation to bourgeoisie of, 483, 487; Romantic view of, 211, 212, 232, 395–96; Seventh Symphony of, 249; Sixteenth Quartet of, 431; Sixth Symphony of, 249; studied by Lissa, 495; style of, determined by social reality, 495; and symbolism, 360, 365, 370; and understanding, 384, 385; unity of musical work in, 212; and the "unspeakable," 325; Wagner's discussion of, 248–49, 250, 252, 260–61

Beethoven (Halm), 396

Beethoven in neuer Deutung (Schering), 359

Beethoven und die Dichtung (Schering), 359

"Beethovens Instrumentalmusik" (Hoffmann), 210–12

Bekker, Paul, 398

Bell, Clive, 368

Bellezza della volgar poesia, La (Crescimbeni), 137–38

"Bellini" (Wagner), 252–53, 257

Benda, Georg, 192

Benjamin, Walter, 472

Benz, Richard, 406

Berg, Alban, 380, 426, 475

Bergson, Henri, 440, 443, 444, 476

Berlinger, Joseph, 203–4, 205–6

Beschützte Orchestre, Das (Mattheson), 61

Besseler, Heinrich, 400–401

Betrachtungen über das Erhaben und das Naive in den schönen Wissenschaften (Mendelssohn), 189

Betrachtungen über die Quellen und die

Verbindungen der schönen Künste und Wissenschaften (Mendelssohn), 188–89
Beurtheilung der Gottschedischen Dichtkunst (Meier), 184
Biedermann, Der, 181
Birken, Sigmund von, 51
Birnbaum, Johann Abraham, 75
Blainville, Charles H., 168
Blaukopf, Kurt, 506–7, 508–9
Blicke eines Tonkünstlers in die Musik der Geister (Dalberg), 126
Bloch, Ernst, 483, 491
Bodmer, Johann, 181
Boethius, 8
Boileau, Nicolas, 81, 93, 156, 177; on clarity, 80, 85; on love in opera, 49–50
Boileau-Despréaux, Nicolas. *See* Boileau, Nicolas
Börne, Ludwig, 207
Bouhours, Dominique, 156
Boyé, 94–95, 96, 300
Brahms, Johannes, 475
Brandes, Johann Christian, 192
Brautwahl (Busoni), 400
Breitinger, Johann, 181
Brelet, Gisèle, 443–52
"Briefe an einem Freund über das deutsche Singspie, 'Alceste'" (Wieland), 192
Briefe über die ästhetische Erziehung des Menschen (Schiller), 133–34, 245
Brockes, Barthold Heinrich, 178
Bruckner, Anton, 395
Brutus, 197
Bruyère, Jean de la, 177
Buffoon War, 165–77
Bullough, Edward, 367
Burmeister, Joachim, 39
Busoni, Ferruccio, 398–400, 403, 407
Buttstedt, Johann Heinrich, 61, 75

Caccini, Giulio, 36, 37–38
Cage, John, 434–46
Caldara, Antonio, 165
Calvinists, 52
Calzabigi, Ranieri, 153, 174, 194
Cambert, Robert, 47
Camerata, 34, 38
Candorin, 51
Carriere, Moritz, 330
Carroll, Lewis, 386

Cassirer, Ernst, 353, 360, 369, 370
Castelvetro, Lodovico, 177
Cato, Marcus Porcius, 197
Chabanon, Michel Paul Gui de, 80, 96–98, 108, 120
Chalcidius, 8
Chastellux, François Jean de, 91–92, 172–73
China, ancient, 5, 10, 52
Chladni, Ernst Floreus Friedrich, 322
Chopin, Frédéric François, 482; Polonaise in A Flat Major of, 483
Christianity, 109; and harmonic interpretation, 9; and opera, 52, 53; and sensuality, 509; and theater, 139; and Wagner, 246
Christina, Queen (of Sweden), 45
Cicero, Marcus Tullius, 86, 139, 511n.2; on cosmic harmony, 6–8; and music and oratory, 22, 27
Cicognini, Giacinto Andrea, 43
Classical music, and musical time, 448–51
Classicism, 121, 126, 136, 139, 218, 409, 514n.2; and constructivism, 410–11; and Stravinsky, 408
Clemenza de Tito, La (Metastasio), 164
Clifton, Thomas, 461–64
Climax, 39
Clytemnestra, 169
Combarieu, Jules, 285, 509
Comentarii intorno alla sua istoria della volgar poesia (Crescimbeni), 139
Commentary on Plato's Timaeus (Chalcidius), 8
Commentary on the Dream of Scipio (Macrobius), 8, 511n.2
Commonwealth of Art (Sach), 449
Communism, 472, 488, 496, 497. *See also* Marxism
Comparaison de la musique italienne et de la musique française (Lecerf), 156–58
"Complementation of Music by Poetry, The" (Engel), 336–37
"Complementation of Poetry by Music, The" (Engel), 336, 337–38
"Composite Work of Art and the Individual Arts" (Engel), 338–39, 515n.10
"Composition with Twelve Tones" (Schönberg), 417–20
"Concept of Music, The" (Engel), 335–36
Confessions (Augustine), 437
Connaissance des beautés et des défauts de

Connaissance . . . (continued)
    la poésie et d'eloquence dans la langue
    française (Voltaire), 164–65
Constantinus der Grosse (Hudemann),
    181
Constructivism, 410–11
"Contradictions du langage sériel"
    (Ruwet), 380
Corded Shell, The (Kivy), 353
Corneille, Pierre, 197
Cosmology, 5–6
Counterpoint, 23, 38, 59, 60
Cours de belles-lettres (Batteux), 184, 188
Crescimbeni, Giovanni Maria, 137–38
Critical Reflections on Poetry, Painting
    and Music, 86–87. See also Réflexions
    critiques sur la poësie et sur la peinture
Critik der Urteilskraft. See Critique of
    Judgment
Critique of Judgment (Kant), 126–33,
    206; criticism of, 207; as foundation
    of formalism, 292–93, 296
Critische Musikus, Der (Scheibe), 74,
    182, 186
Critische Musicus an der Spree, Der
    (Marpurg), 186
Cru et le cuit, Le (Lévi-Strauss), 373–75
Cromwell, Oliver, 154
Crousaz, Jean Pierre de, 85–86, 87, 98

Dafne (Peri), 36
Dalberg, Johann Friedrich, 126
Dance, 24, 188; connection of, to music
    and poetry, 112, 493–94, 501; and
    imitation of feelings, 162; Stravin-
    sky's dependence upon, 476; Wagner's
    examination of, 247
Dante, 54
Darwin, Charles, 275–80, 283, 285, 286,
    318–19
David (King of Israel), 65
De la Liberté de la musique (Alem-
    bert), 168
De l'étre musical (Vial), 452–55
De l'expression en musique et de
    l'imitation dans les arts (Morellet),
    92–93
De ordine (Augustine), 85
de Rochemont, 168
Debussy, Claude, 388, 417, 486, 487
Défense du Parallèle (Raguenet), 158

Descartes, René, 76, 80, 81, 116, 310; on
    clarity, 80, 85; and feeling, 84
Descent of Man and Selection in Relation
    to Sex (Darwin), 275–77, 279
Dessoir, Max, 353
Destouches, André Cardinal, 165
De'teatri antichi e moderni (Maffei),
    149–50
Deutsche Aesthetik seit Kant, Die (Hart-
    mann), 342, 347
Devin du village, Le (Rousseau), 167
Dialogo della musica antica e della
    moderna (Galilei), 35, 36, 155
"Dichter und der Komponist, Der" (Hoff-
    mann), 212–15
Dictionnaire de musique (Rousseau), 89,
    95, 170
Diderot, Denis, 89–90, 167, 168–70, 173
Dido, 197
Dilthey, Wilhelm, 353–54, 356–58, 359,
    370, 392
Diogenes, 323
"Discours préliminaire" (Alembert), 89
"Discourse on Music, Painting, and
    Poetry, A" (Harris), 99–100
Discorso sopra la masica (Giustiniani), 40
Discorso . . . sopra la Musica antica, e il
    cantar bene (Bardi), 34
Dodecachordon (Glareanus), 27
Doflein, Erich, 401–4, 405–6
Don Giovanni (Mozart), 240–43
Doni, Giovanni Battista, 42–43
Drama, 22, 44, 46, 190, 249; ancient
    Greek, 42, 51, 139, 145, 170, 181, 189,
    493; and opera, 50, 51; and rhetoric, 22
Dream of Scipio (Cicero), 7–8, 14, 126
Dryden, John, 13, 53–55
Du Bos, Jean Baptiste; influence of,
    76, 186, 187, 188, 189; on musical
    imitation, 86–87, 89, 95, 159, 282
Dufay, Guillaume, 383
Dufrenne, Mikel, 461

Eco, Umberto, 375–77
Eggebrecht, Hans, 382–86, 388–89, 392
Eichendorff, Joseph von, 207
Eigenart des Ästhetischen, Die (Lukács),
    497–506
Eighteenth century, 46; comparison of one
    art with another in, 22; criticism in,
    351; debate over taste in, 41; devel-

opment of musical aesthetics in, 19, 24–25, 59, 91 (*see also* Galant aesthetics); opera in, 44, 45, 52 (*see also* Operatic aesthetics); term *aesthetics* in, 352
Einbildungskraft des Dichters: Bausteine zu einer Poetik, Die (Dilthey), 354
Einfühlung, 360
Einführung in die Musiksoziologie (Rummenhöller), 508
Einleitung in die Geisteswissenschaften (Dilthey), 354
Einleitung in die Musiksoziologie (Adorno), 479–88, 507
Einleitung in die Schönen Wissenschaften (Batteux), 188
Einschränkung der schönen Künste auf Einen einzigen Grundsatz (Batteaux), 116, 185
Einstein, Albert, 15
Eisler, Hanns, 403, 474
Either/Or (Kierkegaard), 240–43, 514n.2
Electra, 163
Eléments d'une esthètique musicale scientifique (Lalo), 431–32
Emotion and Meaning in Music (Meyer), 353
Emotional realism: aesthetic of, 243–44; forecasts of, 239–40; and opera, 239, 241–42, 244, 269, 288 (see also *Opera and Drama*); return to, 398. *See also* Realism
Empfindsamer Stil, 77, 79, 121
Empfindsamkeit, 126
Encyclopédie, 89, 91, 171
Endimione, L' (Guidi), 45
Engel, Gustav, 334–42, 515n.10, 516n.11
Engel, Hans, 506
Engel, J. J., 126
Engels, Friedrich, 488
England, 61, 74; imitation and expression in, 98–115
Enlightenment, 59, 77, 499
Entretiens sur "Le fils naturel": Dorval et moi (Diderot), 168–69
"Entstehen der instrumentalen Symbolwelt, Das" (Schering), 364–66
Entstehung der Hermeneutik, Die (Dilthey), 357
Epulone, L' (Frugoni), 43–44
Er, 3, 6, 14, 126

Eren- Danz- Singe Schauspiele-Entwurf (Höveln), 51
Erigena, Scotus, 8
"Erkenntnis des Tonwerks, Die" (Schering), 359
Erlebnis und die Dichtung, Das (Dilthey), 357
Erwin: Vier Gespräche über das Schöne und die Kunst (Solger), 224–29
Eschenburg, J. J., 103
Esprit de l'art musical, L' (Blainville), 168
Esprit des beaux-arts, L' (Estève), 167
Essai sur le beau, L' (André), 87
Essai sur les révolutions de la musique en France (Marmontel), 174–75
Essai sur l'origine des langues (Rousseau), 89, 90–91
Essai sur l'union de la poésie et de la musique (Chastellux), 172–73
Essay on Musical Expression, An (Avison), 101–3
Essay on Poetry and Music as They Affect the Mind (Beattie), 106–10
Essays: Scientific, Political, and Speculative (Spencer), 282–84
Estève, Pierre, 167
Ethnomusicology, 471
Euler, Leonhard, 516n.11
Euridice, 300
Euridice (Peri), 36, 263
Euripides, 192, 193, 194
"Euripides unter den Abderiten" (Wieland), 194
Europe, Eastern: aesthetics in, 488
Expression, 36, 175, 204; concept of, 83–84; connected with reason and rules, 159; in England, 98–115; in France, 84–98; in Germany, 115–36, 190; and Hausegger, 288–90; as identical in meaning to imitation, 84, 87, 88, 89, 92, 94; and New Objectivity, 401–2, 403, 407; and objectivity, 411; and painting, 401; and Romanticism, 401, 411; in the sixteenth century, 26–41; and Stravinsky, 408, 416; in twentieth century, 353, 389–90, 401, 414
Expression musicale, mise au rang des chimères, L' (Boyé), 94–95
Expression of the Emotions in Man and Animal (Darwin), 277–80

Faltin, Peter, 381
Faustina, 197
Favart, Charles Simon, 190
Fechner, Gustav Theodor, 313–14
Feind, Barthold, 177–78
Ferretti, Paolo, 378
Feuerbach, Ludwig, 246
Ficino, Marsilio, 8
Fidelio (Beethoven), 342
Figaro (Mozart), 323, 400
Fine arts, 20–21; Kant's division into
    three kinds, 131. *See also* Art; Lib-
    eral arts
First Principles (Gurney), 284
Florentine Camerata. *See* Camerata
Florestan, 342
Fludd, Robert, 8
Fontenelle, Bernard le Bovier de, 156
Forkel, Johann Nikolaus, 125
Formalism; abstract, 310–12; and apper-
    ception, 295, 303, 304; concepts of,
    291–92; connection between music
    and religion in, 298; contrasted with
    subjectivity, 291, 320; defined, 292,
    294–95, 299–300; difference between
    music and visual arts in, 297; distinc-
    tion between feelings and moods in,
    314–15; and feelings, 291, 298–99,
    319, 320–21, 330–31; foundations of,
    292, 293, 296; and idealism, 320–21,
    347, 362; and opera, 296, 312, 316; and
    Romantic aesthetics, 298, 319, 347;
    suppression of sensuous qualities in,
    293; twentieth-century descendants of,
    393; unity of art in, 294, 317; and the
    universality of music, 319
Forschende Orchestre, Das (Matthe-
    son), 62
Fouqué, Friedrich Heinrich Karl, Baron
    de la Motte-, 217
Fragen der Musikästhetik (Lissa), 488–97
"Fragments for a Poetics" (Dilthey), 357
"Fragments on the Phenomenology of
    Music" (Schutz), 439–40
France, 61, 145; galant aesthetics in, 74;
    imitation and expression in, 84–98,
    99, 153, 184, 190; influence of, on
    German Enlightenment, 59, 75, 120,
    178; Italian opera criticized in, 47–49
    (*see also* Buffoon War; Opera: contro-
    versy over French and Italian); Italian
    poetry criticized in, 46, 149; natural-

ness in aesthetics of, 80; neoclassical
    aesthetics of, 46; New Objectivity in,
    405; opera in (*see* Opera, French);
    operatic aesthetics in, 145, 153–77
Frauenzimmer Gesprächspiele (Harsdörf-
    fer), 50–51
Frederick the Great (Friedrich II), 150, 186
Freiheit in der Erscheinung (Schiller), 133
French Academy, 156
French Revolution, 134, 177, 245
Freud, Sigmund, 484
Frommel, Gerhard, 410–11
Frugoni, Francesco, 43–44

Gadamer, Hans-Georg, 353
Galant aesthetics, 59–82, 121, 487; an-
    tithesis of, 59–60, 160; conflict with
    Sturm und Drang of, 175; feelings in,
    78–80, 161; in Germany, 59–60, 74,
    75, 193; and Gluck, 174; and imitation,
    80, 120, 153; music as pleasing in,
    77; musical clarity in, 80; and opera,
    59–60, 61; and polyphony, 59, 74–
    75, 91; and rhetoric, 60; and theory
    of affections and temperaments, 81–
    82; variety in, 77–78. *See also* Krause,
    Christian Gottfried; Mattheson,
    Johann
Galen, Claudius, 81
Galilei, Vincenzo, 32, 34, 35, 36, 76, 155
Galileo (Galileo Galilei), 14
Garcin, Laurent, 173
*Gedanken über die Nachahmung der
    griechischen Werke in der Malerei und
    Bildhauerkunst* (Winckelmann), 81
"Gedanken von den Vorzügen der Oper
    vor Tragedien und Comedien" (Hude-
    mann), 181–82
Gedancken von der Oper (Feind), 177–78
"Gegenwart, Gebrauch, Kitsch und Stil"
    (Doflein), 405–6
"General Part of the Philosophy of Art"
    (Schelling), 224
Generalbass in der Composition, Der
    (Heinichen), 74, 116
Germany, 39, 61; composers of seven-
    teenth century in, 76; conflict between
    secular and religious style in, 59–60;
    expression and imitation in, 115–36,
    184–85, 188, 190, 191, 356; galant
    aesthetics in, 59–60, 74, 75, 193 (*see
    also* Mattheson, Johann); Italian opera

criticized in, 186, 191–92, 193–94; literature in, 178, 218; naturalness of aesthetics in, 80; New Objectivity in, 405; opera in (*see* Opera, German); operatic aesthetics in, 177–99; perspective on soul in, 291; philosophical aesthetics of nineteenth century in, 218–38, 459; synthesis of the arts in, 50–51, 53
Gerstenberg, Heinrich Wilhelm von, 191–92
Gesualdo, Don Carlo, Prince of Venosa, 40
Giasone (Cicognini), 43
Giustiniani, Vincenzo, 40–41
Glareanus, Henricus, 27, 28
Glaucon, 10–11
Gluck, Christoph Willibald, 94, 153, 168, 198; criticism of, 174–75; and feelings, 125, 174, 176; and Italian language, 173–74; and operatic reform, 194–96; and poetry, 191, 196; and unity of the work, 176, 218
Glückliche Hand, Die (Schönberg), 411
Goethe, Johann Wolfgang von, 133, 199, 218
Goodman, Nelson, 369, 370
Gottsched, Johann Christoph, 180–81, 182, 183, 184, 187
Grandval, Nicolas Ragot de, 159
Gravina, Gianvincenzo, 45, 140–41
Greece, ancient, 3, 32, 223; arts in, 20–21, 244; drama of, 42, 51, 139, 145, 170, 181, 189, 493; and emotional realism, 240; ethical view of music in, 10; influence of music in, 15, 109; and melody, 222; myths of, 253–54; poetry of, 196; tragedies of, 31, 37, 45, 140, 141, 142, 150, 164, 191, 244–45; writing on music in, 27–28
Greene, David B., 464–69
Grenzen der Musik und Poesie, Die (Ambros), 322–25
Grimm, Friedrich Melchior, Baron von, 165, 166, 171–72
"Grundfragen der Musikästhetik" (Besseler), 401
Guidi, Alessandro, 45
Gurney, Edmund, 280–82, 283–84, 285, 317–19

Halévy, Jacques François, 312

Halm, August, 394–96
Hamburgische Dramaturgie (Lessing), 189–90
Hamlet (Shakespeare), 502
Handel, George Frederick, 13
Hanslick, Eduard, 94, 311, 317, 334, 381; critics of, 322, 330–34, 356; and idealism, 321; and opera, 312; and relation of feelings to, 134, 293, 295, 298–301, 302–3, 313, 331, 333–34, 396; and tonal motion, 313, 333; and Wagner, 314
Harlekin oder Vertheidigung des Groteske-Komischen (Möser), 190–91
Harmonics (Ptolemy), 321
Harmony, 204; and Christianity, 9; cosmic, 3–5, 6–8, 9, 62, 221, 223–24; and expression, 28, 31; as mathematical discipline, 6, 212; and melody, 90–91, 106, 121–22, 167, 472; and phenomenology, 444–46, 449; and poetry, 9–10; Wagner on, 248, 263–65
Harris, James, 99–100, 103
Harsdörffer, Georg Philipp, 50–51
Hartmann, Eduard von, 333, 342–47
Hartmann, Nicolai, 432–34
Hasse, Johann Adolf, 194
Hauptmann, Moritz, 334, 335, 516n.11
Hausegger, Friedrich von, 286–91
Haydn, Franz Joseph, 136, 323, 425; studied by Lissa, 495; style of, determined by social reality, 495; and tone painting, 211, 329
Hédelin, Francois, Abbé d'Aubignac, 182
Hegel, Georg Wilhelm Friedrich, 224, 340, 343, 426, 475, 498; on content, 236–38; on expression, 235–36; and feeling, 326; and idealism, 320, 321; on music and the other arts, 233–35; on music as accompaniment, 236–37; on music as independent, 237–38; and objectivity, 414; and phenomenology, 437; and time, 499
Heidegger, Martin, 461, 464
Heinichen, Johann David, 74, 116
Heinse, Wilhelm, 121, 123–25, 126, 195–99, 239–40
Helden-Gedichte Hans Sachs genannt, Ein (Wernicke), 177
Helmholtz, Hermann, 280, 304–10, 334, 516n.11
Herbart, Johann Friedrich, 293–96, 299, 314, 516n.11

"Herbert Spencer and the Origin of Music" (Newman), 285–86
Hercules, 197
Herder, Johann Gottfried, 124, 216, 322; and emotional realism, 240; and expression, 207–10; and sound, 121–23, 207–10; and speech theory of music, 285
Hermanns Schlacht, Ein Bardiet für die Schaubühne (Klopstock), 191
Hermeneutics, 353–60, 370, 381
Herzensergiessungen eines Kunstliebenden Klosterbruders (Wackenroder), 203, 204
Hesperus (Paul), 126
Heydenreich, Karl Heinrich, 126
Hildegard von Hohenthal (Heinse), 126, 195, 196, 203
Hiller, Johann Adam, 117–20, 187, 192
Hindemith, Paul, 401, 405, 407, 408, 409, 474
Hippocrates, 81
Hippolyte et Aricie, 159
Histoire, L' (Stravinsky), 475
Historisch-Kritische Beyträge zur Aufnahme der Musik (Marpurg), 186, 188
Hoffmann, Ernst Theodor Wilhelm, 203, 207, 217, 218; on church music, 215–16; on opera, 212–15, 268; and Romantic musical aesthetics, 210–17, 240; on the unity of the musical work, 212
Homophony, 39
Honigsheim, Paul, 506
Horace (Quintus Horatius Flaccus), 89, 164, 178, 188, 323; and comparison of the arts, 22, 203
Horn, Franz, 210
Hostinsky, Ottokar, 314–17
Höveln, Konrad von, 51
Huber, Kurt, 359
Hudemann, Ludwig Friedrich, 181–82, 183
Hunold, Christian Friedrich, 177
Husserl, Edmund, 361, 440, 461, 464; on the consciousness of time, 437–39, 441; and Wesensschau, 361
Hutcheson, Francis, 98–99

"Idéal" (Chastellux), 91–92
Idealism, 392; and the Absolute, 320, 322; and formalism, 320–21, 347, 362;

and mathematics, 321; and moods, 291; types of, 347; twentieth-century descendants of, 393
Imitation, 158, 172, 204, 282; in England, 98–115; and feelings, 83–84; in France, 84–98, 99, 153, 184, 190; and galant aesthetics, 80, 120, 153; in Germany, 115–36, 184–85, 188, 190, 191, 356; as identical in meaning to expression, 84, 87, 88, 89, 92, 94; and nature, 35, 159, 162, 191; in opera, 158, 172; and polyphony, 35, 75–76; rejection of, as an aesthetic principle in music, 91–94
Impressionism, 408
Ingarden, Roman, 441–43, 452, 455; criticism of Hartmann by, 433–34
Inherent musical law, 393–97
Inquiry Concerning Beauty, Order, Harmony, Design (Hutcheson), 98–99
Inquiry into the Original of our Ideas of Beauty and Virtue; In Two Treatises (Hutcheson), 98–99
Introduction to the Sociology of Music (Adorno), 474
Iphigénie (Racine), 168–69
Iphigénie en Aulide (Gluck), 173, 174
Istituzioni harmoniche, Le (Zarlino), 27, 35
Italy, 61; development of musical aesthetics in, 19, 39, 40, 59; galant aesthetics in, 74, 76; influence on German music of, 75; opera in, criticized by French, 47–49 (see also Buffoon War; Opera: controversy over French and Italian); opera in, seventeenth century, 42–46, 47, 51, 53; operatic aesthetics in, 137–53; poetry of, criticized by French, 46, 149
Ives, Charles Edward, 434

Jahrbuch Peters, 354
Jakobson, Roman, 379
Jocasta, 163
Jomelli, Niccolò, 194, 195
Jones, William, 105–6
Josquin (Josquin Desprez), 26, 28
Journal de Paris, 176
Journal des savants, 156, 158
Juvenal (Decimus Junius Juvenalis), 323

Kalligone (Herder), 207–10
Kálmán, Emmerich, 480

Kant, Immanuel, 19, 206, 289, 310, 333, 342, 354, 451; aesthetic pleasure and form, 311; on beauty, 129–31, 132–33; beauty and pleasure distinguished by, 129, 134, 292–93, 309; and cognition, 126–33, 292; criticized, 207, 209, 210, 356 (see also *Critik der Urteilskraft,* criticism of); and formalism, 292–93, 296; and idealism, 320, 321; and philosophical aesthetics, 218, 225; on three kinds of fine art, 131–32; time conceived by, 499

Kayser, Hans, 8

Keiser, Reinhard, 52, 61, 178

Kepler, Johannes, 14, 15

Kern Melodischer Wissenschaft (Mattheson), 62

Kierkegaard, Soren, 240–43; operatic aesthetics of, 241–43, 514n.2

Kircher, Athanasius, 8, 81, 104

Kirnberger, J. P., 120

Kivy, Peter, 353

Klavierstück X (Stockhausen), 420

Kleist, Heinrich von, 207

Klopstock, Friedrich Gottlieb, 191

Kneif, Tibor, 506, 507–8

Kolish, Rudolf, 475

König, Johann Ulrich, 178, 181

Kontakte (Stockhausen), 428, 430

Kontrapunkt (Schenker), 394

Körner, Christian Gottfried, 134–35

Körner, Karl Theodor, 134, 207

Köstlin, Karl, 325, 331

Krause, Christian Gottfried, 67–74, 81, 120, 188, 189; on the effects of music, 67–68, 71–72, 73–74, 80; and galant aesthetics, 67–74; music connected to morality by, 72–73; on opera, 67, 70, 186, 187; on the union of the arts, 67, 186–87

Krenek, Ernst, 407–8, 409

Kretzschmar, Hermann, 361; on Beethoven, 356, 384, 385; and hermeneutics, 354–56, 359, 360

Kritische Briefe über die Tonkunst (Marpurg), 120

Kullak, Adolf, 328–29

Kunst und die Revolution, Die. See Art and Revolution

Kunstwerk der Zukunft, Das. See Art-Work of the Future, The

Kurth, Ernst, 396–97

Kurze Enzyklopädie der Philosophie aus praktischen Gesichtspunkten (Herbart), 293, 296

Lacépède, Bernard Germain, 176–77, 199, 217, 263, 267

la Harpe, Jean François de, 175–76

Lalo, Charles, 431–32

Lamprecht, Jacob Friedrich, 181

Langage, musique, poésie (Ruwet), 379

Langer, Susanne, 273, 282; and symbolism, 366–69

Language, 9, 162, 204, 274; music as basis for development of, 276–77; suitability of French to opera, 54, 167, 168, 170, 171, 173–74, 196, 197, 269; suitability of German to opera, 178, 181, 186, 197, 269; suitability of Italian to opera, 170, 173–74, 196, 197, 269

Languages of Art: An Approach to a Theory of Symbols (Goodman), 369, 370

Laokoon (Lessing), 189, 322

Laporte, 453

Lassus, Orlandus, 39

Laws (Plato), 27; effect of music on society, 11–12; ethical view of music in, 10

Lazarus, Moritz, 301–4, 328

Leben der Seele, Das (Lazarus), 301–4

Lecerf de la Viéville, Jean-Laurent, 154, 156–58, 159, 160

"Lectures on the Phenomenology of the Inner Consciousness of Time" (Husserl), 437–39

Lediard, Thomas, 179

Lehre von den Tonempfindungen, Die (Helmholtz), 304–10

Leibnitz, Gottfried Wilhelm, 80, 188, 321, 341

Lenin, Nikolai, 488, 496

Leo, 171

Lessing, Gotthold Ephraim, 188–89, 314, 322; criticized by Wagner, 253

"Letter" (Diderot), 173

"Letter to the Duke of Buckingham" (Saint-Evremond), 47–49, 177

"Letter to the Editor of the Mercure de France" (Gluck)

Lettre sur la musique française (Rousseau), 90–91, 167

Lettre sur "Omphale" (Grimm), 165

Lévi-Strauss, Claude, 373–75; criticism of, 375–77; serialism rejected by, 375–77, 380
Liberal arts, 20, 26. *See also* Art; Fine arts
Liebesverbot, Das (Wagner), 240
Lied von der Erde, Das (Mahler), 467–69
Lippold, Richard, 435
Lipps, Theodor, 360
Lissa, Zofia, 488–97
Listenius, Nicolas, 23–24
Lisuart und Dariolette (Hiller), 192
Locke, John, 62
Lohenstein, D. C. von, 75
Lotze, Hermann, 301
Lucretia, 197
Ludwig, Christian Gottlieb, 181
Lukács, Georg, 472, 475, 497–506
Lully, Jean Baptiste, 49, 65, 155, 163, 165, 168, 170; connected to the ancients, 158, 159–60; and operatic aesthetics, 167
Lutheranism, 52
Luzzoni, 197

Mach, Ernst, 458
Macpherson, James, 192
Macrobius, Ambrosius Theodosius, 8, 511n.2
Madrigals, 29–31, 34, 35, 36
Maffei, Scipione, 149–50
Mahler, Gustav, 384, 385, 427; Eighth symphony of, 465, 466; Fifth symphony of, 465, 466; Ninth symphony of, 465, 466–69; studies on, 465–69, 475, 487; Third symphony of, 465, 466
Mahler, Consciousness and Temporality (Greene), 464–69
Man the Musician: Sound and Symbol, Volume 2 (Zuckerkandl), 459–61
Manet, Edouard, 400
Mannheim Exhibition, 400
Mannheim symphony, 121
Marcel, Gabriel, 452
Marcello, Benedetto, 140, 145–49
Marini, Antonfrancesco, 138
Marinism, 46
Marino, Giambattista, 46
Marmontel, Jean François, 173, 174–75, 190
Marpurg, Friedrich Wilhelm, 120, 186, 188
Martello, Pier-Jacopo, 141–45, 148
Marx, Berhard Adolph, 322

Marx, Karl, 472, 475, 488, 509. *See also* Marxism
Marxism, 506; criticized, 507; culture determined by social class in, 492, 496; infrastructure and superstructure in, 489, 496; and materialism, 489; and mimesis, 498, 505; and the production of art, 489–90; and reality reflected in art, 497, 498; speech-melody in, 493; Western, 472, 474, 475, 496. *See also* Marx
Marxismus und die Fragen der Sprachwissenschaft, Der (Stalin), 488, 489
Mathematics: and beauty, 98; and music, 22, 24, 87, 132, 183, 204–5, 293, 299, 307, 516n.11; and polyphony, 59; vs. rhetoric, 26–31, 35, 60; and Romantic aesthetics, 212
Mattheson, Johann, 59–66, 74, 75; and the aesthetics of visual art, 63, 81; and the affections, 61, 62, 63, 115–16; on clarity, 64, 65, 80; criticism of, 61; galant homme of, 59; on the mathematical view of music, 62, 63; on melodic aesthetics, 62–63, 64–67, 153; on nature and art, 62, 64–66, 75; and opera, 59–60, 61, 178–80, 183; and sense over reason, 60–61, 62
Matthisson, Friedrich von, 133
Mazarin (Mazarino), Jules, 47
Mazarino. *See* Mazarin (Mazarino), Jules
Meaning, 432–34, 471
Meaning of Music, The (Pratt), 353
Measure for Measure (Shakespeare), 240
Medea, 197
Mei, Girolamo, 32–34, 35, 75–76
Meier, Georg Friedrich, 184
Meisterwerk in der Musik (Schenker), 394
Melodie nach ihrem Wesen sowohl als nach ihren Eigenschaften, Die (Nichelmann), 121
Melos, 403, 405
Memoires de Trévoux, 156, 158
Menantes. *See* Hunold, Christian Friedrich
Mendelssohn, Moses, 188–89, 191, 253, 312, 329
Mer, La (Debussy), 388
Merchant of Venice, The (Shakespeare), 13–14
Mercure de France, 173–74
Merleau-Ponty, Maurice, 461, 464
Mermet, Bollioud de, 162

Merope (Maffei), 150
Mersmann, Hans, 506
Metamorphoses (Ovid), 192
Metastasio, Pietro, 142, 149, 175, 197; fictional character of, 196–99; Voltaire on, 163–64; Wieland on, 193, 194
"Méthodes d'analyse en musicologie" (Ruwet), 377–79
Meyer, Leonard, 353
Middle Ages, 288; cosmic harmony during, 8, 62; ethical view of music during, 12; ideological struggle during, 493; noetic harmony during, 8
Midsummer Night's Dream (Shakespeare), 334
Milton, John, 9–10, 181
Minona, oder Die Angelsachsen, ein tragische Melodrama (Gerstenberg), 192
Mizler von Kolof, Lorenz Christoph, 183
Moderna. See *Musica Moderna*
Momente (Stockhausen), 425–26
Monday Club, 67, 186
Monody: conflict with polyphony, 31–39; types of, 43
Montagsklub, 67, 186, 188
Monteverdi, Claudio, 29, 30
Monteverdi, Giulio, 30–31
Morellet, André, 92–94, 95, 96
Morhof, Daniel Georg, 51
Moritz, Karl Philipp, 126, 218
Morris, Charles, 371
Möser, Justus, 190–91
Motte, Houdart de la, 160
Mozart, Wolfgang Amadeus, 126, 136, 211, 403, 408, 502; *Don Giovanni* both Romantic and erotic, 240; effect of music by, 323, 329; *Figaro* by, 323; galant characteristics in music of, 115
Muratori, Lodovico Antonio, 139–40, 148, 183
Muses, 203
Music: aesthetics of (*see* Musical aesthetics); as an art, 20–25, 26; composition of (*see* Musical composition); connected to architecture, 225; effects of, 12–16, 27, 32, 34, 62, 81, 83; ethical view of, 3, 10–16; folk, 494; function of, 270, 274–75, 281, 480–82; harmonic and ethical conceptions of connected, 14; and language, 26–27; and mathematical theory, 22, 24, 87, 132, 183, 204–5, 293, 299, 307, 516n.11 (*see also* Pythagorean musical theory);

metaphysical view of, 3–10, 24; and nature, 35, 301; social history of, 470; sociology of (*see* Sociology of music); speech theory of, 285, 293, 317
Music as Heard: A Study in Applied Phenomenology (Clifton), 461–64
"Music as Part of the World of the Mind" (Engel), 340
Musical aesthetics: first documents of, 26; and visual art, 80–81. *See also* Aesthetics; Music
Music pathology, 83
Music printing, 23
Music sociology. *See* Sociology of music
Music theory, 432
De musica (Augustine), 437
Musica (Listenius), 23–24
Musica antica, 155
Musica ficta, 39–40
Musica moderna, 155
Musica poetica, 39, 60
Musica poetica (Burmeister), 39
Musica practica, 60
Musica reservata, 39–40
Musical composition, 23–24
"Musical Erotic, The" (Kierkegaard), 240–43, 514n.2
Musical Studies (Newman), 285–86
Musicology, 506
Musik, Die (Benz), 406
Musik als Ausdruck, Die (Hausegger), 286–91
Musik im Wandel der Gesellschaft: Grundzüge der Musiksoziologie (Blaukopf), 508–9
"Musikalische Bedeutung: Grenzen und Möglichkeiten einer semiotischen Ästhetik" (Faltin), 381
Musikalische Dialogen (Heinse), 123–25, 196–97
Musikalische Leiden und Freuden (Tieck), 207
Musikalische Patriot, Der (Mattheson), 179
Musikalische Rhythmus als Erkenntnisquelle, Der (Becking), 358
"Musikalische Symbolkunde" (Schering), 361–64
Musikalisch-Kritische Bibliothek (Forkel), 125
Musikalisch-Schöne, Das (Kullak), 328–29
Musikalisch-Schöne und das Gesamt-

*Musikalisch-Schöne . . . (continued)
kunstwerk vom Standpunkt der for-
malen Aesthetik, Das* (Hostinsky),
314–17
"Musikgeschichtliche Wirklichkeit"
(Zenck), 357
"Musikpsychologie in England" (Stumpf),
284
Musiksoziologie (Kneif), 507–8
*Musiksoziologie: Eine Einführung in
die Grundbegriffe mit besonderer
Berücksichtigung der Soziologie der
Tonsysteme* (Blaukopf), 506–7
"Musikwerk, Das" (Ingarden), 442–43
Musurgia universalis (Kircher), 81

Nägeli, Hans-Georg, 296–98, 299, 356
Nationalism: and music, 12
Nature: and art, 24, 35, 62, 64–66, 75,
246–47; and imitation, 35, 159, 162,
191; and music, 35, 301
Neoclassicism: according to Adorno, 475;
French, 177–78, 180–81, 182, 191; Ital-
ian, 177; and New Objectivity, 406,
407–8; and Stravinsky, 408–10, 473
Neoromanticism, 239, 252, 398; and
Stravinsky, 408
Neoplatonism, 8, 126; harmony in, 9
Neue Klassik in der Musik: Zwei Vorträge
(Frommel), 410
"Neue Musik des Jahres, Die" (Doflein),
401–3
*Neue musikalische Theorien und Phan-
tasien* (Schenker), 394
Neue Sachlichkeit. See New Objectivity
" 'Neue Sachlichkeit', in der Musik"
(Strobel), 400
Neu-Eröffnete musikalische Bibliothek
(Mizler), 183
Neu-Eröffnete Orchestre, Das (Matthe-
son), 59, 60–61, 179
Neueste Untersuchung der Singspiele, Die
(Mattheson), 179–80, 183
Neumeister, Erdmann, 177
Neveu de Rameau, Le (Diderot), 89–90,
169–70
New Objectivity: as conformist move-
ment, 407; as related to expressionism,
401–2, 407; in France, 405; in Ger-
many, 405; and materialist philosophy,
406; and neoclassicism, 406, 407–8;
and objectivity, 410; and Romanti-

cism, 401, 402–3, 406; style in, 402;
the term, 400, 401, 409
Newman, Ernest, 285–86
Nichelmann, Christoph, 121
Nicolai, Friedrich, 187–88, 191
Nietzsche, Friedrich Wilhelm, 233, 448
Nineteenth century, 351; German outlook
during, 62; idea of composer during,
24; music aesthetics during, 470; term
"aesthetics" in, 352
Noces villageoises, Les (Stravinsky), 409
Nohl, Herman, 358
Nugent, Thomas, 86
Nuove musiche, Le (Caccini), 36, 37–38

"Objective Judgment of Art" (Engel),
339–40, 516n.11
Objectivism, 291, 320; according to
Adorno, 475; and analysis, 421, 432;
during second half of century, 414; and
expressionism, 401–2, 403, 411; and
feelings, 291; and illusory realism, 412;
music as sound, 434–36; and musical
stratification, 432–34; in 1920s, 398,
403–4; and neoclassicism, 408–10;
and nineteenth-century emotionalism
and realism, 398; and objectivity, 410;
and order and organization, 421, 432;
and Romanticism, 411; and simplicity,
398; as socioaesthetic, 398, 403, 404–
5; and stability of style, 400; and
Stravinsky, 408–14, 473; and two
types of listening, 413. *See also* New
Objectivity
*Objektive Gesetzmässigkeit in der Musik,
Die* (Lissa), 488
*Observations on the Correspondence
between Poetry and Music* (Webb),
103–5
Observations sur la musique (Chabanon),
96–98, 120
*Observations sur notre instinct pour la
musique, et sur son principe* (Rameau),
90, 167
Octet (Stravinsky), 409
Oedipus, 163
Oersted, Hans Christian, 321–22
"Of the Imitative Arts" (Smith), 111–15
*Ökonomische Probleme des Sozialismus
in der UdSSR* (Stalin), 488
Omphale (Destouches), 165

"On Some Disputed Points in Music" (Gurney), 280–81, 318
"On the Conceptual and Nonconceptual Understanding of Music" (Eggebrecht), 382
"On the Different Senses of the Word Imitative, as Applied to Music by the Antients and by the Moderns" (Twining), 110–11
"On the Fetish-Character of Music and the Regression of Listening" (Adorno), 474–75
"On the Morning of Christ's Nativity" (Milton), 9
"On the Situation of Modern Music" (Eisler), 403
"On the Social Situation of Music" (Adorno), 472–74, 479
Oper und Drama. See Opera and Drama
Opera, 25, 38, 501; aesthetics of entertainment in, 46; boredom in, 42, 43, 47–48; and Christianity, 52, 53; controversy over French and Italian, 47–49, 91, 153–60 (see also Buffoon War); in eighteenth century, 44, 45, 52; and emotional realism, 239, 241–42, 244, 269, 288 (see also Opera and Drama), and English language, 53–55; and expressive style, 36; and formalism, 296, 312, 316; in France (see Opera, French); and galant aesthetics, 59–60, 61; in Germany (see Opera, German); influence of French drama on, 46; and the influence of music, 12; in Italy (see Opera, Italian); original aesthetics of, 43; and poetry, 139, 141, 170, 172, 180, 187, 189, 194, 212; recitative vs. aria, 44–45; religious condemnation of, 52, 53; and Romanticism (see Romantic aesthetics, and opera); seventeenth-century changes in, 45; shift from acceptance to criticism of, 45; and singing, 181, 183, 184, 192, 198; and sociology of music, 483–84; subgenres of, 183; unity of musical work in, 212; and verisimilitude, 177–78, 179, 182, 183–84, 187, 193. See also Operatic aesthetics
"Opera" (Rousseau), 170–71
Opera, French: and controversy over French and Italian, 46–49, 91, 153–60 (see also Buffoon War); equated

with ancient, 155–57; and imitation, 190; influence upon German of, 183, 191; influence upon Italian of, 138; and morality, 49–50, 53; and poetry, 189; seventeenth century, 46–50, 53, 139, 142, 150; as spoken drama, 49, 53, 139, 142
Opera, German: contrast between Gluck's reforms and Italian opera, 194–95, 196; and expression, 190; and French influence, 177–78, 183, 191; influence of Italian literature on, 178, 181; and Italian opera, 53, 186, 191–92, 193–94, 196; positive approach in, 180, 187; seventeenth century, 50–55
Opera, Italian: compared to French, 46–49, 91, 153–60 (see also Buffoon War); compared to German, 51, 53; criticized in Germany, 186, 191–92, 193–94, 196; equated with modern, 155–57; French influence upon, 138, 194; and poetry, 189; seventeenth century, 42–46; Venetian, 43–44, 46, 53, 145–46, 149
"Opéra, Les" (Saint-Evremond), 181
Opera and Drama (Wagner), 244, 252–70
"Opera and the Nature of Music" (Wagner), 252
Opéra comique, 170
Opera in musica, Dell' (Planelli), 153
Operatic aesthetics, 91, 126; in France, 145, 153–77; in Germany, 177–99; in Italy, 137–53; and theory of imitation, 120
Opinioni de' cantori (Tosi), 149
De oratore (Cicero), 86
Order and organization, 414–36; and analysis, 421; and composite structure, 431–32; and craftsmanship, 418, 419; and disorder, 420; and electronic music, 419–20, 423, 426, 430; moments in, 425–26; and music in points, groups and masses, 421–23; and musical form, 415; and objectivity, 421, 432; and phases, 420; and preformed material, 418–19; and serialism, 417–19; statistical form in, 423; and tonal order, 418–19; and tone and noise, 429–30; and two kinds of music, 414–15; types of composition in, 423–25; unification of temporal structure, 427–28
Orestes, 163

Orfeo (Calzabigi), 174, 194
"Origin and Function of Music" (Spencer), 270–75, 282–84
Orpheus, 12, 207, 210, 300
Orpheus (Gluck), 94
Ossian, 192
Ovid (Publius Ovidius Naso), 192

Paix de l'opéra, ou Parallèle impartial de la musique française et de la musique italienne, La (Raguenet), 167. See also *Parallèle des Italiens et des Francois en ce qui regarde la musique et les opéra*
Pajama Game, 480
Palestrina, Giovanni Pierluigi da, 26, 216, 491
Pan, 207
Parallèle des anciens et des modernes (Perrault), 154–55
Parallèle des Italiens et des François en ce qui regarde la musique et les opéra (Raguenet), 154–56, 167
Paride (Calzabigi), 174, 194
Passions de l'âme, Les (Descartes), 81, 84, 116
Pastorale d'Issy (Perrin and Cambert), 47
Paul, Jean, 126
Paulli, Wilhelm Adolph, 187
Peirce, Charles, 370–71
Perfetta poesia italiana, Della (Muratori), 139–40
Pergolesi, Giovanni Battista, 126, 165, 171, 195, 197
Peri, Jacopo, 36–37, 152, 263
Perrault, Charles, 154–55, 157
Perrault, Claude, 157
Perrin, Pierre, 47
Perrucci, Andrea, 46
Petit prophète de Boehmischbroda, Le (Grimm), 166
Petrouchka (Stravinsky), 410, 412
Phantasien über die Kunst für Freunde der Kunst (Wackenroder), 203
Phenomenology, 437–69, 471; and analysis of music, 437, 440; and Classical-Romantic duality, 448–50; and coherence and continuity, 465–69; difference between listening and reflection in, 441; and feeling, 461, 462, 464; identity of the musical work in, 442–43; and Mahler, 465–69; melody and harmony in, 444–46, 449; and metaphysics, 455–61; mixed with ontology, 452–55; and motion, 455, 456; and musical ear, 459, 460; and musical thought, 459, 460–61; and musicality, 459–60; and play, 461–62, 463–64; and polyphony, 449–50; psychological duration and musical time in, 446–47; rhythm in, 446; and space, 455, 456–59, 461, 462–63; and temporal constitution, 437–38, 439, 447–52; and temporal extension, 438–39; and time, 455, 456–57, 461, 462; and tone, 455–56, 457; in twentieth century, 437
"Philosophie der Kunst." *See* "Philosophy of Art"
Philosophie der neuen Music (Adorno), 411–14, 475–79
Philosophie der symbolischen Formen, Die (Cassirer), 366
Philosophie des Schönen (Hartmann), 342–47
Philosophie des Unbewussten (Hartmann), 333, 342
Philosophy in a New Key: A Study in the Symbolism of Reason, Rite, and Art (Langer), 273, 366
"Philosophy of Art" (Schelling), 218–24
Piccini, Nicola, 174
Pietists, 52
Pindar, 498
Pins and Needles, 480
Planelli, Antonio, 149, 153
Plato, 20, 31, 35, 65, 85, 139; and Aristotle, 233; auditory pleasure censured by, 34; and beauty, 198, 341; and effects of music, 14, 81, 503; and ethical view of music, 10, 503; and instrumental performance, 21; and metaphysical view of music, 3, 5, 6, 7, 8; and rhythms, 32; and the sensuous, 341, 397; and song, 30, 38; and suprasensible harmony, 8; view of the universe of, 99. See also *Laws; Republic; Timaeus*
Platonic Forms, 25, 394
"Play and the Nature of Dramatic Poetry" (Wagner), 253–57
Pluche, Abbé, 162
Plutarch, 139
Poe, Edgar Allen, 400
"Poème lyrique" (Grimm), 171–72
Poems, Chiefly Translations from Asiatick Languages, together with Two Essays on the Poetry of Eastern Nations and

on the Arts commonly called Imitative (Jones), 105–6
Poetica toscana all'uso (Salvadori), 44–45
Poetics (Aristotle), 27, 44; on expression and imitation, 110, 111, 162, 172; and French criticism, 46; and operative reform, 139, 140, 142; and temporal art, 85; unity of arts in, 21, 84
Poétique de la musique, La (Lacépède), 176–77
Poétique musicale sous forme de six leçons (Stravinsky), 414–15
Poetry, 23, 36, 39, 112, 324; examined by Hostinsky, 316–17; examined by Wagner, 247; and Gluck, 191, 196; harmony in, 9–10; and influence of music, 12; Italian, 46; and Kant, 131–32; and melody, 257–63; and music, 322, 323, 325, 328, 501; and opera, 42, 44, 139, 141, 163, 170, 172, 180, 187, 188–89, 194, 212; and rhetoric, 22; and Romantic opera, 212–14; and theory of imitation, 99, 100
Politics (Aristotle), 27; on expression and imitation, 84, 86, 107, 110, 111, 498
Polyphony, 23; conflict between two types of, in sixteenth century, 27–31, 35, 39; conflict with monody, in sixteenth century, 31–39; in Germany, 59–60, 74; and mathematical rules, 59; and music as imitative art, 35, 75–76; and phenomenology, 449–50; and rhetoric, 35, 60; and solo song, 39; versus galant aesthetics, 59, 74–75
Porpora, Nicola, 197
Postel, Christian Heinrich, 52–53
Postromanticism, 398
Pousseur, Henri, 380
Power of Sound, The (Gurney), 281–82, 283, 317–18
Praetorius, Johann Philipp, 178
Pratique du Théatre (Hédelin), 182
Pratt, Carroll, 353
"Problem of the Identity of the Musical Work, The" (Ingarden), 442–43
Propyläen, Die, 199
Proust, Marcel, 452
Ptolemy (Claudius Ptolemaeus), 8, 321
Puccini, Giacomo, 487
Pygmalion, 323
Pythagoras, 223, 305. *See also* Pythagorean musical theory
Pythagorean musical theory, 5, 6, 7, 27, 51

Quadrio, Francesco Saverio, 149
Quadrivial studies (quadrivium), 6, 20, 26, 35
Quanto certezza habbia da suoi principii la musica (Steffani), 61
Quantz, Johann Joachim, 74, 76, 77–79, 82, 121
Quinault, Philippe, 49, 163, 175, 192; and ancient-modern dichotomy, 155; and feeling, 161; and imitation, 185; operas of, praised, 165
Quintilianus, Aristides, 8, 23
Quintilian (Marcus Fabius Quintilianus), 22, 27, 97, 139

Racine, Jean Baptiste, 168–69, 197
Raguenet, Abbé François, 154–56, 158, 159, 161, 167
Rameau, Jean Philippe, 163, 170, 186, 310; and harmony, 62, 64, 263; operas of, compared to Lully's, 159–61, 165; quarrel with Rousseau about melody and harmony, 90–91, 106, 121–22, 167
Rameau's Nephew, 203
Ramler, Carl Wilhelm, 188
Rational and Social Foundations of Music, The (Weber), 471–72
Rationalism, 83–84, 85
Raw and the Cooked, The (Lévi-Strauss), 373–75
Realism, 83–84, 330, 515n.10. *See also* Emotional realism
Recherches sur l'analogie de la musique avec les arts qui ont pour objet l'imitation du language (Villoteau), 285
Recitatif obligé, 175
Recitativo accompagnato, 175
Reflexions (Mattheson), 61–62
Réflexions critiques sur la poësie et sur la peinture (Du Bos), 76, 86–87, 159, 186, 188
Réflexions d'un patriote sur l'opéra français et sur l'opéra italien (de Rochemont), 168
Réflexions sur l'opéra (Rémond), 161
Reger, Erik, 406–7
Reihe, 420
Rémond de Saint-Mard, Toussaint, 161, 163
Renaissance; and comparison of the arts, 203; ethical view of music in, 12; music aesthetics in, 16, 19, 20–25;

Renaissance (*continued*)
noetic harmony during, 8; rhetoric
during, 22; and stylistic diversity, 154
Representation, 91
Republic (Cicero), 6–7, 511n.2
Republic (Plato): cosmic harmony in, 3–
5, 6, 7; ethical view of music in, 10;
and expression and imitation, 27, 32;
harmonic and ethical conceptions of
music connected in, 14; on song, 30
"Requiem" (Mozart), 323
Revue musicale (Souvtchinsky), 414–15
Rhetoric: and arbitrary signs, 185; and
composition, 60; and galant aesthetics,
60, 64, 65; influence of, in sixteenth
century, 22; vs. mathematics, 26–31,
35, 60; and polyphony, 35, 60
Richter, Jean Paul, 218
Ring des Nibelungen, Der (Wagner), 244
Rinuccini, Ottavio, 36
Rochlitz, Friedrich, 210
Romans: dramatic genres of, 42; and ethical view of music, 12, 109; tragedies
of, 37
Romantic aesthetics, 126, 203–38; and
Beethoven, 395; absence of social considerations in, 207; comparison of arts
in, 203; departure from, 403, 406;
and emotion, 203, 204–6, 217, 230,
239, 298, 319, 403; and expressionism,
411; and formalism, 298, 319, 347;
images evoked by music of, 211–12;
and instrumental music, 121, 215–
16; and literature, 203, 207, 239, 321,
322; and mathematics, 204–5; musical
instruments in, 204, 206; and New
Objectivity, 401, 402–3, 406; and objectivity, 411; and opera, 210, 212–17,
514n.2; paradox in, 205; religion in,
228, 244, 298; and song, 216; style in,
402; and symbolism, 365, 366; unity of
musical work in, 212, 217–18
Romantic music; and musical time, 448–
49
Romantische Harmonik, Die (Kurth),
396–97
Rore, Cipriano de, 34
Du Roullet, François Le Blond, 173–74
Rousseau, Jean-Jacques, 167, 174, 282; on
contrast between French and Italian
opera, 165, 166, 167, 168; fictional
character of, 123–24; and imitation,

80, 89, 90–91, 95, 123; and operatic aesthetics, 170–71; quarrel with
Rameau about melody and harmony,
90–91, 106, 121–22, 167; on Quinault,
165; and speech theory of music, 90–
91, 123, 285; on unsuitability of French
to music, 90, 167, 171
Ruetz, Caspar, 117, 120
Rummenhöller, Peter, 508
Ruwet, Nicholas, 377–81

Sach, Curt, 449
Sacre (Stravinsky), 410
Saggio sopra l'opera in musica (Algarotti),
150–53
Saint Augustine, 397
Saint-Evremond, Charles de, 140, 181,
183; and opera as tragedy, 49, 164;
on singing, 47–49, 138, 139, 163; and
verisimilitude, 177–78, 179
Salvadori, Giuseppe, 44–45
Samson (Voltaire), 181
Satire X (Boileau), 50
Saussure, Ferdinand de, 353, 370–71
Sbarra, Francesco, 43
Scheibe, Johann Adolf, 74–75, 182–83,
186, 190
Schein, Johann Hermann, 365
Schelling, Friedrich Wilhelm Joseph, von,
8, 218–24, 233; on the Absolute, 220–
21; and construction, 219–20; and the
harmony of the sphere, 8, 221; and
idealism, 321; 223–24; and intellectual
intuition, 219; and music differentiated into three unities, 222–23; on
sound, 224
Schenker, Heinrich, 393–94, 396, 431
Schering, Arnold: Beethoven studies of,
359, 360, 365; categories of symbolism
of, 360–61; and duality of voice and
instrument, 364–66; and history of
musical symbolism, 361–64; types of
instrumental music, 365; and types of
symbolism, 362–64
Scherzi musicali (Monteverdi), 30
Schiebeler, Daniel, 192
Schiller, Friedrich von, 245, 289; and
beauty, 133, 134; and feelings, 126, 133,
218; on the idealism of art, 133–34;
and opera as tragedy, 199
"Schlechte Einrichtung des Italienschen

Singgedichts; Warum ahrem Deutsche sie nach?" (Gerstenberg), 191–92
Schlegel, August Wilhelm, 184–85, 219, 321
Schlegel, Friedrich, 184–85
Schlegel, Johann Adolph, 116, 184–85
Schlegel, Johann Elias, 116–17, 120, 183–84
Schloezer, Boris de, 408–9, 455
Schönberg, Arnold, 384, 401, 405; and objectivity, 413; and order, 417, 426; as progressive and expressive, 475, 486; and serialism, 380; studied by Adorno, 411, 473, 475–78, 486
Schöne und die Kunst; Zur Einführung in die Ästhetik, Das (Vischer), 328
Schopenhauer, Arthur, 290, 343, 353, 443; on the composer, 229–30, 394; and the effects of music, 229, 230; and feelings, 230, 290; on melody, 229–30, 232; and music as a universal language, 229, 230–31; on song and opera, 230, 232–33; and Wagner, 233, 448; and the Will, 229, 230, 231, 232
Schriften zur Einleitung in die Philosophie (Herbart), 293–96
Schulz, J. A. P., 120
Schumann, Robert, 203, 207, 312, 329, 356
Schutz, Alfred, 439–41, 452
Schütz, Heinrich, 365
Schweitzer, Anton, 193
Scruton, Roger, 386–92; and aspect perception, 388; and expression, 389–90; and imagination, 390–91; and musical meaning, 391–92; and representation, 370
Seconda parte dell' Artusi (Artusi), 30
Seelewig (Staden), 50
Semiotics, 353, 370–81; and art, 371; and music, 372; and serialism, 375–77, 380; two traditions of, 371
Sémiramis (Voltaire), 163–64, 190
"Sendschreiben eines Freundes an den andern über einige Ausdrücke des Herrn Batteux von der Musik" (Ruetz), 117
Sensation and Intuition: Studies in Psychology and Aesthetics (Sully), 285
Serauky, Walter, 506
Serva padrona, La (Pergolesi), 91, 153, 165
Seventeenth century, 3; development of music aesthetics in, 19–20, 23, 39, 60;

German composers of, 76; influence of music in, 14–15; opera viewed in, 42–55; prima and seconda prattiche fused during, 31; rationalism in, 85; theory of affections and temperaments in, 81–82, 84
Shaftesbury, Earl of, 69, 98, 99
Shakespeare, 177, 212, 240; and connection between motion and feeling, 105; references to influence of music during, 13–14; and the "unspeakable," 325
Shepherds of the Pegnitz, 50, 51
Siebeck, Hermann, 312–13
Silbermann, Alphons, 506, 507
Silence (Cage), 434–35
Simmel, Georg, 509
Singing: and challenges to ars perfecta, 26; criticized, 140; and expression, 96–97, 161, 288; and expressive vocal melody (see Galant aesthetics); innovations in solo, 37–39; and monody, 43; in opera, 161, 181, 183, 184, 192, 198; origins of, 280; and Romantic aesthetics, 216; during sixteenth century, 31–32; Spencer's views on, 270–74; variations of, 40
Singspiel, 193
"Situation des Handwerks (Kriterien der punktuellen Musik)" (Stockhausen), 417–18
Sixteenth century: comparison of one art with another in, 22; conflict of aesthetic principles during, 26–41; development of musical aesthetics in, 19–20, 21–22, 59, 60; fine arts during, 20; interest in expression during, 27; music composition during, 23; resemblance of art and nature during, 24, 35; rhetoric during, 22; song during, 31–32
Smith, Adam, 111–15
Sociology of music: as antithesis of aesthetics, 470; and the avant-garde, 486–87; and catharsis, 498, 500–501, 503, 504; and chamber music, 483, 484; class import of music in, 482–84, 492–93, 495, 496; composite musical arts in, 501–2; and conductor and orchestra, 484; and the consumption of music, 474–75; distinguished from social history of music, 470; and elements in music indifferent to class,

Sociology of music (*continued*)
493, 496; and ethnomusicology, 471;
and feelings and motions, 497, 498,
500–501, 502, 504; and fetishism, 474;
and the function of music, 480–82;
general introductions to the field of,
506–10; and the indefinite objectivity
of musical works, 502–3; interaction
of harmony and melody in, 472; and
intonation, 494–95; and listening, 474,
477, 479, 482–84; and Marxism, 472,
474, 475, 488–97, 498, 505, 506, 507;
mimesis in, 498–99, 503, 505–6; and
music aesthetics, 509; and music and
ideology, 488, 498; and music and
society, 473, 487–88, 491–92, 508;
and music as commodity, 472–73; and
music as element of Marxist superstructure, 492, 495–96; and music
creating a world, 504–5; and musical
criticism, 485; and musical life, 484–
85; and musicology, 506–7, 508–9;
and national style, 485–86; neglected
during nineteenth century, 470–71;
and opera, 483–84; and popular music,
479–81; and production of types of
music, 473–74; and rationalization
of music, 471–72; and realism in
music, 503; sociomusical groups in,
507; speech-melody in, 493–94; and
studies of Beethoven, 495; and studies
of Haydn, 495; and studies of Schönberg, 473, 475–78, 486; and studies of
Stravinsky, 475–78; and tonal systems,
506; in twentieth century, 509–10
Socrates, 10–11
Solger, Karl Wilhelm Ferdinand, 224–29
Song. *See* Singing
Sopplimenti musicali (Zarlino), 35–36
Sound and Symbol (Zuckerkandl), 455–61
*Sound and Symbol: Music and the Exter-
nal World* (Zuckerkandl), 455–59
Souriau, Étienne, 454
Soviet Union: aesthetics of, 488, 494, 495
Souvtchinsky, Pierre, 414–15
Spencer, Herbert, 318; criticism of, 279,
280–82, 283–84, 285–86, 317; and the
function of music, 270, 274–75, 281;
and the origin of music, 270–74, 276,
280, 281, 282–83, 284
Spinoza, Baruch, 76

Spohr, Louis, 312
Stabat mater (Pergolesi), 126
Stade, Friedrich, 331–34
Staden, Sigmund Gottlieb, 50
Stalin, Joseph, 472, 496; and aesthetics,
488, 490; and the superstructure, 489,
491, 495
Steffani, Agostino, 61
Stockhausen, Karlheinz, 417–31, 434;
on composite structure, 431–32; and
craftmenship, 418, 419; and disorder,
420; and electronic music, 419–20,
423, 430; and moments, 425–26;
and music in points, groups and
masses, 421–23; and phases, 420;
and preformed material, 418–19; and
statistical form, 423; and tonal order,
418–19; on tone and noise, 429–30;
types of composition distinguished by,
423–25; and unification of temporal
structure, 427–28
Strauss, Richard, 487
Stravinsky, Igor, 401; and Adorno, 405,
409–10, 411–14, 473, 475–78; and
Classical music, 448, 450–51; and
constructivism, 410–11; dependency
on dance of, 476; and expressionism,
408, 416; music of, compared to primitive music, 451–52; and neoclassicism,
408–10, 473; and objectivity, 408–14,
473; and order, 414–17, 430–31; as
reactionary and antipsychological, 475
Strobel, Heinrich, 400
Structuralism, 432
Strunk, Oliver, 153
Struttura assente, La (Eco), 375–77
Stuckenschmidt, Hans Heinz, 407
Study of Wagner, A (Newman), 285
Stumpf, Carl, 284–85
Sturm und Drang, 121, 175, 195
Subjectivity, 291, 320
Sully, James, 285
Sulzer, Johann Georg, 120, 191
"Symbol in der Musik" (Schering), 360–
61
Symbolism, 353, 359–70; disagreement be-
tween Germanic and Anglo-American
conception of, 368–69; and exem-
plification, 369–70; four categories,
of, 360–61; and hermeneutics, 359–
60; history of musical, 361–64; and

instrumental music, 365–66; and Romanticism, 365, 366; types of, 362–64, 365

Symphonie Anton Bruckners, Die (Halm), 395

System der Ästhetik (Heydenreich), 126

System der transzendentalen Idealismus (Schelling), 219

Taine, Hippolyte Adolphe, 509

Tannhäuser (Wagner), 240

Tartini, Giuseppe, 76, 77

Teatro alla moda, Il (Marcello), 145–49

Teatro italiano (Maffei), 149

Le Temps musical: Essai d'une esthétique nouvelle de la musique (Brelet), 443–52

Terpander, 305

Teseo (Metastasio and Caldara), 165

Teufel ist los, Der (Weisse), 181

Teutsche Merkur, Der (Wieland), 192, 194

Teutsche Rede- bind- und Dicht-Kunst (Birken), 51

Teutschübende Gesellschaft, 178

Texte (Stockhausen), 420–21

Theatralische, geistliche/vermischte und galante Gedichte (König), 178

Theseus, 165

Three Treatises Concerning Art (Harris), 99–100

Through the Looking-Glass (Carroll), 386

Tieck, Ludwig, 206, 207

Tiessen, Heinz, 403

Timaeus (Plato): cosmic harmony in, 5, 6, 7; harmonic and ethical conceptions of music connected in, 14; influence of music in, 14; suprasensible harmony in, 8

Tonwille, Der (Schenker), 394

Tosi, 149

Traetta, 194

Tragedia antica e moderna, Della (Martello), 141–45

Tragedia, Della (Gravina), 140–41

Tragédie lyrique, 155, 164, 165, 166, 168

Traité du beau (Crousaz), 85–86, 98

Traité du mélodrame, ou Réflexions sur la musique dramatique (Garcin), 172–73

Trattato della musica scenica (Doni), 42–43

Tristan (Wagner), 363

Trois chapitres, ou La Vision, Les (Diderot), 167

Twentieth century, 25; American works in, 353; analysis in, 421, 432; feelings and moods rejected in, 351–52; form in, 351, 352; meaning in, 352–53; music aesthetics in, 351–52, 432; objectivity emphasized in, 351, 393; term aesthetics in, 351–52

Two Dissertations, on Poetical, and Musical, Imitation (Twining), 110

Typen der Weltanschauungen, Die (Dilthey), 358

Typische Kunststile in Dichtung und Musik (Nohl), 358

Über das Spezifische der Musik (Lissa), 488, 497

Über die bildende Nachahmung des Schönen (Moritz), 126

Über die Musik und ihre Wirkungen (Chabanon), 120

Über die musikalische Malerei (Engel), 126

"Über die Oper *Undine*" (Weber), 217–18

"Über Grundlagen der Beurteilung gegenwärtiger Musik" (Doflein), 404

"Über Wahrheit und Wahrscheinlichkeit der Kunstwerke" (Goethe), 199

"Ueber Charakterdarstellung in der Musik" (Körner), 134–36

"Ueber die Gründe des Vergnügens, welches die Töne hervorbringen" (Oersted), 321–22

Ueber neue Musik (Krenek), 407–8

Uffenbach, Johann Friedrich, 182, 183

Understanding, 353, 370, 381–92

"Understanding Music" (Beardsley), 369–70

"Understanding Music" (Scruton), 390–91

Unterricht von der Teutschen Sprache und Poesie (Morhof), 51

Untersuchungen zur Ontologie der Kunst (Ingarden), 442–43

Ut, me, sol, re, fa, la, tota musica (Buttstedt), 61

Vaugirard Anonymous, 175–76

Veda, 5

Venetus, Franciscus, 8

Vergil (Publius Vergilius Maro), 93
Versuch einer Anweisung die Flöte traver-
    siere zu spielen (Quantz), 74, 76, 82
Versuch einer Critischen Dichtkunst
    (Gottsched), 181, 183
"Versuch über das deutsche Singspiel und
    einige dahin einschlagende Gegen-
    stände" (Wieland), 193
Versuch über die wahre Art das Clavier zu
    spielen (Bach), 79–80
"Vertheidigung der Opern" (Ramler), 188
Vial, Jeanne, 452–55
Vicentino, Nicola, 27, 28–29
Vico, Giambattista, 358
"Viertes Wäldchen" (Herder), 121–
    23, 210
Viéville, Jean-Laurent Lecerf de la. See
    Lecerf de la Viéville, Jean-Laurent
Vilate, Cartaud de la, 162
Villoteau, 285
Vinci, Leonardo da, 171
Vischer, Friedrich Theodor, 325–28, 331
Vitruvius (Vitruvius Pollio), Marcus, 8
Vivaldi, Antonio, 77
Volcyr, 23
Volkelt, Johannes, 360
Volkommene Capellmeister, Der (Matthe-
    son), 77; and the affections, 115–16;
    and melody, 62–63, 64–67, 75; and
    opera, 179, 180; and visual art, 63, 81
Voltaire, François Marie Arouet de,
    163–65, 181, 190, 269
Vom Musikalisch-Schönen (Hanslick), 94,
    298–301
Vom Musikalisch-Schönen (Stade), 331–
    34
"Vom Musikalisch-Schönen" (Zimmer-
    mann), 311–12
Von der Einheit der Musik (Busoni), 400
Von der Musikalischen Poesie (Krause),
    67–74, 186–87, 511n.9
"Von der Würde derer Singe-Gedichte"
    (Uffenbach), 182
Von deutscher Dichtung und Musik
    (Dilthey), 357
Von zwei Kulturen der Musik (Halm),
    394–95
Vorhanden, 464
Vorlesungen über die Ästhetik (Hegel),
    233
Vorlesungen über die Musik mit Berück-
    sichtigung der Dilettanten (Nägeli),
    296–98
Vorschule der Ästhetik (Fechner), 313–14
Vorschule der Aesthetik (Paul), 126
Vossiche Zeitung, 334

Wackenroder, Wilhelm Heinrich, 121,
    216; and aesthetics in literary works,
    203; on music and emotions, 204, 217;
    and musical instruments, 206–7
Wagner, Richard, 55, 152, 207, 334, 431;
    adumbrations of, 153, 176, 198, 206;
    on art and nature, 246–47; on art of
    ancient Greece, 244–45; and Bach,
    449–50; on Beethoven, 248–49, 250,
    252, 260–61; on Christianity, 246;
    and the combination of the arts, 249–
    50; compared to Schopenhauer, 448;
    on consonants and vowels, 258–60;
    critique of Lessing by, 253; on drama
    as a whole, 267–68; and emotional
    realism, 177, 243–44, 515n.10; on har-
    mony, 248, 263–65; and Hanslick, 314;
    on language, 269; on modulation, 260,
    261–63; on opera, 317, 326, 337–38
    (see also Opera and Drama); on
    the orchestra, 263–67; on the perfect
    artist, 251–52; and phenomenology,
    449–50; on poetic verse and melody,
    257–63; on relationship of poet and
    musician, 268–70; on the role of
    orchestra in drama, 189; and Romanti-
    cism, 239–430, 248–49, 448, 449–50;
    and Schopenhauer, 233; socioaesthet-
    ics of, 398; and speech theory of music,
    281, 285; studied by Adorno, 475; on
    subject matter appropriate to drama,
    253–56; and the "unspeakable," 325;
    variety of aesthetic ideas of, 243
War of the Buffoons. See Buffoon War
Webb, Daniel, 103–5, 299
Weber, Carl Maria von, 217–18
Weber, Max, 471–72, 506, 509
Webern, Anton von, 422; and order, 417,
    426; and punctile music, 419; and
    serialization, 380, 418; studied by
    Adorno, 475
Weill, Kurt, 473
Weisse, Christian, 181
Well-Tempered Clavier, 354, 355

Welt als Wille und Vorstellung, Die (Schopenhauer), 229–33
Werckmeister, Andreas, 61
Wernicke, Christian, 177
Wesen der ästhetischen Anschauung, Das (Siebeck), 312–13
Western Marxism. *See* Marxism
Whistler, James Abbott McNeill, 22
Wich, Cyrill, 179
". . . wie die Zeit vergeht . . ." (Stockhausen), 420, 421
Wieland, Christoph Martin, 192–94
Willaert, 26, 28
Winckelmann, Johann Joachim, 81, 133, 186
Wolff, Christian, 188
"Work of Art in the Age of Mechanical Reproduction" (Benjamin), 472
Wovon lebt die Musik: die Prinzipien der Musiksoziologie (Silbermann), 507

Yasser, Joseph, 506
"Young Classicism" (Busoni), 398–400
Young Germany movement, 239–40

Zarathustra, 399
Zarlino, Gioseffo, 26, 27, 30, 35–36; and expression and harmony, 28, 31
Zeitmasse (Stockhausen), 423–24
Zenck, Hermann, 357
Zeno, Apostolo, 138–39, 142, 150, 197
Zimmermann, Robert, 298, 310–12
Zuckerkandl, Victor, 455–61, 463
Zuhanden, 464
Zur Geschichte der jüngsten Musik (Tiessen), 403
"Zur gesellschaftlichen Lage der Musik" (Adorno), 409–10
"Zur Grundlegung der musikalischen Hermeneutik" (Schering), 359